SPSS-X™ Advanced Statistics Guide

2nd Edition

MARIJA J. NORUŠIS/SPSS INC.

SPSS Inc.
444 N. Michigan Avenue
Chicago, Illinois 60611
312.329.3500

SPSS International B.V.
P.O. Box 115
4200 AC Gorinchem
The Netherlands
Tel. +31.1830.36711
Twx.: 21019 (SPSS NL)
Fax +31.1830.35839

For more information about SPSS^{X}™ and other software produced and distributed by SPSS Inc., please write or call

Marketing Department
SPSS Inc.
444 North Michigan Avenue
Chicago, IL 60611
312/329-3500

In Europe and the Middle East, please write or call

SPSS International B.V.
P.O. Box 115
4200 AC Gorinchem
The Netherlands
Tel. +31.1830.36711
Twx: 21019 (SPSS nl)
Fax: +31.1830.35839

SPSS^{X} Advanced Statistics Guide, 2nd Edition

Printed in the United States of America.

2 3 4 5 6 7 8 9 0 92 91 90 89

ISBN 0-918469-81-3

Library of Congress Catalog Card Number: 88-061671

Preface

'What *can* all that green stuff be?' said Alice.

Although Alice was probably not referring to output flashed on green CRTs or printed on green-tinted paper, many of us feel like visitors to Wonderland when confronted with the complex and sometimes confusing output from statistical software packages. This text is intended to ease some of the bewilderment by annotating and illustrating the output (and input) from the most commonly used SPSS^X multivariate statistical procedures. (The more basic procedures are covered in the *SPSS^X Introductory Statistics Guide.*) Understanding the output available, and the commands needed to obtain that output, should help in choosing the right multivariate procedure for a problem.

THE SPSS^X SYSTEM

The SPSS^X System™ is a comprehensive tool for managing, analyzing, and displaying data. A broad range of statistical analyses and data modification tasks are accomplished with a simple, English-like language. Results can be easily obtained with minimal understanding of computer intricacies.

While this text includes instructions for entering and defining data and for performing basic data transformations, it does not attempt to cover the full range of data and file management facilities available in SPSS^X. For those who want to extend their use of the system beyond the scope of this text, documentation can be found in *SPSS^X User's Guide.* The computational methods used are described in *SPSS Statistical Algorithms.*

VERSIONS OF THE SPSS^X SYSTEM

The system and its documentation are continually being extended. In addition to new features and facilities, the latest release (3.0) contains several changes in command syntax. These syntactical changes include:

- Release 3.0 uses subcommands and keywords instead of the OPTIONS and STATISTICS commands.
- Release 3.0 uses the MATRIX subcommand to handle matrix materials, instead of the OPTIONS commands and READ and WRITE subcommands that handle matrices in earlier releases.

This edition of the *Advanced Statistics Guide* has been updated to include instructions for Release 3.0 and for earlier releases. Check with your computation center for information about the release of SPSS^X being used there, and other documentation available for that release.

USING THIS TEXT

This text is designed to be both a supplement in courses that integrate the teaching of statistics and computing, and a reference for users of the SPSS^X system. Each chapter illustrates a multivariate statistical procedure by describing a problem and the SPSS^X output useful for its solution, followed by information about the SPSS^X commands needed to obtain the analysis.

Exercises at the end of each chapter review the material presented. Emphasis is on understanding the output from the procedure and the commands necessary to produce it. Answers for questions on syntax and statistical concepts are given in

Appendix C. Appendix B contains a brief guide to the features of the SPSS^X system, including instructions for running the basic procedures not described in this text.

ACKNOWLEDGMENTS

Many of the SPSS Inc. staff have contributed generously to the preparation of this manual. I am most grateful to them. My colleague Susan Shott prepared the exercises and operations sections and offered much valuable advice and encouragement. Thanks are also due to the reviewers of various parts of the manuscript. In particular I wish to thank Ken Berk for his many helpful suggestions. Finally I thank Rasa, whose scholarly example inspires me.

—Marija J. Norušis

Contents

1 Beginning Simply 1

2 Modeling Salary: Multiple Linear Regression Analysis 9

3 Predicting Cure and Credit: Discriminant Analysis 73

4 Identifying Dimensions of Communities: Factor Analysis 123

5 Stacking Beers: Cluster Analysis 165

6 Balancing on Beams: Multivariate Analysis of Variance 193

7 Storing Memories: Repeated Measures Analysis of Variance 255

8 Pursuing Happiness: Hierarchical Log-Linear Models 295

9 Reading the Stars: Further Topics in Log-Linear Models 327

A Data Definition and Management 366

B SPSS^X Command Reference 400

C Answers to Exercises 492

Bibliography 515

Index 518

1 Beginning Simply

People, places, and phenomena usually cannot be described by a single dimension. For example, New York cannot be described by latitude, Mother Teresa by net worth, nor motivation by the number of hours worked in a week. Each has a unique character, resulting from the interplay of numerous and varied attributes. To ignore their multidimensional aspect is to ignore their very essence.

In research, many variables are often needed to describe the outcome of an experiment or the components of a construct. For example, a new type of psychotherapy may simultaneously alter many characteristics of the participant—self-confidence, anxiety level, and number of somatic complaints, to list but a few. When the observed variables are interrelated, as is usually the case, statistical analyses that treat the variables one at a time may ignore much useful information.

For example, in psychological literature, "Meehl's paradox" (1950) provides a simple but powerful example of the importance of the joint distribution of variables. Consider two dichotomously scored test items that are designed to differentiate between two groups, say schizophrenics and normals. Suppose that half of the normals and half of the schizophrenics respond yes to each of the items. The naive researcher would probably dismiss both items as having no predictive power. However, if the responses to the two items together are distributed as shown in Figure 1.0, the two groups can be perfectly distinguished. All normal subjects give the same yes or no response to both items, while schizophrenics never give the same response to both items. Thus, it is essential to analyze both items together.

Figure 1.0 Normals and schizophrenics

TABLE 1.1
JOINT DISTRIBUTION OF TWO ITEMS FOR
100 NORMALS AND 100 SCHIZOPHRENICS

	Normals		Schizophrenics	
	Item 2 Response		Item 2 Response	
	Yes	No	Yes	No
Item 1 Response				
Yes	50	0	0	50
No	0	50	50	0

A special class of statistical techniques, called multivariate methods, have been developed for situations in which several interrelated variables are to be examined together. The goals of multivariate analyses can be quite different, though they share many common features. In *multiple linear regression analysis,* a linear model that relates a dependent variable to a set of independent variables is formulated. For example, an employee's current salary may be expressed as a function of years of education, work experience, job classification, and other related attributes. In *discriminant analysis*, equations that distinguish among members of several mutually exclusive groups are developed. For example, good, bad, and questionable credit risks are differentiated on the basis of income, age, size of family, and other demographic characteristics. In *factor analysis*, a set of variables is summarized by a smaller number of constructs. For example, variables that characterize communities are grouped into three factors.

In *log-linear models*, the relationship between the observed number of cases in the cells of a multidimensional crosstabulation and the variables used for classification is explored. For example, the number of people describing themselves as happy is predicted from marital status, health, and income, as well as the interaction among these variables. In *multivariate analysis of variance,* a wide range of hypotheses about the equality of sets of means for different populations can be tested. Thus, the hypothesis that men and women do not differ on mean scores for four tests of motor ability can be studied. In *cluster analysis*, similar groups of objects are formed based on a variety of attributes. Similar beers can be identified using characteristics such as price, sodium and alcohol content, and number of calories.

This manual focuses on the multivariate statistical procedures available in SPSS^X. However, before using these sophisticated procedures, you should examine your data using basic statistical analyses. The remainder of this chapter is, therefore, devoted to a brief overview of some of the basic statistical procedures available in SPSS^X. The SPSS^X syntax for running these procedures is found in Appendix B. For more detailed information on these capabilities, consult the *SPSS^X Introductory Statistics Guide.*

In Chapter 2, the salaries of 474 people employed by a bank engaged in sex discrimination litigation are analyzed using multiple linear regression. In this chapter, we will explore some useful preliminary steps that might be undertaken before regression analysis. The goals are to examine the distributions of the variables, to look for simple associations, and to obtain summary measures. A particularly important concern is to spot anything suspicious—such as points that may be miscoded or stand apart from the other values.

1.1 THE FREQUENCIES PROCEDURE

The SPSS^X FREQUENCIES procedure is a good starting point for initial analysis. It can be used to calculate frequency tables, bar charts, and histograms, as well as a wide variety of other descriptive statistics.

Figure 1.1a is a frequency table produced by SPSS^X FREQUENCIES for employment category. Each distinct value of this variable is printed along with the value label and number and percentage of cases with that value. Unexpected codes in the table may indicate data entry or coding errors.

Figure 1.1a Frequency table from the FREQUENCIES procedure

JOBCAT EMPLOYMENT CATEGORY

VALUE LABEL	VALUE	FREQUENCY	PERCENT	VALID PERCENT	CUM PERCENT
CLERICAL	1	227	47.9	47.9	47.9
OFFICE TRAINEE	2	136	28.7	28.7	76.6
SECURITY OFFICER	3	27	5.7	5.7	82.3
COLLEGE TRAINEE	4	41	8.6	8.6	90.9
EXEMPT EMPLOYEE	5	32	6.8	6.8	97.7
MBA TRAINEE	6	5	1.1	1.1	98.7
TECHNICAL	7	6	1.3	1.3	100.0
	TOTAL	474	100.0	100.0	

Another way to represent the data displayed in Figure 1.1a is with a bar chart, as shown in Figure 1.1b. There is one bar for each value, with the length of the bar proportional to the number of cases observed in that category. The number of cases is also printed.

Figure 1.1b Bar chart from FREQUENCIES

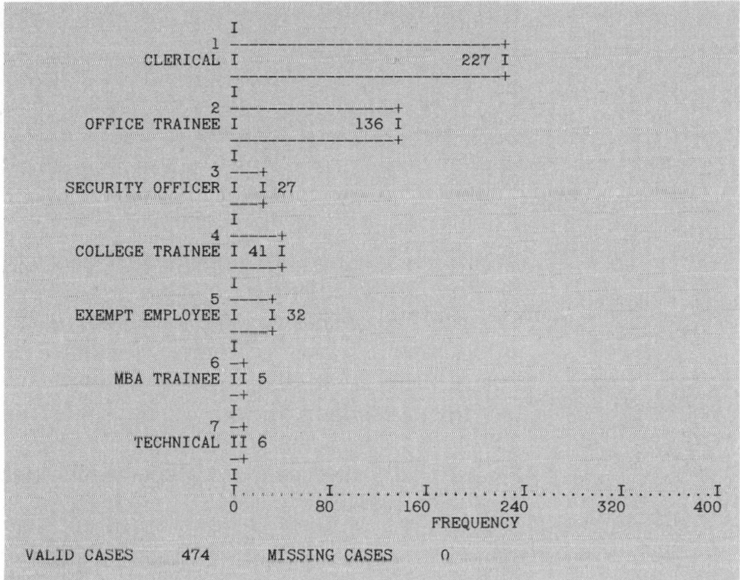

A frequency table or bar chart is a convenient way of summarizing a variable that has a relatively small number of distinct values. For variables that have many different values, such as income or weight, a tally of the number of cases with each observed value may not be very informative. In the worst situation, when all cases have different values, a frequency table is little more than an ordered list of those values.

A histogram is useful for displaying the distribution of variables with many values. The values of the variables are grouped into intervals and the number of cases with values within each interval is tabulated. Figure 1.1c is a histogram of current salary for the bank employees. The first column indicates the number of cases with values within the interval, while the second column gives the interval midpoint. The length of the row of asterisks is proportional to the number of cases with values in the interval. The number of cases represented by each asterisk, printed at the top of the figure, depends on the sample size and the distribution of cases. The distribution of salaries shown in Figure 1.1c is quite asymmetrical, with a tail toward larger salary values.

Figure 1.1c Histogram of salaries from FREQUENCIES

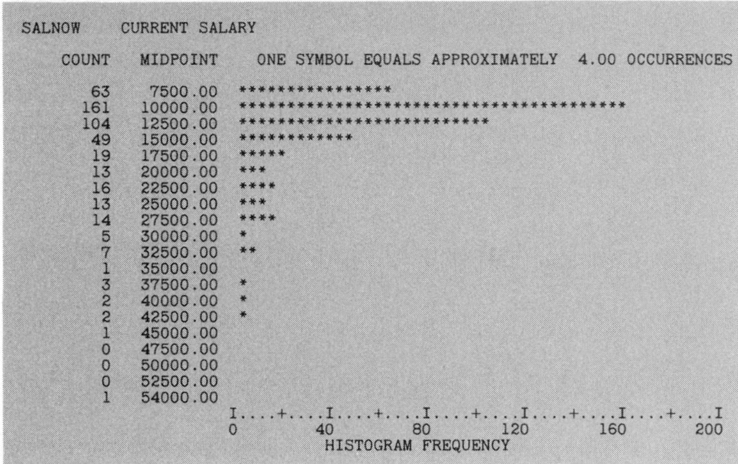

```
SALNOW     CURRENT SALARY

    COUNT    MIDPOINT    ONE SYMBOL EQUALS APPROXIMATELY  4.00 OCCURRENCES

      63      7500.00   ****************
     161     10000.00   ****************************************
     104     12500.00   **************************
      49     15000.00   ************
      19     17500.00   *****
      13     20000.00   ***
      16     22500.00   ****
      13     25000.00   ***
      14     27500.00   ****
       5     30000.00   *
       7     32500.00   **
       1     35000.00
       3     37500.00   *
       2     40000.00   *
       2     42500.00   *
       1     45000.00
       0     47500.00
       0     50000.00
       0     52500.00
       1     54000.00
                        I....+....I....+....I....+....I....+....I....+....I
                        0         40        80        120       160       200
                                  HISTOGRAM FREQUENCY
```

Transformations of variables are often used to modify shapes of distributions so they better comform to those required for various analyses. The SPSS^X COMPUTE command can be used to perform a variety of transformations, such as logs, square roots, and squares, to name a few. For example, taking the natural logs of the current salary variable produces the histogram in Figure 1.1d. Note that the distribution, though still not quite normal, looks better than before.

Figure 1.1d Histogram of transformed variable

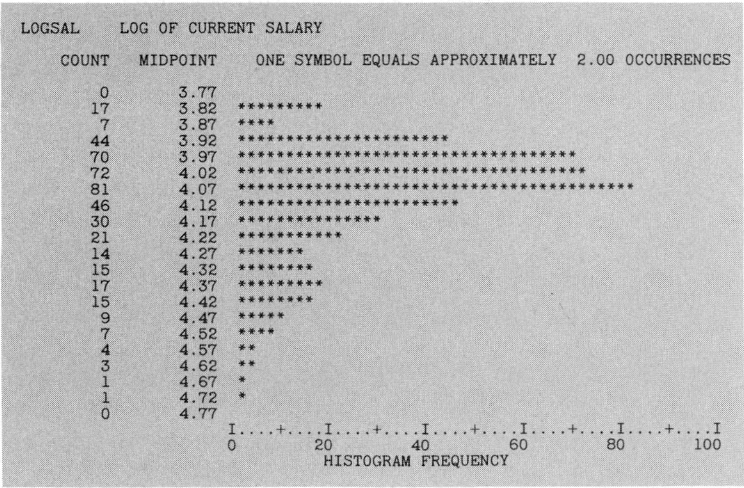

```
LOGSAL     LOG OF CURRENT SALARY

    COUNT    MIDPOINT    ONE SYMBOL EQUALS APPROXIMATELY  2.00 OCCURRENCES

       0         3.77
      17         3.82   *********
       7         3.87   ****
      44         3.92   **********************
      70         3.97   ***********************************
      72         4.02   ************************************
      81         4.07   *****************************************
      46         4.12   ***********************
      30         4.17   ***************
      21         4.22   ***********
      14         4.27   *******
      15         4.32   ********
      17         4.37   *********
      15         4.42   ********
       9         4.47   *****
       7         4.52   ****
       4         4.57   **
       3         4.62   **
       1         4.67   *
       1         4.72   *
       0         4.77
                        I....+....I....+....I....+....I....+....I....+....I
                        0         20        40        60        80        100
                                  HISTOGRAM FREQUENCY
```

Figure 1.1e contains basic descriptive statistics for the current salary variable. The various measures of central tendency, dispersion, and shape summarize the distribution of the variable.

Figure 1.1e Descriptive statistics from FREQUENCIES

```
MEAN        13767.827      STD ERR      313.724      MEDIAN       11550.000
MODE        12300.000      STD DEV     6830.265      VARIANCE  46652514.3
KURTOSIS        5.378      S E KURT       1.996      SKEWNESS         2.125
S E SKEW         .112      RANGE      47700.000      MINIMUM       6300.000
MAXIMUM     54000.000      SUM       6525950.00

VALID CASES       474      MISSING CASES      0
```

1.2 THE CROSSTABS PROCEDURE

The SPSS^X CROSSTABS procedure produces two-way to *n*-way crosstabulations for variables that have a limited number of numeric or string (alphanumeric) values. Cell frequencies, expected frequencies under the assumption of independence, row, column, and total percentages, and a variety of measures of association can also be calculated.

Figure 1.2 shows employment category subdivided by the sex and race of employees. By examining the column percentage (the second entry in the cell), you can see what proportion of cases in each sex-race category falls into each employment category. Additional variables for cross-classification, such as education, can also be included in the table.

In addition to providing substantive information about the relationship among several variables, a crosstabulation can highlight errors in data entry and unusual values that cannot be detected with the FREQUENCIES procedure. For example, a well-paid employee who has not completed grammar school would not be identified as suspicious in FREQUENCIES tables of job classification and education. Jointly, however, the combination is unexpected. Whenever possible, crosstabulations of related variables should be obtained so that anomalies can be identified and corrected before further statistical analysis of the data.

Figure 1.2 Table from the CROSSTABS procedure

```
- - - - - - - - - -   C R O S S T A B U L A T I O N   O F   - - - - - - - - - -
   JOBCAT     EMPLOYMENT CATEGORY
BY  SEXRACE   SEX & RACE CLASSIFICATION
- - - - - - - - - - - - - - - - - - - - - - - - - - - - - - - -  PAGE  1 OF  1

                     SEXRACE
              COUNT  I
            COL PCT  IWHITE    MINORITY WHITE    MINORITY   ROW
                     IMALES    MALES    FEMALES  FEMALES    TOTAL
                     I   1.00I    2.00I    3.00I    4.00I
JOBCAT       --------+--------+--------+--------+--------+
                   1 I    75  I    35  I    85  I    32  I   227
  CLERICAL           I  38.7  I  54.7  I  48.3  I  80.0  I  47.9
                     +--------+--------+--------+--------+
                   2 I    35  I    12  I    81  I     8  I   136
  OFFICE TRAINEE     I  18.0  I  18.8  I  46.0  I  20.0  I  28.7
                     +--------+--------+--------+--------+
                   3 I    14  I    13  I        I        I    27
  SECURITY OFFICER   I   7.2  I  20.3  I        I        I   5.7
                     +--------+--------+--------+--------+
                   4 I    33  I     1  I     7  I        I    41
  COLLEGE TRAINEE    I  17.0  I   1.6  I   4.0  I        I   8.6
                     +--------+--------+--------+--------+
                   5 I    28  I     2  I     2  I        I    32
  EXEMPT EMPLOYEE    I  14.4  I   3.1  I   1.1  I        I   6.8
                     +--------+--------+--------+--------+
                   6 I     3  I     1  I     1  I        I     5
  MBA TRAINEE        I   1.5  I   1.6  I    .6  I        I   1.1
                     +--------+--------+--------+--------+
                   7 I     6  I        I        I        I     6
  TECHNICAL          I   3.1  I        I        I        I   1.3
                     +--------+--------+--------+--------+
             COLUMN      194       64      176       40      474
              TOTAL     40.9     13.5     37.1      8.4    100.0

NUMBER OF MISSING OBSERVATIONS =        0
```

1.3 THE MEANS PROCEDURE

The SPSS^X MEANS procedure can be used to calculate average salaries for groups of employees based on race and sex. Figure 1.3 shows that the average beginning salary for the 474 persons is $6,806. White males have the highest beginning salaries—an average of $8,638—followed by nonwhite males. For each race-sex combination, the average salary, standard deviation, variance, and sample size are printed. The subgroups for which the summary statistics are printed are defined by the values of several variables.

Figure 1.3 Table from the MEANS procedure

```
- - - - - - - - -   D E S C R I P T I O N   O F   S U B P O P U L A T I O N S   - - - - - - - - - -

CRITERION VARIABLE   SALBEG     BEGINNING SALARY
   BROKEN DOWN BY    SEXRACE    SEX & RACE CLASSIFICATION

- - - - - - - - - - - - - - - - - - - - - - - - - - - - - - - - - - - - - - - - - - - - - - - - - - - -

VARIABLE       VALUE  LABEL                       SUM         MEAN     STD DEV   VARIANCE     CASES

FOR ENTIRE POPULATION                       3226250.00   6806.4346   3148.2553 9911511.19      474

SEXRACE         1.00  WHITE MALES           1675680.00   8637.5258   3871.1017 14985428.4      194
SEXRACE         2.00  MINORITY MALES        419424.000   6553.5000   2228.1436 4964624.00       64
SEXRACE         3.00  WHITE FEMALES         939926.000   5340.4886   1225.9605 1502979.07      176
SEXRACE         4.00  MINORITY FEMALES      191220.000   4780.5000    771.4188 595086.923       40

  TOTAL CASES =      474
```

Examining tables containing descriptive statistics for subgroups of cases will help you gain familiarity with the data. As the number of variables on which cases are cross-classified increases, however, the number of cases in each cell rapidly diminishes, making statistically meaningful comparisons difficult.

1.4 THE PLOT PROCEDURE

The relationship between two interval-valued variables can be examined using the SPSS^X PLOT facility. One PLOT option permits points on the scatterplot to be identified by the values of a control variable such as sex. Basic regression statistics can also be printed. PLOT also provides opportunities for detecting unusual observations that may influence subsequent analyses.

Figure 1.4 is a plot of beginning versus current salaries. As expected, beginning and current salaries are linearly related, with current salaries increasing with beginning salaries.

Figure 1.4 Output from the PLOT procedure

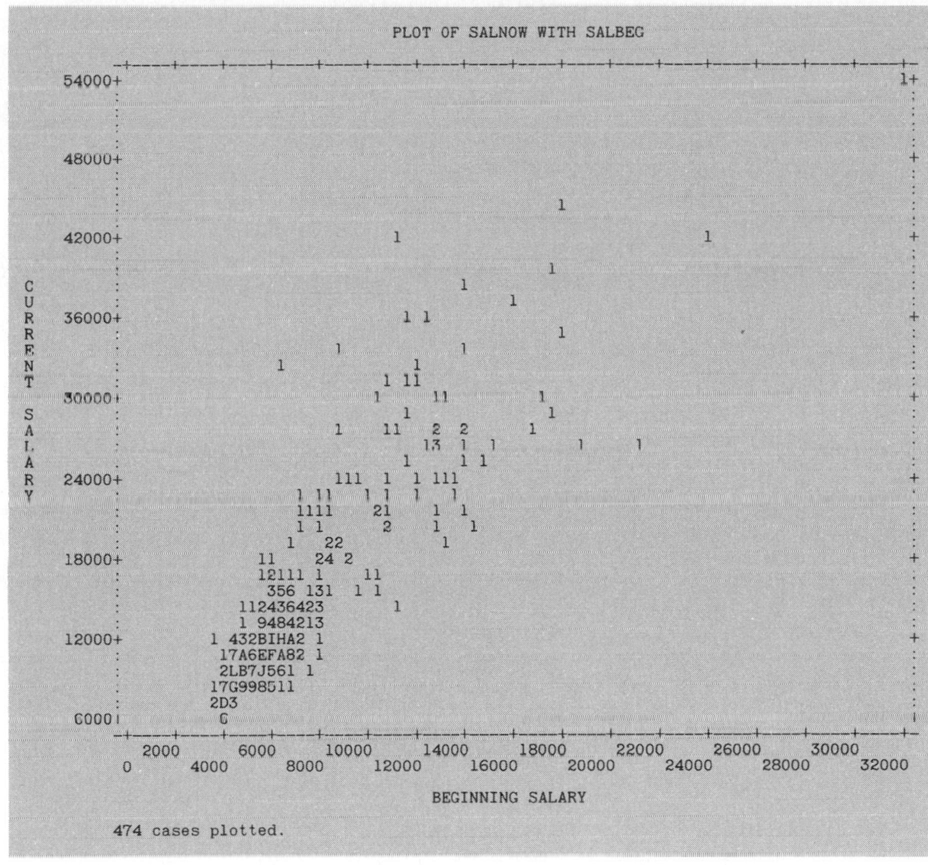

1.5 OTHER PROCEDURES

Examples of output from the most commonly used SPSS^X procedures are presented above. There are many other statistical procedures, however, that have not been illustrated. SPSS^X contains facilities for performing t-tests (procedure T-TEST), calculating analysis of variance tables and multiple comparisons (ONEWAY and ANOVA), obtaining nonparametric tests (NPAR TESTS), and calculating correlation coefficients (CORRELATIONS, PARTIAL CORR, and NONPAR CORR). Summary instructions for running these procedures are in Appendix B. See *SPSS^X User's Guide* for additional statistical capabilities that are not documented in this manual.

2

Multiple Linear Regression Analysis

In this chapter:

Goals:

- To develop an equation that summarizes the relationship between a dependent variable and a set of independent variables.
- To identify the subset of independent variables that are most useful for predicting the dependent variable.
- To predict values for a dependent variable from the values of the independent variables.

Examples:

- Determine the relationship between systolic blood pressure and age, weight, height, cigarettes smoked, and level of physical activity.
- Predict a salesperson's total dollar sales for the year based on years of experience, age, sales territory, years of education, and sex.
- Predict a student's score on the Graduate Record Exam based on undergraduate GPA, IQ score, and major.

How it's done:

A linear model of the form

$$\hat{Y} = B_0 + B_1X_1 + B_2X_2 + \dots + B_nX_n$$

where $\hat{Y}$ is the dependent variable and X_1 to X_n are the independent variables is formulated. The coefficients for the independent variables are chosen so that the sum of the squared differences between the observed and predicted values of the dependent variable based on the model is as small as possible. Various diagnostic plots and statistics are used to identify departures from the model and "unusual" points.

Data considerations:

Each case must have values for the dependent and independent variables. For all combinations of values of the independent variables, the distribution of the dependent variable must be normal with a constant variance. The independent and dependent variables should be measured on an interval scale. (Binary variables satisfy this requirement.) Nominal variables such as religion, major, or region of residence must be recoded to binary (dummy) variables.

General references:

Draper & Smith (1981)
Belsley, Kuh, & Welsch (1980)
Gunst & Mason (1980)

Contents

2.1 LINEAR REGRESSION
2.2 Outliers
2.3 Choosing a Regression Line
2.4 The Standardized Regression Coefficient
2.5 From Samples to Populations
2.6 Estimating Population Parameters
2.7 Testing Hypotheses
2.8 Confidence Intervals
2.9 Goodness of Fit
2.10 The R^2 Coefficient
2.11 Analysis of Variance
2.12 Another Interpretation of R^2
2.13 Predicted Values and Their Standard Errors
2.14 Predicting Mean Response
2.15 Predicting a New Value
2.16 Reading the Casewise Plot
2.17 Searching for Violations of Assumptions
2.18 Residuals
2.19 Linearity
2.20 Equality of Variance
2.21 Independence of Error
2.22 Normality
2.23 Locating Outliers
2.24 Other Unusual Observations: Mahalanobis' Distance
2.25 Influential Cases: Deleted Residuals and Cook's Distance
2.26 When Assumptions Appear To Be Violated
2.27 Coaxing a Nonlinear Relationship to Linearity
2.28 Coping with Skewness
2.29 Stabilizing the Variance
2.30 Transforming the Salary Data
2.31 A Final Comment on Assumptions
2.32 MULTIPLE REGRESSION MODELS
2.33 Predictors of Beginning Salary
2.34 The Correlation Matrix
2.35 Correlation Matrices and Missing Data
2.36 Partial Regression Coefficients
2.37 Determining Important Variables
2.38 Beta Coefficients
2.39 Part and Partial Coefficients
2.40 Variance of the Estimators
2.41 Building a Model
2.42 Adding and Deleting Variables
2.43 Statistics for Variables Not in the Equation
2.44 The "Optimal" Number of Independent Variables
2.45 Procedures for Selecting Variables
2.46 Forward Selection
2.47 Backward Elimination
2.48 Stepwise Selection
2.49 Checking for Violation of Assumptions
2.50 Interpreting the Equation
2.51 Statistics for Unselected Cases
2.52 Problems of Multicollinearity
2.53 Methods of Detection
2.54 SPSS^X and Multicollinearity
2.55 RUNNING PROCEDURE REGRESSION
2.56 Building the Equation
2.57 The VARIABLES and DEPENDENT Subcommands
2.58 The METHOD Subcommand
2.59 The CRITERIA Subcommand
2.60 The STATISTICS Subcommand
2.61 The ORIGIN Subcommand
2.62 The SELECT Subcommand
2.63 The MISSING Subcommand
2.64 The DESCRIPTIVES Subcommand
2.65 Analyzing Residuals
2.66 The RESIDUALS Subcommand
2.67 The CASEWISE Subcommand
2.68 The SCATTERPLOT Subcommand
2.69 The PARTIALPLOT Subcommand
2.70 The SAVE Subcommand
2.71 The REGWGT Subcommand
2.72 The MATRIX Subcommand
2.73 The WIDTH Subcommand
2.74 EXERCISES

2 Modeling Salary: Multiple Linear Regression Analysis

The 1964 Civil Rights Act prohibits discrimination in the workplace based on sex or race. Employers who violate the act, by unfair hiring or advancement, are liable to prosecution. Numerous lawsuits have been filed on behalf of women, blacks, and other groups on these grounds.

The courts have ruled that statistics can be used as *prima facie* evidence of discrimination. Many lawsuits depend heavily on complex statistical analyses, which attempt to demonstrate that similarly qualified individuals are not treated equally (Roberts, 1980). In this chapter, employee records for 474 individuals hired between 1969 and 1971 by a bank engaged in Equal Employment Opportunity litigation are analyzed. A mathematical model is developed that relates beginning salary and salary progression to various employee characteristics such as seniority, education, and previous work experience. One objective is to determine whether sex and race are important predictors of salary.

The technique used to build the model is linear regression analysis, one of the most versatile data analysis procedures. Regression can be used to summarize data as well as to study relations among variables.

2.1 LINEAR REGRESSION

Before examining a model that relates beginning salary to several other variables, consider the relationship between beginning salary and current (as of March 1977) salary. For employees hired during a similar time period, beginning salary should serve as a reasonably good predictor of salary at a later date. Although superstars and underachievers might progress differently from the group as a whole, salary progression should be similar for the others. The scatterplot of beginning salary and current salary produced by the PLOT procedure and shown in Figure 2.1 supports this hypothesis.

Figure 2.1 Scatterplot of beginning and current salaries

```
PLOT VERTICAL=MIN(0) /HORIZONTAL=MIN(0) /VSIZE=35
   /CUTPOINTS=EVERY(3) /SYMBOLS='.+*#@@@@@@'
   /PLOT=SALNOW WITH SALBEG
```

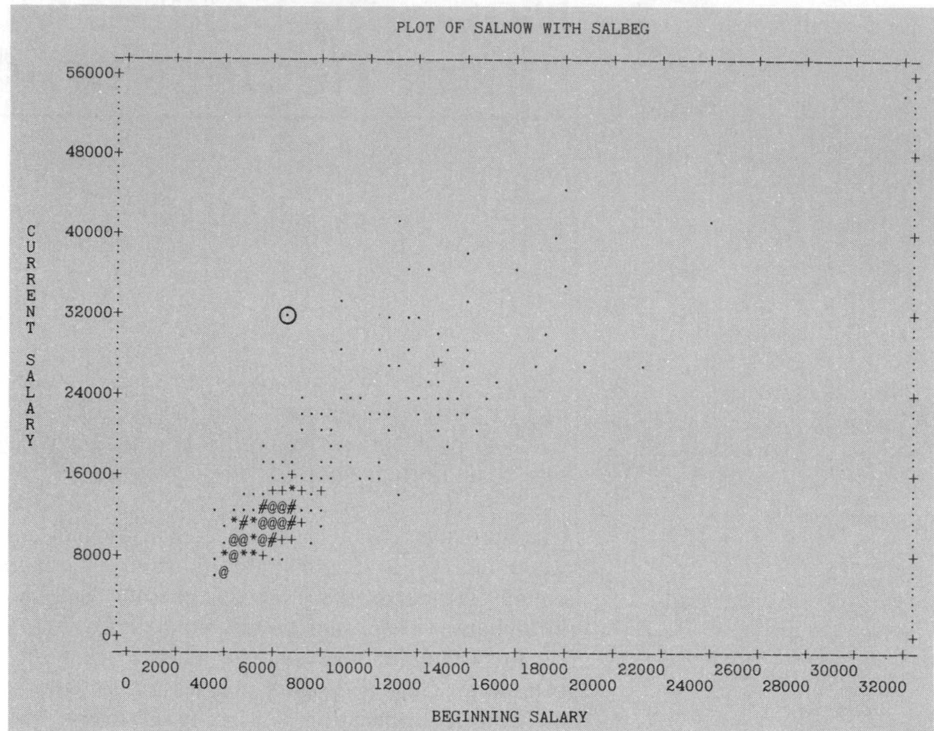

A scatterplot may suggest what type of mathematical functions would be appropriate for summarizing the data. A variety of functions are useful in fitting models to data. Parabolas, hyperbolas, polynomials, trigonometric functions, and many more are potential candidates. For the scatterplot in Figure 2.1, current salaries tend to increase linearly with increases in beginning salary. If the plot indicates that a straight line is not a good summary measure of the relationship, you should consider other possibilities, including attempts to transform the data to achieve linearity (see Section 2.27).

2.2 Outliers

A plot may also indicate the presence of points suspiciously different from the others. Examine such observations, termed *outliers*, carefully to see if they result from errors in gathering, coding, or entering data. The circled point in Figure 2.1 appears to be an outlier. Though neither the value of beginning salary ($6,300) nor the value of current salary ($32,000) is unique, jointly they are unusual.

The treatment of outliers can be difficult. If the point is really incorrect, due to coding or entry problems, you should correct it and rerun the analysis. If there is no apparent explanation for the outlier, consider interactions with other variables as a possible explanation. For example, the outlier may represent an employee who was hired as a low-paid clerical worker while pursuing an MBA degree. After graduation, a rapid rise in position was possible, making education the variable that explains the unusual salary characteristics of the employee.

2.3 Choosing a Regression Line

Since current salary tends to increase linearly with beginning salary, a straight line can be used to summarize the relationship. The equation for the line is

$$\text{predicted current salary} = B_0 + B_1(\text{beginning salary}) \qquad \textbf{Equation 2.3a}$$

The *slope* (B_1) is the dollar change in the fitted current salary for a dollar change in the beginning salary. The *intercept* (B_0) is the theoretical estimate of current salary if there were a beginning salary of 0.

However, the observed data points do not all fall on a straight line but cluster about it. Many lines can be drawn through the data points; the problem is to select among them. The method of *least squares* results in a line that minimizes the sum of squared vertical distances from the observed data points to the line. Any other line has a larger sum. Figure 2.3a shows the least-squares line superimposed on the salary scatterplot. Several vertical distances from points to the line are also shown.

Figure 2.3a Regression line for beginning and current salaries

```
PLOT FORMAT=REGRESSION
  /VERTICAL=MIN(0) /HORIZONTAL=MIN(0) /VSIZE=35
  /CUTPOINTS=EVERY(3) /SYMBOLS='.+*#@@@@@@'
  /PLOT=SALNOW WITH SALBEG
```

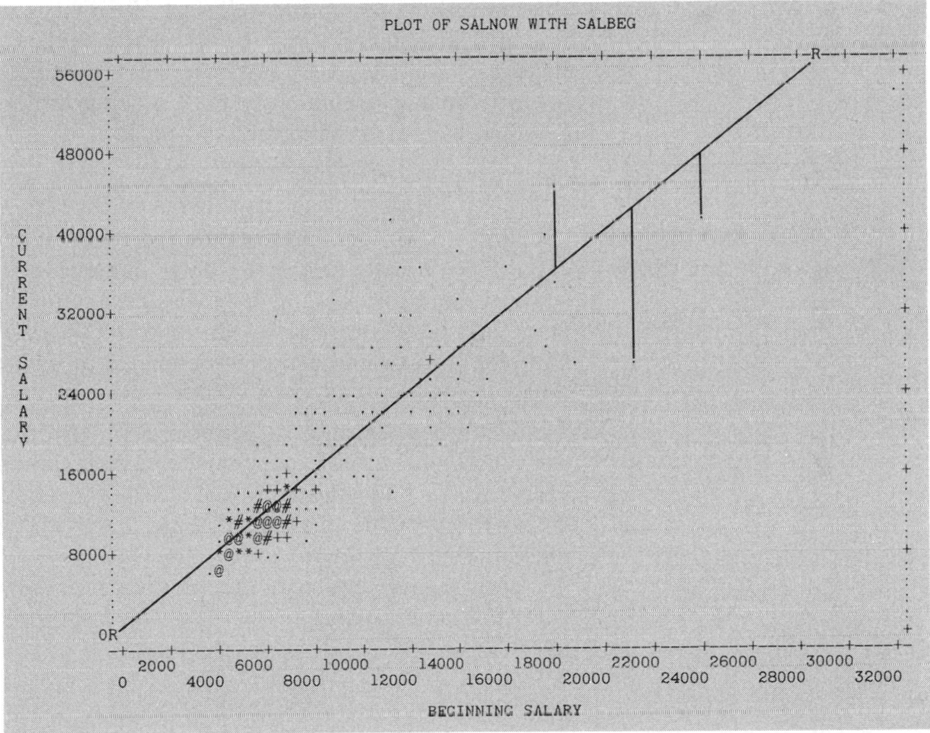

You can use the SPSS^X REGRESSION procedure to calculate the least-squares line. For the data in Figure 2.1, that line is

predicted current salary = 771.28 + 1.91(beginning salary) **Equation 2.3b**

The slope and intercept values are shown in the column labeled B in the output shown in Figure 2.3b.

Figure 2.3b Statistics for variables in the equation

```
REGRESSION VARIABLES=SALBEG, SALNOW
  /DEPENDENT=SALNOW
  /METHOD=ENTER SALBEG
```

```
----------------- Variables in the Equation ------------------

Variable              B         SE B       Beta         T  Sig T

SALBEG          1.90945       .04741     .88012    40.276  .0000
(Constant)    771.28230    355.47194                2.170  .0305
```

2.4 The Standardized Regression Coefficient

The *standardized regression coefficient*, labeled Beta in Figure 2.3b, is defined as

$$BETA = B_1 \frac{S_X}{S_Y}$$ **Equation 2.4**

Multiplying the regression coefficient (B_1) by the ratio of the standard deviation of the independent variable (S_X) to the standard deviation of the dependent variable (S_Y) results in a dimensionless coefficient. In fact, the Beta coefficient is the slope of the least-squares line when both X and Y are expressed as Z scores. The Beta coefficient is further discussed in Section 2.38.

2.5 From Samples to Populations

Generally, more is sought in regression analysis than a description of observed data. One usually wishes to draw inferences about the relationship of the variables in the population from which the sample was taken. How are beginning and current salaries related for all employees, not just those included in the sample? To draw inferences about population values based on sample results, the following assumptions are needed:

Normality and Equality of Variance. For any fixed value of the independent variable X, the distribution of the dependent variable Y is normal, with mean $\mu_{Y/X}$ (the mean of Y for a given X) and a constant variance of σ^2 (see Figure 2.5). This assumption specifies that not all employees with the same beginning salary have the same current salary. Instead, there is a normal distribution of current salaries for each beginning salary. Though the distributions have different means, they have the same variance σ^2.

Figure 2.5 Regression assumptions

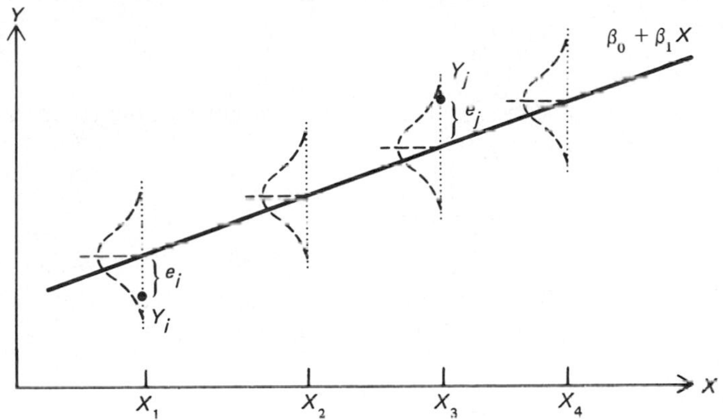

Independence. The *Y*'s are statistically independent of each other. That is, observations are in no way influenced by other observations. For example, observations are *not* independent if they are based on repeated measurements from the same experimental unit. If three observations are taken from each of four families, the twelve observations are not independent.

Linearity. The mean values $\mu_{Y/X}$ all lie on a straight line, which is the population regression line. This line is drawn in Figure 2.5. An alternative way of stating this assumption is that the linear model is correct.

When there is a single independent variable, the model can be summarized by

$$Y_i = \beta_0 + \beta_1 X_i + e_i$$ **Equation 2.5**

The population parameters (values) for the slope and intercept are denoted by β_1 and β_0. The term e_i, often called an error or disturbance, is the difference between the observed value of Y_i and the subpopulation mean at the point X_i. The e_i are assumed to be normally distributed, independent, random variables with a mean of 0 and variance of σ^2 (see Figure 2.5).

2.6 Estimating Population Parameters

Since β_0 and β_1 are unknown population parameters, they must be estimated from the sample. The least-squares coefficients B_0 and B_1, discussed in Section 2.3, are used to estimate the population parameters.

However, the slope and intercept estimated from a single sample typically differ from the population values and vary from sample to sample. To use these estimates for inference about the population values, the sampling distributions of the two statistics are needed. When the assumptions of linear regression are met, the sampling distributions of B_0 and B_1 are normal with means of β_0 and β_1.

The standard error of B_0 is

$$\sigma_{B_0} = \sigma \sqrt{\frac{1}{N} + \frac{\bar{X}^2}{(N-1)S_X{}^2}}$$ **Equation 2.6a**

where $S_X{}^2$ is the sample variance of the independent variable. The standard error of B_1 is

$$\sigma_{B_1} = \frac{\sigma}{\sqrt{(N-1)S_X{}^2}}$$ **Equation 2.6b**

Since the population variance of the errors, σ^2, is not known, it must also be estimated. The usual estimate of σ^2 is

$$S^2 = \frac{\sum_{i=1}^{N} (Y_i - B_0 - B_1X_i)^2}{N-2}$$ **Equation 2.6c**

The positive square root of σ^2 is termed the *standard error of the estimate,* or the standard deviation of the residuals. (The reason for this name is discussed in Section 2.15.) The estimated standard errors of the slope and intercept are printed in the third column (labeled SE B) in Figure 2.3b.

2.7 Testing Hypotheses

A frequently tested hypothesis is that there is no linear relationship between X and Y—that the slope of the population regression line is 0. The statistic used to test this hypothesis is

$$t = \frac{B_1}{S_{B_1}}$$ **Equation 2.7a**

The distribution of the statistic, when the assumptions are met and the hypothesis of no linear relationship is true, is Student's t distribution with $N-2$ degrees of freedom. The statistic for testing the hypothesis that the intercept is 0 is

$$t = \frac{B_0}{S_{B_0}}$$ **Equation 2.7b**

Its distribution is also Student's t with $N-2$ degrees of freedom.

These t statistics and their two-tailed observed significance levels are displayed in the last two columns of Figure 2.3b. The small observed significance level (less than 0.00005) associated with the slope for the salary data supports the hypothesis that beginning and current salary are linearly related.

2.8 Confidence Intervals

A statistic calculated from a sample provides a point estimate of the unknown parameter. A point estimate can be thought of as the single best guess for the population value. While the estimated value from the sample is typically different from the value of the unknown population parameter, the hope is that it isn't too far away. Based on the sample estimate, it is possible to calculate a range of values that, with a designated likelihood, includes the population value. Such a range is called a *confidence interval*. For example, as shown in Figure 2.8, the 95% confidence interval for β_1, the population slope, is 1.816 to 2.003.

Figure 2.8 Confidence intervals

```
REGRESSION VARIABLES=SALBEG, SALNOW
  /STATISTICS=CI
  /DEPENDENT=SALNOW
  /METHOD=ENTER SALBEG
```

Variable	95% Confdnce Intrvl B	
SALBEG	1.81629	2.00261
(Constant)	72.77921	1469.78540

Ninety-five percent confidence means that, if repeated samples are drawn from a population under the same conditions and 95% confidence intervals are calculated, 95% of the intervals will contain the unknown parameter β_1. Since the parameter value is unknown, it is not possible to determine whether or not a particular interval contains it.

2.9 Goodness of Fit

An important part of any statistical procedure that builds models from data is establishing how well the model actually fits. This topic encompasses the detection of possible violations of the required assumptions in the data being analyzed. Sections 2.10 through 2.16 are limited to the question of how close to the fitted line the observed points fall. Subsequent sections discuss other assumptions and tests for their violation.

2.10 The R^2 Coefficient

A commonly used measure of the goodness of fit of a linear model is R^2, sometimes called the *coefficient of determination*. It can be thought of in a variety of ways. Besides being the square of the correlation coefficient between variables X and Y, it is the square of the correlation coefficient between Y, the observed value of the dependent variable, and $\hat{Y}$, the predicted value of Y from the fitted line. If for each employee one computes (based on the coefficients in the output in Figure 2.3b) the predicted salary

predicted current salary = 771.28 + 1.91(beginning salary) **Equation 2.10a**

and then calculates the square of the Pearson correlation coefficent between predicted current salary and observed current salary, R^2 is obtained. If all the observations fall on the regression line, R^2 is 1. If there is no linear relationship between the dependent and independent variables, R^2 is 0.

Note that R^2 is a measure of the goodness of fit of a particular model and that an R^2 of 0 does not necessarily mean that there is no association between the variables. Instead, it indicates that there is no *linear relationship*.

In the output in Figure 2.10, R^2 is labeled R Square; its square root is called Multiple R. The sample R^2 tends to be an optimistic estimate of how well the model fits the population. The model usually does not fit the population as well as it fits the sample from which it is derived. The statistic *adjusted* R^2 attempts to correct R^2 to more closely reflect the goodness of fit of the model in the population. Adjusted R^2 is given by

$$R_a{}^2 = R^2 - \frac{p(1 - R^2)}{N - p - 1}$$ **Equation 2.10b**

where p is the number of independent variables in the equation (1 in the salary example).

Figure 2.10 Summary statistics for the equation

```
REGRESSION VARIABLES=SALBEG, SALNOW
  /DEPENDENT=SALNOW
  /METHOD=ENTER SALBEG
```

```
Multiple R              .88012      Analysis of Variance
R Square                .77461                          DF      Sum of Squares       Mean Square
Adjusted R Square       .77413      Regression           1   17092967800.01931 17092967800.0193
Standard Error      3246.14226      Residual           472    4973671469.79484    10537439.55465

                                    F =      1622.11776       Signif F =  .0000
```

2.11 Analysis of Variance

To test the hypothesis of no linear relationship between X and Y, several equivalent statistics can be computed. When there is a single independent variable, the hypothesis that the population R^2 is 0 is identical to the hypothesis that the population slope is 0. The test for $R^2_{pop}=0$ is usually obtained from the *analysis of variance* (ANOVA) table (see Figure 2.11a).

Figure 2.11a Analysis of variance table

```
REGRESSION VARIABLES=SALBEG, SALNOW
  /DEPENDENT=SALNOW
  /METHOD=ENTER SALBEG
```

```
Analysis of Variance
                    DF      Sum of Squares       Mean Square
Regression           1   17092967800.01931 17092967800.0193
Residual           472    4973671469.79484    10537439.55465

F =      1622.11776       Signif F =  .0000
```

The total observed variability in the dependent variable is subdivided into two components—that which is attributable to the regression (labeled Regression) and that which is not (labeled Residual). Consider Figure 2.11b. For a particular point, the distance from Y_i to $\bar{Y}$ (the mean of the Y's) can be subdivided into two parts.

$$Y_i - \bar{Y} = (Y_i - \hat{Y}_i) + (\hat{Y}_i - \bar{Y})$$ **Equation 2.11a**

Figure 2.11b Components of variability

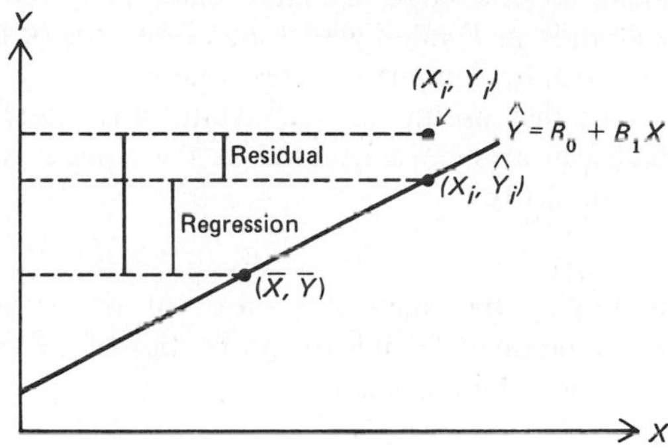

The distance from Y_i, the observed value, to $\hat{Y}_i$, the value predicted by the regression line, or $Y_i - \hat{Y}_i$, is 0 if the regression line passes through the point. It is called the *residual from the regression.* The second component $(\hat{Y}_i - \bar{Y})$ is the distance from the regression line to the mean of the Y's. This distance is "explained" by the regression in that it represents the improvement in the estimate of the dependent variable achieved by the regression. Without the regression, the mean of the dependent variable $(\bar{Y})$ is used as the estimate. It can be shown that

$$\sum_{i=1}^{N} (Y_i - \bar{Y})^2 = \sum_{i=1}^{N} (Y_i - \hat{Y}_i)^2 + \sum_{i=1}^{N} (\hat{Y}_i - \bar{Y})^2$$ **Equation 2.11b**

The first quantity following the equals sign is called the *residual sum of squares* and the second quantity is the *regression sum of squares.* The sum of these is called the *total sum of squares.*

The analysis of variance table displays these two sums of squares under the heading Sum of Squares (Figure 2.11a). The Mean Square for each entry is the Sum of Squares divided by the degrees of freedom (DF). If the regression assumptions are met, the ratio of the mean square regression to the mean square residual is distributed as an F statistic with p and $N-p-1$ degrees of freedom. F serves to test how well the regression model fits the data. If the probability associated with the F statistic is small, the hypothesis that $R^2_{pop}=0$ is rejected. For this example, the F statistic is

$$F = \frac{\text{MEAN SQUARE REGRESSION}}{\text{MEAN SQUARE RESIDUAL}} = 1622$$ **Equation 2.11c**

The observed significance level (SIGNIF F) is less than 0.00005.

The square root of the F value (1622) is 40.28, which is the value of the t statistic for the slope in Figure 2.3b. The square of a t value with k degrees of freedom is an F value with 1 and k degrees of freedom. Therefore, either t or F values can be computed to test that $\beta_i=0$.

Another useful summary statistic is the standard error of the estimate, S, which can also be calculated as the square root of the residual mean square (Section 2.15).

2.12 Another Interpretation of R^2

Partitioning the sum of squares of the dependent variable allows another interpretation of R^2. It is the proportion of the variation in the dependent variable "explained" by the model.

$$R^2 = 1 - \frac{\text{RESIDUAL SUM OF SQUARES}}{\text{TOTAL SUM OF SQUARES}} = 0.775 \quad \textbf{Equation 2.12a}$$

Similarly, adjusted R^2 is

$$R_a^2 = 1 - \frac{\text{RESIDUAL SUM OF SQUARES}/(N - p - 1)}{\text{TOTAL SUM OF SQUARES}/(N - 1)} \quad \textbf{Equation 2.12b}$$

where p is the number of independent variables in the equation (1 in the salary example).

2.13 Predicted Values and Their Standard Errors

By comparing the observed values of the dependent variable to the values predicted by the regression equation, you can learn a good deal about how well a model and the various assumptions fit the data (see the discussion of residuals beginning with Section 2.17). Predicted values are also of interest when the results are used to predict new data. You may wish to predict the mean Y for all cases with a given value of X, denoted X_0, or to predict the value of Y for a single case. For example, you can predict either the mean salary for all employees with a beginning salary of $10,000 or the salary for a particular employee with a beginning salary of $10,000. In both situations, the predicted value

$$\hat{Y}_0 = B_0 + B_1X_0 = 771 + 1.91 \times 10{,}000 = 19{,}871 \quad \textbf{Equation 2.13}$$

is the same. What differs is the standard error.

2.14 Predicting Mean Response

The estimated standard error for the predicted mean Y at X_0 is

$$S_{\hat{Y}} = S\sqrt{\frac{1}{N} + \frac{(X_0 - \overline{X})^2}{(N-1)S_X{}^2}} \quad \textbf{Equation 2.14a}$$

The equation for the standard error shows that the smallest value occurs when X_0 is equal to $\overline{X}$, the mean of X. The larger the distance from the mean, the greater the standard error. Thus, the mean of Y for a given X is better estimated for central values of the observed X's than for outlying values. Figure 2.14a is a plot from the PLOT procedure of the standard errors of predicted mean salaries for different values of beginning salary.

Figure 2.14a Standard errors for predicted mean responses

```
REGRESSION VARIABLES=SALBEG, SALNOW
  /DEPENDENT=SALNOW
  /METHOD=ENTER SALBEG
  /SAVE=SEPRED(SE)
PLOT CUTPOINTS=EVERY(20) /SYMBOLS='*'
      /PLOT=SE WITH SALBEG
```

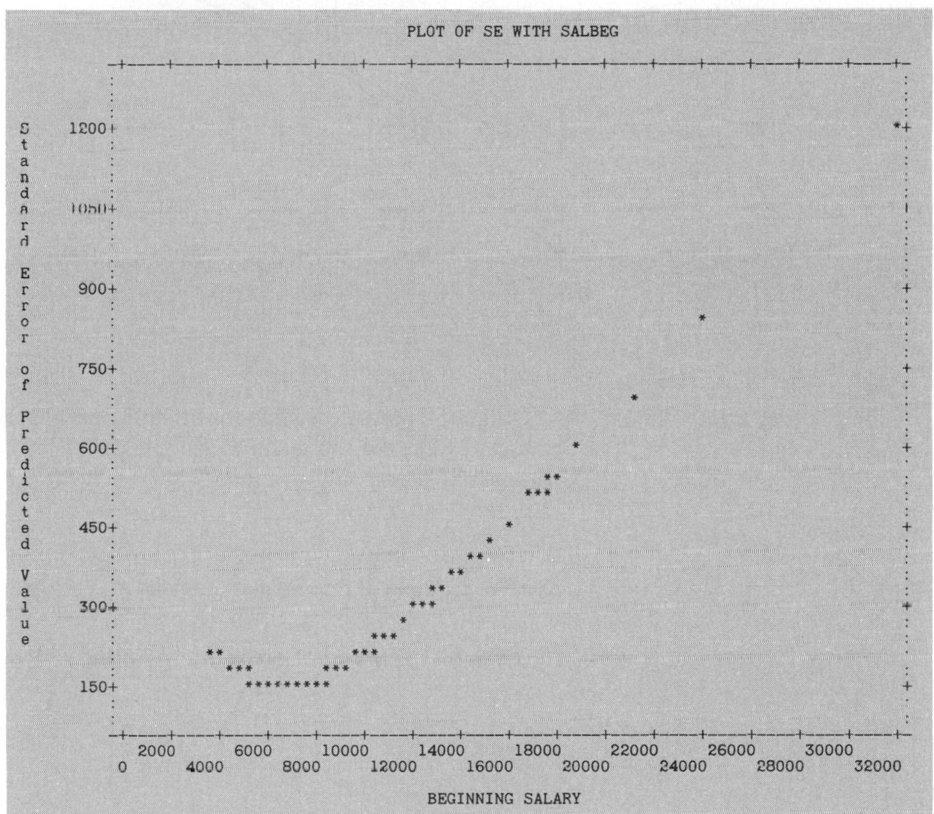

Prediction intervals for the mean predicted salary are calculated in the standard way. The 95% confidence interval at X_0 is

$$\hat{Y} \pm t_{\left(1-\frac{\alpha}{2},N-2\right)} S_{\hat{Y}}$$ **Equation 2.14b**

Figure 2.14b shows a typical 95% confidence band for predicted mean responses. It is narrowest at the mean of X and increases as the distance from the mean $(X_0-\overline{X})$ increases.

Figure 2.14b 95% confidence band for mean prediction

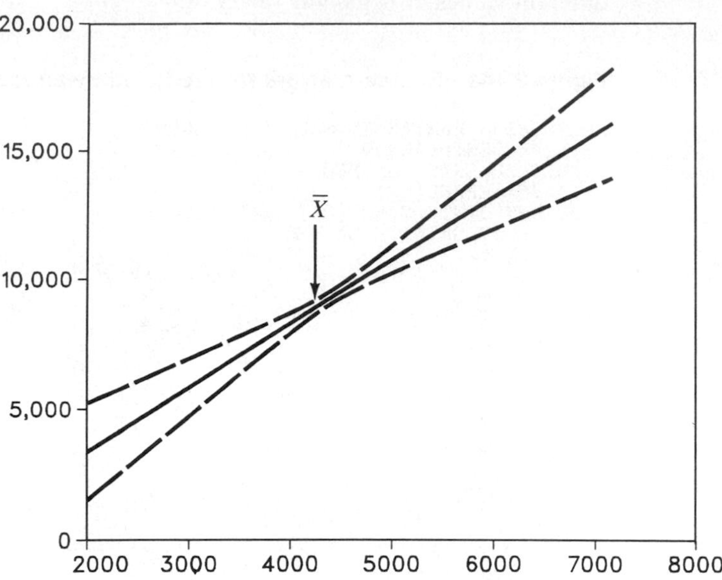

2.15 Predicting a New Value

Although the predicted value for a single new observation at X_0 is the same as the predicted value for the mean at X_0, the standard error is not. The two sources of error when predicting an individual observation are illustrated in Figure 2.15. They are

1 The individual value may differ from the population mean of Y for X_0.

2 The estimate of the population mean at X_0 may differ from the population mean.

Figure 2.15 Sources of error in predicting individual observations

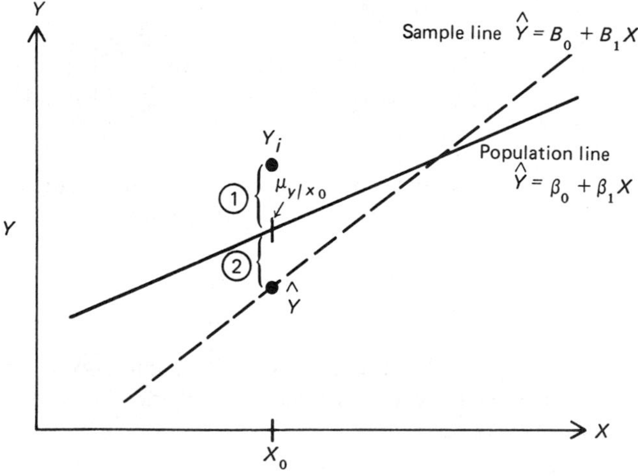

When estimating the mean response, only the second error component is considered. The variance of the individual prediction is the variance of the mean prediction plus the variance of Y_i for a given X. This can be written as

$$S^2_{ind\hat{Y}} = S^2_{\hat{Y}} + S^2 = S^2\left(1 + \frac{1}{N} + \frac{(X_0 - \overline{X})^2}{(N-1)S_X{}^2}\right) \qquad \textbf{Equation 2.15a}$$

Prediction intervals for the new observation are obtained by substituting S_{indY} for S_Y in the equation for the confidence intervals for the mean given in Section 2.14. If the sample size is large, the terms $1/N$ and

$$\frac{(X_0 - \overline{X})^2}{(N-1)S_X{}^2} \qquad \textbf{Equation 2.15b}$$

are negligible. In that case, the standard error is simply S, which explains the name *standard error of the estimate* for S (see Section 2.6).

2.16 Reading the Casewise Plot

Figure 2.16 shows the output from the beginning and end of a plot of the salary data. The sequence number of the case and an optional labeling variable (SEXRACE) are listed first, followed by the plot of standardized residuals, the observed (SALNOW), predicted (PRED), and residual (RESID) values, and, finally, the standard error of the mean prediction (SEPRED). The variance of an individual prediction can be obtained by adding S^2 to the square of each of the standard error values. You can generate predicted values and the standard errors of the mean responses in the REGRESSION procedure, and you can display both of these values for all cases or for a subset of cases along with a casewise plot.

Figure 2.16 Casewise plot with predicted values and standard errors

```
REGRESSION VARIABLES=SALBEG,SALNOW
  /DEPENDENT=SALNOW
  /METHOD=ENTER SALBEG
  /RESIDUALS=ID(SEXRACE)
  /CASEWISE=ALL DEPENDENT PRED RESID SEPRED
```

```
Casewise Plot of Standardized Residual

*: Selected   M: Missing

                 -3.0             0.0              3.0
Case # SEXRACE    0:...............:...............:0  SALNOW      *PRED     *RESID   *SEPRED
     1       1    .               *.                .   16080 16810.6600  -730.6600  167.1489
     2       1    .       *        .                .   41400 46598.0758 -5198.0758  828.6655
     3       1    .                .  *             .   21960 20247.6695  1712.3305  219.3531
     4       1    .                .  *             .   19200 17383.4949  1816.5051  174.0406
     5       1    .      *         .                .   28350 33995.7076 -5645.7076  523.9021
     6       1    .                .  *             .   27250 25586.4910  1663.5090  329.1520
     7       1    .                .  *             .   16080 13946.4854  2133.5146  149.1662
     8       1    .                .    *           .   14100 11082.3108  3017.6892  163.3307
     9       1    .                .  *             .   12420 10394.9089  2025.0911  171.0096
    10       1    .               *.                .   12300 12800.8156  -500.8156  151.0211
    11       1    .                .   *            .   15720 12800.8156  2919.1844  151.0211
    12       1    .           *    .                .    8880 12227.9807 -3347.9807  153.9241
   ...
   ...
   ...
   470       4    .                *                .    9420  9592.9401  -172.9401  181.5927
   471       4    .                .*               .    9780  9134.6721   645.3279  188.3196
   472       4    .              * .                .    7680  9249.2391 -1569.2391  186.5956
   473       4    .              * .                .    7380  8561.8372 -1181.8372  197.3294
   474       4    .            *   .                .    8340 10738.6099 -2398.6099  166.9964
Case # SEXRACE    0:...............:...............:0  SALNOW      *PRED     *RESID   *SEPRED
                 -3.0             0.0              3.0
```

2.17 Searching for Violations of Assumptions

You usually don't know in advance whether a model such as linear regression is appropriate. Therefore, it is necessary to conduct a search focused on residuals to look for evidence that the necessary assumptions are violated.

2.18 Residuals

In model building, a *residual* is what is left after the model is fit. It is the difference between an observed value and the value predicted by the model.

$$E_i = Y_i - B_0 - B_1X_i = Y_i - \hat{Y}_i \qquad \textbf{Equation 2.18}$$

In regression analysis, the true errors e_i are assumed to be independent normal values with a mean of 0 and a constant variance of σ^2. If the model is appropriate for the data, the observed residuals E_i, which are estimates of the true errors e_i, should have similar characteristics.

If the intercept term is included in the equation, the mean of the residuals is always 0, so it provides no information about the true mean of the errors. Since the sum of the residuals is constrained to be 0, they are *not* strictly independent. However, if the number of residuals is large when compared to the number of independent variables, the dependency among the residuals can be ignored for practical purposes.

The relative magnitudes of residuals are easier to judge when they are divided by estimates of their standard deviations. The resulting standardized residuals are expressed in standard deviation units above or below the mean. For example, the fact that a particular residual is −5198.1 provides little information. If you know that its standardized form is −3.1, you know not only that the observed value is less than the predicted value but also that the residual is larger than most in absolute value.

Residuals are sometimes adjusted in one of two ways. The *standardized residual* for case *i* is the residual divided by the sample standard deviation of the residuals. Standardized residuals have a mean of 0 and a standard deviation of 1. The *Studentized residual* is the residual divided by an estimate of its standard deviation that varies from point to point, depending on the distance of X_i from the mean of X. Usually standardized and Studentized residuals are close in value, but not always. The Studentized residual reflects more precisely differences in the true error variances from point to point.

2.19 Linearity

For the bivariate situation, a scatterplot is a good means for judging how well a straight line fits the data. Another convenient method is to plot the residuals against the predicted values. If the assumptions of linearity and homogeneity of variance are met, there should be no relationship between the predicted and residual values. You should be suspicious of any observable pattern.

For example, fitting a least-squares line to the data in the two left-hand plots in Figure 2.19a yields the residual plots shown on the right. The two residual plots show patterns since straight lines do not fit the data well. Systematic patterns between the predicted values and the residuals suggest possible violations of the linearity assumption. If the assumption was met, the residuals would be randomly distributed in a band about the horizontal straight line through 0, as shown in Figure 2.19b.

Figure 2.19a Standardized residuals scatterplots

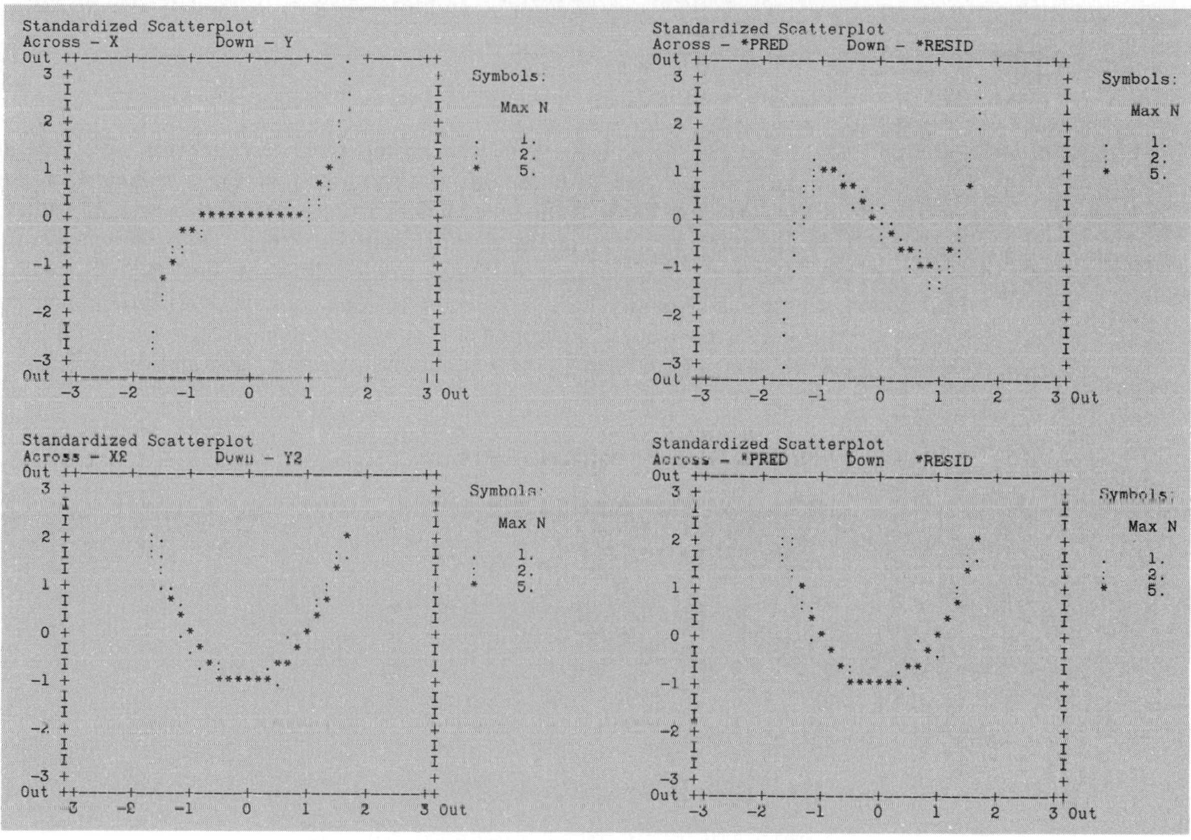

Figure 2.19b Randomly distributed residuals

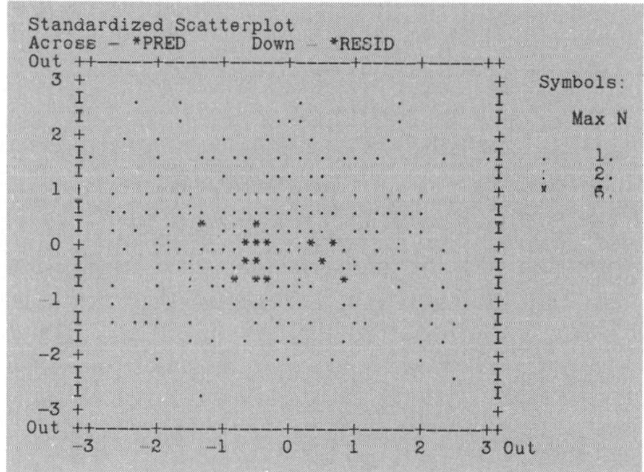

Residuals can also be plotted against individual independent variables. Again, if the assumptions are met, you should see a horizontal band of residuals. Consider plotting the residuals against independent variables not in the equation as well. If the residuals are not randomly distributed, you may want to include the variable in the equation for a multiple regression model (see Sections 2.32 through 2.54).

2.20 Equality of Variance

You can also use the previously described plots to check for violations of the equality of variance assumption. If the spread of the residuals increases or decreases with values of the independent variables or with predicted values, you should question the assumption of constant variance of *Y* for all values of *X*.

Figure 2.20 is a plot of the Studentized residuals against the predicted values for the salary data. The spread of the residuals increases with the magnitude of the predicted values, suggesting that the variability of current salaries increases with salary level. Thus, the equality of variance assumption appears to be violated.

Figure 2.20 Unequal variance

```
REGRESSION VARIABLES=SALBEG,SALNOW
  /DEPENDENT=SALNOW
  /METHOD=ENTER SALBEG
  /SCATTERPLOT=(*SRESID,*PRED)
```

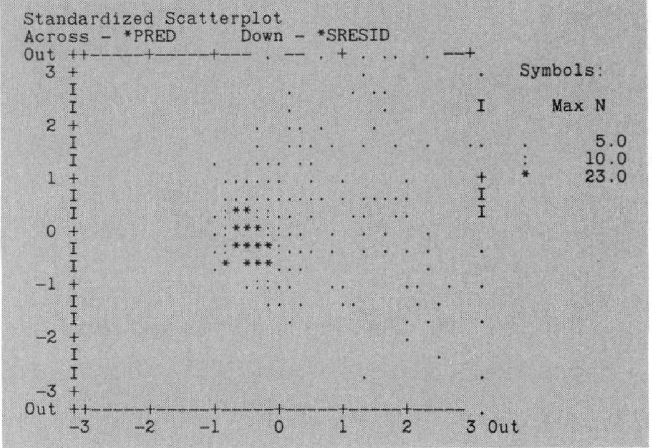

2.21 Independence of Error

Whenever the data are collected and recorded sequentially, you should plot residuals against the sequence variable. Even if time is not considered a variable in the model, it could influence the residuals. For example, suppose you are studying survival time after surgery as a function of complexity of surgery, amount of blood transfused, dosage of medication, and so forth. In addition to these variables, it is also possible that the surgeon's skill increased with each operation and that a patient's survival time is influenced by the number of prior patients treated. The plot of residuals corresponding to the order in which patients received surgery shows a shorter survival time for earlier patients than for later patients (see Figure 2.21). If sequence and the residual are independent, you should not see a discernable pattern.

Figure 2.21 Casewise serial plot

```
Casewise Plot of Studentized Residual

                      -3.0        0.0        3.0          LIFE      *PRED     *RESID   *SRESID
  Case #     TIME      O:.........:.........:O
      1     70012       . *        .         .         15.0000   19.5624   -4.5624   -2.2598
      2     78055       . *        .         .         13.5000   17.8974   -4.3974   -2.1856
      3     78122       .  *       .         .          9.9000   13.8390   -3.9390   -1.9871
      4     78134       .    *     .         .         15.5000   18.5218   -3.0218   -1.4997
      5     78233       .   *      .         .         35.0000   38.2933   -3.2933   -1.7466
      6     78298       .     *    .         .         14.7000   16.6487   -1.9487    -.9720
      7     78344       .      *   .         .         34.8000   36.0040   -1.2040    -.6258
      8     79002       .       *  .         .         20.8000   20.0111    -.0111    -.0055
      9     79008       .          . *       .         15.9000   14.8796    1.0204     .5123
     10     79039       .          *         .         22.0000   21.6436     .3564     .1762
     11     79101       .          .  *      .         13.7000   11.7578    1.9422     .9910
     12     79129       .          .  *      .         14.2000   11.4456    2.7544    1.4082
     13     79178       .          .   *     .         33.2000   30.3847    2.8153    1.4144
     14     79188       .          .   *     .         26.2000   22.4761    3.7239    1.8401
     15     79189       .          .    *    .         37.4000   33.2984    4.1016    2.0920
    ...
```

The *Durbin-Watson* statistic, a test for sequential correlation of adjacent error terms, is defined as

$$D = \frac{\sum_{t=2}^{N} (E_t - E_{t-1})^2}{\sum_{t=1}^{N} E_t^2} \qquad \textbf{Equation 2.21}$$

The differences between successive residuals tend to be small when error terms are positively correlated and large when error terms are negatively correlated. Thus, small values of D indicate positive correlation and large values of D indicate negative correlation. Consult tables of the D statistic for bounds upon which significance tests can be based (Neter & Wasserman, 1974).

2.22 Normality

The distribution of residuals may not appear to be normal for reasons other than actual nonnormality: misspecification of the model, nonconstant variance, a small number of residuals actually available for analysis, etc. Therefore, you should pursue several lines of investigation. One of the simplest is to construct a histogram of the residuals such as the one shown in Figure 2.22a for the salary data.

Figure 2.22a Histogram of Studentized residuals

```
REGRESSION VARIABLES=SALBEG,SALNOW
  /DEPENDENT=SALNOW
  /METHOD=ENTER SALBEG
  /RESIDUALS=HISTOGRAM(SRESID)
```

```
Histogram - Studentized Residual

   N  Exp N       (* = 2 Cases,    . : = Normal Curve)
   7    .37   Out ****
   2    .73  3.00 *
   4   1.85  2.67 :*
   2   4.23  2.33 *.
   6   8.65  2.00 ***.
  12  15.85  1.67 ****** .
   7  26.01  1.33 ****       .
  18  38.23  1.00 *********        .
  35  50.34   .67 ******************        .
  63  59.38   .33 ******************************:**
  87  62.74   .00 ******************************:**************
 114  59.38  -.33 ******************************:***************************
  64  50.34  -.67 *************************:*******
  32  38.23 -1.00 ****************       .
   9  26.01 -1.33 *****       .
   6  15.85 -1.67 ***     .
   1   8.65 -2.00 *   .
   1   4.23 -2.33 *.
   2   1.85 -2.67 :
   0    .73 -3.00
   2    .37   Out *
```

The REGRESSION histogram contains a tally of the observed number of residuals (labeled N) in each interval and the number expected in a normal distribution with the same mean and variance as the residuals (Exp N). The first and last intervals (Out) contain residuals more than 3.16 standard deviations from the mean. Such residuals deserve examination. A histogram of expected *N*'s is superimposed on that of the observed *N*'s. Expected frequencies are indicated by a period. When observed and expected frequencies overlap, a colon is displayed. However, it is unreasonable to expect the observed residuals to be exactly normal—some deviation is expected because of sampling variation. Even if the errors are normally distributed in the population, sample residuals are only approximately normal.

In the histogram in Figure 2.22a, the distribution does not seem normal since there is an exaggerated clustering of residuals toward the center and a straggling tail toward large positive values. Thus, the normality assumption may be violated.

Another way to compare the observed distribution of residuals to that expected under the assumption of normality is to plot the two cumulative distributions against each other for a series of points. If the two distributions are identical, a straight line results. By observing how points scatter about the expected straight line, you can compare the two distributions.

Figure 2.22b is a cumulative probability plot of the salary residuals. Initially, the observed residuals are below the straight line, since there is a smaller number of large negative residuals than expected. Once the greatest concentration of residuals is reached, the observed points are above the line, since the observed cumulative proportion exceeds the expected.

Figure 2.22b A normal probability (P-P) plot

```
REGRESSION VARIABLES=SALBEG,SALNOW
  /DEPENDENT=SALNOW
  /METHOD=ENTER SALBEG
  /RESIDUALS=HISTOGRAM(SRESID) NORMPROB
```

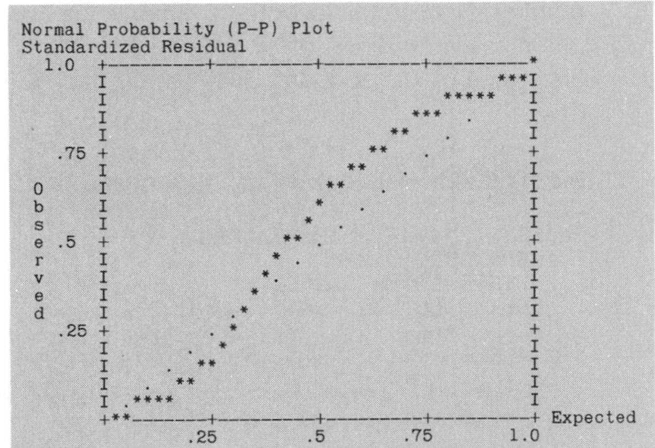

2.23 Locating Outliers

You can spot outliers readily on residual plots since they are cases with very large positive or negative residuals. In the histogram, cases with values greater than +3.16 or less than −3.16 appear in the interval labeled Out. In the scatterplots, they appear on the borders of the plot, again labeled Out. Since you usually want more information about outliers, you can use the casewise plotting facility to display identification numbers and a variety of other statistics for cases having residuals beyond a specified cutoff point.

Figure 2.23 lists information for the nine cases with Studentized residuals greater than 3 in absolute value. Only two of these nine employees have current salaries less than those predicted by the model (Cases 67 and 122), while the others have larger salaries. The second column contains identifier information that indicates that all outliers are white males (SEXRACE=1). They all have large salaries, an average of $33,294, while the average for the sample is only $13,767. Thus, there is some evidence that the model may not fit well for the highly paid cases.

Figure 2.23 Casewise plot of residuals outliers

```
REGRESSION VARIABLES=SALBEG,SALNOW
  /DEPENDENT=SALNOW
  /METHOD=ENTER SALBEG
  /CASEWISE=PLOT(SRESID)
  /RESIDUALS=ID(SEXRACE)
```

```
Casewise Plot of Studentized Residual

Outliers = 3.     *: Selected   M: Missing

                  -6.          -3.  3.          6.
   Case # SEXRACE  0:............:  :............:0   SALNOW       *PRED       *RESID
      24        1  .             .. *             .    28000  17383.4949  10616.5051
      60        1  .             ..              *.    32000  12800.8156  19199.1844
      67        1  .            * ..              .    26400  37043.1894 -10643.1894
     114        1  .             ..  *            .    38800  27511.2163  11288.7837
     122        1  .     *       ..               .    26700  40869.7266 -14169.7266
     123        1  .             ..  *            .    36250  24639.4039  11610.5961
     129        1  .             ..          *    .    33500  17383.4949  16116.5051
     149        1  .             ..               *    41500  21782.8671  19717.1329
     177        1  .             ..     *         .    36500  23295.1513  13204.8487

     9 Outliers found.
```

2.24 Other Unusual Observations: Mahalanobis' Distance

In Section 2.2, an employee was identified as an outlier because the combination of values for beginning and current salaries was atypical. This case, which is Case 60, shows up in Figure 2.23 since it has a large value for the Studentized residual. Another unusual employee (Case 56) has a beginning salary of $31,992. Since the average beginning salary for the entire sample is only $6,806 and the standard deviation is 3148, the case is eight standard deviations above the mean. But since the Studentized residual is not large, this case does not appear in Figure 2.23.

However, cases that have unusual values for the independent variables can have a substantial impact on the results of analysis and should be identified. One measure of the distance of cases from average values of the independent variables is *Mahalanobis' distance*. In the case of a regression equation with a single independent variable, it is the square of the standardized value of X:

$$D_i = \left(\frac{X_i - \bar{X}}{S_X}\right)^2 \qquad \textbf{Equation 2.24}$$

Thus, for Case 56, the Mahalanobis' distance shown in Figure 2.24 is 64 (8^2). When there is more than one independent variable—where Mahalanobis' distance is most valuable—the computations are more complex.

Figure 2.24 Mahalanobis' distances

```
REGRESSION VARIABLES=SALBEG,SALNOW
  /DEPENDENT=SALNOW
  /METHOD=ENTER SALBEG
  /RESIDUALS=OUTLIERS(MAHAL) ID(SEXRACE)
```

```
Outliers - Mahalanobis' Distance

  Case #  SEXRACE        *MAHAL

     56       1        63.99758
      2       1        29.82579
    122       1        20.32559
     67       1        14.99121
    132       1        12.64145
     55       1        12.64145
    415       2        11.84140
      5       1        11.32255
    172       1        10.49188
     23       1        10.46720
```

2.25 Influential Cases: Deleted Residuals and Cook's Distance

Certain observations in a set of data can have a large influence on estimates of the parameters. Figure 2.25a shows such a point. The regression line obtained for the data is quite different if the point is omitted. However, the residual for the circled point is not particularly large when the case (Case 8) is included in the computations and does not therefore arouse suspicion (see the plot in Figure 2.25b).

Figure 2.25a Influential observation

```
REGRESSION VARIABLES=X,Y
  /STATISTICS=DEFAULTS CI
  /DEPENDENT=Y /METHOD=ENTER X
  /SCATTERPLOT=(Y,X)
```

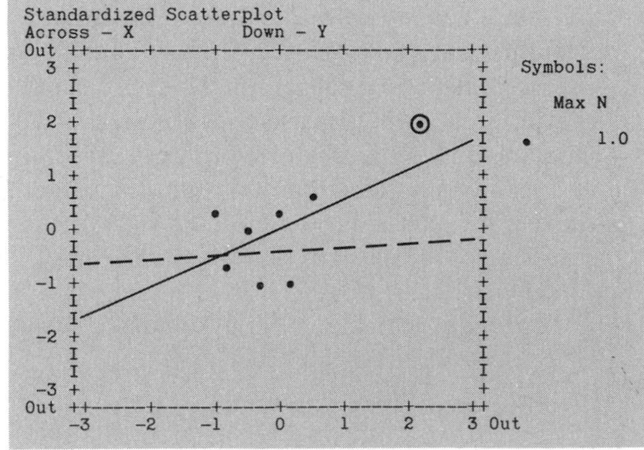

One way to identify an influential case is to compare the residuals for a case when the suspected case is included in the equation and when it is not. The *adjusted predicted value* (ADJPRED) for case i when it is not included in the computation of the regression line is

$$\hat{Y}_i^{(i)} = B_0^{(i)} + B_1^{(i)} X_i \qquad \textbf{Equation 2.25a}$$

where the superscript i indicates that the ith case is excluded. The residual calculated for a case when it is not included is called the *deleted residual* (DRESID), computed as

$$Y_i - \hat{Y}_i^{(i)} \qquad \textbf{Equation 2.25b}$$

The deleted residual can be divided by its standard error to produce the *Studentized deleted residual* (SDRESID).

Although the difference between the deleted and ordinary residual for a case is useful as an index of the influence of that case, this measure does not reflect changes in residuals of other observations when the ith case is deleted. *Cook's distance* does consider changes in all residuals when case i is omitted (Cook, 1977). It is defined as

$$C_i = \frac{\sum_{j=1}^{N} (\hat{Y}_j^{(i)} - \hat{Y}_j)^2}{(p + 1)S^2} \qquad \textbf{Equation 2.25c}$$

The casewise plot for the data in Figure 2.25a is shown in Figure 2.25b. The line for Case 8 describes the circled point. It has neither a very large Studentized residual nor a very large Studentized deleted residual. However, the deleted residual is 5.86 ($Y-ADJPRED=12-6.14$), which is somewhat larger than the ordinary residual (1.24). The large Mahalanobis' distance identifies the case as having an X value far from the mean, while the large Cook's D identifies the case as an influential point.

Figure 2.25b Casewise plot to study influential observation

```
REGRESSION VARIABLES=X,Y
  /STATISTICS=DEFAULTS CI
  /DEPENDENT=Y /METHOD=ENTER X
  /CASEWISE=ALL DEPENDENT RESID SRESID DRESID ADJPRED MAHAL COOK
```

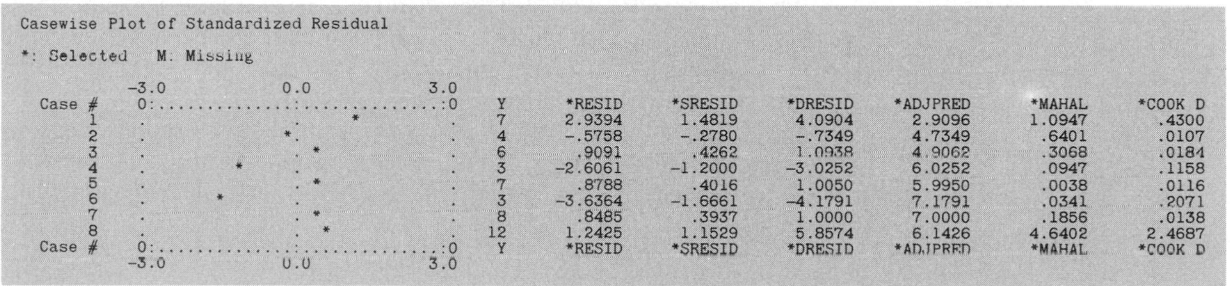

```
Casewise Plot of Standardized Residual

*: Selected   M: Missing

          -3.0          0.0          3.0
 Case #    O:.............:.............:O   Y     *RESID    *SRESID    *DRESID   *ADJPRED     *MAHAL    *COOK D
      1    .              .     *       .    7     2.9394     1.4819     4.0904     2.9096     1.0947      .4300
      2    .             *.             .    4     -.5758     -.2780     -.7349     4.7349      .6401      .0107
      3    .              . *           .    6      .9091      .4262     1.0938     4.9062      .3068      .0184
      4    .       *      .             .    3    -2.6061    -1.2000    -3.0252     6.0252      .0947      .1158
      5    .              . *           .    7      .8788      .4016     1.0050     5.9950      .0038      .0116
      6    .     *        .             .    3    -3.6364    -1.6661    -4.1791     7.1791      .0341      .2071
      7    .              . *           .    8      .8485      .3937     1.0000     7.0000      .1856      .0138
      8    .              .  *          .   12     1.2425     1.1529     5.8574     6.1426     4.6402     2.4687
 Case #    O:.............:.............:O   Y     *RESID    *SRESID    *DRESID   *ADJPRED     *MAHAL    *COOK D
          -3.0          0.0          3.0
```

The regression coefficients with and without Case 8 are shown in Figures 2.25c and 2.25d. Both $B_0^{(8)}$ and $B_1^{(8)}$ are far removed from B_0 and B_1, since Case 8 is an influential point.

Figure 2.25c Regression results from all cases

```
REGRESSION VARIABLES=X,Y
  /STATISTICS=DEFAULTS CI
  /DEPENDENT=Y /METHOD=ENTER X
```

Variables in the Equation

Variable	B	SE B	95% Confdnce Intrvl B		Beta	T	Sig T
X	.51514	.21772	-.01759	1.04788	.69476	2.366	.0558
(Constant)	3.54547	1.41098	.09294	6.99799		2.513	.0457

Figure 2.25d Regression coefficients without Case 8

```
REGRESSION VARIABLES=X,Y
  /SELECT=CASEID NE 8
  /STATISTICS=DEFAULTS CI
  /DEPENDENT=Y /METHOD=ENTER X
```

Variables in the Equation

Variable	B	SE B	95% Confdnce Intrvl B		Beta	T	Sig T
X	.07141	.42738	-1.02719	1.17000	.07451	.167	.8739
(Constant)	5.14294	1.91132	.22982	10.05606		2.691	.0433

2.26 When Assumptions Appear To Be Violated

When evidence of violation of assumptions appears, you can pursue one of two strategies. You can either formulate an alternative model, such as weighted least squares, or you can transform the variables so that the current model will be more adequate. For example, taking logs, square roots, or reciprocals can stabilize the variance, achieve normality, or linearize a relationship.

2.27 Coaxing a Nonlinear Relationship to Linearity

To try to achieve linearity, you can transform either the dependent or independent variables, or both. If you alter the scale of independent variables, linearity can be achieved without any effect on the distribution of the dependent variable. Thus, if the dependent variable is normally distributed with constant variance for each value of X, it remains so.

When you transform the dependent variable, its distribution is changed. This new distribution must then satisfy the assumptions of the analysis. For example, if logs of the values of the dependent variable are taken, log Y—not the original Y—must be normally distributed with constant variance.

The choice of transformations depends on several considerations. If the form of the true model governing the relationship is known, it should dictate the choice. For instance, if it is known that $\hat{Y}=AC^X$ is an adequate model, taking logs of both sides of the equation results in

$$\log \hat{Y}_i = \underbrace{(\log A)}_{[B_0]} + \underbrace{(\log C)}_{[B_1]} X_i$$

Equation 2.27

Thus log Y is linearly related to X.

Figure 2.27 A transformed relationship

```
REGRESSION VARIABLES=Y,LOGY,X
   /DEPENDENT=Y /ENTER=X
   /SCATTERPLOT=(Y,X)
   /DEPENDENT=LOGY /ENTER=X
   /SCATTERPLOT=(LOGY,X)
```

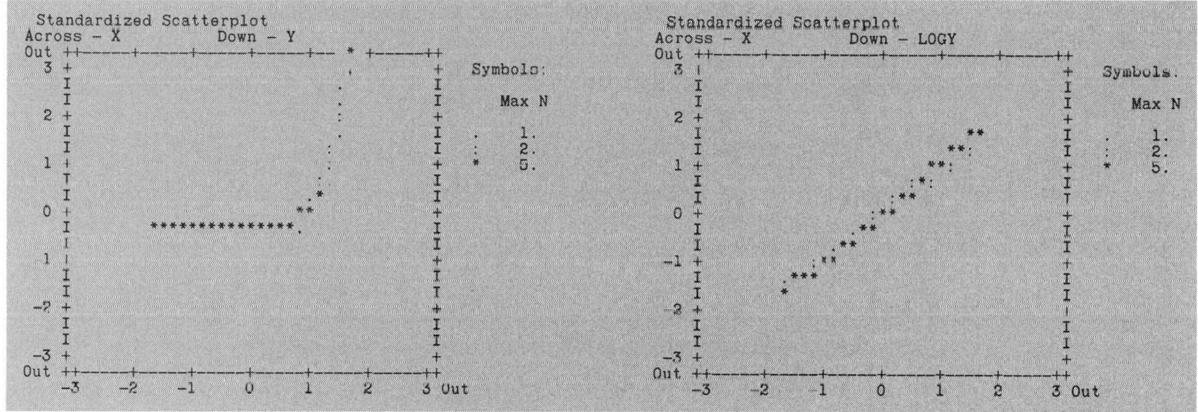

If the true model is not known, you should choose the transformation by examining the plotted data. Frequently, a relationship appears nearly linear for part of the data but is curved for the rest. The first plot in Figure 2.27 is an example. Taking the log of the dependent variable results in the second plot—an improved linear fit.

Other transformations that may diminish curvature are the square root of Y and $-1/Y$. The choice depends, to a certain extent, on the severity of the problem.

2.28 Coping with Skewness

When the distribution of residuals is positively skewed, the log transformation of the dependent variable is often helpful. For negatively skewed distributions, the square transformation is common. It should be noted that the F tests used in regression hypothesis testing are usually quite insensitive to moderate departures from normality.

2.29 Stabilizing the Variance

If the variance of the residuals is not constant, you can try a variety of remedial measures:

- When the variance is proportional to the mean of Y for a given X, use the square root of Y if all Y_i are positive.
- When the standard deviation is proportional to the mean, try the logarithmic transformation.
- When the standard deviation is proportional to the square of the mean, use the reciprocal of Y.
- When Y is a proportion or rate, the arc sine transformation may stabilize the variance.

2.30 Transforming the Salary Data

The assumptions of constant variance and normality appear to be violated with the salary data (see Figures 2.20 and 2.22a). A regression equation using logs of beginning and current salary was developed to obtain a better fit to the assumptions. Figure 2.30a is a scatterplot of Studentized residuals against predicted values when logs of both variables are used in the regression equation.

Figure 2.30a Scatterplot of transformed salary data

```
COMPUTE LOGBEG=LG10(SALBEG)
COMPUTE LOGNOW=LG10(SALNOW)
REGRESSION VARIABLES=LOGBEG,LOGNOW
  /DEPENDENT=LOGNOW
  /METHOD=ENTER LOGBEG
  /SCATTERPLOT=(*SRESID,*PRED)
```

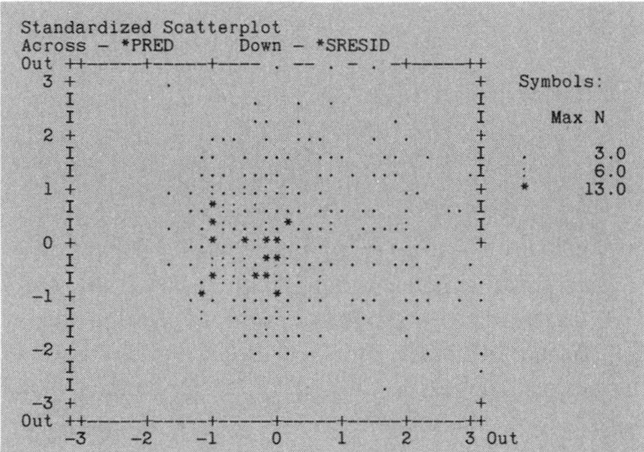

Compare Figures 2.20 and 2.30a and note the improvement in the behavior of the residuals. The spread no longer increases with increasing salary level. Also compare Figures 2.22a and 2.30b and note that the distribution in Figure 2.30b is nearly normal.

Figure 2.30b Histogram of transformed salary data

```
COMPUTE LOGBEG=LG10(SALBEG)
COMPUTE LOGNOW=LG10(SALNOW)
REGRESSION VARIABLES=LOGBEG,LOGNOW
  /DEPENDENT=LOGNOW
  /METHOD=ENTER LOGBEG
  /RESIDUALS=HISTOGRAM(SRESID)
```

```
Histogram - Studentized Residual

 N Exp N       (* = 1 Cases,    . : = Normal Curve)
 3   .37   Out ***
 1   .73  3.00 :
 3  1.85  2.67 *:*
 4  4.23  2.33 ***:
10  8.65  2.00 ********:*
14 15.85  1.67 ************** .
21 26.01  1.33 *********************    .
31 38.23  1.00 *******************************      .
48 50.34   .67 ************************************************ .
55 59.38   .33 *******************************************************   .
63 62.74   .00 **************************************************************:
64 59.38  -.33 **********************************************************:*****
62 50.34  -.67 *************************************************:************
44 38.23 -1.00 *************************************:******
28 26.01 -1.33 *************************:**
14 15.85 -1.67 ************** .
 7  8.65 -2.00 ******* .
 1  4.23 -2.33 *  .
 1  1.85 -2.67 *.
 0   .73 -3.00 .
 0   .37   Out
```

For the transformed data, the multiple R increases slightly to 0.8864, and the outlier plot contains only four cases (compare with Figures 2.10 and 2.23). Thus, the transformation appears to have resulted in a better model.

2.31 A Final Comment on Assumptions

Rarely are assumptions not violated in one way or another in regression analysis and other statistical procedures. However, this is not a justification for ignoring the assumptions. Cranking out regressions with little thought to possible departures from the necessary assumptions can lead to problems in interpreting and applying results. Significance levels, confidence intervals, and other results are sensitive to certain types of violations and cannot be interpreted in the usual fashion if serious departures exist.

By carefully examining residuals and, if need be, using transformations or other methods of analysis, you are in a much better position to pursue analyses that solve the problems you are investigating. Even if everything isn't perfect, you can at least knowledgeably gauge the possible extent of difficulties.

2.32 MULTIPLE REGRESSION MODELS

Beginning salary seems to be a good predictor of current salary, given the evidence shown above. Nearly 80% ($R^2 = 0.77$ from Figure 2.10) of the observed variability in current salaries can be explained by beginning salary levels. But how do variables such as education level, years of experience, race, and sex affect the salary level at which one enters the company?

2.33 Predictors of Beginning Salary

Multiple linear regression extends bivariate regression by incorporating multiple independent variables. The model can be expressed as:

$$Y_i = \beta_0 + \beta_1 X_{1i} + \beta_2 X_{2i} + \ldots + \beta_p X_{pi} + e_i \qquad \textbf{Equation 2.33}$$

The notation X_{pi} indicates the value of the pth independent variable for case i. Again, the β terms are unknown parameters and the e_i terms are independent random variables that are normally distributed with mean 0 and constant variance σ^2. The model assumes that there is a normal distribution of the dependent variable for every combination of the values of the independent variables in the model. For example, if child's height is the dependent variable and age and maternal height are the independent variables, it is assumed that for every combination of age and maternal height there is a normal distribution of children's heights and, though the means of these distributions may differ, all have the same variance.

2.34 The Correlation Matrix

One of the first steps in calculating an equation with several independent variables is to calculate a correlation matrix for all variables, as shown in Figure 2.34. The variables are the log of beginning salary, years of education, sex, years of work experience, race, and age in years. Variables sex and race are represented by *indicator variables,* that is, variables coded as 0 or 1. SEX is coded 1 for female and 0 for male, and MINORITY is coded 1 for nonwhite and 0 for white.

Figure 2.34 The correlation matrix

```
COMPUTE LOGBEG=LG10(SALBEG)
REGRESSION
  /DESCRIPTIVES=CORR
  /VARIABLES=LOGBEG,EDLEVEL,SEX,WORK,MINORITY,AGE
  /DEPENDENT=LOGBEG
  /METHOD=ENTER EDLEVEL TO AGE
```

	LOGBEG	EDLEVEL	SEX	WORK	MINORITY	AGE
LOGBEG	1.000	.686	-.548	.040	-.173	-.048
EDLEVEL	.686	1.000	-.356	-.252	-.133	-.281
SEX	-.548	-.356	1.000	-.165	-.076	.052
WORK	.040	-.252	-.165	1.000	.145	.804
MINORITY	-.173	-.133	-.076	.145	1.000	.111
AGE	-.048	-.281	.052	.804	.111	1.000

The matrix shows the correlations between the dependent variable (LOGBEG) and each independent variable, as well as the correlations between the independent variables. Particularly note any large intercorrelations between the independent variables, since such correlations can substantially affect the results of multiple regression analysis.

2.35 Correlation Matrices and Missing Data

For a variety of reasons, data files frequently contain incomplete observations. Respondents in surveys scrawl illegible responses or refuse to answer certain questions. Laboratory animals die before experiments are completed. Patients fail to keep scheduled clinic appointments. Thus, before computing the correlation matrix, you must usually decide what to do with cases that have missing values for some of the variables.

Before even considering possible strategies, you should determine whether there is evidence that the missing-value pattern is not random. That is, are there reasons to believe that missing values for a variable are related to the values of that variable or other variables? For example, people with low incomes may be less willing to report their financial status than more affluent people. This may be even more pronounced for people who are poor but highly educated.

One simple method of exploring such possibilities is to subdivide the data into two groups—those observations with missing data on a variable and those with complete data—and examine the distributions of the other variables in the file across these two groups. The SPSS^X procedures CROSSTABS and T-TEST are particularly useful for this. For a discussion of more sophisticated methods for detecting nonrandomness, see Frane (1976).

If it appears that the data are not missing randomly, use great caution in attempting to analyze the data. It may be that no satisfactory analysis is possible, especially if there are only a few cases.

If you are satisfied that the missing data are random, several strategies are available. First, if the same few variables are missing for most cases, consider excluding those variables from the analysis. Since this luxury is not usually available, you can alternatively keep all variables but eliminate the cases with missing values on any of them. This is termed *listwise* missing-value treatment since a case is eliminated if it has a missing value on any variable in the list.

If many cases have missing data for some variables, listwise missing-value treatment may eliminate too many cases and leave you with a very small sample. One common technique is to calculate the correlation coefficient between a pair of variables based on all cases with complete information for the two variables, regardless of whether the cases have missing data on any other variable. For example, if a case has values only for variables 1, 3, and 5, it is used only in computations involving variable pairs 1 and 3, 1 and 5, and 3 and 5. This is *pairwise* missing-value treatment.

Several problems can arise with pairwise matrices, one of which is inconsistency. There are some relationships between coefficients that are impossible but may occur when different cases are used to estimate different coefficients. For example, if age and weight and age and height have a high positive correlation, it is impossible in the same sample for height and weight to have a high negative correlation. However, if the same cases are not used to estimate all three coefficients, such an anomaly can occur.

Another problem with pairwise matrices is that no single sample size can be obtained since each coefficient may be based on a different number of cases. In addition, significance levels obtained from analyses based on pairwise matrices must be viewed with caution, since little is known about hypothesis testing in such situations.

Missing-value problems should not be treated lightly. You should always select a missing-value treatment based on careful examination of the data and not leave the choices up to system defaults. In this example, complete information is available for all cases, so missing values are not a problem.

2.36 Partial Regression Coefficients

The summary output when all independent variables are included in the multiple regression equation is shown in Figure 2.36a. The *F* test associated with the analysis of variance table is a test of the null hypothesis that

$$\beta_1=\beta_2=\beta_3=\beta_4=\beta_5=0$$ **Equation 2.36a**

In other words, it is a test of whether there is a linear relationship between the dependent variable and the entire set of independent variables.

Figure 2.36a Statistics for the equation and analysis of variance table

```
COMPUTE LOGBEG=LG10(SALBEG)
REGRESSION VARIABLES=SALBEG LOGBEG EDLEVEL SEX WORK MINORITY AGE
  /DEPENDENT=LOGBEG
  /METHOD=ENTER EDLEVEL TO AGE
```

```
Multiple R           .78420      Analysis of Variance
R Square             .61498                         DF      Sum of Squares      Mean Square
Adjusted R Square    .61086      Regression          5             6.83039          1.36608
Standard Error       .09559      Residual          468             4.27638           .00914

                                 F =      149.50125       Signif F =  .0000
```

The statistics for the independent variables in Figure 2.36b are parallel to those obtained in regression with a single independent variable (see Figure 2.3b). In multiple regression, the coefficients labeled B are called *partial regression coefficients* since the coefficient for a particular variable is adjusted for other independent variables in the equation. The equation that relates the predicted log of beginning salary to the independent variables is

$$\text{LOGBEG} = 3.3853 + 0.00102(\text{AGE}) - 0.10358(\text{SEX}) - 0.05237(\text{MINORITY}) + 0.03144(\text{EDLEVEL}) + 0.00161(\text{WORK})$$

Equation 2.36b

Since the dependent variable is in log units, the coefficients can be approximately interpreted in percentage terms. For example, the coefficient of −0.104 for the SEX variable when females are coded as 1 indicates that female salaries are estimated to be about 10% less than male salaries, after statistical adjustment for age, education, work history, and minority status.

Figure 2.36b Statistics for variables in the equation

```
COMPUTE LOGBEG=LG10(SALBEG)
REGRESSION VARIABLES=LOGBEG EDLEVEL SEX WORK MINORITY AGE
  /DEPENDENT=LOGBEG
  /METHOD=ENTER EDLEVEL TO AGE
```

------------------ Variables in the Equation ------------------

Variable	B	SE B	Beta	T	Sig T
AGE	.00102	6.6132E-04	.07811	1.535	.1254
SEX	-.10358	.01032	-.33699	-10.038	.0000
MINORITY	-.05237	.01084	-.14157	-4.832	.0000
EDLEVEL	.03144	1.7480E-03	.59195	17.988	.0000
WORK	.00161	9.2407E-04	.09143	1.740	.0826
(Constant)	3.38530	.03323		101.866	.0000

2.37 Determining Important Variables

In multiple regression, one sometimes wants to assign relative importance to each independent variable. For example, you might want to know whether education is more important in predicting beginning salary than previous work experience. There are two possible answers, depending on which of the following questions is asked:

- How important are education and work experience when each one is used alone to predict beginning salary?
- How important are education and work experience when they are used to predict beginning salary along with other independent variables in the regression equation?

The first question is answered by looking at the correlation coefficients between salary and the independent variables. The larger the absolute value of the correlation coefficient, the stronger the linear association. Figure 2.34 shows that education correlates more highly with the log of salary than does previous work experience (0.686 and 0.040, respectively). Thus, you would assign more importance to education as a predictor of salary.

The answer to the second question is considerably more complicated. When the independent variables are correlated among themselves, the unique contribution of each is difficult to assess. Any statement about an independent variable is contingent upon the other variables in the equation. For example, the regression coefficient (*B*) for work experience is 0.0007 when it is the sole independent variable in the equation, compared to 0.00161 when the other four independent variables are also in the equation. The second coefficient is more than twice the size of the first.

2.38 Beta Coefficients

It is also inappropriate to interpret the *B*'s as indicators of the relative importance of variables. The actual magnitude of the coefficients depends on the units in which the variables are measured. Only if all independent variables are measured in the same units—years, for example—are their coefficients directly comparable. When variables differ substantially in units of measurement, the sheer magnitude of their coefficients does not reveal anything about relative importance.

One way to make regression coefficients somewhat more comparable is to calculate *Beta* weights, which are the coefficients of the independent variables when all variables are expressed in standardized (*Z*-score) form (see Figure 2.36b). The Beta coefficients can be calculated directly from the regression coefficients using

$$BETA_k = B_k\left(\frac{S_k}{S_Y}\right)$$

Equation 2.38

where S_k is the standard deviation of the *k*th independent variable.

However, the values of the Beta coefficients, like the *B*'s, are contingent on the other independent variables in the equation. They are also affected by the correlations of the independent variables and do not in any absolute sense reflect the importance of the various independent variables.

2.39 Part and Partial Coefficients

Another way of assessing the relative importance of independent variables is to consider the increase in R^2 when a variable is entered into an equation that already contains the other independent variables. This increase is

$$R^2_{change} = R^2 - R^2_{(i)}$$

Equation 2.39a

where $R^2_{(i)}$ is the square of the multiple correlation coefficent when all independent variables except the *i*th are in the equation. A large change in R^2 indicates that a variable provides unique information about the dependent variable that is not available from the other independent variables in the equation. The signed square root of the increase is called the *part correlation coefficient.* It is the correlation between *Y* and X_i when the linear effects of the other independent variables have been removed from X_i. If all independent variables are uncorrelated, the change in R^2 when a variable is entered into the equation is simply the square of the correlation coefficient between that variable and the dependent variable.

The output in Figure 2.39 shows that the addition of years of education to an equation that contains the other four independent variables results in a change in R^2 of 0.266 ($.51593^2$). The square of the part coefficient tells only how much R^2 increases when a variable is added to the regression equation. It does not indicate what proportion of the unexplained variation this increase constitutes. If most of the variation had been explained by the other variables, a small part correlation is all that is possible for the remaining variable. It may therefore be difficult to compare part coefficients.

Figure 2.39 Zero-order, part, and partial correlation coefficients

```
COMPUTE LOGBEG=LG10(SALBEG)
REGRESSION VARIABLES=LOGBEG,EDLEVEL,SEX,WORK,MINORITY,AGE
  /STATISTICS=R CHA BCOV ZPP F
  /DEPENDENT=LOGBEG
  /METHOD=ENTER AGE /ENTER SEX /ENTER MINORITY /ENTER WORK /ENTER EDLEVEL
```

```
Variable(s) Entered on Step Number 5..     EDLEVEL    EDUCATIONAL LEVEL

Multiple R              .78420
R Square                .61498             R Square Change       .26619
Adjusted R Square       .61086             F Change           323.55404
Standard Error          .09559             Signif F Change       .0000

F =       149.50125           Signif F =  .0000


------------- Variables in the Equation --------------

Variable        Correl Part Cor  Partial           F  Sig F

AGE            -.04780   .04404   .07080       2.357  .1254
SEX            -.54802  -.28792  -.42090     100.761  .0000
MINORITY       -.17284  -.13860  -.21799      23.349  .0000
WORK            .03994   .04990   .08015       3.026  .0826
EDLEVEL         .68572   .51593   .63934     323.554  .0000
(Constant)                                 10376.613  .0000
```

A coefficient that measures the proportional reduction in variation is

$$Pr_i^2 = \frac{R^2 - R_{(i)}^2}{1 - R_{(i)}^2} \qquad \textbf{Equation 2.39b}$$

The numerator is the square of the part coefficient; the denominator is the proportion of unexplained variation when all but the ith variable are in the equation. The signed square root of Pr_i^2 is the *partial correlation coefficient*. It can be interpreted as the correlation between the ith independent variable and the dependent variable when the linear effects of the other independent variables have been removed from both X_i and Y. Since the denominator of Pr_i^2 is always less than or equal to 1, the part correlation coefficient is never larger in absolute value than the partial correlation coefficient.

Plots of the residuals of Y and X_i, when the linear effects of the other independent variables have been removed, are a useful diagnostic aid. They are discussed in Section 2.49.

2.40 Variance of the Estimators

The variability of the estimated regression coefficients must also be considered in evaluating the relative importance of the independent variables. Coefficients with large standard errors are unreliable and may differ markedly from sample to sample. It is a dangerous practice to identify variables as important for prediction based only on their significant individual t values.

When the independent variables are correlated among themselves, the parameter estimates are correlated as well. High intercorrelations among the variables can affect the regression estimates in several ways. The estimated variance of the regression coefficient for the ith independent variable is

$$S_{B_i}^2 = \frac{S^2}{(1 - R_i^2)(N - 1)S_i^2} \qquad \textbf{Equation 2.40}$$

Here, R_i^2 is the squared multiple correlation when the ith independent variable is considered the dependent variable and the regression equation between it and the other independent variables is calculated. A large value of R_i^2 indicates that the ith independent variable is almost a linear function or combination of the other independent variables. The proportion of variability not explained by the other variables is, as before, $1-R_i^2$. This quantity is usually called the *tolerance* of the variable. As can be seen from Equation 2.40, for a fixed sample size and standard error S, the smaller the tolerance the larger the standard error of the coefficient. Small tolerance values can also cause computational problems for regression solutions. SPSS^X displays the tolerances as shown in Figure 2.40a.

Figure 2.40a Tolerances

```
COMPUTE LOGBEG=LG10(SALBEG)
REGRESSION VARIABLES=LOGBEG,EDLEVEL,SEX,WORK,MINORITY,AGE
  /STATISTICS=TOLERANCE
  /DEPENDENT=LOGBEG
  /METHOD=ENTER AGE /ENTER SEX /ENTER MINORITY /ENTER WORK /ENTER EDLEVEL
```

Variable	Tolerance
AGE	.31792
SEX	.72998
MINORITY	.95839
WORK	.29784
EDLEVEL	.75966

The variance-covariance matrix and the correlation matrix of the parameter estimates are shown in Figure 2.40b. The entries on the diagonal are the variances of the coefficients. The correlations are displayed above the diagonal and the covariances are displayed below. Note the high correlations between the coefficients for work experience and age (-0.80753). Very small and very large values are displayed in scientific notation. The exponent follows the letter "E." For example, 4.373E$-$07 is 0.0000004373.

Figure 2.40b Variance-covariance output

```
COMPUTE LOGBEG=LG10(SALBEG)
REGRESSION VARIABLES=LOGBEG,EDLEVEL,SEX,WORK,MINORITY,AGE
  /STATISTICS=BCOV
  /DEPENDENT=LOGBEG
  /METHOD=ENTER AGE /ENTER SEX /ENTER MINORITY /ENTER WORK /ENTER EDLEVEL
```

Var-Covar Matrix of Regression Coefficients (B)
Below Diagonal: Covariance Above: Correlation

	AGE	SEX	MINORITY	WORK	EDLEVEL
AGE	4.373E-07	-.28621	-.00722	-.80753	.00388
SEX	-1.953E-06	1.065E-04	.10271	.38399	.40581
MINORITY	-5.175E-08	1.140E-05	1.174E-04	-.04290	.13519
WORK	-4.935E-07	3.661E-06	-4.296E-07	8.539E-07	.18683
EDLEVEL	4.480E-09	7.320E-06	2.561E-06	3.018E-07	3.056E-06

2.41 Building a Model

Our selection of the five variables to predict beginning salary has been arbitrary to some extent. It is unlikely that all relevant variables have been identified and measured. Instead, some relevant variables have no doubt been excluded, while others that were included may not be very important determinants of salary level. This is not unusual; one must try to build a model from available data, as voluminous or scanty as the data may be. Before considering several formal procedures for model building, we will examine some of the consequences of adding and deleting variables from regression equations. The SPSS^X statistics for variables not in the equation are also described.

2.42 Adding and Deleting Variables

The first step in Figure 2.42 shows the equation and summary statistics when years of education is the sole independent variable and log of beginning salary is the dependent variable. Consider the second step in the same figure, when another variable, sex, is added. The value displayed as R Square Change in the second step is the change in R^2 when sex is added. R^2 for education alone is 0.47021, so R^2_{change} is 0.57598−0.47021, or 0.10577.

Figure 2.42 Adding a variable to the equation

```
COMPUTE LOGBEG=LG10(SALBEG)
REGRESSION VARIABLES=LOGBEG,EDLEVEL,SEX
  /STATISTICS=DEFAULTS CHANGE
  /DEPENDENT=LOGBEG
  /METHOD=ENTER EDLEVEL /ENTER SEX
```

```
Beginning Block Number  1.  Method:  Enter      EDLEVEL

Variable(s) Entered on Step Number  1..    EDLEVEL    EDUCATIONAL LEVEL

Multiple R           .68572                                        Analysis of Variance
R Square             .47021        R Square Change     .47021                          DF        Sum of Squares        Mean Square
Adjusted R Square    .46909        F Change         418.92011      Regression           1              5.22252            5.22252
Standard Error       .11165        Signif F Change     .0000       Residual           472              5.88425             .01247

------------------ Variables in the Equation ------------------     ------------ Variables not in the Equation ------------

Variable             B         SE B        Beta         T  Sig T    Variable      Beta In  Partial  Min Toler        T  Sig T

EDLEVEL         .036424     .001780     .685719    20.468  .0000    SEX        -.348017 -.446811    .873274   -10.839  .0000
(Constant)     3.310013     .024551               134.821  .0000

End Block Number   1   All requested variables entered.

                    * * * * * * * * * * * * * * * * * * * * * * * * * * * * * * *

Beginning Block Number  2.  Method:  Enter      SEX

Variable(s) Entered on Step Number  2..    SEX        SEX OF EMPLOYEE

Multiple R           .75893                                        Analysis of Variance
R Square             .57598        R Square Change     .10577                          DF        Sum of Squares        Mean Square
Adjusted R Square    .57418        F Change         117.48552      Regression           2              6.39725            3.19863
Standard Error       .09999        Signif F Change     .0000       Residual           471              4.70951             .01000

------------------ Variables in the Equation ------------------

Variable             B         SE B        Beta         T  Sig T

EDLEVEL         .029843     .001705     .561830    17.498  .0000
SEX            -.106966     .009869    -.348017   -10.839  .0000
(Constant)     3.447542     .025386               135.806  .0000

End Block Number   2   All requested variables entered.
```

The null hypothesis that the true population value for the change in R^2 is 0 can be tested using

$$F_{change} = \frac{R^2_{change}(N - p - 1)}{q(1 - R^2)} = \frac{(0.1058)\,(474\text{-}2\text{-}1)}{1(1\text{-}0.5760)} = 117.48 \qquad \textbf{Equation 2.42}$$

where N is the number of cases in the equation, p is the total number of independent variables in the equation, and q is the number of variables entered at this step. Sometimes, this is referred to as a *partial F test.* Under the hypothesis that the true change is 0, the significance of the value labeled F Change can be obtained from the F distribution with q and $N-p-1$ degrees of freedom.

The hypothesis that the real change in R^2 is 0 can also be formulated in terms of the β parameters. When only the ith variable is added in a step, the hypothesis that the change in R^2 is 0 is equivalent to the hypothesis that β_i is 0. The F value printed for the change in R^2 is the square of the t value displayed for the test of the coefficient, as shown in Figure 2.42. For example, the t value for sex from Figure 2.42 is -10.839. This value squared is 117.48, the value displayed for F Change.

When q independent variables are entered in a single step, the test that R^2 is 0 is equivalent to the simultaneous test that the coefficients of all q variables are 0. For example, if sex and age were added in the same step to the regression equation that contains education, the F test for R^2 change would be the same as the F test which tests the hypothesis that $\beta_{sex}=\beta_{age}=0$.

Entering sex into the equation with education has effects in addition to changing R^2. For example, note the decrease in magnitude of the regression coefficient for education from Step 1 to Step 2 (from 0.03642 to 0.02984) in Figure 2.42. This is attributable to the correlation between sex and level of education.

When highly intercorrelated independent variables are included in a regression equation, results may appear anomalous. The overall regression may be significant while none of the individual coefficients are significant. The signs of the regression coefficients may be counterintuitive. High correlations between independent variables inflate the variances of the estimates, making individual coefficients quite unreliable without adding much to the overall fit of the model. The problem of linear relationships between independent variables is discussed further in Sections 2.52 through 2.54.

2.43 Statistics for Variables Not in the Equation

When you have independent variables that have not been entered into the equation, you can examine what would happen if they were entered at the next step. Statistics describing these variables are shown in Figure 2.43. The column labeled Beta In is the standardized regression coefficient that would result if the variable were entered into the equation at the next step. The F test and level of significance are for the hypothesis that the coefficient is 0. (Remember that the partial F test and the t test for the hypothesis that a coefficient is 0 are equivalent.) The partial correlation coefficient with the dependent variable adjusts for the variables already in the equation.

Figure 2.43 Coefficients for variables not in the equation

```
COMPUTE LOGBEG=LG10(SALBEG)
REGRESSION VARIABLES=LOGBEG,EDLEVEL,SEX,WORK,MINORITY,AGE
  /STATISTICS=OUTS F
  /DEPENDENT=LOGBEG
  /METHOD=FORWARD
```

```
------------- Variables not in the Equation -------------
Variable      Beta In   Partial   Min Toler        F  Sig F

WORK           .14425    .20567     .77382    20.759  .0000
MINORITY      -.12902   -.19464     .84758    18.507  .0000
AGE            .13942    .20519     .80425    20.659  .0000
```

From statistics calculated for variables not in the equation, you can decide what variable should be entered next. This process is detailed in Section 2.45.

2.44 The "Optimal" Number of Independent Variables

Having seen what happens when sex is added to the equation containing education (Figure 2.42), consider now what happens when the remaining three independent variables are entered one at a time in no particular order. Summary output is shown in Figure 2.44. Step 5 shows the statistics for the equation with all independent variables entered. Step 3 describes the model with education, sex, and work experience as the independent variables.

Figure 2.44 All independent variables in the equation

```
COMPUTE LOGBEG=LG10(SALBEG)
REGRESSION VARIABLES=LOGBEG,EDLEVEL,SEX,WORK,AGE,MINORITY
  /STATISTICS=HISTORY F
  /DEPENDENT=LOGBEG
  /METHOD=ENTER EDLEVEL /ENTER SEX /ENTER WORK /ENTER AGE /ENTER MINORITY
```

Summary table

Step	MultR	Rsq	AdjRsq	F(Eqn)	SigF	RsqCh	FCh	SigCh		Variable	BetaIn	Correl	
1	.6857	.4702	.4691	418.920	.000	.4702	418.920	.000	In:	EDLEVEL	.6857	.6857	EDUCATIONAL LEVEL
2	.7589	.5760	.5742	319.896	.000	.1058	117.486	.000	In:	SEX	-.3480	-.5480	SEX OF EMPLOYEE
3	.7707	.5939	.5913	229.130	.000	.0179	20.759	.000	In:	WORK	.1442	.0399	WORK EXPERIENCE
4	.7719	.5958	.5923	172.805	.000	.0019	2.149	.143	In:	AGE	.0763	-.0478	AGE OF EMPLOYEE
5	.7842	.6150	.6109	149.501	.000	.0192	23.349	.000	In:	MINORITY	-.1416	-.1728	MINORITY CLASSIFICATION

Examination of Figure 2.44 shows that R^2 never decreases as independent variables are added. This is always true in regression analysis. However, this does not necessarily mean that the equation with more variables better fits the population. As the number of parameters estimated from the sample increases, so does the goodness of fit to the sample as measured by R^2. For example, if a sample contains six cases, a regression equation with six parameters fits the sample exactly, even though there may be no true statistical relationship at all between the dependent variable and the independent variables.

As indicated in Section 2.10, the sample R^2 in general tends to overestimate the population value of R^2. Adjusted R^2 attempts to correct the optimistic bias of the sample R^2. Adjusted R^2 does not necessarily increase as additional variables are added to an equation and is the preferred measure of goodness of fit because it is not subject to the inflationary bias of unadjusted R^2. This statistic is shown in the column labeled AdjRsq in the output.

Although adding independent variables increases R^2, it does not necessarily decrease the standard error of the estimate. Each time a variable is added to the equation, a degree of freedom is lost from the residual sum of squares and one is gained for the regression sum of squares. The standard error may increase when the decrease in the residual sum of squares is very slight and not sufficient to make up for the loss of a degree of freedom for the residual sum of squares. The F value for the test of the overall regression decreases when the regression sum of squares does not increase as fast as the degrees of freedom for the regression.

Including a large number of independent variables in a regression model is never a good strategy, unless there are strong, previous reasons to suggest that they all should be included. The observed increase in R^2 does not necessarily reflect a better fit of the model in the population. Including irrelevant variables increases the standard errors of all estimates without improving prediction. A model with many variables is often difficult to interpret.

On the other hand, it is important not to exclude potentially relevant independent variables. The following sections describe various procedures for selecting variables to be included in a regression model. The goal is to build a concise model that makes good prediction possible.

2.45 Procedures for Selecting Variables

You can construct a variety of regression models from the same set of variables. For instance, you can build seven different equations from three independent variables: three with only one independent variable, three with two independent variables, and one with all three. As the number of variables increases, so does the number of potential models (ten independent variables yield 1,023 models).

Although there are procedures for computing all possible regression equations, several other methods do not require as much computation and are more frequently used. Among these procedures are forward selection, backward elimination, and stepwise regression. None of these variable selection procedures is "best" in any absolute sense; they merely identify subsets of variables that, for the sample, are good predictors of the dependent variable.

2.46 Forward Selection

In *forward selection*, the first variable considered for entry into the equation is the one with the largest positive or negative correlation with the dependent variable. The F test for the hypothesis that the coefficient of the entered variable is 0 is then calculated. To determine whether this variable (and each succeeding variable) is entered, the F value is compared to an established criterion. You can specify one of two criteria in SPSS^X. One criterion is the minimum value of the F statistic that a variable must achieve in order to enter, called *F-to-enter* (keyword FIN), with a default value of 3.84. The other criterion you can specify is the probability associated with the F statistic, called *probability of F-to-enter* (keyword PIN), with a default of 0.05. In this case, a variable enters into the equation only if the probability associated with the F test is less than or equal to the default 0.05 or the value you specify. By default, the probability of F-to-enter is the criterion used.

These two criteria are not necessarily equivalent. As variables are added to the equation, the degrees of freedom associated with the residual sum of squares decrease while the regression degrees of freedom increase. Thus, a fixed F value has different significance levels depending on the number of variables currently in the equation. For large samples, the differences are negligible.

The actual significance level associated with the F-to-enter statistic is not the one usually obtained from the F distribution, since many variables are being examined and the largest F value is selected. Unfortunately, the true significance level is difficult to compute since it depends not only on the number of cases and variables but also on the correlations between independent variables.

If the first variable selected for entry meets the criterion for inclusion, forward selection continues. Otherwise, the procedure terminates with no variables in the equation. Once one variable is entered, the statistics for variables not in the equation are used to select the next one. The partial correlations between the dependent variable and each of the independent variables not in the equation, adjusted for the independent variables in the equation, are examined. The variable with the largest partial correlation is the next candidate. Choosing the variable with the largest partial correlation in absolute value is equivalent to selecting the variable with the largest F value.

If the criterion is met, the variable is entered into the equation and the procedure is repeated. The procedure stops when there are no other variables that meet the entry criterion.

To include a specific number of independent variables in the equation, you can specify the number of steps and SPSS^X selects only the first n variables that meet entry requirements. Another criterion that is always checked before a variable is entered is the tolerance, which is discussed in Section 2.54.

Figure 2.46a shows output generated from a forward-selection procedure using the salary data. The default entry criterion is PIN=0.05. In the first step, education (variable EDLEVEL) is entered since it has the highest correlation with beginning salary. The significance level associated with education is less than 0.0005, so it certainly meets the criterion for entry.

Figure 2.46a Summary statistics for forward selection

```
COMPUTE LOGBEG=LG10(SALBEG)
REGRESSION VARIABLES=LOGBEG,EDLEVEL,SEX,WORK,MINORITY,AGE
  /STATISTICS=HISTORY F
  /DEPENDENT=LOGBEG
  /METHOD=FORWARD
```

Step	MultR	Rsq	AdjRsq	F(Eqn)	SigF	RsqCh	FCh	SigCh		Variable	BetaIn	Correl
1	.6857	.4702	.4691	418.920	.000	.4702	418.920	.000	In:	EDLEVEL	.6857	.6857
2	.7589	.5760	.5742	319.896	.000	.1058	117.486	.000	In:	SEX	-.3480	-.5480
3	.7707	.5939	.5913	229.130	.000	.0179	20.759	.000	In:	WORK	.1442	.0399
4	.7830	.6130	.6097	185.750	.000	.0191	23.176	.000	In:	MINORITY	-.1412	-.1728

To see how the next variable, SEX, was selected, look at the statistics shown in Figure 2.46b for variables not in the equation when only EDLEVEL is in the equation. The variable with the largest partial correlation is SEX. If entered at the next step, it would have an F value of approximately 117 for the test that its coefficient is 0. Since the probability associated with the F is less than 0.05, variable sex is entered in the second step.

Figure 2.46b Status of the variables at the first step

```
COMPUTE LOGBEG=LG10(SALBEG)
REGRESSION VARIABLES=LOGBEG,EDLEVEL,SEX,WORK,MINORITY,AGE
  /STATISTICS=F
  /DEPENDENT=LOGBEG
  /METHOD=FORWARD
```

------------------ Variables in the Equation ------------------

Variable	B	SE B	Beta	F	Sig F
EDLEVEL	.03642	1.7796E-03	.68572	418.920	.0000
(Constant)	3.31001	.02455		18176.773	.0000

------------- Variables not in the Equation -------------

Variable	Beta In	Partial	Min Toler	F	Sig F
SEX	-.34802	-.44681	.87327	117.486	.0000
WORK	.22747	.30241	.93632	47.408	.0000
MINORITY	-.08318	-.11327	.98234	6.121	.0137
AGE	.15718	.20726	.92113	21.140	.0000

Once variable SEX enters at Step 2, the statistics for variables not in the equation must be examined (see Figure 2.43). The variable with the largest absolute value for the partial correlation coefficient is now years of work experience. Its F value is 20.759 with a probability less than 0.05, so variable work is entered in the next step. The same process takes place with variable minority and it is entered, leaving age as the only variable out of the equation. However, as shown in Figure 2.46c, the significance level associated with the age coefficient F value is 0.1254, which is too large for entry. Thus, forward selection yields the summary table for the four steps shown in Figure 2.46a.

Figure 2.46c The last step

```
COMPUTE LOGBEG=LG10(SALBEG)
REGRESSION VARIABLES=LOGBEG,EDLEVEL,SEX,WORK,MINORITY,AGE
  /STATISTICS=F
  /DEPENDENT=LOGBEG
  /METHOD=FORWARD
```

------------- Variables not in the Equation -------------					
Variable	Beta In	Partial	Min Toler	F	Sig F
AGE	.07811	.07080	.29784	2.357	.1254

2.47 Backward Elimination

While forward selection starts with no independent variables in the equation and sequentially enters them, *backward elimination* starts with all variables in the equation and sequentially removes them. Instead of entry criteria, removal criteria are specified.

Two removal criteria are available in SPSS^X. The first is the minimum F value (FOUT) that a variable must have in order to remain in the equation. Variables with F values less than this *F-to-remove* are eligible for removal. The second criterion available is the maximum probability of F-to-remove (keyword POUT) a variable can have. The default FOUT value is 2.71 and the default POUT value is 0.10. The default criterion is POUT.

Figure 2.47a Backward elimination at the first step

```
COMPUTE LOGBEG=LG10(SALBEG)
REGRESSION VARIABLES=LOGBEG,EDLEVEL,SEX,WORK,MINORITY,AGE
  /STATISTICS=COEFF ZPP F
  /DEPENDENT=LOGBEG
  /METHOD=BACKWARD
```

------------- Variables in the Equation -------------								
Variable	B	SE B	Beta	Correl	Part Cor	Partial	F	Sig F
AGE	1.01540E-03	6.6132E-04	.07811	-.04780	.04404	.07080	2.357	.1254
SEX	-.10358	.01032	-.33699	-.54802	-.28792	-.42090	100.761	.0000
MINORITY	-.05237	.01084	-.14157	-.17284	-.13860	-.21799	23.349	.0000
EDLEVEL	.03144	1.7480E-03	.59195	.68572	.51593	.63934	323.554	.0000
WORK	1.60751E-03	9.2407E-04	.09143	.03994	.04990	.08015	3.026	.0826
(Constant)	3.38530	.03323					10376.613	.0000

Look at the salary example again, this time constructing the model with backward elimination. The output in Figure 2.47a is from the first step, in which all variables are entered into the equation. The variable with the smallest partial correlation coefficient, age, is examined first. Since the probability of its F (0.1254) is greater than the default POUT criterion value of 0.10, variable AGE is removed.

Figure 2.47b Backward elimination at the last step

```
COMPUTE LOGBEG=LG10(SALBEG)
REGRESSION VARIABLES=LOGBEG,EDLEVEL,SEX,WORK,MINORITY,AGE
  /STATISTICS=COEFF ZPP F
  /DEPENDENT=LOGBEG
  /METHOD=BACKWARD
```

Variables in the Equation								
Variable	B	SE B	Beta	Correl	Part Cor	Partial	F	Sig F
SEX	-.09904	9.9010E-03	-.32223	-.54802	-.28733	-.41933	100.063	.0000
MINORITY	-.05225	.01085	-.14125	-.17284	-.13828	-.21700	23.176	.0000
EDLEVEL	.03143	1.7506E-03	.59176	.68572	.51577	.63827	322.412	.0000
WORK	2.75324E-03	5.4582E-04	.15659	.03994	.14489	.22685	25.444	.0000
(Constant)	3.41195	.02838					14454.046	.0000

The equation is then recalculated without AGE, producing the statistics shown in Figure 2.47b. The variable with the smallest partial correlation is MINORITY. However, its significance is less than the 0.10 criterion, so backward elimination stops. The equation resulting from backward elimination is the same as the one from forward selection. This is not always the case, however. Forward- and backward-selection procedures can give different results, even with comparable entry and removal criteria.

2.48 Stepwise Selection

Stepwise selection of independent variables is really a combination of backward and forward procedures and is probably the most commonly used method. The first variable is selected in the same manner as in forward selection. If the variable fails to meet entry requirements (either FIN or PIN), the procedure terminates with no independent variables in the equation. If it passes the criterion, the second variable is selected based on the highest partial correlation. If it passes entry criteria, it also enters the equation.

From this point, stepwise selection differs from forward selection: the first variable is examined to see whether it should be removed according to the removal criterion (FOUT or POUT) as in backward elimination. In the next step, variables not in the equation are examined for entry. After each step, variables already in the equation are examined for removal. Variables are removed until none remain that meet the removal criterion. To prevent the same variable from being repeatedly entered and removed, PIN must be less than POUT (or FIN greater than FOUT). Variable selection terminates when no more variables meet entry and removal criteria.

In the salary example, stepwise selection with the default criteria results in the same equation produced by both forward selection and backward elimination (see Figure 2.48).

The three procedures do not always result in the same equation, though you should be encouraged when they do. The model selected by any method should be carefully studied for violations of the assumptions. It is often a good idea to develop several acceptable models and then choose among them based on interpretability, ease of variable acquisition, parsimony, and so forth.

2.49 Checking for Violation of Assumptions

The procedures discussed in Sections 2.17 through 2.22 for checking for violations of assumptions in bivariate regression apply in the multivariate case as well. Residuals should be plotted against predicted values as well as against each independent variable. The distribution of residuals should be examined for normality.

Figure 2.48 Stepwise output

```
COMPUTE LOGBEG=LG10(SALBEG)
REGRESSION VARIABLES=LOGBEG EDLEVEL SEX WORK MINORITY AGE
  /STATISTICS=R COEFF OUTS F
  /DEPENDENT=LOGBEG
  /METHOD=STEPWISE
```

```
                              * * * * * * * * * * * * * * * * * * * * * * * * * * * * * * *

Listwise Deletion of Missing Data

Equation Number 1    Dependent Variable..   LOGBEG

Beginning Block Number  1.  Method:  Stepwise

Variable(s) Entered on Step Number  1..    EDLEVEL    EDUCATIONAL LEVEL

Multiple R           .68572
R Square             .47021
Adjusted R Square    .46909
Standard Error       .11165

F =     418.92011        Signif F =  .0000

---------------- Variables in the Equation -----------------        ------------- Variables not in the Equation -------------

Variable             B        SE B       Beta          F  Sig F        Variable      Beta In  Partial  Min Toler         F  Sig F

EDLEVEL         .03642  1.7796E-03     .68572    418.920  .0000        SEX          -.34802  -.44681     .87327   117.486  .0000
(Constant)     3.31001      .02455             18176.773  .0000        WORK          .22747   .30241     .93632    47.408  .0000

                              * * * * * * * * * * * * * * * * * * * * * * * * * * * * * * *

Variable(s) Entered on Step Number  2..    SEX        SEX OF EMPLOYEE

Multiple R           .75893
R Square             .57598
Adjusted R Square    .57418
Standard Error       .09999

F =     319.89574        Signif F =  .0000

---------------- Variables in the Equation -----------------        ------------- Variables not in the Equation -------------

Variable             B        SE B       Beta          F  Sig F        Variable      Beta In  Partial  Min Toler         F  Sig F

EDLEVEL         .02984  1.7055E-03     .56183    306.191  .0000        WORK          .14425   .20567     .77382    20.759  .0000
SEX            -.10697  9.8686E-03    -.34802    117.486  .0000        MINORITY     -.12902  -.19464     .84758    18.507  .0000
(Constant)     3.44754      .02539             18443.284  .0000        AGE           .13942   .20519     .80425    20.659  .0000

                              * * * * * * * * * * * * * * * * * * * * * * * * * * * * * * *

Variable(s) Entered on Step Number  3..    WORK       WORK EXPERIENCE

Multiple R           .77066
R Square             .59391
Adjusted R Square    .59132
Standard Error       .09796

F =     229.13001        Signif F =  .0000

---------------- Variables in the Equation -----------------        ------------- Variables not in the Equation -------------

Variable             B        SE B       Beta          F  Sig F        Variable      Beta In  Partial  Min Toler         F  Sig F

EDLEVEL         .03257  1.7749E-03     .61321    336.771  .0000        MINORITY     -.14125  -.21700     .75967    23.176  .0000
SEX            -.09403      .01008    -.30594     87.099  .0000        AGE           .07633   .06754     .29839     2.149  .1433
WORK        2.53616E-03 5.5664E-04     .14425     20.759  .0000
(Constant)     3.38457      .02845             14150.645  .0000

                              * * * * * * * * * * * * * * * * * * * * * * * * * * * * * * *

Variable(s) Entered on Step Number  4..    MINORITY   MINORITY CLASSIFICATION

Multiple R           .78297
R Square             .61304
Adjusted R Square    .60974
Standard Error       .09573

F =     185.74958        Signif F =  .0000

---------------- Variables in the Equation -----------------        ------------- Variables not in the Equation -------------

Variable             B        SE B       Beta          F  Sig F        Variable      Beta In  Partial  Min Toler         F  Sig F

EDLEVEL         .03143  1.7506E-03     .59176    322.412  .0000        AGE           .07811   .07080     .29784     2.357  .1254
SEX            -.09904  9.9010E-03    -.32223    100.063  .0000
WORK        2.75324E-03 5.4582E-04     .15659     25.444  .0000
MINORITY       -.05225      .01085    -.14125     23.176  .0000
(Constant)     3.41195      .02838             14454.046  .0000

End Block Number   1   PIN =     .050 Limits reached.
```

Several additional residual plots may be useful for multivariate models. One of these is the partial regression plot. For the *j*th independent variable, it is obtained by calculating the residuals for the dependent variable when it is predicted from all the independent variables excluding the *j*th and by calculating the residuals for the *j*th independent variable when it is predicted from all of the other independent variables. This removes the linear effect of the other independent variables from both variables. For each case, these two residuals are plotted against each other.

A partial regression plot for educational level for the regression equation that contains work experience, minority, sex, and educational level as the independent

Figure 2.49a Partial regression plot from PLOT

```
COMPUTE LOGBEG=LG10(SALBEG)
REGRESSION VARIABLES=LOGBEG SEX MINORITY EDLEVEL WORK
  /DEPENDENT=LOGBEG
  /METHOD=ENTER MINORITY SEX WORK
  /SAVE=RESID(RES1)
  /DEPENDENT=EDLEVEL
  /METHOD=ENTER MINORITY SEX WORK
  /SAVE=RESID(RES2)
PLOT FORMAT=REGRESSION /PLOT=RES1 WITH RES2
```

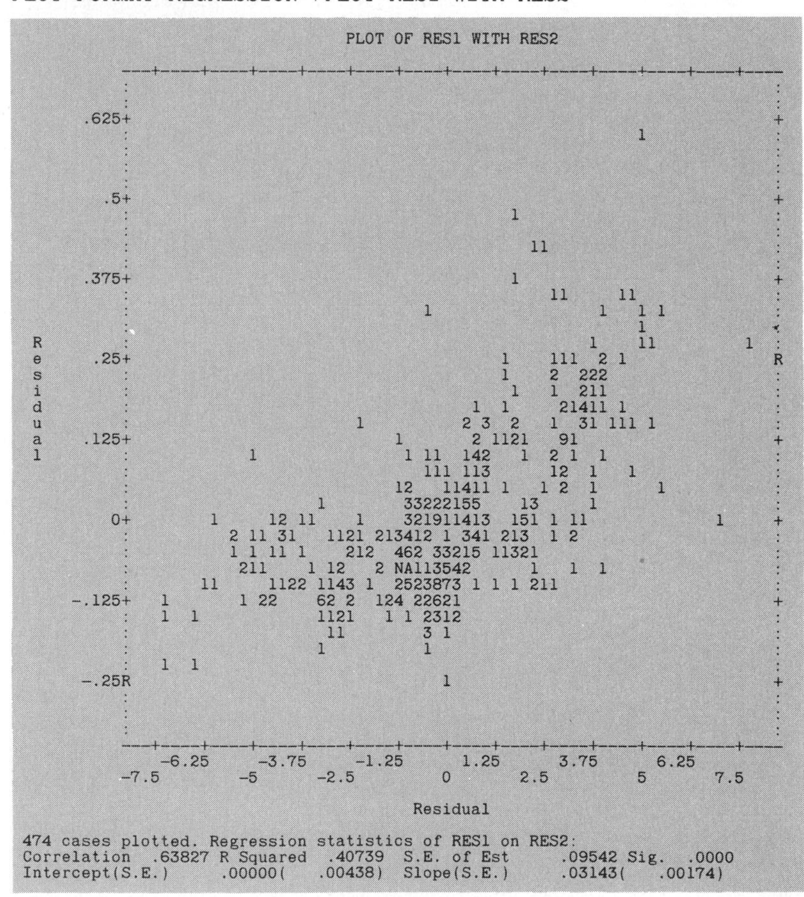

variables is shown in Figure 2.49a. (Summary statistics for the regression equation with all independent variables are displayed in the last step of Figure 2.48.)

Several characteristics of the partial regression plot make it a particularly valuable diagnostic tool. The slope of the regression line for the two residual variables (0.03143) is equal to the coefficient for the EDLEVEL variable in the multiple regression equation after the last step (Step 4 in Figure 2.48). Thus, by examining the bivariate plot, you can conveniently identify points that are "influential" in the determination of the particular regression coefficient (see Sections 2.23 through 2.25). The correlation coefficient between the two residuals, 0.638, is the partial correlation coefficient coefficient discussed in Section 2.39. The residuals from the least-squares line in Figure 2.49a are equal to the residuals from the final multiple regression equation, which includes all the independent variables.

The partial regression plot also helps you assess inadequacies of the selected model and violations of the underlying assumptions. For example, the partial regression plot of educational level does not appear to be linear, suggesting that an additional term, such as years of education squared, might also be included in the model. This violation is much easier to spot using the partial regression plot than the plot of the independent variable against the residual from the equation with all independent variables. Figures 2.49b and 2.49c show the residual scatterplot and partial regression plot produced by the REGRESSION procedure. Note that the nonlinearity is much more apparent in the partial regression plot.

Figure 2.49b Residual scatterplot from REGRESSION

```
COMPUTE LOGBEG=LG10(SALBEG)
REGRESSION VARIABLES=LOGBEG SEX MINORITY EDLEVEL WORK
  /DEPENDENT=LOGBEG
  /METHOD=STEPWISE
  /SCATTERPLOT=(*RESID, EDLEVEL)
```

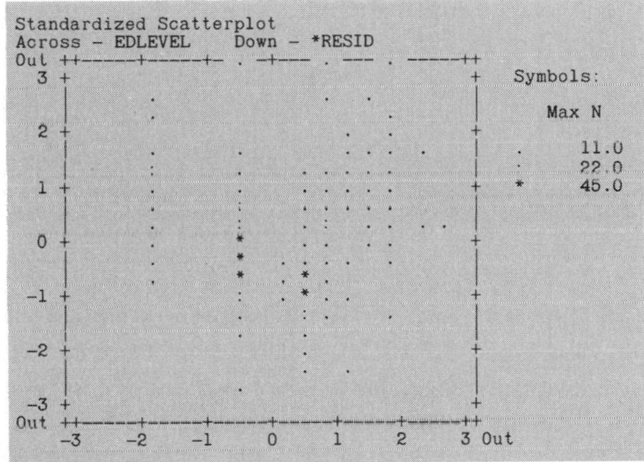

Figure 2.49c Partial regression plot from REGRESSION

```
COMPUTE LOGBEG=LG10(SALBEG)
REGRESSION VARIABLES=LOGBEG SEX MINORITY EDLEVEL WORK
  /DEPENDENT=LOGBEG
  /METHOD=STEPWISE
  /PARTIALPLOT=EDLEVEL
```

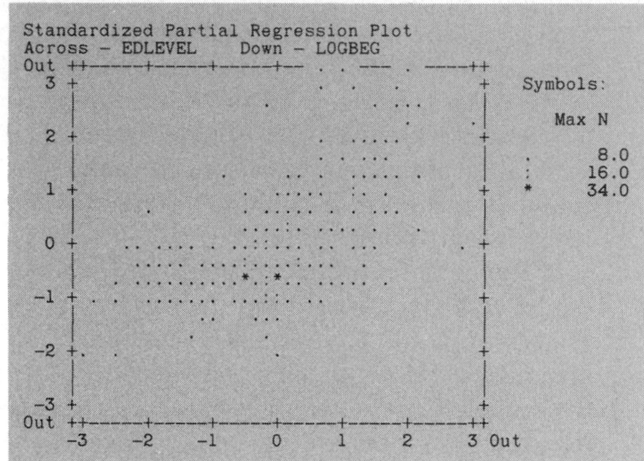

Figure 2.49d contains the summary statistics when the number of years of education squared is included in the multiple regression equation. The multiple R^2 increases from 0.61 (Step 4 in Figure 2.48) to 0.71, a significant improvement.

Figure 2.49d The regression equation with education squared

```
COMPUTE LOGBEG=LG10(SALBEG)
COMPUTE ED2=EDLEVEL*EDLEVEL
REGRESSION VARIABLES=LOGBEG SEX MINORITY EDLEVEL ED2 WORK
  /DEPENDENT=LOGBEG
  /METHOD=ENTER
```

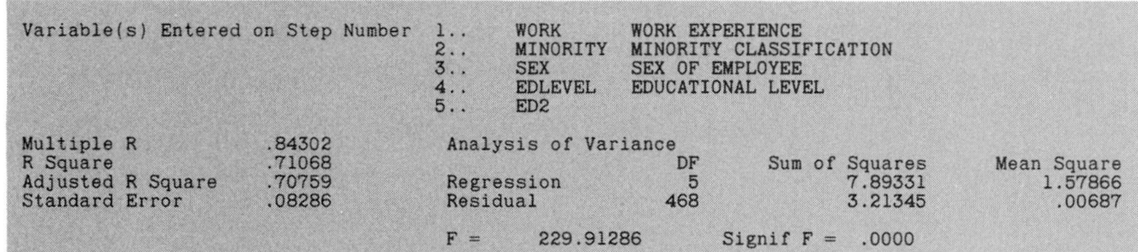

```
Variable(s) Entered on Step Number  1..   WORK      WORK EXPERIENCE
                                    2..   MINORITY  MINORITY CLASSIFICATION
                                    3..   SEX       SEX OF EMPLOYEE
                                    4..   EDLEVEL   EDUCATIONAL LEVEL
                                    5..   ED2

Multiple R           .84302       Analysis of Variance
R Square             .71068                        DF      Sum of Squares      Mean Square
Adjusted R Square    .70759       Regression        5             7.89331          1.57866
Standard Error       .08286       Residual        468             3.21345           .00687

                                  F =     229.91286        Signif F =  .0000
```

The casewise plot of cases with residuals greater than 3 in absolute value is shown in Figure 2.49e. An additional statistic shown with this plot is the centered leverage (*LEVER), which is a measure of the influence of a point. The centered leverage ranges from $-1/N$ to $(N-1)/N$, where N is the number of observations. The mean value for the centered leverage is N/p, where p is the number of independent variables in the equation. The Mahalanobis' distance previously described is obtained by multiplying the leverage value by $N-1$. A leverage of $-1/N$ identifies a point with no influence on the fit, while a point with a leverage of $(N-1)/N$ indicates that a degree of freedom has been devoted to fitting the data point. See Belsley, Kuh, and Welsch (1980) for further details.

Figure 2.49e Casewise plot of outliers

```
COMPUTE LOGBEG=LG10(SALBEG)
COMPUTE ED2=EDLEVEL*EDLEVEL
REGRESSION VARIABLES=LOGBEG SEX MINORITY EDLEVEL ED2 WORK
  /DEPENDENT=LOGBEG
  /METHOD=ENTER
  /CASEWISE=PRED RESID MAHAL COOK LEVER OUTLIERS(3)
```

```
Casewise Plot of Standardized Residual

Outliers = 3.    *: Selected   M: Missing

        -6.          -3.  3.          6.
 Case #  0:............:  :............:0      *PRED     *RESID     *LEVER     *MAHAL    *COOK D
     2   .            ..            *  .     3.9303     .4499     .0042     2.0100     .0316
    56   .            ..     *         .     4.1478     .3572     .0210     9.9449     .0751
    67   .            ..     *         .     3.9303     .3484     .0042     2.0100     .0190
   122   .            ..      *        .     3.9465     .3758     .0103     4.8777     .0437
   283   .            ..*              .     3.8276     .2516     .0066     3.1029     .0136
   402   .            ..      *        .     3.7578     .3725     .0141     6.6804     .0565
   415   .            ..     *         .     3.8888     .3577     .0106     5.0249     .0406

    7 Outliers found.
```

2.50 Interpreting the Equation

The multiple regression equation estimated above suggests several findings. Education appears to be the best predictor of beginning salary, at least among the variables included in this study (Figure 2.47a). The sex of the employee also appears to be important. Women are paid less than men since the sign of the regression coefficient is negative (men are coded 0 and women are coded 1). Years of prior work experience and race are also related to salary, but when education and sex are included in the equation, the effect of experience and race is less striking.

Do these results indicate that there is sex discrimination at the bank? Not necessarily. It is well recognized that all education is not equally profitable. Master's degrees in business administration and political science are treated quite differently in the marketplace. Thus, a possible explanation of the observed results is that women enter areas that are just not very well paid. Although this may suggest inequities in societal evaluation of skills, it does not necessarily imply discrimination at the bank. Further, many other potential job-related skills or qualifications are not included in the model. Also, some of the existing variables, such as age, may make nonlinear as well as linear contributions to the fit. Such contributions can often be approximated by including new variables that are simple functions of the existing one. For example, the age values squared may improve the fit.

2.51 Statistics for Unselected Cases

As previously noted, a model usually fits the sample from which it is derived better than it fits the population. A sometimes useful strategy for obtaining an estimate of how well the model fits the population is to split the sample randomly into two parts. One part is then used to estimate the model, while the remaining cases are reserved for testing the goodness of fit.

It is also sometimes interesting to split the data on some characteristics of the sample. For example, you can develop the salary equation for males alone and then apply it to females to see how well it fits. For example, Figure 2.51 shows histograms of residuals for males (denoted as selected cases) and females (unselected cases). Note that the females' salaries are too large when predicted from the male equation since most of the residuals are negative. The multiple *R* for the females is 0.45596, which is smaller than the 0.73882 for males (stepwise selection was used).

Figure 2.51 Histograms for males (selected) and females (unselected)

```
COMPUTE LOGBEG=LG10(SALBEG)
COMPUTE ED2=EDLEVEL*EDLEVEL
REGRESSION WIDTH=90
  /SELECT SEX EQ 0
  /VARIABLES=LOGBEG,EDLEVEL,ED2,SEX,WORK,MINORITY,AGE
  /DEPENDENT=LOGBEG
  /METHOD=STEPWISE
  /RESIDUALS=HISTOGRAM
```

```
Histogram - Standardized Residual
- Selected Cases
 N Exp N        (* = 1 Cases,     . : = Normal Curve)
 6   .20   Out ******
 0   .40  3.00
 0  1.01  2.67 .
 1  2.30  2.33 *.
 1  4.71  2.00 *   .
 6  8.63  1.67 ******  .
 7 14.16  1.33 *******      .
14 20.81  1.00 **************      .
24 27.40   .67 ************************  .
36 32.32   .33 *******************************:****
39 34.15   .00 *********************************:*****
48 32.32  -.33 *******************************:****************
41 27.40  -.67 **************************:**************
17 20.81 -1.00 *****************   .
12 14.16 -1.33 ************ .
 3  8.63 -1.67 ***     .
 0  4.71 -2.00     .
 2  2.30 -2.33 *:
 1  1.01 -2.67 :
 0   .40 -3.00
 0   .20   Out


Histogram - Standardized Residual
- Unselected Cases
 N Exp N        (X = 1 Cases,     . : = Normal Curve)
 0   .17   Out
 0   .33  3.00
 0   .84  2.67 .
 0  1.93  2.33  .
 0  3.94  2.00   .
 1  7.22  1.67 X     .
 2 11.85  1.33 XX         .
 2 17.42  1.00 XX              .
 3 22.94   .67 XXX                   .
 5 27.06   .33 XXXXX                     .
23 28.59   .00 XXXXXXXXXXXXXXXXXXXXXXX     .
23 27.06  -.33 XXXXXXXXXXXXXXXXXXXXXXX   .
36 22.94  -.67 XXXXXXXXXXXXXXXXXXXXXX:XXXXXXXXXXXXX
49 17.42 -1.00 XXXXXXXXXXXXXXXX:XXXXXXXXXXXXXXXXXXXXXXXXXXXXXXXX
20 11.85 -1.33 XXXXXXXXXXX:XXXXXXXX
14  7.22 -1.67 XXXXXX:XXXXXXX
15  3.94 -2.00 XXX:XXXXXXXXXXX
15  1.93 -2.33 X:XXXXXXXXXXXXX
 4   .84 -2.67 :XXX
 0   .33 -3.00
 4   .17   Out XXXX
```

2.52 Problems of Multicollinearity

Preceding sections deal with the consequences of correlated independent variables in regression analysis. The estimates of the β's and the sum of squares attributable to each variable are dependent on the other variables in the equation. Variances of the estimators also increase when independent variables are interrelated. This may result in a regression equation with a significant R^2, although virtually none of the coefficients is significantly different from 0. If any independent variable is a perfect linear combination of other independent variables, the correlation matrix is *singular* and a unique, unbiased least-squares solution does not exist.

Although situations involving singularities do occur, they are not as common as those involving near-singularities—variables that are almost linear combinations of other independent variables. These variables are often called *multicollinear*.

2.53 Methods of Detection

Multicollinearities can be detected in several ways. Large coefficients in the correlation matrix always signal the presence of multicollinearity. However, multicollinearity can exist even when none of the correlation coefficients is very large.

One of the most frequently used indicators of interdependency between variables is the tolerance (see Section 2.40). If the variable has a large R^2—or equivalently a small tolerance—when it is predicted from the other independent variables, a potentially troublesome situation exists. Not only are the variances of the estimators inflated, but computational problems can occur.

2.54 SPSS^X and Multicollinearity

In the SPSS^X REGRESSION procedure, various steps are taken to warn you of multicollinearity. Before an independent variable is entered into the equation, its tolerance with other independent variables already in the equation is calculated.

It is possible for a variable not in the equation to have an acceptable tolerance level but when entered to cause the tolerance of other variables already in the equation to become unacceptably small (Berk, 1977; Frane, 1977). Thus, the tolerances of all the variables in the equation are recomputed at each step. If either the tolerance of the variable or the tolerance of any variable already in the equation is less than 0.01, a warning is issued and the variable is not entered unless the default TOLERANCE criterion has been altered.

In SPSS^X, you can display both the tolerance of a variable and the minimum tolerance of all independent variables in the equation if the variable were entered.

2.55 RUNNING PROCEDURE REGRESSION

The REGRESSION procedure provides five equation-building methods: forward selection, backward elimination, stepwise selection, forced entry, and forced removal. The subcommands for residual analysis help detect influential data points, outliers, and violations of the regression model assumptions.

2.56 Building the Equation

To build a simple regression model, you must specify three required subcommands: a VARIABLES subcommand that names the variables to be analyzed, a DEPENDENT subcommand that indicates the dependent variable, and a METHOD subcommand that names the method to be used. For example, to build the simple bivariate model of beginning salary and current salary discussed earlier in the chapter, specify

```
REGRESSION VARIABLES=SALBEG SALNOW
  /DEPENDENT=SALNOW
  /METHOD-ENTER SALBEG
```

The beginning (SALBEG) and current (SALNOW) salaries are named, with the latter specified as the dependent variable. The ENTER keyword enters beginning salary into the equation. The output produced from this command is shown in Figures 2.3b, 2.10, and 2.11a.

2.57 The VARIABLES and DEPENDENT Subcommands

The VARIABLES subcommand lists all variables needed for the regression analysis, including those that are named on the DEPENDENT and METHOD subcommands. As of Release 2.1 of SPSS^X, there can be only one VARIABLES subcommand per REGRESSION command, and it must be specified before the DEPENDENT and METHOD subcommands. (Earlier releases permit multiple VARIABLES subcommands, one for each DEPENDENT and METHOD subcommand pair.)

For example, to run both the bivariate and multivariate examples that have been developed in this chapter, specify

```
REGRESSION VARIABLES=SALBEG SALNOW LOGBEG
           EDLEVEL SEX WORK MINORITY AGE
  /DEPENDENT=SALNOW
  /METHOD=ENTER SALBEG
  /DEPENDENT=LOGBEG
  /METHOD=ENTER EDLEVEL TO AGE
```

The first DEPENDENT subcommand defines a single equation with SALNOW as the dependent variable, and the METHOD subcommand requests that SALBEG be entered into the equation. The second DEPENDENT subcommand defines another equation, with LOGBEG as the dependent variable. The associated METHOD subcommand requests that the variables EDLEVEL to AGE be entered into the equation. The TO convention for naming consecutive variables used in the second METHOD subcommand refers to the order in which the variables are named on the VARIABLES subcommand. See Figures 2.36a and 2.36b for the output from the second equation.

Usually only one variable is named as a dependent variable on a DEPENDENT subcommand. If you name more than one dependent variable, SPSS^X develops an equation for the first variable, then for the second, and so on.

2.58 The METHOD Subcommand

At least one METHOD subcommand must immediately follow each DEPENDENT subcommand, specifying the method to be used in developing the regression equation. The available methods are

FORWARD *Forward variable selection.* Variables are entered one at a time based on entry criteria (Section 2.46).

BACKWARD *Backward variable elimination.* All variables are entered and then removed one at a time based on removal criteria (Section 2.47).

STEPWISE *Stepwise variable entry and removal.* Variables are examined at each step for entry or removal (Section 2.48).

ENTER *Forced entry.* The variables named are entered in a single step. The default variable list is all independent variables.

REMOVE (varlist) *Forced removal.* The variables named are removed in a single step. REMOVE must have an accompanying variable list.

TEST (varlist) *Test indicated subsets of independent variables.* TEST offers an easy way to test a variety of models using R^2 change and its test of significance as the criterion for the "best" model. TEST must have an accompanying variable list.

A variable list is required with the REMOVE and TEST keywords and is optional for the other METHOD keywords. The default variable list for methods FORWARD, BACKWARD, STEPWISE, and ENTER includes all variables named on the VARIABLES subcommand that are not named on the preceding

DEPENDENT subcommand. For example, to request the backward-elimination method discussed in Section 2.47, specify

```
REGRESSION VARIABLES=LOGBEG EDLEVEL SEX WORK MINORITY AGE
  /DEPENDENT=LOGBEG
  /METHOD=BACKWARD
```

The METHOD subcommand keyword was introduced with Release 2.1 of SPSS^X. This keyword is not recognized in Releases 1 and 2 of SPSS^X and is optional in 2.1 and later releases. However, all releases will accept the following specification as equivalent to the one above:

```
REGRESSION VARIABLES=LOGBEG EDLEVEL SEX WORK MINORITY AGE
  /DEPENDENT=LOGBEG
  /BACKWARD
```

You can specify multiple METHOD subcommands. For example, you might want to force one variable into the equation first and then enter the remaining variables in a forward-selection fashion, as in

```
REGRESSION VARIABLES=LOGBEG EDLEVEL SEX WORK MINORITY AGE
  /DEPENDENT=LOGBEG
  /METHOD=ENTER EDLEVEL
  /METHOD=FORWARD SEX TO AGE
```

2.59 The CRITERIA Subcommand

You can control the statistical criteria by which REGRESSION chooses variables for entry into or removal from an equation with the CRITERIA subcommand. Place the CRITERIA subcommand after the VARIABLES subcommand and before the DEPENDENT subcommand. A CRITERIA subcommand affects any subsequent DEPENDENT and METHOD subcommands and remains in effect until overridden with another CRITERIA subcommand.

The CRITERIA keywords are

DEFAULTS *PIN(0.05), POUT(0.10), and TOLERANCE(0.01).* These are the defaults if no CRITERIA subcommand is specified. If criteria have been changed, DEFAULTS restores the default values.

PIN(value) *Probability of* F*-to-enter.* Use to override the default value of 0.05.

POUT(value) *Probability of* F*-to-remove.* Use to override the default value of 0.10.

FIN(value) F*-to-enter.* The default value is 3.84. FIN and PIN are mutually exclusive.

FOUT(value) F*-to-remove.* The default value is 2.71. FOUT and POUT are mutually exclusive.

TOLERANCE(value) *Tolerance.* The default value in Release 3.0 is 0.0001. In earlier releases it is 0.01. All variables must pass both tolerance and minimum tolerance tests before entering the equation. (See Sections 2.40, 2.53, and 2.54.)

MAXSTEPS(n) *Maximum number of steps.* For the STEPWISE method, the default is twice the number of independent variables. For the FORWARD and BACKWARD methods, the default maximum is the number of variables meeting the PIN and POUT or FIN and FOUT criteria. The MAXSTEPS value applies to the total model. The default value for the total model is the sum of the maximum number of steps over each method in the model.

For example, to change stepwise entry and removal criteria to FIN and FOUT and use their default values of 3.84 and 2.71, respectively, specify

```
REGRESSION VARIABLES=LOGBEG EDLEVEL SEX WORK MINORITY AGE
  /CRITERIA=FIN,FOUT
  /DEPENDENT=LOGBEG
  /METHOD=STEPWISE
```

2.60 The STATISTICS Subcommand

By default, REGRESSION displays the four sets of statistics described for keywords R, ANOVA, COEFF, and OUTS below. These statistics are shown in Figures 2.3b, 2.10, and 2.11a for the bivariate equation, and in Figures 2.36a and 2.36b for the multivariate equation. You can specify exactly which statistics you want displayed by any of the following keywords on the STATISTICS subcommand.

DEFAULTS R, *ANOVA, COEFF, and OUTS.* These statistics are displayed when the STATISTICS subcommand is omitted or if no keywords are specified on the subcommand. If you specify statistics keywords on a STATISTICS subcommand, the default statistics will not appear unless you specify them explicitly, either individually, or with the DEFAULTS keyword.

ALL *All statistics except* F, *LINE, and END.*

R *Multiple* R. Displays multiple R, R^2, adjusted R^2, and the standard error. (See Figure 2.10.)

ANOVA *Analysis of variance table.* Displays degrees of freedom, sums of squares, mean squares, F value for multiple R, and the observed significance level of F. (See Figure 2.11a.)

CHA *Displays change in* R^2 *between steps,* F *value for change in* R^2, *and* significance of F. (See Figure 2.42.)

BCOV *Variance-covariance matrix.* Displays a matrix with covariances above the diagonal, correlations below the diagonal, and variances on the diagonal. (See Figure 2.40b.)

XTX *Sweep matrix.*

COND *Condition number bounds.* Prints the lower and upper bounds for the condition number of the submatrix of the sweep matrix that contains independent variables already entered. (Berk, 1977)

COEFF *Statistics for variables in the equation.* Displays regression coefficient B, standard error of B, standardized coefficient Beta, t value for B, and two-tailed significance level of t.

OUTS *Statistics for variables not in the equation* that have been named on the VARIABLES subcommand. Statistics are Beta if the variable were entered, t value for Beta, significance level of t, partial correlation with the dependent variable controlling for variables in the equation, and minimum tolerance.

ZPP *Zero-order, part, and partial correlation.* (See Figure 2.39.)

CI *Confidence intervals.* Displays the 95% confidence interval for the unstandardized regression coefficient. (See Figure 2.8.)

SES *Approximate standard error of the standardized regression coefficients.* (Meyer and Younger, 1976)

TOL *Tolerance.* Displays tolerance for variables in the equation and, for variables not in the equation, the tolerance a variable would have if it were the only variable entered next. (See Figure 2.40a.)

F F *value for* B *and significance of* F. Displayed instead of t for COEFF and OUTS. (See, for example, Figures 2.46b, 2.46c, 2.47a, and 2.47b.)

LINE *Summary line for each step in step methods.* Displays a single summary line for each step in BACKWARD, FORWARD, or STEPWISE methods and the default or requested statistics at the end of each method block (BACKWARD, FORWARD, STEPWISE, ENTER, REMOVE, or TEST).

HISTORY *Step history.* Displays a summary report with a summary line for each method (ENTER, REMOVE, or TEST, if the equation changes) or step if the method entails steps (FORWARD, BACKWARD, or STEPWISE). If history is the only statistic requested, COEFF is displayed for the final equation. (See Figures 2.44 and 2.46a.)

END *One summary line per step or method block.* Displays a summary line per step for BACKWARD, FORWARD, or STEPWISE, and one summary line per block for ENTER, REMOVE, or TEST, if the equation changes.

The STATISTICS subcommand must appear before the DEPENDENT subcommand that initiates the equation and remains in effect until overridden by another STATISTICS subcommand. For example, to produce the output in Figure 2.8, specify

```
REGRESSION VARIABLES=SALBEG SALNOW
  /STATISTICS=CI
  /DEPENDENT=SALNOW
  /METHOD=ENTER SALBEG
```

To produce the output for the multivariate example shown in Figure 2.42, specify

```
REGRESSION VARIABLES=LOGBEG EDLEVEL SEX WORK MINORITY AGE
  /STATISTICS=R CHANGE COEFF
  /DEPENDENT=LOGBEG
  /METHOD=ENTER EDLEVEL
  /METHOD=ENTER SEX
```

2.61 The ORIGIN Subcommand

The regression model contains a constant term. You can use the ORIGIN subcommand to suppress this term and obtain regression through the origin. The NOORIGIN subcommand, which is the default, requests that equations include a constant term.

Place the ORIGIN or NOORIGIN subcommand between the VARIABLES subcommand and the DEPENDENT subcommand for the equation. For example,

```
REGRESSION VARIABLES=SALBEG SALNOW,EDLEVEL
  /DEPENDENT=SALNOW
  /METHOD=ENTER SALBEG
    /ORIGIN
    /DEPENDENT=SALBEG
    /METHOD=ENTER EDLEVEL
```

requests two equations, the first with a constant term (the default) and the second with regression through the origin.

There are no specifications for the ORIGIN and NOORIGIN subcommands. Once specified, the ORIGIN subcommand remains in effect until NOORIGIN is requested.

2.62 The SELECT Subcommand

Use the SELECT subcommand to select a subset of cases for computing the regression equation. Only selected cases contribute to the correlation coefficients and to the regression equation. Residuals and predicted values are calculated and reported separately for both selected and unselected cases. The SELECT subcommand can precede or immediately follow the VARIABLES subcommand and is in effect for the entire REGRESSION command. The form of the SELECT subcommand is

/SELECT= varname relation value

The *relation* can be EQ, NE, LT, LE, GT, or GE.

For example, to generate separate residuals histograms for males and females based on the equation developed for males alone (SEX=0), as shown in Figure 2.51, specify

```
REGRESSION SELECT SEX EQ 0
  /VARIABLES=LOGBEG EDLEVEL SEX WORK MINORITY AGE
  /DEPENDENT=LOGBEG
  /METHOD=STEPWISE
  /RESIDUALS=HISTOGRAM
```

2.63 The MISSING Subcommand

Use the MISSING subcommand to specify the treatment of cases with missing values. If the MISSING subcommand is omitted, a case with user- or system-missing values for any variable named on the VARIABLES subcommand is excluded from the computation of the correlation matrix on which all analyses are based. The MISSING subcommand can precede or immediately follow the VARIABLES subcommand and is in effect for the entire REGRESSION command.

The available keywords are

LISTWISE *Delete cases with missing values listwise.* Only cases with valid values for all variables listed on the VARIABLES subcommand are included in analyses. If INCLUDE is also specified, only cases with system-missing values are deleted listwise. LISTWISE is the default.

PAIRWISE *Delete cases with missing values pairwise.* Cases with complete data on the pair of variables being correlated are used to compute the correlation coefficient. If INCLUDE is also specified, only cases with system-missing values are deleted pairwise.

MEANSUBSTITUTION *Replace missing values with the variable mean.* All cases are used for computations, with the mean of a variable substituted for missing observations. If INCLUDE is also specified, user-missing values are included in the computation of the means and only system-missing values are substituted.

INCLUDE *Include all cases with user-missing values.* Only cases with system-missing values are excluded.

2.64 The DESCRIPTIVES Subcommand

You can request a variety of descriptive statistics with the DESCRIPTIVES subcommand. These statistics are displayed for all variables specified on the VARIABLES subcommand, regardless of which variables you specify for computations. Descriptive statistics are based on all valid cases for each variable if you have specified PAIRWISE or MEANSUB on the MISSING subcommand. Otherwise, only cases that are included in the computation of the correlation matrix are used. If you specify the DESCRIPTIVES subcommand without any keywords, the statistics listed for keyword DEFAULTS are displayed. If you name any statistics on DESCRIPTIVES, only those explicity requested are displayed.

The following descriptive statistics are available:

DEFAULTS *MEAN, STDDEV, and CORR.* This is the default if DESCRIPTIVES is specified without any keywords.

MEAN *Variable means.*

STDDEV *Variable standard deviations.*

VARIANCE *Variable variances.*

CORR *Correlation matrix.*

SIG *One-tailed significance levels for the correlation coefficients.*

BADCORR *Correlation matrix only if some coefficients cannot be computed.*

COV *Covariance matrix.*

XPROD *Cross-product deviations from the mean.*

N *Number of cases used to compute the correlation coefficients.*

ALL *All descriptive statistics.*

For example, to produce the correlation matrix shown in Figure 2.34, specify

```
REGRESSION DESCRIPTIVES=CORR
  /VARIABLES=LOGBEG EDLEVEL SEX WORK MINORITY AGE
  /DEPENDENT=LOGBEG
  /METHOD=ENTER EDLEVEL TO AGE
```

2.65 Analyzing Residuals

Once you have built an equation, REGRESSION can calculate twelve temporary variables containing several types of residuals, predicted values, and related measures. You can use these variables to detect outliers and influential data points and to examine the regression assumptions described in Sections 2.17 through 2.22.

The following temporary variables are available for the analysis of residuals.

PRED *Unstandardized predicted values.* (See Section 2.13.)

ZPRED *Standardized predicted values.* (See Section 2.13.)

SEPRED *Standard errors of the predicted values.* (See Section 2.14.)

RESID *Unstandardized residuals.* (See Section 2.18.)

ZRESID *Standardized residuals.* (See Section 2.18.)

SRESID *Studentized residuals.* (See Section 2.18.)

MAHAL *Mahalanobis' distance.* (See Section 2.21.)

ADJPRED *Adjusted predicted values.* (See Section 2.25.)

DRESID *Deleted residuals.* (See Section 2.25.)

SDRESID *Studentized deleted residuals.* (See Section 2.25.)

COOK *Cook's distances.* (See Section 2.25.)

LEVER *Leverage values.* (See Section 2.49.)

Residuals analysis is specified with four subcommands: RESIDUALS, CASEWISE, PARTIALPLOT, and SCATTERPLOT. You can specify these subcommands in any order, but you cannot specify more than one of each per equation, and they must immediately follow the last METHOD subcommand that completes an equation. The residuals subcommands affect only the equation they follow. Requesting any residuals analysis always produces descriptive statistics on at least four of the temporary variables (PRED, ZPRED, RESID, and ZRESID).

All variables are standardized before plotting. If an unstandardized version of a variable is requested, the standardized version is plotted.

2.66 The RESIDUALS Subcommand

Use the RESIDUALS subcommand to obtain the statistics and plots listed below. Specifying the RESIDUALS subcommand without any specifications produces the display described for keyword DEFAULTS. If any keywords are specified on RESIDUALS, *only* the displays for those keywords are produced.

DEFAULTS *HISTOGRAM(ZRESID), NORMPROB(ZRESID), OUTLIERS plots(ZRESID), SIZE(SMALL), and DURBIN.* These plots are produced if RESIDUALS is specified without any specifications.

HISTOGRAM(tempvars) *Histogram of standardized temporary variables named.* The default temporary variable is ZRESID. Other variables that can be plotted are PRED, RESID, ZPRED, DRESID, ADJPRED, SRESID, and SDRESID. (See Figure 2.22a.)

NORMPROB(tempvars) *Normal probability (P-P) plot of standardized values.* The default variable is ZRESID. Other variables that can be plotted are PRED, RESID, ZPRED, and DRESID. (See Figure 2.22b.)

SIZE(plotsize) *Plot sizes.* The plot size can be specified as SMALL or LARGE. The default is LARGE if the display width is at least 120 and the page length is at least 55.

OUTLIERS(tempvars) *The ten most extreme values for the temporary variables named.* The default temporary variable is ZRESID. Other variables can be RESID, DRESID, SRESID, SDRESID MAHAL, and COOK. (See Figure 2.24.)

DURBIN *Durbin-Watson test statistic.* (See Section 2.21.)

ID(varname) *Identification labels for casewise and outlier plots.* Cases are labeled with values of the variable named after the ID keyword. By default, the plots are labeled with the sequential case number. ID also labels the CASEWISE list of cases. (See Figures 2.23 and 2.24.)

POOLED *Pooled plots and statistics when the SELECT subcommand is in effect.* All cases in the active file are used. The default is separate reporting of residuals statistics and plots for selected and unselected cases.

For example, to produce the output shown in Figures 2.22a, 2.22b, and 2.24, specify

```
REGRESSION VARIABLES=SALBEG SALNOW
  /DEPENDENT=SALNOW
  /METHOD=ENTER SALBEG
  /RESIDUALS=HISTOGRAM(SRESID) NORMPROB
             OUTLIERS(MAHAL) ID(SEXRACE)
```

2.67 The CASEWISE Subcommand

You can display a casewise plot of one of the temporary variables accompanied by a listing of the values of the dependent and the temporary variables. The plot can be requested for all cases or limited to outliers. Specifying the CASEWISE subcommand without keywords produces the output listed for DEFAULTS.

The following may be specified on the CASEWISE subcommand.

DEFAULTS *OUTLIERS(3), PLOT(ZRESID), DEPENDENT, PRED, and RESID.* This is the default if CASEWISE is specified without any keywords.

OUTLIERS(value) *Limit plot to outliers greater than or equal to the standardized absolute value of the plotted variable.* The default value is 3. (See Figure 2.23.)

ALL *Include all cases in the casewise plot.* Produces a plot of all cases, including outliers. The keyword OUTLIERS is ignored when ALL is specified.

PLOT(tempvar) *Plot the standardized values of the temporary variable named.* The default variable is ZRESID. The other variables that can be plotted are RESID, DRESID, SRESID, and SDRESID. (See Figure 2.23.)

varlist *List values of the DEPENDENT and temporary variables named.* Any temporary variable, including LEVER, can be listed. The defaults are DEPENDENT (the dependent variable), PRED, and RESID. (See Figures 2.16 and 2.23.)

For example, to produce the casewise plot shown in Figure 2.16, specify

```
REGRESSION VARIABLES=SALBEG SALNOW
  /DEPENDENT=SALNOW
  /METHOD=ENTER SALBEG
  /RESIDUALS=ID(SEXRACE)
  /CASEWISE=ALL DEPENDENT PRED RESID SEPRED
```

To plot outliers whose absolute values are equal to or greater than 3 based on ZRESID, you need only specify the CASEWISE subcommand. To base the plot on Studentized residuals and label it with an ID variable, as shown in Figure 2.23, specify

```
REGRESSION VARIABLES=SALBEG SALNOW
  /DEPENDENT=SALNOW
  /METHOD=ENTER SALBEG
  /RESIDUALS=ID(SEXRACE)
  /CASEWISE=PLOT(SRESID)
```

If you request more variables than will fit on the page width set either with the SET WIDTH command or the WIDTH subcommand in REGRESSION, your output will be truncated. (See Section 2.73).

2.68 The SCATTERPLOT Subcommand

Use the SCATTERPLOT subcommand to generate scatterplots for the variables in the equation. You must name at least one pair of variables on the SCATTERPLOT subcommand. Optionally, you can specify the SIZE keyword to control the size of the plots. All scatterplots are standardized.

The specifications for SCATTERPLOT are

(varname,varname) *The pair of variables to be plotted.* Available variables are PRED, RESID, ZPRED, ZRESID, DRESID, ADJPRED, SRESID, SDRESID, and any variable named on the VARIABLES subcommand. Temporary variables should be preceded by an asterisk on this subcommand.

SIZE(plotsize) *Plot sizes.* Plotsize can be SMALL or LARGE. The default is SMALL.

The first variable named inside the parentheses is plotted on the vertical (*Y*) axis, and the second is plotted on the horizontal (*X*) axis. For example, to generate the scatterplot shown in Figure 2.20, specify

```
REGRESSION VARIABLES=SALBEG SALNOW
  /DEPENDENT=SALNOW
  /METHOD=ENTER SALBEG
  /SCATTERPLOT=(*SRESID,*PRED)
```

To produce a scatterplot for SRESID and PRED based on the logarithmic transformation of both the dependent and independent variables, as shown in Figure 2.30a, use the SCATTERPLOT subcommand above along with the following transformation commands:

```
COMPUTE LOGBEG=LG10(SALBEG)
COMPUTE LOGNOW=LG10(SALNOW)
REGRESSION VARIABLES=LOGBEG,LOGNOW
  /DEPENDENT=LOGNOW
  /METHOD=ENTER LOGBEG
  /SCATTERPLOT=(*SRESID,*PRED)
```

To produce more than one scatterplot, simply add pairs of variable names in parentheses, as in

```
  /SCATTERPLOT=(*SRESID,*PRED)(SALBEG,*PRED)
```

2.69 The PARTIALPLOT Subcommand

Use the PARTIALPLOT subcommand to generate partial residual plots. Partial residual plots are scatterplots of the residuals of the dependent variable and an independent variable when both variables are regressed on the rest of the independent variables.

If no variable list is given on the PARTIALPLOT subcommand, a partial residual plot is produced for every independent variable in the equation. Plots are displayed in descending order of the standard error of *B*. All plots are standardized.

The specifications on the PARTIALPLOT subcommand are

varlist *Independent variables to be used in partial residual plot.* At least two independent variables must be in the equation for a partial residual plot to be produced. You can specify the keyword ALL to obtain the default plots for every independent variable in the equation.

SIZE(plotsize) *Plot sizes.* The plot size can be specified as SMALL or LARGE. The default plotsize is SMALL.

2.70 The SAVE Subcommand

Use the SAVE subcommand to save any or all of the 12 temporary variables described in Section 2.65. The format is the name of the temporary variable followed by a valid variable name in parentheses, as in

```
FILE HANDLE BANK/NAME='BANK SPSSXFIL'
GET FILE=BANK
REGRESSION VARIABLES=SALBEG, SALNOW
  /DEPENDENT=SALNOW
  /METHOD=ENTER SALBEG
  /SAVE=SEPRED(SE)
PLOT CUTPOINTS=EVERY(20) /SYMBOLS='.'
     /PLOT=SE WITH SALBEG
```

This example saves the standard errors of the predicted values with variable name SE. Then the PLOT procedure is used to plot the standard errors against the values of the independent variable SALBEG. Figure 2.14a shows the plot.

2.71 The REGWGT Subcommand

The REGWGT subcommand specifies a variable for estimating weighted least-squares models. The only specification on REGWGT is the name of the single variable containing the weights, as in

```
REGRESSION VARIABLES=IQ TO ACHIEVE/ REGWGT=WGT_1
             /DEPENDENT=VARY/ METHOD=ENTER/ SAVE=PRED(P) RESID(R)
```

The weights of the named variable must correspond in number and order to the cases to which they apply. REGWGT must follow the VARIABLES subcommand and precede the DEPENDENT subcommand.

2.72 The MATRIX Subcommand

Procedure REGRESSION can read and write matrix materials, which can be processed more quickly than cases. When MATRIX is used, it must be the first subcommand specified. Use the following keywords to specify matrix input and output:

OUT *Write matrix materials.* After OUT, in parentheses specify either a name for the matrix file or * to replace the active file with the matrix. The mean, standard deviation, and number of cases used to compute each coefficient are also written with the matrix. (With releases before 3.0, use the /READ subcommand instead.)

IN *Read matrix materials.* After IN, in parentheses specify either the name of the matrix file to read or * to read the matrix materials from the active file. (With releases before 3.0, use the /WRITE subcommand instead.)

See *SPSS^X User's Guide* for complete instructions on using matrix materials with REGRESSION.

2.73 The WIDTH Subcommand

You can use the WIDTH subcommand to control the width of the display produced by the REGRESSION procedure. The default is the width specified on the SET command. The WIDTH subcommand in REGRESSION overrides the width specified on SET.

Changing the width may affect the appearance of your output. For example, if you reduce the width, the equation and ANOVA statistics shown in Figure 2.10 might be displayed separately (as in Figure 2.11a) instead of side-by-side. A smaller page width limits the number of statistics that can be displayed in a summary line and may also cause casewise output to be truncated (see Section 2.67). Specifying a smaller page width may also reduce the size of scatter and normal-probability plots in the residuals output.

2.74 EXERCISES

Syntax

1. The following REGRESSION commands contain syntax errors. Write the correct commands.

   a.
   ```
   REGRESSION VARIABLES=IQ TO ACHIEVE
     /METHOD=STEPWISE /DEPENDENT=ACHIEVE
   ```
   b.
   ```
   REGRESSION DESCRIPTIVES=
     MEAN STDDEV /VARIABLES=IQ TO ACHIEVE
     /DEPENDENT=ACHIEVE /METHOD STEPWISE
     /CRITERIA=MAXSTEPS(3)
   ```
   c.
   ```
   REGRESSION VARIABLES=IQ TO ACHIEVE/
     METHOD=ENTER
   ```
   d.
   ```
   REGRESSION VARS=IQ TO ACHIEVE /DEP=ACHIEVE
     /SCATTER(*RES, *PRE) /METHOD=STEP
   ```

2. A researcher wants to predict the frequency of illness (ILLFREQ) using the following variables:

   ```
   JOBSATIS STRESS INCOME HOMEOWNR RACE EXERCISE SEX DIETYPE OVERWGHT
   PETS AGE
   ```

   Write the REGRESSION command that produces a stepwise regression only for people who are married or living with a partner (MARITAL=1). In this command, specify all of the following:

   a. All default regression statistics.

   b. A casewise plot of standardized residuals with absolute values greater than 2.

   c. Descriptive statistics for each variable.

3. What is wrong with the following REGRESSION commands?

   a.
   ```
   REGRESSION VARIABLES = COLLPERF GPA IQ SAT PSYCHTST PARINCOM
                          FAMILY PAREDUC SPORTS RECREATN
     /DEPENDENDT = COLLPERF /METHOD=STEPWISE /METHOD=REMOVE
   ```
   b.
   ```
   REGRESSION VARIABLES=SAVINGS TO GROWTH
     /DEPENDENT=SAVINGS /METHOD=ENTER
     /SCATTERPLOT=(RESID,PRED)
   ```
   c.
   ```
   REGRESSION DESCRIPTIVES
     /VARIABLES=WGHTLOSS MOTIVATN SEX FAMILY PROGRAM RACE
                DIETYPE ROUGHAGE EXERCISE MARITAL
     /DEPENDENT=WGHTLOSS
     /METHOD=ENTER OVERWGHT /METHOD=STEPWISE
   ```
   d.
   ```
   REGRESSION VARIABLES INCOME EDUCATN PAREDUC PARINCOM SEX RACE
                        URBAN COLLPERF FIELD/
     DEPENDENT INCOME/
      STATISTICS ALL/
       METHOD ENTER/
        CASEWISE ALL PRED SEPRED/
   ```

4. A company manager wants to predict SALES using the following variables:

```
DISTRICT PCTHOMES PCTBUSNS BUSNTYP AVGINCOM PCTSNGLE
CATALOGS SALESPN TVADS RADIOADS NEWSPADS
```

   Write the REGRESSION command needed to obtain an analysis that includes all of the following:
   a. Forward selection.
   b. Regression coefficients.
   c. A step history.
   d. Confidence intervals for the regression coefficients.
   e. A histogram of the residuals.
   f. A scatterplot of the residuals with the fitted values.
5. A researcher wants to use a tolerance criterion value of 0.001 rather than 0.0001. Does the REGRESSION command below accomplish this?

```
REGRESSION VARIABLES = MATHTEST IQ MTHANXTY SEX OCCUPATN EDUCATN
  /STATISTICS = TOLERANCE(.001)
  /DEPENDENT = MATHTEST
  /METHOD = BACKWARD
```

Statistical Concepts

1. Why is the hypothesis $\beta_1=\beta_2= \ldots =\beta_k=0$ of interest?
2. What assumptions are you checking when you examine a casewise serial plot (a plot of residuals in time sequence)?
3. What null hypotheses are tested by the following statistics:
   a. $F = \dfrac{\text{MEAN SQUARE REGRESSION}}{\text{MEAN SQUARE RESIDUAL}}$ b. $F_{change} = \dfrac{R^2_{change}(N - p - 1)}{q(1 - R^2)}$
4. Is the following regression output possible if a variable is added at each step and none is dropped from the equation?

STEP	MULTR	RSQ
1	0.5821	0.3388
2	0.6164	0.3799
3	0.6025	0.3630
4	0.6399	0.4095

5. A researcher writes his own regression analysis program. The program produces the following regression line and confidence band. Do you think the new computer program is working properly?

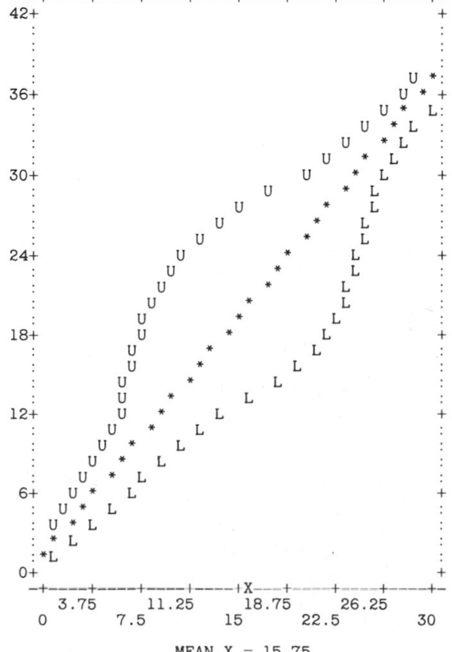

6. For what values of X can you make the best (least variable) predictions of the mean of Y at X? For what values of X can you make the best predictions of new values of Y?

7. What violations of assumptions, if any, are suggested by the following plots:

a. 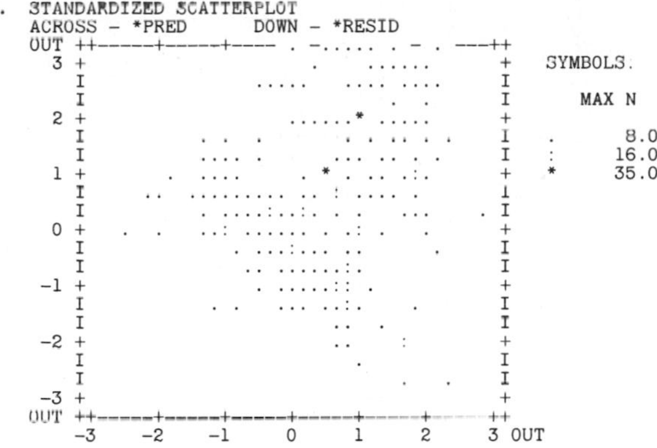

b. 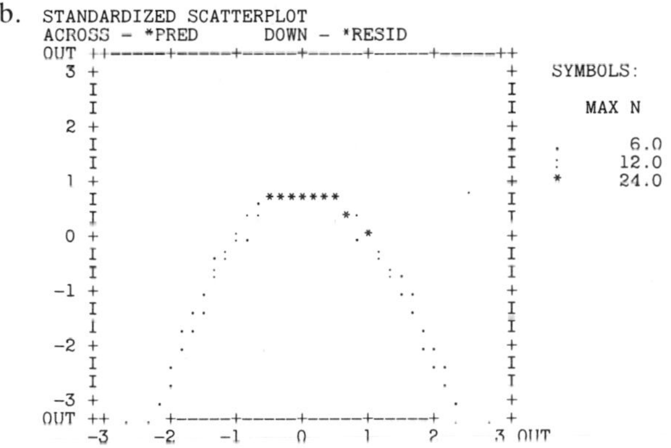

c. 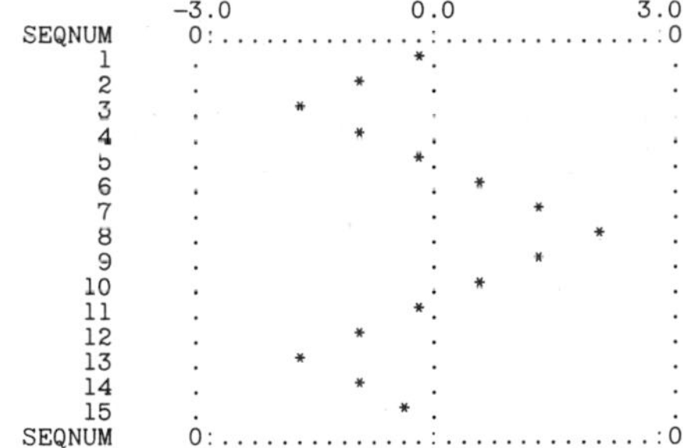

d.

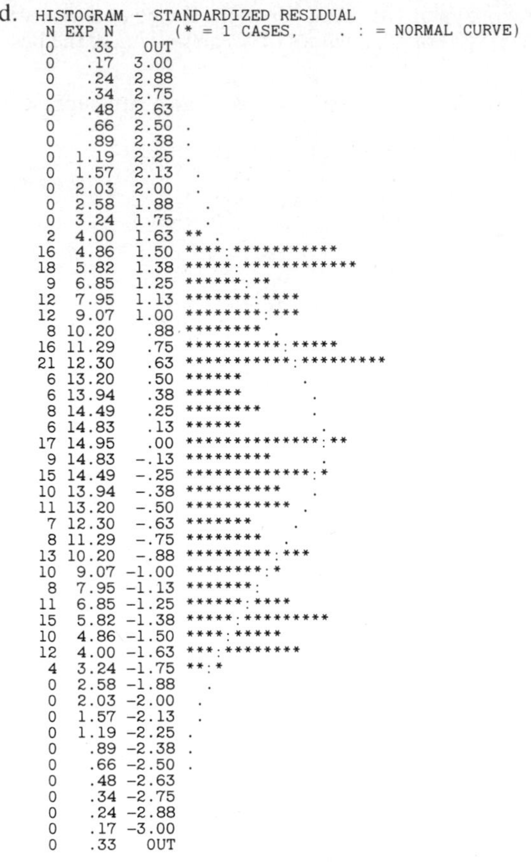
HISTOGRAM - STANDARDIZED RESIDUAL
N EXP N (* = 1 CASES, . : = NORMAL CURVE)
0 .33 OUT
0 .17 3.00
0 .24 2.88
0 .34 2.75
0 .48 2.63
0 .66 2.50
0 .89 2.38
0 1.19 2.25
0 1.57 2.13
0 2.03 2.00
0 2.58 1.88
0 3.24 1.75
2 4.00 1.63
16 4.86 1.50
18 5.82 1.38
9 6.85 1.25
12 7.95 1.13
12 9.07 1.00
8 10.20 .88
16 11.29 .75
21 12.30 .63
6 13.20 .50
6 13.94 .38
8 14.49 .25
6 14.83 .13
17 14.95 .00
9 14.83 -.13
15 14.49 -.25
10 13.94 -.38
11 13.20 -.50
7 12.30 -.63
8 11.29 -.75
13 10.20 -.88
10 9.07 -1.00
8 7.95 -1.13
11 6.85 -1.25
15 5.82 -1.38
10 4.86 -1.50
12 4.00 -1.63
4 3.24 -1.75
0 2.58 -1.88
0 2.03 -2.00
0 1.57 -2.13
0 1.19 -2.25
0 .89 -2.38
0 .66 -2.50
0 .48 -2.63
0 .34 -2.75
0 .24 -2.88
0 .17 -3.00
0 .33 OUT

e.

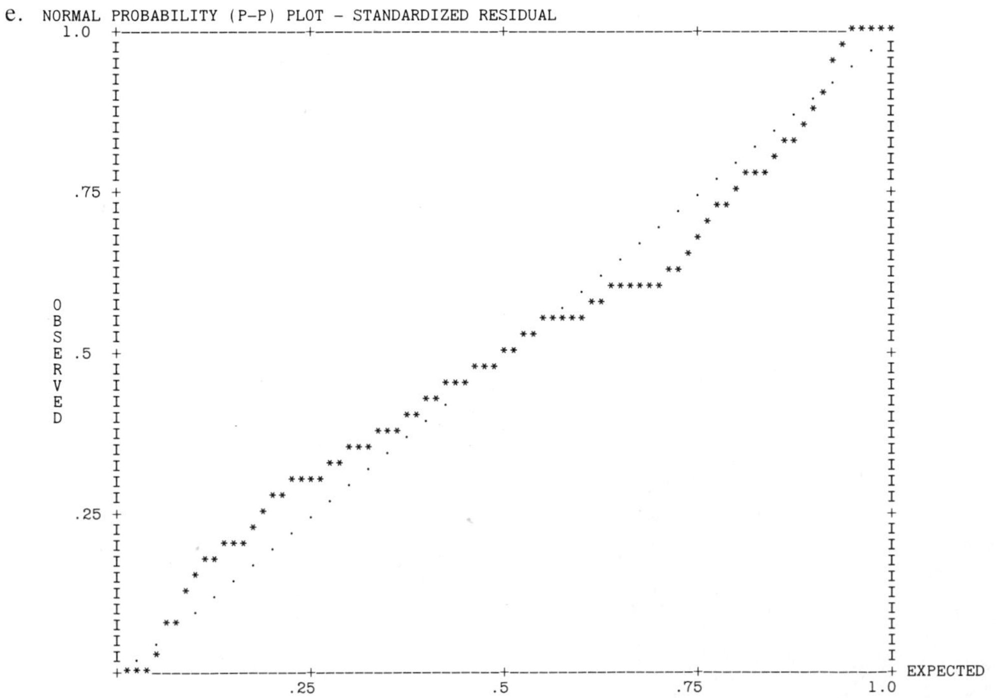
NORMAL PROBABILITY (P-P) PLOT - STANDARDIZED RESIDUAL
1.0
.75
OBSERVED
.5
.25
.25
.5
.75
1.0
EXPECTED

8. From the following statistics for variables not in the equation, determine which variable is entered next if forward variable selection with an F-to-enter of 3.84 is used.

------------- VARIABLES NOT IN THE EQUATION -------------

VARIABLE	BETA IN	PARTIAL	MIN TOLER	F	SIG F
AGE	.18107	.22453	.92113	25.005	.0000
SEX	-.26483	.31974	.87327	53.637	.0000
MINORITY	-.07477	-.09575	.98234	4.358	.0374
WORK	.21888	.27364	.93632	38.122	.0000

9. From the following statistics for variables in the equation, determine which variable is removed next if backward elimination with a FOUT of 3 is used.

----------- IN ------------

VARIABLE	F	SIG F
WORK	1.217	.2705
MINORITY	13.822	.0002
SEX	45.159	.0000
EDLEVEL	238.736	.0000
AGE	4.696	.0307
(CONSTANT)	7.935	.0051

10. Suppose you obtain the following correlation matrix while running the REGRESSION procedure:

P E A R S O N   C O R R E L A T I O N   C O E F F I C I E N T S

	X1	X2	X3	X5	X4	Y
X1	1.0000 (0) P=*****	-0.0003 (300) P=0.498	0.0206 (300) P=0.361	-0.1384 (300) P=0.008	0.9999 (300) P=0.000	0.3595 (300) P=0.000
X2	-0.0003 (300) P=0.498	1.0000 (0) P=*****	-0.0262 (300) P=0.325	-0.0741 (300) P=0.100	-0.0003 (300) P=0.498	-0.0025 (300) P=0.483
X3	0.0206 (300) P=0.361	-0.0262 (300) P=0.325	1.0000 (0) P=*****	0.0364 (300) P=0.265	0.0206 (300) P=0.361	0.0322 (300) P=0.289
X5	-0.1384 (300) P=0.008	-0.0741 (300) P=0.100	0.0364 (300) P=0.265	1.0000 (0) P=*****	-0.1384 (300) P=0.008	-0.0083 (300) P=0.443
X4	0.9999 (300) P=0.000	-0.0003 (300) P=0.498	0.0206 (300) P=0.361	-0.1384 (300) P=0.008	1.0000 (0) P=*****	0.3595 (300) P=0.000
Y	0.3595 (300) P=0.000	-0.0025 (300) P=0.483	0.0322 (300) P=0.289	-0.0083 (300) P=0.443	0.3595 (300) P=0.000	1.0000 (0) P=*****

When you try to enter the variable X4 into an equation that already contains the variables X1 to X3, you get the following message:

```
FOR BLOCK NUMBER  2    TOLERANCE = 0.0001 LIMITS REACHED.
NO VARIABLES ENTERED FOR THIS BLOCK.
```

What does this message mean? Why does it occur?

11. Fill in the missing information in the following table and calculate R^2:

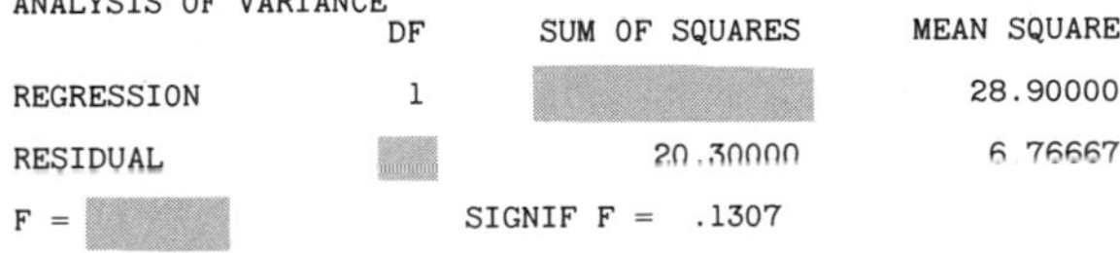

ANALYSIS OF VARIANCE

	DF	SUM OF SQUARES	MEAN SQUARE
REGRESSION	1		28.90000
RESIDUAL		20.30000	6.76667

F =   SIGNIF F = .1307

12. Below are regression statistics and values of the independent and dependent variables for five cases. Fill in the missing information in the casewise plot.

```
------------------ VARIABLES IN THE EQUATION ------------------

VARIABLE              B          SE B        BETA          T   SIG T

X               1.70000        .82260      .76642      2.067   .1307
(CONSTANT)      4.30000       2.72825                  1.576   .2131
```

```
CASEWISE PLOT OF STANDARDIZED RESIDUAL

*: SELECTED    M: MISSING
```

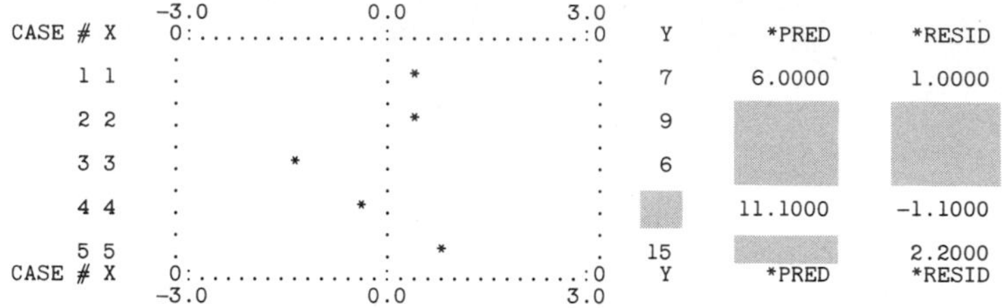

```
          -3.0           0.0          3.0
CASE # X   0:.............:.............:0    Y       *PRED      *RESID
      1 1  .              .  *          .     7      6.0000      1.0000
      2 2  .              .  *          .     9
      3 3  .     *        .             .     6
      4 4  .            * .             .           11.1000     -1.1000
      5 5  .              .    *        .    15                  2.2000
CASE # X   0:.............:.............:0    Y       *PRED      *RESID
          -3.0           0.0          3.0
```

13. Fill in the missing information in the following table:

```
------------------ VARIABLES IN THE EQUATION ------------------

VARIABLE              B          SE B          T   SIG T

WORK           23.77950      21.55603              .2705
MINORITY     -939.85580                   -3.718   .0002
SEX         -1617.52918     240.70102     -6.720   .0000
EDLEVEL                      40.77734     15.451   .0000
AGE            33.43079      15.42695              .0307
(CONSTANT)  -2183.78652                   -2.817   .0051
```

14. A regression analysis was performed for the data below, producing an S^2 of 11.005 and the following regression equation:

$\hat{Y}_i = 0.042 + (1.539)X_i$

SEQNUM	X	Y
1	0.15	0.41
2	1.24	0.32
3	2.23	6.92
4	6.85	12.45
5	3.87	1.03
6	0.64	2.17

When the first case is dropped and the regression analysis is performed again, the following equation results:

$\hat{Y}_i = -0.031 + (1.554)X_i$

When the fourth case is dropped and the first case included again, the regression equation obtained is:

$\hat{Y}_i = 1.493 + (0.416)X_i$

a. Calculate Cook's distance for Cases 1 and 4.

b. Which case is more influential, judging from Cook's distance?

c. Sketch a scatterplot of Y vs X. Draw the regression line with and without Case 4. Does this scatterplot help explain why one of the cases in (b) was influential? Why or why not?

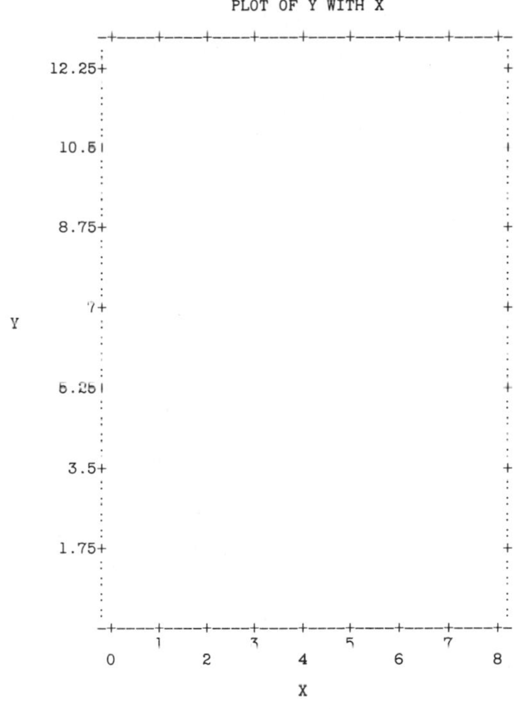

15. A regression of INCOME on AGE was performed, and the mean and standard deviation of AGE were determined to be 43.5 and 10.84.

a. For each case shown below, find the Mahalanobis' distance.

SEQNUM	AGE	MAHALANOBIS' DISTANCE
2	27	
3	60	
4	41	
5	76	

b. Which case is the most unusual, judging from the Mahalanobis distance?

16. Two variables, X1 and X2, are uncorrelated, and a regression of Y on X1 and X2 produced the following standardized regression coefficients:

VARIABLE	BETA
X1	1.75
X2	-2.11

Is it possible to determine, from this equation, which variable would be most important, by itself, for predicting Y? Why or why not?

17. The REGRESSION command shown below is syntactically correct, but it would be a bad idea to use it. Why?

```
REGRESSION DESCRIPTIVES
  /VARIABLES=DOGSCORE TRAINTM BREED METHOD DIET PLAY
             OWNRTIME FAMSIZE AGE
  /CRITERIA=FIN(2.5) FOUT(3)
  /DEPENDENT=DOGSCORE /METHOD=STEPWISE
  /RESIDUALS=HISTOGRAM(ZRESID) NORMPROB
  /SCATTERPLOT=(*ZRESID,*PRED)
```

3

Discriminant Analysis

In this chapter:

Goals:

- To classify cases into one of several mutually exclusive groups on the basis of various characteristics.
- To establish which characteristics are important for distinguishing among the groups.
- To evaluate the accuracy of the classification.

Examples:

- Predict which offenders are going to jump bail on the basis of severity of crime, age, number of previous offenses, and family income.
- Predict success or failure of a business on the basis of number of employees, earnings-to-profits ratio, net assets, and years in existence.
- Predict which people are likely to buy a product on the basis of income, place of residence, number of children, and education of head of household.
- Predict which people should be admitted to a coronary care unit on the basis of duration and location of chest pain, lab results, and family history of heart disease.

How it's done:

Based on a set of cases for which group membership is known, linear combinations of the characteristics are formed and serve as the basis for assigning cases to groups. The coefficients for the linear combinations are so chosen that they result in the "best" separation among the groups. The accuracy of the classification can be estimated by applying the model to cases for whom group membership is known and comparing predicted group membership to actual.

Data considerations:

Each case must have a value for the group variable (which may be unknown for some of the cases) and values for the characteristics used for classification. For cases used in developing the equation, group membership must be known. Additional cases for whom group membership is not known can also be included, and these will be classified using the model. The grouping variable can be nominal or ordinal. The classification variables are assumed to be from a multivariate normal distribution.

General references:

Kleinbaum & Kupper (1978)
Tatsuoka (1971)
Lachenbruch (1975)

Contents

3.1 INVESTIGATING RESPIRATORY DISTRESS SYNDROME
3.2 Selecting Cases for the Analysis
3.3 Analyzing Group Differences
3.4 Wilks' Lambda
3.5 Correlations
3.6 Estimating the Coefficients
3.7 Calculating the Discriminant Score
3.8 Bayes' Rule
3.9 Prior Probability
3.10 Conditional Probability
3.11 Posterior Probability
3.12 Classification Output
3.13 Classification Summary
3.14 Histograms of Discriminant Scores
3.15 Estimating Misclassification Rates
3.16 The Expected Misclassification Rate
3.17 Other Discriminant Function Statistics
3.18 Interpreting the Discriminant Function Coefficients
3.19 Function-Variable Correlations
3.20 Fisher's Classification Function Coefficients
3.21 Relationship to Multiple Regression Analysis
3.22 VARIABLE SELECTION METHODS
3.23 A Stepwise Selection Example
3.24 Variable Selection Criteria
3.25 The First Step
3.26 Statistics for Variables Not in the Model
3.27 The Second Step
3.28 The Last Step
3.29 Summary Tables
3.30 Other Criteria for Variable Selection
3.31 Rao's V
3.32 Mahalanobis' Distance
3.33 Between-Groups F
3.34 Sum of Unexplained Variance
3.35 THREE-GROUP DISCRIMINANT ANALYSIS
3.36 The Number of Functions
3.37 Classification
3.38 Additional Statistics
3.39 Testing the Significance of the Discriminant Functions
3.40 Classification with One Function
3.41 The Variables
3.42 WHEN ASSUMPTIONS ARE VIOLATED
3.43 RUNNING PROECDURE DISCRIMINANT
3.44 The GROUPS Subcommand
3.45 The VARIABLES Subcommand
3.46 The ANALYSIS Subcommand
3.47 The METHOD Subcommand
3.48 Inclusion Levels
3.49 The MAXSTEPS Subcommand
3.50 Setting Statistical Criteria
3.51 The FUNCTIONS Subcommand
3.52 The SELECT Subcommand
3.53 The PRIORS Subcommand
3.54 The SAVE Subcommand
3.55 The MISSING Subcommand
3.56 The MATRIX Subcommand
3.57 The HISTORY Subcommand
3.58 The ROTATE subcommand
3.59 The CLASSIFY Subcommand
3.60 The STATISTICS Subcommand
3.61 The PLOT Subcommand
3.62 EXERCISES

3 Predicting Cure and Credit: Discriminant Analysis

Gazing into crystal balls is not the exclusive domain of soothsayers. Judges, college admissions counselors, bankers, and many other professionals must foretell outcomes such as parole violation, success in college, and creditworthiness.

An intuitive strategy is to compare the characteristics of a potential student or credit applicant to those of cases whose success or failure is already known. Based on similarities and differences a prediction can be made. Often this is done subjectively, using only the experience and wisdom of the decision maker. However, as problems grow more complex and the consequences of bad decisions become more severe, a more objective procedure for predicting outcomes is often desirable.

Before considering statistical techniques, let's summarize the problem. Based on a collection of variables, such as yearly income, age, marital status, and total worth, we wish to distinguish among several mutually exclusive groups, such as good credit risks and bad credit risks. The available data are the values of the variables for cases whose group membership is known, that is, cases who have proven to be good or bad credit risks. We also wish to identify the variables that are important for distinguishing among the groups and to develop a procedure for predicting group membership for new cases whose group membership is undetermined.

Discriminant analysis, first introduced by Sir Ronald Fisher, is the statistical technique most commonly used to investigate this set of problems. The concept underlying discriminant analysis is fairly simple. Linear combinations of the independent, sometimes called predictor, variables are formed and serve as the basis for classifying cases into one of the groups.

For the linear discriminant function to be "optimal," that is, to provide a classification rule that minimizes the probability of misclassification, certain assumptions about the data must be met. Each group must be a sample from a multivariate normal population, and the population covariance matrices must all be equal. Section 3.42 discusses tests for violations of the assumptions and the performance of linear discriminant analysis when assumptions are violated.

Sections 3.2 through 3.34 cover the basics of discriminant analysis and the output from SPSS^X DISCRIMINANT using a two-group example. Extending this type of analysis to include more than two groups is discussed beginning in Section 3.35.

3.1 INVESTIGATING RESPIRATORY DISTRESS SYNDROME

Respiratory Distress Syndrome (RDS) is one of the leading causes of death in premature infants. Although intensive research has failed to uncover its causes, a variety of physiological disturbances, such as insufficient oxygen uptake and high blood acidity, are characteristic of RDS. These are usually treated by administering oxygen and buffers to decrease acidity. However, a substantial proportion of RDS infants fail to survive.

P. K. J. van Vliet and J. M. Gupta (1973) studied 50 infants with a diagnosis of RDS based on clinical signs and symptoms and confirmed by chest x-ray. For each case they report the infant's outcome—whether the infant died or survived—as well as values for eight variables that might be predictors of outcome. Table 3.1 gives the SPSS^X names and descriptions of these variables.

Table 3.1 Possible predictors of survival

Variable name	Description
SURVIVAL	Infant's outcome. Coded 1 if infant died, 2 if survived.
SEX	Infant's sex. Coded 0 for females, 1 for males.
APGAR	Score on the APGAR test, which measures infant's responsiveness. Scores range from 0 to 10.
AGE	The gestational age of the infant measured in weeks. Values of 36 to 38 are obtained for full-term infants.
TIME	Time, measured in minutes, that it took the infant to begin breathing spontaneously.
WEIGHT	Birthweight measured in kilograms.
PH	The acidity level of the blood, measured on a scale from 0 to 14.
TREATMNT	Type of buffer adminstered (buffer neutralizes acidity). Coded 1 for THAM, 0 for sodium carbonate.
RESP	Indicates whether respiratory therapy was initiated. Coded 0 for no, 1 for yes.

Some dichotomous variables such as SEX are included among the predictor variables. Although, as previously indicated, the linear discriminant function requires that the predictor variables have a multivariate normal distribution, the function has been shown to perform fairly well in a variety of other situations (see Section 3.42).

In this example, we will use discriminant analysis to determine whether the variables listed in Table 3.1 distinguish between infants who recover from RDS and those who do not. If high-risk infants can be identified early, special monitoring and treatment procedures may be instituted for them. It is also of interest to determine which variables contribute most to the separation of infants who survive from those who do not.

3.2 Selecting Cases for the Analysis

The first step in discriminant analysis is to select cases to be included in the computations. A case is excluded from the analysis if it contains missing information for the variable that defines the groups or for any of the predictor variables.

If many cases have missing values for at least one variable, the actual analysis will be based on a small subset of cases. This may be troublesome for two reasons. First, estimates based on small samples are usually quite variable. Second, if the cases with missing values differ from those without missing values, the resulting estimates may be too biased. For example, if highly educated people are more likely to provide information on the variables used in the analysis, selecting cases with complete data will result in a sample that is highly educated. Results obtained from such a sample might differ from those that would be obtained if people at all educational levels were included. Therefore, it is usually a good strategy to examine cases with missing values to see whether there is evidence that missing values are associated with some particular characteristics of the cases. If there are many missing values for some variables, you should consider the possibility of eliminating those variables from the analysis.

Figure 3.2 shows the entire SPSS^X job (run in an IBM CMS environment) and the output produced by DISCRIMINANT after all the data have been processed. The first line of the output indicates how many cases are eligible for inclusion. The second line indicates the number of cases excluded from analysis because of missing values for the predictor variables or the variable that defines the groups. In this example, two cases with missing values are excluded from the analysis. If you use the WEIGHT command (see Appendix B), DISCRIMINANT prints the sum of the weights in each group and the actual number of cases.

Figure 3.2 Case summary

```
TITLE 'INFANT SURVIVAL EXAMPLE--2-GROUP DISCRIMINANT'
DATA LIST /CASEID 1-2 SURVIVAL 4 TREATMNT 6 TIME 8-10(1)
  WEIGHT 12-15(3) APGAR 17-18 SEX 20 AGE 22-23 PH 33-35(2) RESP 37
VARIABLE LABELS SURVIVAL 'INFANT SURVIVAL'
  TREATMNT 'TREATMNT ADMINISTERED'
  TIME 'TIME TO SPONTANEOUS RESPIRATION'
  WEIGHT 'BIRTHWEIGHT IN KILOGRAMS'
  APGAR 'APGAR SCORE'
  SEX 'SEX OF INFANT'
  PH 'PH LEVEL'
  RESP 'RESPIRATORY THERAPY'
MISSING VALUES RESP(9)
VALUE LABELS TREATMNT 1'THAM' 0'SODIUM BICARBONATE'
  /SEX 0'FEMALE' 1'MALE' /RESP 1'YES' 0'NO' 9'NO ANSWER'
  /SURVIVAL 2'SURVIVE' 1'DIE'
DISCRIMINANT GROUPS=SURVIVAL(1,2)
  /VARIABLES=TREATMNT TO RESP
```

```
ON GROUPS DEFINED BY SURVIVAL   INFANT SURVIVAL

              50 (UNWEIGHTED) CASES WERE PROCESSED.
               2 OF THESE WERE EXCLUDED FROM THE ANALYSIS.
                 0 HAD MISSING OR OUT-OF-RANGE GROUP CODES.
                 2 HAD AT LEAST ONE MISSING DISCRIMINATING VARIABLE.
                 0 HAD BOTH.
              48 (UNWEIGHTED) CASES WILL BE USED IN THE ANALYSIS.

NUMBER OF CASES BY GROUP

                  NUMBER OF CASES
  SURVIVAL  UNWEIGHTED      WEIGHTED  LABEL

      1          26            26.0  DIE
      2          22            22.0  SURVIVE

    TOTAL        48            48.0
```

3.3 Analyzing Group Differences

Although the variables are interrelated and we will need to employ statistical techniques that incorporate these dependencies, it is often helpful to begin analyzing the differences between groups by examining univariate statistics.

Figure 3.3a contains the means for the eight independent variables for infants who died (Group 1) and who survived (Group 2), along with the corresponding standard deviations. The last row of each table, labeled TOTAL, contains the means and standard deviations calculated when all cases are combined into a single sample.

Figure 3.3a Group means and standard deviations

```
DISCRIMINANT GROUPS=SURVIVAL(1,2)
  /VARIABLES=TREATMNT TO RESP
  /STATISTICS MEAN STDDEV
```
[1]

GROUP MEANS

SURVIVAL	TREATMNT	TIME	WEIGHT	APGAR	SEX	AGE	PH	RESP
1	0.38462	2.88462	1.70950	5.50000	0.65385	32.38462	7.17962	0.65385
2	0.59091	2.31818	2.36091	6.31818	0.68182	34.63636	7.34636	0.27273
TOTAL	0.47917	2.62500	2.00806	5.87500	0.66667	33.41667	7.25604	0.47917

GROUP STANDARD DEVIATIONS

SURVIVAL	TREATMNT	TIME	WEIGHT	APGAR	SEX	AGE	PH	RESP
1	0.49614	3.48513	0.51944	2.77489	0.48516	3.11226	0.08502	0.48516
2	0.50324	3.70503	0.62760	2.69720	0.47673	2.71759	0.60478	0.45584
TOTAL	0.50485	3.56027	0.65353	2.74152	0.47639	3.12051	0.41751	0.50485

From Figure 3.3a you can see that 38% of the infants who died were treated with THAM, 65% were male, and 65% received respiratory therapy. (When a variable is coded 0 or 1, the mean of the variable is the proportion of cases with a value of 1.) Infants who died took longer to breathe spontaneously, weighed less, and had lower APGAR scores than infants who survived.

Figure 3.3b shows significance tests for the equality of group means for each variable. The *F* values and their significance, shown in columns 3 and 4, are the same as those calculated from a one-way analysis of variance with survival as the grouping variable. For example, the *F* value in Figure 3.3c, which is an analysis of variance table for WEIGHT from procedure ONEWAY (see Appendix F), is 15.49, the same as shown for WEIGHT in Figure 3.3b. (When there are two groups, the *F* value is just the square of the *t* value from the two-sample *t* test.) The significance level is 0.0003. If the observed significance level is small (less than 0.05), the hypothesis that all group means are equal is rejected.

Figure 3.3b Tests for univariate equality of group means

```
DISCRIMINANT GROUPS=SURVIVAL(1,2)
  /VARIABLES=TREATMNT TO RESP
  /STATISTICS MEAN STDDEV UNIVF
```
[2]

WILKS' LAMBDA (U-STATISTIC) AND UNIVARIATE F-RATIO
WITH 1 AND 46 DEGREES OF FREEDOM

VARIABLE	WILKS' LAMBDA	F	SIGNIFICANCE
TREATMNT	0.95766	2.034	0.1606
TIME	0.99358	.297	0.5883
WEIGHT	0.74810	15.490	0.0003
APGAR	0.97742	1.063	0.3080
SEX	0.99913	.040	0.8419
AGE	0.86798	6.997	0.0111
PH	0.95956	1.939	0.1705
RESP	0.85551	7.769	0.0077

[1]With releases before 3.0, replace the DISCRIMINANT command with the following:

```
DISCRIMINANT GROUPS=SURVIVAL(1,2)
  /VARIABLES=TREATMNT TO RESP
STATISTICS 1 2
```

[2]With releases before 3.0, replace the DISCRIMINANT command with the following:

```
DISCRIMINANT GROUPS=SURVIVAL(1,2)
  /VARIABLES=TREATMNT TO RESP
STATISTICS 1 2 6
```

Figure 3.3c ONEWAY analysis of variance table for WEIGHT

```
ONEWAY WEIGHT BY SURVIVAL(1,2)
  /MISSING LISTWISE
```
[3]

```
- - - - - - - - - - - - - - - - - - - - - - - - - - - O N E W A Y - - - - - - - - - - - - - - - - - - - -

   VARIABLE  WEIGHT       BIRTHWEIGHT IN KILOGRAMS
BY VARIABLE  SURVIVAL     INFANT SURVIVAL
                                         ANALYSIS OF VARIANCE

          SOURCE               D.F.    SUM OF SQUARES     MEAN SQUARES       F RATIO    F PROB.
   BETWEEN GROUPS                1          5.0566           5.0566          15.489     0.0003
   WITHIN GROUPS                46         15.0171           0.3265
   TOTAL                        47         20.0737
```

3.4 Wilks' Lambda

Another statistic displayed in Figure 3.3b is Wilks' lambda, sometimes called the *U* statistic (see Section 3.17). When variables are considered individually, lambda is the ratio of the within-groups sum of squares to the total sum of squares. For example, Figure 3.3c shows the sums of squares for variable WEIGHT. The ratio of the within-groups sum of squares (15.02) to the total sum of squares (20.07) is 0.748, the value for Wilks' lambda for WEIGHT in Figure 3.3b.

A lambda of 1 occurs when all observed group means are equal. Values close to 0 occur when within-groups variability is small compared to the total variability, that is, when most of the total variability is attributable to differences between the means of the groups. Thus, large values of lambda indicate that group means do not appear to be different, while small values indicate that group means do appear to be different. From Figure 3.3b, WEIGHT, AGE, and RESP are the variables whose means are most different for survivors and nonsurvivors.

3.5 Correlations

Since interdependencies among the variables affect most multivariate analyses, it is worth examining the correlation matrix of the predictor variables. Figure 3.5a is the pooled within-groups correlation matrix. WEIGHT and AGE have the largest correlation coefficient, 0.84. This is to be expected, since weight increases with gestational age. Section 3.19 discusses some of the possible consequences of including highly correlated variables in the analysis.

A *pooled within-groups* correlation matrix is obtained by averaging the separate covariance matrices for all groups and then computing the correlation matrix. A *total* correlation matrix is obtained when all cases are treated as if they are from a single sample.

Figure 3.5a Pooled within-groups correlation matrix

```
DISCRIMINANT GROUPS=SURVIVAL(1,2)
  /VARIABLES=TREATMNT TO RESP
  /STATISTICS MEAN STDDEV UNIVF CORR
```
[4]

POOLED WITHIN-GROUPS CORRELATION MATRIX

	TREATMNT	TIME	WEIGHT	APGAR	SEX	AGE	PH	RESP
TREATMNT	1.00000							
TIME	0.01841	1.00000						
WEIGHT	0.09091	-0.21244	1.00000					
APGAR	-0.03394	-0.50152	0.22161	1.00000				
SEX	-0.03637	-0.12982	0.19500	-0.02098	1.00000			
AGE	0.05749	-0.20066	0.84040	0.36329	-0.00129	1.00000		
PH	-0.08307	0.09102	0.12436	-0.07197	-0.03156	0.00205	1.00000	
RESP	-0.00774	-0.06994	-0.02394	0.16123	0.26732	-0.06828	0.03770	1.00000

[3]With releases before 3.0, replace the ONEWAY command with the following:

```
ONEWAY WEIGHT BY SURVIVAL(1,2)
OPTIONS 2
```

[4]With releases before 3.0, replace the DISCRIMINANT command with the following:

```
DISCRIMINANT GROUPS=SURVIVAL(1,2)
  /VARIABLES=TREATMNT TO RESP
STATISTICS 1 2 6 4
```

The total and pooled within-groups correlation matrices can be quite different. For example, Figure 3.5b shows a plot of two hypothetical variables for three groups. When each group is considered individually, the correlation coefficient is close to 0. Averaging, or pooling, these individual estimates also results in a coefficient close to 0. However, the correlation coefficient computed for all cases combined (total) is 0.97, since groups with larger *X* values also have larger *Y* values.

Figure 3.5b Hypothetical variable plot for three groups

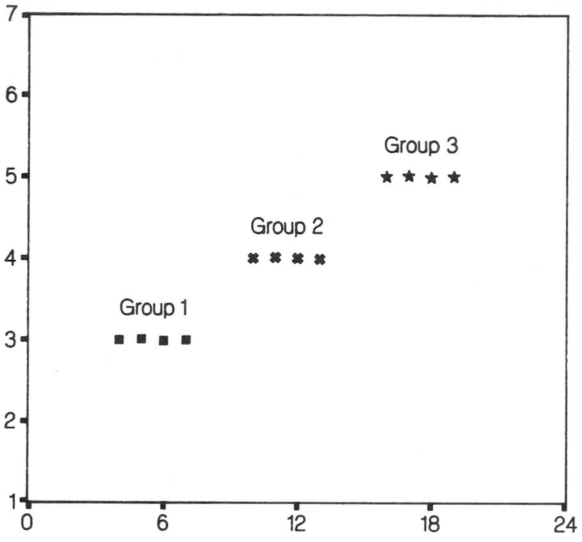

3.6 Estimating the Coefficients

Descriptive statistics and univariate tests of significance provide basic information about the distributions of the variables in the groups and help identify some differences among the groups. However, in discriminant analysis and other multivariate statistical procedures, the emphasis is on analyzing the variables together, not one at a time. By considering the variables simultaneously, we are able to incorporate important information about their relationships.

In discriminant analysis, a linear combination of the independent variables is formed and serves as the basis for assigning cases to groups. Thus, information contained in multiple independent variables is summarized in a single index. For example, by finding a weighted average of variables such as age, weight, and APGAR score, you can obtain a score that distinguishes infants who survive from those who do not. In discriminant analysis, the weights are estimated so that they result in the "best" separation between the groups.

The linear discriminant equation

$$D = B_0 + B_1X_1 + B_2X_2 + \ldots + B_pX_p \qquad \textbf{Equation 3.6a}$$

is similar to the multiple linear regression equation. The *X*'s are the values of the independent variables and the *B*'s are coefficients estimated from the data. If a linear discriminant function is to distinguish infants who die from those who survive, the two groups must differ in their *D* values.

Therefore, the *B*'s are chosen so that the values of the discriminant function differ as much as possible between the groups, or that for the discriminant scores the ratio

$$\left(\frac{\text{between-groups sum of squares}}{\text{within-groups sum of squares}}\right) \qquad \textbf{Equation 3.6b}$$

is a maximum. Any other linear combination of the variables will have a smaller ratio.

The actual mechanics of computing the coefficients, especially if there are more than two groups, is somewhat involved (see Morrison, 1967; Tatsuoka, 1971).

The coefficients for the eight variables listed in Table 3.1 are shown in Figure 3.6. Small and large values are sometimes printed in scientific notation. For example, the number 0.0003678 might be printed as 0.368D−03.

Figure 3.6 Unstandardized discriminant function coefficients

```
DISCRIMINANT GROUPS=SURVIVAL(1,2)
  /VARIABLES=TREATMNT TO RESP
  /STATISTICS MEAN STDDEV UNIVF CORR RAW
```
[5]

```
UNSTANDARDIZED CANONICAL DISCRIMINANT FUNCTION COEFFICIENTS

                 FUNC  1

TREATMNT         .4311545
TIME             .0367127
WEIGHT          2.044035
APGAR            .1264302
SEX              .0069983
AGE             -.2180711
PH               .4078705
RESP           -1.244539
(CONSTANT)      -.2309344
```

3.7 Calculating the Discriminant Score

Based on the coefficients in Figure 3.6, it is possible to calculate the discriminant score for each case. For example, Figure 3.7a contains the value of each variable for the first five cases in the data file. The discriminant score for Case 1 is obtained by multiplying the unstandardized coefficients by the values of the variables, summing these products, and adding the constant. For Case 1, the discriminant score is

$$\begin{aligned} D_1 = {} & 0.431(1) + 0.0367(2) + 2.044(1.05) + 0.126(5) + 0.007(0) \\ & - 0.218(28) + 0.408(7.09) - 1.244(0) - 0.231 = -0.16 \end{aligned} \qquad \textbf{Equation 3.7}$$

Figure 3.7a Values of the variables for the first five cases

```
COMPUTE SCORE=.431*TREATMNT + .0367*TIME + 2.04*WEIGHT + .126*APGAR
                + .007*SEX - .218*AGE + .408*PH - 1.24*RESP - .231
FORMAT SCORE(F6.3)
LIST CASES=5 /VARIABLES=TREATMNT TO RESP SURVIVAL SCORE
  /FORMAT=NUMBERED
```

```
   TREATMNT TIME WEIGHT APGAR SEX AGE   PH RESP SURVIVAL  SCORE

1       1    2.0  1.050     5   0   28 7.09   0       1    -.166
2       1    2.0  1.175     4   0   28 7.11   1       1   -1.269
3       1     .5  1.230     7   0   29 7.24   9       1      .
4       1    4.0  1.310     4   1   29 7.13   1       1   -1.123
5       1     .5  1.500     8   1   32 7.23   1       1    -.973

NUMBER OF CASES READ =       5   NUMBER OF CASES LISTED =       5
```

[5]With releases before 3.0, replace the DISCRIMINANT command with the following:

```
DISCRIMINANT GROUPS=SURVIVAL(1,2)
  /VARIABLES=TREATMNT TO RESP
STATISTICS 1 2 6 4 11
```

Figure 3.7b contains basic descriptive statistics for the discriminant scores in the two groups. The mean score for all cases combined is 0 and the pooled within-groups variance is 1. This is always true for discriminant scores calculated by SPSS^X.

Figure 3.7b Descriptive statistics from procedure MEANS

```
DISCRIMINANT GROUPS=SURVIVAL(1,2)
  /VARIABLES=TREATMNT TO RESP
  /SAVE=SCORES=DISCORE
VARIABLE LABELS DISCORE1 'DISCRIMINANT SCORE'
MEANS TABLES=DISCORE1 BY SURVIVAL
  /STATISTICS ANOVA6
```

```
CRITERION VARIABLE   DISCORE1   DISCRIMINANT SCORE
    BROKEN DOWN BY   SURVIVAL   INFANT SURVIVAL

- - - - - - - - - - -  A N A L Y S I S   O F   V A R I A N C E  - - - - - - - - - - -

   VALUE  LABEL                        SUM        MEAN     STD DEV   SUM OF SQ   CASES

       1  DIE                   -18.525394  -.7125152    .9055960  20.5026022      26
       2  SURVIVE               18.5253943   .8420634   1.1018901  25.4973978      22

WITHIN GROUPS TOTAL              0.0000000  0.0000000   1.0000000  46.0000000      48
```

3.8 Bayes' Rule

Using the discriminant score, it is possible to obtain a rule for classifying cases into one of the two groups. The technique used in SPSS^X DISCRIMINANT is based on Bayes' rule. The probability that a case with a discriminant score of D belongs to group i is estimated by

$$P(G_i|D) = \frac{P(D|G_i)P(G_i)}{\sum_{i=1}^{g} P(D|G_i)P(G_i)} \qquad \textbf{Equation 3.8}$$

Sections 3.9 through 3.11 describe the various components of this equation and their relationships.

3.9 Prior Probability

The *prior probability,* represented by $P(G_i)$, is an estimate of the likelihood that a case belongs to a particular group when no information about it is available. For example, if 30% of infants with RDS die, the probability that an infant with RDS will die is 0.3.

The prior probability can be estimated in several ways. If the sample is considered representative of the population, the observed proportions of cases in each group can serve as estimates of the prior probabilities. In this example, 26 out of 48 cases for whom all information is available, or 54%, belong to Group 1 (nonsurvivors), and 22 (46%) belong to Group 2 (survivors). The prior probability of belonging to Group 1, then, is 0.54, and the prior probability of belonging to Group 2 is 0.46.

Often samples are chosen so that they include a fixed number of observations per group. For example, if deaths from RDS were rare, say occurring once per 100 RDS births, even reasonably large samples of RDS births would result in a small number of cases in the nonsurvivor group. Therefore, an investigator might include the same number of survivors and nonsurvivors in the study. In such

[6] With releases before 3.0, replace the MEANS command with the following two commands:

```
BREAKDOWN TABLES=DISCORE1 BY SURVIVAL
STATISTICS 1
```

situations, the prior probability of group membership can be estimated from other sources, such as hospital discharge records.

When all groups are equally likely, or when no information about the probability of group membership is known, equal prior probabilities for all groups may be selected. Since each case must belong to one of the groups, the prior probabilities must sum to 1.

Although prior probabilities convey some information about the likelihood of group membership, they ignore the attributes of the particular case. For example, an infant who is known to be very sick based on various criteria is assigned the same probability of dying as is an infant known to be healthier.

3.10 Conditional Probability

To take advantage of the additional information available for a case in developing a classification scheme, we need to assess the likelihood of the additional information under different circumstances. For example, if the discriminant function scores are normally distributed for each of two groups and the parameters of the distributions can be estimated, it is possible to calculate the probability of obtaining a particular discriminant function value of D if the case is a member of Group 1 or Group 2.

This probability is called the *conditional probability* of D given the group and is denoted by $P(D|G_i)$. To calculate this probability, the case is assumed to belong to a particular group and the probability of the observed score given membership in the group is estimated.

3.11 Posterior Probability

The conditional probability of D given the group gives an idea of how likely the score is for members of a particular group. However, when group membership is unknown, what is really needed is an estimate of how likely membership in the various groups is, given the available information. This is called the *posterior probability* and is denoted by $P(G_i|D)$. It can be estimated from $P(D|G_i)$ and $P(G_i)$ using Bayes' rule. A case is classified, based on its discriminant score D, in the group for which the posterior probability is the largest. That is, it is assigned to the most likely group based on its discriminant score. (See Tatsuoka, 1971, for further information.)

3.12 Classification Output

Figure 3.12 is an excerpt from the SPSS^X output that lists classification information for each case for a group of cases whose membership is known. The first column (labeled CASE SEQNUM) is the sequence number of the case in the file. The next column (MIS VAL) contains the number of variables with missing values for that case. Cases with missing values are not used in estimating the coefficients and are not included in the output shown in Figure 3.12 (note the absence of cases 3 and 28). However, those two cases with missing values could have been classified and included in the table by substituting group means for missing values. The third column (SEL) indicates whether a case has been excluded from the computations using the SELECT subcommand.

Figure 3.12 Classification output

```
DISCRIMINANT GROUPS=SURVIVAL(1,2)
  /VARIABLES=TREATMNT TO RESP
  /STATISTICS MEAN STDDEV UNIVF CORR RAW
  /PLOT CASES 7
```

CASE SEQNUM	MIS VAL	SEL	ACTUAL GROUP	HIGHEST PROBABILITY GROUP	P(D/G)	P(G/D)	2ND HIGHEST GROUP	P(G/D)	DISCRIMINANT SCORES...
1			1	1	0.5821	0.5873	2	0.4127	-0.1622
2			1	1	0.5776	0.8884	2	0.1116	-1.2695
4			1	1	0.6814	0.8637	2	0.1363	-1.1230
5			1	1	0.7962	0.8334	2	0.1666	-0.9708
6			1	1	0.9080	0.7367	2	0.2633	-0.5970
7			1 **	2	0.4623	0.5164	1	0.4836	0.1070
8			1	1	0.8433	0.7112	2	0.2888	-0.5149
9			1	1	0.6581	0.8695	2	0.1305	-1.1551
10			1	1	0.4577	0.5134	2	0.4866	0.0302
11			1	1	0.6087	0.6017	2	0.3983	-0.2006
12			1	1	0.1722	0.9655	2	0.0345	-2.0775
13			1	1	0.1140	0.9750	2	0.0250	-2.2930
14			1	1	0.3430	0.9360	2	0.0640	-1.6607
15			1	1	0.7983	0.6923	2	0.3077	-0.4569
16			1	1	0.7008	0.6482	2	0.3518	-0.3283
17			1	1	0.2090	0.9593	2	0.0407	-1.9687
18			1	1	0.1128	0.9752	2	0.0248	-2.2982
19			1	1	0.4383	0.9178	2	0.0822	-1.4875
20			1 **	2	0.9418	0.7493	1	0.2507	0.7690
21			1	1	0.7384	0.6658	2	0.3342	-0.3786
22			1 **	2	0.5161	0.5495	1	0.4505	0.1927
23			1	1	0.5399	0.8967	2	0.1033	-1.3255
24			1	1	0.4409	0.5026	2	0.4974	0.0582
25			1 **	2	0.8126	0.8288	1	0.1712	1.0791
26			1	1	0.7050	0.6502	2	0.3498	-0.3339
27			1	1	0.5804	0.5864	2	0.4136	-0.1597
29			2 **	1	0.4595	0.5146	2	0.4854	0.0272
30			2	2	0.8552	0.7160	1	0.2840	0.6596
31			2	2	0.6172	0.6062	1	0.3938	0.3423
32			2	2	0.6928	0.6443	1	0.3557	0.4469
33			2	2	0.8887	0.8063	1	0.1937	0.9820
34			2	2	0.6169	0.8793	1	0.1207	1.3423
35			2	2	0.6823	0.8635	1	0.1365	1.2514
36			2	2	0.7755	0.6824	1	0.3176	0.5568
37			2	2	0.6368	0.8746	1	0.1254	1.3143
38			2	2	0.0874	0.9795	1	0.0205	2.5512
39			2	2	0.1236	0.9735	1	0.0265	2.3821
40			2	2	0.0181	0.9925	1	0.0075	3.2050
41			2	2	0.9033	0.7349	1	0.2651	0.7206
42			2 **	1	0.5613	0.8920	2	0.1080	-1.2934
43			2 **	1	0.5270	0.5560	2	0.4440	-0.0799
44			2 **	1	0.3851	0.9281	2	0.0719	-1.5810
45			2	2	0.5574	0.5735	1	0.4265	0.2553
46			2	2	0.7718	0.8401	1	0.1599	1.1321
47			2	2	0.6792	0.6377	1	0.3623	0.4286
48			2	2	0.9649	0.7819	1	0.2181	0.8861
49			2	2	0.5742	0.8891	1	0.1109	1.4040
50			2	2	0.4533	0.9148	1	0.0852	1.5920

For cases included in the computation of the discriminant function, actual group membership is known and can be compared to that predicted using the discriminant function. The group to which a case actually belongs is listed in the column labeled ACTUAL GROUP. The most-likely group for a case based on the discriminant analysis (the group with the largest posterior probability) is listed in the column labeled HIGHEST GROUP. Cases that are misclassified using the discriminant function are flagged with asterisks next to the actual group number.

The next value listed is the probability of a case's discriminant score, or one more extreme, if the case is a member of the most-likely group.

The larger posterior probabilities of membership in the two groups P(G|*D*) follow in Figure 3.12. When there are only two groups, both probabilities are given since one is the highest and the other the second highest. The probabilities 0.5873 and 0.4127 sum to 1 since a case must be a member of one of the two groups.

---

[7]With releases before 3.0, replace the DISCRIMINANT command with the following:

```
DISCRIMINANT GROUPS=SURVIVAL(1,2)
  /VARIABLES=TREATMNT TO RESP
STATISTICS 1 2 6 4 11 14
```

3.13 Classification Summary

You can obtain the number of misclassified cases by counting the number of cases with asterisks in Figure 3.12. In this example, 8 cases out of 48 are classified incorrectly.

More detailed information on the results of the classification phase is available from the output in Figure 3.13, sometimes called the "Confusion Matrix." For each group, this output shows the numbers of correct and incorrect classifications. In this example only the cases with complete information for all predictor variables are included in the classification results table. Correctly classified cases appear on the diagonal of the table since the predicted and actual groups are the same. For example, of 26 cases in Group 1, 22 were predicted correctly to be members of Group 1 (84.6%), while 4 (15.4%) were assigned incorrectly to Group 2. Similarly, 18 out of 22 (81.8%) of the Group 2 cases were identified correctly, and 4 (18.2%) were misclassified. The overall percentage of cases classified correctly is 83.3% (40 out of 48).

Figure 3.13 Classification results

```
DISCRIMINANT GROUPS=SURVIVAL(1,2)
  /VARIABLES=TREATMNT TO RESP
  /STATISTICS MEAN STDDEV UNIVF CORR RAW TABLE
  /PLOT CASES
```
[8]

CLASSIFICATION RESULTS -

ACTUAL GROUP		NO. OF CASES	PREDICTED GROUP MEMBERSHIP 1	2
GROUP DIE	1	26	22 84.6%	4 15.4%
GROUP SURVIVE	2	22	4 18.2%	18 81.8%

PERCENT OF "GROUPED" CASES CORRECTLY CLASSIFIED: 83.33%

3.14 Histograms of Discriminant Scores

To see how much the two groups overlap and to examine the distribution of the discriminant scores, it is often useful to plot the discriminant function scores for the groups. Figure 3.14a is a histogram of the scores for each group separately. Four symbols (either 1's or 2's) represent one case. (The number of cases represented by a symbol depends on the number of cases used in an analysis.) The row of 1's and 2's underneath the plot denote to which group scores are assigned.

The average score for a group is called the group centroid and is indicated on each plot as well as in Figure 3.14b. These values are the same as the means in Figure 3.7b. On the average, infants who died have smaller discriminant function scores than infants who survived. The average value for Group 1 infants who died is −0.71, whereas the average value for those who survived is 0.84.

---

[8]With releases before 3.0, replace the DISCRIMINANT command with the following:

```
DISCRIMINANT GROUPS=SURVIVAL(1,2)
  /VARIABLES=TREATMNT TO RESP
STATISTICS 1 2 6 4 11 14 13
```

Figure 3.14a Histograms of discriminant scores

```
DISCRIMINANT GROUPS=SURVIVAL(1,2)
  /VARIABLES=TREATMNT TO RESP
  /STATISTICS MEAN STDDEV UNIVF CORR RAW TABLE
  /PLOT CASES SEPARATE 9
```

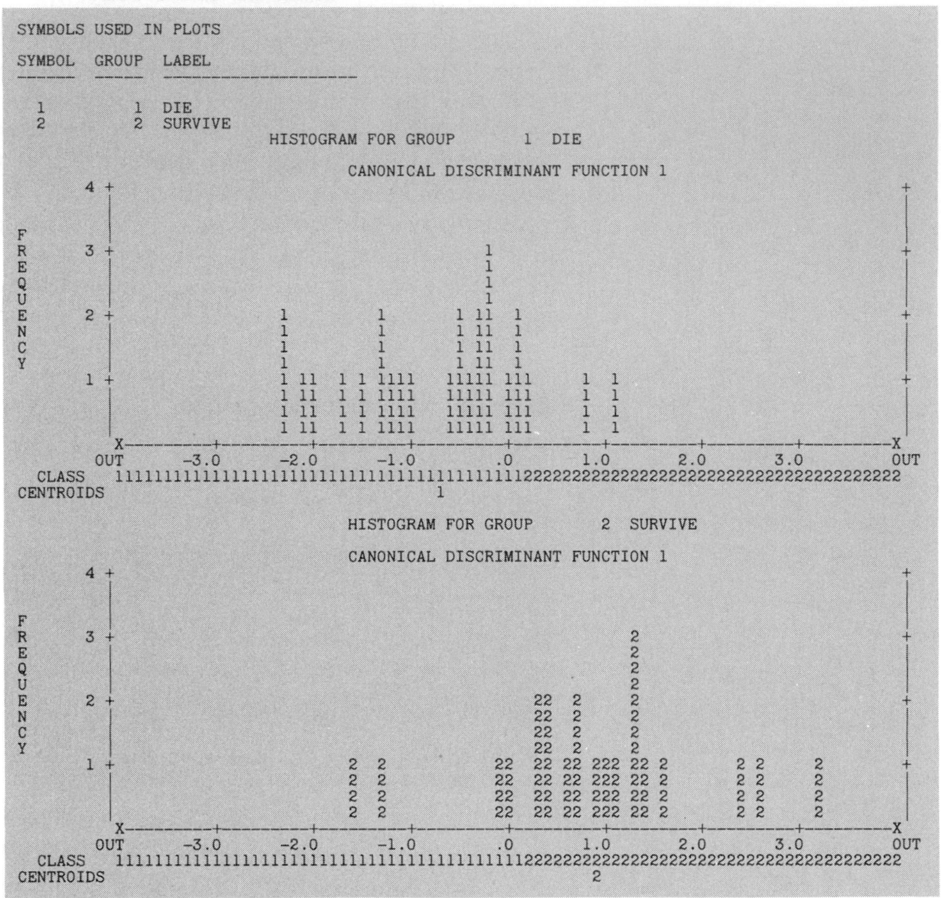

Figure 3.14b Discriminant functions evaluated at group means

```
DISCRIMINANT GROUPS=SURVIVAL(1,2)
  /VARIABLES=TREATMNT TO RESP
  /STATISTICS MEAN STDDEV UNIVF CORR RAW TABLE
  /PLOT CASES SEPARATE 9
```

```
CANONICAL DISCRIMINANT FUNCTIONS EVALUATED AT GROUP MEANS (GROUP CENTROIDS)

  GROUP      FUNC  1

    1      -0.71252
    2       0.84206
```

In Figure 3.14a we note that three Group 1 cases clearly fall into the Group 2 classification region, whereas four Group 1 cases are misclassified. Of the two cases that have values around 0.1, one (Case 7) has a classification probability for Group 1 of 0.48, while the other (Case 24) has a value of 0.503. Thus Case 7 is

[9]With releases before 3.0, replace the DISCRIMINANT command with the following:

```
DISCRIMINANT GROUPS=SURVIVAL(1,2)
  /VARIABLES=TREATMNT TO RESP
STATISTICS 1 2 6 4 11 14 13 16
```

misclassified, although on the plot it appears to be correctly classified because the boundary between the two territories falls within an interval attributed to group 1.

The combined distribution of the scores for the two groups is shown in Figure 3.14c. Again four symbols represent a case, and you can see the amount of overlap between the two groups. For example, the interval with midpoint −1.3 has three cases, two from Group 1 and one from Group 2.

Figure 3.14c All-groups stacked histogram canonical discriminant function

```
DISCRIMINANT GROUPS=SURVIVAL(1,2)
  /VARIABLES=TREATMNT TO RESP
  /STATISTICS MEAN STDDEV UNIVF CORR RAW TABLE
  /PLOT CASES SEPARATE COMBINED
```
[10]

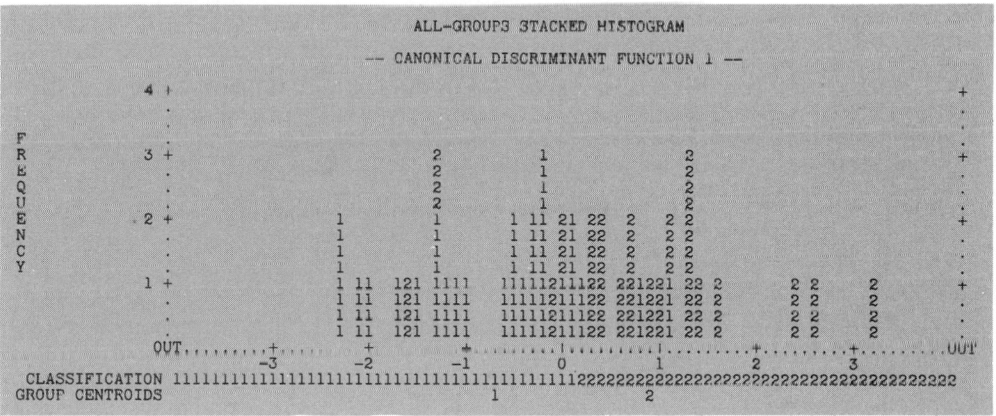

3.15 Estimating Misclassification Rates

Recall from Chapter 2 that a model usually fits the sample from which it is derived better than it will fit another sample from the same population. Thus, the percentage of cases classified correctly by the discriminant function is an inflated estimate of the true performance in the population, just as R^2 is an overly optimistic estimate of a model's fit in regression.

There are several ways to obtain a better estimate of the true misclassification rate. If the sample is large enough to be randomly split into two parts, you can use one to derive the discriminant function and the other to test it. Since the same cases are not used for both estimating the function and testing it, the observed error rate in the "test" sample should better reflect the function's effectiveness. However, this method requires large sample sizes and does not make good use of all of the available information.

Another technique for obtaining an improved estimate of the misclassification rate is the "jackknife," sometimes called the leaving-one-out method. It involves leaving out each of the cases in turn, calculating the function based on the remaining n-1 cases, and then classifying the left-out case. Again, since the case which is being classified is not included in the calculation of the function, the observed (or apparent) misclassification rate is a less-biased estimate of the true one.

[10]With releases before 3.0, replace the DISCRIMINANT command with the following:

```
DISCRIMINANT GROUPS=SURVIVAL(1,2)
  /VARIABLES=TREATMNT TO RESP
STATISTICS 1 2 6 4 11 14 13 16 15
```

When one of the groups is much smaller than the other, a highly correct classification rate can occur even when most of the "minority" group cases are misclassified. The smaller group—adopters of a new product, diseased individuals, or parole violators—are, however, often of particular interest, and their correct classification is of paramount importance. The desired result is not to minimize the overall misclassification rate but to identify most cases of the smaller group. For example, by judging everyone to be disease-free in a cancer-screening program, the error rate will be very small, since few people actually have the disease. However, the results are useless since the goal is to identify the diseased individuals.

The result of different classification rules for identifying "minority" cases can be examined by ranking all cases on the value of their discriminant score, and determining how many "minority" cases are in the various deciles. If most of the cases of interest are at the extremes of the distribution, a good rule for identifying them can be obtained at the expense of increasing the number of misclassified cases from the larger group. If the intent of the discriminant analysis is to identify persons to receive promotional materials for a new product, or undergo further screening procedures, this is a fairly reasonable tactic. Unequal costs for misclassification can also be incorporated into the classification rule by adjusting the prior probabilities to reflect them. For further discussion see Lachenbruch (1975).

3.16 The Expected Misclassification Rate

The percentage of cases classified correctly is often taken as an index of the effectiveness of the discriminant function. When evaluating this measure it is important to compare the observed misclassification rate to that expected by chance alone. For example, if there are two groups with equal prior probabilities, assigning cases to groups based on the outcome of a flip of a fair coin, that is, heads allocate to Group 1 and tails allocate to Group 2, results in an expected misclassification rate of 50%. A discriminant function with an observed misclassification rate of 50% is performing no better than chance. In fact, if the rate is based on the sample used for deriving the function, it is probably doing worse.

As the number of groups with equal prior probabilities increases, the percentage of cases that can be classified correctly by chance alone decreases. If there are 10 groups, only 10% of the cases would be expected to be classified correctly by chance. Observed misclassification rates should always be viewed in light of results expected by chance.

3.17 Other Discriminant Function Statistics

The percentage of cases classified correctly is one indicator of the effectiveness of the discriminant function. Another indicator of effectiveness of the function is the actual discriminant scores in the groups. A "good" discriminant function is one that has much between-groups variability when compared to within-groups variability. In fact, the coefficients of the discriminant function are chosen so that the ratio of the between-groups sum of squares to the within-groups sum of squares is as large as possible. Any other linear combination of the predictor variables will have a smaller ratio.

Figure 3.17a Analysis of variance table from MEANS for discriminant score

```
DISCRIMINANT GROUPS=SURVIVAL(1,2)
  /VARIABLES=TREATMNT TO RESP
  /SAVE=SCORES=DISCORE
VARIABLE LABELS DISCORE1 'DISCRIMINANT SCORE'
MEANS TABLES=DISCORE1 BY SURVIVAL
  /STATISTICS ANOVA[11]
```

```
CRITERION VARIABLE   DISCORE1   DISCRIMINANT SCORE
   BROKEN DOWN BY    SURVIVAL   INFANT SURVIVAL

* * * * * * * * * * * * * * * * * * * * * * * * * * * * * * * * * * * *
*                  A N A L Y S I S   O F   V A R I A N C E                *
* * * * * * * * * * * * * * * * * * * * * * * * * * * * * * * * * * * *

                         SUM OF                   MEAN
SOURCE                   SQUARES        D.F.      SQUARE          F         SIG.

BETWEEN GROUPS           28.7992          1       28.7992     28.7992      .0000

WITHIN GROUPS            46.0000         46        1.0000

                   ETA =  .6205    ETA SQUARED =   .3850
* * * * * * * * * * * * * * * * * * * * * * * * * * * * * * * * * * * *
```

Figure 3.17a is an analysis of variance table from procedure MEANS using the discriminant scores as the dependent variable and the group variable as the independent or classification variable. Figure 3.17b shows a variety of statistics based on the analysis of variance table. For example the eigenvalue in Figure 3.17b. is simply the ratio of the between-groups to within-groups sums of squares. Thus, from Figure 3.17a it is

$$\text{eigenvalue} = \frac{\text{between-groups ss}}{\text{within-groups ss}} = \frac{28.8}{46.0} = 0.626 \qquad \textbf{Equation 3.17a}$$

Large eigenvalues are associated with "good" functions. The next two entries in Figure 3.17b, percent of variance and cumulative percent are always 100 for the two-group situation. (See Section 3.38 for further explanation.)

Figure 3.17b Canonical discriminant functions

```
DISCRIMINANT GROUPS=SURVIVAL(1,2)
  /VARIABLES=TREATMNT TO RESP
```

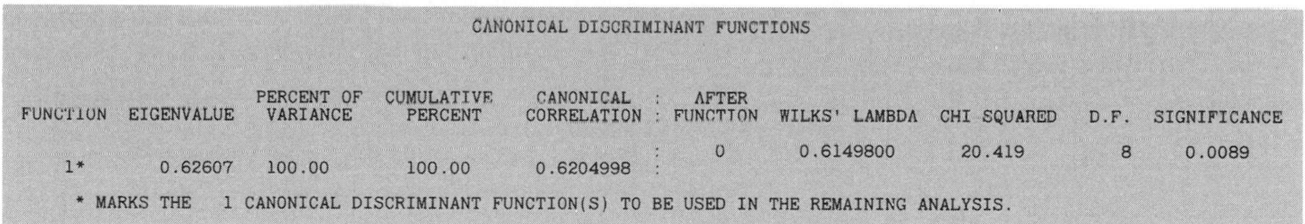

CANONICAL DISCRIMINANT FUNCTIONS

FUNCTION	EIGENVALUE	PERCENT OF VARIANCE	CUMULATIVE PERCENT	CANONICAL CORRELATION	:	AFTER FUNCTION	WILKS' LAMBDA	CHI SQUARED	D.F.	SIGNIFICANCE
					:	0	0.6149800	20.419	8	0.0089
1*	0.62607	100.00	100.00	0.6204998	:					

* MARKS THE 1 CANONICAL DISCRIMINANT FUNCTION(S) TO BE USED IN THE REMAINING ANALYSIS.

The *canonical correlation* is a measure of the degree of association between the discriminant scores and the groups. It is equivalent to eta from the oneway analysis of variance, in which the discriminant score is the dependent variable and

[11]With releases before 3.0, replace the MEANS command with the following two commands:

```
BREAKDOWN TABLES=DISCORE1 BY SURVIVAL
STATISTICS 1
```

group is the independent variable. Remember eta^2 is the ratio of the between-groups sum of squares to the total sum of squares and represents the proportion of the total variance attributable to differences among the groups. Thus, from Figure 3.17a, eta is

$$eta = \sqrt{\frac{28.8}{74.8}} = 0.620$$ **Equation 3.17b**

In the two-group situation, the canonical correlation is simply the usual Pearson correlation coefficient between the discriminant score and the group variable, which is coded 0 and 1.

For the two-group case, Wilks' lambda is the ratio of the within-groups sum of squares to the total sum of squares. It is the proportion of the total variance in the discriminant scores not explained by differences among groups (lambda plus eta^2 sum to 1.) From Figure 3.17a, lambda is

$$\lambda = \frac{46}{74.8} = 0.615$$ **Equation 3.17c**

As indicated in Section 3.38, small values of lambda are associated with functions that have much variability between groups and little variability within groups. A lambda of 1 occurs when the mean of the discriminant scores is the same in all groups and there is no between-groups variability.

A test of the null hypothesis that in the populations from which the samples are drawn there is no difference between the group means can be based on Wilks' lambda. Lambda is transformed to a variable which has approximately a chi-square distribution. Figure 3.17b shows that a lambda of 0.615 is transformed to a chi-square value of 20.42 with 8 degrees of freedom. The observed significance level is 0.0089. Thus, it appears unlikely that infants who die from RDS and those who survive have the same means on the discriminant function.

It is important to remember that even though Wilks' lambda may be statistically significant, it provides little information about the effectiveness of the discriminant function in classification. It only provides a test of the null hypothesis that the population means are equal. Small differences may be statistically significant but still not permit good discrimination among the groups. If the means and covariance matrices are equal, of course, discrimination is not possible.

3.18 Interpreting the Discriminant Function Coefficients

Table 3.18 contains the standardized and unstandardized discriminant function coefficients for the RDS example. The unstandardized coefficients are the multipliers of the variables when they are expressed in the original units. As in multiple regression, the standardized coefficients are used when the variables are standardized to a mean of 0 and a standard deviation of 1.

Table 3.18 Standardized and unstandardized discriminant function coefficients

Variable	Unstandardized	Standardized
TREATMNT	0.43115	0.21531
TIME	0.03671	0.13170
WEIGHT	2.04404	1.16789
APGAR	0.12643	0.34638
SEX	0.00700	0.00337
AGE	−0.21807	−0.64084
PH	0.40787	0.16862
RESP	−1.24454	−0.58743
(CONSTANT)	−0.23093	

The interpretation of the coefficients is also similar to that in multiple regression. Since the variables are correlated, it is not possible to assess the importance of an individual variable. The value of the coefficient for a particular variable depends on the other variables included in the function.

It is sometimes tempting to interpret the magnitudes of the coefficients as indicators of the relative importance of variables. Variables with large coefficients are thought to contribute more to the overall discriminant function. However, the magnitude of the unstandardized coefficients is not a good index of relative importance when the variables differ in the units in which they are measured. For example, the gestational age (variable AGE) is measured in weeks and ranges from 28 to 39 weeks, while the pH level ranges from 6.85 to 7.37. When the absolute values of the unstandardized coefficients are ranked from largest to smallest, age (−0.22) has a rank of 5. However, when the coefficients are standardized to adjust for the unequal means and standard deviations of the independent variables, the coefficient for age (−0.64) is the second largest.

The actual signs of the coefficients are arbitrary. The negative coefficients for age and respiratory therapy could just as well be positive if the signs of the other coefficients were reversed.

By looking at the groups of variables which have coefficients of different signs, we can determine which variable values result in large and small function values. For example, since respiratory therapy is usually initiated for infants who are in considerable distress, it is a bad omen for survival. Values of 1 for the RESP variable will decrease the function value. Infants who weigh more usually have better-developed lungs and are more likely to survive. Thus, larger weights increase the function. Large function values are associated with survival, while small function values are associated with death.

3.19 Function-Variable Correlations

Another way to assess the contribution of a variable to the discriminant function is to examine the correlations between the values of the function and the values of the variables. The computation of the coefficients is straightforward. For each case the value of the discriminant function is computed, and the Pearson correlation coefficients between it and the original variables are obtained.

Separate correlation matrices can be calculated for each group and the results combined to obtain a *pooled within-groups* correlation matrix like that in Figure 3.19. Or all of the cases can be considered together and a *total* correlation matrix calculated. The total correlation coefficients are larger than the corresponding within-groups correlations. However, the relative magnitudes will be similar. Variables with high total correlations will also have high pooled within-groups correlations.

Figure 3.19 Pooled within-groups correlations

```
STRUCTURE MATRIX:

POOLED WITHIN-GROUPS CORRELATIONS BETWEEN DISCRIMINATING VARIABLES
                                   AND CANONICAL DISCRIMINANT FUNCTIONS
(VARIABLES ORDERED BY SIZE OF CORRELATION WITHIN FUNCTION)

              FUNC  1

WEIGHT         0.73338
RESP          -0.51940
AGE            0.49290
TREATMNT       0.26572
PH             0.25946
APGAR          0.19210
TIME          -0.10157
SEX            0.03738
```

Figure 3.19 indicates that variable WEIGHT has the highest correlation with the discriminant function. RESP has the second largest correlation in absolute value. The negative sign indicates that small function values are associated with the presence of respiratory therapy (coded 1) and larger values are associated with the absence of respiratory therapy. These results are similar to those obtained from the standardized coefficients.

However, if you compare Table 3.18 and Figure 3.19, you will notice that AGE, which has a negative standardized coefficient, is positively correlated with the discriminant function. Similarly, TIME, which has a positive standardized coefficient, has a negative correlation with the discriminant score. This occurs because WEIGHT and AGE, as expected, are highly correlated. The correlation coefficient is 0.84 from Figure 3.5a. Thus, the contribution of AGE and WEIGHT is shared and the individual coefficients are not meaningful. You should exercise care when attempting to interpret the coefficients, since correlations between variables affect the magnitudes and signs of the coefficients.

3.20 Fisher's Classification Function Coefficients

In Table 3.18, the linear discriminant function coefficients are those that maximize the ratio of between-groups to within-groups sum of squares. These coefficients are sometimes called the canonical discriminant function coefficients since they are identical to those obtained from canonical correlation analysis when maximally correlated linear combinations of the group membership variables and predictor variables are formed (see Tatsuoka, 1971).

Another set of coefficients, sometimes called Fisher's linear discriminant function coefficients or classification coefficients, can be used directly for classification. A set of coefficients is obtained for each group and a case is assigned to the group for which it has the largest discriminant score. The classification results are identical for both methods if all canonical discriminant functions are used (see Kshirsagar & Arseven, 1975; Green, 1979).

3.21 Relationship to Multiple Regression Analysis

Two-group linear discriminant analysis is closely related to multiple linear regression analysis. If the binary grouping variable is considered the dependent variable and the predictor variables are the independent variables, the multiple regression coefficients in Table 3.21 are obtained. Comparison of these coefficients to the discriminant function coefficients shows that the two sets of coefficients are proportional. The discriminant coefficients can be obtained by multiplying the regression coefficients by 4.04. The exact constant of proportionality varies from data set to data set, but the two sets of coefficients are always proportional. This is true only for two-group discriminant analysis.

Table 3.21 Regression and discriminant coefficients

Variable	B Regression	B Discriminant	Ratio
RESP	−0.3082	−1.2445	4.04
TIME	0.0091	0.0367	4.04
PH	0.1010	0.4079	4.04
TREATMNT	0.1068	0.4311	4.04
SEX	0.0017	0.0070	4.04
AGE	−0.0540	−0.2180	4.04
APGAR	0.0313	0.1264	4.04
WEIGHT	0.5062	2.0040	4.04

3.22 VARIABLE SELECTION METHODS

In many situations discriminant analysis, like multiple regression analysis, is used as an exploratory tool. In order to arrive at a good model, a variety of potentially useful variables are included in the data set. It is not known in advance which of these variables are important for group separation and which are, more or less, extraneous. One of the desired end-products of the analysis is identification of the "good" predictor variables. All of the caveats for variable selection procedures in multiple regression discussed in Chapter 2 apply to discriminant analysis as well. If you have not read Chapter 2, you are advised to do so before continuing with this chapter.

The three most commonly used algorithms for variable selection—forward entry, stepwise selection, and backward elimination—are available in DISCRIMINANT. The principles are the same as in multiple regression. What differs are the actual criteria for variable selection. In the following example, only minimization of Wilks' lambda will be considered. Some others are discussed in Sections 3.30 through 3.34.

3.23 A Stepwise Selection Example

Since stepwise variable selection algorithms combine the features of forward selection and backward elimination, output from the stepwise method will be discussed. Remember that in a stepwise method the first variable included in the analysis has the largest acceptable value for the selection criterion. After the first variable is entered, the value of the criterion is reevaluated for all variables not in the model, and the variable with the largest acceptable criterion value is entered next. At this point, the variable entered first is reevaluated to determine whether it meets the removal criterion. If it does, it is removed from the model.

The next step is to examine the variables not in the equation for entry, followed by examination of the variables in the equation for removal. Variables are removed until none remain that meet the removal criterion. Variable selection terminates when no more variables meet entry or removal criteria.

3.24 Variable Selection Criteria

Figure 3.24 is output from the beginning of a stepwise variable selection job, listing the criteria in effect. As mentioned previously, several criteria are available for variable selection (see Section 3.22). This example uses minimization of Wilks' lambda. Thus, at each step the variable that results in the smallest Wilks' lambda for the discriminant function is selected for entry.

Figure 3.24 Stepwise variable selection

```
DISCRIMINANT GROUPS=SURVIVAL(1,2)
  /VARIABLES=TREATMNT TO RESP
  /METHOD=WILKS
```

```
STEPWISE VARIABLE SELECTION

    SELECTION RULE:  MINIMIZE WILKS' LAMBDA
    MAXIMUM NUMBER OF STEPS..................        16
    MINIMUM TOLERANCE LEVEL.................. 0.00100
    MINIMUM F TO ENTER......................   1.0000
    MAXIMUM F TO REMOVE.....................   1.0000
```

Each entry or removal of a variable is considered a step. The maximum number of steps permitted in an analysis is either twice the number of independent variables (the default) or a user-specified value.

As in multiple regression, if there are independent variables that are linear combinations of other independent variables, a unique solution is not possible. To prevent computational difficulties the tolerance of a variable is checked before it is entered into a model. The tolerance is a measure of the degree of linear association between the independent variables. For the *i*th independent variable, it is $1-R_i^2$, where R_i^2 is the squared multiple correlation coefficient when the *i*th independent variable is considered the dependent variable and the regression equation between it and the other independent variables is calculated. Small values for the tolerance indicate that the *i*th independent variable is almost a linear combination of the other independent variables. Variables with small tolerances (by default, less than 0.001) are not permitted to enter the analysis. Also, if entry of a variable would cause the tolerance of a variable already in the model to drop to an unacceptable level (0.001 by default), the variable is not entered. The smallest acceptable tolerance for a particular analysis is shown in Figure 3.24.

The significance of the change in Wilks' lambda when a variable is entered or removed from the model can be based on an *F* statistic. Either the actual value of *F* or its significance level can be used as the criterion for variable entry and removal. These two criteria are not necessarily equivalent since a fixed *F* value has different significance levels depending on the number of variables in the model at any step. The actual significance levels associated with the *F*-to-enter and *F*-to-remove statistics are not those usually obtained from the *F* distribution, since many variables are examined and the largest and smallest *F* values selected. The true significance level is difficult to compute since it depends on many factors, including the correlations between the independent variables.

3.25 The First Step

Before the stepwise selection algorithm begins, at Step 0, basic information about the variables is printed, as shown in Figure 3.25a. The tolerance and minimum tolerance are 1, since there are no variables in the model. (The tolerance is based only on the independent variables in the model. The minimum tolerance, which is the smallest tolerance for any variable in the equation if the variable under consideration is entered, is also based only on the variables in the equation.) The *F*-to-enter in Figure 3.25a is equal to the *F* test for equality of group means in Figure 3.3b. The univariate Wilks' lambda is also the same.

Figure 3.25a Output at Step 0

```
DISCRIMINANT GROUPS=SURVIVAL(1,2)
  /VARIABLES=TREATMNT TO RESP
  /METHOD=WILKS
  /STATISTICS FPAIR[12]
```

------------------- VARIABLES NOT IN THE ANALYSIS AFTER STEP 0 -------------------

VARIABLE	TOLERANCE	MINIMUM TOLERANCE	F TO ENTER	WILKS' LAMBDA
TREATMNT	1.0000000	1.0000000	2.0335	0.9576649
TIME	1.0000000	1.0000000	0.2971	0.9935822
WEIGHT	1.0000000	1.0000000	15.4890	0.7480967
APGAR	1.0000000	1.0000000	1.0628	0.9774175
SEX	1.0000000	1.0000000	0.0402	0.9991259
AGE	1.0000000	1.0000000	6.9967	0.8679783
PH	1.0000000	1.0000000	1.9388	0.9595576
RESP	1.0000000	1.0000000	7.7693	0.8555062

The WEIGHT variable has the smallest Wilks' lambda, and correspondingly the largest *F*-to-enter, so it is the first variable entered into the equation. When WEIGHT is entered, as shown in Figure 3.25b, the Wilks' lambda and corresponding *F* are the same as in Figures 3.3b and 3.25a. The degrees of freedom for the Wilks' lambda printed in Figure 3.25b are for its untransformed (not converted to an *F*) distribution.

[12]With releases before 3.0, replace the DISCRIMINANT command with the following:

```
DISCRIMINANT GROUPS=SURVIVAL(1,2)
  /VARIABLES=TREATMNT TO RESP
  /METHOD=WILKS
STATISTICS 5
```

After each step, SPSSX prints a table showing the variables in the model (see Figure 3.25c). When only one variable is in the model, this table contains no new information. The *F*-to-remove corresponds to that in Figure 3.25b since it represents the change in Wilks' lambda if WEIGHT is removed. The last column usually contains the value of Wilks' lambda if the variable is removed. However, since removal of WEIGHT results in a model with no variables, no value is printed at the first step.

Figure 3.25b Summary statistics for Step 1

```
AT STEP   1, WEIGHT    WAS INCLUDED IN THE ANALYSIS.

                                       DEGREES OF FREEDOM  SIGNIF.   BETWEEN GROUPS
WILKS' LAMBDA            0.74810         1     1       46.0
EQUIVALENT F            15.4894                1       46.0  0.0003
```

Figure 3.25c Variables in the analysis after Step 1

```
---------------- VARIABLES IN THE ANALYSIS AFTER STEP   1 ----------------

VARIABLE  TOLERANCE  F TO REMOVE   WILKS' LAMBDA

WEIGHT    1.0000000     15.489
```

SPSSX also prints a test of differences between pairs of groups after each step. When there are only two groups, the *F* value printed is the same as that for Wilks' lambda for the overall model, as shown in Figures 3.25c and 3.25d.

Figure 3.25d *F* values and significance at Step 1

```
F STATISTICS AND SIGNIFICANCES BETWEEN PAIRS OF GROUPS AFTER STEP    1
EACH F STATISTIC HAS    1 AND        46.0 DEGREES OF FREEDOM.

                   GROUP          1
                        DIE
   GROUP

       2  SURVIVE          15.489
                           0.0003
```

3.26 Statistics for Variables Not in the Model

Also printed at each step is a set of summary statistics for variables not yet in the model. From Figure 3.26, RESP is the variable which results in the smallest Wilks' lambda for the model if it is entered next. Note that the Wilks' lambda calculated is for the variables WEIGHT and RESP jointly. Its *F*-test is a multivariate significance test for group differences.

The *F* value for the change in Wilks' lambda when a variable is added to a model which contains *p* independent variables is

$$F_{change} = \left(\frac{n - g - p}{g - 1}\right)\left(\frac{(1 - \lambda_{p+1}/\lambda_p)}{\lambda_{p+1}/\lambda_p}\right) \qquad \textbf{Equation 3.26a}$$

where n is the total number of cases, g is the number of groups, λ_p is Wilks' lambda before adding the variable, and λ_{p+1} is Wilks' lambda after inclusion.

If variable RESP is entered into the model containing variable WEIGHT, Wilks' lambda is 0.669. The lambda for WEIGHT alone is 0.748 (see Figure 3.25b). The *F* value for the change, called *F*-to-enter, is from Equation 3.26a:

$$F = \frac{(48 - 2 - 1)(1 - 0.669/0.748)}{(2 - 1)(0.669/0.748)} = 5.31 \qquad \textbf{Equation 3.26b}$$

This is the value for RESP in Figure 3.26.

Figure 3.26 Variables not in the analysis after Step 1

```
---------------- VARIABLES NOT IN THE ANALYSIS AFTER STEP   1 ---------------

                          MINIMUM
VARIABLE  TOLERANCE  TOLERANCE  F TO ENTER    WILKS' LAMBDA

TREATMNT  0.9917361  0.9917361   0.8420         0.73435
TIME      0.9548707  0.9548707   0.0648         0.74702
APGAR     0.9508910  0.9508910   0.0193         0.74777
SEX       0.9619762  0.9619762   0.2444         0.74406
AGE       0.2937327  0.2937327   1.0931         0.73035
PH        0.9845349  0.9845349   0.6060         0.73816
RESP      0.9994270  0.9994270   5.3111         0.66912
```

3.27 The Second Step

Figure 3.27 shows the output when RESP is entered into the model. Wilks' lambda for the model is the same as Wilks' lambda for RESP in Figure 3.26. If WEIGHT is removed from the current model, leaving only RESP, the resulting Wilks' lambda is 0.855, the entry for WEIGHT in the second part of Figure 3.27. The *F* value associated with the change in lambda, *F*-to-remove, is 12.5, which is also printed in Figure 3.27.

$$F\text{-to-remove} = \frac{(48 - 2 - 1)(1 - 0.669/0.855)}{(1)(0.669/0.855)} = 12.5 \qquad \textbf{Equation 3.27}$$

Since the *F*-to-remove for all the variables in the model is larger than the default value of 1, none are removed.

Figure 3.27 RESP included in analysis at Step 2

```
AT STEP   2, RESP      WAS INCLUDED IN THE ANALYSIS.

                                          DEGREES OF FREEDOM  SIGNIF.   BETWEEN GROUPS
WILKS' LAMBDA           0.66912            2     1        46.0
EQUIVALENT F            11.1260                  2        45.0  0.0001

---------------- VARIABLES IN THE ANALYSIS AFTER STEP    2 ---------------

VARIABLE  TOLERANCE  F TO REMOVE   WILKS' LAMBDA

WEIGHT    0.9994270    12.535         0.85551
RESP      0.9994270    5.3111         0.74810

---------------- VARIABLES NOT IN THE ANALYSIS AFTER STEP    2 ---------------

                          MINIMUM
VARIABLE  TOLERANCE  TOLERANCE  F TO ENTER    WILKS' LAMBDA

TREATMNT  0.9917051  0.9911962   0.71594         0.65841
TIME      0.9492383  0.9492383   0.53176         0.66904
APGAR     0.9231403  0.9231403   0.25589         0.66526
SEX       0.8879566  0.8879566   0.19884         0.66882
AGE       0.2914116  0.2914116   1.37830         0.64880
PH        0.9828797  0.9828797   0.66764         0.65912

F STATISTICS AND SIGNIFICANCES BETWEEN PAIRS OF GROUPS AFTER STEP    2
EACH F STATISTIC HAS    2 AND         45.0 DEGREES OF FREEDOM.
```

After WEIGHT and RESP have both been included in the model, the next variable that would result in the smallest Wilks' lambda if entered is AGE. Its *F*-to-enter is 1.38, and the resulting model lambda is 0.649. Thus, AGE is entered in Step 3.

3.28 The Last Step

After AGE is entered, all *F*-to-remove values are still greater than 1 so no variables are removed. All variables not in the model after Step 3 have *F*-to-enter values less than 1, so none are eligible for inclusion and variable selection stops (see Figure 3.28).

Figure 3.28 Output for Step 3

```
AT STEP   3, AGE        WAS INCLUDED IN THE ANALYSIS.

                                     DEGREES OF FREEDOM  SIGNIF.    BETWEEN GROUPS
WILKS' LAMBDA          0.64880         3    1        46.0
EQUIVALENT F           7.93913              3        44.0  0.0002

---------------- VARIABLES IN THE ANALYSIS AFTER STEP   3 ----------------

VARIABLE  TOLERANCE  F TO REMOVE   WILKS' LAMBDA

WEIGHT    0.2926088    8.1466          0.76893
AGE       0.2914116    1.3783          0.66912
RESP      0.9916294    5.5307          0.73035

---------------- VARIABLES NOT IN THE ANALYSIS AFTER STEP   3 ----------------

                      MINIMUM
VARIABLE  TOLERANCE  TOLERANCE  F TO ENTER      WILKS' LAMBDA

TREATMNT  0.9904436  0.2907779   0.61371           0.63967
TIME      0.9469645  0.2907135   0.00023           0.64880
APGAR     0.8055887  0.2543036   0.92868           0.63509
SEX       0.8086141  0.2548962   0.04585           0.64811
PH        0.9482218  0.2778589   0.34965           0.64357

F STATISTICS AND SIGNIFICANCES BETWEEN PAIRS OF GROUPS AFTER STEP    3
EACH F STATISTIC HAS   3 AND        44.0 DEGREES OF FREEDOM.
```

3.29 Summary Tables

After the last step, SPSS^{X} prints a summary table (see Figure 3.29). For each step this table lists the action taken (entry or removal) and the resulting Wilks' lambda and its significance level. Note that although inclusion of additional variables results in a decrease in Wilks' lambda, the observed significance level does not necessarily decrease since it depends both on the value of lambda and on the number of independent variables in the model.

Figure 3.29 Summary table

```
                              SUMMARY TABLE

        ACTION          VARS   WILKS'
STEP ENTERED REMOVED     IN    LAMBDA    SIG.   LABEL

  1  WEIGHT               1    .74810   .0003   BIRTHWEIGHT IN KILOGRAMS
  2  RESP                 2    .66912   .0001   RESPIRATORY LEVEL
  3  AGE                  3    .64880   .0002   GESTATION AGE
```

Table 3.29 shows the percentage of cases classified correctly at each step of the analysis. The model with variables WEIGHT, RESP, and AGE classifies almost 80% of the cases correctly, while the complete model with eight variables classifies 83% of the cases correctly. Including additional variables does not substantially improve classification. In fact, sometimes the percentage of cases classified correctly actually decreases if poor predictors are included in the model.

Table 3.29 Cases correctly classified by step

Variables included	Percent correctly classified
WEIGHT	68.00
WEIGHT, RESP	75.00
WEIGHT, RESP, AGE	79.17
All Eight Variables	83.33

3.30 Other Criteria for Variable Selection

In previous sections, variables were included in the model based on Wilks' lambda. At each step, the variable that resulted in the smallest Wilks' lambda was selected. Other criteria besides Wilks' lambda are sometimes used for variable selection.

3.31 Rao's V

Rao's V, also known as the Lawley-Hotelling trace, is defined as

$$V = (n - g) \sum_{i=1}^{p} \sum_{j=1}^{p} w_{ij}^* \sum_{k=1}^{g} n_k (\overline{X}_{ik} - \overline{X}_i)(\overline{X}_{jk} - \overline{X}_j) \qquad \textbf{Equation 3.31}$$

where p is the number of variables in the model, g is the number of groups, n_k is the sample size in the kth group, $\overline{X}_{ik}$ is the mean of the ith variable for the kth group, $\overline{X}_i$ is the mean of the ith variable for all groups combined, and w_{ij}^* is an element of the inverse of the within-groups covariance matrix. The larger the differences between group means, the larger Rao's V.

One way to evaluate the contribution of a variable is to see how much it increases Rao's V when it is added to the model. The sampling distribution of V is approximately a chi-square with $p(g - 1)$ degrees of freedom. A test of the significance of the change in Rao's V when a variable is included can also be based on the chi-square distribution. It is possible for a variable to actually decrease Rao's V when it is added to a model.

3.32 Mahalanobis' Distance

Mahalanobis' distance, D^2, is a generalized measure of the distance between two groups. (See Chapter 2 for an example using Mahalanobis' distance in regression analysis.) The distance between groups a and b is defined as

$$D_{ab}^2 = (n - g) \sum_{i=1}^{p} \sum_{j=1}^{p} w_{ij}^* (\overline{X}_{ia} - \overline{X}_{ib})(\overline{X}_{ja} - \overline{X}_{jb}) \qquad \textbf{Equation 3.32}$$

where p is the number of variables in the model, $\overline{X}_{ia}$ is the mean for the ith variable in group a, and w_{ij}^* is an element from the inverse of the within-groups covariance matrix.

When Mahalanobis' distance is the criterion for variable selection, the Mahalanobis' distances between all pairs of groups are calculated first. The variable that has the largest D^2 for the two groups that are closest (have the smallest D^2 initially) is selected for inclusion.

3.33 Between-Groups F

A test of the null hypothesis that the two sets of population means are equal can be based on Mahalanobis' distance. The corresponding F statistic is

$$F = \frac{(n-1-p)n_1n_2}{p(n-2)(n_1+n_2)} D^2_{ab} \qquad \textbf{Equation 3.33}$$

This F value can also be used for variable selection. At each step the variable chosen for inclusion is the one with the largest F value. Since the Mahalanobis' distance is weighted by the sample sizes when the between-groups F is used as the criterion for stepwise selection, the results from the two methods may differ.

3.34 Sum of Unexplained Variance

As mentioned previously, two-group discriminant analysis is analogous to multiple regression in which the dependent variable is either 0 or 1, depending on the group to which a case belongs. In fact, the Mahalanobis' distance and R^2 are proportional. Thus

$$R^2 = cD^2 \qquad \textbf{Equation 3.34}$$

For each pair of groups, *a* and *b*, the unexplained variation from the regression is $1 - R^2_{ab}$, where R^2_{ab} is the square of the multiple correlation coefficient when a variable coded as 0 or 1 (depending on whether the case is a member of *a* or *b*) is considered the dependent variable.

The sum of the unexplained variation for all pairs of groups can also be used as a criterion for variable selection. The variable chosen for inclusion is the one that minimizes the sum of the unexplained variation.

3.35 THREE-GROUP DISCRIMINANT ANALYSIS

The previous example used discriminant analysis to distinguish between members of two groups. This section presents a three-group discriminant example. The basics are the same as in two-group discriminant analysis, although there are several additional considerations.

One of the early applications of discriminant analysis in business was for credit-granting decisions. Many different models for extending credit based on a variety of predictor variables have been proposed. Churchill (1979) describes the case of the Consumer Finance Company, which must screen credit applicants. It has available for analysis 30 cases known to be poor, equivocal, and good credit risks. For each case, the annual income (in thousands of dollars), the number of credit cards, the number of children, and the age of the household head are known. The task is to use discriminant analysis to derive a classification scheme for new cases based on the available data.

3.36 The Number of Functions

With two groups, it is possible to derive one discriminant function that maximizes the ratio of between- to within-groups sums of squares. When there are three groups, two discriminant functions can be calculated. The first function, as in the two-group case, has the largest ratio of between-groups to within-groups sums of squares. The second function is uncorrelated with the first and has the next largest ratio. In general, if there are *k* groups, $k - 1$ discriminant functions can be computed. They are all uncorrelated with each other and maximize the ratio of between-groups to within-groups sums of squares, subject to the constraint of being uncorrelated.

Figure 3.36a contains the two sets of unstandardized discriminant function coefficients for the credit risk example. Based on these coefficients it is possible to compute two scores for each case, one for each function. Consider, for example, the first case in the file with an annual income of $9,200, 2 credit cards, 3 children, and a 27-year-old head of household. For Function 1, the discriminant score is

$$D_{11} = -14.47 + 0.33(9.2) + 0.13(2) + 0.24(27) + 0.15(3) = -4.2 \qquad \textbf{Equation 3.36}$$

The discriminant score for Function 2 is obtained the same way, using the coefficients for the second function. Figure 3.36b shows the discriminant scores and other classification information.

Figure 3.36a Unstandardized canonical discriminant function coefficients

```
DISCRIMINANT GROUPS=RISK(1,3) /VARIABLES=INCOME TO CHILDREN
  /STATISTICS RAW
```
[13]

```
UNSTANDARDIZED CANONICAL DISCRIMINANT FUNCTION COEFFICIENTS

              FUNC  1        FUNC  2

INCOME       .3257077      -.2251991
CREDIT       .1344126      -.0055648
AGEHEAD      .2444825       .1497008
CHILDREN     .1497964       .1778159
(CONSTANT) -14.46811      -2.540298
```

Figure 3.36b Classification output

```
DISCRIMINANT GROUPS=RISK(1,3) /VARIABLES=INCOME TO CHILDREN
  /STATISTICS RAW
  /PLOT CASES
```
[14]

```
 CASE   MIS          ACTUAL       HIGHEST PROBABILITY       2ND HIGHEST        DISCRIMINANT
SEQNUM  VAL   SEL     GROUP        GROUP P(D/G) P(G/D)      GROUP P(G/D)        SCORES...

   1                    1              1 0.8229 0.9993          2 0.0007      -4.1524    -0.0479
   2                    1              1 0.2100 0.9999          2 0.0001      -4.7122    -1.3738
   3                    1              1 0.7864 0.9885          2 0.0115      -3.3119     0.5959
   4                    1              1 0.8673 0.9718          2 0.0282      -2.9966    -0.0155
   5                    1              1 0.7610 0.9646          2 0.0354      -2.9464     0.3933
   6                    1              1 0.8797 0.9865          2 0.0135      -3.2056    -0.4530
   7                    1              1 0.7589 0.9995          2 0.0005      -4.2685    -0.1243
   8                    1              1 0.5684 0.9812          2 0.0188      -3.1762     0.9402
   9                    1              1 0.8191 0.9980          2 0.0020      -3.7851    -0.6398
  10                    1              1 0.7160 0.9336          2 0.0664      -2.7267     0.0973
  11                    2              2 0.9923 0.9938          1 0.0060      -0.3287    -0.0043
  12                    2              2 0.7764 0.9922          1 0.0076      -0.3718    -0.5939
  13                    2              2 0.6003 0.9938          3 0.0059       0.5383     0.6958
  14                    2              2 0.2482 0.6334          1 0.3666      -1.7833     0.8513
  15                    2              2 0.5867 0.9856          3 0.0143       0.7262    -0.0908
  16                    2              2 0.5199 0.9770          3 0.0229       0.8454    -0.0539
  17                    2              2 0.5355 0.9788          3 0.0211       0.8312     0.1126
  18                    2              2 0.3812 0.7845          1 0.2155      -1.5451     0.6993
  19                    2              2 0.9734 0.9961          1 0.0036      -0.1879     0.3225
  20                    2              2 0.2789 0.7086          1 0.2914      -1.5878    -0.8148
  21                    3              3 0.8476 0.9977          2 0.0023       3.2486     0.0529
  22                    3              3 0.3037 1.0000          2 0.0000       4.2453     1.4329
  23                    3              3 0.4273 0.9996          2 0.0004       3.6041    -1.3365
  24                    3              3 0.0973 0.9997          2 0.0003       3.6535    -2.2021
  25                    3              3 0.5946 0.9861          2 0.0139       2.7974    -0.1220
  26                    3              3 0.2355 0.9988          2 0.0012       3.4655     1.6148
  27                    3 **           2 0.0585 0.7055          3 0.2945       1.6111     1.5539
  28                    3              3 0.2221 1.0000          2 0.0000       5.5428     0.0977
  29                    3              3 0.0510 1.0000          2 0.0000       4.2979    -2.4410
  30                    3              3 0.1170 1.0000          2 0.0000       5.6787     0.8533
```

3.37 Classification

When there is one discriminant function, classification of cases into groups is based on the values for the single function. When there are several groups, a case's values on all functions must be considered simultaneously.

Figure 3.37a contains group means for the two functions. Group 1 has negative means for both functions, Group 2 has a negative mean for Function 1 and a positive mean for Function 2, while Group 3 has a positive mean on Function 1 and a slightly negative mean on Function 2.

Figure 3.37a Canonical discriminant function—group means

```
CANONICAL DISCRIMINANT FUNCTIONS EVALUATED AT GROUP MEANS (GROUP CENTROIDS)

    GROUP        FUNC  1       FUNC  2

      1        -3.52816      -0.06276
      2        -0.28634       0.11238
      3         3.81449      -0.04962
```

[13]With releases before 3.0, replace the DISCRIMINANT command with the following:

```
DISCRIMINANT GROUPS=RISK(1,3)  /VARIABLES=INCOME TO CHILDREN
STATISTICS 11
```

[14]With releases before 3.0, replace the DISCRIMINANT command with the following:

```
DISCRIMINANT GROUPS=RISK(1,3)  /VARIABLES=INCOME TO CHILDREN
STATISTICS 11 14
```

Figure 3.37b shows the territorial map for the three groups on the two functions. The mean for each group is indicated by an asterisk (*). The numbered boundaries mark off the combination of function values that result in the classification of the cases into the three groups. All cases with values that fall into the region bordered by the 3's are classified into the third group, those that fall into the region bordered by 2's are assigned to the second group, and so on.

Figure 3.37b Territorial map

```
DISCRIMINANT GROUPS=RISK(1,3) /VARIABLES=INCOME TO CHILDREN
  /STATISTICS RAW
  /PLOT CASES MAP
```
[15]

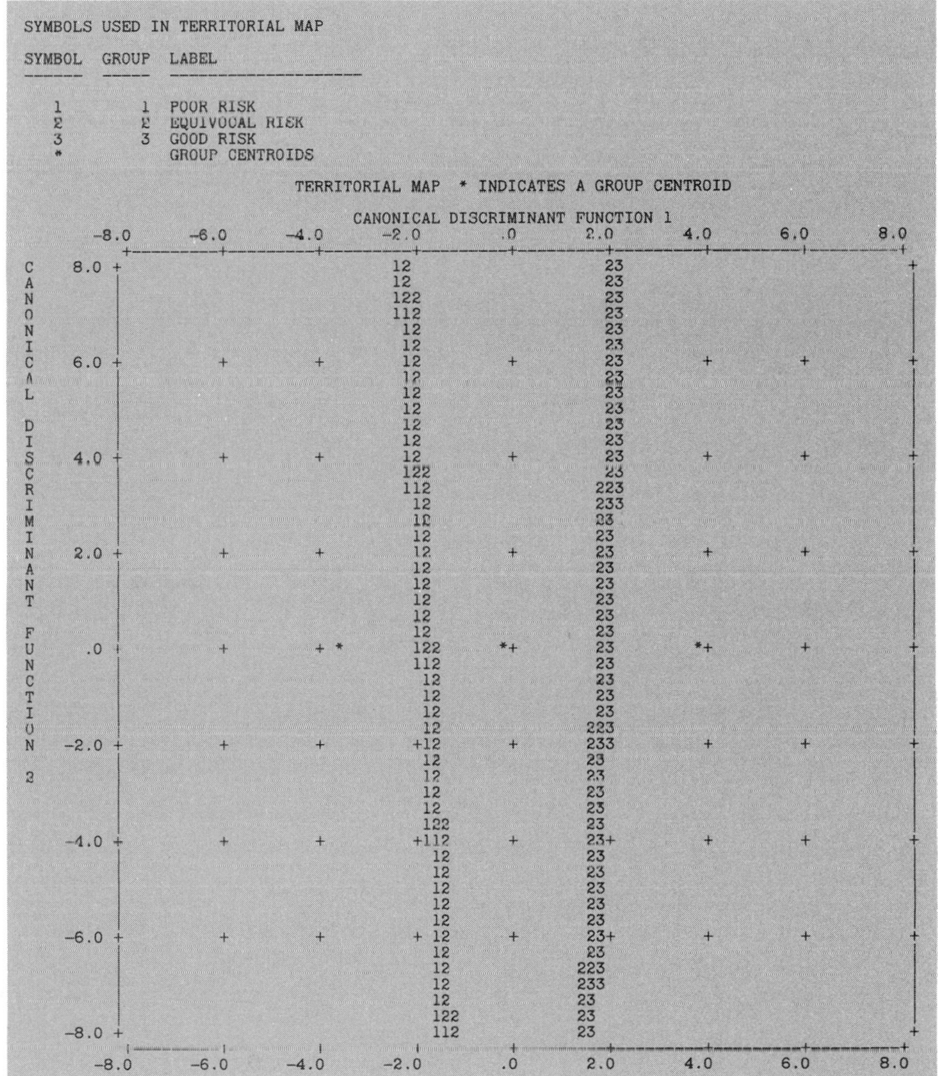

```
SYMBOLS USED IN TERRITORIAL MAP

SYMBOL  GROUP  LABEL
------  -----  --------------------

  1       1    POOR RISK
  2       2    EQUIVOCAL RISK
  3       3    GOOD RISK
  *            GROUP CENTROIDS

                          TERRITORIAL MAP  * INDICATES A GROUP CENTROID

                               CANONICAL DISCRIMINANT FUNCTION 1
      -8.0      -6.0      -4.0      -2.0       .0       2.0       4.0       6.0       8.0
        +---------+---------+---------+---------+---------+---------+---------+---------+
C   8.0 +                            12                  23                             +
A       |                            12                  23                             |
N       |                            122                 23                             |
O       |                            112                 23                             |
N       |                             12                 23                             |
I       |                             12                 23                             |
C   6.0 +         +         +         12         +       23         +         +         +
A       |                             12                 23                             |
L       |                             12                 23                             |
        |                             12                 23                             |
D       |                             12                 23                             |
I       |                             12                 23                             |
S   4.0 +         +         +         12         +       23         +         +         +
C       |                             122                23                             |
R       |                             112               223                             |
I       |                              12               233                             |
M       |                              12                23                             |
I       |                              12                23                             |
N   2.0 +         +         +          12        +       23         +         +         +
A       |                              12                23                             |
N       |                              12                23                             |
T       |                              12                23                             |
        |                              12                23                             |
F       |                              12                23                             |
U    .0 +         +         + *        122      *+       23        *+         +         +
N       |                              112               23                             |
C       |                               12               23                             |
T       |                               12               23                             |
I       |                               12               23                             |
O       |                               12              223                             |
N  -2.0 +         +         +          +12       +      233         +         +         +
        |                               12              23                              |
2       |                               12              23                              |
        |                               12              23                              |
        |                               12              23                              |
        |                              122              23                              |
   -4.0 +         +         +         +112       +      23+         +         +         +
        |                               12              23                              |
        |                               12              23                              |
        |                               12              23                              |
        |                               12              23                              |
        |                               12              23                              |
   -6.0 +         +         +         + 12       +      23+         +         +         +
        |                               12              23                              |
        |                               12             223                              |
        |                               12             233                              |
        |                               12             23                               |
        |                              122             23                               |
   -8.0 +                              112             23                               +
        +---------+---------+---------+---------+---------+---------+---------+---------+
      -8.0      -6.0      -4.0      -2.0       .0       2.0       4.0       6.0       8.0
```

[15]With releases before 3.0, replace the DISCRIMINANT command with the following:

```
DISCRIMINANT GROUPS=RISK(1,3)  /VARIABLES=INCOME TO CHILDREN
STATISTICS 11 14 10
```

Figure 3.37c is a plot of the values of the two discriminant scores for each case. Cases are identified by their group number. When several cases fall into the same plotting location, only the symbol of the last case is printed.

Figure 3.37c All-groups scatterplot

```
DISCRIMINANT GROUPS=RISK(1,3) /VARIABLES=INCOME TO CHILDREN
  /STATISTICS RAW
  /PLOT CASES MAP COMBINED 16
```

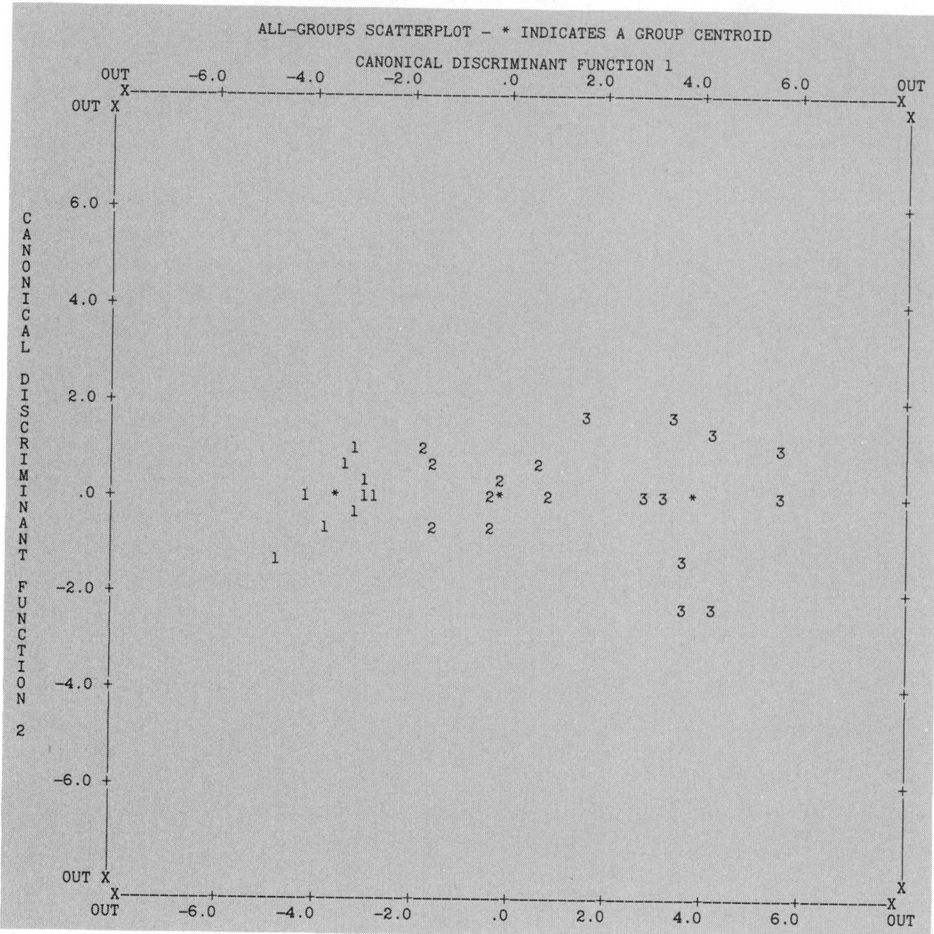

From Figures 3.36b and 3.37c you can see approximately how many cases are misclassified. For example, the case at the (1.6, 1.6) coordinates is denoted by a 3 but falls into the Group 2 region.

Figure 3.37d is the summary of the classification results. The diagonal elements are the number of cases classified correctly into the groups. For

---

[16] With releases before 3.0, replace the DISCRIMINANT command with the following:

```
DISCRIMINANT GROUPS=RISK(1,3)  /VARIABLES=INCOME TO CHILDREN
STATISTICS 11 14 10 15
```

example, all poor and equivocal risks are classified correctly (10 out of 10 in each group). One of the good risks is misclassified as an equivocal risk. The overall percentage of cases classified correctly is the sum of the number of cases classified correctly in each group divided by the total number of cases. In this example, 29 out of 30 cases (96.7%) are classified correctly. These results may differ slightly from those obtained by counting plotted points in Figure 3.37c, since a single point in the plot may represent multiple cases.

Figure 3.37d Classification table

```
DISCRIMINANT GROUPS=RISK(1,3) /VARIABLES=INCOME TO CHILDREN
 /STATISTICS RAW TABLE
 /PLOT CASES MAP COMBINED
```
[17]

```
CLASSIFICATION RESULTS -

                            NO. OF     PREDICTED GROUP MEMBERSHIP
   ACTUAL GROUP             CASES         1            2            3
--------------------       ------     --------     --------     --------

GROUP          1              10         10            0            0
POOR RISK                              100.0%         0.0%         0.0%

GROUP          2              10          0           10            0
EQUIVOCAL RISK                           0.0%       100.0%         0.0%

GROUP          3              10          0            1            9
GOOD RISK                                0.0%        10.0%        90.0%

PERCENT OF "GROUPED" CASES CORRECTLY CLASSIFIED:  96.67%

CLASSIFICATION PROCESSING SUMMARY

         30 CASES WERE PROCESSED.
          0 CASES WERE EXCLUDED FOR MISSING OR OUT-OF-RANGE GROUP CODES.
          0 CASES HAD AT LEAST ONE MISSING DISCRIMINATING VARIABLE.
         30 CASES WERE USED FOR PRINTED OUTPUT.
```

3.38 Additional Statistics

When more than one discriminant function is derived, several statistics other than those discussed in Section 3.17 are of interest. Consider Figure 3.38a. For each function, the eigenvalue is the ratio of between-groups to within-groups sums of squares. From Figure 3.38b (the analysis of variance tables for the two functions), the eigenvalue for Function 1 is 10.03 (270.8/27). For Function 2, it is 0.007 (0.19/27).

Figure 3.38a Additional statistics

```
DISCRIMINANT GROUPS=RISK(1,3) /VARIABLES=INCOME TO CHILDREN
```

```
                                    CANONICAL DISCRIMINANT FUNCTIONS

                        PERCENT OF  CUMULATIVE     CANONICAL   :   AFTER
FUNCTION  EIGENVALUE     VARIANCE     PERCENT    CORRELATION   : FUNCTION  WILKS' LAMBDA  CHI-SQUARED   D.F.  SIGNIFICANCE

                                                               :    0       0.0900296       61.394        8      0.0000
   1*      10.02971       99.93        99.93      0.9535910    :    1       0.9930012       .17910        3      0.9809
   2*       0.00705        0.07       100.00      0.0836587    :

   * MARKS THE   2 CANONICAL DISCRIMINANT FUNCTIONS REMAINING IN THE ANALYSIS.
```

[17] With releases before 3.0, replace the DISCRIMINANT command with the following:

```
DISCRIMINANT GROUPS=RISK(1,3)  /VARIABLES=INCOME TO CHILDREN
STATISTICS 11 14 10 15 13
```

Figure 3.38b ONEWAY analysis of variance for the two functions

```
DISCRIMINANT GROUPS=RISK(1,3) /VARIABLES=INCOME TO CHILDREN
  /SAVE=SCORES=DISCORE
ONEWAY DISCORE1 DISCORE2 BY RISK(1,3)
```

```
- - - - - - -  - - - - - - - - - - - O N E W A Y - - - - - - - - - - - - - - - -

      Variable  DISCORE1    FIRST DISCRIMINANT SCORE
   By Variable  RISK

                                 ANALYSIS OF VARIANCE

                                 SUM OF             MEAN                 F        F
        SOURCE            D.F.   SQUARES            SQUARES              RATIO    PROB.

BETWEEN GROUPS              2    270.8023           135.4011        135.4011    .0000

WITHIN GROUPS              27     27.0000             1.0000

TOTAL                      29    297.8023
- - - - - - -  - - - - - - - - - - - O N E W A Y - - - - - - - - - - - - - - - -

      Variable  DISCORE2    SECOND DISCRIMINANT SCORE
   By Variable  RISK

                                 ANALYSIS OF VARIANCE

                                 SUM OF             MEAN                 F        F
        SOURCE            D.F.   SQUARES            SQUARES              RATIO    PROB.

BETWEEN GROUPS              2       .1903              .0951           .0951    .9095

WITHIN GROUPS              27     27.0000             1.0000

TOTAL                      29     27.1903
```

The canonical correlation for a function is the square root of the between-groups to total sums of squares. When squared, it is the proportion of total variability "explained" by differences between groups. For example, for Function 1 the canonical correlation is

$$\sqrt{\frac{270.8}{297.8}} = 0.953$$ **Equation 3.38a**

When two or more functions are derived, it may be of interest to compare their merits. One frequently encountered criterion is the percentage of the total between-groups variability attributable to each function. Remember from the two-group example that the canonical discriminant functions are derived so that the pooled within-groups variance is 1. (This is seen in Figure 3.38b by the value of 1 for the within-groups mean square.) Thus, each function differs only in the between-groups sum of squares.

The first function always has the largest between-groups variability. The remaining functions have successively less between-groups variability. From Figure 3.38a, Function 1 accounts for 99.93% of the total between-groups variability:

Equation 3.38b

$$\frac{\text{Between Groups SS for Function 1}}{\text{Between Groups SS for Function 1} + \text{Between Groups SS for Function 2}}$$

$$= 0.9993$$

Function 2 accounts for the remaining 0.07% of the between-groups variability. These values are listed in the column labeled PERCENT OF VARIANCE in Figure 3.38a. The next column, CUMULATIVE PERCENT, is simply the sum of the percentage of variance of that function and the preceding ones.

3.39 Testing the Significance of the Discriminant Functions

When there are no differences among the populations from which the samples are selected, the discriminant functions reflect only sampling variability. A test of the null hypothesis that, in the population, the means of all discriminant functions in all groups are really equal and 0 can be based on Wilks' lambda. Since several functions must be considered simultaneously, Wilks' lambda is not just the ratio of the between-groups to within-groups sums of squares but is the product of the univariate Wilks' lambda for each function. For example, the Wilks' lambda for both functions considered simultaneously is, from Figure 3.38b:

$$\Lambda = \left(\frac{27}{297.8}\right)\left(\frac{27}{27.19}\right) = 0.09 \qquad \textbf{Equation 3.39}$$

The significance level of the observed Wilks' lambda can be based on a chi-square transformation of the statistic. The value of lambda and its associated chi-square value, the degrees of freedom, and the significance level are shown in the second half of Figure 3.38a in the first row. Since the observed significance level is less than 0.00005, the null hypothesis that the means of both functions are equal in the three populations can be rejected.

When more than one function is derived, you can successively test the means of the functions by first testing all means simultaneously and then excluding one function at a time, testing the means of the remaining functions at each step. Using such successive tests, it is possible to find that a subset of discriminant functions accounts for all differences and that additional functions do not reflect true population differences, only random variation.

As shown in Figure 3.38a, DISCRIMINANT prints Wilks' lambda and the associated statistics as functions are removed successively. The column labeled AFTER FUNCTION contains the number of the last function removed. The 0 indicates that no functions are removed, while a value of 2 indicates that the first two functions have been removed. For this example, the Wilks' lambda associated with Function 2 after Function 1 has been removed is 0.993. Since it is the last remaining function, the Wilks' lambda obtained is just the univariate value from Figure 3.38b. The significance level associated with the second function is 0.981, indicating that it does not contribute substantially to group differences. This can also be seen in Figure 3.37c, since only the first function determines the classification boundaries. All three groups have similar values for Function 2.

Figure 3.39 is a classification map that illustrates the situation in which both functions contribute to group separation. In other words, a case's values on both functions are important for classification. For example, a case with a value of -2 for the first discriminant function will be classified into Group 2 if the second function is negative and into Group 1 if the second function is positive.

Figure 3.39 Territorial map

```
TITLE INFANT SURVIVAL EXAMPLE--3-GROUP DISCRIMINANT
IF (ANY($CASENUM,1,2,3,4,5,6,18,22,23)) SURVIVAL=2
VALUE LABELS SURVIVAL 3'SURVIVE' 1'DIE' 2'DIE LATER'
RECODE SURVIVAL (2=2) (1=3) (0=1)
DISCRIMINANT GROUPS=SURVIVAL(1,3)
  /VARIABLES=TREATMNT TO RESP
  /PLOT MAP[18]
```

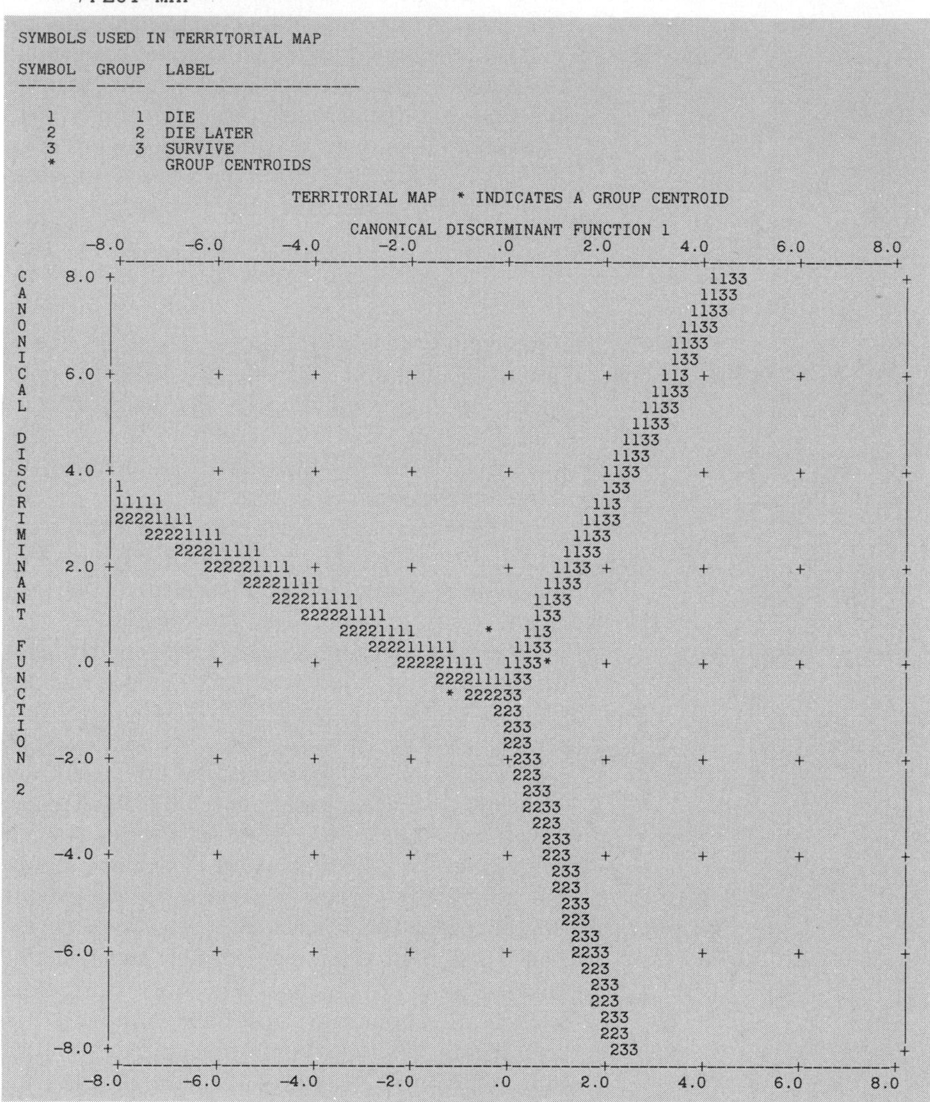

3.40 Classification with One Function

Instead of using all available functions to classify cases into groups, you can restrict the functions to the subset that has substantial between-groups variability. Eliminating weak functions should result in a more stable classification rule, since some of the sampling variability is removed.

When only one discriminant function is used to classify the credit risk cases, 96.67% of the cases are still classified correctly, as shown in Figure 3.40a.

[18]With releases before 3.0, replace the DISCRIMINANT command with the following:

```
DISCRIMINANT GROUPS=SURVIVAL(1,3)
  /VARIABLES=TREATMNT TO REST
STATISTICS 10
```

Figure 3.40a Classification table

```
DISCRIMINANT GROUPS=RISK(1,3) /VARIABLES=INCOME TO CHILDREN
   /FUNCTIONS= 1
   /STATISTICS RAW TABLE
   /PLOT CASES MAP COMBINED 19
```

CLASSIFICATION RESULTS -

ACTUAL GROUP	NO. OF CASES	PREDICTED GROUP MEMBERSHIP 1	2	3
GROUP 1 POOR RISK	10	10 100.0%	0 0.0%	0 0.0%
GROUP 2 EQUIVOCAL RISK	10	0 0.0%	10 100.0%	0 0.0%
GROUP 3 GOOD RISK	10	0 0.0%	1 10.0%	9 90.0%

PERCENT OF "GROUPED" CASES CORRECTLY CLASSIFIED: 96.67%

Figure 3.40b shows the all-groups histogram for the single discriminant function. Large negative values are associated with poor risks, large positive values with good risks, and small positive and negative values with equivocal risks.

Figure 3.40b All-groups histogram

```
DISCRIMINANT GROUPS=RISK(1,3) /VARIABLES=INCOME TO CHILDREN
   /FUNCTIONS=1
   /STATISTICS RAW TABLE
   /PLOT CASES MAP COMBINED 19
```

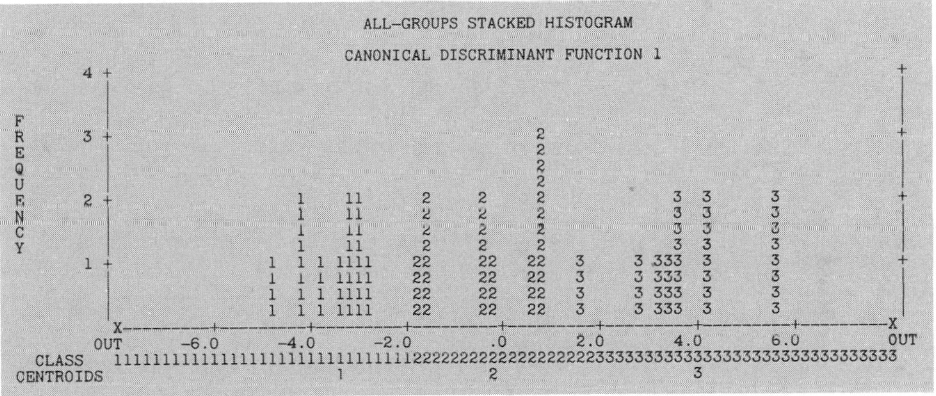

3.41 The Variables

To assess the contribution of each variable to the discriminant functions, you can compute standardized coefficients. From Figure 3.41a, income and age of the household head appear to be the variables with the largest standardized coefficients.

Figure 3.41a Standardized canonical discriminant functions

```
DISCRIMINANT GROUPS=RISK(1,3) /VARIABLES=INCOME TO CHILDREN
```

STANDARDIZED CANONICAL DISCRIMINANT FUNCTION COEFFICIENTS

	FUNC 1	FUNC 2
INCOME	0.89487	-0.61872
CREDIT	0.31363	-0.01298
AGEHEAD	0.84508	0.51746
CHILDREN	0.22936	0.27226

[19]With releases before 3.0, replace the DISCRIMINANT command with the following:

```
DISCRIMINANT GROUPS=RISK(1,3) /VARIABLES=INCOME TO CHILDREN
   /FUNCTIONS= 1
STATISTICS 11 14 10 15 13
```

Another way to examine the contributions of the variables is to examine the correlation coefficients between the variables and the functions, as shown in Figure 3.41b. To help you interpret the functions, variables with large coefficients for a particular function are grouped together. These groupings are indicated with asterisks.

Figure 3.41b Pooled within-groups correlation matrix

```
DISCRIMINANT GROUPS=RISK(1,3) /VARIABLES=INCOME TO CHILDREN
   /STATISTICS RAW TABLE CORR
   /PLOT CASES MAP COMBINED 20
```

```
STRUCTURE MATRIX:

POOLED WITHIN-GROUPS CORRELATIONS BETWEEN DISCRIMINATING VARIABLES
                                    AND CANONICAL DISCRIMINANT FUNCTIONS
(VARIABLES ORDERED BY SIZE OF CORRELATION WITHIN FUNCTION)

              FUNC  1     FUNC  2

CREDIT        0.22728*    0.19774

INCOME        0.48482    -0.84832*
AGEHEAD       0.58577     0.72023*
CHILDREN     -0.00069     0.38568*
```

3.42 WHEN ASSUMPTIONS ARE VIOLATED

As previously indicated, the linear discriminant function minimizes the probability of misclassification if in each group the variables are from multivariate normal distributions and the covariance matrices for all groups are equal. A variety of tests for multivariate normality are available (see Andrews, 1973). A simple tactic is to examine first the distributions of each of the variables individually. If the variables are jointly distributed as a multivariate normal, it follows that each is individually distributed normally. Therefore, if any of the variables have markedly non-normal distributions, there is reason to suspect that the multivariate normality assumption is violated. However, if all variables are normally distributed, the joint distribution is not necessarily multivariate normal.

There are several ways to test equality of the group covariance matrices. DISCRIMINANT prints Box's *M* test, which is based on the determinants of the group covariance matrices. As shown in Figure 3.42, the significance probability is based on an *F* transformation. A small probability might lead us to reject the null hypothesis that the covariance matrices are equal. However, when sample sizes in

Figure 3.42 Test of equality of group covariance matrices

```
DISCRIMINANT GROUPS=SURVIVAL(1,2)
  /VARIABLES=TREATMNT TO RESP /MAXSTEPS=1
  /METHOD=WILKS
  /STATISTICS BOXM 21
```

```
TEST OF EQUALITY OF GROUP COVARIANCE MATRICES USING BOX'S M

  THE RANKS AND NATURAL LOGARITHMS OF DETERMINANTS PRINTED ARE THOSE
  OF THE GROUP COVARIANCE MATRICES.

   GROUP LABEL                      RANK   LOG DETERMINANT

      1 DIE                           3       -1.722152
      2 SURVIVE                       3       -1.902866
    POOLED WITHIN-GROUPS
    COVARIANCE MATRIX                 3       -1.698666

  BOX'S M        APPROXIMATE F   DEGREES OF FREEDOM   SIGNIFICANCE
   4.8753            .75422          6,       14168.3      0.6058
```

[20]With releases before 3.0, replace the DISCRIMINANT command with the following:

```
DISCRIMINANT GROUPS=RISK(1,3)  /VARIABLES=INCOME TO CHILDREN
STATISTICS 11 14 10 15 13 4
```

[21]With releases before 3.0, replace the DISCRIMINANT command with the following:

```
DISCRIMINANT GROUPS=SURVIVAL(1,2)
   /VARIABLES=TREATMNT TO REST  /MAXSTEPS=1
   /METHOD=WILKS
STATISTICS 7
```

the groups are large, the significance probability may be small even if the group covariance matrices are not too dissimilar. The test is also sensitive to departures from multivariate normality. That is, it tends to call matrices unequal if the normality assumption is violated.

If the covariance matrices are unequal but the joint distribution of the variables is multivariate normal, the optimum classification rule is the quadratic discriminant function. However, if the covariance matrices are not too dissimilar the linear discriminant function performs quite well, especially if the sample sizes are small (Wahl & Kronmal, 1977). Simulation studies suggest that with small sample sizes the quadratic rule can perform quite poorly. Since DISCRIMINANT uses the discriminant function values to classify cases, not the original variables, it is not possible to obtain the optimum quadratic rule. (When covariance matrices are assumed identical, classification based on the original variables and all canonical functions are equivalent.) However, results obtained using the functions and their covariance matrices might not be too different from those obtained using covariance matrices for the original variables (Tatsuoka, 1971).

In situations where the independent variables are all binary (yes-no, male-female) or a mixture of continuous and discrete variables, the linear discriminant function is not optimal. A variety of nonparametric procedures as well as special procedures for binary variables are available (see Hand, 1981; Goldstein & Dillon, 1978). In the case of dichotomous variables, most evidence suggests that the linear discriminant function often performs reasonably well (Gilbert, 1981; Moore, 1973).

3.43 RUNNING PROCEDURE DISCRIMINANT

DISCRIMINANT provides six methods for obtaining discriminant functions: forced entry and five stepwise procedures. You can use the discriminant functions to classify cases, and you can assess the accuracy of these classifications by examining classification results tables, plots of classified cases, and other statistical output provided by DISCRIMINANT.

Only two subcommands are required to obtain discriminant functions using the forced-entry method: the GROUPS subcommand, which specifies the grouping variable; and the VARIABLES subcommand, which specifies the predictor variables. These subcommands produce the eigenvalue and Wilks' lambda for each function, the standardized discriminant-function coefficients, the pooled within-groups correlations between the discriminant scores and the predictor variables, and the group centroids. To obtain unstandardized discriminant functions and coefficients, you must use the STATISTICS subcommand (see Section 3.56).

3.44 The GROUPS Subcommand

Use the GROUPS subcommand to specify the grouping variable and its range of values. For example, the subcommand

```
/GROUPS=RISK(1,3)
```

indicates that RISK is the grouping variable, with integer values from 1 to 3. This command produces a three-group analysis. If there were no cases for one of the specified RISK values, DISCRIMINANT would perform a two-group analysis.

Cases with values outside the range specified for the grouping variable are not used to obtain the discriminant functions. However, such cases are classified into one of the existing groups if classification is requested.

You can specify only one GROUPS subcommand per DISCRIMINANT command.

3.45 The VARIABLES Subcommand

List all variables to be used as predictor variables on the VARIABLES subcommand. You can specify only numeric variables, and you can use only one VARIABLES subcommand per DISCRIMINANT command. For example, the command

```
DISCRIMINANT GROUPS=SURVIVAL(1,2)
  /VARIABLES=TREATMNT SEX APGAR AGE TIME WEIGHT PH RESP
```

produces the output in Figures 3.2 and 3.17b.

3.46 The ANALYSIS Subcommand

The ANALYSIS subcommand is useful when you want several discriminant analyses, each with the same grouping variable but different predictor variables. Name all variables to be used in your analysis on the VARIABLES subcommand, and then use the ANALYSIS subcommand to specify subsets of these variables for particular analyses. In this way, you can specify several analyses on a single DISCRIMINANT command.

The variable list on the ANALYSIS subcommand follows the usual SPSS^X conventions for variable lists with one exception: the TO keyword refers to the order of variables on the VARIABLES subcommand, not their order on the active file. You can use the keyword ALL to refer to all variables listed on the VARIABLES subcommand.

The following command produces two discriminant analyses, both with RISK as the grouping variable:

```
DISCRIMINANT GROUPS=RISK(1,3)
  /VARIABLES=INCOME CREDIT AGEHEAD CHILDREN
  /ANALYSIS=INCOME CREDIT
  /ANALYSIS=INCOME TO CHILDREN
```

The first analysis uses INCOME and CREDIT as the predictor variables. The second analysis uses INCOME, CREDIT, AGEHEAD, and CHILDREN as the predictor variables.

3.47 The METHOD Subcommand

Use the METHOD subcommand to specify the method for selecting variables for inclusion in the discriminant analysis. Specify METHOD after the ANALYSIS subcommand (or after the VARIABLES subcommand if ANALYSIS is not used). Each METHOD subcommand applies only to the previous ANALYSIS subcommand when multiple ANALYSIS subcommands are used.

DIRECT *Forced entry.* All variables in the VARIABLES or ANALYSIS subcommand are entered simultaneously (if they satisfy tolerance criteria). This is the default. (See Sections 3.1 through 3.21.)

WILKS *Stepwise analysis based on minimizing the overall Wilks' lambda.* (See Sections 3.24 through 3.29.)

RAO *Stepwise analysis based on maximizing the increase in Rao's V.* (See Section 3.31.)

MAHAL *Stepwise analysis based on maximizing Mahalanobis' distance between the two closest groups.* (See Section 3.32.)

MAXMINF *Stepwise analysis based on maximizing the smallest* F *ratio for pairs of groups.* (See Section 3.33.)

MINRESID *Stepwise analysis based on minimizing the sum of unexplained variation between groups.* (See Section 3.34.)

To obtain forced entry, do not specify a METHOD subcommand, or specify

```
DISCRIMINANT GROUPS=SURVIVAL(1,2)
  /VARIABLES=SEX APGAR AGE TIME WEIGHT PH TREATMNT RESP
  /METHOD=DIRECT
```

The following command produces a stepwise analysis based on Wilks' lambda:

```
DISCRIMINANT GROUPS=RISK(1,3)
  /VARIABLES=INCOME CREDIT AGEHEAD CHILDREN
  /METHOD=WILKS
```

3.48 Inclusion Levels

When you specify a stepwise method, you can use the ANALYSIS subcommand to control the order in which variables are considered for entry. By default, variables are examined for entry or removal on the basis of their partial *F* values. To control the order in which sets of variables are examined, specify an inclusion level in parentheses following the sets of variables on the ANALYSIS subcommand. The inclusion level can be any integer between 0 and 99, as in

```
DISCRIMINANT GROUPS=SURVIVAL(1,2)
  /VARIABLES=SEX APGAR AGE TIME WEIGHT PH TREATMNT RESP
  /ANALYSIS=SEX APGAR TIME PH(2) WEIGHT AGE RESP TREATMNT(1)
  /METHOD=WILKS
```

The inclusion level controls the order in which variables are entered, the way in which they are entered, and whether or not they should be considered for removal, according to the rules outlined below. All variables must still pass the tolerance criterion to be entered.

- Variables with higher inclusion levels are considered for entry before variables with lower levels. Variables do not have to be ordered by their inclusion level on the subcommand itself.
- Variables with even inclusion levels are entered together.
- Variables with odd inclusion levels are entered one variable at a time according to the stepwise method specified on the METHOD subcommand.
- Only variables with an inclusion level of 1 may be considered for removal. To make a variable with a higher inclusion level eligible for removal, name it twice on the ANALYSIS subcommand, first specifying the desired inclusion level and then an inclusion level of 1.
- An inclusion level of 0 prevents a variable from being entered, although an entry criterion is computed and printed.
- The default inclusion level is 1.

Example of Backwards Elimination and Forward Selection. For example, to perform backward elimination of variables, all variables must first be entered. Those meeting criteria for removal can then be eliminated. The command

```
DISCRIMINANT GROUPS=SURVIVAL(1,2)
  /VARIABLES=SEX TP RESP
  /ANALYSIS SEX TO RESP(2)
            SEX TO RESP(1)
  /METHOD=WILKS
```

enters all variables meeting the tolerance criteria and then removes those meeting removal criteria.

3.49 The MAXSTEPS Subcommand

By default, the maximum number of steps in a stepwise analysis is twice the number of variables considered for inclusion. Use the MAXSTEPS subcommand to decrease the maximum. Specify MAXSTEPS after the METHOD subcommand. The form of MAXSTEPS is MAXSTEPS=*n* where *n* is the maximum number of steps desired. MAXSTEPS applies only to the previous ANALYSIS subcommand.

3.50 Setting Statistical Criteria

Several subcommands are available to override the default statistical criteria for discriminant analysis. Specify these subcommands, in any order, after the METHOD subcommand. These subcommands apply only to the previous ANALYSIS subcommand.

TOLERANCE=n *Tolerance level.* The default tolerance level is .001. You can reset it to any decimal number between 0 and 1. This sets the minimum tolerance as well as the tolerance for individual variables. (See Section 3.24.)

FIN=n F*-to-enter.* The default *F*-to-enter is 1.0. You may reset it to any nonnegative number. (See Section 3.24.)

FOUT=n F*-to-remove.* The default *F*-to-remove is 1.0. You may reset it to any nonnegative number. (See Section 3.24.)

PIN=n *Probability of* F*-to-enter.* There is no default value, since *F*-to-enter is the default criterion used for selection. Use PIN to maintain a fixed significance level as the entry criterion. You can specify any number between 0 and 1. (See Section 3.24.)

POUT=n *Probability of* F*-to-remove.* There is no default value, since *F*-to-remove is the default criterion used for selection. Use POUT to maintain a fixed significance level as the removal criterion. You can specify any number between 0 and 1. (See Section 3.24.)

VIN=n *Rao's* V*-to-enter.* The default value is 0. (See Section 3.31)

For example, the following command requests two discriminant analyses:

```
DISCRIMINANT GROUPS=RISK(1,3)
  /VARIABLES=INCOME CREDIT AGEHEAD CHILDREN
  /ANALYSIS=INCOME CREDIT
  /TOLERANCE=.01
  /ANALYSIS=INCOME TO CHILDREN
  /METHOD=RAO
  /VIN=.01
```

The first requests a forced entry with the tolerance criterion reset to 0.01, and the second requests a stepwise analysis based on Rao's *V*, with the increase in Rao's *V* required to be at least 0.01 for entry.

3.51 The FUNCTIONS Subcommand

By default, DISCRIMINANT calculates all discriminant functions available. To reduce the number of functions obtained, specify FUNCTIONS=*nf* where *nf* is the number of functions desired. FUNCTIONS applies only to the previous ANALYSIS subcommand.

3.52 The SELECT Subcommand

Use the SELECT subcommand to select a subset of cases for computing basic statistics and coefficients. You can then use these coefficients to classify either all the cases or only the unselected cases.

The specification for the SELECT subcommand is a variable name followed by a value in parentheses. Only cases with the specified value on the selection variable are used during the analysis phase. The value must be an integer, as in

```
DISCRIMINANT GROUPS=TYPE(1,5) /VARIABLES=A TO H
  /SELECT=LASTYEAR(81)
```

This command limits the analysis phase to cases containing the value 81 for variable LASTYEAR. The SELECT subcommand must precede the first ANALYSIS subcommand. It remains in effect for all analyses.

When you use the SELECT subcommand, DISCRIMINANT by default reports classification statistics separately for selected and unselected cases. To limit classification to unselected cases, use the CLASSIFY subcommand described in Section 3.55.

3.53 The PRIORS Subcommand

By default, DISCRIMINANT assumes the prior probabilities of group membership to be equal. You can specify other prior probabilities with the PRIORS subcommand. It follows the ANALYSIS subcommand and applies only to the previous ANALYSIS subcommand. You can specify any of the following:

EQUAL *Equal prior probabilities.* This is the default specification.

SIZE *Sample proportion of cases actually falling into each group.*

value list *User-specified list of probabilities.* These must sum to 1, and there must be as many probabilities as there are groups.

For example, the command

```
DISCRIMINANT GROUPS=RISK(1,3)
  /VARIABLES=INCOME CREDIT AGEHEAD CHILDREN
  /PRIORS=.2 .4 .4
```

specifies a prior probability of 0.2 for the first RISK group and 0.4 for the second and third groups.

3.54 The SAVE Subcommand

Much of the casewise information produced by the PLOT subcommand (Section 3.36) can be added to the active file. The SAVE subcommand specifies the type of information to be saved and the variable names assigned to each piece of information. Three different types of variables can be saved using the following keywords:

CLASS *Save a variable containing the predicted group value.*

PROBS *Save posterior probabilities of group membership for each case.* For example, if you have three groups, the first probability is the probability of the case being in Group 1 given its discriminant scores, the second probability is its probability of being in Group 2, and the third probability is its probability of being in Group 3. Since DISCRIMINANT produces more than one probability, a *rootname* used to create a set of variables of the form alpha1 to alpha*n* must be supplied. The rootname cannot exceed seven characters.

SCORES *Save the discriminant scores.* The number of scores equals the number of functions derived. As with the PROBS parameter, the designated rootname is used to create a set of variables.

Consider the following example:

```
DISCRIMINANT GROUPS=RISK(1,3)
  /VARIABLES=INCOME CREDIT AGEHEAD CHILDREN
  /SAVE CLASS=PRDCLAS SCORES=SCORE PROBS=PRB
```

Since the number of groups is 3, DISCRIMINANT writes out the 6 variables illustrated in Table 3.54.

Table 3.54 Saved casewise results

Name	Description
PRDCLAS	Predicted Group
SCORE1	Discriminant score for Function 1
SCORE2	Discriminant score for Function 2
PRB1	Probability of being in Risk Group 1
PRB2	Probability of being in Risk Group 2
PRB3	Probability of being in Risk Group 3

Only the types of variables specified are saved. You can specify the keywords in any order, but the order in which the variables are added to the file is fixed. The group variable (CLASS) is always written first, followed by discriminant scores (SCORES), and probabilities (PROBS). Variable labels are provided automatically for the newly saved variables. Any value labels defined for the group variable are also saved for the predicted-group variable.

The SAVE subcommand applies only to the previous ANALYSIS subcommand. If there are multiple analyses and you want to save casewise materials from each, use multiple SAVE subcommands. Be sure to use a different rootname.

3.55 The MISSING Subcommand

By default, cases missing on any of the variables named on the VARIABLES subcommand and cases out of range or missing on the GROUPS subcommand are not used during the analysis phase. Use the following keyword with the MISSING subcommand:

INCLUDE *Include missing values.* User-missing values are treated as valid values. Only the system-missing value is treated as missing. (With releases before 3.0, use the command OPTION 1.)

3.56 The MATRIX Subcommand

DISCRIMINANT reads and writes matrix materials so an analysis performed on one file can be used to classify another file. Assume you have two files: the first file contains group codes and variables used to classify groups; the second contains only the variables used to classify groups. You can use the first file to produce matrix materials that can then be used along with the variables in the second file to classify the cases in the second file. Use the following keywords to specify matrix input and output:

OUT *Write matrix materials.* After OUT, in parentheses specify either a name for the matrix file or * to replace the active file with the matrix. (With releases before 3.0, use the command OPTION 2.)

IN *Read matrix materials.* After IN, in parentheses specify either the name of the matrix file to read or * to read the matrix materials from the active file. (With releases before 3.0, use the command OPTION 3.)

3.57 The HISTORY Subcommand

The HISTORY subcommand has two keywords to reduce the amount of output produced during stepwise analysis.

NOSTEP *Suppress printing of step-by-step output.* The default, STEP, prints step-by-step output. (With releases before 3.0, use the command OPTION 4.)

NOEND *Suppress printing of the summary table.* The default, END, prints the summary table. (With Release 2.2, use the subcommand /PRINT NOTABLE. With releases before 2.2, use the command OPTION 5.)

These keywords only affect printing, not the computation of intermediate results.

3.58 The ROTATE Subcommand

The pattern and structure matrices printed during the analysis phase can be rotated to facilitate interpretation of results.

COEFF *Rotate pattern matrix.* (With releases before 3.0, use the command OPTION 6.)

STRUCTURE *Rotate structure matrix.* (With releases before 3.0, use the command OPTION 7.)

Neither keyword affects the classification of cases since the rotation is orthogonal.

3.59 The CLASSIFY Subcommand

Four keywords related to the classification phase are available.

MEANSUB *Substitute means for missing values during classification.* Cases with missing values are not used during analysis. During classification, means are substituted for missing values and cases containing missing values are classified. (With releases before 3.0, use the command OPTION 8.)

UNSELECTED *Classify only unselected cases.* If you use the SELECT subcommand, by default DISCRIMINANT classifies all nonmissing cases. Two sets of classification results are produced, one for the selected cases and one for the nonselected cases. UNSELECTED suppresses the classification phase for cases selected via the SELECT subcommand. (With releases before 3.0, use the command OPTION 9.)

UNCLASSIFIED *Classify only unclassified cases.* Cases whose values on the grouping variable fall outside the range specified on the GROUPS subcommand are considered initially unclassified. During classification, these ungrouped cases are classified as a separate entry in the classification results table. UNCLASSIFIED suppresses classification of cases that fall into the range specified on the GROUPS subcommand and classifies only cases falling outside the range. (With releases before 3.0, use the command OPTION 10.)

CLASSIFY *Use separate-group covariance matrices of the discriminant functions for classification.* By default, DISCRIMINANT uses the pooled within-groups covariance matrix to classify cases. CLASSIFY uses the separate-group covariance matrices for classification. However, since classification is based on the discriminant functions and not the original variables, this option is not equivalent to quadratic discrimination (Tatsuoka, 1971). (With releases before 3.0, use the command OPTION 11.)

3.60 The STATISTICS Subcommand

You can request optional statistics by using the following keywords on the STATISTICS subcommand:

MEAN *Means.* Requests total and group means for all variables named on the ANALYSIS subcommand. (See Section 3.3.) (With releases before 3.0, use the command STATISTIC 1.)

STDDEV *Standard deviations.* Requests total and group standard deviations for all variables named on the ANALYSIS subcommand. (See Section 3.3.) (With releases before 3.0, use the command STATISTIC 2.)

COV *Pooled within-groups covariance matrix.* (With releases before 3.0. use the command STATISTIC 3.)

CORR *Pooled within-groups correlation matrix.* (See Sections 3.5 and 3.41.) (With releases before 3.0, use the command STATISTIC 4.)

FPAIR *Matrix of pairwise* F *ratios.* Requests the *F* ratio for each pair of groups. The *F*'s are for significance tests for the Mahalanobis' distances between groups. This statistic is available only with stepwise methods. (See Section 3.25.) (With releases before 3.0, use the command STATISTIC 5.)

UNIVF *Univariate* F *ratios.* Requests *F* for each variable. This is a one-way analysis of variance test for equality of group means for a single predictor variable. (See Section 3.3.) (With releases before 3.0, use the command STATISTIC 6.)

BOXM *Box's* M *test.* Tests the equality of group covariance matrices. (See Section 3.42.) (With releases before 3.0, use the command STATISTIC 7.)

GCOV *Group covariance matrices.* (With releases before 3.0, use the command STATISTIC 8.)

TCOV *Total covariance matrix.* (With releases before 3.0, use the command STATISTIC 9.)

RAW *Unstandardized discriminant functions and coefficients.* (See Sections 3.6 and 3.36.) (With releases before 3.0, use the command STATISTIC 11.)

COEFF *Classification function coefficients.* Although DISCRIMINANT does not directly use these coefficients to classify cases, you can use them to classify other samples. (With releases before 3.0, use the command STATISTIC 12.)

TABLE *Obtain the classification results table.* For example, the following commands request the classification table shown in Figure 3.13. (With releases before 3.0, use the command STATISTIC 13.)

```
DISCRIMINANT GROUPS=SURVIVAL(1,2)
  /VARIABLES=TREATMNT SEX APGAR AGE TIME WEIGHT PH RESP
  /STATISTICS TABLE
```

ALL *All statistics available for DISCRIMINANT.* (With releases before 3.0, use the command STATISTICS ALL.)

3.61 The PLOT Subcommand

Two types of classification plots are available, and a territorial map is available when there is more than one discriminant function (see Sections 3.37 and 3.39). If you have at least two functions, you can obtain separate-groups and all-groups scatterplots with the axes defined by the first two functions (see Section 3.37). If you have only one function, separate-groups and all-groups histograms are available (see Section 3.14). You can also obtain casewise information that includes the observed group, the classified group, group membership probabilities, and discriminant scores (see Figures 3.12 and 3.36b).

To obtain any of these plots, use the following keywords on the PLOT subcommand:

MAP *Territorial map.* (See Sections 3.37 and 3.46.) (With releases before 3.0, use the command STATISTIC 10.)

COMBINED *All-groups scatterplot or histogram.* (See Sections 3.14, 3.37, and 3.40.) (With releases before 3.0, use the command STATISTIC 15.)

SEPARATE *Separate-groups scatterplot or histogram.* (See Section 3.14.) (With releases before 3.0, use the command STATISTIC 16.)

CASES *Discriminant scores and classification information.* (See Sections 3.12 and 3.36.) (With releases before 3.0, use the command STATISTIC 14.)

ALL *All plots available for DISCRIMINANT.* (Not available before Release 3.0.)

3.62 EXERCISES

Syntax

1. The DISCRIMINANT command shown below contains several errors. Find them, and rewrite a correct command.

```
DISCRIMINANT GROUPS=CRMEVICT(1,3)
   /VARIABLES SES SEX RACE NBRHOOD DEMEANOR MARTIAL AGE PBLCTRAN INCOME
   /METHOD=DIRECT
   /ANALYSIS=SES SEX RACE NBRHOOD DEMEANOR MARTIAL AGE PBLCTRAN INCOME
   /TOLERANCE=0.05
   /METHOD=WILKS
   /PRIORS=0.5 0.3 0.3
   /STATISTICS=TABLE
   /PLOT=CASES
```
[22]

2. A department store manager wants a discriminant analysis to distinguish between good, poor, and equivocal credit risks (RISK) based on the following variables:

   `INCOME CREDIT AGEHEAD CHILDREN JOBTIME RESTIME HOMEOWNR`

   The risk variable is coded as 1=poor risk, 2=equivocal risk, and 3=good risk. Write the DISCRIMINANT command necessary to obtain a discriminant analysis that includes all of the following:

   a. Stepwise analysis, with selection based on the Mahalanobis' distance.
   b. A tolerance criterion value of 0.01.
   c. Box's M test.
   d. Prior probabilitites of 0.5 for the good credit risks, 0.2 for the equivocal credit risks, and 0.3 for the poor credit risks.
   e. A classification results table.
   f. A territorial map and separate-groups scatterplots.

3. A sociologist wants to discriminate between emotionally expressive (EMOTION=1) and emotionally reserved (EMOTION=2) people, using the following variables:

   `ETHNIC SEX IQ SES EMOTINDX INCOME EDUCATN`

   Write the DISCRIMINANT command needed to produce a discriminant analysis that includes all of the following:

   a. Stepwise analysis, with selection based on Wilks' lambda, and the probability of F-to-enter and the probability of F-to-remove both set at 0.01.

---

[22]With releases before 3.0, replace the DISCRIMINANT command with the following:

```
DISCRIMINANT GROUPS=CRMEVICT(1,3)
   /VARIABLES SES SEX RACE NBRHOOD DEMEANOR MARTIAL AGE PBLCTRAN INCOME
   /METHOD=DIRECT
   /ANALYSIS=SES SEX RACE NBRHOOD DEMEANOR MARTIAL AGE PBLCTRAN INCOME
   /TOLERANCE=0.05
   /METHOD=WILKS
   /PRIORS=0.5 0.3 0.3
STATISTICS 13, 14
```

b. Unstandardized discriminant-function coefficients.
c. Prior probabilities equal to the sample proportions of cases falling into the two EMOTION groups.
d. A classification results table.
e. Group membership probabilities for all the cases.

4. Find the syntax errors in the following DISCRIMINANT commands.

a.
```
DISCRIMINANT GROUPS=GRADUATE(1,2)
  /VARIABLES=GPA PAREDUC PARINCOM FINAID MAJOR SAT MARITAL SEX RACE
  /METHOD=RAO
  /TOLERANCE=.01
  /GROUPS=GRADEMPL(1,3)
  /METHOD=WILKS
```

b.
```
DISCRIMINANT GROUPS=CARDIAC(1,3)
  /VARIABLES=OVERWGHT AGE DIET FAMHIST JOBSATIS OTHERILL
  /ANALYSIS=OVERWGHT AGE DIET FAMHIST OTHERILL
  /PRIORS=SIZE
  /ANALYSIS=OVERWGHT AGE DIET FAMHIST EXERCISE OTHERILL
  /PRIORS=SIZE
```

c.
```
DISCRIMINANT GROUPS=SEXISM(1,4)
  /VARIABLES=EDUCATN INCOME RACE SEX MARITAL DAUGHTER
        FAMILY WOMNWORK AGE
  /ANALYSIS=EDUCATN TO AGE
  /PRIORS=.5 .2 .2
```

d.
```
DISCRIMINANT GROUPS=EFFCIENT(1)
  /VARIABLES=SUPERVSN FLEXTIME STRESS DIVRSITY BREAKS
        TRAINING INTEREST BONUS
  /ANALYSIS=SUPERVSN TO BONUS
  /FUNCTIONS=3
  /METHOD=WILKS
```

Statistical Concepts

1. Consider the discriminant-function coefficients and variable values shown below. For the cases shown, calculate the discriminant scores. (The constant is −10.31.)

```
UNSTANDARDIZED CANONICAL DISCRIMINANT FUNCTION COEFFICIENTS

              FUNC  1

IQ                .22
EDUC              .95
SAT               .10
TESTSCOR          .35
GRA              1.52
```

CASE SEQ	IQ	EDUC	SAT	TESTSCORE	GPA	DISCRIMINANT SCORE
1	115	12	580	59	3.2	??
2	121	14	780	45	3.9	??
3	127	12	720	52	2.0	??

2. A researcher obtained standardized discriminant-function coefficients and found that the two largest coefficients (in absolute value) were 0.89 for EDUCATN and 0.54 for INCOME. He concluded from this that EDUCATN taken by itself is more important than INCOME taken by itself. Was this a reasonable interpretation? Why or why not?

3. Consider the analysis of variance table shown below for the scores of a discriminant function used to distinguish between persons convicted of violent crimes and those convicted of non-violent crimes.

SOURCE	SUM OF SQUARES	D.F.	MEAN SQUARE
BETWEEN GROUPS	37.814	1	37.814
WITHIN GROUPS	81.000	81	1.000

From this table, obtain and interpret the following statistics:

a. Eta^2
b. Eigenvalue
c. Wilks' lambda

4. A two-group discriminant analysis and a multiple regression analysis resulted in the following (incomplete) table. (The regression coefficients in the table were obtained by treating the grouping variable as the dependent variable.) Fill in the missing entries.

VARIABLE	B DISCRIMINANT	B REGRESSION
WEIGHT	-.8963	-.3543
HEIGHT	??	.0215
AGE	??	-1.1446
BLOODPRS	??	-1.6852

5. A stepwise discriminant analysis, using minimization of Wilks' lambda as the entry criterion (*F*-to-enter=1) and the default tolerance level of 0.001, is performed. After the third step, the following statistics are obtained for all variables not in the equation. Which variable, if any, will be entered next?

VARIABLE	TOLERANCE	MINIMUM TOLERANCE	F TO ENTER	WILKS' LAMBDA
X1	.6884	.5713	1.2354	.5213
X2	.1029	.0002	3.1762	.2165
X3	.2275	.1986	1.0271	.6679
X4	.0007	.0005	2.0542	.2911
X5	.1269	.0828	2.0038	.3052
X6	.1736	.1411	0.8512	.7490

6. A new computer program for discriminant analysis produced the following output. Do you think the program is working properly? Give your reasoning.

ETASQ	EIGENVALUE	CANONICAL CORRELATION	WILKS' LAMBDA
0.5013	-0.3218	0.5289	1.0326

7. Indicate whether each of following statements is true or false:
   a. Using the same sample for both estimating and testing discriminant coefficients results in a good estimate of the true error rate.
   b. The greater the between-groups variability for a discriminant function, the better the function.
   c. The smaller the eigenvalue for a discriminant function, the better the function.
   d. The smaller the Wilks' lambda for a discriminant function, the better the function.
   e. If the Wilks' lambda for a function is highly statistically significant, this indicates that the function will be very effective for classification.
   f. Discriminant function coefficients are difficult to interpret when the discriminating variables are correlated.

8. Consider the summary table shown below for a stepwise discriminant analysis. Which variables are included in the final discriminant function?

SUMMARY TABLE

STEP	ACTION ENTERED	ACTION REMOVED
1	X10	
2	X3	
3	X1	
4		X10
5	X9	
6	X7	
7		X9

9. A discriminant analysis is performed in an attempt to classify skulls as male or female. Based on the information given below, find P(Female|Discriminant score D), and P(Male|Discriminant score D). (Assume that P(Female)=0.5.) Classify each of the cases shown as male or female based on these probabilities.

CASE SEQ	P(D|FEMALE)	P(D|MALE)	P(FEMALE|D)	P(MALE|D)	GROUP CLASSIFICATION
8	.250	.513			
9	.814	.711			
10	.358	.226			
11	.402	.409			
12	.003	.178			

10. Two discriminant functions, each with four variables, are being considered in a two-group analysis. Histograms of their discriminant scores are shown below. Which function, if either, do you prefer? Why?

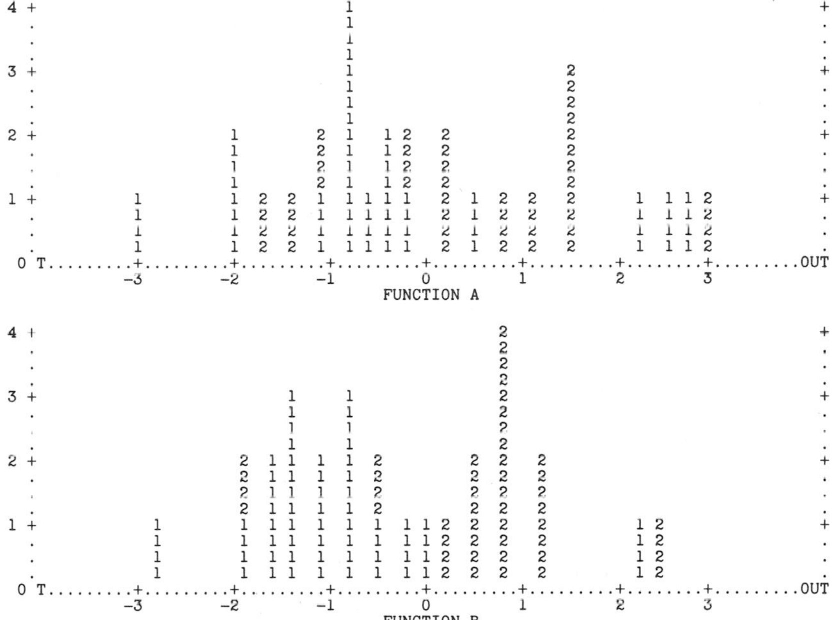

11. Two discriminant functions, one with five variables (Function A), and one with two variables (Function B), have been developed for a data set. Fill in the missing entries in the classification tables, and indicate which function you would prefer for classifying new cases. Why do you prefer this function?

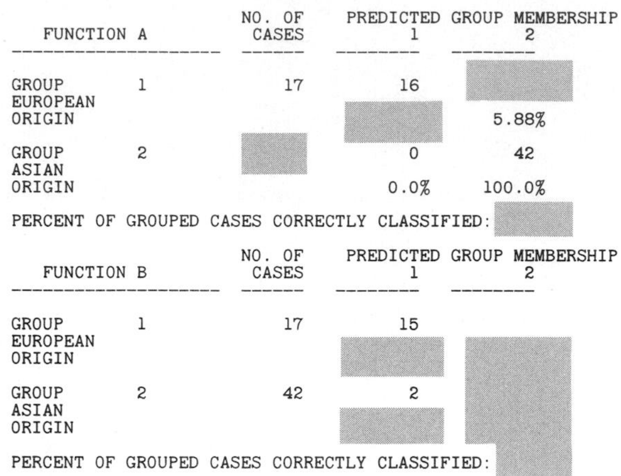

FUNCTION A		NO. OF CASES	PREDICTED GROUP MEMBERSHIP 1	2
GROUP EUROPEAN ORIGIN	1	17	16	
				5.88%
GROUP ASIAN ORIGIN	2		0	42
			0.0%	100.0%

PERCENT OF GROUPED CASES CORRECTLY CLASSIFIED:

FUNCTION B		NO. OF CASES	PREDICTED GROUP MEMBERSHIP 1	2
GROUP EUROPEAN ORIGIN	1	17	15	
GROUP ASIAN ORIGIN	2	42	2	

PERCENT OF GROUPED CASES CORRECTLY CLASSIFIED:

12. Consider the classification table shown below.

ACTUAL GROUP (1)		NO. OF CASES	PREDICTED GROUP MEMBERSHIP 1	2	3	4
GROUP FREQUENT PRODUCT USER	1	20	15	4	1	0
			75.0%	20.0%	5.0%	0.0%
GROUP OCCASIONAL PRODUCT USER	2	20	0	16	3	1
			0.0%	80.0%	15.0%	5.0%
GROUP INFREQUENT PRODUCT USER	3	20	0	1	18	1
			0.0%	5.0%	90.0%	5.0%
GROUP NON-USER OF PRODUCT	4	30	0	5	13	12
			0.0%	16.67%	43.33%	40.0%

a. What is the overall misclassification rate?

b. Suppose 10% of the population are frequent users of the product. If you were primarily interested in identifying these users, would this discriminant analysis be useful to you?

13. The following are analysis of variance tables for three discriminant functions in a four-group analysis.

FUNCTION 1

SOURCE	SUM OF SQUARES	D.F.	MEAN SQUARE
BETWEEN GROUPS	261.848	3	87.283
WITHIN GROUPS	54.000	54	1.000
TOTAL	315.848	57	

FUNCTION 2

SOURCE	SUM OF SQUARES	D.F.	MEAN SQUARE
BETWEEN GROUPS	92.105	3	30.702
WITHIN GROUPS	54.000	54	1.000
TOTAL	146.105	57	

FUNCTION 3

SOURCE	SUM OF SQUARES	D.F.	MEAN SQUARE
BETWEEN GROUPS	47.663	3	15.888
WITHIN GROUPS	54.000	54	1.000
TOTAL	101.663	57	

a. Fill in the entries in the table below.

CANONICAL DISCRIMINANT FUNCTIONS

FUNCTION	EIGENVALUE	PERCENT OF VARIANCE	CUMULATIVE PERCENT	CANONICAL CORRELATION	:	AFTER FUNCTION	WILKS' LAMBDA
1					:		
2					:		
3					:		

b. Which functions, if any, are candidates for elimination?

14. Indicate whether each of the following is true or false:
    a. If histograms indicate that all of the variables in a discriminant analysis are, for each group, normally distributed, you can be fairly sure that the assumption of multivariate normality is satisfied.
    b. Classification functions should be kept even when they add only slightly to classification accuracy, since even a small gain in accuracy is worth keeping.
    c. Box's M test depends heavily on the assumption of mutivariate normality.
    d. The percentage of cases classified correctly cannot decrease if another variable is added to the model.
    e. The use of different criteria for stepwise variable selection will always produce different discriminant models.
    f. It is possible for the total and pooled within-group correlation matrices for the discriminating variables to be dramatically different.

15. Are the histograms shown below appropriate for checking the assumption of multivariate normality? If so, what do they indicate about this assumption?

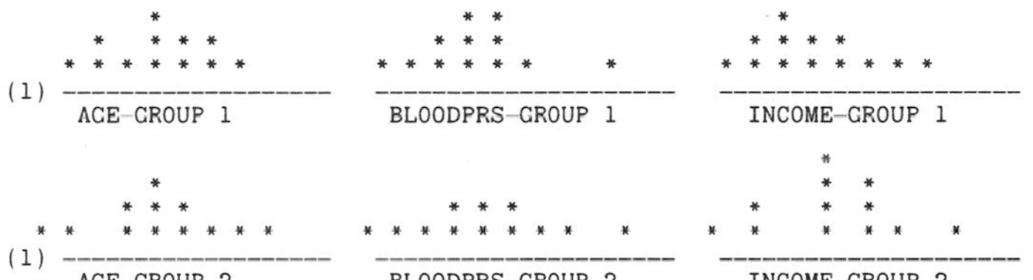

16. A forward-selection discriminant analysis for 150 observations and two groups is performed. At the 7th step, the one remaining variable, PRODUCT (a score measuring product loyalty), is considered for entry. Without PRODUCT, the Wilks' lambda for the function is 0.4163; with it, Wilks' lambda is 0.2982. What is the F-to-enter for PRODUCT? Should PRODUCT be included in the discriminant function (if it satifies the tolerance criteria)?

17. A three-group discriminant analysis produced the classification boundaries and discriminant scores shown below. Classify the cases shown, based on the boundaries and discriminant scores.

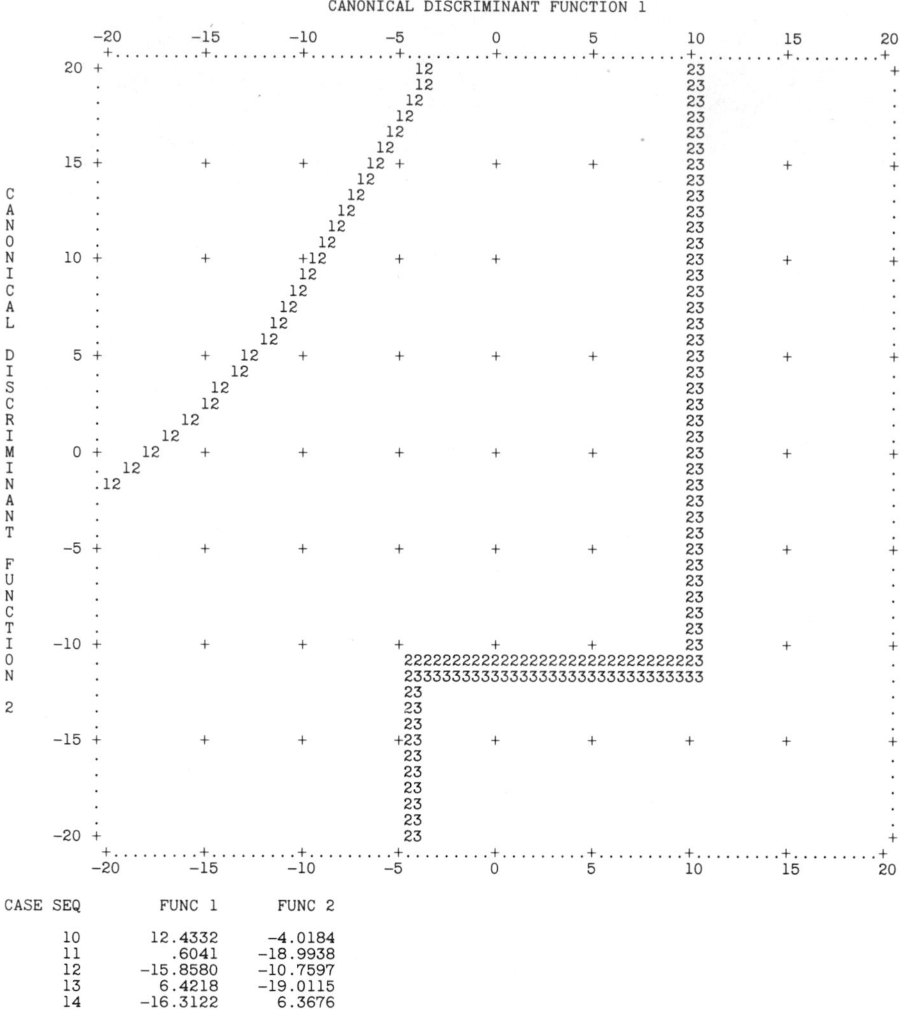

CASE SEQ	FUNC 1	FUNC 2
10	12.4332	-4.0184
11	.6041	-18.9938
12	-15.8580	-10.7597
13	6.4218	-19.0115
14	-16.3122	6.3676

4

Factor Analysis

In this chapter:

Goals:

- To identify underlying constructs or "factors" that explain the correlations among a set of variables.
- To test hypotheses about the structure of variables.
- To summarize a large number of variables with a smaller number of "derived" variables.
- To determine the number of dimensions required to represent a set of variables.

Examples:

- Determine the dimensions on which consumers rate coffees. These might be heartiness, genuineness, and freshness.
- "Explain" the correlations in a battery of tests on the basis of factors that measure overall intelligence and mathematical and verbal skills.
- Determine the characteristics of leaders. These might be efficiency, likeability, and respect.

How it's done:

Each variable is expressed as a linear combination of a small number of common factors, which are shared by all variables, and a unique factor that is specific to that variable. The correlations between the variable arise from the "sharing" of the common factors. The common factors in turn are estimated as linear combinations of the original variables. To improve the interpretability of the factors, solutions can be rotated. A good factor solution is both simple and meaningful.

Data considerations:

Since the correlation matrix between all pairs of variables serves as the starting point for factor analysis, the level of measurement of the variables must be such that the correlation coefficient is an acceptable summary statistic. If there are many cases with missing values for a subset of variables, eliminating cases with missing values for any variables in the analysis may leave few remaining cases. A correlation matrix with each coefficient computed from all cases with nonmissing values for that pair of variables may be used. However, this may produce a correlation matrix with inconsistencies.

General references:

Kim & Mueller (1978)
Harman (1967)
Afifi & Clark (1984)

Contents

4.1 THE FACTOR ANALYSIS MODEL
4.2 Ingredients of a Good Factor Analysis Solution
4.3 STEPS IN A FACTOR ANALYSIS
4.4 Examining the Correlation Matrix
4.5 Factor Extraction
4.6 The Three Factors
4.7 More on the Factor Matrix
4.8 The Reproduced Correlation Matrix
4.9 Some Additional Considerations
4.10 Methods for Factor Extraction
4.11 Goodness of Fit of the Factor Model
4.12 Summary of the Extraction Phase
4.13 The Rotation Phase
4.14 Factor Loading Plots
4.15 Interpreting the Factors
4.16 Oblique Rotation
4.17 Factor Pattern and Structure Matrices
4.18 Algorithm for Oblique Rotation
4.19 Factor Scores
4.20 RUNNING PROCEDURE FACTOR
4.21 Global and Analysis Block Subcommands
4.22 Subcommand Order
4.23 The VARIABLES Subcommand
4.24 The MISSING Subcommand
4.25 The WIDTH Subcommand
4.26 The ANALYSIS Subcommand
4.27 The EXTRACTION Subcommand
4.28 The DIAGONAL Subcommand
4.29 The CRITERIA Subcommand
4.30 Rotating Factors
4.31 The PRINT Subcommand
4.32 The FORMAT Subcommand
4.33 The PLOT Subcommand
4.34 The SAVE Subcommand
4.35 The MATRIX Subcommand
4.36 EXERCISES

4 Identifying Dimensions of Communities: Factor Analysis

What are creativity, love, and altruism? Unlike variables such as weight, blood pressure, and temperature, they cannot be measured on a scale, sphygmomanometer, or thermometer, in units of pounds, millimeters of mercury, or degrees Fahrenheit. Instead they can be thought of as unifying constructs or labels that characterize responses to related groups of variables. For example, answers of "strongly agree" to items such as he (or she) sends me flowers, listens to my problems, reads my manuscripts, laughs at my jokes, and gazes deeply into my soul, may lead one to conclude that the love "factor" is present. Thus, love is not a single measurable entity but a construct which is derived from measurement of other, directly observable variables. Identification of such underlying dimensions or factors greatly simplifies the description and understanding of complex phenomena, such as social interaction. For example, postulating the existence of something called "love" explains the observed correlations between the responses to numerous and varied situations.

Factor analysis is a statistical technique used to identify a relatively small number of factors that can be used to represent relationships among sets of many interrelated variables. For example, variables such as scores on a battery of aptitude tests may be expressed as a linear combination of factors that represent verbal skills, mathematical aptitude, and perceptual speed. Variables such as consumer ratings of products in a survey can be expressed as a function of factors such as product quality and utility. Factor analysis helps identify these underlying, not directly observable, constructs.

A huge number of variables can be used to describe a community—degree of industrialization, commercial activity, population, mobility, average family income, extent of home ownership, birth rate, and so forth. However, descriptions of what is meant by the term "community" might be greatly simplified if it were possible to identify underlying dimensions, or factors, of communities. This was attempted by Jonassen and Peres (1960), who examined 82 community variables from 88 counties in Ohio. This chapter uses a subset of their variables (shown in Table 4.0) to illustrate the basics of factor analysis.

Table 4.0 Community variables

POPSTABL	population stability
NEWSCIRC	weekly per capita local newspaper circulation
FEMEMPLD	percentage of females 14 years or older in labor force
FARMERS	percentage of farmers and farm managers in labor force
RETAILNG	per capita dollar retail sales
COMMERCL	total per capita commercial activity in dollars
INDUSTZN	industrialization index
HEALTH	health index
CHLDNEGL	total per capita expenditures on county aid to dependent children
COMMEFFC	index of the extent to which a community fosters a high standard of living
DWELGNEW	percentage of dwelling units built recently
MIGRNPOP	index measuring the extent of in- and out-migration
UNEMPLOY	unemployment index
MENTALIL	extent of mental illness

4.1 THE FACTOR ANALYSIS MODEL

The basic assumption of factor analysis is that underlying dimensions, or factors, can be used to explain complex phenomena. Observed correlations between variables result from their sharing these factors. For example, correlations between test scores might be attributable to such shared factors as general intelligence, abstract reasoning skill, and reading comprehension. The correlations between the community variables might be due to factors like amount of urbanization, the socioeconomic level or welfare of the community, and the population stability. The goal of factor analysis is to identify the not-directly-observable factors based on a set of observable variables.

The mathematical model for factor analysis appears somewhat similar to a multiple regression equation. Each variable is expressed as a linear combination of factors which are not actually observed. For example, the industrialization index might be expressed as

$$\text{INDUSTZN} = a(\text{URBANISM}) + b(\text{WELFARE}) + c(\text{INFLUX}) + U_{\text{INDUSTZN}} \qquad \textbf{Equation 4.1a}$$

This equation differs from the usual multiple regression equation in that URBANISM, WELFARE, and INFLUX are not single independent variables. Instead, they are labels for groups of variables that characterize these concepts. These groups of variables constitute the factors. Usually, the factors useful for characterizing a set of variables are not known in advance but are determined by factor analysis.

URBANISM, WELFARE, and INFLUX are called *common factors,* since all variables are expressed as functions of them. The U in Equation 4.1a is called a *unique factor,* since it represents that part of the industrialization index that cannot be explained by the common factors. It is unique to the industrialization index variable.

In general, the model for the ith standardized variable is written as

$$X_i = A_{i1}F_1 + A_{i2}F_2 + \ldots + A_{ik}F_k + U_i \qquad \textbf{Equation 4.1b}$$

where the F's are the common factors, the U is the unique factor, and the A's are the constants used to combine the k factors. The unique factors are assumed to be uncorrelated with each other and with the common factors.

The factors are inferred from the observed variables and can be estimated as linear combinations of them. For example, the estimated urbanism factor is expressed as

$$\text{URBANISM} = C_1\ \text{POPSTABL} + C_2\ \text{NEWSCIRC} + \ldots + C_{14}\ \text{MENTALIL}$$ **Equation 4.1c**

While it is possible that all of the variables contribute to the urbanism factor, we hope that a only subset of variables characterizes urbanism, as indicated by their large coefficients. The general expression for the estimate of the *j*th factor F_j is

$$F_j = \sum_{i=1}^{p} W_{ji} X_i = W_{j1} X_1 + W_{j2} X_2 + \ldots + W_{jp} X_p$$ **Equation 4.1d**

The W_i's are known as factor score coefficients, and p is the number of variables.

4.2 Ingredients of a Good Factor Analysis Solution

Before examining the mechanics of a factor analysis solution, let's consider the characteristics of a successful factor analysis. One goal is to represent relationships among sets of variables parsimoniously. That is, we would like to explain the observed correlations using as few factors as possible. If many factors are needed, little simplification or summarization occurs. We would also like the factors to be meaningful. A good factor solution is both simple and interpretable. When factors can be interpreted, new insights are possible. For example, if liquor preferences can be explained by such factors as sweetness and regional tastes (Stoetzel, 1960), marketing strategies can reflect this.

4.3 STEPS IN A FACTOR ANALYSIS

Factor analysis usually proceeds in four steps.

- First, the correlation matrix for all variables is computed, as in Figure 4.4a. Variables that do not appear to be related to other variables can be identified from the matrix and associated statistics. The appropriateness of the factor model can also be evaluated. At this step you should also decide what to do with cases that have missing values for some of the variables (see Chapter 2 for a discussion of missing values).
- In the second step, factor extraction—the number of factors necessary to represent the data and the method of calculating them—must be determined. At this step, you also ascertain how well the chosen model fits the data.
- The third step, rotation, focuses on transforming the factors to make them more interpretable.
- At the fourth step, scores for each factor can be computed for each case. These scores can then be used in a variety of other analyses.

4.4 Examining the Correlation Matrix

The correlation matrix for the 14 community variables is shown in Figure 4.4a. Since one of the goals of factor analysis is to obtain "factors" that help explain these correlations, the variables must be related to each other for the factor model to be appropriate. If the correlations between variables are small, it is unlikely that they share common factors. Figure 4.4a shows that almost half the coefficients are greater than 0.3 in absolute value. All variables, except the extent of mental illness, have large correlations with at least one of the other variables in the set.

Figure 4.4a Correlation matrix and matrix input

```
UNNUMBERED
MATRIX DATA VARIABLES =    POPSTABL NEWSCIRC FEMEMPLD FARMERS RETAILNG
  COMMERCL INDUSTZN HEALTH CHLDNEGL COMMEFFC DWELGNEW MIGRNPOP UNEMPLOY
  MENTALIL
  /N=88
BEGIN DATA
1.
-.175 1.
etc.
END DATA
FACTOR MATRIX = IN (CORR *)
  /PRINT=CORRELATION
```
[1]

CORRELATION MATRIX:

	POPSTABL	NEWSCIRC	FEMEMPLD	FARMERS	RETAILNG	COMMERCL	INDUSTZN	HEALTH	CHLDNEGL	COMMEFFC	DWELGNEW	MIGRNPOP
POPSTABL	1.00000											
NEWSCIRC	-.17500	1.00000										
FEMEMPLD	-.27600	.61600	1.00000									
FARMERS	.36900	-.62500	-.63700	1.00000								
RETAILNG	-.12700	.62400	.73600	-.51900	1.00000							
COMMERCL	-.06900	.65200	.58900	-.30600	.72700	1.00000						
INDUSTZN	-.10600	.71200	.74200	-.54500	.78500	.91100	1.00000					
HEALTH	-.14900	-.03000	.24100	-.06800	.10000	.12300	.12900	1.00000				
CHLDNEGL	-.03900	-.17100	-.58900	.25700	-.55700	-.35700	-.42400	-.40700	1.00000			
COMMEFFC	-.00500	.10000	.47100	-.21300	.45200	.28700	.35700	.73200	-.66000	1.00000		
DWELGNEW	-.67000	.18800	.41300	-.57900	.16500	.03000	.20300	.29000	-.13800	.31100	1.00000	
MIGRNPOP	-.47600	-.08600	.06400	-.19800	.00700	-.06800	-.02400	.08300	.14800	.06700	.50500	1.00000
UNEMPLOY	.13700	-.37300	-.68900	.45000	-.65000	-.42400	-.52800	-.34800	.73300	-.60100	-.26600	.18100
MENTALIL	.23700	.04600	-.23700	.12100	-.19000	-.05500	-.09500	-.27900	.24700	-.32400	-.26600	-.30700

	UNEMPLOY	MENTALIL
UNEMPLOY	1.00000	
MENTALIL	.21700	1.00000

Bartlett's test of sphericity can be used to test the hypothesis that the correlation matrix is an identity matrix. That is, all diagonal terms are 1 and all off-diagonal terms are 0. The test requires that the data be a sample from a multivariate normal population. From Figure 4.4b, the value of the test statistic for sphericity (based on a chi-square transformation of the determinant of the correlation matrix) is large and the associated significance level is small, so it appears unlikely that the population correlation matrix is an identity. If the hypothesis that the population correlation matrix is an identity cannot be rejected because the observed significance level is large, you should reconsider the use of the factor model.

Figure 4.4b Test-statistic for sphericity

```
FACTOR MATRIX = IN (CORR *)
  /PRINT=CORRELATION  KMO  AIC
```
[2]

```
KAISER-MEYER-OLKIN MEASURE OF SAMPLING ADEQUACY =  .76968

BARTLETT TEST OF SPHERICITY = 946.15313, SIGNIFICANCE =     .00000
```

---

[1]With releases before 3.0, replace all of the commands with the following commands:

```
UNNUMBERED
INPUT PROGRAM
N OF CASES 88
NUMERIC POPSTABL NEWSCIRC FEMEMPLD FARMERS RETAILNG COMMERCL INDUSTZN
  HEALTH CHLDNEGL COMMEFFC DWELGNEW MIGRNPOP UNEMPLOY MENTALIL
INPUT MATRIX FREE
END INPUT PROGRAM
FACTOR READ=CORRELATION TRIANGLE
  /VARIABLES=POPSTABL TO MENTALIL
  /PRINT=CORRELATION
BEGIN DATA
1.
-.175 1.
etc.
END DATA
```

[2]With releases before 3.0, whenever you see the line

```
FACTOR MATRIX = IN (CORR *)
```

always replace it with the following two lines:

```
FACTOR READ=CORRELATION TRIANGLE
  /VARIABLES=POPSTABL TO MENTALIL
```

Another indicator of the strength of the relationship among variables is the partial correlation coefficient. If variables share common factors, the partial correlation coefficients between pairs of variables should be small when the linear effects of the other variables are eliminated. The partial correlations are then estimates of the correlations between the unique factors and should be close to zero when the factor analysis assumptions are met. (Recall that the unique factors are assumed to be uncorrelated with each other.)

The negative of the partial correlation coefficient is called the anti-image correlation. The matrix of anti-image correlations is shown in Figure 4.4c. If the proportion of large coefficients is high, you should reconsider the use of the factor model.

Figure 4.4c Anti-image correlation matrix

```
FACTOR MATRIX = IN (CORR *)
  /PRINT=CORRELATION KMO AIC
```

ANTI-IMAGE CORRELATION MATRIX:

	POPSTABL	NEWSCIRC	FEMEMPLD	FARMERS	RETAILNG	COMMERCL	INDUSTZN	HEALTH	CHLDNEGL	COMMEFFC	DWELGNEW	MIGRNPOP
POPSTABL	.58174											
NEWSCIRC	.01578	.82801										
FEMEMPLD	.10076	-.24223	.90896									
FARMERS	.03198	.43797	-.00260	.73927								
RETAILNG	.14998	-.14295	-.12037	.16426	.86110							
COMMERCL	.20138	-.27622	.20714	-.49344	-.19535	.68094						
INDUSTZN	-.23815	.08231	-.32790	.41648	-.04602	-.85499	.75581					
HEALTH	.26114	-.02839	-.02332	.05845	.38421	-.16150	.08627	.59124				
CHLDNEGL	.10875	.24685	.27281	-.03446	.13062	.07043	-.07979	.02899	.87023			
COMMEFFC	-.39878	.05772	.03017	-.16386	-.33700	.09427	-.06742	-.70853	.19554	.68836		
DWELGNEW	.55010	.04505	.00403	.33470	.20078	.13831	-.13726	.07480	-.04008	-.30434	.70473	
MIGRNPOP	.20693	.22883	-.06689	.11784	-.15886	-.07421	.06501	.07460	-.10809	-.14292	-.24074	.61759
UNEMPLOY	-.17774	-.05946	.18631	-.12699	.19591	-.01262	-.02503	-.02904	-.33523	.19240	.02181	-.38208
MENTALIL	-.08437	-.10058	.07770	.03053	.07842	-.02921	-.00056	.06821	-.04163	.04728	-.02505	.20487

	UNEMPLOY	MENTALIL
UNEMPLOY	.87230	
MENTALIL	-.02708	.88390

MEASURES OF SAMPLING ADEQUACY (MSA) ARE PRINTED ON THE DIAGONAL.

The Kaiser-Meyer-Olkin measure of sampling adequacy is an index for comparing the magnitudes of the observed correlation coefficients to the magnitudes of the partial correlation coefficients. It is computed as

$$\text{KMO} = \frac{\sum\sum_{i \neq j} r_{ij}^2}{\sum\sum_{i \neq j} r_{ij}^2 + \sum\sum_{i \neq j} a_{ij}^2}$$

Equation 4.4a

where r_{ij} is the simple correlation coefficient between variables *i* and *j*, and a_{ij} is the partial correlation coefficient between variables *i* and *j*. If the sum of the squared partial correlation coefficients between all pairs of variables is small when compared to the sum of the squared correlation coefficients, the KMO measure is close to 1. Small values for the KMO measure indicate that a factor analysis of the variables may not be a good idea, since correlations between pairs of variables cannot be explained by the other variables. Kaiser (1974) characterizes measures in the 0.90's as marvelous, in the 0.80's as meritorious, in the 0.70's as middling, in the 0.60's as mediocre, in the 0.50's as miserable, and below 0.5 as unacceptable. The value of the overall KMO statistic for this example is shown in Figure 4.4b. Since it is close to 0.8, we can comfortably proceed with the factor analysis.

A measure of sampling adequacy can be computed for each individual variable in a similar manner. Instead of including all pairs of variables in the summations, only coefficients involving that variable are included. For the *i*th variable, the measure of sampling adequacy is

$$MSA_i = \frac{\sum_{j \neq i} r_{ij}^2}{\sum_{j \neq i} r_{ij}^2 + \sum_{j \neq i} a_{ij}^2}$$

Equation 4.4b

These measures of sampling adequacy are printed on the diagonals of Figure 4.4c. Again, reasonably large values are needed for a good factor analysis. Thus, you might consider eliminating variables with small values for the measure of sampling adequacy.

The squared multiple correlation coefficient between a variable and all other variables is another indication of the strength of the linear association among the variables. These values are shown in the column labeled "COMMUNALITY" in Figure 4.9a. The extent of mental illness variable has a small multiple R^2, suggesting that it should be eliminated from the set of variables being analyzed. It will be kept in the analysis for illustrative purposes.

4.5 Factor Extraction

The goal of the factor extraction step is to determine the factors. In this example, we will obtain estimates of the initial factors from principal components analysis. Other methods for factor extraction are described in Section 4.10. In principal components analysis, linear combinations of the observed variables are formed. The first principal component is the combination that accounts for the largest amount of variance in the sample. The second principal component accounts for the next largest amount of variance and is uncorrelated with the first. Successive components explain progressively smaller portions of the total sample variance, and all are uncorrelated with each other.

It is possible to compute as many principal components as there are variables. If all principal components are used, each variable can be exactly represented by them, but nothing has been gained since there are as many factors (principal components) as variables. When all factors are included in the solution, all of the variance of each variable is accounted for, and there is no need for a unique factor in the model. The proportion of variance accounted for by the common factors, or the *communality* of a variable, is 1 for all the variables, as shown in Figure 4.5a. In general, principal components analysis is a separate technique from factor analysis. That is, it can be used whenever uncorrelated linear combinations of the observed variables are desired. All it does is transform a set of correlated variables to a set of uncorrelated variables (principal components).

To help us decide how many factors we need to represent the data, it is helpful to examine the percentage of total variance explained by each. The total variance is the sum of the variance of each variable. For simplicity, all variables and factors are expressed in standardized form, with a mean of 0 and a standard deviation of 1. Since there are 14 variables and each is standardized to have a variance of 1, the total variance is 14 in this example.

Figure 4.5a contains the initial statistics for each factor. The total variance explained by each factor is listed in the column labeled EIGENVALUE. The next column contains the percentage of the total variance attributable to each factor. For example, the linear combination formed by Factor 2 has a variance of 2.35, which is 16.8% of the total variance of 14. The last column, the cumulative percentage, indicates the percentage of variance attributable to that factor and those that precede it in the table. Note that the factors are arranged in descending order of variance explained. Note also that although variable names and factors are displayed on the same line, there is no correspondence between the lines in the two halves of the table. The first two columns provide information about the individual variables, while the last four columns describe the factors.

Figure 4.5a Initial statistics

```
FACTOR MATRIX = IN (CORR *)
```

```
EXTRACTION  1  FOR ANALYSIS  1, PRINCIPAL-COMPONENTS ANALYSIS (PC)


INITIAL STATISTICS:

VARIABLE      COMMUNALITY  *  FACTOR   EIGENVALUE   PCT OF VAR   CUM PCT
                           *
POPSTABL        1.00000    *     1       5.70658       40.8        40.8
NEWSCIRC        1.00000    *     2       2.35543       16.8        57.6
FEMEMPLD        1.00000    *     3       2.00926       14.4        71.9
FARMERS         1.00000    *     4        .89745        6.4        78.3
RETAILNG        1.00000    *     5        .75847        5.4        83.8
COMMERCL        1.00000    *     6        .53520        3.8        87.6
INDUSTZN        1.00000    *     7        .50886        3.6        91.2
HEALTH          1.00000    *     8        .27607        2.0        93.2
CHLDNEGL        1.00000    *     9        .24511        1.8        94.9
COMMEFFC        1.00000    *    10        .20505        1.5        96.4
DWELGNEW        1.00000    *    11        .19123        1.4        97.8
MIGRNPOP        1.00000    *    12        .16982        1.2        99.0
UNEMPLOY        1.00000    *    13        .10000         .7        99.7
MENTALIL        1.00000    *    14        .03946         .3       100.0
```

Figure 4.5a shows that almost 72% of the total variance is attributable to the first three factors. The remaining eleven factors together account for only 28.1% of the variance. Thus, a model with three factors may be adequate to represent the data.

Several procedures have been proposed for determining the number of factors to use in a model. One criterion suggests that only factors that account for variances greater than 1 (the eigenvalue is greater than 1) should be included. Factors with a variance less than 1 are no better than a single variable, since each variable has a variance of 1. Although this is the default criterion in SPSS^X FACTOR, it is not always a good solution (see Tucker, Koopman, & Linn, 1969).

Figure 4.5b is a plot of the total variance associated with each factor. Typically, the plot shows a distinct break between the steep slope of the large factors and the gradual trailing off of the rest of the factors. This gradual trailing off is called the *scree* (Cattell, 1966) because it resembles the rubble that forms at the foot of a mountain. Experimental evidence indicates that the scree begins at the *k*th factor, where *k* is the true number of factors. From the scree plot, it again appears that a three-factor model should be sufficient for the community example.

Figure 4.5b Scree plot

```
FACTOR MATRIX = IN (CORR *)
  /PLOT=EIGEN
```

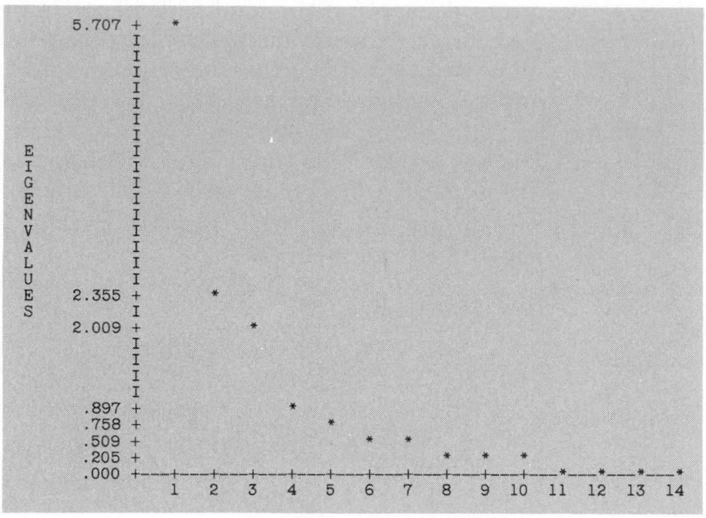

4.6 The Three Factors

Figure 4.6 contains the coefficients that relate the variables to the three factors. The figure shows that the industrialization index can be expressed as

$$\text{INDUSTZN} = 0.844F_1 + 0.300F_2 + 0.238F_3$$ **Equation 4.6a**

Similarly, the health index is

$$\text{HEALTH} = 0.383F_1 - 0.327F_2 - 0.635F_3$$ **Equation 4.6b**

Figure 4.6 Factor matrix

```
FACTOR MATRIX = IN (CORR *)
```

FACTOR MATRIX:

	FACTOR 1	FACTOR 2	FACTOR 3
POPSTABL	-.30247	.68597	-.36451
NEWSCIRC	.67238	.28096	.49779
FEMEMPLD	.89461	.01131	.08063
FARMERS	-.68659	.20002	-.40450
RETAILNG	.85141	.24264	.09351
COMMERCL	.72503	.39394	.19896
INDUSTZN	.84436	.29956	.23775
HEALTH	.38347	-.32718	-.63474
CHLDNEGL	-.67430	-.12139	.52896
COMMEFFC	.63205	-.15540	-.64221
DWELGNEW	.45886	-.73940	.18706
MIGRNPOP	.07894	-.74371	.24335
UNEMPLOY	-.78714	-.09777	.30110
MENTALIL	-.30025	.45463	.27134

Each row of Figure 4.6 contains the coefficients used to express a standardized variable in terms of the factors. These coefficients are called *factor loadings*, since they indicate how much weight is assigned to each factor. Factors with large coefficients (in absolute value) for a variable are closely related to the variable. For example, Factor 1 is the factor with the largest loading for the INDUSTZN variable. The matrix of factor loadings is called the *factor pattern* matrix.

When the estimated factors are uncorrelated with each other (orthogonal), the factor loadings are also the correlations between the factors and the variables. Thus, the correlation between the health index and Factor 1 is 0.383. Similarly, there is a slightly smaller correlation (−0.327) between the health index and Factor 2. The matrix of correlations between variables and factors is called the *factor structure* matrix. When the factors are orthogonal, the factor structure matrix and the factor pattern matrix are equivalent. As shown in Figure 4.6, such a matrix is labeled the factor matrix in SPSS^X output.

4.7 More on the Factor Matrix

There is yet another interpretation of the factor matrix in Figure 4.6. Whether the factors are orthogonal or not, the factor loadings are the standardized regression coefficients in the multiple regression equation with the original variable as the dependent variable and the factors as the independent variables. If the factors are uncorrelated, the values of the coefficients are not dependent on each other. They represent the unique contribution of each factor, and are the correlations between the factors and the variable.

To judge how well the three-factor model describes the original variables, we can compute the proportion of the variance of each variable explained by the three-factor model. Since the factors are uncorrelated, the total proportion of variance explained is just the sum of the variance proportions explained by each factor.

Consider, for example, the health index. Factor 1 accounts for 14.7% of the variance for this variable. This is obtained by squaring the correlation coefficient for Factor 1 and HEALTH (0.383). Similarly, Factor 3 explains 40.3% ($(-0.635)^2$) of the variance. The total percentage of variance in the health index accounted for by this three-factor model is therefore 65.7% (14.7 + 10.7 + 40.3). The proportion of variance explained by the common factors is called the *communality* of the variable.

The communalities for the variables are shown in Figure 4.7, together with the percentage of variance accounted for by each of the retained factors. This table is labeled as "final statistics," since it shows the communalities and factor statistics after the desired number of factors has been extracted. When factors are estimated using the method of principal components, the factor statistics are the same in the tables labeled as initial and final. However, the communalities are different since all of the variances of the variables are not explained when only a subset of factors is retained.

Figure 4.7 Communality of variables

```
FACTOR MATRIX = IN (CORR *)
```

```
FINAL STATISTICS:

VARIABLE      COMMUNALITY  *  FACTOR   EIGENVALUE   PCT OF VAR   CUM PCT
                           *
POPSTABL         .69491    *     1      5.70658        40.8        40.8
NEWSCIRC         .77882    *     2      2.35543        16.8        57.6
FEMEMPLD         .80696    *     3      2.00926        14.4        71.9
FARMERS          .67503    *
RETAILNG         .79253    *
COMMERCL         .72044    *
INDUSTZN         .85921    *
HEALTH           .65699    *
CHLDNEGL         .74921    *
COMMEFFC         .83607    *
DWELGNEW         .79226    *
MIGRNPOP         .61855    *
UNEMPLOY         .71981    *
MENTALIL         .37047    *
```

Communalities can range from 0 to 1, with 0 indicating that the common factors explain none of the variance, and 1 indicating that all the variance is explained by the common factors. The variance that is not explained by the common factors is attributed to the unique factor and is called the *uniqueness* of the variable.

4.8 The Reproduced Correlation Matrix

One of the basic assumptions of factor analysis is that the observed correlation between variables is due to the sharing of common factors. Therefore, the estimated correlations between the factors and the variables can be used to estimate the correlations between the variables. In general, if factors are orthogonal, the estimated correlation coefficient for variables i and j is

$$r_{ij} = \sum_{f=1}^{k} r_{fi} r_{fj} = r_{1i} r_{1j} + r_{2i} r_{2j} + \ldots r_{ki} r_{kj}$$ **Equation 4.8a**

where k is the number of common factors, and r_{fi} is the correlation between the fth factor and the ith variable.

From Figure 4.6 and Equation 4.8a, the estimated correlation coefficient for HEALTH and COMMEFFC, based on the three-factor model, is

$$r_{8,10} = (0.38)(0.63) + (-0.33)(-0.16) + (-0.63)(-0.64) = 0.70.$$ **Equation 4.8b**

Figure 4.4a shows that the observed correlation coefficient between HEALTH and COMMEFFC is 0.73, so the difference between the observed correlation coefficient and that estimated from the model is about −0.03. This difference is called a residual.

The estimated correlation coefficients and the residuals are shown in Figure 4.8. The residuals are listed above the diagonal and the estimated correlation coefficients are below the triangle. The values with asterisks (on the diagonal) are the communalities discussed in Section 4.7.

Below the matrix is a message indicating how many residuals are greater than 0.05 in absolute value. In the community example, less than half (46%) are greater than 0.05 in absolute value. The magnitudes of the residuals indicate how well the fitted model reproduces the observed correlations. If the residuals are large, the model does not fit the data well and should probably be reconsidered.

Figure 4.8 Estimated correlations and residuals

```
FACTOR MATRIX = IN (CORR *)
  /PRINT=DEFAULT REPR
```

REPRODUCED CORRELATION MATRIX:

	POPSTABL	NEWSCIRC	FEMEMPLD	FARMERS	RETAILNG	COMMERCL	INDUSTZN	HEALTH	CHLDNEGL
POPSTABL	.69491*	.01709	.01623	-.12332	-.00183	-.04741	.03056	-.03994	.03312
NEWSCIRC	-.19209	.77882*	-.02883	-.01820	-.06320	-.04521	-.05824	.12005	.05318
FEMEMPLD	-.29223	.64483	.80696*	.00758	-.03597	-.08012	-.03593	-.04718	-.02704
FARMERS	.49232	-.60680	-.64458	.67503*	.05486	.19348	.07098	.00398	.03227
RETAILNG	-.12517	.68720	.77197	-.57386	.79253*	.00449	.02008	-.08775	-.00290
COMMERCL	-.02159	.69721	.66912	-.49948	.73149	.72044*	.13350	.10014	.07447
INDUSTZN	-.13656	.77024	.77793	-.61598	.81382	.77750	.85921*	.05413	.05596
HEALTH	-.10906	-.15005	.28818	-.07198	.18775	.02286	.07487	.65699*	.14761
CHLDNEGL	-.07212	-.22418	-.56196	.22473	-.55410	-.43147	-.47996	-.55461	.74921*
COMMEFFC	-.06368	.06163	.51190	-.20527	.44037	.26927	.33444	.70086	-.74703
DWELGNEW	-.71418	.19390	.41722	.53861	.22076	.07863	.21042	.29914	-.12070
MIGRNPOP	-.62274	-.03474	.08183	-.30139	-.09049	-.18732	-.09828	.11013	.10577
UNEMPLOY	.06126	-.40684	-.68101	.39909	-.66575	-.54931	-.62233	-.46098	.70191
MENTALIL	.30378	.06093	-.24158	.18733	-.11995	.01539	-.05282	-.43612	.29080

	COMMEFFC	DWELGNEW	MIGRNPOP	UNEMPLOY	MENTALIL
POPSTABL	.05868	.04418	.14674	.07574	-.06678
NEWSCIRC	.03837	-.00590	.06126	.03384	-.01493
FEMEMPLD	-.04090	-.00422	.01783	-.00799	.00458
FARMERS	-.00773	.04039	.10339	.05091	-.06633
RETAILNG	.01163	-.06376	.09749	.01575	-.07005
COMMERCL	.01773	-.04863	.11932	.12531	-.07039
INDUSTZN	.02256	-.00742	.07428	.09433	-.04218
HEALTH	.03114	-.00914	-.03613	.11298	.15712
CHLDNEGL	.08703	-.01730	-.01777	.03109	-.04380
COMMEFFC	.83607*	.02621	.05782	.07469	.11068
DWELGNEW	.28479	.79226*	-.12664	-.03343	.15717
MIGRNPOP	.00918	.63164	.61855*	.09715	-.01121
UNEMPLOY	-.67569	-.23257	.08385	.71981*	-.05659
MENTALIL	-.43468	-.42317	-.29579	.27359	.37047*

THERE ARE 42 (46.0%) RESIDUALS (ABOVE DIAGONAL) THAT ARE > 0.05

4.9 Some Additional Considerations

If a method other than principal components analysis is used to extract the initial factors, there are differences in parts of the factor output. Consider, for example, Figure 4.9a, which contains the initial statistics obtained when the maximum-likelihood algorithm is used.

Figure 4.9a Maximum-likelihood extractions

```
FACTOR MATRIX = IN (CORR *)
  /PRINT=DEFAULT REPR
  /EXTRACTION=ML
```

INITIAL STATISTICS:

VARIABLE	COMMUNALITY	*	FACTOR	EIGENVALUE	PCT OF VAR	CUM PCT
		*				
POPSTABL	.62385	*	1	5.70658	40.8	40.8
NEWSCIRC	.71096	*	2	2.35543	16.8	57.6
FEMEMPLD	.77447	*	3	2.00926	14.4	71.9
FARMERS	.74519	*	4	.89745	6.4	78.3
RETAILNG	.79259	*	5	.75847	5.4	83.8
COMMERCL	.90987	*	6	.53520	3.8	87.6
INDUSTZN	.92914	*	7	.50886	3.6	91.2
HEALTH	.66536	*	8	.27607	2.0	93.2
CHLDNEGL	.67007	*	9	.24511	1.8	94.9
COMMEFFC	.79852	*	10	.20505	1.5	96.4
DWELGNEW	.72576	*	11	.19123	1.4	97.8
MIGRNPOP	.50560	*	12	.16982	1.2	99.0
UNEMPLOY	.72549	*	13	.10202	.7	99.7
MENTALIL	.23825	*	14	.03946	.3	100.0

Regardless of the algorithm used, by default the number of factors to be retained is determined by the principal components solution because it is easily obtainable. Thus most of the output in Figure 4.9a is identical to that displayed in Figure 4.5a. The only exception is the column of communalities. In the principal components solution, all initial communalities are listed as 1's. In all other solutions, the initial estimate of the communality of a variable is the multiple R^2 from the regression equation that predicts that variable from all other variables. These initial communalities are used in the estimation algorithm.

When a method other than principal components analysis is used to estimate the final factor matrix, the percentage of variance explained by each final factor is usually different. Figure 4.9b contains the final statistics from a maximum-likelihood solution. The final three factors extracted explain only 63% of the total variance, as compared to 72% for the first three principal components. The first factor accounts for 35.5% of the total variance, as compared to 40.8% for the first principal component.

Figure 4.9b Maximum-likelihood final statistics

```
FACTOR MATRIX = IN (CORR *)
  /PRINT=DEFAULT REPR
  /EXTRACTION=ML
```

FINAL STATISTICS:

VARIABLE	COMMUNALITY	*	FACTOR	EIGENVALUE	PCT OF VAR	CUM PCT
		*				
POPSTABL	.52806	*	1	4.96465	35.5	35.5
NEWSCIRC	.57439	*	2	2.17833	15.6	51.0
FEMEMPLD	.75057	*	3	1.67661	12.0	63.0
FARMERS	.56808	*				
RETAILNG	.72089	*				
COMMERCL	.87128	*				
INDUSTZN	.96817	*				
HEALTH	.33383	*				
CHLDNEGL	.78341	*				
COMMEFFC	.62762	*				
DWELGNEW	.87445	*				
MIGRNPOP	.35074	*				
UNEMPLOY	.70833	*				
MENTALIL	.15977	*				

The proportion of the total variance explained by each factor can be calculated from the factor matrix. The proportion of the total variance explained by Factor 1 is calculated by summing the proportions of variance of each variable attributable to Factor 1. Figure 4.9c, the factor matrix for the maximum-likelihood solution, shows that Factor 1 accounts for $(-0.16)^2$ of the POPSTABL variance, 0.72^2 of the NEWSCIRC variance, 0.81^2 of the FEMEMPLD variance, and so on for the other variables. The total variance attributable to Factor 1 is therefore

Equation 4.9

$$\text{Total variance for Factor 1} = (-0.16)^2 + 0.72^2 + 0.81^2 + (-0.59)^2 + 0.83^2 + 0.89^2 + 0.97^2 + 0.20^2 + (-0.52)^2 + 0.44^2 + 0.27^2 + (-0.00)^2 + (-0.62)^2 + (-0.15)^2 = 4.96$$

This is the eigenvalue displayed for Factor 1 in Figure 4.9b.

Figure 4.9c Maximum-likelihood factor matrix

```
FACTOR MATRIX = IN (CORR *)
  /PRINT=DEFAULT REPR
  /EXTRACTION=ML
```

FACTOR MATRIX:

	FACTOR 1	FACTOR 2	FACTOR 3
POPSTABL	-.16474	-.62235	-.33705
NEWSCIRC	.71934	-.04703	.23394
FEMEMPLD	.80703	.27934	-.14573
FARMERS	-.58607	-.43787	-.18130
RETAILNG	.83267	.00538	-.16588
COMMERCL	.88945	.27142	.08063
INDUSTZN	.97436	-.10452	.08869
HEALTH	.19912	.35743	-.40795
CHLDNEGL	-.51856	-.17816	.69481
COMMEFFC	.44351	.33795	-.56277
DWELGNEW	.27494	.86373	.22983
MIGRNPOP	-.00353	.49141	.33052
UNEMPLOY	-.62354	-.25283	.50558
MENTALIL	-.14756	-.33056	.16948

4.10 Methods for Factor Extraction

Several different methods can be used to obtain estimates of the common factors. These methods differ in the criterion used to define "good fit." Principal axis factoring proceeds much as principal components analysis, except that the diagonals of the correlation matrix are replaced by estimates of the communalities. At the first step, squared multiple correlation coefficients can be used as initial estimates of the communalities. Based on these, the requisite number of factors is extracted. The communalities are reestimated from the factor loadings, and factors are again extracted with the new communality estimates replacing the old. This continues until negligible change occurs in the communality estimates.

The method of unweighted least squares produces, for a fixed number of factors, a factor pattern matrix that minimizes the sum of the squared differences between the observed and reproduced correlation matrices (ignoring the diagonals). The generalized least-squares method minimizes the same criterion; however, correlations are weighted inversely by the uniqueness of the variables. That is, correlations involving variables with high uniqueness are given less weight than correlations involving variables with low uniqueness.

The maximum-likelihood method produces parameter estimates that are the most likely to have produced the observed correlation matrix if the sample is from a multivariate normal distribution. Again, the correlations are weighted by the inverse of the uniqueness of the variables, and an iterative algorithm is employed.

The alpha method considers the variables in a particular analysis to be a sample from the universe of potential variables. It maximizes the alpha reliability of the factors. This differs from the previously described methods, which consider the cases to be a sample from some population and the variables to be fixed. With alpha factor extraction, the eigenvalues can no longer be obtained as the sum of the squared factor loadings and the communalities for each variable are not the sum of the squared loadings on the individual factors. See Harman (1967) and Kim and Mueller (1978) for discussions of the different factor estimation algorithms.

4.11 Goodness of Fit of the Factor Model

When factors are extracted using generalized least squares or maximum-likelihood estimation and it is assumed that the sample is from a multivariate normal population, it is possible to obtain goodness-of-fit tests for the adequacy of a k-factor model. For large sample sizes, the goodness-of-fit statistic tends to be distributed as a chi-squared variate. In most applications, the number of common factors is not known, and the number of factors is increased until a reasonably good fit is obtained—that is, until the observed significance level is no longer small. The statistics obtained in this fashion are not independent and the true significance level is not the same as the observed significance level at each step.

The value of the chi-squared goodness-of-fit statistic is directly proportional to the sample size. The degrees of freedom are a function of only the number of common factors and the number of variables. (For the chi-squared statistic to have positive degrees of freedom, the number of common factors cannot exceed the largest integer satisfying

$$m < 0.5\left(2p + 1 - \sqrt{8p + 1}\right) \qquad \text{Equation 4.11}$$

where m is the number of common factors to be extracted and p is the number of variables). For large sample sizes, the goodness-of-fit test may cause rather small discrepancies in fit to be deemed statistically significant, resulting in a larger number of factors being extracted than is really necessary.

Table 4.11 contains the goodness-of-fit statistics for maximum-likelihood extraction for different numbers of common factors. Using this criterion, six common factors are needed to adequately represent the community data.

Table 4.11 Goodness-of-fit statistics

Number of factors	Chi-square statistic	Iterations required	Significance
3	184.8846	13	0.0000
4	94.1803	8	0.0000
5	61.0836	11	0.0010
6	27.3431	15	0.1985

4.12 Summary of the Extraction Phase

In the factor extraction phase, the number of common factors needed to adequately describe the data is determined. This decision is based on eigenvalues and percentage of the total variance accounted for by different numbers of factors. A plot of the eigenvalues (the scree plot) is also helpful in determining the number of factors.

4.13 The Rotation Phase

Although the factor matrix obtained in the extraction phase indicates the relationship between the factors and the individual variables, it is usually difficult to identify meaningful factors based on this matrix. Often the variables and factors do not appear correlated in any interpretable pattern. Most factors are correlated with many variables. Since one of the goals of factor analysis is to identify factors that are substantively meaningful (in the sense that they summarize sets of closely related variables) the *rotation* phase of factor analysis attempts to transform the initial matrix into one that is easier to interpret.

Consider Figure 4.13a, which is a factor matrix for four hypothetical variables. From the factor loadings, it is difficult to interpret any of the factors, since the variables and factors are intertwined. That is, all factor loadings are quite high, and both factors explain all of the variables.

Figure 4.13a Hypothetical factor matrix

```
FACTOR MATRIX:

              FACTOR  1      FACTOR  2

V1              .50000         .50000
V2              .50000        -.40000
V3              .70000         .70000
V4            -.60000          .60000
```

Figure 4.13b Rotated hypothetical factor matrix

```
ROTATED FACTOR MATRIX:
              FACTOR  1      FACTOR  2

V1              .70684        -.01938
V2              .05324        -.63809
V3              .98958        -.02713
V4              .02325         .84821
```

In the factor matrix in Figure 4.13b, variables V1 and V3 are highly related to Factor 1, while V2 and V4 load highly on Factor 2. By looking at what variables V2 and V4 have in common (such as a measurement of job satisfaction, or a characterization of an anxious personality), we may be able to identify Factor 2. Similar steps can be taken to identify Factor 1. The goal of rotation is to transform complicated matrices like that in Figure 4.13a into simpler ones like that in Figure 4.13b.

Consider Figure 4.13c, which is a plot of variables V1 to V4 using the factor loadings in Figure 4.13a as the coordinates, and Figure 4.13d, which is the corresponding plot for Figure 4.13b. Note that Figure 4.13c would look exactly like Figure 4.13d if the dotted lines were rotated to be the reference axes. When the axes are maintained at right angles, the rotation is called orthogonal. If the axes are not maintained at right angles, the rotation is called oblique. Oblique rotation is discussed in Section 4.16.

Figure 4.13c Prior to rotation

```
FACTOR VARIABLES=V1 V2 V3 V4
  /ROTATION=NOROTATE
  /PLOT=ROTATION(1,2)
```

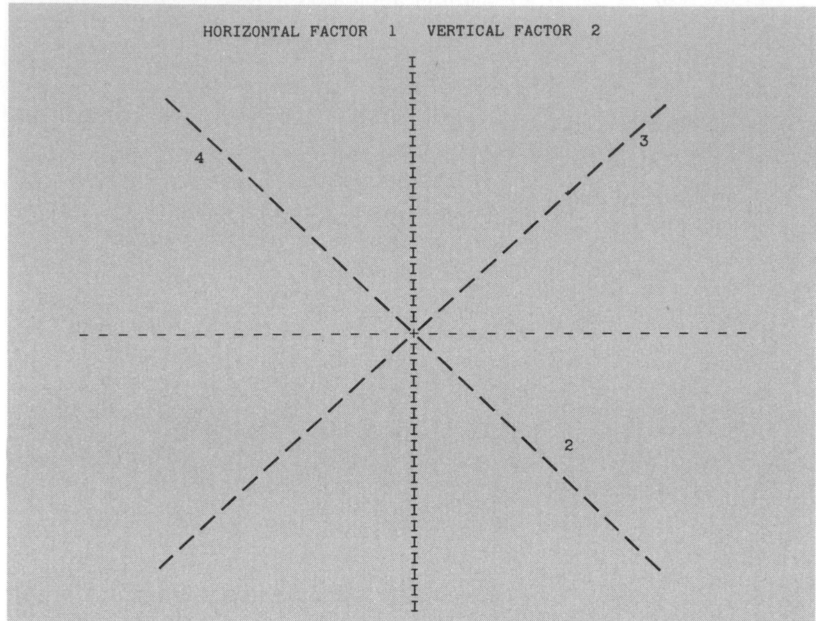

The purpose of rotation is to achieve a simple structure. This means that we would like each factor to have nonzero loadings for only some of the variables. This helps us interpret the factors. We would also like each variable to have nonzero loadings for only a few factors, preferably one. This permits the factors to be differentiated from each other. If several factors have high loadings on the same variables, it is difficult to ascertain how the factors differ.

Rotation does not affect the goodness of fit of a factor solution. That is, although the factor matrix changes, the communalities and the percentage of total variance explained do not change. The percentage of variance accounted for by each of the factors does, however, change. Rotation redistributes the explained variance for the individual factors. Different rotation methods may actually result in the identification of somewhat different factors.

A variety of algorithms are used for orthogonal rotation to a simple structure. The most commonly used method is the *varimax* method, which attempts to minimize the number of variables that have high loadings on a factor. This should enhance the interpretability of the factors.

Figure 4.13d Orthogonal rotation

```
FACTOR VARIABLES=V1 V2 V3 V4
  /ROTATION=VARIMAX
  /PLOT=ROTATION(1,2)
```

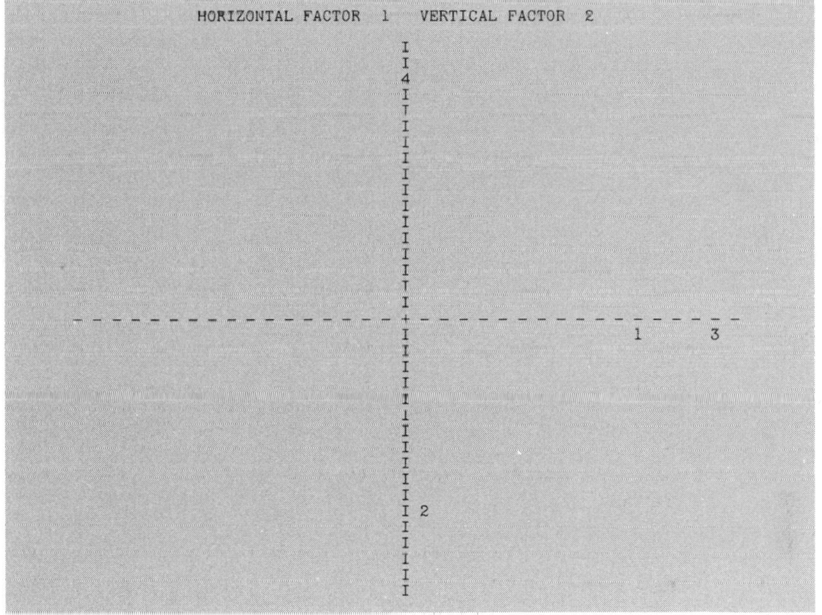

The *quartimax* method emphasizes simple interpretation of variables, since the solution minimizes the number of factors needed to explain a variable. A quartimax rotation often results in a general factor with high-to-moderate loadings on most variables. This is one of the main shortcomings of the quartimax method.

The *equamax* method is a combination of the varimax method, which simplifies the factors, and the quartimax method, which simplifies variables.

Consider Figure 4.13e, which shows the factor matrices for the community data before rotation and again after a varimax (and quartimax and equamax) orthogonal rotation procedure.

The unrotated factor matrix is difficult to interpret. Many variables have moderate-size correlations with several factors. After rotation, the number of large and small factor loadings increases. Variables are more highly correlated with single factors. Interpretation of the factors also appears possible. For example, the first factor shows string positive correlation with newspaper circulation, percentage of females in the labor force, sales, commercial activity, and the

Figure 4.13e Factor matrices for community data

```
FACTOR MATRIX = IN (CORR *)
  /EXTRACT=PC
  /ROTATION=VARIMAX
  /ROTATION=QUARTIMAX
  /ROTATION=EQUAMAX
```

FACTOR MATRIX (unrotated):

	FACTOR 1	FACTOR 2	FACTOR 3
POPSTABL	-.30247	.68597	-.36451
NEWSCIRC	.67238	.28096	.49779
FEMEMPLD	.89461	.01131	.08063
FARMERS	-.68659	.20002	-.40450
RETAILNG	.85141	.24264	.09351
COMMERCL	.72503	.39394	.19896
INDUSTZN	.84436	.29956	.23775
HEALTH	.38347	-.32718	-.63474
CHLDNEGL	-.67430	-.12139	.52896
COMMEFFC	.63205	-.15540	-.64221
DWELGNEW	.45886	-.73940	.18706
MIGRNPOP	.07894	-.74371	.24335
UNEMPLOY	-.78714	-.09777	.30110
MENTALIL	-.30025	.45463	.27134

ROTATED FACTOR MATRIX (varimax):

	FACTOR 1	FACTOR 2	FACTOR 3
POPSTABL	-.13553	.00916	-.82247
NEWSCIRC	.86634	-.14256	.08920
FEMEMPLD	.78248	.37620	.23055
FARMERS	-.65736	-.04537	-.49077
RETAILNG	.83993	.29454	.01705
COMMERCL	.83432	.11068	-.11000
INDUSTZN	.91325	.15773	.01730
HEALTH	-.05806	.79424	.15101
CHLDNEGL	-.39791	-.75492	.14486
COMMEFFC	.21186	.88794	.05241
DWELGNEW	.17484	.22931	.84208
MIGRNPOP	-.12119	-.00660	.77706
UNEMPLOY	-.57378	-.62483	.01311
MENTALIL	.03133	-.47460	-.37979

ROTATED FACTOR MATRIX (quartimax):

	FACTOR 1	FACTOR 2	FACTOR 3
POPSTABL	-.14884	.00769	-.82018
NEWSCIRC	.85549	-.20254	.07706
FEMEMPLD	.81105	.32272	.21214
FARMERS	-.66736	-.00515	-.47920
RETAILNG	.85885	.23432	-.00105
COMMERCL	.83802	.04963	-.12529
INDUSTZN	.92229	.09267	.00000
HEALTH	.00097	.79832	.14028
CHLDNEGL	-.44778	-.72272	.16242
COMMEFFC	.27508	.87127	.03590
DWELGNEW	.20527	.22763	.83565
MIGRNPOP	-.10781	.01249	.77896
UNEMPLOY	-.61627	-.58226	.03168
MENTALIL	-.00897	-.48069	-.37326

ROTATED FACTOR MATRIX (equamax):

	FACTOR 1	FACTOR 2	FACTOR 3
POPSTABL	-.12961	.01218	-.82338
NEWSCIRC	.86917	-.12003	.09470
FEMEMPLD	.77037	.39514	.23949
FARMERS	-.65223	-.05898	-.49613
RETAILNG	.83157	.31678	.02580
COMMERCL	.83185	.13387	-.10273
INDUSTZN	.90854	.18199	.02554
HEALTH	-.08047	.79116	.15682
CHLDNEGL	-.37857	-.76645	.13585
COMMEFFC	.18756	.89284	.06103
DWELGNEW	.16236	.22710	.84518
MIGRNPOP	-.12675	-.01613	.77603
UNEMPLOY	-.55688	-.64006	.00379
MENTALIL	.04688	-.47050	-.38327

industrialization index. It also shows a strong negative correlation with the number of farmers. Thus Factor 1 might be interpreted as measuring something like "urbanism." The second factor is positively correlated with health and a high standard of living and negatively correlated with aid to dependent children, unemployment, and mental illness. This factor describes the affluence or welfare of a community. The last factor is associated with the instability or influx of a community. Thus, communities may be fairly well characterized by three factors—urbanism, welfare, and influx.

4.14 Factor Loading Plots

A convenient means of examining the success of an orthogonal rotation is to plot the variables using the factor loadings as coordinates. In Figure 4.14a, the variables are plotted using Factors 1 and 2 after varimax rotation of the two

Figure 4.14a Varimax-rotated solution

```
SET WIDTH=80
FACTOR MATRIX = IN (CORR *)
  /ROTATION=VARIMAX
  /PLOT=ROTATION(1,2)
```

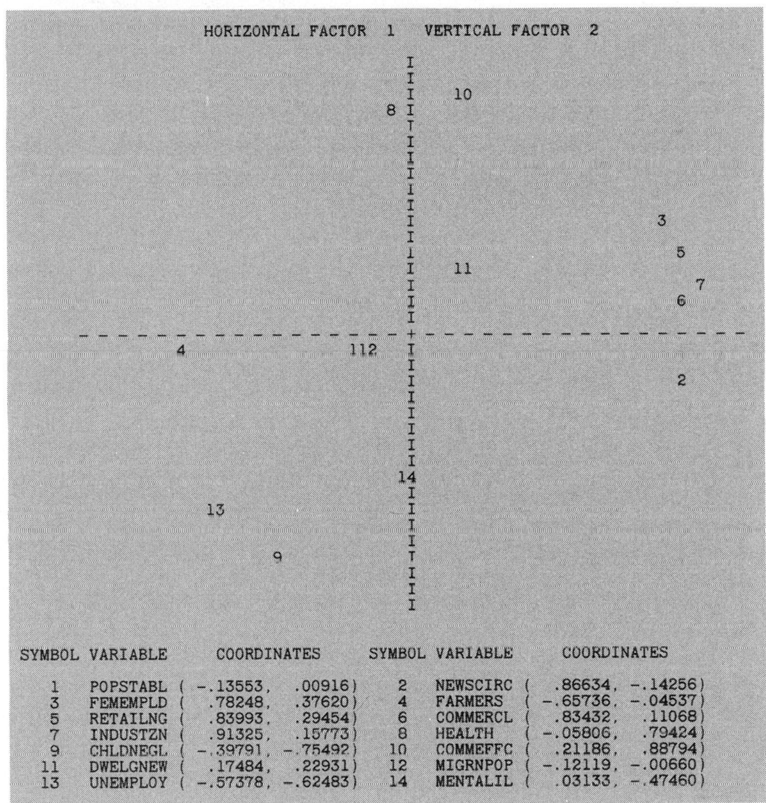

SYMBOL	VARIABLE	COORDINATES	SYMBOL	VARIABLE	COORDINATES
1	POPSTABL	(-.13553, .00916)	2	NEWSCIRC	(.86634, -.14256)
3	FEMEMPLD	(.78248, .37620)	4	FARMERS	(-.65736, -.04537)
5	RETAILNG	(.83993, .29454)	6	COMMERCL	(.83432, .11068)
7	INDUSTZN	(.91325, .15773)	8	HEALTH	(-.05806, .79424)
9	CHLDNEGL	(-.39791, -.75492)	10	COMMEFFC	(.21186, .88794)
11	DWELGNEW	(.17484, .22931)	12	MIGRNPOP	(-.12119, -.00660)
13	UNEMPLOY	(-.57378, -.62483)	14	MENTALIL	(.03133, -.47460)

factors. The plotted numbers represent the number of the variable; e.g., 7 represents the seventh variable (INDUSTZN). The coordinates correspond to the factor loadings in Figure 4.13e for the varimax-rotated solution. The coordinates are also listed under each plot (these have been omitted in Figure 4.14b). In Figure 4.14b, the variables are plotted using Factors 1 and 2 before rotation.

Figure 4.14b Unrotated solution

```
SET WIDTH=80
FACTOR MATRIX = IN (CORR *)
  /ROTATION=NOROTATE
  /PLOT=ROTATION(1,2)
```

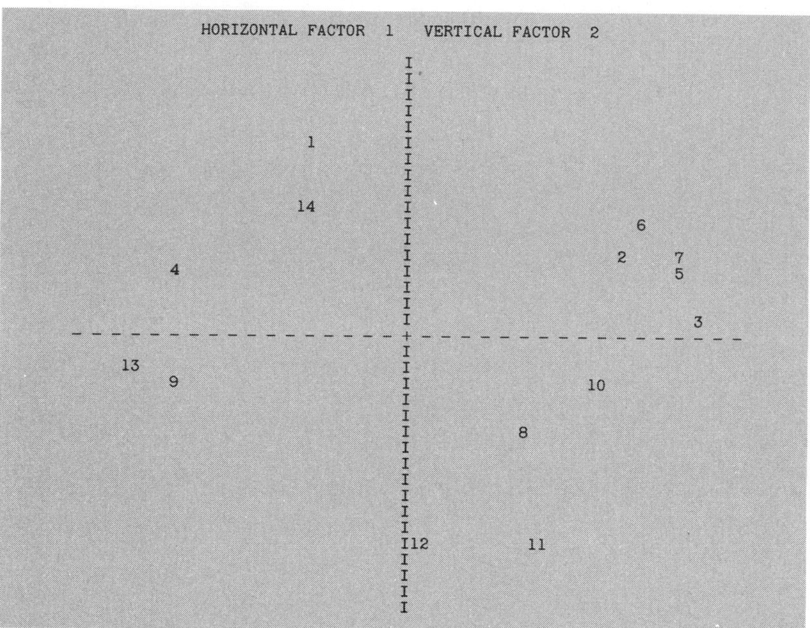

If a rotation has achieved a simple structure, clusters of variables should occur near the ends of the axes and at their intersection. Variables at the end of an axis are those that have high loadings on only that factor. Variables near the origin of the plot have small loadings on both factors. Variables that are not near the axes are explained by both factors. If a simple structure has been achieved, there should be few, if any, variables with large loadings on more than one factor.

4.15 Interpreting the Factors

To identify the factors, it is necessary to group the variables that have large loadings for the same factors. Plots of the loadings, as discussed in Section 4.14, are one way of determining the clusters of variables. Another convenient strategy is to sort the factor pattern matrix so that variables with high loadings on the same factor appear together, as shown in Figure 4.15a. Small factor loadings can be omitted from such a table. In Figure 4.15b, no loadings less than 0.5 in absolute value are displayed. Note that the mental illness variable, as expected, does not correlate highly with any of the factors.

Figure 4.15a Sorted loadings

```
FACTOR MATRIX = IN (CORR *)
  /FORMAT=SORT
  /ROTATION=VARIMAX
```

```
ROTATED FACTOR MATRIX:

              FACTOR  1     FACTOR  2     FACTOR  3

INDUSTZN        .91325        .15773        .01730
NEWSCIRC        .86634       -.14256        .08920
RETAILNG        .83993        .20454        .01705
COMMERCL        .83432        .11068       -.11000
FEMEMPLD        .78248        .37620        .23055
FARMERS        -.65736       -.04537       -.49077

COMMEFFC        .21186        .88794        .05241
HEALTH         -.05806        .79424        .15101
CHLDNEGL       -.39791       -.75492        .14486
UNEMPLOY       -.57378       -.62483        .01311
MENTALIL        .03133       -.47460       -.37979
DWELGNEW        .17484        .22931        .84208
POPSTABL       -.13553        .00916       -.82247
MIGRNPOP       -.12119       -.00660        .77706
```

Figure 4.15b Sorted and blanked loadings

```
FACTOR MATRIX = IN (CORR *)
  /FORMAT=SORT BLANK(.5)
  /ROTATION=VARIMAX
```

```
ROTATED FACTOR MATRIX:

              FACTOR  1     FACTOR  2     FACTOR  3

INDUSTZN        .91325
NEWSCIRC        .86634
RETAILNG        .83993
COMMERCL        .83432
FEMEMPLD        .78248
FARMERS        -.65736

COMMEFFC                      .88794
HEALTH                        .79424
CHLDNEGL                     -.75492
UNEMPLOY       -.57378       -.62483
MENTALIL

DWELGNEW                                    .84208
POPSTABL                                   -.82247
MIGRNPOP                                    .77706
```

4.16 Oblique Rotation

Orthogonal rotation results in factors that are uncorrelated. Although this is an appealing property, sometimes allowing for correlations among factors simplifies the factor pattern matrix. Consider Figure 4.16a, which is a plot of the factor loadings for six variables. Note that if the axes went through the points (the solid line), a simpler factor pattern matrix would result than with an orthogonal rotation (the dotted lines). Factor pattern matrices for both rotations are shown in Figure 4.16b.

Figure 4.16a Plot of factor loadings

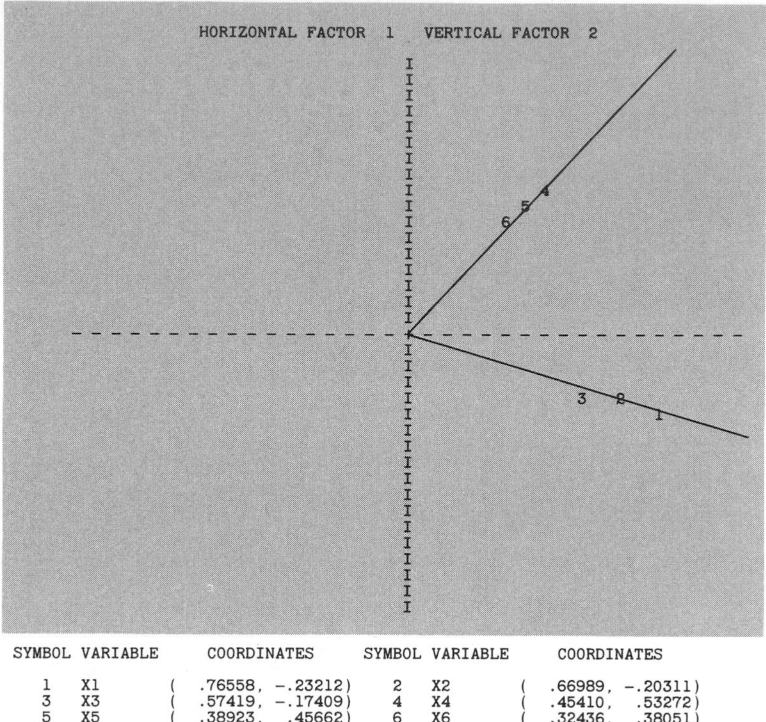

Figure 4.16b Rotated varimax and oblique factor loadings

ROTATED FACTOR MATRIX varimax:

	FACTOR 1	FACTOR 2
X1	.78313	.16345
X2	.68523	.14302
X3	.58734	.12259
X4	.14302	.68523
X5	.12259	.58734
X6	.10215	.48945

PATTERN MATRIX oblique:

	FACTOR 1	FACTOR 2
X1	.80000	.00000
X2	.70000	.00000
X3	.60000	.00000
X4	.00000	.70000
X5	.00000	.60000
X6	.00000	.50000

There are several reasons why oblique rotation has come into favor. It is unlikely that influences in nature are uncorrelated. And even if they are uncorrelated in the population, they need not be so in the sample. Thus, oblique rotations have often been found to yield substantively meaningful factors.

4.17 Factor Pattern and Structure Matrices

Oblique rotation preserves the communalities of the variables, as does orthogonal rotation. When oblique rotation is used, however, the factor loadings and factor variable correlations are no longer identical. The factor loadings are still partial regression coefficients, but since the factors are correlated, they are no longer equal to the simple factor variable correlations. (Remember that the regression coefficients depend on the interrelationships of the independent variables when these are correlated.) Therefore, separate factor loading and factor structure matrices are displayed as part of the output.

4.18 Algorithm for Oblique Rotation

The method for oblique rotation available in SPSS^X is called OBLIMIN. A parameter called δ (delta) controls the extent of obliqueness. When δ is zero, the factors are most oblique. For negative values of δ, the factors become less oblique as δ becomes more negative. Harman (1967) recommends that δ be either zero or negative.

The factor loadings for the communities data after an oblique rotation are shown in the factor pattern matrix in Figure 4.18a. The loadings are no longer constrained to a range from -1 to $+1$. The correlations between the factors and variables are shown in Figure 4.18b, the factor structure matrix.

Figure 4.18a Factor pattern matrix

```
FACTOR MATRIX = IN (CORR *)
  /FORMAT=SORT
  /ROTATION=OBLIMIN
```

PATTERN MATRIX:

	FACTOR 1	FACTOR 2	FACTOR 3
INDUSTZN	.91577	.02882	-.04731
NEWSCIRC	.90594	-.06987	.26053
COMMERCL	.84325	.15024	-.01504
RETAILNG	.82253	.03760	-.19782
FEMEMPLD	.74906	-.17274	-.27862
FARMERS	-.65969	.46636	-.06041
POPSTABL	-.12570	.82380	-.06787
DWELGNEW	.13426	-.82258	-.17248
MIGRNPOP	-.13720	-.78724	.03070
COMMEFFC	.09940	.02770	-.88775
HEALTH	-.16689	-.08909	-.81993
CHLDNEGL	-.31128	-.22218	.73693
UNEMPLOY	-.50651	-.08531	.57387
MENTALIL	.10140	.34462	.47495

Figure 4.18b Factor structure matrix

STRUCTURE MATRIX:

	FACTOR 1	FACTOR 2	FACTOR 3
INDUSTZN	.92553	-.04717	-.27457
RETAILNG	.86963	-.05222	-.40031
NEWSCIRC	.84545	-.10235	.02205
COMMERCL	.83566	.08423	-.20712
FEMEMPLD	.83252	-.26822	-.49178
FARMERS	-.67979	.50798	.17096
DWELGNEW	.24017	-.85671	-.32064
POPSTABL	-.17101	.82390	.07829
MIGRNPOP	-.08527	-.77258	-.04400
COMMEFFC	.32149	-.10314	-.90901
HEALTH	.04692	-.19032	-.79016
CHLDNEGL	-.48053	-.09623	.78468
UNEMPLOY	-.64496	.03280	.68993
MENTALIL	-.04466	.40290	.49721

The correlation matrix for the factors is in Figure 4.18c. Note that there are small correlations between all three factors. In the case of an orthogonal rotation, the factor correlation matrix is an identity matrix: that is, there are 1's on the diagonal and 0's elsewhere.

Figure 4.18c Factor correlation matrix

```
FACTOR CORRELATION MATRIX:

            FACTOR  1    FACTOR  2    FACTOR  3

FACTOR  1    1.00000
FACTOR  2    -.07580      1.00000
FACTOR  3    -.25253       .13890      1.00000
```

The oblique rotation resulted in the same grouping of variables as did the orthogonal rotation. The interpretation of the factors does not change based on it.

4.19 Factor Scores

Since one of the goals of factor analysis is to reduce a large number of variables to a smaller number of factors, it is often desirable to estimate factor scores for each case. The factor scores can be used in subsequent analyses to represent the values of the factors. Plots of factor scores for pairs of factors are useful for detecting unusual observations.

Recall from Section 4.1 that a factor can be estimated as a linear combination of the original variables. That is, for case k, the score for the jth factor is estimated as

$$\hat{F}_{jk} = \sum_{i=1}^{p} W_{ji} X_{ik}$$ **Equation 4.19a**

where X_{ik} is the standardized value of the ith variable for case k and W_{ji} is the factor score coefficient for the jth factor and the ith variable. Except for principal components analysis, exact factor scores cannot be obtained. Estimates are obtained instead.

There are several methods for estimating factor score coefficients. Each has different properties and results in different scores (see Tucker, 1971; Harman, 1967). The three methods available in SPSS^X FACTOR (Anderson-Rubin, regression, and Bartlett) all result in scores with a mean of 0. The Anderson-Rubin method always produces uncorrelated scores with a standard deviation of 1, even when the original factors are estimated to be correlated. The regression factor scores (the default) have a variance equal to the squared multiple correlation between the estimated factor scores and the true factor values. (These are shown on the diagonal in Figure 4.19b.) Regression method factor scores can be correlated even when factors are assumed to be orthogonal. If principal components extraction is used, all three methods result in the same factor scores, which are no longer estimated but are exact.

Figure 4.19a contains the factor score coefficients used to calculate regression method factor scores for the community data. The correlation matrix for the estimated scores is shown in Figure 4.19b.

Figure 4.19a Factor coefficient matrix

```
FACTOR MATRIX = IN (CORR *)
  /PRINT FSCORES/EXT=ML/ROT=VARI
```

FACTOR SCORE COEFFICIENT MATRIX:

	FACTOR 1	FACTOR 2	FACTOR 3
POPSTABL	-.00150	.03191	-.15843
NEWSCIRC	.05487	-.06095	.03524
FEMEMPLD	.01729	.14014	.05328
FARMERS	-.01797	.00113	-.11462
RETAILNG	.03728	.09460	-.03577
COMMERCL	.20579	-.11667	-.10723
INDUSTZN	.77285	-.27024	.00882
HEALTH	-.02786	.09971	-.00161
CHLDNEGL	.08404	-.44657	.16521
COMMEFFC	-.05030	.23211	-.03623
DWELGNEW	-.05117	.07034	.68792
MIGRNPOP	.00029	-.03198	.09778
UNEMPLOY	.03856	-.26435	.05378
MENTALIL	.01264	-.04224	-.01691

Figure 4.19b Covariance matrix for estimated regression factor scores

```
FACTOR MATRIX = IN (CORR *)
  /PRINT FSCORES/EXT=ML/ROT=VARI
```

COVARIANCE MATRIX FOR ESTIMATED REGRESSION FACTOR SCORES:

	FACTOR 1	FACTOR 2	FACTOR 3
FACTOR 1	.96763		
FACTOR 2	.03294	.87641	
FACTOR 3	.00042	.02544	.89452

To see how factor scores are calculated, consider Table 4.19 which contains standardized values for the original 14 variables for 5 counties, and factor score values for the three factors. For each factor, the factor scores are obtained by multiplying the standardized values by the corresponding factor score coefficients. Thus, for Adams county the value for Factor 1 is −1.328.

$$-.00150 \times -.36 + .05487 \times -.93 + .01729 \times -1.06 + \ldots$$
$$+.01264 \times -.76 = -1.328$$
Equation 4.19b

Table 4.19 Standardized values and factor scores

	County				
Variable	**Adams**	**Butler**	**Crawford**	**Cuyahoga**	**Hamilton**
POPSTABL	−0.36	−1.49	2.44	−0.13	−0.30
NEWSCIRC	−0.93	0.39	−0.26	2.04	1.17
FEMEMPLD	−1.06	0.41	0.24	1.30	1.03
FARMERS	2.20	−0.67	0.01	−0.93	−0.90
RETAILNG	−1.41	0.49	0.58	1.15	1.07
COMMERCL	−0.89	−0.30	−0.07	1.58	2.02
INDUSTZN	−1.14	−0.11	0.03	1.53	1.85
HEALTH	−0.25	−0.56	−1.32	−0.36	−1.17
CHLDNEGL	−1.26	0.79	−0.61	0.63	0.99
COMMEFFC	−0.20	0.78	−0.87	−0.78	−1.66
DWELGNEW	−0.52	0.52	−1.09	−0.01	−0.22
MIGRNPOP	−0.98	0.16	−0.60	0.63	1.13
UNEMPLOY	−0.75	−0.36	−0.44	1.56	0.76
MENTALIL	−0.76	−0.77	−0.46	−0.14	0.61
Factor			**Scores**		
Factor 1	−1.328	−0.089	0.083	1.862	2.233
Factor 2	0.897	0.027	0.197	−1.362	−1.79
Factor 3	−0.830	0.831	−1.290	0.342	0.226

4.20 RUNNING PROCEDURE FACTOR

A variety of extraction and rotation techniques are available in the SPSS^X FACTOR procedure. The extraction methods available include principal components analysis (Section 4.5) and the maximum-likelihood factor method (Section 4.9). The factor rotation methods are varimax, equamax, quartimax, and oblimin.

You can also request scree plots and factor loading plots to help in selecting and interpreting factors. FACTOR will accept a correlation matrix or a factor loading matrix as input, as well as the original values of your variables for cases.

4.21 Global and Analysis Block Subcommands

There are two types of FACTOR subcommands: global and analysis block. Global subcommands are specified once and are in effect for the entire FACTOR procedure. Analysis block subcommands apply only to the ANALYSIS subcommand that precedes them.

The global subcommands are VARIABLES, MISSING, and WIDTH. The VARIABLES subcommand identifies the subset of variables from the active file available for analysis by FACTOR. The MISSING subcommand provides several alternative missing-value treatments. WIDTH controls the width of the display.

An analysis block begins with an ANALYSIS subcommand, which names a subset of variables from the list specified on the VARIABLES subcommand. If you omit the ANALYSIS subcommand, all variables named on the VARIABLES subcommand are used.

Analysis block subcommands include EXTRACTION, ROTATION, CRITERIA, SAVE, etc. You also can tailor the statistics displayed for an analysis block by specifying the PRINT subcommand to request optional statistics, the FORMAT subcommand to reformat factor loading and structure matrices, and the PLOT subcommand to obtain scree plots and factor loading plots.

The extraction phase is initiated with the EXTRACTION subcommand. (A principal components analysis is performed if there is no EXTRACTION subcommand.) The CRITERIA subcommand controls the number of factors selected in subsequent extractions, and the DIAGONAL subcommand supplies initial diagonal values for principal axis factoring.

The rotation phase is initiated with the ROTATION subcommand, which specifies the rotation method to use. The default varimax rotation is obtained if you omit both EXTRACTION and ROTATION. No rotation occurs if EXTRACTION is specified without ROTATION. The CRITERIA subcommand controls subsequent rotation, as well as extraction, criteria.

Optional subcommands are available to write and read matrices for FACTOR.

4.22 Subcommand Order

The global subcommands VARIABLES and MISSING must be the first specifications. If the MATRIX subcommand is used, it must appear before the analysis block. The remaining subcommands can appear in any logical order.

Within an analysis block, the placement of CRITERIA is important, as it affects all extractions and rotations that follow. Once specified, a CRITERIA subcommand is in effect for the remainder of the FACTOR procedure. However, you can specify more than one CRITERIA subcommand.

4.23 The VARIABLES Subcommand

The VARIABLES subcommand lists the variables to analyze. If you do not specify a subsequent EXTRACTION or ROTATION subcommand, the default principal components analysis with varimax rotation is produced. Thus, the command

```
FACTOR VARIABLES=POPSTABL NEWSCIRC FEMEMPLD FARMERS RETAILNG COMMERCL
  INDUSTZN HEALTH CHLDNEGL COMMEFFC DWELGNEW MIGRNPOP UNEMPLOY MENTALIL
```

or, if the variables exist on that order on the active file, the command

```
FACTOR VARIABLES=POPSTABL TO MENTALIL
```

produces the output shown in Figures 4.5a, 4.6, and 4.7.

VARIABLES is the only required subcommand and must be placed before all other subcommands except MISSING, WIDTH, and MATRIX. Only variables named on the VARIABLES subcommand can be referred to in subsequent subcommands. You can specify only one VARIABLES subcommand on a FACTOR command.

4.24 The MISSING Subcommand

FACTOR results are based on the correlation matrix for the variables listed on the VARIABLES subcommand. Use the MISSING subcommand to specify the missing-value treatment for this matrix. If you omit the MISSING subcommand, or include it with no specifications, missing values are deleted listwise.

LISTWISE *Delete missing values listwise.* Only cases with valid values on all variables on the VARIABLES subcommand are used. This is the default.

PAIRWISE *Delete missing values pairwise.* Cases with complete data on each pair of variables correlated are used.

MEANSUB *Replace missing values with the variable mean.* This includes both user-missing and system-missing values.

INCLUDE *Include missing values.* Cases with user-missing values are treated as valid observations. System-missing values are excluded from analysis.

For example, the command

```
FACTOR VARIABLES=IQ GPA TESTSCOR STRESS SAT PSYCHTST
  /MISSING=PAIRWISE
```

requests a default analysis that uses pairwise missing-value treatment in calculating the correlation matrix.

You can specify only one MISSING subcommand per FACTOR command. The MISSING subcommand must be placed before all other subcommands except VARIABLES and WIDTH. MISSING is ignored with matrix input.

4.25 The WIDTH Subcommand

The WIDTH subcommand controls the display width for factor output. For example, the subcommand

```
/WIDTH=80
```

requests output that is 80 characters wide. The value on WIDTH must be an integer. This value overrides the one specified on the SET command. You can specify only one WIDTH subcommand per FACTOR command. The WIDTH subcommand can be placed anywhere.

4.26 The ANALYSIS Subcommand

The ANALYSIS subcommand allows you to perform analyses on subsets of variables named on the VARIABLES subcommand. For example, the command

```
FACTOR VARIABLES=POPSTABL TO MENTALIL
  /ANALYSIS=FEMEMPLD FARMERS INDUSTZN HEALTH CHILDNEGL DWELGNEW
  /ANALYSIS=POPSTABL NEWSCIRC FEMEMPLD COMMERCL UNEMPLOY MENTALIL
```

requests two default principal components analyses. The first uses variables FEMEMPLD, FARMERS, INDUSTZN, HEALTH, CHLDNEGL, and DWELGNEW, and the second uses variables POPSTABL, NEWSCIRC, FEMEMPLD, COMMERCL, UNEMPLOY, and MENTALIL.

If you do not include the ANALYSIS subcommand, FACTOR uses all of the variables listed on the VARIABLES subcommand for the analysis and produces the following message:

```
>NOTE    11284
>Since the ANALYSIS subcommand is not used, all variables on the VARIABLES
>subcommand will be used for the first analysis.
```

The TO keyword in a variable list on the ANALYSIS subcommand refers to the order of variables on the VARIABLES subcommand, not to their order in the file. Otherwise, the usual SPSS^X conventions for variable lists are followed. You can use the keyword ALL to refer to all of the variables listed on the VARIABLES subcommand.

If you follow the VARIABLES subcommand with another analysis block subcommand prior to the ANALYSIS subcommand, you implicitly initiate an analysis block. For example, the command

```
FACTOR VARIABLES=POPSTABL TO MENTALIL
  /PRINT=DEFAULTS CORRELATIONS
  /ANALYSIS=FEMEMPLD FARMERS INDUSTZN HEALTH CHILDNEGL DWELGNEW
  /ANALYSIS=POPSTABL NEWSCIRC FEMEMPLD COMMERCL UNEMPLOY MENTALIL
```

requests three analyses. The first uses all variables and prints the correlation matrix along with the defaults, and the second and third use different subsets of the variable list and print only the defaults.

4.27 The EXTRACTION Subcommand

To specify the extraction method, use the EXTRACTION subcommand with one of the keywords shown below.

PC *Principal components analysis.* This is the default.

PAF *Principal axis factoring.*

ML *Maximum likelihood.*

ALPHA *Alpha factoring.*

IMAGE *Image factoring.*

ULS *Unweighted least squares.*

GLS *Generalized least squares.*

You can specify more than one EXTRACTION subcommand. For example, the command

```
FACTOR VARIABLES=IQ GPA TESTSCOR STRESS SAT PSYCHTST
  /EXTRACTION=ML
  /EXTRACTION=PC
```

produces output based on two extraction methods—maximum likelihood and principal components. You can specify multiple EXTRACTION subcommands in each analysis block to produce output for different extraction methods for subsets of variables named on the VARIABLES subcommand.

If you use the EXTRACTION subcommand without a subsequent ROTATION subcommand, the factor pattern matrix is not rotated (see Section 4.30).

4.28 The DIAGONAL Subcommand

Use the DIAGONAL subcommand to specify initial diagonal values in conjunction with principal axis factoring (EXTRACTION=PAF). You can specify any one of the following:

value list *Diagonal values.* User-supplied diagonal values are used only for principal axis factoring.

DEFAULT *1's on the diagonal for principal components or initial communality estimates on the diagonal for factor methods.*

You must supply the same number of diagonal values as there are variables in the analysis. For example, the command

```
FACTOR VARIABLES=IQ GPA TESTSCOR SAT EDYEARS
  /DIAGONAL=.55 .45 .35 .40 .50
  /EXTRACTION=PAF
```

assigns five diagonal values for the specified principal axis factoring. You can use the prefix *n* and an asterisk to indicate replicated values. For example, 5*0.80 is the same as specifying 0.80 five times.

4.29 The CRITERIA Subcommand

Use CRITERIA to control criteria for extractions and rotations that follow the subcommand.

FACTORS(nf) *Number of factors extracted.* The default is the number of eigenvalues greater than MINEIGEN (see below).

MINEIGEN(eg) *Minimum eigenvalue used to control the number of factors.* The default value is 1.

ITERATE(ni) *Number of iterations for the factor solution.* The default value is 25.

ECONVERGE(e1) *Convergence criterion for extraction.* The default value is 0.001.

RCONVERGE(e2) *Convergence criterion for rotation.* The default value is 0.0001.

KAISER *Kaiser normalization in rotation.* This is the default.

NOKAISER *No Kaiser normalization.*

DELTA(d) *Value of delta for direct oblimin rotation.* The default value is 0.

DEFAULT *Use default values for all criteria.*

Once specified, criteria stay in effect for the procedure until explicitly overridden. For example, the command

```
FACTOR VARIABLES=IQ GPA TESTSCOR STRESS SAT PSYCHTST
  /CRITERIA=FACTORS(2)
  /ANALYSIS=ALL
  /CRITERIA=DEFAULT
```

produces two factor analyses for the same set of variables. The first analysis limits the number of factors extracted to 2, and the second extracts all factors whose eigenvalue is greater than 1.

4.30 Rotating Factors

Four rotation methods are available in FACTOR: varimax, equamax, quartimax, and oblimin (see Section 4.13). When both the EXTRACTION and ROTATION subcommands are omitted, the factors are rotated using the varimax method. However, if EXTRACTION is specified but ROTATION is not, the factors are not rotated. To specify a rotation method other than these defaults, use the ROTATION subcommand.

VARIMAX *Varimax rotation.* This is the default if both EXTRACTION and ROTATION are omitted.

EQUAMAX *Equamax rotation.*

QUARTIMAX *Quartimax rotation.*

OBLIMIN *Direct oblimin rotation.*

NOROTATE *No rotation.* This is the default if EXTRACTION is specified but ROTATION is not.

OBLIMIN uses a default delta value of 0. Use the CRITERIA subcommand to change this default (see Section 4.29).

To obtain a factor loading plot based on unrotated factors, use the PLOT subcommand (see Section 4.33) and specify NOROTATE in the ROTATION subcommand, as in

```
FACTOR VARIABLES=IQ GPA TESTSCOR STRESS SAT PSYCHTST
  /PLOT=EIGEN ROTATION(1,2)
  /ROTATION=NOROTATE
```

You can specify more than one rotation for a given extraction by using multiple ROTATION subcommands. See Section 4.29 for information on controlling rotation criteria.

4.31 The PRINT Subcommand

By default, the statistics listed below under INITIAL, EXTRACTION, and ROTATION are printed. Use the PRINT subcommand to request additional statistics. If you specify PRINT, only those statistics explicity named are displayed. You can use only one PRINT subcommand for each analysis block.

UNIVARIATE *Numbers of valid observations, means, and standard deviations for the variables named on the ANALYSIS subcommand.*

INITIAL *Initial communalities, eigenvalues, and percentage of variance explained.* (See Sections 4.5 and 4.7.)

CORRELATION *Correlation matrix for the variables named on the ANALYSIS subcommand.*

SIG *Significance levels of correlations.* These are one-tailed probabilities.

DET *The determinant of the correlation matrix.*

INV *The inverse of the correlation matrix.*

AIC *The anti-image covariance and correlation matrices.*

KMO *The Kaiser-Meyer-Olkin measure of sampling adequacy and Bartlett's test of sphericity.* (See Section 4.4.)

EXTRACTION *Communalities, eigenvalues, and rotated factor loadings.* (See Sections 4.5 through 4.10.)

REPR *Reproduced correlations and their residuals.* (See Section 4.8.)

ROTATION *Rotated factor pattern and structure matrices, factor transformation matrix, and factor correlation matrix.* (See Sections 4.13.)

FSCORE *The factor score coefficient matrix.* By default, this is based on a regression solution.

DEFAULT *INITIAL, EXTRACTION, and ROTATION statistics.* If you use the EXTRACTION subcommand without a subsequent ROTATION subcommand, only the statistics specified by INITIAL and EXTRACTION are displayed by default.

ALL *All available statistics.*

For example,

```
FACTOR VARIABLES=POPSTABL TO MENTALIL
  /PRINT=REPR
```

produced the output in Figure 4.8.

4.32 The FORMAT Subcommand

Use the FORMAT subcommand to reformat the display of the factor loading and structure matrices to help you interpret the factors (see Section 4.15). You can use only one FORMAT subcommand per analysis block. The following keywords may be specified on FORMAT:

SORT *Order the factor loadings by magnitude.*

BLANK(n) *Suppress coefficients lower in absolute value than* n.

DEFAULT *Turn off blanking and sorting.*

For example, the command

```
FACTOR VARIABLES=POPSTABL TO MENTALIL
  /FORMAT=SORT BLANK(.5)
```

produced the output in Figure 4.15b.

4.33 The PLOT Subcommand

To obtain a scree plot (Section 4.5) or a factor loading plot (Section 4.14), use the PLOT subcommand with the following keywords:

EIGEN *Scree plot.* Plots the eigenvalues in descending order.

ROTATION(n1 n2) *Factor loading plot.* The specifications *n*1 and *n*2 refer to the factors used as the axes. Several pairs of factors in parentheses can be specified on one ROTATION specification. A plot is displayed for each pair of factor numbers enclosed in parentheses.

You can specify only one PLOT subcommand per analysis block. Plots are based on rotated factors. To get an unrotated factor plot, you must explicitly specify NOROTATE on the ROTATION subcommand (see Section 4.30).

The plots in Figures 4.5b and 4.14a can be augmented with two additional factor plots by specifying

```
FACTOR VARIABLES=POPSTABL TO MENTALIL
  /PLOT=EIGEN ROTATION(1 2)(1 3)(2 3)
```

4.34 The SAVE Subcommand

Use the SAVE subcommand to compute and save factor scores on the active file. (Factor scores cannot be produced from matrix input.) The specifications on the SAVE subcommand include the method for calculating factor scores, how many factor scores to calculate, and a *rootname* to be used in naming the factor scores.

First, choose one of the following method keywords (see Section 4.19):

REG *The regression method.* This is the default.

BART *The Bartlett method.*

AR *The Anderson-Rubin method.*

Next, specify within parentheses the number of desired factor scores and a rootname up to seven characters long to be used in naming the scores. The maximum number of scores equals the order of the factor solution. You can use keyword ALL to calculate factor scores for all extracted factors.

FACTOR uses the rootname to name the factor scores sequentially, as in root1, root2, root3, etc. If you are calculating factor scores for a many-factor solution, make sure that the rootname is short enough to accommodate the number of the highest-order factor score variable. When FACTOR saves the variables on the active file, it automatically supplies a variable label indicating the method used to calculate it, its positional order, and the analysis number.

For example, the following FACTOR command saves factor scores for a study of abortion items:

```
FACTOR VARIABLES=ABDEFECT TO ABSINGLE
  /MISSING=MEANSUB
  /CRITERIA=FACTORS(2)
  /EXTRACTION=ULS
  /ROTATION=VARIMAX
  /SAVE AR (ALL FSULS)
```

FACTOR calculates two factor scores named FSULS1 and FSULS2 using the Anderson-Rubin method and saves them on the active file.

You can use multiple SAVE subcommands for an extraction. For example,

```
FACTOR VARIABLES=ABDEFECT TO ABSINGLE
  /MISSING=MEANSUB
  /EXTRACTION=ULS
  /ROTATION=VARIMAX
  /SAVE AR (ALL FSULS)
  /SAVE BART (ALL BFAC)
```

saves two sets of factor scores. The first set is computed using the Anderson-Rubin method and the second is computed using the Bartlett method.

4.35 The MATRIX Subcommand

The MATRIX subcommand allows FACTOR to read matrix materials written by procedures that generate matrices with Pearson correlation coefficients and write matrix materials in the form of either a correlation matrix or a factor-loading matrix. This subcommand must always appear before the analysis block.

The MATRIX subcommand has two keywords, IN and OUT, which specify whether the matrix is to be read or written, along with the matrix type and filename in parentheses. If you use both of the keywords IN and OUT, you can specify them in either order.

With MATRIX=IN, the VARIABLES subcommand should not be used. If it is used, it must come *after* the MATRIX subcommand, or it is ignored. For correlation matrix input, the ANALYSIS subcommand may specify a subset of the variables in the matrix. For factor matrix input, MATRIX IN reads all the variables in the matrix; it cannot read a subset. For either type of matrix input, the ANALYSIS subcommand defaults to the entire set of variables and may be omitted.

The keywords IN and OUT each have the same four options:

(COR=file) *Read the correlation matrix from a system file or write it to a system file.* The name of the file follows the equal sign. (With releases before 3.0, use the subcommand /READ CORRELATION or /WRITE CORRELATION.)

(COR=*) *Read the correlation matrix from the active file or write it to the active file.* With keyword OUT, the matrix materials replace the active file. (With releases before 3.0, use the subcommand /READ CORRELATION or /WRITE CORRELATION.)

(FAC=file) *Read the factor-loading matrix from a system file or write it to a system file.* The name of the file follows the equals sign. (With releases before 3.0, use the subcommand /READ FACTOR or /WRITE FACTOR.)

(FAC=*) *Read the factor-loading matrix from the active file or write it to the active file.* With keyword OUT, the matrix materials replace the active file. (With releases before 3.0, use the subcommand /READ FACTOR or /WRITE FACTOR.)

FACTOR writes only CORR values for correlation matrix materials and FACTOR values for factor-loading matrix materials. It neither reads nor writes additional statistics with its matrix materials. (When FACTOR reads matrix materials, it skips vectors that represent mean, standard deviation, and N values.)

In the example below, FACTOR reads a factor-loading matrix from a file called FACLOAD:

```
FACTOR MATRIX IN (FAC=facload)
```

In the example below, FACTOR writes a correlation matrix, which replaces the active file:

```
FACTOR MATRIX OUT (COR=*)
```

4.36 EXERCISES

Syntax

1. Consider these variables:

```
PCTHOMES PASTSALE DSTRCTYP AVGINCOM PCTBUSNS BUSNSTYP PCTFAMLY
AVGAGE AVGEDUC PRICE
```

   Write the FACTOR command needed to obtain a factor analysis that includes all of the following:

   a. Maximum-likelihood extraction of factors.
   b. A scree plot.
   c. A factor loading plot based on the unrotated factors.
   d. Oblimin rotation with delta equal to −0.5.
   e. Default initial, extraction, and rotation statistics, and the reproduced correlation matrix.

2. Find the syntax errors in the FACTOR commands below, and if possible, write a correct version of the command.

   a.
```
FACTOR ANALYSIS=IQ GPA TESTSCOR STRESS SAT PSYCHTST
   /EXTRACTION=ML
   /ROTATION=VARIMAX
   /ANALYSIS=TESTSCOR ANXIETY DEPRESSN HOSTILTY CONFDNCE PASTSCOR
   /EXTRACTION=ML
   /ROTATION=EQUAMAX
```

   b.
```
FACTOR VARIABLES=IQ GPA TESTSCOR STRESS SAT PSYCHTST NBRHOOD
   /ANALYSIS=IQ GPA TESTSCOR STRESS SAT PSYCHTST
   /PLOT=ROTATION(2,3)
   /ANALYSIS=IQ GPA TESTSCOR STRESS SAT SES NBRHOOD
   /ROTATION=EQUAMAX
```

   c.
```
FACTOR VARIABLES=IQ GPA TESTSCOR STRESS SAT SES NBRHOOD
   /ANALYSIS=IQ GPA SAT TO TESTSCOR SES
   /ANALYSIS=IQ GPA TESTSCOR STRESS SES NBRHOOD
```

   d.
```
FACTOR VARIABLES=IQ GPA TESTSCOR STRESS SAT PSYCHTST NBRHOOD SES
   /EXTRACTION=ML
   /ROTATION=OBLIMIN
   /PRINT=REPR KMO
   /PLOT=SCREE
```

3. Consider these variables:

```
DRUGUSE PEERS FAMSTABL NBRHOOD SCHLACHV ALCOHOL ALIENATN RECREATN
SPORTS SES AGE CRIME
```

   Write a command that performs a factor analysis that includes all of the following:

   a. Principal components extraction.
   b. Quartimax rotation.
   c. The correlation matrix.
   d. Eigenvalues.
   e. The rotated factor pattern matrix.

4. a. What is wrong with the FACTOR command shown below?

```
FACTOR VARIABLES=IQ GPA TESTSCOR SAT EDUCATN
   /EXTRACTION=ML
   /VARIABLES=IQ GPA TESTSCOR SAT EDUCATN SES NBRHOOD
   /EXTRACTION=ML
```

   b. What is the intent of this command? What is the correct command needed to carry it out?

5. A researcher wished to conduct two factor analyses, one using the default extraction criteria, and the other using extraction based on a minimum eigenvalue of 1.5. Will the FACTOR command shown below produce the analyses she wants?

```
FACTOR VARIABLES=DISTURBS PCTHOMES POLICE TEMP MINGOVT TOTLPOP
                 PCTBUSNS BUSNSTYP MINBUSNS RENT DENSITY CRIME
  /ANALYSIS=ALL
  /CRITERIA=MINEIGEN(1.5)
  /ANALYSIS=ALL
```

6. Consider these variables:

```
WORDLNTH PARLNTH VOCAB COMPRHSN TOPIC INTEREST BCKGRND IQ EDUCATN
```

Write the FACTOR command needed to obtain a factor analysis that includes all of the following:

a. A factor analysis with principal components extraction and quartimax rotation.
b. A factor analysis with maximum-likelihood extraction and varimax rotation.
c. Scree plots for each analysis.
d. Two factor loading plots for each analysis, one with Factors 1 and 2 as the axes and the other with Factors 3 and 4 as the axes.

Statistical Concepts

1. A factor analysis done by a marketing firm produced the factor loadings shown below. Interpret each factor—that is, describe what each factor represents.

	FACTOR 1	FACTOR 2	
MAGAZINE	-.7347	.0398	Type of magazines read
IQ	.0146	.1128	IQ score
OCCSTAT	.0852	.8521	Status of occupation
NBRHOOD	-.0513	-.7952	Type of neighborhood living in
RECREATN	.8707	-.0667	Main recreation interest
EDUCATN	-.0283	.8901	Level of education
INCOME	.1002	.6724	Level of income
POLITACT	.1964	-.0783	Degree of political activity
SPORT	.7095	.0332	Interest in professional sports
CULTURE	-.8948	-.0427	Interest in plays, concerts, etc.

2. Consider the factor pattern matrix shown below:

	FACTOR 1	FACTOR 2	FACTOR 3	
VERBAL	.64453	-.03421	-.03381	Verbal score
MATH	.89116	.07376	.00010	Math score
LOGIC	.91583	-.05229	.08890	Logic score
GPA	.14429	.12238	-.05362	Grade point average
SAT	.18742	.32156	-.12154	Standard aptitude test
SES	.08321	.91842	.14885	Socio-economic status
EDUCATN	.09312	.96593	-.10436	Education level
TESTSCOR	.41127	.34432	-.14892	Test score
STRESS	.08552	.06648	.95422	Stress level
PSYCHTST	.11383	.11524	.89989	Psychology test
IQ	.00077	-.08321	.24661	IQ score

a. Write the factor models for TESTSCOR and PSYCHTST.
b. Interpret each factor—that is, describe what each factor represents.

3. a. Complete the following table:

VARIABLE	COMMUNALITY	FACTOR	EIGENVALUE	PCT OF VAR	CUM PCT
AGE	1.00000	1	2.27		
MEDHIST	1.00000	2	2.05		
BLOODPRS	1.00000	3	1.73		
WEIGHT	1.00000	4	.64		
IQ	1.00000	5	.15		
PSYCHTST	1.00000	6	.10		
STRESS	1.00000	7	.07		

b. Sketch a scree plot based on the table above.

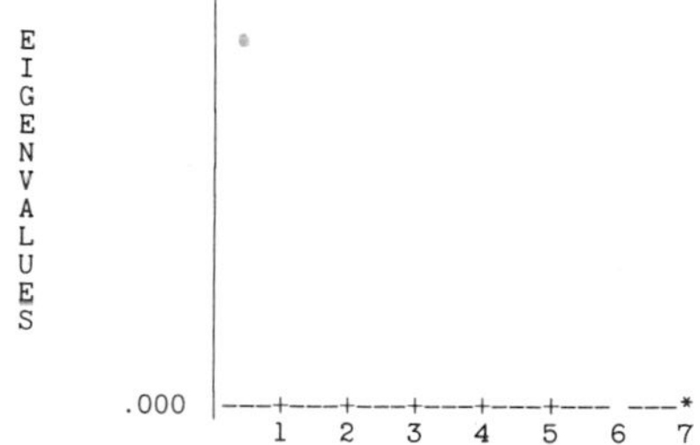

c. Which factors would you use, and why?

4. Three different rotations produced the three sets of factor loadings shown below:

	ROTATION 1			ROTATION 2			ROTATION 3	
	FACTOR 1	FACTOR 2		FACTOR 1	FACTOR 2		FACTOR 1	FACTOR 2
X1	.11530	.82214	X1	-.76540	.20311	X1	-.72702	.61164
X2	-.76229	-.63161	X2	.03274	-.65421	X2	-.81423	-.24321
X3	-.69730	.71154	X3	-.88478	-.09951	X3	-.60819	.71522
X4	.78143	.62776	X4	.03681	.85342	X4	.71828	.62192
X5	-.76318	-.56422	X5	-.04577	.71923	X5	-.79945	.50163
X6	.44319	.52813	X6	.42384	-.49288	X6	.11281	.10554
X7	.09335	-.06210	X7	-.07344	-.06119	X7	-.09282	-.12812
X8	.12144	-.09666	X8	-.09952	-.00345	X8	.13230	-.03941
X9	.74222	-.56585	X9	.91237	-.03186	X9	.73359	-.50152

a. For each set of loadings, plot the variables using the factor loadings as coordinates.

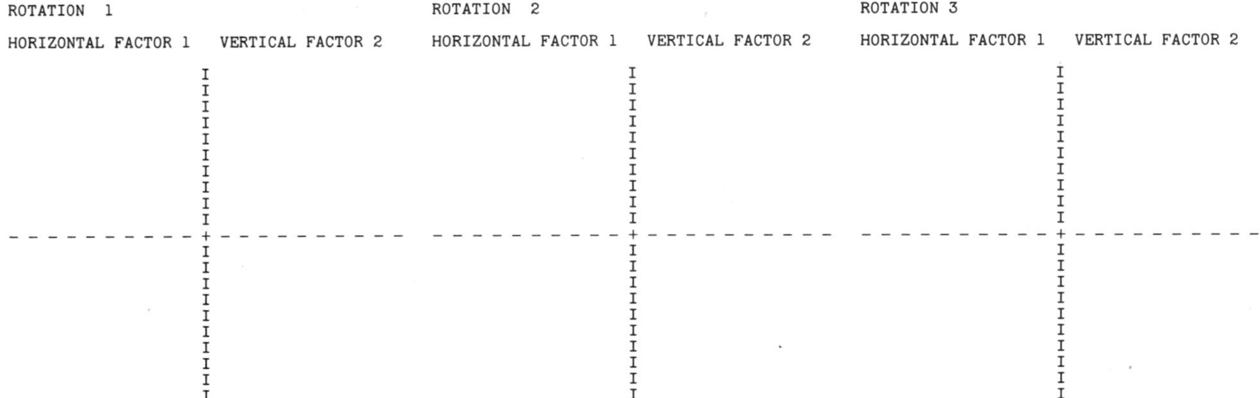

b. Which rotation do you prefer? Why?

5. A new computer program has produced the following factor structure matrix for two orthogonal factors. Would you use this program?

FACTOR MATRIX:

	FACTOR 1	FACTOR 2
X1	.71023	.38771
X2	-.20498	.86179
X3	-.63766	-.33652
X4	-.39724	.08751
X5	1.04930	.05166
X6	.65462	-.11647

6. Below are two factor correlation matrices, one for orthogonal factors before oblique rotation, and the other for the same factors after oblique rotation. Which is the matrix for the factors after rotation?

FACTOR CORRELATION MATRIX:

	FACTOR 1	FACTOR 2	FACTOR 3
FACTOR 1	1.00000	.76000	.34000
FACTOR 2	.76000	1.00000	.28000
FACTOR 3	.34000	.28000	1.00000

FACTOR CORRELATION MATRIX:

	FACTOR 1	FACTOR 2	FACTOR 3
FACTOR 1	1.00000	.00000	.00000
FACTOR 2	.00000	1.00000	.00000
FACTOR 3	.00000	.00000	1.00000

7. Using the table shown below, rank the variables in terms of the amount of variance explained by the common factors.

VARIABLE	COMMUNALITY	FACTOR	EIGENVALUE	PCT OF VAR	CUM PCT
INCOME	.75204	1	3.10020	38.7	38.7
AGE	.09423	2	2.06981	25.9	64.6
URBAN	.84189	3	2.00548	25.1	89.7
OCCUPATN	.90143				
EDUCATN	.72054				
PASTSALE	.93876				
SEX	.52210				
RECREATN	.64771				

8. Table 1 below shows final statistics for a factor model before oblique rotation, and Table 2 shows final statistics for the same factors after oblique rotation. Can you fill in the missing entries in Table 2? If so, complete the table.

TABLE 1

VARIABLE	COMMUNALITY	FACTOR	EIGENVALUE	PCT OF VAR	CUM PCT
BLOODPRS	.70247	1	6.58630	73.1	73.1
WEIGHT	.79956	2	2.03521	22.6	95.7
HEIGHT	.61546				
AGE	.83597				
MEDHIST	.91422				
STRESS	.86176				
DIET	.81345				
EKG	.59606				
PSYCHIST	.80264				

TABLE 2

VARIABLE	COMMUNALITY	FACTOR	EIGENVALUE	PCT OF VAR	CUM PCT
BLOODPRS		1			
WEIGHT		2			
HEIGHT					
AGE	.83597				
MEDHIST					
STRESS					
DIET					
EKG					
PSYCHIST					

9. Indicate whether the following statements are true or false:
   a. A highly negative factor loading for a variable indicates that the variable is an important component of the factor.
   b. Principal components are useful primarily because they are almost always interpretable.
   c. The second unrotated factor can never explain more of the total variance than the first unrotated factor.
   d. The method you use to determine the number of factors depends on the method you use for factor extraction.
   e. Oblique rotation sometimes affects the goodness of fit of a factor model.
   f. The percentage of variance accounted for by each factor usually depends on the method of factor extraction.

10. Figure 1 below shows the factor pattern matrix for a factor model before orthogonal rotation. Figure 2 shows the factor pattern matrix for the same factors after orthogonal rotation. Can you fill in the missing entries in Figure 2?

FIGURE 1

	FACTOR 1	FACTOR 2
CREDIT	.038	.773
RESLNGTH	.702	.042
HOMEOWNR	.753	-.068
JOBLNGTH	.862	.112
PASTCRED	.403	.692
INCOME	.698	.456

FIGURE 2

	FACTOR 1	FACTOR 2
CREDIT		.72314
RESLNGTH		
HOMEOWNR		
JOBLNGTH		
PASTCRED		
INCOME	.04458	

11. A three-factor model was fitted to a data set, resulting in the factor loadings shown below. Use these factor loadings to complete the table of communalities.

FACTOR MATRIX:

	FACTOR 1	FACTOR 2	FACTOR 3
DEPRESSN	.070	.702	-.050
ANXIETY	-.087	.810	.074
STRESS	.216	.733	.326
CONFDNCE	.027	-.049	-.882
PERFORM	-.080	.063	-.742
AGGRESSN	.879	.131	.011
HOSTILTY	.917	.178	-.078
AUTHORTN	.909	-.065	.062

FINAL STATISTICS

VARIABLE	COMMUNALITY
DEPRESSN	
ANXIETY	
STRESS	
CONFDNCE	
PERFORM	
AGGRESSN	
HOSTILTY	
AUTHORTN	

12. Consider the factor pattern matrix shown below. Calculate the total variance explained by each factor, and use this information to complete the table.

FACTOR MATRIX:

	FACTOR 1	FACTOR 2	FACTOR 3
PROGOVT	.036	.921	-.048
INCOME	.742	.121	.203
EDUCATN	.921	.095	-.161
RACE	.938	-.020	.053
UNEMPLOY	.176	.143	.878
HOMEOWNR	.232	-.215	.902
CONSERV	-.054	.953	-.032

FINAL STATISTICS

VARIABLE	COMMUNALITY	FACTOR	EIGENVALUE	PCT OF VAR	CUM PCT
PROGOVT	.852	1			
INCOME	.606	2			
EDUCATN	.883	3			
RACE	.883				
UNEMPLOY	.822				
HOMEOWNR	.914				
CONSERV	.912				

13. Consider the factor pattern matrix and the variable correlation matrix shown below:

FACTOR MATRIX:

	FACTOR 1	FACTOR 2
X1	.892	.325
X2	.511	.120
X3	.632	.436
X4	.349	.804

CORRELATION MATRIX:

	X1	X2	X3	X4
X1	1.000*	.537	.900	.558
X2	.537	1.000*	.335	.268
X3	.900	.335	1.000*	.610
X4	.558	.268	.610	1.000*

a. Assuming that the two factors are orthogonal, compute the estimated correlation coefficients for variables X1 to X4, based on the two-factor model:

ESTIMATED CORRELATIONS

	X1	X2	X3	X4
X1				
X2				
X3				
X4				

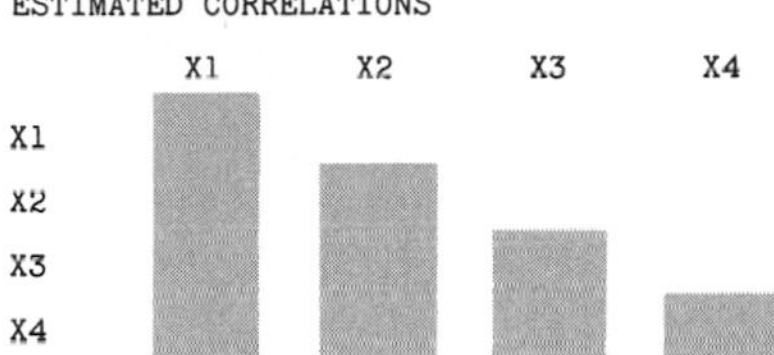

b. Compute the differences between the observed correlation coefficients and the estimated coefficients obtained in (a).

RESIDUALS

	X1	X2	X3	X4
X1	******			
X2		******		
X3			******	
X4				******

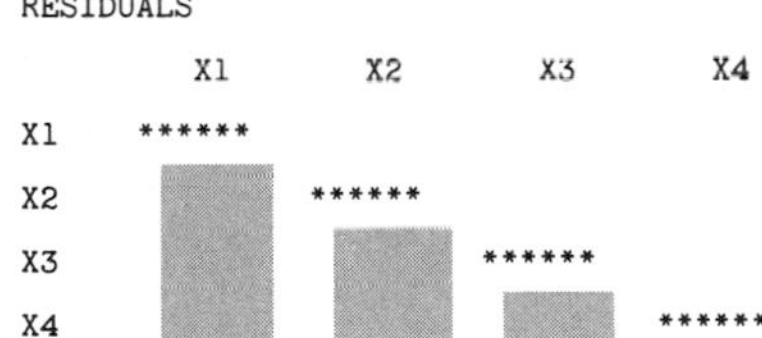

c. How many of the residuals calculated in (b) are greater than 0.05 in absolute value?

d. How well does the two-factor model fit the data?

5

Cluster Analysis

In this chapter:

Goals:

- To identify relatively homogeneous groups of cases based on selected attributes.
- To classify variables into homogeneous groups.

Examples:

- Group cities into homogeneous clusters so that comparable cities can be selected to test various marketing strategies.
- Cluster skulls excavated from various archeological digs into the civilizations from which they originated.
- Group television shows into homogeneous categories based on viewer characteristics. This can be used to identify segments for marketing.
- Identify subgroups of patients with similar disease profiles based on a variety of signs and symptoms.

How it's done:

Measures that compute the similarity or distance between all pairs of objects are computed. Based on these, similar objects are grouped into clusters using one of several criteria for cluster formation. The clustering algorithm terminates when all objects are merged into a single cluster.

Data considerations:

Variables must be measured on at least an ordinal scale so that distance or similarity criteria can be computed. Special similarity measures can be computed for binary variables. If the variables to be used for the cluster analysis are measured in different units, such as pounds, numbers of children, and income in dollars, some type of standardization of the variables prior to analysis should be considered.

General references:

Romesburg (1984)
Everitt (1977)
Anderberg (1973)

Contents

5.1 CLUSTER ANALYSIS
5.2 Basic Steps
5.3 How Alike are the Cases?
5.4 Forming Clusters
5.5 Agglomerative Clustering
5.6 Criteria for Combining Clusters
5.7 Back to the Example
5.8 Icicle Plots
5.9 The Agglomeration Schedule
5.10 The Dendrogram
5.11 Some Additional Displays and Modifications
5.12 More on Calculating Distances and Similarities
5.13 Methods for Combining Clusters
5.14 Clustering Variables
5.15 RUNNING PROCEDURE CLUSTER
5.16 Specifying the Variables
5.17 The METHOD Subcommand
5.18 The MEASURE Subcommand
5.19 The PRINT Subcommand
5.20 The PLOT Subcommand
5.21 The ID Subcommand
5.22 The MISSING Subcommand
5.23 The MATRIX Subcommand
5.24 The SAVE Subcommand
5.25 EXERCISES

5 Stacking Beers: Cluster Analysis

Despite the old adage that opposites attract, it appears instead that likes cluster together. Birds of a feather, yuppies, and many other animate and inanimate objects that share similar characteristics are found together. By studying such clusters, one can determine the charactersitics the objects share, as well as those in which they differ. In statistics, the search for relatively homogeneous groups of objects is called *cluster analysis*.

5.1 CLUSTER ANALYSIS

In biology, cluster analysis is used to classify animals and plants. This is called numerical taxonomy. In medicine, cluster analysis is used to identify diseases and their stages. For example, by examining patients who are diagnosed as depressed, one finds that there are several distinct subgroups of patients with different types of depression. In marketing, cluster analysis is used to identify persons with similar buying habits. By examining their characteristics, one may be able to target future marketing strategies more efficiently. See Romesburg (1984) for more examples of the use of cluster analysis.

Although both cluster analysis and discriminant analysis classify objects or cases into categories, discriminant analysis requires you to know group membership for the cases used to derive the classification rule. For example, if you are interested in distinguishing among several disease groups, cases with known diagnoses must be available. Then, based on cases whose group membership is known, discriminant analysis derives a rule for allocating undiagnosed patients. In cluster analysis, group membership for all cases is unknown. In fact, even the number of groups is often unknown. The goal of cluster analysis is to identify homogeneous groups or clusters.

In this chapter the fundamentals of cluster analysis are illustrated using a subset of data presented in a Consumer Reports (1983) survey of beer. Each of 20 beers is characterized in terms of cost per 12 ounces, alcohol content, sodium content, and the number of calories per 12 ounce serving. From these variables is it possible to identify several distinct subgroups of beer?

5.2 Basic Steps

As in other statistical procedures, a number of decisions must be made before one embarks on the actual analysis. Which variables will serve as the basis for cluster formation? How will the distance between cases be measured? What criteria will be used for combining cases into clusters?

Selecting the variables to include in an analysis is always crucial. If important variables are excluded, poor or misleading findings may result. For example, in a regression analysis of salary, if variables such as education and experience are not included, the results may be questionable. In cluster analysis, the initial choice of variables determines the characteristics that can be used to identify subgroups. If one is interested in clustering schools within a city and does not include variables like the number of students or the number of teachers, size is automatically excluded as a criterion for establishing clusters. By excluding all measures of taste or quality from the beer data, only physical characteristics and price will determine which beers are deemed similar.

5.3 How Alike are the Cases?

The concepts of distance and similarity are basic to many statistical techniques. Distance is a measure of how far apart two objects are, and similarity measures closeness. Distance measures are small and similarity measures are large for cases that are similar. In cluster analysis, these concepts are especially important, since cases are grouped on the basis of their "nearness." There are many different definitions of distance and similarity. Selection of a distance measure should be based both on the properties of the measure and on the algorithm for cluster formation. See Section 5.12 for further discussion of distance measures.

To see how a simple distance measure is computed, consider Table 5.3a, which shows the values of calories and cost for two of the beers. There is a 13-calorie and 5-cent difference between the two beers. This information can be combined into a single index or distance measure in many different ways. A commonly used index is the *squared Euclidean distance,* which is the sum of the squared differences over all of the variables. In this example, the squared Euclidean distance is 13^2+5^2, or 194.

Table 5.3a Values of calories and cost for two beers

	Calories	Cost
Budweiser	144	43
Lowenbrau	157	48

The squared Euclidean distance has the disadvantage that it depends on the units of measurement for the variables. For example, if the cost were given as pennies per ounce instead of per twelve ounces, the distance measure would change. Another disadvantage is that when variables are measured on different scales, as in this example, variables that are measured in larger numbers will contribute more to the distance than variables that are recorded in smaller numbers. For example, the 13-calorie difference contributes much more to the distance score than does the 5-cent difference in cost.

One means of circumventing this problem is to express all variables in standardized form. That is, all variables have a mean of 0 and a standard deviation of 1. This is not always the best strategy, however, since the variability of a particular measure can provide useful information (see Sneath & Sokal, 1973).

Table 5.3b shows the Z scores for calories and cost for Budweiser and Lowenbrau based on the means and standard deviations for all twenty beers. The squared Euclidean distance based on the standardized variables is $(0.38-0.81)^2+(-0.46-(-0.11))^2$, or 0.307. The differences in calories and cost are now weighted equally.

Table 5.3b *Z* scores for the calories and cost variables

	Calories	Cost
Budweiser	0.38	-0.46
Lowenbrau	0.81	-0.11

5.4 Forming Clusters

Just as there are many methods for calculating distances between objects, there are many methods for combining objects into clusters. A commonly used method for forming clusters is hierarchical cluster analysis, using one of two methods: agglomerative, or divisive. In *agglomerative* hierarchical clustering, clusters are formed by grouping cases into bigger and bigger clusters until all cases are members of a single cluster. *Divisive* hierarchical clustering starts out with all cases grouped into a single cluster and splits clusters until there are as many clusters as there are cases. For a discussion of nonhierarchical clustering methods, see Everitt (1980).

5.5 Agglomerative Clustering

Before discussing the rules for forming clusters, consider what happens during the steps of agglomerative hierarchical cluster analysis. At the first step all cases are considered separate clusters: there are as many clusters as there are cases. At the second step, two of the cases are combined into a single cluster. At the third step, either a third case is added to the cluster already containing two cases, or two additional cases are merged into a new cluster. At every step, either individual cases are added to clusters or already existing clusters are combined. Once a cluster is formed, it cannot be split; it can only be combined with other clusters. Thus, hierarchical clustering methods do not allow cases to separate from clusters to which they have been allocated. For example, if two beers are deemed members of the same cluster at the first step, they will always be members of the same cluster, although they may be combined with additional cases at a later step.

5.6 Criteria for Combining Clusters

There are many criteria for deciding which cases or clusters should be combined at each step. All of these criteria are based on a matrix of either distances or similarities between pairs of cases. One of the simplest methods is *single linkage*, sometimes called "nearest neighbor." The first two cases combined are those that have the smallest distance (or largest similarity) between them. The distance between the new cluster and individual cases is then computed as the minimum distance between an individual case and a case in the cluster. The distances between cases that have not been joined do not change. At every step, the distance between two clusters is the distance between their two closest points.

Another commonly used method is called *complete linkage*, or the "furthest neighbor" technique. In this method, the distance between two clusters is calculated as the distance between their two furthest points. Other methods for combining clusters available in SPSS^X are described in Section 5.12.

5.7 Back to the Example

Before considering other distance measures and methods of combining clusters, consider Figure 5.7a, which was produced by the SPSS[X] PROXIMITIES procedure. This figure contains the matrix of squared Euclidean distance coefficients for all possible pairs of the 20 beers, based on standardized calories, sodium, alcohol, and cost. The listing of the original and standardized values for these variables is shown in Figure 5.7b.

Figure 5.7a The squared Euclidean distance coefficient matrix

```
DATA LIST FREE /RATING * BEER (A21) ORIGIN AVAIL
    PRICE COST CALORIES SODIUM ALCOHOL CLASS LIGHT
FORMAT RATING ORIGIN AVAIL CLASS LIGHT (F1) PRICE COST (F4.2)
    CALORIES (F3) SODIUM (F2) ALCOHOL (F3.2)
PROXIMITIES COST CALORIES SODIUM ALCOHOL
  /STANDARDIZE = VAR Z/ MEASURE=SEUCLID/ID=BEER/PRINT PROX
BEGIN DATA
[data goes here]
END DATA
```

Squared Euclidean Dissimilarity Coefficient Matrix

Case	BUDWEISE	SCHLITZ	LOWENBRA	KRONENBO	HEINEKEN	OLD MILW	AUGSBERG	STROHS B
SCHLITZ	.4922							
LOWENBRA	.3749	.5297						
KRONENBO	7.0040	8.2298	4.8424					
HEINEKEN	6.1889	7.0897	4.4835	.8700				
OLD MILW	2.5848	1.6534	3.7263	17.0154	15.2734			
AUGSBERG	4.0720	1.8735	3.1573	12.1251	11.5371	3.1061		
STROHS B	3.3568	1.5561	3.6380	14.8000	12.0038	1.3526	2.0742	
MILLER L	3.0662	5.4473	4.9962	11.4721	9.5339	7.4577	13.3723	9.6850
BUDWEISE	3.9181	6.8702	5.8179	11.5391	10.0663	8.9551	15.7993	11.5019
COORS	.2474	.3160	.7568	8.4698	6.8353	1.8432	3.6498	1.9953
COORS LI	2.5940	4.1442	4.4322	12.1519	9.1534	5.4981	11.2604	6.4385
MICHELOB	1.1281	2.8432	1.7663	5.9995	4.9519	6.0530	9.0610	6.8673
BECKS	5.6782	5.3399	4.2859	4.2382	1.6427	11.5628	8.6397	7.0724
KIRIN	8.3245	10.1947	6.6075	.7483	.6064	19.5528	16.0117	16.9620
PABST EX	16.4081	19.7255	20.8463	33.3380	28.0650	17.6015	32.1339	20.5466
HAMMS	.5952	.6788	1.4051	10.0509	7.9746	1.6159	4.3782	1.8230
HEILEMAN	1.9394	.6307	2.1757	11.9216	9.5828	1.2688	1.7169	.3092
OLYMPIA	13.1887	17.6915	16.7104	23.2048	19.8574	19.0673	30.9530	22.3479
SCHLITZ	4.4010	7.4360	6.2635	10.8241	9.1372	10.4511	16.4825	12.7426

Case	MILLER L	BUDWEISE	COORS	COORS LI	MICHELOB	BECKS	KIRIN	PABST EX
BUDWEISE	.9349							
COORS	3.4745	4.5082						
COORS LI	.6999	1.5600	2.2375					
MICHELOB	1.6931	1.3437	1.6100	1.6536				
BECKS	10.2578	10.9762	5.1046	7.8646	5.4275			
KIRIN	10.2201	10.3631	9.6179	10.9556	5.9694	4.1024		
PABST EX	8.6771	6.9127	15.2083	7.1851	12.2231	24.6793	29.7992	
HAMMS	3.3828	4.2251	.1147	1.8315	1.7851	5.6395	10.9812	13.1806
HEILEMAN	7.3607	9.4595	1.0094	4.9491	5.0762	5.9553	13.7962	20.0105
OLYMPIA	4.6046	3.0565	13.4011	5.3477	7.9175	20.5149	19.3851	2.8209
SCHLITZ	.3069	.7793	5.1340	1.5271	1.9902	10.8954	9.0403	9.0418

Case	HAMMS	HEILEMAN	OLYMPIA
HEILEMAN	1.0802		
OLYMPIA	12.3170	20.1156	
SCHLITZ	5.1327	10.0114	3.6382

Figure 5.7b Original and standardized values for the 20 beers from procedure LIST

```
DESCRIPTIVES CALORIES SODIUM ALCOHOL COST
  /SAVE 1
FORMATS ZCALORIE TO ZCOST (F4.2)
LIST VARIABLES=ID BEER CALORIES SODIUM ALCOHOL COST ZCALORIE TO ZCOST
```

ID	BEER	CALORIES	SODIUM	ALCOHOL	COST	ZCALORIE	ZSODIUM	ZALCOHOL	ZCOST
1	BUDWEISER	144	15	4.7	.43	.38	.01	.34	-.46
2	SCHLITZ	151	19	4.9	.43	.61	.62	.61	-.46
3	LOWENBRAU	157	15	4.9	.48	.81	.01	.61	-.11
4	KRONENBOURG	170	7	5.2	.73	1.24	-1.2	1.00	1.62
5	HEINEKEN	152	11	5.0	.77	.65	-.60	.74	1.90
6	OLD MILWAUKEE	145	23	4.6	.28	.42	1.22	.21	-1.5
7	AUGSBERGER	175	24	5.5	.40	1.41	1.38	1.40	-.67
8	STROHS BOHEMIAN STYLE	149	27	4.7	.42	.55	1.83	.34	-.53
9	MILLER LITE	99	10	4.3	.43	-1.1	-.75	-.18	-.46
10	BUDWEISER LIGHT	113	8	3.7	.44	-.64	-1.1	-.97	-.39
11	COORS	140	18	4.6	.44	.25	.46	.21	-.39
12	COORS LIGHT	102	15	4.1	.46	-1.0	.01	-.45	-.25
13	MICHELOB LIGHT	135	11	4.2	.50	.09	-.60	-.32	.02
14	BECKS	150	19	4.7	.76	.58	.62	.34	1.83
15	KIRIN	149	6	5.0	.79	.55	-1.4	.74	2.04
16	PABST EXTRA LIGHT	68	15	2.3	.38	-2.1	.01	-2.8	-.81
17	HAMMS	136	19	4.4	.43	.12	.62	.05	-.46
18	HEILEMANS OLD STYLE	144	24	4.9	.43	.38	1.38	.61	-.46
19	OLYMPIA GOLD LIGHT	72	6	2.9	.46	-2.0	-1.4	-2.0	-.25
20	SCHLITZ LIGHT	97	7	4.2	.47	-1.2	-1.2	-.82	-.18

NUMBER OF CASES READ = 20 NUMBER OF CASES LISTED = 20

The first entry in Figure 5.7a is the distance between Case 1 and Case 2, Budweiser and Schlitz. This can be calculated from the standardized values in Figure 5.7b as

$$D^2 = (0.38-0.61)^2+(0.01-0.62)^2 + (0.34-0.61)^2+(-0.46-(-0.46))^2 = 0.49$$

Equation 5.7

Since the distance between pairs of cases is symmetric (that is, the distance between Case 3 and Case 4 is the same as the distance between Case 4 and Case 3), only the lower half of the distance matrix is displayed.

5.8 Icicle Plots

Once the distance matrix has been calculated, the actual formation of clusters can commence. Figure 5.8a summarizes a cluster analysis that uses the complete linkage method. This type of figure is sometimes called a vertical icicle plot because it resembles a row of icicles hanging from eaves.

The columns of Figure 5.8a correspond to the objects being clustered. They are identified both by a sequential number ranging from 1 to the number of cases and, when possible, by the labels of the objects. Thus, the first column corresponds to beer number 19, Olympia Gold Light, while the last column corresponds to the first beer in the file, Budweiser. In order to follow the sequence of steps in the cluster analysis, the figure is read from bottom to top.

As previously described, all cases are considered initially as individual clusters. Since there are twenty beers in this example, there are 20 clusters. At the first step the two "closest" cases are combined into a single cluster, resulting in 19 clusters. The bottom line of Figure 5.8a shows these 19 clusters. Each case is represented by a single X separated by blanks. The two cases that have been merged into a single cluster, Coors and Hamms, do not have blanks separating them. Instead they are represented by consecutive *X*'s. The row labeled 18 in Figure 5.8a corresponds to the solution at the next step, when 18 clusters are present. At this step Miller Lite and Schlitz Light are merged into a single cluster.

[1]With releases before 3.0, replace the DESCRIPTIVES command with the following:

```
CONDESCRIPTIVE CALORIES SODIUM ALCOHOL COST
OPTION 3
```

Figure 5.8a Vertical icicle plot for the 20 beers

```
DATA LIST FREE /RATING * BEER (A21) ORIGIN AVAIL
     PRICE COST CALORIES SODIUM ALCOHOL CLASS LIGHT
FORMAT RATING ORIGIN AVAIL CLASS LIGHT (F1) PRICE COST (F4.2)
     CALORIES (F3) SODIUM (F2) ALCOHOL (F3.2)
PROXIMITIES COST CALORIES SODIUM ALCOHOL
   /STANDARDIZE = VAR Z/ MEASURE=SEUCLID/ID=BEER/PRINT PROX
   /MATRIX=OUT (*)
BEGIN DATA
[data goes here]
END DATA

NUMERIC BEER1 TO BEER20
CLUSTER /MATRIX=IN (*)
      /ID=BEER
      /METHOD=COMPLETE
      /PLOT=VICICLE²
```

```
Vertical Icicle Plot using Complete Linkage

   (Down) Number of Clusters  (Across) Case Label and number

    O  P  M  C  B  S  M  B  K  H  K  A  H  S  O  H  C  S  L  B
    L  A  I  O  U  C  I  E  I  E  R  U  E  T  L  A  O  C  O  U
    Y  B  C  O  D  H  L  C  R  I  O  G  I  R  D  M  O  H  W  D
    M  S  H  R  W  L  L  K  I  N  N  S  L  O     M  R  L  E  W
    P  T  E  S  E  I  E  S  N  E  E  B  E  H  M  S  S  I  N  E
    I     L     I  T  R        K  N  E  M  S  I        T  B  I
    A  E  O  L  S  Z           E  B  R  A     L        Z  R  S
       X  B  I  E     L        N  O  G  N  B  W           A  E
    G  T     G  R  L  I           U  E  S  O  A           U  R
    O  R  L  H     I  T           R  R     H  U
    L  A  I  T  L  G  E           G     O  E  K
    D     G     I  H                    L  M  E
       L  H     G  T                    D  I  E
    L  I  T     H                          A
    I  G        T                       S  N
    G  H                                T
    H  T                                Y  S
    T                                   L  T
                                        E  Y
                                           L

    1  1  1  1  1  2     1  1           1        1  1
    9  6  3  2  0  0  9  4  5  5  4  7  8  8  6  7  1  2  3  1
 1 +XXXXXXXXXXXXXXXXXXXXXXXXXXXXXXXXXXXXXXXXXXXXXXXXXXXXXXXXXX
 2 +XXXX  XXXXXXXXXXXXXXXXXXXXXXXXXXXXXXXXXXXXXXXXXXXXXXXXXXXX
 3 +XXXX  XXXXXXXXXXXXXXXXXXXXXXXXX  XXXXXXXXXXXXXXXXXXXXXXXXX
 4 +XXXX  XXXXXXXXXXXXX  XXXXXXXXXX  XXXXXXXXXXXXXXXXXXXXXXXXX
 5 +XXXX  XXXXXXXXXXXXX  XXXXXXXXXX  XXXXXXXXXX  XXXXXXXXXXXXX
 6 +XXXX  XXXXXXXXXXXXX  X  XXXXXXX  XXXXXXXXXX  XXXXXXXXXXXXX
 7 +XXXX  XXXXXXXXXXXXX  X  XXXXXXX  X  XXXXXXX  XXXXXXXXXXXXX
 8 +X  X  XXXXXXXXXXXXX  X  XXXXXXX  X  XXXXXXX  XXXXXXXXXXXXX
 9 +X  X  X  XXXXXXXXXX  X  XXXXXXX  X  XXXXXXX  XXXXXXXXXXXXX
10 +X  X  X  X  XXXXXXX  X  XXXXXXX  X  XXXXXXX  XXXXXXXXXXXXX
11 +X  X  X  X  XXXXXXX  X  XXXXXXX  X  XXXXXXX  XXXX  XXXXXXX
12 +X  X  X  X  XXXXXXX  X  XXXXXXX  X  XXXX  X  XXXX  XXXXXXX
13 +X  X  X  X  X  XXXX  X  XXXXXXX  X  XXXX  X  XXXX  XXXXXXX
14 +X  X  X  X  X  XXXX  X  XXXX  X  X  XXXX  X  XXXX  XXXXXXX
15 +X  X  X  X  X  XXXX  X  X  X  X  X  XXXX  X  XXXX  XXXXXXX
16 +X  X  X  X  X  XXXX  X  X  X  X  X  XXXX  X  XXXX  X  XXXX
17 +X  X  X  X  X  XXXX  X  X  X  X  X  XXXX  X  XXXX  X  X  X
18 +X  X  X  X  X  XXXX  X  X  X  X  X  X  X  X  XXXX  X  X  X
19 +X  X  X  X  X  X  X  X  X  X  X  X  X  X  X  XXXX  X  X  X
```

[2]With releases before 3.0, replace all of the commands with the following commands:

```
DATA LIST FREE /RATING * BEER (A21) ORIGIN AVAIL
     PRICE COST CALORIES SODIUM ALCOHOL CLASS LIGHT
FORMAT RATING ORIGIN AVAIL CLASS LIGHT (F1) PRICE COST (F4.2)
     CALORIES (F3) SODIUM (F2) ALCOHOL (F3.2)

FILE HANDLE PROX/ NAME = 'PROX MATRIX'
PROCEDURE OUTPUT OUTFILE=PROX
PROXIMITIES COST CALORIES SODIUM ALCOHOL
   /STANDARDIZE = VAR Z/ MEASURE=SEUCLID/ID=BEER/PRINT PROX
   /WRITE
BEGIN DATA
[data goes here]
END DATA

NUMERIC BEER1 TO BEER20
INPUT MATRIX  FILE = PROX/FREE
CLUSTER BEER1 TO BEER20/READ
      /ID=BEER
      /METHOD=COMPLETE
      /PLOT=VICICLE
```

As previously described, all cases are considered initially as individual clusters. Since there are twenty beers in this example, there are 20 clusters. At the first step the two "closest" cases are combined into a single cluster, resulting in 19 clusters. The bottom line of Figure 5.8a shows these 19 clusters. Each case is represented by a single X separated by blanks. The two cases that have been merged into a single cluster, Coors and Hamms, do not have blanks separating them. Instead they are represented by consecutive *X*'s. The row labeled 18 in Figure 5.8a corresponds to the solution at the next step, when 18 clusters are present. At this step Miller Lite and Schlitz Light are merged into a single cluster. Thus, at this point there are 18 clusters, 16 consisting of individual beers and 2 consisting of pairs of beers. At each subsequent step an additional cluster is formed by joining either a case to an already existing multicase cluster, two separate cases into a single cluster, or two multicase clusters.

For example, the row labeled 5 in Figure 5.8a corresponds to a solution that has five clusters. Beers 19 and 16, the very light beers, form one cluster; beers 13, 12, 10, 20, and 9 form the next. These beers, Michelob Light, Coors Light, Budweiser Light, Schlitz Light, and Miller Light, are all light beers, but not as light as the two in the first cluster. The third cluster consists of Becks, Kirin, Heineken, and Kronenbourg. These are all imported beers. Although no variable in this example explicitly indicates whether beers are domestic or imported, the cost variable (see Figure 5.7b) causes the imported beers to cluster together since they are quite a bit more expensive than the domestic ones. A fourth cluster consists of Augsberger, Heilemans Old Style, Strohs Bohemian Style, and Old Milwaukee. Inspection of Figure 5.8b shows that all of these beers are distinguished by high sodium content. The last cluster consists of five beers, Hamms, Coors, Schlitz, Lowenbrau, and Budweiser. These beers share the distinction of being average. That is, they are neither particulary high nor particularly low on the variables measured. Note from Figure 5.8b that, based on the standard deviations, beers in the same cluster, when compared to all beers, are more homogeneous on the variables measured.

Figure 5.8b Cluster characteristics

```
CLUSTER ZCALORIE ZSODIUM ZALCOHOL ZCOST
   /ID=BEER
   /SAVE CLUSTER(5)
   /METHOD=COMPLETE(CLUSMEM)
TABLES OBSERVATION= COST CALORIES ALCOHOL SODIUM
   /FTOTAL=TOTAL
   /FORMAT=CWIDTH(10,9)
   /TABLE= CLUSMEM5+TOTAL BY CALORIES +COST+ALCOHOL+SODIUM
   /STATISTICS=MEAN STDDEV
```

	CALORIES		COST		ALCOHOL		SODIUM	
	Mean	Standard Deviation	Mean	Standard Deviation	Mean	Standard Deviation	Mean	Standard Deviation
CLUSMEM5								
1	146	8	.44	.02	4.70	.21	17	2
2	155	10	.76	.03	4.97	.21	11	6
3	153	15	.38	.07	4.92	.40	25	2
4	109	16	.46	.03	4.10	.23	10	3
5	70	3	.42	.06	2.60	.42	11	6
TOTAL	132	30	.50	.14	4.44	.76	15	7

Cluster formation continues in Figure 5.8a until all cases are merged into a single cluster, as shown in the first row. Thus, all steps of the cluster analysis are displayed in Figure 5.8a. If we were clustering people instead of beers, the last row would be individual persons, higher up they would perhaps merge into families, these into neighborhoods, and so forth. Often there is not one single, meaningful cluster solution, but many, depending on what is of interest.

5.9 The Agglomeration Schedule

The results of the cluster analysis are summarized in the *agglomeration schedule* in Figure 5.9, which contains the number of cases or clusters being combined at each stage. The first line is Stage 1, the 19-cluster solution. Beers 11 and 17 are combined at this stage, as shown in the columns labeled "Clusters Combined." The squared Euclidean distance between these two beers is displayed in the column labeled "Coefficient." Since this is the first step, this coefficient is identical to the distance measure in Figure 5.7a for Cases 11 and 17. The last column indicates at which stage another case or cluster is combined with this one. For example, at the tenth stage, Case 1 is merged with Cases 11 and 17 into a single cluster. The column entitled "Stage Cluster 1st Appears" indicates at which stage a cluster is first formed. For example, the entry of 4 at Stage 5 indicates that Case 1 was first involved in a merge in the previous step (Stage 4). From the line for Stage 4, you can see that, at this point, Case 1 was involved in a merge with Case 3. From the last column of Stage 5 we see that the new cluster (Cases 1, 2, and 3) is next involved in a merge at Stage 10, where the cases combine with Cases 11 and 17.

Figure 5.9 Agglomeration schedule using complete linkage

```
CLUSTER /MATRIX=IN (*)³
 /ID=BEER
 /PRINT=SCHEDULE
 /METHOD=COMPLETE
```

Agglomeration Schedule using Complete Linkage

Stage	Clusters Combined Cluster 1	Cluster 2	Coefficient	Stage Cluster 1st Appears Cluster 1	Cluster 2	Next Stage
1	11	17	.114700	0	0	10
2	9	20	.306900	0	0	8
3	8	18	.309230	0	0	9
4	1	3	.374860	0	0	5
5	1	2	.529700	4	0	10
6	5	15	.606380	0	0	7
7	4	5	.870020	0	6	15
8	9	10	.934910	2	0	11
9	6	8	1.352619	0	3	14
10	1	11	1.405149	5	1	16
11	9	12	1.559990	8	0	12
12	9	13	1.990199	11	0	17
13	16	19	2.820900	0	0	19
14	6	7	3.106110	9	0	16
15	4	14	4.238159	7	0	17
16	1	6	4.378200	10	14	18
17	4	9	12.151939	15	12	18
18	1	4	19.552826	16	17	19
19	1	16	33.338028	18	13	0

The information in Figure 5.9 that is not available in the icicle plot is the value of the distance between the two most dissimilar points of the clusters being combined at each stage. By examining these values, you can get an idea of how unlike the clusters being combined are. Small coefficients indicate that fairly homogeneous clusters are being merged. Large coefficients indicate that clusters containing quite dissimilar members are being combined. The actual value depends on the clustering method and the distance measure used.

These coefficients can also be used for guidance in deciding how many clusters are needed to represent the data. One usually wishes to stop agglomeration as soon as the increase between two adjacent steps becomes large. For example, in Figure 5.9 there is a fairly large increase in the value of the distance measure from a four-cluster to a three-cluster solution (Stages 16 and 17).

---

[3]With releases before 3.0, always replace the line

```
CLUSTER /MATRIX=IN (*)
```

with the following line:

```
CLUSTER BEER1 TO BEER20/READ
```

5.10 The Dendrogram

Another way of visually representing the steps in a hierarchical clustering solution is with a display called a *dendrogram*. The dendrogram shows the clusters being combined and the values of the coefficients at each step. The dendrogram produced by the SPSS^X CLUSTER procedure does not plot actual distances but rescales them to numbers between 0 and 25. Thus, the ratio of the distances between steps is preserved. The scale displayed at the top of the figure does not correspond to actual distance values.

To understand how a dendrogram is constructed, consider a simple four-beer example. Figure 5.10a contains the icicle plot for the clustering of Kirin, Becks, Old Milwaukee, and Budweiser. From the icicle plot, you can see that at the first step Budweiser and Old Milwaukee are combined, at the second step Becks and Kirin are merged, and all four beers are merged into a single cluster at the last step.

Figure 5.10a Vertical icicle plot for the four-beer example

```
CLUSTER /MATRIX=IN (*)
 /ID=BEER
 /METHOD=COMPLETE
 /PLOT=VICICLE
```

```
Vertical Icicle Plot using Complete Linkage

   (Down) Number of Clusters  (Across) Case Label and number

     K  B  O  B
     I  E  L  U
     R  C  D  D
     I  K     W
     N  S  M  E
           I  I
           L  S
           W  E
           A  R
           U
           K
           E
           E

     4  3  2  1
   1 +XXXXXXXXXX
   2 +XXXX  XXXX
   3 +X  X  XXXX
```

The distances at which the beers are combined are shown in the agglomeration schedule in Figure 5.10b. From this schedule, we see that the distance between Budweiser and Old Milwaukee is 2.017 when they are combined. Similarly when Becks and Kirin are combined, their distance is 6.323. Since the method of complete linkage is used, the distance coefficient displayed for the last stage is the largest distance between a member of the Budweiser-Milwaukee cluster and a member of the Becks-Kirin cluster. This distance is 16.789.

Figure 5.10b Agglomeration schedule for the four-beer example

```
CLUSTER /MATRIX=IN (*)
 /ID=BEER
 /PRINT=SCHEDULE
 /METHOD=COMPLETE
```

Agglomeration Schedule using Complete Linkage

Stage	Clusters Combined Cluster 1	Cluster 2	Coefficient	Stage Cluster 1st Appears Cluster 1	Cluster 2	Next Stage
1	1	2	2.017019	0	0	3
2	3	4	6.323440	0	0	3
3	1	3	16.789215	1	2	0

The information in Figure 5.10b is displayed in the dendrogram in Figure 5.10c, which is read from left to right. Vertical lines denote joined clusters. The position of the line on the scale indicates the distance at which clusters were joined. Since the distances are rescaled to fall in the range of 1 to 25, the largest distance, 16.8, corresponds to the value of 25. The smallest distance, 2.017, corresponds to the value 1. Thus, the second distance (6.32) corresponds to a value of about 8. Note that the ratio of the rescaled distances is, after the first, the same as the ratios of the original distances.

The first two clusters that are joined are Budweiser and Old Milwaukee. They are connected by a line that is 1 unit from the origin since this is the rescaled distance between these points. When Becks and Kirin are joined, the line that connects them is 8 units from the origin. Similarly, when these two clusters are merged into a single cluster, the line that connects them is 25 units from the origin. Thus, the dendrogram indicates not only which clusters are joined but also the distance at which they are joined.

Figure 5.10c Dendrogram for the four-beer example

```
CLUSTER /MATRIX=IN (*)
 /ID=BEER
 /METHOD=COMPLETE
 /PLOT=DENDROGRAM
```

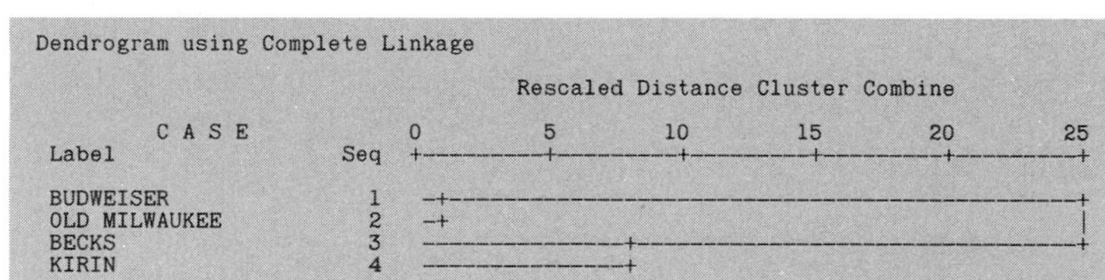

```
Dendrogram using Complete Linkage

                                Rescaled Distance Cluster Combine

         C A S E          0         5        10        15        20        25
 Label               Seq  +---------+---------+---------+---------+---------+

 BUDWEISER             1   -+-----------------------------------------------+
 OLD MILWAUKEE         2   -+                                               |
 BECKS                 3   ---------------+---------------------------------+
 KIRIN                 4   ---------------+
```

Figure 5.10d contains the dendrogram for the complete 20-beer example. Since many of the distances at the beginning stages are similar in magnitude, one cannot tell the sequence in which some of the early clusters are formed. However, at the last three stages the distances at which clusters are being combined are fairly large. Looking at the dendrogram, it appears that the five-cluster solution (very light beers, light beers, imported beers, high-sodium beers, and "average" beers) may be appropriate since it is easily interpretable and occurs before the distances at which clusters are combined become too large.

Figure 5.10d Dendrogram using complete linkage for the 20 beers

```
CLUSTER /MATRIX IN (*)
 /ID=BEER
 /METHOD=COMPLETE
 /PLOT-DENDROGRAM
```

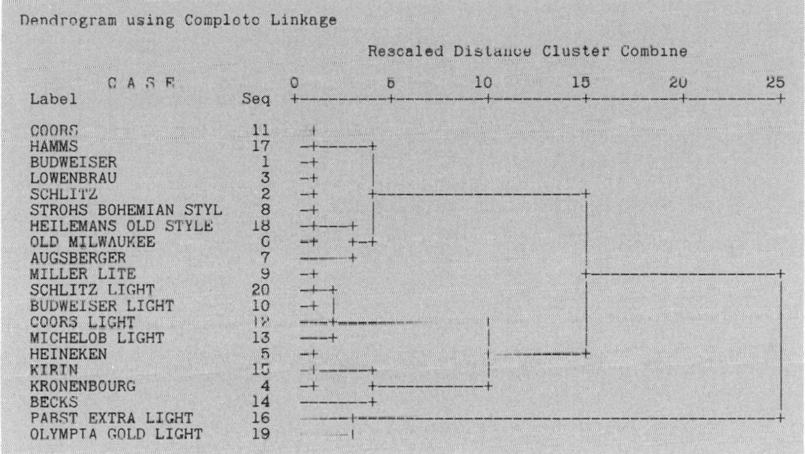

5.11 Some Additional Displays and Modifications

The agglomeration schedule, the icicle plot, and the dendrogram illustrate the results produced by a hierarchical clustering solution. Several variations of these plots may also be useful. For example, when there are many cases, the initial steps of the cluster analysis may not be of particular interest. You might want to display solutions for only certain numbers of clusters. Or you might want to see the results at every *k*th step. Figure 5.11a contains the icicle plot of results at every fifth step.

Figure 5.11a Icicle plot with results at every fifth step

```
CLUSTER /MATRIX IN (*)
 /ID=BEER
 /METHOD=COMPLETE
 /PLOT=VICICLE(1,19,5)
```

```
Vertical Icicle Plot using Complete Linkage

  (Down) Number of Clusters  (Across) Case Label and number

    O  P  M  C  B  S  M  B  K  H  K  A  H  S  O  H  C  S  L  B
    L  A  I  O  U  C  I  E  I  E  R  U  E  T  L  A  O  C  O  U
    Y  B  C  O  D  H  L  C  R  I  O  G  I  R  D  M  O  H  W  D
    M  S  H  R  W  L  L  K  I  N  N  S  L  O     M  R  L  E  W
    P  T  E  S  E  I  E  S  N  E  E  B  E  H  M  S  S  I  N  E
    I     L     I  T  R        K  N  E  M  S  I        T  B  I
    A  E  O  L  S  Z           E  B  R  A     L        Z  R  S
       X  B  I  E     L        N  O  G  N  B  W           A  E
    G  T     G  R  L  I           U  E  S  O  A           U  R
    O  R  L  H     I  T           R  R     H  U
    L  A  I  T  L  G  E           G     O  E  K
    D     G     I  H                    L  M  E
       L  H     G  T                    D  I  E
    L  I  T     H                          A
    I  G        T                       S  N
    G  H                                T
    H  T                                Y  S
    T                                   L  T
                                        E  Y
                                           L

    1  1  1  1  1  2     1  1           1        1  1
    9  6  3  2  0  0  9  4  5  5  4  7  8  8  6  7  1  2  3  1
 1 +XXXXXXXXXXXXXXXXXXXXXXXXXXXXXXXXXXXXXXXXXXXXXXXXXXXXXXXXXX
 6 +XXXX  XXXXXXXXXXXXX  X  XXXXXXX  XXXXXXXXXX  XXXXXXXXXXXXX
11 +X  X  X  X  XXXXXXX  X  XXXXXXX  X  XXXXXXX  XXXX  XXXXXXX
16 +X  X  X  X  X  XXXX  X  X  X  X  X  XXXX  X  XXXX  X  XXXX
```

When there are many cases, all of them may not fit across the top of a single page. In this situation it may be useful to turn the icicle plot on its side. This is called a horizontal icicle plot. Figure 5.11b contains the horizontal icicle plot corresponding to Figure 5.8a.

Figure 5.11b Horizontal icicle plot

```
CLUSTER /MATRIX=IN (*)
 /ID=BEER
 /METHOD=COMPLETE
 /PLOT=HICICLE
```

```
Horizontal Icicle Plot Using Complete Linkage

                             Number of Clusters

                                      1111111111
          C A S E            1234567890123456789
 Label                   Seq +++++++++++++++++++

 OLYMPIA GOLD LIGHT       19 XXXXXXXXXXXXXXXXXXX
                             XXXXXXX
                             XXXXXXX
 PABST EXTRA LIGHT        16 XXXXXXXXXXXXXXXXXXX
                             X
                             X
 MICHELOB LIGHT           13 XXXXXXXXXXXXXXXXXXX
                             XXXXXXXX
                             XXXXXXXX
 COORS LIGHT              12 XXXXXXXXXXXXXXXXXXX
                             XXXXXXXXX
                             XXXXXXXXX
 BUDWEISER LIGHT          10 XXXXXXXXXXXXXXXXXXX
                             XXXXXXXXXXXX
                             XXXXXXXXXXXX
 SCHLITZ LIGHT            20 XXXXXXXXXXXXXXXXXXX
                             XXXXXXXXXXXXXXXXXX
                             XXXXXXXXXXXXXXXXXX
 MILLER LITE               9 XXXXXXXXXXXXXXXXXXX
                             XXX
                             XXX
 BECKS                    14 XXXXXXXXXXXXXXXXXXX
                             XXXXX
                             XXXXX
 KIRIN                    15 XXXXXXXXXXXXXXXXXXX
                             XXXXXXXXXXXXXX
                             XXXXXXXXXXXXXX
 HEINEKEN                  5 XXXXXXXXXXXXXXXXXXX
                             XXXXXXXXXXXXX
                             XXXXXXXXXXXXX
 KRONENBOURG               4 XXXXXXXXXXXXXXXXXXX
                             XX
                             XX
 AUGSBERGER                7 XXXXXXXXXXXXXXXXXXX
                             XXXXXX
                             XXXXXX
 HEILEMANS OLD STYLE      18 XXXXXXXXXXXXXXXXXXX
                             XXXXXXXXXXXXXXXXX
                             XXXXXXXXXXXXXXXXX
 STROHS BOHEMIAN STYL      8 XXXXXXXXXXXXXXXXXXX
                             XXXXXXXXXXX
                             XXXXXXXXXXX
 OLD MILWAUKEE             6 XXXXXXXXXXXXXXXXXXX
                             XXXX
                             XXXX
 HAMMS                    17 XXXXXXXXXXXXXXXXXXX
                             XXXXXXXXXXXXXXXXXXX
                             XXXXXXXXXXXXXXXXXXX
 COORS                    11 XXXXXXXXXXXXXXXXXXX
                             XXXXXXXXXX
                             XXXXXXXXXX
 SCHLITZ                   2 XXXXXXXXXXXXXXXXXXX
                             XXXXXXXXXXXXXXX
                             XXXXXXXXXXXXXXX
 LOWENBRAU                 3 XXXXXXXXXXXXXXXXXXX
                             XXXXXXXXXXXXXXXX
                             XXXXXXXXXXXXXXXX
 BUDWEISER                 1 XXXXXXXXXXXXXXXXXXX
```

Although the composition of clusters at any stage can be discerned from the icicle plots, it is often helpful to display the information in tabular form. Figure 5.11c contains the cluster memberships for the cases at different stages of the solution. From Figure 5.11c, you can easily tell which clusters cases belong to in the two- to five-cluster solutions.

Figure 5.11c Cluster membership at different stages

```
CLUSTER /MATRIX=IN (*)
 /ID=BEER
 /PRINT=CLUSTER(2,5)
 /METHOD=COMPLETE
```

Cluster Membership of Cases using Complete Linkage

		Number of Clusters			
Label	Case	5	4	3	2
BUDWEISER	1	1	1	1	1
SCHLITZ	2	1	1	1	1
LOWENBRAU	3	1	1	1	1
KRONENBOURG	4	2	2	2	1
HEINEKEN	5	2	2	2	1
OLD MILWAUKEE	6	3	1	1	1
AUGSBERGER	7	3	1	1	1
STROHS BOHEMIAN STYL	8	3	1	1	1
MILLER LITE	9	4	3	2	1
BUDWEISER LIGHT	10	4	3	2	1
COORS	11	1	1	1	1
COORS LIGHT	12	4	3	2	1
MICHELOB LIGHT	13	4	3	2	1
BECKS	14	2	2	2	1
KIRIN	15	2	2	2	1
PABST EXTRA LIGHT	16	5	4	3	2
HAMMS	17	1	1	1	1
HEILEMANS OLD STYLE	18	3	1	1	1
OLYMPIA GOLD LIGHT	19	5	4	3	2
SCHLITZ LIGHT	20	4	3	2	1

5.12 More on Calculating Distances and Similarities

There are many methods for estimating the distance or similarity between two cases. But even before these measures are computed, you must decide whether the variables need to be rescaled. When the variables have different scales, such as cents and calories, and they are not standardized, any distance measure will reflect primarily the contributions of variables measured in the large units. For example, the beer data variables were standardized prior to cluster analysis to have a mean of 0 and a standard deviation of 1. Besides standardization to Z-scores, variables can be standardized by dividing by just the standard deviation, the range, the mean, or the maximum. See Romesburg (1984) or Anderberg (1973) for further discussion.

Based on the transformed data it is possible to calculate many different types of distance and similarity measures. Different distance and similarity measures weight data characteristics differently. The choice among the measures should be based on which differences or similarities in the data are important for a particular application. For example, if one is clustering animal bones, what may matter is not the actual differences in bone size but relationships among the dimensions, since we know that even animals of the same species differ in size. Bones with the same relationship between length and diameter should be judged as similar, regardless of their absolute magnitudes. See Romesburg (1984) for further discussion.

The most commonly used distance measure, the squared Euclidean distance, has been discussed previously. Sometimes its square root, the Euclidean distance, is also used. A distance measure that is based on the absolute values of differences is the *city-block* or *Manhattan* distance. For two cases it is just the sum of the absolute differences of the values for all variables. Since the differences are not squared, large differences are not weighted as heavily as in the squared Euclidean distances. The *Chebychev* distance defines the distance between two cases as the maximum absolute difference in the values over all variables. Thus, it ignores much of the available information.

When variables are binary, special distance and similarity measures are required. Many are based on the familiar measures of association for contingency tables. See Appendix B for further description of the numerous measures computed by the SPSS^X PROXIMITIES procedure.

5.13 Methods for Combining Clusters

Many methods can be used to decide which cases or clusters should be combined at each step. In general, clustering methods fall into three groups: linkage methods, error sums of squares or variance methods, and centroid methods. All are based on either a matrix of distances or a matrix of similarities between pairs of cases. The methods differ in how they estimate distances between clusters at successive steps. Since the merging of clusters at each step depends on the distance measure, different distance measures can result in different cluster solutions for the same clustering method. See Milligan (1980) for comparisons of the performance of some of the different clustering methods.

One of the simplest methods for joining clusters is *single linkage,* sometimes called "nearest neighbor." The first two cases combined are those with the smallest distance, or greatest similarity, between them. The distance between the new cluster and individual cases is then computed as the minimum distance between an individual case and a case in the cluster. The distances between cases that have not been joined do not change. At every step the distance between two clusters is taken to be the distance between their two closest points.

Another commonly used method is called *complete linkage,* or the "furthest neighbor" technique. In this method the distance between two clusters is calculated as the distance between their two furthest points.

The *average linkage between groups method,* often called UPGMA (unweighted pair-group method using arithmetic averages), defines the distance between two clusters as the average of the distances between all pairs of cases in which one member of the pair is from each of the clusters. For example, if Cases 1 and 2 form cluster A and Cases 3, 4, and 5 form cluster B, the distance between clusters A and B is taken to be the average of the distances between the following pairs of cases: (1,3) (1,4) (1,5) (2,3) (2,4) (2,5). This differs from the linkage methods in that it uses information about all pairs of distances, not just the nearest or the furthest. For this reason it is usually preferred to the single and complete linkage methods for cluster analysis.

The UPGMA method considers only distances between pairs of cases in different clusters. A variant of it, *the average linkage within groups,* combines clusters so that the average distance between all cases in the resulting cluster is as small as possible. Thus, the distance between two clusters is taken to be the average of the distances between all possible pairs of cases in the resulting cluster.

Another frequently used method for cluster formation is *Ward's method.* For each cluster the means for all variables are calculated. Then for each case the squared Euclidean distance to the cluster means is calculated. These distances are summed for all of the cases. At each step, the two clusters that merge are those that result in the smallest increase in the overall sum of the squared within-cluster distances.

The *centroid method* calculates the distance between two clusters as the distance between their means for all of the variables. One disadvantage of the centroid method is that the distance at which clusters are combined can actually decrease from one step to the next. Since clusters merged at later stages are more dissimilar than those merged at early stages, this is an undesirable property.

In the centroid method, the centroid of a merged cluster is a weighted combination of the centroids of the two individual clusters, where the weights are proportional to the sizes of the clusters. In the *median method,* the two clusters being combined are weighted equally in the computation of the centroid, regardless of the number of cases in each. This allows small groups to have equal effect on the characterization of larger clusters into which they are merged. Squared Euclidean distances should be used with both centroid and median methods.

Some of the above methods, such as single and complete linkage and the average distances between and within clusters, can be used with similarity or distance measures. Other methods require particular types of distance measures. In particular, the median, centroid, and Ward's methods should use squared Euclidean distances. When similarity measures are used, the criteria for combining is reversed. That is, clusters with large similarity-based measures are merged.

5.14 Clustering Variables

In the previous example, the units used for cluster analysis were individual cases (the different brands of beer). Cluster analysis can also be used to find homogeneous groups of variables. For example, consider the 14 community variables described in Chapter 4. We could use cluster analysis to group the 88 counties included in the study and then examine the resulting clusters to establish the characteristics they share. Another approach is to cluster the 14 variables used to describe the communities. In this case, the unit used for analysis is the variable. The distance or similarity measures are computed for all pairs of variables. (Distances can be calculated in the PROXIMITIES procedure.)

Figure 5.14 contains the results of clustering the community variables using the absolute value of the correlation coefficient as a measure of similarity. The absolute value of the coefficient is used since it is a measure of the strength of the relationship. The sign indicates only the direction. If you want clusters for positively correlated variables only, the sign of the coefficient should be maintained.

Figure 5.14 Cluster analysis of the community variables

```
MATRIX DATA VARIABLES=POPSTABL NEWSCIRC FEMEMPLD FARMERS RETAILNG
   COMMERCL INDUSTZN HEALTH CHLDNEGL COMMEFFC DWELGNEW MIGRNPOP
   UNEMPLOY MENTALIL
   /CONTENTS=PROX
   /N=88
BEGIN DATA
1.
-.175 1.
-.276 .616 1.
.369 -.625 -.637 1.
-.127 .624 .736 -.519 1.
-.069 .652 .589 -.306 .727 1.
-.106 .712 .742 -.545 .785 .911 1.
-.149 -.030 .241 -.068 .100 .123 .129 1.
-.039 -.171 -.589 .257 -.557 -.357 -.424 -.407 1.
-.005 .100 .471 -.213 .452 .287 .357 .732 -.660 1.
-.670 .188 .413 -.579 .165 .030 .203 .290 -.138 .311 1.
-.476 -.086 .064 -.198 .007 -.068 -.024 .083 .148 .067 .505 1.
.137 -.373 -.689 .450 -.650 -.424 -.528 -.348 .733 -.601 -.266 .181 1.0
.237 .046 -.237 .121 -.190 -.055 -.095 -.279 .247 -.324 -.266 -.307 .217
1.
END DATA
PROXIMITIES  /MATRIX IN (*)
   /MEASURE = NONE ABSOLUTE
   /MATRIX OUT (*)
CLUSTER /MATRIX IN (*)⁴
```

```
Vertical Icicle Plot using Average Linkage (Between Groups)

   (Down) Number of Clusters  (Across) Case Label and number

      U  C  C  H  F  I  C  R  F  N  M  M  D  P
      N  H  O  E  A  N  O  E  E  E  E  I  W  O
      E  L  M  A  R  D  M  T  M  W  N  G  E  P
      M  D  M  L  M  U  M  A  E  S  T  R  L  S
      P  N  E  T  E  S  E  I  M  C  A  N  G  T
      L  E  F  H  R  T  R  L  P  I  L  P  N  A
      O  G  F     S  Z  C  N  L  R  I  O  E  B
      Y  L  C        N  L  G  D  C  L  P  W  L

      1     1                    1  1  1
      3  9  0  8  4  7  6  5  3  2  4  2  1  1
   1 +XXXXXXXXXXXXXXXXXXXXXXXXXXXXXXXXXXXXXXXX
   2 +XXXXXXXXXXXXXXXXXXXXXXXXXXXX  XXXXXXXXXX
   3 +XXXXXXXXXXXXXXXXXXXXXXXXXXXX  X  XXXXXXX
   4 +XXXXXXXXXX  XXXXXXXXXXXXXXXX  X  XXXXXXX
   5 +XXXXXXXXXX  XXXXXXXXXXXXXXXX  X  X  XXXX
   6 +XXXX  XXXX  XXXXXXXXXXXXXXXX  X  X  XXXX
   7 +XXXX  XXXX  X  XXXXXXXXXXXXX  X  X  XXXX
   8 +XXXX  XXXX  X  XXXXXXXXXX  X  X  X  XXXX
   9 +XXXX  XXXX  X  XXXXXXXXXX  X  X  X  X  X
  10 +XXXX  XXXX  X  XXXXXXX  X  X  X  X  X  X
  11 +XXXX  X  X  X  XXXXXXX  X  X  X  X  X  X
  12 +X  X  X  X  X  XXXXXXX  X  X  X  X  X  X
  13 +X  X  X  X  X  XXXX  X  X  X  X  X  X  X
```

The clustering procedure is the same whether variables or cases are clustered. It starts out with as many clusters as there are variables. At each successive step, variables or clusters of variables are merged, as shown in the icicle plot in Figure 5.14.

---

[4]With releases before 3.0, replace all of the commands with the following commands:

```
INPUT PROGRAM
N OF CASES 88
NUMERIC POPSTABL NEWSCIRC FEMEMPLD FARMERS RETAILNG COMMERCL INDUSTZN
  HEALTH CHLDNEGL COMMEFFC DWELGNEW MIGRNPOP UNEMPLOY MENTALIL
INPUT MATRIX FREE
END FILE
END INPUT PROGRAM
FILE HANDLE PROX/ NAME ='CORR MATRIX'
PROCEDURE OUTPUT OUTFILE=PROX
PROXIMITIES  POPSTABL TO MENTALIL
   /READ = SIMILAR TRIANGULAR
   /MEASURE = NONE ABSOLUTE
   /WRITE
BEGIN DATA
1.
-.175 1.
etc.
END DATA
INPUT MATRIX FILE=PROX
CLUSTER POPSTABL TO MENTALIL/READ SIMILAR
```

Consider the four-cluster solution. The HEALTH, COMMEFFC, CHLDNEGL, and UNEMPLOY variables form one cluster, the FARMERS, INDUSTZN, COMMERCL, RETAILNG, FEMEMPLD, and NEWSCIRC variables form the second cluster, MENTALIL is a cluster by itself, and the fourth cluster is MIGRNPOP, DWELGNEW, and POPSTABL.

For readers of Chapter 4, this solution should appear familiar. The groupings of the variables are exactly those established by the factor analysis. The first cluster is the WELFARE factor, the second the URBANISM, and the fourth INFLUX. In both cases the extent of mental illness does not appear to be related to the remainder of the variables.

This is not a chance occurrence. Although factor analysis has an underlying theoretical model and cluster analysis is much more ad hoc, both identify related groups of variables. However, factor analysis allows variables to be either positively or negatively related to a factor. Cluster analysis can be restricted to search only for positive associations between variables. Thus, if the absolute values of the correlation coefficients are not taken, variables that correlate negatively with a factor do not appear in the same cluster with variables that correlate positively. For example, the FARMERS variable would not appear with the other urbanism variables. Factor analysis and cluster analysis need not always arrive at the same variable groupings, but it is comforting when they do.

5.15 RUNNING PROCEDURE CLUSTER

Use the CLUSTER procedure to obtain hierarchical clusters for cases when the number of cases is not too large. Variables can also be clustered if the data are in the appropriate format (for example, if you have a correlation matrix or some other measure of distance). CLUSTER provides several measures of dissimilarity and allows you to specify missing-value treatment. A matrix of similarity or dissimilarity coefficients can be entered and used to cluster cases or variables.

Procedure PROXIMITIES, described in Appendix B, is useful for computing a wide variety of distance and similarity coefficients for either cases or variables. Options for standardizing matrix data are also available. The CLUSTER procedure does not allow for data standardizations. Proximity matrices from procedure PROXIMITIES can be used in the CLUSTER procedure, as well as in other procedures that permit matrix input.

An alternative to using PROXIMITIES to calculate squared Euclidean distances for standardized variables is to standardize variables in DESCRIPTIVES and read them into CLUSTER using the following commands:

```
DESCRIPTIVES CALORIES SODIUM ALCOHOL COST
  /SAVE 5
CLUSTER ZCALORIE ZSODIUM ZALCOHOL ZCOST
```

The results are the same.

5.16 Specifying the Variables

The first specification on CLUSTER is a list of variables to use in computing similarities or distances between cases, as in

```
CLUSTER ZCALORIE ZSODIUM ZALCOHOL ZCOST
```

The variable list is the only required specification and must precede any optional subcommands. When a matrix is read, the variable list should be omitted. These variables are then clustered.

[5]With releases before 3.0, replace the DESCRIPTIVES command with the following:

```
CONDESCRIPTIVE CALORIES SODIUM ALCOHOL COST
OPTION 3
```

5.17 The METHOD Subcommand

The METHOD subcommand specifies the clustering method. If you do not specify a method, CLUSTER uses the average-linkage between-groups method (see Section 5.13). You can use more than one method on a single matrix.

BAVERAGE *Average linkage between groups (UPGMA).* This is the default.

WAVERAGE *Average linkage within groups.*

SINGLE *Single linkage or nearest neighbor.*

COMPLETE *Complete linkage or furthest neighbor.*

CENTROID *Centroid clustering (UPGMC).* Squared Euclidean distances should be used with this method.

MEDIAN *Median clustering (WPGMC).* Squared Euclidean distances should be used with this method.

WARD *Ward's method.* Squared Euclidean distances should be used with this method.

For example, the command

```
CLUSTER ZCALORIE ZSODIUM ZALCOHOL ZCOST
  /METHOD=SINGLE COMPLETE
```

requests clustering with both the single and complete methods.

5.18 The MEASURE Subcommand

Use the MEASURE subcommand to specify the distance measure to use for clustering cases (see Section 5.3 and 5.12). If you omit MEASURE, CLUSTER uses squared Euclidean distances. You can specify only one distance measure.

MEASURE has the following keywords:

SEUCLID *Squared Euclidean distances.* This is the default. This measure should be used with the centroid, median, and Ward's methods of clustering. The distance between two cases is the sum of the squared differences in values for each variable:

$$\text{Distance}(X, Y) = \sum_i (X_i - Y_i)^2$$

EUCLID *Euclidean distances.* The distance between two cases is the square root of the sum of the squared differences in values for each variable:

$$\text{Distance}(X, Y) = \sqrt{\sum_i (X_i - Y_i)^2}$$

COSINE *Cosine of vectors of variables.* This is a pattern similarity measure:

$$\text{Similarity}(X, Y) = \frac{\sum_i (X_i Y_i)}{\sqrt{\sum_i (X_i^2) \sum_i (Y_i^2)}}$$

BLOCK *City-block or Manhattan distances.* The distance between two cases is the sum of the absolute differences in values for each variable:

$$\text{Distance}(X, Y) = \sum_i |X_i - Y_i|$$

CHEBYCHEV *Chebychev distance metric.* The distance between two cases is the maximum absolute difference in values for any variable:

$$\text{Distance}(X, Y) = MAX_i |X_i - Y_i|$$

POWER(p,r) *Distances in an absolute power metric.* The distance between two cases is the *r*th root of the sum of the absolute differences to the *p*th power in values on each variable.

$$\text{Distance}(X, Y) = \left(\sum_i (X_i - Y_i)^p\right)^{1/r}$$

Appropriate selection of integer parameters *p* and *r* yields Euclidean, squared Euclidean, Minkowski, city-block, minimum, maximum, and many other distance metrics.

DEFAULT *Same as SEUCLID.*

5.19 The PRINT Subcommand

CLUSTER automatically displays the clustering method, the similarity or distance measure used for clustering, and the number of cases. Use the PRINT subcommand to obtain additional output. The agglomeration schedule is displayed by default if you do not specify PRINT. If you specify PRINT, you must request SCHEDULE explicitly.

SCHEDULE *Agglomeration schedule.* Display the order in which and distances at which clusters combine to form new clusters as well as the last cluster level at which a case (or variable) joined the cluster (see Figures 5.9 and 5.10b). This is the default.

CLUSTER(min,max) *Cluster membership. Min* and *max* specify the minimum and maximum numbers of clusters in the cluster solutions. For each case, CLUSTER displays an identifying label and values indicating which cluster the case belongs to in a given cluster solution (see Figure 5.11c). For example, PRINT=CLUSTER(3,5) displays the clusters to which each case belongs when three, four, and five clusters are produced. Cases are identified by case number plus the value of any string variable specified on the ID subcommand (see Section 5.21).

DISTANCE *Matrix of distances or similarities between items.* The type of matrix produced (similarities or dissimilarities) depends upon the measure selected. With a large number of clustered cases, DISTANCE uses considerable computer processing time.

NONE *No display output.* Use PRINT=NONE when you want to suppress all display output, such as when you are using SAVE.

5.20 The PLOT Subcommand

CLUSTER produces the verticle icicle plot by default. Use the PLOT subcommand to obtain a horizontal icicle plot or a dendrogram. When you specify PLOT, only the requested plots are produced.

VICICLE[(min,max,inc)] *Verticle icicle plot. Min* and *max* specify the minimum and maximum numbers of cluster solutions to plot, and *inc* specifies the increment to use between cluster levels. Min, max, and inc must be integers. By default, the increment is 1 and all cluster solutions are plotted. For example, PLOT = VICICLE (2,10,2) plots cluster solutions with two, four, six, eight, and ten clusters. VICICLE is the default. (See Figures 5.8a, 5.10a, and 5.11a.)

HICICLE[(min,max,inc)] *Horizontal icicle plot.* Has the same specifications as VICICLE. (See Figure 5.11b.)

DENDROGRAM *Dendrogram.* The dendrogram is scaled by the joining distances of the clusters. (See Figures 5.10c and 5.10d.)

NONE *No display output.* Use PLOT=NONE to suppress all plots.

If there is insufficient memory to plot a dendrogram or icicle plot, CLUSTER performs the cluster analysis, skips the plot, and displays an error message. To obtain a plot when this occurs, request more memory or specify an increment for VICICLE or HICICLE.

5.21 The ID Subcommand

By default, CLUSTER identifies cases by case number. Name a string variable on the ID subcommand to identify cases with string values. For example, the subcommand

```
/ID=BEER
```

produces the beer-name labels in Figures 5.8a, 5.10a, 5.10c, 5.10d, 5.11a, 5.11b, and 5.11c.

5.22 The MISSING Subcommand

CLUSTER uses listwise deletion as the default missing-value treatment. A case with missing values for any clustering variable is excluded from the analysis. Use the MISSING subcommand to treat user-defined missing values as valid.

INCLUDE *Include user-missing values.*

LISTWISE *Delete cases with missing values listwise.* This is the default.

Cases with system-missing values for clustering variables are never included in the analysis.

5.23 The MATRIX Subcommand

The CLUSTER procedure can read and write proximity-type matrix materials. The MATRIX subcommand has the following two keywords:

OUT *Write matrix materials.* After OUT, in parentheses specify either a name for the matrix file or * to replace the active file with the matrix. (With releases before 3.0, use the subcommand /WRITE or /WRITE DISTANCE.)

IN *Read matrix materials.* After IN, in parentheses specify either the name of the matrix file to read or * to read the matrix materials from the active file. (With releases before 3.0, use either the subcommand /READ SIMILAR to read a matrix of similarity values, or /READ TRIANGLE to read the lower triangle of a square matrix, or /READ LOWER to read the lower triangle of a square matrix without the diagonal.)

5.24 The SAVE Subcommand

You can use the SAVE subcommand to save cluster memberships at specified cluster levels as new variables on the active file. You must specify a rootname for each cluster method for which you wish to save cluster membership, as in

```
CLUSTER A B C
  /METHOD=BAVERAGE(CLUSMEM)
  /SAVE=CLUSTERS(3,5)
```

This command saves each case's cluster memberships for the three-, four-, and five-cluster solutions. The new variables derive their names from the rootname CLUSMEM and would appear on the active file in the order CLUSMEM5, CLUSMEM4, and CLUSMEM3. CLUSTER prints the names of variables it adds to the active file.

5.25 EXERCISES

Syntax

1. Find the errors in the following CLUSTER commands:

a.
```
CLUSTER WORDLNTH SENTLNTH DESCRIPT CHARDVEL SUBPLOTS
        SUBCHARS MORALIZE DIGRESSN
   /METHOD=MEDIAN
   /MEASURE=COSINE
```

b.
```
CLUSTER ABDMPAIN CHSTPAIN NAUSEA DYSPNEA VOMITING ATAXIA FEVER
   /METHOD=BAVERAGE WAVERAGE COMPLETE
   /MEASURE=POWER(.5,.25)
   /PRINT=SCHEDULE CLUSTER(5,1)
   /PLOT=VICICLE(1,5)
   /ID=DISORDER
```

c.
```
CLUSTER DIFFCLTY LOGIC INTUITN FAMILRTY CREATVTY
   /METHOD=WARD
   /MEASURE=POWER(2,1)
   /PRINT=CLUSTER(1,10) DISTANCE SCHEDULE
   /PLOT=HICICLE(1,3.5,.5)
   /MISSING=MEANSUB
```

d.
```
CLUSTER WINSALES SPRSALES SUMSALES FALSALES TOTSALES
        EQPSALES SUPSALES NUMSALES
   /METHOD=COMPLETE SINGLE
   /MEASURE=EUCLID BLOCK
   /PRINT=CLUSTER(1,10,2)
   /MISSING=INCLUDE
```

2. Correct the following CLUSTER command:

```
CLUSTER SWEETNES TARNESS SALTINES BTTRNESS CALORIES PROTEIN
        CARBHYDR FAT PALTBLTY
   /METHOD=BAVERAGE WAVERAGE SINGEL COMPLETE
   /MEASURE=DEFAULT
   /PRINT=SCHEDULE CLUSTER(1,9) DISTANCE HICICLE(1,9,1) DENDROGRAM
   /ID=TYPE
   /MATRIX=IN(*)
```
[6]

3. An ornithologist wants a cluster analysis using the following variables for a sample of 85 birds:

```
WINGSPAN BEAKCURV BEAKWDTH MIGRLNTH MATELNTH FSHDIET INSDIET GRNDIET
```

The plan calls for three clustering methods (average linkage within groups, nearest neighbor, and farthest neighbor), with an icicle plot and the distance measure

$$\text{Distance (X, Y)} = \left[\sum_i (X_i - Y_i)^4\right]^{1/4}$$

The output should include cluster memberships for 5 to 20 clusters, but no other results. The names of the birds are in variable BIRDS and should appear on the output. Write the CLUSTER command for this study.

4. A sociologist studying popular culture wants to see if 60 automobiles can be clustered according to the following variables.

```
WEIGHT LENGTH WIDTH HGHTLEN WINDOWS CHROME DOODADS
```

The study calls for two cluster analyses, one using the nearest neighbor method and Euclidean distances, and the other using farthest neighbor and city-block distances. Both analyses should include an agglomeration schedule and cluster memberships along with an icicle plot for clusters 5 through 10. Will the following CLUSTER command accomplish the tasks?

```
CLUSTER WEIGHT LENGTH WIDTH HGHTLEN WINDOWS CHROME DOODADS
   /METHOD SINGLE
   /MEASURE EUCLID
   /METHOD COMPLETE
   /MEASURE BLOCK
   /PRINT CLUSTER(5,10)
   /PLOT HICICLE(5,10,1)
```

---

[6] With releases before 3.0, replace the CLUSTER command with the following:

```
CLUSTER SWEETNES TARNESS SALTINES BTTRNESS CALORIES PROTEIN
        CARBHYDR FAT PALTBLTY
  /METHOD=BAVERAGE WAVERAGE SINGEL COMPLETE
  /MEASURE=DEFAULT
  /PRINT=SCHEDULE CLUSTER(1,9) DISTANCE HICICLE(1,9,1) DENDROGRAM
  /ID=TYPE
  /READ=SIMILAR LOWER
```

Statistical Concepts

1. Consider the following four cases:

CASE	OBEDENCE	GUARDING	HUNTING	ONEPERSN
1	1.4	-0.6	-0.9	-0.2
2	-3.1	0.8	2.4	1.9
3	1.5	1.8	-0.3	2.2
4	2.1	2.6	-0.6	2.0

   a. Compute the matrix of squared Euclidean distance coefficients:

```
Squared Euclidean Dissimilarity Coefficient Matrix

   Case          1            2            3

     2
     3
     4
```

   b. Which of these four cases would be combined first into a cluster?

2. Using the vertical icicle plot below and assuming agglomerative clustering, describe the clusters at
   a. Step 7.
   b. Step 5.
   c. Step 3.

```
Vertical Icicle Plot using Complete Linkage

   (Down) Number of Clusters  (Across) Case Label and number

   S  B  F  C  C  M  C  E  G  M
   W  L  A  O  O  O  H  D  O  O
   I  U  R  T  L  N  E  A  U  Z
   S  E  M  T  B  T  D  M  D  Z
   S     E  A  Y  E  D     A  A
         R  G     R  A        R
         S  E     E  R        E
                  Y           L
                              L
                  J           A
                  A
                  C
                  K
   1
   0  9  5  4  7  8  6  3  2  1
1 +XXXXXXXXXXXXXXXXXXXXXXXXXXXX
2 +XXXX  XXXXXXXXXXXXXXXXXXXXXX
3 +XXXX  XXXX  XXXXXXXXXXXXXXXX
4 +XXXX  XXXX  X  XXXXXXXXXXXXX
5 +XXXX  XXXX  X  XXXX  XXXXXXX
6 +X  X  XXXX  X  XXXX  XXXXXXX
7 +X  X  XXXX  X  X  X  XXXXXXX
8 +X  X  X  X  X  X  X  XXXXXXX
9 +X  X  X  X  X  X  X  XXXX  X
```

3. a. Fill in the missing entries in the agglomeration schedule below:

Agglomeration Schedule using Complete Linkage

Stage	Clusters Combined Cluster 1	Clusters Combined Cluster 2	Coefficient	Stage Cluster 1st Appears Cluster 1	Stage Cluster 1st Appears Cluster 2	Next Stage
1	2	3	.494757			
2	1	2	.582524			
3	4	5	1.146706			
4	6	8	1.247115			
5	9	10	1.912980			
6	1	6	3.659030			
7	1	7	6.030436			
8	1	4	16.585556			
9	1	9	25.452454			

   b. At what stage would you stop merging cases into clusters?

4. a. Based on the following icicle plot and agglomeration schedule, complete the dendrogram below. Do not rescale the distances.

Agglomeration Schedule using Complete Linkage

Stage	Clusters Combined Cluster 1	Cluster 2	Coefficient	Stage Cluster 1st Appears Cluster 1	Cluster 2	Next Stage
1	3	4	.800757	0	0	4
2	1	2	.863292	0	0	5
3	5	6	1.595673	0	0	4
4	3	5	10.366976	1	3	5
5	1	3	14.717737	2	4	0

Vertical Icicle Plot using Complete Linkage

```
   (Down) Number of Clusters  (Across) Case Label and number

     E  P  B  C  V  P
     N  H  I  H  E  H
     G  Y  O  E  T  Y
     I  S  C  M  R  S
     N  I  H  I  N  I
     E  C  M  S  A  C
     E  S  S  T  R  A
     R  T  T     N  N

     6  5  4  3  2  1
  1 +XXXXXXXXXXXXXXXX
  2 +XXXXXXXXXX  XXXX
  3 +XXXX  XXXX  XXXX
  4 +X  X  XXXX  XXXX
  5 +X  X  XXXX  X  X
```

Dendrogram using Complete Linkage

```
                              Rescaled Distance Cluster Combine

         C A S E              0         5        10        15        20        25
  Label              Seq     +---------+---------+---------+---------+---------+

  CHEMIST              3   -
  BIOCHMST             4
  PHYSICST             5   -
  ENGINEER             6   -
  PHYSICAN             1   -
  VETRNARN             2   -
```

b. How many clusters would you recommend?

5. a. Use the distance matrix shown below and agglomerative hierarchical clustering with the farthest neighbor technique to construct an agglomeration schedule and an icicle plot.

Squared Euclidean Dissimilarity Coefficient Matrix

Case	1	2	3	4
2	5.81			
3	1.42	15.84		
4	.56	2.07	15.18	
5	9.61	.68	2.76	13.21

Agglomeration Schedule using Complete Linkage

Stage	Clusters Combined Cluster 1	Cluster 2	Coefficient	Stage Cluster 1st Appears Cluster 1	Cluster 2	Next Stage
1						
2						
3						
4						

Vertical Icicle Plot using Complete Linkage

```
   (Down) Number of Clusters  (Across) Case Label and number

     3  5  2  4  1
  1 +XXXXXXXXXXXXX
  2 +X  X  X  X  X
  3 +X  X  X  X  X
  4 +X  X  X  X  X
```

b. How many clusters would you recommend?

6. If a program designed to do agglomerative hierarchical clustering produced the following icicle plot, would you trust it?

```
    1  1  1     1     1        1     1
    5  2  6  7  1  4  4  6  5  0  9  3  8  2  3  1
 1 +XXXXXXXXXXXXXXXXXXXXXXXXXXXXXXXXXXXXXXXXXXXXXX
 2 +XXXXXXXXXX  XXXXXXXXXXXXXXXXXXXXXXXXXXXXXXXXXX
 3 +XXXXXXXXXX  XXXX  XXXXXXXXXXXXXXXXXXXXXXXXXXXX
 4 +XXXX  XXXX  XXXX  XXXXXXXXXXXXXXXXXXXXXXXXXXXX
 5 +X  X  XXXX  XXXX  XXXXXXXXXXXXXXXXXXXXXXXXXXXX
 6 +X  X  XXXX  XXXX  XXXXXXX  XXXXXXXXXXXXXXXXXXX
 7 +X  X  X  X  XXXX  XXXXXXX  XXXXXXXXXXXXX  XXXX
 8 +X  X  X  X  XXXX  XXXXXXX  XXXX  XXXXXXX  XXXX
 9 +X  X  X  X  X  X  XXXXXXX  XXXX  XXXXXXXXXXXXX
10 +X  X  X  X  X  X  XXXX  X  XXXX  XXXXXXXXXXXXX
11 +X  X  X  X  X  X  XXXX  X  XXXX  XXXXXXX  XXXX
12 +X  X  X  X  X  X  XXXX  X  X  X  XXXXXXX  XXXX
13 +X  X  X  X  X  X  XXXX  X  X  X  XXXXXXX  X  X
14 +X  X  X  X  X  X  XXXX  X  X  X  XXXX  X  X  X
15 +X  X  X  X  X  X  X  X  X  X  X  XXXX  X  X  X
```

7. Indicate whether the following statements are true or false:
   a. The choice of variables for clustering has little effect on the clusters obtained.
   b. The nearest neighbor and farthest neighbor clustering techniques will always produce different clusters.
   c. The squared Euclidean distance between two cases depends on the order in which the cases are considered. That is, the distance between Case 5 and Case 11 can differ if the distance is calculated between Case 11 and Case 5.
   d. Small distance coefficients in the agglomeration schedule indicate that fairly dissimilar clusters or cases are being merged.
   e. A dendrogram always indicates the stages at which clusters are formed.
   f. Standardization of the clustering variables has no effect on clustering.
8. Consider the following icicle plot:

```
Horizontal Icicle Plot Using Complete Linkage

                                   Number of Clusters

             C A S E               123456789
 Label                        Seq  +++++++++

 MOBY DICK                      9  XXXXXXXXX
                                   XXX
                                   XXX
 ODYSSEY                        4  XXXXXXXXX
                                   X
                                   X
 GREAT EXPECTATIONS            10  XXXXXXXXX
                                   XXXXX
                                   XXXXX
 OLIVER TWIST                   6  XXXXXXXXX
                                   XX
                                   XX
 TOM JONES                      5  XXXXXXXXX
                                   XXXX
                                   XXXX
 MADAM BOVARY                   7  XXXXXXXXX
                                   XXXXXXXX
                                   XXXXXXXX
 PORTRAIT OF A LADY             8  XXXXXXXXX
                                   XXXXXXXXX
                                   XXXXXXXXX
 ANNA KARENINA                  3  XXXXXXXXX
                                   XXXXXXX
                                   XXXXXXX
 BLEAK HOUSE                    2  XXXXXXXXX
                                   XXXXXX
                                   XXXXXX
 CANDIDE                        1  XXXXXXXXX
```

Based on this plot, complete the cluster membership table below.

Cluster Membership of Cases using Complete Linkage

Label	Case	Number of Clusters 6	5	4	3	2
CANDIDE	1					
BLEAK HOUSE	2					
ANNA KARENINA	3					
ODYSSEY	4					
TOM JONES	5					
OLIVER TWIST	6					
MADAM BOVARY	7					
PORTRAIT OF A LADY	8					
MOBY DICK	9					
GREAT EXPECTATIONS	10					

6

Multivariate Analysis of Variance

In this chapter:

Goals:

- To test hypotheses about the relationship between a set of interrelated dependent variables and one or more classification or grouping variables.
- To identify the subset of dependent variables contributing to differences among groups.

Examples:

- Compare four instructional methods based on student achievement levels, satisfaction, anxiety, and long-term retention of material.
- Evaluate the effectiveness of three types of chemotherapy and two dosages of radiation based on length of patient survival, length of time the patient is disease free, and quality of life.
- Compare five new ice-cream flavors on the basis of amount consumed, preference rating, and estimate of price.

How it's done:

The variability in the dependent variables is subdivided into two components: that attributable to differences between groups (the hypothesis sums of squares matrix), and that attributable to variability within groups (the error sums of squares matrix). Various test statistics that compare the magnitudes of these two matrices are computed.

Data considerations:

Each case has a set of dependent variables and one or more discrete grouping variables. The dependent variables are measured only once for each case. The multivariate analysis of variance model requires that for each group the dependent variables are from a multivariate normal distribution and that the variance-covariance matrices are equal for all groups.

General references:

Finn (1974)
Bock (1975)
Morrison (1967)

Contents

6.1 MULTIVARIATE ANALYSIS OF VARIANCE
6.2 Assumptions
6.3 One-Sample Hotelling's T^2
6.4 Descriptive Statistics
6.5 Further Displays for Checking Assumptions
6.6 Normal Plots
6.7 Another Plot
6.8 Bartlett's Test of Sphericity
6.9 Testing Hypotheses
6.10 Univariate Tests
6.11 The Two-Sample Multivariate T-Test
6.12 Tests of Homogeneity of Variance
6.13 Hotelling's T^2 for Two Independent Samples
6.14 Univariate Tests
6.15 Discriminant Analysis
6.16 Parameter Estimates
6.17 A Multivariate Factorial Design
6.18 Principal Components Analysis
6.19 Tests of Multivariate Differences
6.20 Testing the Effects
6.21 Discriminant Analysis
6.22 Testing for Differences Among Field Dependence and Sex Categories
6.23 Stepdown ***F*** Tests
6.24 Different Types of Sums of Squares
6.25 Problems with Empty Cells
6.26 Examining Residuals
6.27 Predicted Means
6.28 Some Final Comments
6.29 RUNNING PROCEDURE MANOVA
6.30 Specifying Factors and the Structure of the Data
6.31 The Dependent Variable List
6.32 The Factor List
6.33 The Covariate List
6.34 The ANALYSIS Subcommand
6.35 The DESIGN Subcommand
6.36 Specifying Effects
6.37 Specifying Nested Designs
6.38 Specifying Error Terms
6.39 The ERROR Subcommand
6.40 The WSFACTORS Subcommand
6.41 The WSDESIGN Subcommand
6.42 The MEASURE Subcommand
6.43 The TRANSFORM Subcommand
6.44 The RENAME Subcommand
6.45 The METHOD Subcommand
6.46 The PARTITION Subcommand
6.47 The CONTRAST Subcommand
6.48 The PRINT and NOPRINT Subcommands
6.49 The PCOMPS Subcommand
6.50 The DISCRIM Subcommand
6.51 The OMEANS Subcommand
6.52 The PMEANS Subcommand
6.53 The RESIDUALS Subcommand
6.54 The PLOT Subcommand
6.55 The MATRIX Subcommand
6.56 The MISSING Subcommand
6.57 The CRITERIA Subcommand
6.58 EXERCISES

6 Balancing on Beams: Multivariate Analysis of Variance

"Tilted" houses featured in amusement parks capitalize on the challenge of navigating one's way in the presence of misleading visual cues. It's difficult to maintain balance when walls are no longer parallel and rooms assume strange shapes. We are all dependent on visual information to guide movement, but the extent of this dependence has been found to vary considerably.

Based on a series of experiments, Witkin (1954) classified individuals into two categories: those who can ignore misleading visual cues, termed field independent, and those who cannot, termed field dependent. Field dependence has been linked to a variety of psychological characteristics such as self-image and intelligence. Psychologists theorize that it derives from childhood socialization patterns—field-dependent children learn to depend on highly structured environments while field independent children learn to cope with ambiguous situations.

In this chapter, the relationship between field dependence, sex, and various motor abilities is examined, using data reported by Barnard (1973). Students (63 female and 71 male) from the College of Southern Idaho were administered a test of field independence, the rod and frame test. On the basis of this test, subjects were classified as field dependent, field independent, or intermediate. Four tests of motor ability were also conducted: two tests of balance, a test of gross motor skills, and a test of fine motor skills.

For the balance test, subjects were required to maintain balance while standing on one foot on a rail. Two trials for each of two conditions, eyes open and eyes closed, were administered and the average number of seconds a subject maintained balance under each condition was recorded. Gross motor coordination was assessed with the side-stepping test. For this test, three parallel lines are drawn four feet apart on the floor and a subject stands on the middle line. At the start signal the subject must sidestep to the left until the left foot crosses the left line. He or she then sidesteps to the right until the right line is crossed. A subject's score is the average number of lines crossed in three ten second trials. The Purdue Pegboard Test was used to quantify fine motor skills. Subjects are required to place small pegs into pegholes using only the left hand, only the right hand, and then both hands simultaneously. The number of pegs placed in two 30-second trials for each condition was recorded and the average over six trials calculated.

The experiment described above is fairly typical of many investigations. There are several "classification" or independent variables, sex and field independence in this case, and a dependent variable. The goal of the experiment is to examine the relationship between the classification variables and the dependent variable. For example, is motor ability related to field dependence? Does the relationship differ for men and women? Analysis of variance techniques are usually used to answer these questions, as discussed in the *SPSS^X Introductory Statistics Guide.*

MANOVA was designed and programmed by Philip Burns of Northwestern University.

In this experiment, however, the dependent variable is not a single measure but four different scores obtained for each student. Although ANOVA tests can be computed separately for each of the dependent variables, this approach ignores the interrelation among the dependent variables. As explained in the previous chapters, substantial information may be lost when correlations between variables are ignored. For example, several bivariate regression analyses cannot substitute for a multiple regression model which considers the independent variables jointly. Only when the independent variables are uncorrelated with each other are the bivariate and multivariate regression results equivalent. Similarly, analyzing multiple two dimensional tables cannot substitute for an analysis that considers the variables simultaneously.

6.1 MULTIVARIATE ANALYSIS OF VARIANCE

The extension of univariate analysis of variance to the case of multiple dependent variables is termed *multivariate analysis of variance,* abbreviated as MANOVA. Univariate analysis of variance is just a special case of MANOVA, the case with a single dependent variable. The hypotheses tested with MANOVA are similar to those tested with ANOVA. The difference is that sets(sometimes called a vector) of means replace the individual means specified in ANOVA. In a one-way design, for example, the hypothesis tested is that the populations from which the groups are selected have the same means for all dependent variables. Thus, the hypothesis might be that the population means for the four motor-ability variables are the same for the three field dependence categories.

6.2 Assumptions

For the case of a single dependent variable, two assumptions are necessary for the proper application of the ANOVA test: the groups must be random samples from normal populations with the same variance. Similar assumptions are necessary for MANOVA. Since we are dealing with several dependent variables, however, we must make assumptions about their joint distribution, that is, the distribution of the variables considered together. The extension of the ANOVA assumptions to MANOVA requires that the dependent variables have a multivariate normal distribution with the same variance-covariance matrix in each group. A variance-covariance matrix, as its name indicates, is a square arrangement of elements, with the variances of the variables on the diagonal, and the covariances of pairs of variables off the diagonal. A variance-covariance matrix can be transformed into a correlation matrix by dividing each covariance by the standard deviations of the two variables. Later sections of the chapter will present tests for these assumptions.

6.3 One-Sample Hotelling's T^2

Before considering more complex generalizations of ANOVA techniques, let's consider the simple one-sample *t* test and its extension to the case of multiple dependent variables. As you will recall, the one-sample *t* test is used to test the hypothesis that the sample originates from a population with a known mean. For example, you might want to test the hypothesis that schizophrenics do not differ in mean IQ from the general population, which is assumed to have a mean IQ of 100. If additional variables such as reading comprehension, mathematical aptitude, and motor dexterity are also to be considered, a test that allows comparison of several observed means to a set of constants is required.

A test developed by Hotelling, called Hotelling's T^2, is often used for this purpose. It is the simplest example of MANOVA. To illustrate this test and introduce some of the SPSS^X MANOVA output, we will use the field-dependence and motor-ability data to test the hypothesis that the observed sample comes from a population with specified values for the means of the four tests. That is, we will assume that normative data are available for the four tests and we will test the hypothesis that our sample is from a population having the normative means.

For illustrative purposes, the standard values are taken to be 13 seconds for balancing with eyes open, 3 seconds for balancing with eyes closed, 18 lines for the side-stepping test, and 10 pegs for the pegboard test. Since SPSS^X MANOVA automatically tests the hypothesis that a set of means is equal to 0, the normative values must be subtracted from the observed scores and the hypothesis that the differences are 0 is tested.

Figure 6.3 contains the message displayed by SPSS^X MANOVA when the cases are processed. It indicates the number of cases to be used in the analysis as well as the number of cases to be excluded. In this example, 134 cases will be included in the analysis. SPSS^X also indicates whether any cases contain missing values for the variables being analyzed or have independent-variable (factor) values outside of the designated range. Such cases are excluded from the analysis.

Since the hypothesis being tested involves only a test of a single sample, all observations are members of one "cell," in ANOVA terminology. If two independent samples, for example males and females, were compared, two "cells" would exist. The last line of Figure 6.3 indicates how many different MANOVA models have been specified.

Figure 6.3 Case information

```
COMPUTE BALOMEAN=MEAN(TEST1,TEST2)-13
COMPUTE BALCMEAN=MEAN(TEST3,TEST4)-3
COMPUTE SSTMEAN=MEAN(TEST5,TEST6)-18
COMPUTE PP=MEAN(TEST7,TEST8)-10
MANOVA BALOMEAN BALCMEAN SSTMEAN PP
  /DESIGN
```

```
134 cases accepted.
  0 cases rejected because of out-of-range factor values.
  0 cases rejected because of missing data.
  1 non-empty cells.

  1 design will be processed.
```

6.4 Descriptive Statistics

One of the first steps in any statistical analysis, regardless of how simple or complex it may be, is examination of the individual variables. This preliminary screening provides information about a variable's distribution and permits identification of unusual or outlying values.

Of course, when multivariate analyses are undertaken, it is not sufficient just to look at the characteristics of the variables individually. Information about their joint distribution must also be obtained. Similarly, identification of outliers must be based on the joint distribution of variables. For example, a height of six feet is not very unusual, and neither is a weight of 100 pounds nor being a man. A six-foot-tall male who weighs 100 pounds, however, is fairly atypical and needs to be identified to ascertain that the values have been correctly recorded, and if so, to gauge the effect of such a lean physique on subsequent analyses. (Remember the discussion in Chapter 2 on Mahalanobis' and Cook's distance and deleted residuals.)

Figure 6.4 contains means, standard deviations, and confidence intervals for each of the four motor-ability variables after the normative values have been subtracted. The sample exceeds the norm for balancing with eyes closed and peg insertion and is poorer than the norm for balancing with eyes open and side-stepping. The only confidence interval that includes 0 is for the balancing-with-eyes-closed variable.

Figure 6.4 Cell means and standard deviations

```
MANOVA BALOMEAN BALCMEAN SSTMEAN PP
  /PRINT=CELLINFO(MEANS)
  /DESIGN
```

```
Cell Means and Standard Deviations
Variable .. BALOMEAN           Balance Test - Eyes Open
                                             Mean    Std. Dev.          N   95 percent Conf. Interval

For entire sample                        -1.53993      5.86007        134     -2.54123       -.53862

- - - - - - - - - - - - - - - - - - - - - - - - - - - - - - - - - - - - - - - - - - - - - - - - -

Variable .. BALCMEAN           Balance Test - Eyes Closed
                                             Mean    Std. Dev.          N   95 percent Conf. Interval

For entire sample                          .14291      1.40488        134      -.09714        .38296

- - - - - - - - - - - - - - - - - - - - - - - - - - - - - - - - - - - - - - - - - - - - - - - - -

Variable .. SSTMEAN            Sidestepping Test
                                             Mean    Std. Dev.          N   95 percent Conf. Interval

For entire sample                        -2.59701      2.68137        134     -3.05518      -2.13885

- - - - - - - - - - - - - - - - - - - - - - - - - - - - - - - - - - - - - - - - - - - - - - - - -

Variable .. PP                 Purdue Pegboard Test
                                             Mean    Std. Dev.          N   95 percent Conf. Interval

For entire sample                         4.97264      1.49466        134      4.71724       5.22803
```

The 95% confidence intervals that are printed are individual confidence intervals. This means that no adjustment has been made for the fact that the confidence intervals for several variables have been computed. We have 95% confidence that each of the individual intervals contains the unknown parameter value. We do not have 95% confidence that *all* intervals considered jointly contain the unknown parameters. The distinction here is closely related to the problem of multiple comparisons in ANOVA.

When many tests are done, the chance that some observed differences appear to be statistically significant when there are no true differences in the populations increases with the number of comparisons made. To protect against calling too many differences "real" when in fact they are not, the criterion for how large a difference must be before it is considered "significant" is made more stringent. That is, larger differences are required, depending on the number of comparisons made. The larger the number of comparisons, the greater the observed difference must be. Similarly, if a confidence region that simultaneously contains values of observed population parameters with a specified overall confidence level is to be constructed, the confidence interval for each variable must be wider than that needed if only one variable is considered.

6.5 Further Displays for Checking Assumptions

Although the summary statistics presented in Figure 6.4 provide some information about the distributions of the dependent variables, more detailed information is often desirable. Figure 6.5 is a stem-and-leaf plot of the peg-board variable after the normative values have been subtracted. Stem-and-leaf plots provide a convenient way to examine the distribution of a variable.

In Figure 6.5, the numbers to the left of the dotted line are called the *stem*, while those to the right are the *leaves*. Each case is represented by a leaf. For example, the first line of the plot is for a case with a value of 1.2 and a case with a value of 1.3. The stem, 1, is the same for both cases while the values of the leaves (2 and 3) differ. When there are several cases with the same values, the leaf value is repeated. For example, there are two cases with a value of 2.7 and four cases with a value of 2.8. In this example, each stem value occurs twice, once for cases with leaves 0 through 4, and once for cases with leaves 5 through 9. This is not always the case, since the stem values depends on the actual data. In this example, the decimal point for each case occurs between the value of the stem and the leaf. This also is not always the case. SPSS^X MANOVA scales the variables so that the stem-and-leaf plot is based on the number of significant digits. Since the purpose of the plot is to display the distribution of the variable, the actual scale is not important.

Figure 6.5 Stem-and-leaf plot—pegboard test

```
MANOVA BALOMEAN BALCMEAN SSTMEAN PP
  /PLOT=STEMLEAF
  /DESIGN
```

```
Stem-and-leaf display for variable .. PP

     1 . 23
     1 . 8
     2 . 033
     2 . 778888
     3 . 02333
     3 . 555555577777778888
     4 . 002222222223
     4 . 5555555557777778888
     5 . 00000222222333
     5 . 555555557777788888
     6 . 0000222223333
     6 . 5577777778
     7 . 00000223
     7 . 5778
     8 . 2
     8 .
     9 . 3
```

One assumption needed for hypothesis testing in MANOVA is the assumption that the dependent variables have a multivariate normal distribution. If variables have a multivariate normal distribution, each one taken individually must be normally distributed. (However, variables that are normally distributed individually will not necessarily have a multivariate normal distribution when considered together.) The stem-and-leaf plots for each variable allows us to assess the reasonableness of the normality assumption, since if any distribution appears to be markedly nonnormal, the assumption of multivariate normality is likely to be violated.

6.6 Normal Plots

Although the stem-and-leaf plot gives a rough idea of the normality of the distribution of a variable, other plots that are especially designed for assessing normality can also be obtained. For example, we can assess normality using a normal probability plot, which is obtained by ranking the observed values of a variable from smallest to largest and then pairing each value with an expected normal value for a sample of that size from a standard normal distribution.

Figure 6.6a is a normal probability plot of the peg-board variable. The symbols represent the number of cases that fall in the same position on the plot. If the observed scores are from a normal distribution, the plot in should be approximately a straight line. Since the distribution of the peg-board scores appeared fairly normal in the stem-and-leaf plot (Figure 6.5), the normal probability plot should be fairly linear, and it is.

Figure 6.6a Normal probability plot—pegboard test

```
MANOVA BALOMEAN BALCMEAN SSTMEAN PP
  /PLOT=NORMAL
  /DESIGN
```

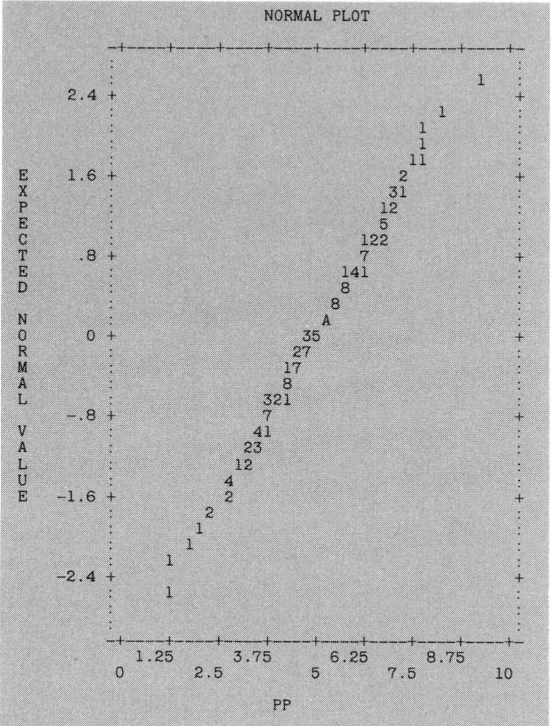

To further assess the linearity of the normal probability plot, we can calculate the difference between the observed point and the expected point under the assumption of normality and plot this difference for each case. If the observed sample is from a normal distribution, these differences should be fairly close to 0 and be randomly distributed.

Figure 6.6b is a plot of the differences for the normal probability plot shown in Figure 6.6a. This plot is called a detrended normal plot since the trend in Figure 6.6a, the straight line, has been removed. Note that the values fall roughly in a horizontal band about 0, though there appears to be some pattern. Also notice the two outliers, one in the lower-right corner and the other in the upper-left corner. These correspond to the smallest and largest observations in the sample and indicate that the observed distribution doesn't have quite as much spread in the tails as expected. For the smallest value, the deviation from the expected line is positive, indicating that the smallest value is not quite as small as would be expected. For the largest value, the value is not as large as would be expected.

Since most of the points cluster nicely around 0, this small deviation is probably not of too much concern. Nonetheless, it is usually a good idea to check outlying points to ascertain that they have been correctly recorded and entered. If the distribution of a variable appears markedly nonnormal, transformation of the data should be considered.

Figure 6.6b Detrended normal plot—pegboard test

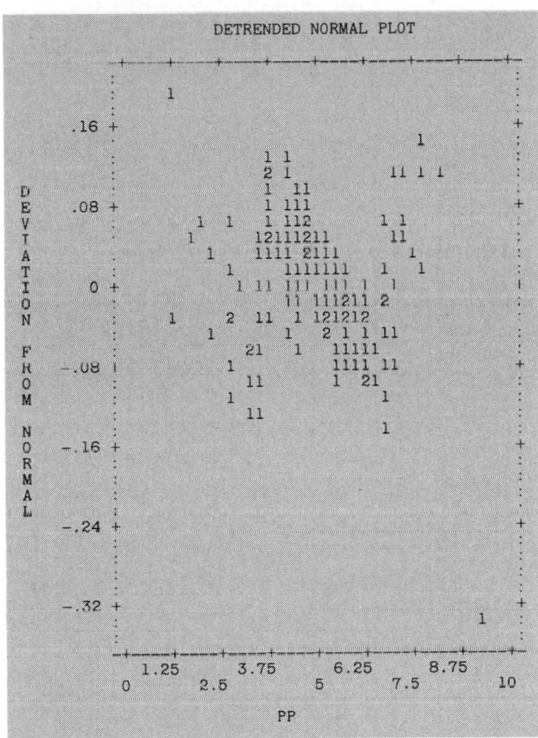

6.7 Another Plot

To get a little more practice in interpreting the previously described plots, consider Figure 6.7a, which is the plot for the balancing-with-eyes-closed variable. From this stem-and-leaf plot, you can see that the distribution of the data is skewed to the right. That is, there are several large values that are quite removed from the rest.

Figure 6.7a Stem-and-leaf plot—balance variable

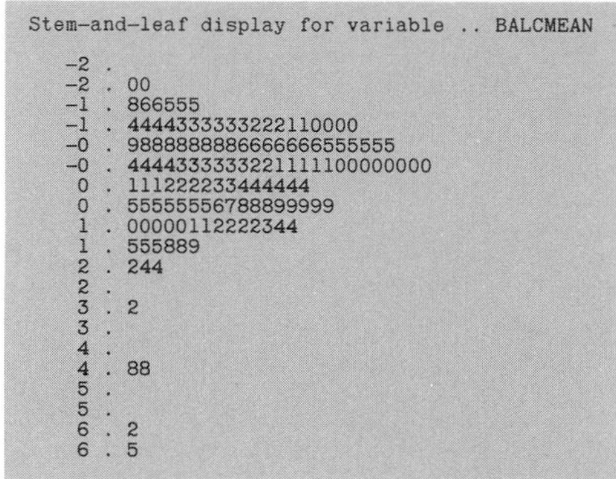

```
Stem-and-leaf display for variable .. BALCMEAN

   -2 .
   -2 . 00
   -1 . 866555
   -1 . 44443333322211 0000
   -0 . 98888888866666665555 55
   -0 . 444433333221111100000000
    0 . 111222233444444
    0 . 555555567888 99999
    1 . 00000112222344
    1 . 555889
    2 . 244
    2 .
    3 . 2
    3 .
    4 .
    4 . 88
    5 .
    5 .
    6 . 2
    6 . 5
```

Figure 6.7b is the corresponding normal probability plot. Note that the plot is no longer linear but is curved, especially for larger values of the variable. This downward curve indicates that the observed values are larger than predicted by the corresponding expected normal values. This is also seen in the stem-and-leaf plot. The detrended normal plot for this variable is shown in Figure 6.7c, which shows that there is a definite pattern to the deviations. The values no longer cluster in a horizontal band about 0. A transformation might be considered.

Figure 6.7b Normal probability plot—balance variable

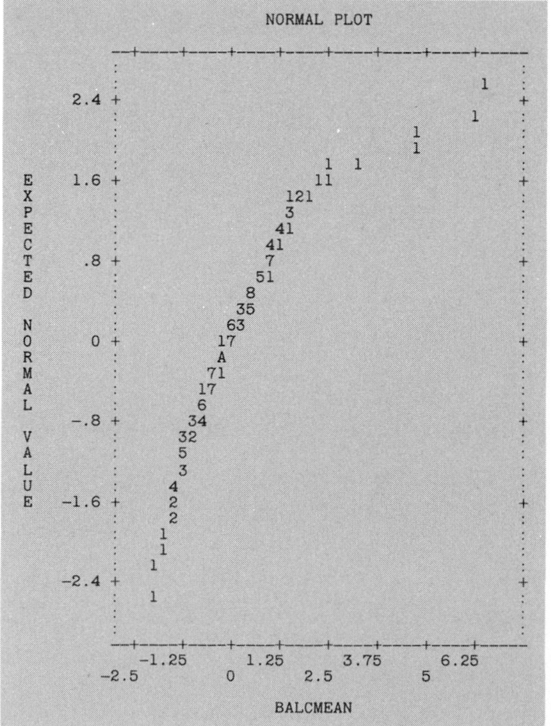

Figure 6.7c Detrended normal plot—balance variable

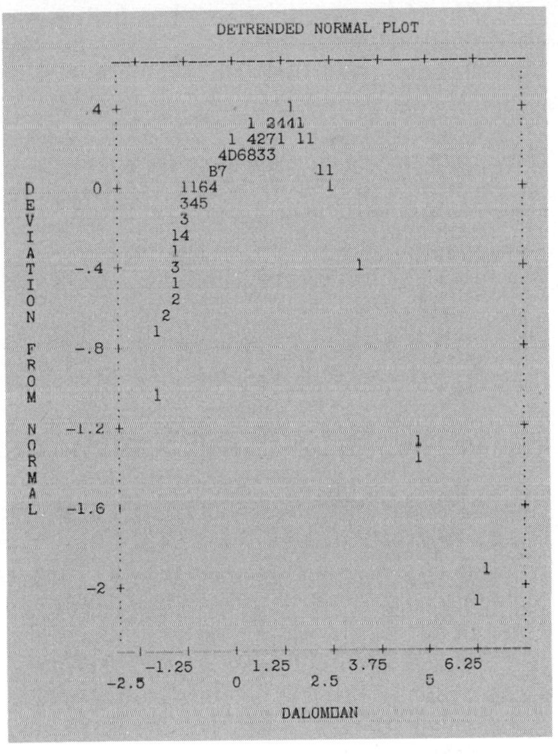

6.8 Bartlett's Test of Sphericity

Since there is no reason to use the multivariate analysis of variance procedure if the dependent variables are not correlated, it is useful to examine the correlation matrix of the dependent variables. If the variables are independent, the observed correlation matrix is expected to have small off-diagonal elements. Bartlett's test of sphericity can be used to test the hypothesis that the population correlation matrix is an identity matrix, that is, all diagonal terms are 1 and all off-diagonal terms are 0.

The test is based on the determinant of the within-cells correlation matrix. A determinant that is close in value to 0 indicates that one or more of the variables can almost be expressed as a linear function of the other dependent variables. Thus the hypothesis that the variables are independent is rejected if the determinant is small. Figure 6.8a contains output from Bartlett's test of sphericity. The determinant is displayed first, followed by a transformation of the determinant (which has a chi-square distribution). Since the observed significance level is small (less than 0.0005), the hypothesis that the population correlation matrix is an identity matrix is rejected.

Figure 6.8a Bartlett's test of sphericity

```
MANOVA BALOMEAN BALCMEAN SSTMEAN PP
  /PRINT=ERROR(COR)
  /DESIGN
```

```
Statistics for WITHIN CELLS correlations

Determinant =                          .82942
Bartlett test of sphericity =    24.46993 with 6 D. F.
Significance =                           .000
```

A graphical test of the hypothesis that the correlation matrix is an identity matrix is described by Everitt (1978). The observed correlation coefficients are transformed using Fisher's Z-transform, and then a half-normal plot of the transformed coefficients is obtained. A half-normal plot is very similar to the normal plot described above. The only difference is that both positive and negative values are treated identically. If the population correlation matrix is an identity matrix, the plot should be fairly linear and the line should pass through the origin.

Figure 6.8b is the plot of the transformed correlation coefficients for the correlation matrix in Figure 6.4. The plot shows deviations from linearity, suggesting that the dependent variables are not independent, a result also indicated by Bartlett's test.

Figure 6.8b A half-normal plot of the correlation coefficients

```
MANOVA BALOMEAN BALCMEAN SSTMEAN PP
  /PLOT=ZCORR
  /DESIGN
```

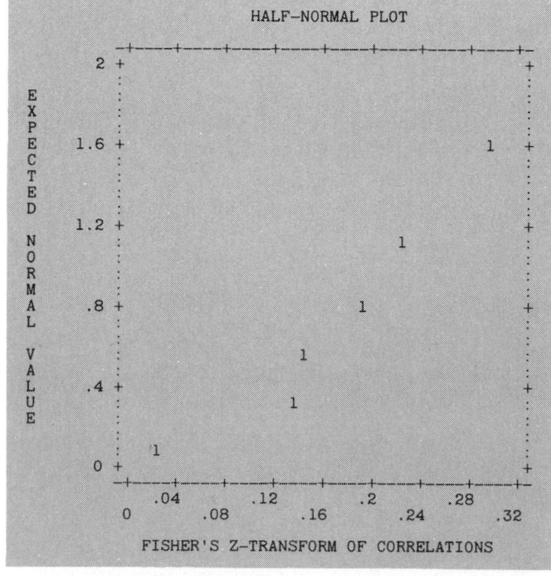

6.9 Testing Hypotheses

Once the distributions of the variables have been examined, we are ready to test the hypothesis that there is no difference between the population means and the hypothesized values. To test the various hypotheses of interest, SPSS^X MANOVA computes a design matrix whose columns correspond to the various effects in the model (see Section 6.16). Figure 6.9a shows the table displayed by SPSS^X MANOVA containing the names of the effects to be tested and their corresponding columns in the design matrix. In the one-sample MANOVA design, there is only one effect, labeled the CONSTANT.

Figure 6.9a The effects matrix

```
MANOVA BALOMEAN BALCMEAN SSTMEAN PP
  /PRINT=DESIGN
  /DESIGN¹
```

```
Correspondence between Effects and Columns of BETWEEN-Subjects Design 1

 Starting  Ending
  Column   Column   Effect Name

     1        1     CONSTANT
```

To understand how the statistic for testing the hypothesis that all differences are 0 is constructed, recall the one-sample t test. The statistic for testing the hypothesis that the population mean is some known constant, which we will call μ_0, is

$$t = \frac{\bar{X} - \mu_0}{S/\sqrt{N}} \qquad \textbf{Equation 6.9a}$$

where $\bar{X}$ is the sample mean and S is the standard deviation. The numerator of the t value is a measure of how much the sample mean differs from the hypothesized value, while the denominator is a measure of how variable the sample mean is.

When you simultaneously test the hypothesis that several population means do not differ from a specified set of constants, a statistic that considers all variables together is required. Hotelling's T^2 statistic is usually used for this purpose. It is computed as

$$T^2 = N(\underset{\sim}{\bar{X}} - \underset{\sim}{\mu_0})' S^{-1} (\underset{\sim}{\bar{X}} - \underset{\sim}{\mu_0}) \qquad \textbf{Equation 6.9b}$$

where S^{-1} is the inverse of the variance-covariance matrix of the dependent variables and $\underset{\sim}{X} - \underset{\sim}{\mu_0}$ is the vector of differences between the sample means and the hypothesized constants. The two matrices upon which Hotelling's T^2 is based can be displayed by SPSS^X MANOVA. The matrix that contains the differences between the observed sample means and the hypothesized values is shown in Figure 6.9b.

Figure 6.9b The hypothesis sum of squares and cross-products matrix

```
MANOVA BALOMEAN BALCMEAN SSTMEAN PP
  /PRINT=SIGNIF(HYPOTH)
  /DESIGN
```

```
EFFECT .. CONSTANT

Adjusted Hypothesis Sum-of-Squares and Cross-Products

               BALOMEAN    BALCMEAN     SSTMEAN          PP

BALOMEAN        317.764
BALCMEAN        -29.490       2.737
SSTMEAN         535.894     -49.733     903.761
PP            -1026.103      95.226   -1730.477    3313.433
```

[1]With releases before 2.2, replace the MANOVA command with the following:

```
MANOVA BALOMEAN BALCMEAN SSTMEAN PP
  /DESIGN
```

The diagonal elements are just the squares of the sample means minus the hypothesized values, multiplied by the sample size. For example, from Figure 6.4, the difference between the eyes-open balance score and the hypothesized value is −1.54. Squaring this difference and multiplying it by the sample size of 134, we get 317.76, the entry for BALOMEAN in Figure 6.9b. The off-diagonal elements are the product of the differences for the two variables, multiplied by the sample size. For example, the cross-products entry for the BALOMEAN and BALCMEAN is, from Figure 6.4, $-1.54 \times 0.14 \times 134 = -29.49$. For a fixed sample size, as the magnitude of the differences between the sample means and hypothesized values increases, so do the entries of this sums-of-squares and cross-products matrix.

The matrix whose entries indicate how much variability there is in the dependent variables is called the within-cells sum-of-squares and cross-products matrix. It is designated as S in the previous formula and is shown in Figure 6.9c. The diagonal entries are (N−1) times the variance of the dependent variables. For example, the entry for the pegboard variable is, from Figure 6.4, $1.49^2 \times (133) = 297.12$. The off-diagonal entries are the sums of the cross-products for the two variables. For example, for variables X and Y the cross-product is

$$CPSS_{xy} = \sum_{i=1}^{N} (X_i - \bar{X})(Y_i - \bar{Y}) \qquad \textbf{Equation 6.9c}$$

To compute Hotelling's T^2, the inverse of this within-cells sums-of-squares matrix is required, as well as the hypothesis sums-of-squares matrix in Figure 6.9b. The significance level associated with T^2 can be obtained from the *F* distribution. Figure 6.9d contains the value of Hotelling's T^2 divided by (N−1), its transformation to a variable that has an *F* distribution, and the degrees of freedom associated with the *F* statistic. Since there are four dependent variables in this example, the hypothesis degrees of freedom are 4, while the remaining degrees of freedom, 130, are associated with the error sums of squares. Since the observed significance level is small (less than 0.0005), the null hypothesis that the population means do not differ from the hypothesized constants is rejected.

Figure 6.9c Within-cells sum-of-squares and cross-products matrix

```
MANOVA BALOMEAN BALCMEAN SSTMEAN PP
  /PRINT=ERROR(SSCP)
  /DESIGN
```

WITHIN CELLS Sum-of-Squares and Cross-Products

	BALOMEAN	BALCMEAN	SSTMEAN	PP
BALOMEAN	4567.274			
BALCMEAN	311.080	262.501		
SSTMEAN	459.656	94.833	956.239	
PP	26.795	40.782	70.422	297.122

Figure 6.9d Hotelling's statistic

```
MANOVA BALOMEAN BALCMEAN SSTMEAN PP
  /DESIGN
```

Multivariate Tests of Significance (S = 1, M = 1 , N = 64)

Test Name	Value	Approx. F	Hypoth. DF	Error DF	Sig. of F
Hotellings	13.20587	429.19091	4.00	130.00	.000

6.10 Univariate Tests

When the hypothesis of no difference is rejected, it is often informative to examine the univariate test results to get some idea of where the differences may be. Figure 6.10a contains the univariate results for the four dependent variables. The hypothesis and error sums of squares are the diagonal terms in Figures 6.9b and 6.9c. The mean squares are obtained by dividing the sums of squares by their degrees of freedom, 1 for the hypothesis sums of squares and 133 for the error sums of squares. The ratio of the two mean squares is displayed in the column labeled F. These *F* values are nothing more than the squares of one-sample *t* values. Thus, from Figure 6.4, the mean difference for the BALOMEAN variable is −1.54 and the standard deviation is 5.86. The corresponding *t* value is

$$t = \frac{-1.54}{5.86/\sqrt{134}} = -3.04 \qquad \textbf{Equation 6.10}$$

Squaring this produces the value 9.25, which is the entry in Figure 6.10a. From Figure 6.10a, we can see that the balancing-with-eyes-closed variable is the only one whose *t* value is not significant. This is to be expected, since it has a 95% confidence interval that includes 0. The significance levels for the univariate statistics are not adjusted for the fact that several comparisons are being made and thus should be used with a certain amount of caution. For a discussion of the problem of multiple comparisons, see Miller, 1981, or Burns, 1984.

Figure 6.10 Univariate *F* tests

```
MANOVA BALOMEAN BALCMEAN SSTMEAN PP
  /PRINT=SIGNIF(UNIV)
  /DESIGN
```

Univariate F-tests with (1,133) D. F.

Variable	Hypoth. SS	Error SS	Hypoth. MS	Error MS	F	Sig. of F
BALOMEAN	317.76355	1567.27368	317.76355	34.34040	9.25334	.003
BALCMEAN	2.73673	262.50070	2.73673	1.97369	1.38661	.241
SSTMEAN	903.76111	956.23869	903.76111	7.18976	125.70107	.000
PP	3313.43322	297.12189	3313.43322	2.23400	1483.18463	.000

6.11 The Two-Sample Multivariate T-Test

In the previous sections, we were concerned with testing the hypothesis that the sample was drawn from a population with a particular set of means. There was only one sample involved, though there were several dependent variables. In this section, we will consider the multivariate generalization of the two-sample *t* test. The hypothesis that men and women do not differ on the four motor-ability variables will be tested.

Figure 6.11a contains descriptive statistics for each variable according to sex. The female subjects are coded as *1*'s, and the males are coded as *2*'s. Males appear to maintain balance with eyes open longer than females and cross more lines in the stepping test.

Figure 6.11a Cell means and standard deviations

```
MANOVA BALOMEAN BALCMEAN SSTMEAN PP BY SEX(1,2)
  /PRINT=CELLINFO(MEANS)
  /DESIGN
```

```
Cell Means and Standard Deviations
Variable .. BALOMEAN           Balance Test - Eyes Open
     Factor          Code                    Mean     Std. Dev.        N   95 percent Conf. Interval
 SEX             Female                   9.74841      5.70718        63      8.31108      11.18575
 SEX             Male                    12.97887      5.60544        71     11.65209      14.30566
For entire sample                        11.46007      5.86007       134     10.45877      12.46138
- - - - - - - - - - - - - - - - - - - - - - - - - - - - - - - - - - - - - - - - - - - - - - - - - -
Variable .. BALCMEAN           Balance Test - Eyes Closed
     Factor          Code                    Mean     Std. Dev.        N   95 percent Conf. Interval
 SEX             Female                   3.19127      1.51789        63      2.80899       3.57355
 SEX             Male                     3.10000      1.30589        71      2.79090       3.40910
For entire sample                         3.14291      1.40488       134      2.90286       3.38296
- - - - - - - - - - - - - - - - - - - - - - - - - - - - - - - - - - - - - - - - - - - - - - - - - -
Variable .. SSTMEAN            Sidestepping Test
     Factor          Code                    Mean     Std. Dev.        N   95 percent Conf. Interval
 SEX             Female                  14.09524      2.25477        63     13.52738      14.66309
 SEX             Male                    16.56338      2.50053        71     15.97151      17.15524
For entire sample                        15.40298      2.68137       134     14.94482      15.86115
- - - - - - - - - - - - - - - - - - - - - - - - - - - - - - - - - - - - - - - - - - - - - - - - - -
Variable .. PP                 Purdue Pegboard Test
     Factor          Code                    Mean     Std. Dev.        N   95 percent Conf. Interval
 SEX             Female                  15.46561      1.45270        63     15.09975      15.83146
 SEX             Male                    14.53521      1.40094        71     14.20361      14.86681
For entire sample                        14.97263      1.49465       134     14.71724      15.22803
```

Another way to visualize the distribution of scores in each of the groups is with box-and-whisker plots, as shown in Figure 6.11b for the two balance variables. The upper and lower boundaries of the boxes are the upper and lower quartiles. The box length is the interquartile distance and the box contains the middle 50% of values in a group. The asterisk (*) inside the box identifies the group median. The larger the box, the greater the spread of the observations. The lines emanating from each box (the whiskers) extend to the smallest and largest observations in a group that are less than one interquartile range from the end of the box. These are marked with an *X*. Any points outside of this range but less than one-and-a-half interquartile ranges from the end of the box are marked with *O*'s for outlying. Points more than 1.5 interquartile distances away are marked with *E*'s for extreme. If there are multiple points at a single position, the number of points is also displayed.

Figure 6.11b

```
MANOVA BALOMEAN BALCMEAN SSTMEAN PP BY SEX(1,2)
  /PLOT=BOXPLOTS
  /DESIGN
```

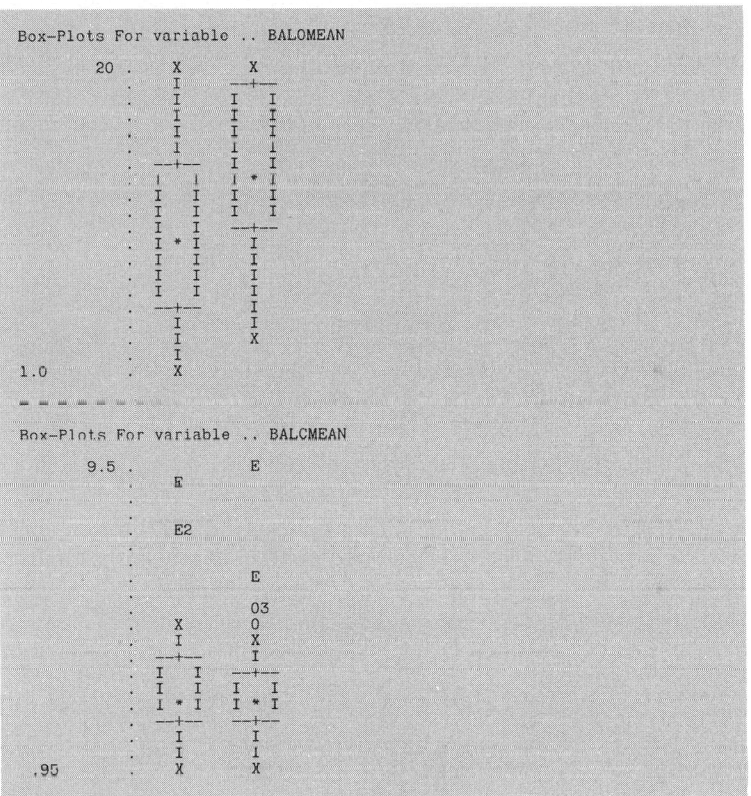

6.12 Tests of Homogeneity of Variance

In the one-sample Hotelling's T^2 test, there was no need to worry about the homogeneity of the variance-covariance matrices since there was only one matrix. In the two-sample test, there are two matrices (one for each group) and tests for their equality are necessary.

The variance-covariance matrices are shown in Figure 6.12a. They are computed for each group using the means of the variables within that group. Thus, each matrix indicates how much variability there is in a group. Combining these individual matrices into a common variance-covariance matrix results in the pooled matrix displayed in Figure 6.12b.

Figure 6.12a Variance-covariance matrices for BALOMEAN and BALCMEAN

```
MANOVA BALOMEAN BALCMEAN SSTMEAN PP BY SEX(1,2)
  /PRINT=CELLINFO(COV)
  /DESIGN
```

```
Cell Number .. 1

Variance-Covariance matrix

              BALOMEAN     BALCMEAN      SSTMEAN           PP

BALOMEAN        32.572
BALCMEAN         3.391        2.304
SSTMEAN           .427         .556        5.084
PP               1.437         .367        1.309        2.110

- - - - - - - - - -

Cell Number .. 2

Variance-Covariance matrix

              BALOMEAN     BALCMEAN      SSTMEAN           PP

BALOMEAN        31.421
BALCMEAN         1.581        1.705
SSTMEAN          2.386         .970        6.253
PP                .543         .217         .942        1.963
```

Figure 6.12b Pooled matrix

```
Pooled within-cells variance-covariance matrix

              BALOMEAN     BALCMEAN      SSTMEAN           PP

BALOMEAN        31.962
BALCMEAN         2.431        1.987
SSTMEAN          1.466         .775        5.704
PP                .963         .287        1.114        2.032
```

Figure 6.12c contains two homogeneity-of-variance tests (Cochrans C and the Bartlett-Box F) for each variable individually. The significance levels indicate that there is no reason to reject the hypotheses that the variances in the two groups are equal. Although these univariate tests are a convenient starting point for examining the equality of the covariance matrices, they are not sufficient. A test that simultaneously considers both the variances and covariances is required.

Figure 6.12c Univariate homogeneity of variance tests

```
MANOVA BALOMEAN BALCMEAN SSTMEAN PP BY SEX(1,2)
  /PRINT=HOMOGENEITY(COCHRAN BARTLETT)
  /DESIGN
```

```
Univariate Homogeneity of Variance Tests

Variable .. BALOMEAN              Balance Test - Eyes Open

     Cochrans C(66,2) =                            .50899, P = 1.000 (approx.)
     Bartlett-Box F(1,51762) =                     .02113, P =  .884

Variable .. BALCMEAN              Balance Test - Eyes Closed

     Cochrans C(66,2) =                            .57466, P = 1.000 (approx.)
     Bartlett-Box F(1,51762) =                    1.48033, P =  .224

Variable .. SSTMEAN               Sidestepping Test

     Cochrans C(66,2) =                            .55154, P = 1.000 (approx.)
     Bartlett-Box F(1,51762) =                     .69437, P =  .405

Variable .. PP                    Purdue Pegboard Test

     Cochrans C(66,2) =                            .51813, P = 1.000 (approx.)
     Bartlett-Box F(1,51762) =                     .08603, P =  .769
```

Box's *M* test, which is based on the determinants of the variance-covariance matrices in each cell as well as of the pooled variance-covariance matrix, provides a multivariate test for the homogeneity of the matrices. However, Box's *M* test is very sensitive to departures from normality. The significance level can be based on either an *F* or a χ^2 statistic, and both approximations are given in the output, as shown in Figure 6.12d. Given the result of Box's *M* test, there appears to be no reason to suspect the homogeneity-of-dispersion-matrices assumption.

Figure 6.12d Homogeneity of dispersion matrices

```
MANOVA BALOMEAN BALCMEAN SSTMEAN PP BY SEX(1,2)
  /PRINT=HOMOGENEITY(COCHRAN BARTLETT BOXM)
  /DESIGN
```

```
Cell Number .. 1

Determinant of variance-covariance matrix =          538.89601
LOG(Determinant) =                                     6.28952

- - - - - - - - - -

Cell Number .. 2

Determinant of variance-covariance matrix =          522.34684
LOG(Determinant) =                                     6.25833

- - - - - - - - - -

Determinant of pooled variance-covariance matrix          557.40536
LOG(Determinant) =                                          6.32329

- - - - - - - - - - - - - - - - - - - - - - - - - - - - - - - - - - -

Multivariate test for Homogeneity of Dispersion matrices

Boxs M =                           6.64101
F with (10,80608) DF =              .64228, P =   .779 (Approx.)
Chi-Square with 10 DF =            6.42361, P =   .779 (Approx.)
```

6.13 Hotelling's T^2 for Two Independent Samples

The actual statistic for testing the equality of several means with two independent samples is also based on Hotelling's T^2. The formula is

$$T^2 = \frac{N_1 N_2}{N_1 + N_2} (\underset{\sim}{\bar{X}}_1 - \underset{\sim}{\bar{X}}_2)' S^{-1} (\underset{\sim}{\bar{X}}_1 - \underset{\sim}{\bar{X}}_2) \qquad \textbf{Equation 6.13a}$$

where $\underset{\sim}{\bar{X}}_1$ is the vector of means for the first group (females), $\underset{\sim}{\bar{X}}_2$ is the vector for the second group (males), and S^{-1} is the inverse of the pooled within-groups covariance matrix. The statistic is somewhat similar to the one described for the one-sample test in Section 6.9.

Again, two matrices are used in the computation of the statistic. The pooled within-groups covariance matrix has been described previously and is displayed in Figure 6.12b. The second matrix is the adjusted hypothesis sum-of-squares and cross-products matrix. It is displayed under the heading EFFECT .. SEX and in Figure 6.13a. The entries in this matrix are the weighted squared differences of the group means from the combined mean. For example, the entry for the balancing-with-eyes-open variable is

$$SS = 63(9.75-11.46)^2 + 71(12.98-11.46)^2 = 348.36 \qquad \textbf{Equation 6.13b}$$

where, from Figure 6.11a, 9.75 is the mean value for the 63 females, 12.98 is the value for the 71 males, and 11.46 is the mean for the entire sample. The first off-diagonal term for balancing with eyes open (BALOMEAN) and eyes closed (BALCMEAN) is similarly

$$SS = (9.75-11.46)(3.19-3.14)63 + (12.98-11.46)(3.10-3.14)71 = -9.84$$ **Equation 6.13c**

The diagonal terms should be recognizable to anyone familiar with analysis of variance methodology. They are the sums of squares due to groups for each variable.

Figure 6.13a Adjusted hypothesis sums of squares and cross-products matrix

```
MANOVA BALOMEAN BALCMEAN SSTMEAN PP BY SEX(1,2)
  /PRINT=SIGNIF(HYPOTH)
  /DESIGN
```

```
EFFECT .. SEX

Adjusted Hypothesis Sum-of-Squares and Cross-Products

              BALOMEAN    BALCMEAN     SSTMEAN          PP

BALOMEAN       348.356
BALCMEAN        -9.842        .278
SSTMEAN        266.151      -7.520     203.345
PP            -100.329       2.835     -76.653      28.895
```

Figure 6.13b contains the value of Hotelling's T^2 statistic divided by $N-2$ for the test of the hypothesis that men and women do not differ on the motor-ability test scores. The significance level is based on the F distribution with 4 and 129 degrees of freedom. The observed significance level is small (less than 0.0005), so the null hypothesis that men and women perform equally well on the motor-ability tests is rejected.

Figure 6.13b

```
MANOVA BALOMEAN BALCMEAN SSTMEAN PP BY SEX(1,2)
  /PRINT=SIGNIF(HYPOTH MULTIV)
  /DESIGN
```

```
Multivariate Tests of Significance (S = 1, M = 1 , N = 63 1/2)

Test Name           Value   Approx. F  Hypoth. DF    Error DF   Sig. of F

Hotellings         .66953   21.59224        4.00      129.00        .000
```

6.14 Univariate Tests

To get some idea of where the differences between men's and women's scores occur, the univariate tests for the individual variables may be examined. These are the same as the F values from one-way analyses of variance. In the case of two groups, the F values are just the squares of the two-sample t values.

Figure 6.14

```
MANOVA BALOMEAN BALCMEAN SSTMEAN PP BY SEX(1,2)
  /PRINT=SIGNIF(HYPOTH MULTIV UNIV)
  /DESIGN
```

```
EFFECT .. SEX (CONT.)

Univariate F-tests with (1,132) D. F.

Variable     Hypoth. SS     Error SS  Hypoth. MS      Error MS           F   Sig. of F

BALOMEAN      348.35572   4218.91817   348.35572      31.96150    10.89923        .001
BALCMEAN         .27807    262.22270      .27807       1.98654      .13998        .709
SSTMEAN       203.34512    752.89249   203.34512       5.70373    35.65125        .000
PP             28.89544    268.22570    28.89544       2.03201    14.22011        .000
```

From Figure 6.14, we can see that there are significant univariate tests for all variables except balancing with eyes closed. Again, the significance levels are not adjusted for the fact that four tests, rather than one, are being performed.

6.15 Discriminant Analysis

In Chapter 3, we considered the problem of finding the best linear combination of variables for distinguishing among several groups. Coefficients for the variables are chosen so that the ratio of between-groups sums of squares to total sums of squares is as large as possible. Although the equality of means hypotheses tested in MANOVA may initially appear quite unrelated to the discriminant problem, the two procedures are closely related. In fact, MANOVA can be viewed as a problem of first finding linear combinations of the dependent variables that best separate the groups and then testing whether these new variables are significantly different for the groups. For this reason, the usual discriminant analysis statistics can be obtained as part of the SPSSˣ MANOVA output.

Figure 6.15a contains the eigenvalues and canonical correlation for the canonical discriminant function that separates males and females. Remember that the eigenvalue is the ratio of the between-groups sum of squares to the within-groups sum of squares, while the square of the canonical correlation is the ratio of the between-groups sums of squares to the total sum of squares. Thus, about 40% of the variablility in the discriminant scores is attributable to between-group differences ($0.633^2 = 0.401$).

Figure 6.15a Eigenvalue and canonical correlation

```
MANOVA BALOMEAN BALCMEAN SSTMEAN PP BY SEX(1,2)
  /PRINT=SIGNIF(HYPOTH MULTIV UNIV EIGEN)
  /DESIGN
```

Eigenvalues and Canonical Correlations

Root No.	Eigenvalue	Pct.	Cum. Pct.	Canon. Cor.
1	.670	100.000	100.000	.633

As discussed in Chapter 3, when there are two groups Wilks' lambda, can be interpreted as a measure of the proportion of total variability not explained by group differences. As shown in Figure 6.15b, almost 60% of the observed variability is not explained by the group differences. The hypothesis that in the population there are no difference between the group means can be tested using Wilks' lambda. Lambda is transformed to a variable that has an *F* distribution. For the two-group situation, the *F* value for Wilks' lambda is identical to that given for Hotelling's T^2 (Figure 6.13b).

Figure 6.15b Wilks' lambda

```
MANOVA BALOMEAN BALCMEAN SSTMEAN PP BY SEX(1,2)
  /PRINT=SIGNIF(HYPOTH MULTIV UNIV EIGEN DIMENR)
  /DESIGN
```

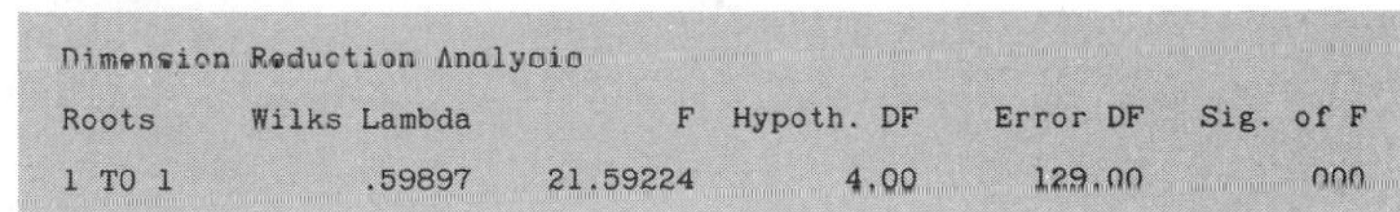

Dimension Reduction Analysis

Roots	Wilks Lambda	F	Hypoth. DF	Error DF	Sig. of F
1 TO 1	.59897	21.59224	4.00	129.00	.000

Both raw and standardized discriminant function coefficients can be displayed by SPSSˣ MANOVA. The raw coefficents are the multipliers of the dependent variables in their original units, while the standardized coefficients are the multipliers of the dependent variables when the latter have been standardized to a mean of 0 and a standard deviation of 1. Both sets of coefficients are displayed in Figure 6.15c.

Figure 6.15c Raw and standardized discriminant function coefficients

```
MANOVA BALOMEAN BALCMEAN SSTMEAN PP BY SEX(1,2)
  /DISCRIM=RAW STAN²
  /DESIGN
```

```
EFFECT .. SEX (CONT.)

Raw discriminant function coefficients

          Function No.

Variable               1

BALOMEAN           -.075
BALCMEAN            .192
SSTMEAN            -.369
PP                  .492

- - - - - - - - - - - - - - - - - - - - - - - - - - - - - - - - - - - -

Standardized discriminant function coefficients

          Function No.

Variable               1

BALOMEAN           -.422
BALCMEAN            .271
SSTMEAN            -.881
PP                  .701
```

The side-stepping and pegboard scores have the largest standardized coefficients and, as you will recall from Figure 6.9a, they also have the largest univariate *F*'s, suggesting that they are important for separating the two groups. Of course, when variables are correlated, the discriminant function coefficients must be interpreted with care, since highly correlated variables "share" the discriminant weights.

The correlation coefficients for the discriminant scores and each dependent variable are somewhat less likely to be strongly influenced by the correlations between the variables. These coefficients, sometimes called *structure coefficients,* are displayed in Figure 6.15d. Once again, the side-stepping test and the pegboard test are most highly correlated with the discriminant function, while the correlation coefficient between balancing with eyes closed and the discriminant function is near 0. Again, balancing with eyes closed had a nonsignificant univariate *F*.

Figure 6.15d Correlations between dependent variables and canonical variables

```
MANOVA BALOMEAN BALCMEAN SSTMEAN PP BY SEX(1,2)
  /DISCRIM=RAW STAN COR³
  /DESIGN
```

```
Correlations between DEPENDENT and canonical variables

          Canonical Variable

Variable               1

BALOMEAN           -.351
BALCMEAN            .040
SSTMEAN            -.635
PP                  .401
```

An additional statistic displayed as part of the discriminant output in MANOVA is an estimate of the effect for the canonical variable. Consider Figure

[2]With releases before 2.2, replace the MANOVA command with the following:

```
MANOVA BALOMEAN BALCMEAN SSTMEAN PP BY SEX(1,2)
  /PRINT=DISCRIM(RAW STAN)
  /DESIGN
```

[3]With releases before 2.2, replace the MANOVA command with the following:

```
MANOVA BALOMEAN BALCMEAN SSTMEAN PP BY SEX(1,2)
  /PRINT=DISCRIM(RAW STAN CORR)
  /DESIGN
```

6.15e (from procedure DISCRIMINANT), which gives the average canonical function scores for the two groups. We can estimate the effect of a canonical variable by measuring its average distance from 0 across all groups. In this example the average distance is $(0.86 + 0.77) / 2 = 0.81$, as shown in Figure 6.15f. Canonical variables with small effects do not contribute much to separation between groups.

Figure 6.15e Average canonical function scores from DISCRIMINANT

```
DISCRIMINANT GROUPS=SEX(1,2)
  /VARIABLES=BALOMEAN SSTMEAN BALCMEAN PP
  /METHOD=DIRECT
```

```
CANONICAL DISCRIMINANT FUNCTIONS EVALUATED AT GROUP MEANS (GROUP CENTROIDS)

   GROUP       FUNC   1

     1         -0.86214
     2          0.76500
```

Figure 6.15f Estimates of effects for canonical variables

```
MANOVA BALOMEAN BALCMEAN SSTMEAN PP BY SEX(1,2)
  /DISCRIM=RAW STAN COR ESTIM⁴
  /DESIGN
```

```
Estimates of effects for canonical variables

          Canonical Variable

 Parameter           1

      2           .814
```

6.16 Parameter Estimates

As for most other statistical techniques, there is for MANOVA a mathematical model that expresses the relationship between the dependent variable and the independent variables. Recall, for example, that in a univariate analysis of variance model with four groups, the mean for each group can be expressed as

$$\begin{aligned} Y_{.1} &= \mu + \alpha_1 + E_{.1} \\ Y_{.2} &= \mu + \alpha_2 + E_{.2} \\ Y_{.3} &= \mu + \alpha_3 + E_{.3} \\ Y_{.4} &= \mu + \alpha_4 + E_{.4} \end{aligned}$$

Equation 6.16a

In matrix form this can be written as

$$\begin{bmatrix} Y_{.1} \\ Y_{.2} \\ Y_{.3} \\ Y_{.4} \end{bmatrix} = \begin{bmatrix} 1 & 1 & 0 & 0 & 0 \\ 1 & 0 & 1 & 0 & 0 \\ 1 & 0 & 0 & 1 & 0 \\ 1 & 0 & 0 & 0 & 1 \end{bmatrix} \begin{bmatrix} \mu \\ \alpha_1 \\ \alpha_2 \\ \alpha_3 \\ \alpha_4 \end{bmatrix} + \begin{bmatrix} E_{.1} \\ E_{.2} \\ E_{.3} \\ E_{.4} \end{bmatrix}$$

Equation 6.16b

or

$$Y_{.} = A\Theta^* + E$$

Equation 6.16c

Since the Θ matrix has more columns than rows, it does not have a unique inverse. We are unable to estimate five parameters (μ and α_1 to α_4) on the basis of four sample means. Instead we can estimate four linear combinations, termed contrasts, of the parameters (see Finn, 1974).

[4]With releases before 2.2, replace the MANOVA command with the following:

```
MANOVA BALOMEAN BALCMEAN SSTMEAN PP BY SEX(1,2)
  /PRINT=DISCRIM(RAW STAN CORR ESTIM)
  /DESIGN
```

Several types of contrasts are available in SPSS^X MANOVA, resulting in different types of parameter estimates. Deviation contrasts, the default, estimate each parameter as its difference from the overall average for that parameter. This results in parameter estimates of the form $\mu_j - \mu.$ Deviation contrasts do not require any particular ordering of the factor levels.

Simple contrasts are useful when one of the factor levels is a comparison or control group. All parameter estimates are then expressed as a deviation from the value of the control group. When factor levels have an underlying metric, orthogonal polynomial contrasts may be used to determine whether group means are related to the values of the factor level. For example, if three doses of an agent are administered (10 units, 20 units, and 30 units), you can test whether response is related to dose in a linear or quadratic fashion.

Figure 6.16 contains parameter estimates corresponding to the default deviation contrasts. For each dependent variable, the entry under CONSTANT is just the unweighted average of the means in the two groups. For example, from Figure 6.11a, we see that the mean for balancing with eyes open is 9.748 for females and 12.979 for males. The estimate for the average time balanced with eyes open, the constant term in Figure 6.16, is 11.364, the average of 12.979 and 9.748.

Figure 6.16 Parameter estimates

```
Estimates for BALOMEAN
CONSTANT
 Parameter          Coeff.        Std. Err.        T-Value      Sig. of T    Lower 95% CL    Upper 95% CL
         1   11.3636424853           .48926       23.22635           .000        10.39584        12.33144
SEX
 Parameter          Coeff.        Std. Err.        T-Value      Sig. of T    Lower 95% CL    Upper 95% CL
         2   -1.6152302168           .48926       -3.30140           .001        -2.58303         -.64743
- - - - - - - - - - - - - - - - - - - - - - - - - - - - - - - - - - - - - - - - - - - - - - - - - - - -
Estimates for BALCMEAN
CONSTANT
 Parameter          Coeff.        Std. Err.        T-Value      Sig. of T    Lower 95% CL    Upper 95% CL
         1    3.1456344691           .12198       25.78916           .000         2.90436         3.38691
SEX
 Parameter          Coeff.        Std. Err.        T-Value      Sig. of T    Lower 95% CL    Upper 95% CL
         2     .0456348936           .12198         .37413           .709         -.19564          .28691
- - - - - - - - - - - - - - - - - - - - - - - - - - - - - - - - - - - - - - - - - - - - - - - - - - - -
Estimates for SSTMEAN
CONSTANT
 Parameter          Coeff.        Std. Err.        T-Value      Sig. of T    Lower 95% CL    Upper 95% CL
         1   15.3293073837           .20668       74.16860           .000        14.92047        15.73814
SEX
 Parameter          Coeff.        Std. Err.        T-Value      Sig. of T    Lower 95% CL    Upper 95% CL
         2   -1.2340700907           .20668       -5.97087           .000        -1.64291         -.82523
- - - - - - - - - - - - - - - - - - - - - - - - - - - - - - - - - - - - - - - - - - - - - - - - - - - -
Estimates for PP
CONSTANT
 Parameter          Coeff.        Std. Err.        T-Value      Sig. of T    Lower 95% CL    Upper 95% CL
         1   15.0004079854           .12336      121.59533           .000        14.75638        15.24443
SEX
 Parameter          Coeff.        Std. Err.        T-Value      Sig. of T    Lower 95% CL    Upper 95% CL
         2     .4651977655           .12336        3.77096           .000          .22117          .70922
```

There are two estimates for the sex parameter, one for females and one for males. The output includes only values for the first parameter (females), since the value for the second parameter is just the negative of the value for the first. The sex effect for females is estimated as the difference between the mean score of females and the overall unweighted mean. For balancing with eyes open it is 9.75 − 11.36 = −1.61, the value displayed in Figure 6.16. Confidence intervals and t tests for the null hypothesis that a parameter value is 0 can also be calculated. Again, these are calculated on a parameter-by-parameter basis and do not offer an overall protection level against Type 1 errors. Note that the t values displayed for each parameter are equal to the square root of the F values displayed for the univariate F tests in Figure 6.14.

6.17 A Multivariate Factorial Design

So far we have considered two very simple multivariate designs, generalizations of the one- and two-sample t tests to the case of multiple dependent variables. We are now ready to examine a more complex design. Recall that in the experiment conducted by Barnard, the hypothesis of interest concerned the relationship among field dependence, sex, and motor abilities. Since subjects are classified into one of three field-dependence categories—low, intermediate, and high—we have a two-way factorial design with three levels of field dependence and two categories of sex.

Figure 6.17a contains the location of the effects in the design matrix. The number of columns required by each effect equals its degrees of freedom. Thus, there is one column for sex, two for field-dependence, and two for the sex-by-field-dependence interaction.

Figure 6.17a Correspondence table

```
MANOVA BALCMEAN BY SEX(1,2) FIELD(1,3) WITH BALOMEAN
  /PRINT=DESIGN
  /DESIGN 5
```

```
Correspondence between Effects and Columns of BETWEEN-Subjects Design 1

 Starting  Ending
  Column   Column    Effect Name

    1         1      CONSTANT
    2         2      SEX
    3         4      FIELD
    5         6      SEX BY FIELD
```

When orthogonal contrasts are requested for a factor, that is, when the sum of the products of corresponding coefficients for any two contrasts is zero, the numbers in the columns of the design matrix are the coefficients of the contrasts, except for scaling. When nonorthogonal contrasts, such as "deviation" or "simple," are requested for a factor, the columns of the matrix are not the contrast coefficients but are the "basis" for the contrast requested (see Bock, 1975; Finn, 1974). The actual parameter estimates always correspond to the contrast requested.

Descriptive statistics are available for each cell in the design. Some additional plots may also be useful. Plotting the mean of a variable for all cells in the design, as shown in Figure 6.17b, gives an idea of the spread of the means. The top row of numbers indicates how many cell means there are in each interval. You can see from the plot that there are two cells with means close to 14 seconds, three cells with means less than 10 seconds, and 1 cell with a mean in between.

[5]With releases before 2.2, replace the MANOVA command with the following:

```
MANOVA BALCMEAN BY SEX(1,2) FIELD(1,3) WITH BALOMEAN
  /DESIGN
```

Figure 6.17b Distribution of cell means for BALOMEAN

```
MANOVA BALCMEAN BY SEX(1,2) FIELD(1,3) WITH BALOMEAN
  /PLOT=CELLPLOTS
  /DESIGN
```

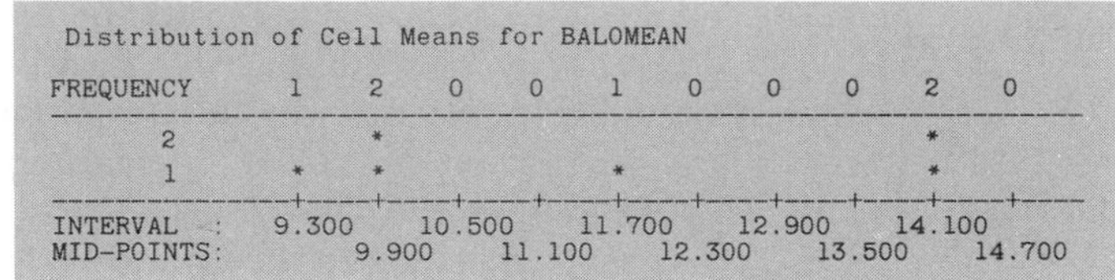

```
Distribution of Cell Means for BALOMEAN
FREQUENCY        1    2    0    0    1    0    0    0    2    0
-----------------------------------------------------------------
        2             *                                  *
        1        *    *              *                   *
---------------+----+----+----+----+----+----+----+----+----+----
INTERVAL   :   9.300     10.500    11.700    12.900    14.100
MID-POINTS:         9.900     11.100    12.300    13.500    14.700
```

Although both univariate and multivariate analyses of variance require equal variances in the cells, there are many situations in which cell means and standard deviations, or cell means and variances, are proportional. Figure 6.17c shows plots of cell means versus cell variances and cell standard deviations. There appears to be no relationship between the means and the measures of variability. If patterns were evident, transformations of the dependent variables might be used to stabilize the variances.

Figure 6.17c Plots of cell means, cell variances, and cell standard deviations

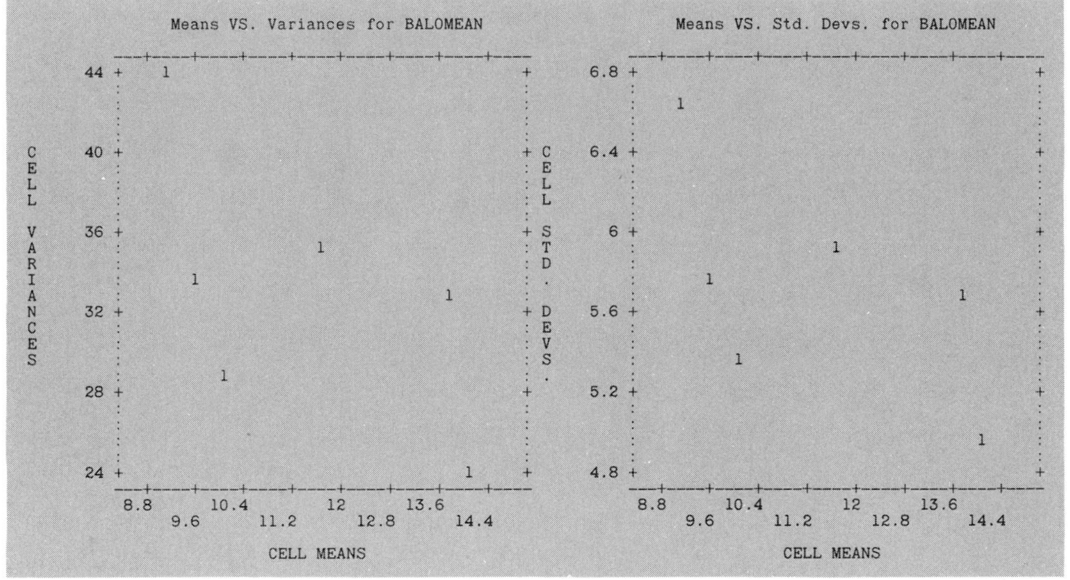

6.18 Principal Components Analysis

Bartlett's test of sphericity provides information about the correlations among the dependent variables by testing the hypothesis that the correlation matrix is an identity matrix. Another way to examine dependencies among the dependent variables is to perform a principal components analysis of their within-cells correlation or covariance matrix (see Chapter 4 for a discussion of principal components analysis). If principal components analysis reveals that one of the variables can be expressed as a linear combination of the others, the error sums-of-squares and cross-products matrix will be singular and a unique inverse cannot be obtained.

Figure 6.18a contains the within-cells correlation matrix for the two-way factorial design. The eigenvalues and percent of variance explained by each are shown in Figure 6.18b. The first two principal components account for about two-thirds of the total variance, and the remaining two components account for the rest. None of the eigenvalues is close enough to 0 to cause concern about the error matrix being singular.

Figure 6.18a Within-cells correlation matrix

```
MANOVA BALOMEAN BALCMEAN SSTMEAN PP BY SEX(1,2) FIELD(1,3)
  /PRINT=ERROR(COR)
  /METHOD=SSTYPE(UNIQUE)
  /DESIGN
```

WITHIN CELLS Correlations with Std. Devs. on Diagonal

	BALOMEAN	BALCMEAN	SSTMEAN	PP
BALOMEAN	5.675			
BALCMEAN	.300	1.415		
SSTMEAN	.115	.243	2.393	
PP	.111	.143	.347	1.438

Figure 6.18b Eigenvalues and percent of variance

```
MANOVA BALOMEAN BALCMEAN SSTMEAN PP BY SEX(1,2) FIELD(1,3)
  /PCOMPS=COR 6
  /METHOD=SSTYPE(UNIQUE)
  /DESIGN
```

Eigenvalues of WITHIN CELLS correlation matrix

	Eigenvalue	Pct of Var	Cum Pct
1	1.636	40.903	40.903
2	1.028	25.695	66.598
3	.723	18.064	84.662
4	.614	15.338	100.000

Figure 6.18c contains the loadings, which in this case are equivalent to correlations, between the principal components and dependent variables. The components can be rotated, as shown in Figure 6.18d, to increase interpretability. Each variable loads highly on only one of the components, suggesting that none is redundant or highly correlated with the others. When there are many dependent variables, a principal components analysis may indicate how the variables are related to each other. This information is useful for establishing the number of unique dimensions being measured by the dependent variables.

Figure 6.18c Correlations between principal components and dependent variable

```
MANOVA BALOMEAN BALCMEAN SSTMEAN PP BY SEX(1,2) FIELD(1,3)
  /PCOMPS=COR ROTATE(VARIMAX)7
  /METHOD=SSTYPE(UNIQUE)
  /DESIGN
```

Normalized principal components

Variables	Components 1	2	3	4
BALOMEAN	-.552	-.631	-.487	.246
BALCMEAN	-.669	-.415	.494	-.368
SSTMEAN	-.699	.416	.276	.512
PP	-.628	.534	-.406	-.394

[6]With releases before 2.2, replace the MANOVA command with the following:

```
MANOVA BALOMEAN BALCMEAN SSTMEAN PP BY SEX(1,2) FIELD (1,3)
  /PRINT=PRINCOMPS(CORR)
  /METHOD=SSTYPE(UNIQUE)
  /DESIGN
```

[7]With releases before 2.2, replace the MANOVA command with the following:

```
MANOVA BALOMEAN BALCMEAN SSTMEAN PP BY SEX(1,2) FIELD (1,3)
  /PRINT=PRINCOMPS(CORR ROTATE(VARIMAX))
  /METHOD=SSTYPE(UNIQUE)
  /DESIGN
```

Figure 6.18d Rotated correlations between components and dependent variable

VARIMAX rotated correlations between components and DEPENDENT variable

Dep. Var.	Can. Var. 1	2	3	4
BALOMEAN	.987	.048	.147	.045
BALCMEAN	.150	.060	.980	.115
SSTMEAN	.046	.174	.116	.977
PP	.048	.982	.059	.171

6.19 Tests of Multivariate Differences

Once the preliminary steps of examining the distribution of the variables for outliers, nonnormality, and inequality of variances have been taken and no significant violations have been found, hypothesis testing can begin. In the one- and two-sample test, Hotelling's T^2, a multivariate generalization of the univariate t value, is used. For more complicated designs, an extension of the familiar analysis of variance F test to the multivariate case is needed.

The univariate F tests in ANOVA are the ratios of the hypothesis mean squares to the error mean squares. When there is more than one dependent variable, there is no longer a single number that represents the hypothesis and error sums of squares. Instead, as shown in Section 6.9, there are matrices for the hypothesis and error sums of squares and cross-products. These matrices must be combined into some type of test statistic.

Most multivariate test statistics are based on the determinant of HE^{-1}, where H is the hypothesis sums-of-squares and cross-products matrix and E^{-1} is the inverse of the error sums-of-squares and cross-products matrix. The determinant is a measure of the generalized variance, or dispersion, of a matrix. This determinant can be calculated as the product of the eigenvalues of a matrix, since each eigenvalue represents a portion of the generalized variance. In fact, the process of extracting eigenvalues can be viewed as a principal components analysis on the HE^{-1} matrix.

There are a variety of test statistics for evaluating multivariate differences based on the eigenvalues of HE^{-1}. Four of the most commonly used tests are displayed by SPSS^X MANOVA:

- Pillai's Trace

$$V = \sum_{i=1}^{s} \frac{1}{1 + \lambda_i} \qquad \textbf{Equation 6.19a}$$

- Wilks' Lambda

$$W = \prod_{i=1}^{s} \frac{1}{1 + \lambda_i} \qquad \textbf{Equation 6.19b}$$

- Hotelling's Trace

$$T = \sum_{i=1}^{s} \lambda_i \qquad \textbf{Equation 6.19c}$$

- Roy's Largest Root

$$R = \frac{\lambda_{MAX}}{1 + \lambda_{MAX}} \qquad \textbf{Equation 6.19d}$$

where λ_{max} is the largest eigenvalue, λ_i is the ith eigenvalue, and s is the number of nonzero eigenvalues of HE^{-1}.

Although the exact distributions of the four criteria differ, they can be transformed into statistics that have approximately an *F* distribution. Tables of the exact distributions of the statistics are also available.

When there is a single dependent variable, all four criteria are equivalent to the ordinary ANOVA *F* statistic. When there is a single sample or two independent samples with multiple dependent variables, they are all equivalent to Hotelling's T^2. In both situations, the transformed statistics are distributed exactly as *F*'s.

Two concerns dictate the choice of the multivariate criterion—power and robustness. That is, the test statistic should detect differences when they exist and not be much affected by departures from the assumptions. For most practical situations, when differences among groups are spread along several dimensions, the ordering of the test criteria in terms of decreasing power is Pillai's, Wilks', Hotelling's, and Roy's. Pillai's trace is also the most robust criterion. That is, the significance level based on it is reasonably correct even when the assumptions are violated. This is important since a test that results in distorted significance levels in the presence of mild violations of homogeneity of covariance matrices or multivariate normality is of limited use (Olson, 1976).

6.20 Testing the Effects

Since our design is a two-by-three factorial (two sexes and three categories of field dependence), there are three effects to be tested: the sex and field-dependence main effects and the sex-by-field-dependence interaction. As in univariate analysis of variance, the terms are tested in reverse order. That is, higher-order effects are tested before lower-order ones, since it is difficult to interpret lower-order effects in the presence of higher order interactions. For example, if there is a sex-by-field-dependence interaction, testing for sex and field-dependence main effects is not particularly useful and can be misleading.

SPSS^X MANOVA displays separate output for each effect. Figure 6.20a shows the label displayed on each page to identify the effect being tested. The hypothesis sums-of-squares and cross-products matrix can be displayed for each effect. The same error matrix (the pooled within-cells sums-of-squares and cross-products matrix) is used to test all effects and is displayed only once before the effect-by-effect output. Figure 6.20b contains the error matrix for the factorial design. Figure 6.20c is the hypothesis sums-of-squares and cross-product matrix. These two matrices are the ones involved in the computation of the test statistic displayed in Figure 6.20d.

Figure 6.20a Label for effect being tested

```
EFFECT .. SEX BY FIELD
```

Figure 6.20b Error sums-of-squares and cross-products matrix

```
MANOVA BALOMEAN BALCMEAN SSTMEAN PP BY SEX(1,2) FIELD(1,3)
  /PRINT=ERROR(SSCP)
  /DESIGN
```

WITHIN CELLS Sum-of-Squares and Cross-Products

	BALOMEAN	BALCMEAN	SSTMEAN	PP
BALOMEAN	4122.152			
BALCMEAN	308.514	256.229		
SSTMEAN	200.021	105.499	733.148	
PP	115.981	37.339	152.895	264.837

Figure 6.20c Hypothesis sums-of-squares and cross-products matrix

```
MANOVA BALOMEAN BALCMEAN SSTMEAN PP BY SEX(1,2) FIELD(1,3)
  /PRINT=SIGNIF(HYPOTH)
  /DESIGN
```

Adjusted Hypothesis Sum-of-Squares and Cross-Products

	BALOMEAN	BALCMEAN	SSTMEAN	PP
BALOMEAN	18.102			
BALCMEAN	8.236	3.773		
SSTMEAN	2.495	.552	13.523	
PP	-.004	.213	-4.857	1.790

Figure 6.20d Multivariate tests of significance

```
MANOVA BALOMEAN BALCMEAN SSTMEAN PP BY SEX(1,2) FIELD(1,3)
  /PRINT=SIGNIF(HYPOTH MULTIV)
  /DESIGN
```

Multivariate Tests of Significance (S = 2, M = 1/2, N = 61 1/2)

Test Name	Value	Approx. F	Hypoth. DF	Error DF	Sig. of F
Pillais	.05245	.84827	8.00	252.00	.561
Hotellings	.05410	.83848	8.00	248.00	.570
Wilks	.94813	.84339	8.00	250.00	.565

Roys largest root criterion = .03668

The first line of Figure 6.20d contains the values of the parameters (S, M, N) used to find significance levels in tables of the exact distributions of the statistics. For the first three tests, the value of the test statistic is given, followed by its transformation to a statistic that has approximately an *F* distribution. The next two columns contain the numerator (hypothesis) and denominator (error) degrees of freedom for the *F* statistic. The observed significance level (the probability of observing a difference at least as large as the one found in the sample when there is no difference in the populations) is given in the last column. All of the observed significance levels are large, causing us not to reject the hypothesis that the sex-by-field-dependence interaction is 0. There is no straightforward transformation for Roy's largest root criterion to a statistic with a known distribution, so only the value of the largest root is displayed.

Since the multivariate results are not statistically significant, there is no reason to examine the univariate results shown in Figure 6.20e. When the multivariate results are significant, however, the univariate statistics may help determine which variables contribute to the overall differences. The univariate *F* tests for the SEX-by-FIELD interaction are the same as the *F*'s for SEX by FIELD in a two-way ANOVA. Figure 6.20f contains a two-way analysis of variance for the balancing-with-eyes-open (BALOMEAN) variable. The within-

Figure 6.20e Univariate *F* tests

```
MANOVA BALOMEAN BALCMEAN SSTMEAN PP BY SEX(1,2) FIELD(1,3)
  /PRINT=SIGNIF(HYPOTH MULTIV UNIV)
  /DESIGN
```

EFFECT .. SEX BY FIELD (CONT.)

Univariate F-tests with (2,128) D. F.

Variable	Hypoth. SS	Error SS	Hypoth. MS	Error MS	F	Sig. of F
BALOMEAN	18.10216	4122.15198	9.05108	32.20431	.28105	.755
BALCMEAN	3.77316	256.22940	1.88658	2.00179	.94244	.392
SSTMEAN	13.52285	733.14820	6.76143	5.72772	1.18047	.310
PP	1.78987	264.83723	.89493	2.06904	.43254	.650

cells sum of squares is identical to the diagonal entry for BALOMEAN in Figure 6.20b. Similarly, the SEX BY FIELD sum of squares is identical to the diagonal entry for BALOMEAN in Figure 6.20c. The F value for the interaction term, 0.281, is the same as in the first line of Figure 6.20e.

Figure 6.20f Two-way analysis of variance

```
MANOVA BALOMEAN BY SEX(1,2) FIELD(1,3)
  /METHOD=SSTYPE(UNIQUE)
  /DESIGN
```

Tests of Significance for BALOMEAN using UNIQUE Sums of Squares

Source of Variation	Sum of Squares	DF	Mean Square	F	Sig. of F
WITHIN CELLS	4122.15108	128	32.20431		
CONSTANT	16042.04632	1	16042.04632	498.13348	.000
SEX	389.32559	1	389.32559	12.08924	.001
FIELD	55.18943	2	27.59471	.85686	.427
SEX BY FIELD	18.10216	2	9.05108	.28105	.755

6.21 Discriminant Analysis

As discussed in Section 6.15 for the two-group situation, the MANOVA problem can also be viewed as one of finding the linear combinations of the dependent variables that best separate the categories of the independent variables. For main effects, the analogy with discriminant analysis is clear: What combinations of the variables distinguish men from women and what combinations distinguish the three categories of field dependence? When interaction terms are considered, we must distinguish among the six (two sex and three field-dependence) categories jointly. This is done by finding the linear combination of variables that maximizes the ratio of the hypothesis to error sums-of-squares. Since the interaction effect is not significant, there is no particular reason to examine the discriminant analysis results. However, we will consider them for illustrative purposes.

Figure 6.21a contains the standardized discriminant function coefficients for the interaction term. The number of functions that can be derived is equal to the degrees of freedom for that term if it is less than the number of dependent variables. The two variables that have the largest standardized coefficients are the side-stepping test and the Purdue Pegboard Test. All warnings concerning the interpretation of coefficients when variables are correlated apply in this situation as well. However, the magnitude of the coefficients may give us some idea of the variables contributing most to group differences.

Figure 6.21a Standardized discriminant function coefficients

```
MANOVA BALOMEAN BALCMEAN SSTMEAN PP BY SEX(1,2) FIELD(1,3)
  /DISCRIM=STAN ALPHA(1) 8
  /METHOD=SSTYPE(UNIQUE)
  /DESIGN
```

EFFECT .. SEX BY FIELD (CONT.)

Standardized discriminant function coefficients

Variable	Function No. 1	2
BALOMEAN	.026	-.273
BALCMEAN	-.195	-.901
SSTMEAN	.988	.024
PP	-.739	.153

As discussed in Chapter 3, a measure of the strength of the association between the discriminant functions and the grouping variables is the canonical correlation coefficient. Its square is the proportion of variability in the discrimi-

[8] With releases before 2.2, replace the MANOVA command with the following:

```
MANOVA BALOMEAN BALCMEAN SSTMEAN PP BY SEX(1,2) FIELD (1,3)
  /PRINT=DISCRIM(STAN ALPHA(1))
  /METHOD=SSTYPE(UNIQUE)
  /DESIGN
```

nant function scores "explained" by the independent variables. All multivariate significance tests, which were expressed as functions of the eigenvalues in Section 6.19, can also be expressed as functions of the canonical correlations.

Figure 6.21b contains several sets of statistics for the discriminant functions. The entry under eigenvalues is the dispersion associated with each function. The next column is the percentage of the total dispersion associated with each function. (It is obtained by dividing each eigenvalue by the sum of all eigenvalues and multiplying by 100.) The last column contains the canonical correlation coefficients. The results in Figure 6.21b are consistent with the results of the multivariate significance tests. Both the eigenvalues and canonical correlation coefficients are small, indicating that there is no interaction effect.

Figure 6.21b Eigenvalues and canonical correlations

```
MANOVA BALOMEAN BALCMEAN SSTMEAN PP BY SEX(1,2) FIELD(1,3)
  /PRINT=SIGNIF(EIGEN)
  /METHOD=SSTYPE(UNIQUE)
  /DESIGN
```

```
EFFECT .. SEX BY FIELD

- - - - - - - - - - - - - - - - - - - - - - - - - - - - - - - -

Eigenvalues and Canonical Correlations

Root No.    Eigenvalue        Pct.    Cum. Pct.  Canon. Cor.

       1          .038      70.391      70.391         .192
       2          .016      29.609     100.000         .126
```

When more than one discriminant function can be derived, you should examine how many functions contribute to group differences. The same tests for successive eigenvalues described in Chapter 3 can be obtained from SPSS^X MANOVA. The first line in Figure 6.21c is a test of the hypothesis that all eigenvalues are equal to 0. The value for Wilks' lambda in the first line of Figure 6.21c is equal to the test of multivariate differences in Figure 6.20d. Successive lines in Figure 6.21c correspond to tests of the hypothesis that all remaining functions are equal in the groups. These tests allow you to assess the number of dimensions on which the groups differ.

Figure 6.21c Dimension reduction analysis

```
MANOVA BALOMEAN BALCMEAN SSTMEAN PP BY SEX(1,2) FIELD(1,3)
  /PRINT=SIGNIF(EIGEN DIMENR)
  /METHOD=SSTYPE(UNIQUE)
  /DESIGN
```

```
EFFECT .. SEX BY FIELD

- - - - - - - - - - - - - - - - - - - - - - - - - - - - - - - - - - - - - - - - - - - - - -

Dimension Reduction Analysis

Roots          Wilks Lambda           F       Hypoth. DF        Error DF        Sig. of F

1 TO 2             .94813       .84339            8.00          250.00              .565
2 TO 2             .98424       .67273            3.00          126.00              .570
```

6.22 Testing for Differences Among Field Dependence and Sex Categories

Since the field-dependence-by-sex interaction term is not significant, the main effects can be tested. Figure 6.22a contains the multivariate tests of significance for the field-dependence variable. All four criteria indicate that there is not sufficient evidence to reject the null hypothesis that the means of the motor-ability variables do not differ for the three categories of field dependence.

Figure 6.22a Multivariate tests of significance for FIELD

```
MANOVA BALOMEAN BALCMEAN SSTMEAN PP BY SEX(1,2) FIELD(1,3)
  /PRINT=SIGNIF(EIGEN DIMENR MULTIV)
  /METHOD=SSTYPE(UNIQUE)
  /DESIGN
```

```
EFFECT .. FIELD
- - - - - - - - - - - - - - - - - - - - - - - - - - - - - - - - - - - - - - - -

Multivariate Tests of Significance (S = 2, M = 1/2, N = 61 1/2)

Test Name         Value      Approx. F     Hypoth. DF      Error DF     Sig. of F

Pillais           .04152       .66780          8.00         252.00         .720
Hotellings        .04244       .65789          8.00         248.00         .728
Wilks             .95889       .66285          8.00         250.00         .724
Roys              .02533
```

The multivariate tests of significance for the sex variable are shown in Figure 6.22b. All four criteria indicate that there are significant differences between men and women on the motor-ability variables. Compare Figure 6.22b with Figure 6.13b, which contains Hotelling's statistic for the two-group situation. Note that although the two statistics are close in value—0.669 when SEX is considered alone and 0.609 when SEX is included in a model containing field dependence and the sex-by-field-dependence interaction—they are not identical. The reason is that in the second model the sex effect is "adjusted" for the other effects in the model (see Section 6.24).

Figure 6.22b Multivariate tests of significance for SEX

```
EFFECT .. SEX
...
Multivariate Tests of Significance (S = 1, M = 1 , N = 61 1/2)

Test Name         Value   Approx. F  Hypoth. DF    Error DF   Sig. of F

Pillais          .37871    19.04870        4.00      125.00        .000
Hotellings       .60956    19.04870        4.00      125.00        .000
Wilks            .62129    19.04870        4.00      125.00        .000

Roys largest root criterion =         .37871
```

6.23 Stepdown *F* Tests

If the dependent variables are ordered in some fashion, it is possible to test for group differences of variables adjusting for effects of other variables. This is termed a *stepdown* procedure. Consider Figure 6.23a, which contains the stepdown tests for the motor-ability variables. The first line is just a univariate *F* test for the balancing-with-eyes-open variable. The value is the same as that displayed in Figure 6.23b, which contains the univariate *F* tests. The next line in Figure 6.23a is the univariate *F* test for balancing with eyes closed when balancing with eyes open is taken to be a covariate. That is, differences in balancing with eyes open are eliminated from the comparison of balancing with eyes closed. Figure 6.23c is the ANOVA table for the BALCMEAN variable when BALOMEAN is treated as the covariate. Note that the *F* value of 1.76 for SEX in Figure 6.23c is identical to that for BALCMEAN in Figure 6.23a.

Figure 6.23a Stepdown tests

```
MANOVA BALOMEAN BALCMEAN SSTMEAN PP BY SEX(1,2) FIELD(1,3)
  /PRINT=SIGNIF(EIGEN DIMENR MULTIV STEPDOWN)
  /METHOD=SSTYPE(UNIQUE)
  /DESIGN
```

```
EFFECT .. SEX
...

Roy-Bargman Stepdown F - tests

Variable     Hypoth. MS     Error MS Step-Down F  Hypoth. DF     Error DF    Sig. of F

BALOMEAN      389.32559     32.20431     12.08924            1          128         .001
BALCMEAN        3.24111      1.83574      1.76556            1          127         .186
SSTMEAN       149.80319      5.46262     27.42333            1          126         .000
PP             44.19749      1.84899     23.90357            1          125         .000
```

Figure 6.23b Univariate *F* tests

```
MANOVA BALOMEAN BALCMEAN SSTMEAN PP BY SEX(1,2) FIELD(1,3)
  /PRINT=SIGNIF(EIGEN DIMENR MULTIV STEPDOWN UNIV)
  /METHOD=SSTYPE(UNIQUE)
  /DESIGN
```

```
EFFECT .. SEX
...

Univariate F-tests with (1,128) D. F.

Variable     Hypoth. SS     Error SS  Hypoth. MS     Error MS            F   Sig. of F

BALOMEAN      389.32559   4122.15198   389.32559     32.20431     12.08924        .001
BALCMEAN         .16537    256.22940      .16537      2.00179       .08261        .774
SSTMEAN       172.11227    733.14820   172.11227      5.72772     30.04900        .000
PP             23.56111    264.83723    23.56111      2.06904     11.38746        .001
```

Figure 6.23c ANOVA table for BALCMEAN with BALOMEAN as the covariate

```
MANOVA BALOMEAN BALCMEAN SSTMEAN PP BY SEX(1,2) FIELD(1,3)
  /ANALYSIS=BALCMEAN WITH BALOMEAN
  /METHOD=SSTYPE(UNIQUE)
  /DESIGN
```

```
Tests of Significance for BALCMEAN using UNIQUE Sums of Squares

Source of Variation          SS      DF        MS         F  Sig of F

WITHIN CELLS            233.139     127     1.836
Regression               23.090       1    23.090    12.578      .001
CONSTANT                135.459       1   135.459    73.790      .000
SEX                       3.241       1     3.241     1.766      .186
FIELD                     2.398       2     1.199      .653      .522
SEX BY FIELD              2.630       2     1.315      .716      .490
```

The third line of Figure 6.23a, the test for the side-stepping variable, is adjusted for both the balancing-with-eyes-open variable and the balancing-with-eyes-closed variable. Similarly, the last line, the Purdue Pegboard Test score, has balancing with eyes open, balancing with eyes closed, and the side-stepping test as covariates. Thus each variable in Figure 6.23a is adjusted for variables that precede it in the table.

The order in which variables are displayed on the stepdown tests in MANOVA output depends only on the order in which the variables are specified for the procedure. If this order is not meaningful, the stepdown tests that result will not be readily interpretable or meaningful.

6.24 Different Types of Sums of Squares

When there is more than one factor and unequal numbers of cases in each cell in univariate analysis of variance, the total sums of squares cannot be partitioned into additive components for each effect. That is, the sums of squares for all effects do not add up to the total sums of squares. Differences between factor means are "contaminated" by the effects of the other factors.

There are many different algorithms for calculating the sums of squares for unbalanced data. Different types of sums of squares correspond to tests of different hypotheses. Two frequently used methods for calculating the sums of squares are the regression method, in which an effect is adjusted for all other effects in the model, and the sequential method, in which an effect is adjusted only for effects that precede it in the model.

In multivariate analysis of variance, unequal sample sizes in the cells lead to similar problems. Again, different procedures for calculating the requisite statistics are available. SPSS^X MANOVA offers two options—the regression solution (requested by keyword UNIQUE) and the sequential solution (requested by keyword SEQUENTIAL). All output displayed in this chapter is obtained from the regression solution, the default (see Milliken & Johnson, 1984).

For any connected design, the hypotheses associated with the sequential sums of squares are weighted functions of the population cell means, with weights depending on the cell frequencies (see Searle, 1971). For designs in which every cell is filled, it can be shown that the hypotheses corresponding to the regression model sums of squares are the hypotheses about the unweighted cell means. With empty cells, the hypotheses will depend on the pattern of missingness. In such cases, you can display the solution matrix, which contains the coefficients of the linear combinations of the cell means being tested.

6.25 Problems with Empty Cells

When there are no observations in one or more cells in a design, the analysis is greatly complicated. This is true for both univariate and multivariate designs. Empty cells results in the inability to estimate uniquely all of the necessary parameters. Hypotheses that involve parameters corresponding to the empty cells usually cannot be tested. Thus, the output from an analysis involving empty cells should be treated with caution (see Freund, 1980; Milliken & Johnson 1984).

6.26 Examining Residuals

Residuals—the differences between observed values and those predicted from a model—provide information about the adequacy of fit of the model and the assumptions. Previous chapters have discussed residual analysis for regression and log-linear models. The same techniques are appropriate for analysis of variance models as well.

In the two-factor model with interactions, the equation is

$$\hat{Y}_{ij} = \hat{\mu} + \hat{\alpha}_i + \hat{\beta}_j + \hat{\gamma}_{ij}$$ **Equation 6.26a**

where $\hat{Y}_{ij}$ is the predicted value for the cases in the *i*th category of the first variable and the *j*th category of the second. As before, $\hat{\mu}$ is the grand mean, $\hat{\alpha}_i$ the effect of the *i*th category of the first variable, $\hat{\beta}_j$ is the effect of the *j*th category of the second variable, and $\hat{\gamma}_{ij}$ is their interaction.

Consider Figure 6.26a, which contains deviation parameter estimates for the balancing-with-eyes-open variable. From this table, the predicted value for females in the low field-dependence category is

$$\hat{Y}_{11} = 11.42 - 1.78 - 0.97 + 0.51 = 9.18$$ **Equation 6.26b**

Similarly, the predicted value for males in the high field-dependence category is

$$\hat{Y}_{23} = 11.42 + 1.78 + 0.53 + 0.09 = 13.82$$ **Equation 6.26c**

Note that only independent parameter estimates are displayed and the other estimates must be derived from these. (For the main effects these can be requested with the keyword NEGSUM.) For example, the parameter estimate displayed for the sex variable is for the first category, females. The estimate for males is the negative of the estimate for females, since the two values must sum to 0. The value for the third category of field dependence is 0.53, the negative of the sum of the values for the first two categories. The two parameter estimates displayed for the interaction effects are for females with low field dependence and females with medium field dependence. The remaining estimates can be easily calculated. For example, the value for males in the low field-dependence category is −0.51, the negative of that for females. Similarly, the value for females in the high field-dependence category is −0.087, the negative of the sum of the values for females in low and medium field-dependence categories.

Figure 6.26a Parameter estimates

```
MANOVA BALOMEAN BALCMEAN SSTMEAN PP BY SEX(1,2) FIELD(1,3)
  /PRINT=PARAMETERS(ESTIM)
  /ANALYSIS=BALOMEAN
  /METHOD=SSTYPE(UNIQUE)
  /DESIGN
```

```
Estimates for BALOMEAN
CONSTANT
 Parameter          Coeff.       Std. Err.        T-Value      Sig. of T   Lower 95% CL   Upper 95% CL

         1   11.4196871137          .51166       22.31890           .000       10.40728       12.43209
SEX
 Parameter          Coeff.       Std. Err.        T-Value      Sig. of T   Lower 95% CL   Upper 95% CL

         2   -1.7790198740          .51166       -3.47696           .001       -2.79143        -.76661
FIELD
 Parameter          Coeff.       Std. Err.        T-Value      Sig. of T   Lower 95% CL   Upper 95% CL

         3    -.9744643265          .74485       -1.30827           .193       -2.44828         .49935
         4     .4457273663          .70743         .63006           .530        -.95405        1.84551
SEX BY FIELD
 Parameter          Coeff.       Std. Err.        T-Value      Sig. of T   Lower 95% CL   Upper 95% CL

         5     .5145659802          .74485         .69083           .491        -.95925        1.98838
         6    -.4273043037          .70743        -.60402           .547       -1.82709         .97248
```

Figure 6.26b contains an excerpt of some cases in the study and their observed and predicted values for the balancing-with-eyes-open variable. The fourth column is the residual, the difference between the observed and predicted values. The residuals can be standardized by dividing each one by the error standard deviation (Column 5).

Figure 6.26b Observed and predicted values

```
MANOVA BALOMEAN BALCMEAN SSTMEAN PP BY SEX(1,2) FIELD(1,3)
  /ANALYSIS=BALOMEAN
  /RESIDUALS=CASEWISE PLOT⁹
  /METHOD-SSTYPE(UNIQUE)
  /DESIGN
```

```
Observed and Predicted Values for Each Case

Dependent Variable.. BALOMEAN              Balance Test - Eyes Open

Case No.        Observed    Predicted  Raw Resid.  Std Resid.

    1            4.000       10.082      -6.082      -1.072
    2            8.850        9.181       -.331       -.058
    3           10.000        9.659        .341        .060
    4            3.550       10.082      -6.532      -1.151
    5            2.800        9.659      -6.859      -1.209
    6           14.500        9.659       4.841        .853
    .              .            .            .           .
    .              .            .            .           .
    .              .            .            .           .
  127            5.000       13.815      -8.815      -1.553
  128           20.000       11.710       8.290       1.461
  129           20.000       13.815       6.185       1.090
  130           19.000       11.710       7.290       1.285
  131           16.150       14.072       2.078        .366
  132           20.000       14.072       5.928       1.045
    .              .            .            .           .
    .              .            .            .           .
```

As in regression analysis, a variety of plots are useful for checking the assumptions. Figure 6.26c is a plot of the observed and predicted values for the BALOMEAN variable. The cases fall into six rows for the predicted values, since all cases in the same cell have the same predicted value. Residuals are plotted against the predicted values in Figure 6.26d and against the case numbers in Figure 6.26e. The plot against the case numbers is useful if the data are gathered and entered into the file sequentially. Any patterns in this plot lead to suspicions that the data are not independent of each other. Of course, if the data have been sorted before being entered, a pattern is to be expected.

Figure 6.26c Plot of observed and predicted values

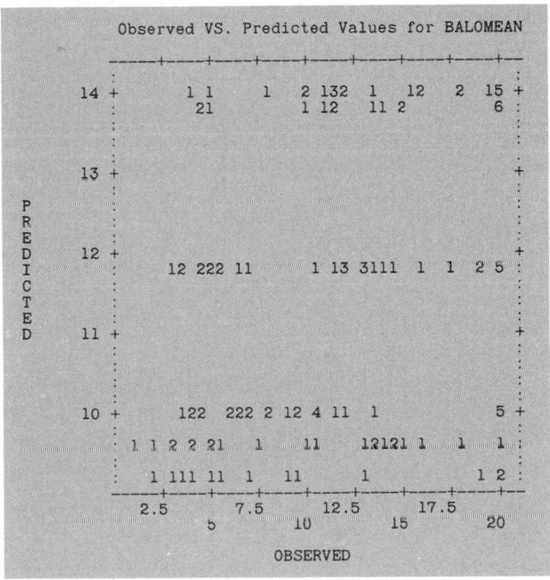

⁹With releases before 2.2, replace the MANOVA command with the following:

```
MANOVA BALOMEAN BALCMEAN SSTMEAN PP BY SEX(1,2) FIELD(1,3)
  /ANALYSIS=BALOMEAN
  /PRINT=POBS
  /PLOT=POBS
  /METHOD=SSTYPE(UNIQUE)
  /DESIGN
```

Figure 6.26d Plot of predicted and residual values

```
           Predicted Values VS. Std Resid. for BALOMEAN

          ---+----+----+----+----+----+----+----+----
         :                                         :
         :    2                                    :
         :    1  1  5                              :
     1.6 +                                         +
         :       1            5                    :
         :                    2                    :
         :       1                         6 5     :
         :       1            1              1     :
R     .8 +       3                                 +
E        :    1  3  1         1              2     :
S        :                    2                    :
I        :          2         3              3     :
D        :       1            1            2       :
U      0 +    2  1  5         3            2       +
A        :          2         2              1     :
L        :       1  2                        2     :
S        :    1     2                      3 4     :
         :    1     3                      1 1     :
     -.8 +    1  3  1         1              1     +
         :    2  2  2         1                    :
         :    1  1  3         4              1     :
         :    1  2            2                    :
         :       1            3                    :
    -1.6 +                                 3 1     +
         :                                   1     :
         :                                         :
          ---+----+----+----+----+----+----+----+----
          8.8       10.4        12      13.6
              9.6        11.2       12.8       14.4

                        PREDICTED
```

Figure 6.26e Plot of case numbers and residuals

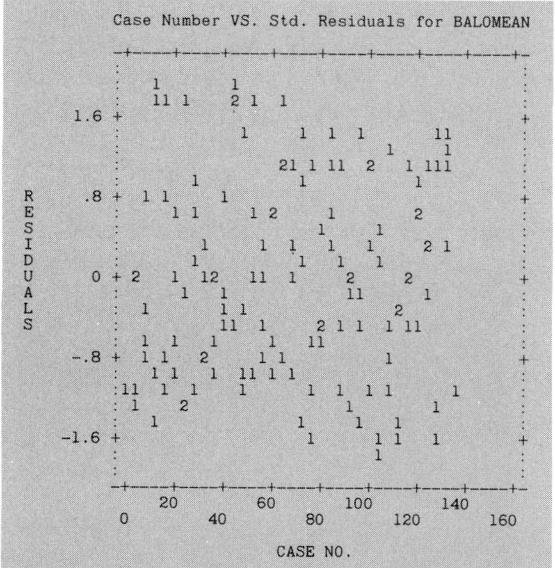

If the assumption of multivariate normality is met, the distribution of the residuals for each variable should be approximately normal. Figure 6.26f is a normal plot of the residuals for the balancing-with-eyes-open variable, while Figure 6.26g is the detrended normal plot of the same variable. Both of these plots suggest that there may be reason to suspect that the distribution of the residuals is not normal.

Figure 6.26f Normal plot of residuals

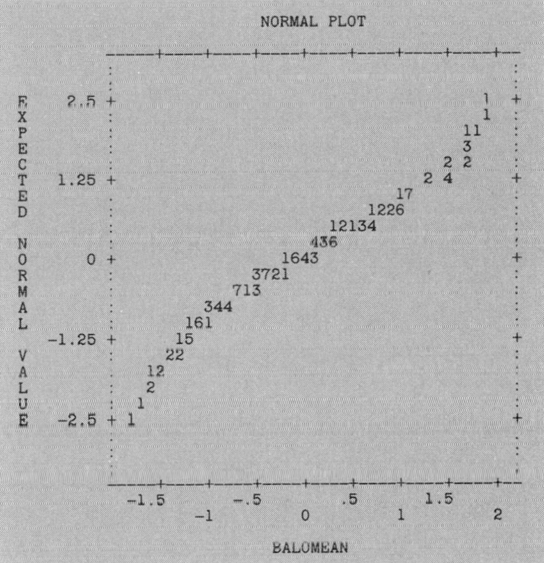

Figure 6.26g Detrended normal plot

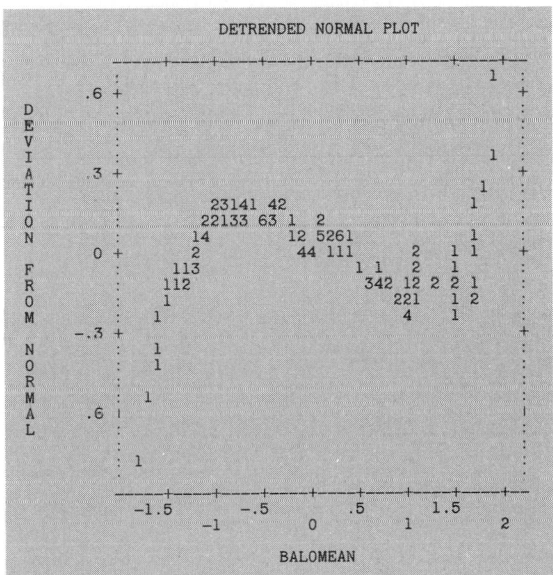

6.27 Predicted Means

Figure 6.27a shows a table that contains observed and predicted means for all cells in the design, as well as residuals, for the balancing-with-eyes-open variable. The first column of the table, labeled "Obs. Mean," is the observed mean for that cell. The next value, labeled "Adj. Mean" is the mean predicted from the model adjusted for the covariates. The column labeled "Est. Mean" contains the predicted means without correcting for covariates. When covariates are present, the differences between the adjusted and estimated means provide an indication of the effectiveness of the covariate adjustment (see Finn, 1974). For a complete factorial design without covariates the observed, adjusted and estimated means will always be equal.The difference between them, the residual, will also be equal to 0.

If the design is not a full-factorial model, the observed means and those predicted using the parameter estimates will differ. Consider Figure 6.27b, which contains a table of means for the main-effects-only model. The observed cell means are no longer equal to those predicted by the model. The difference between the observed and estimated mean is shown in the column labeled "Raw Resid." The residual divided by the error standard deviation is shown in the column labeled "Std. Resid." From this table it is possible to identify cells for which the model does not fit well.

Figure 6.27a Table of predicted means

```
MANOVA BALOMEAN BALCMEAN SSTMEAN PP BY SEX (1,2) FIELD (1,3)
  /METHOD=SSTYPE (UNIQUE)
  /PMEANS (TABLES (SEX BY FIELD))[10]
  /DESIGN
```

```
Adjusted and Estimated Means
Variable .. BALOMEAN

      Factor           Code              Obs. Mean    Adj. Mean     Est. Mean     Raw Resid.    Std. Resid.

 SEX                     1
  CAT                      1               9.18077      9.18077       9.18077        .00000        .00000
  CAT                      2               9.65909      9.65909       9.65909        .00000        .00000
  CAT                      3              10.08214     10.08214      10.08214        .00000        .00000

 SEX                     2
  CAT                      1              11.70968     11.70968      11.70968        .00000        .00000
  CAT                      2              14.07174     14.07174      14.07174        .00000        .00000
  CAT                      3              13.81471     13.81471      13.81471        .00000        .00000
```

It is also possible to obtain various combinations of the adjusted means. For example, Figure 6.27b contains the combined adjusted means for the SEX and FIELD variables for the main effects design. The means are labeled as unweighted, since the sample sizes in the cells are not used when means are combined over the categories of a variable.

Figure 6.27b Table of predicted means

```
MANOVA BALOMEAN BALCMEAN SSTMEAN PP BY SEX (1,2) FIELD (1,3)
  /METHOD=SSTYPE (UNIQUE)
  /PMEANS (TABLES (SEX, FIELD))[11]
  /DESIGN SEX FIELD
```

```
Adjusted and Estimated Means
Variable .. BALOMEAN

      Factor           Code              Obs. Mean    Adj. Mean     Est. Mean     Raw Resid.    Std. Resid.

 SEX                     1
  CAT                      1               9.18077      8.40954       8.40954        .77123        .13590
  CAT                      2               9.65909     10.06240      10.06240       -.40331       -.07107
  CAT                      3              10.08214     10.12332      10.12332       -.04118       -.00726

 SEX                     2
  CAT                      1              11.70968     12.03310      12.03310       -.32342       -.05699
  CAT                      2              14.07174     13.68596      13.68596        .38578        .06798
  CAT                      3              13.81471     13.74688      13.74688        .06783        .01195

Combined Adjusted Means for SEX                        Combined Adjusted Means for FIELD
Variable .. BALOMEAN                                   Variable .. BALOMEAN


          SEX                                                 FIELD

            1        UNWGT.        9.53176                       1        UNWGT.      10.22132

            2        UNWGT.       13.15531                       2        UNWGT.      11.87418

                                                                 3        UNWGT.      11.93510
```

[10]With releases before 2.2, replace the MANOVA command with the following:

```
MANOVA BALOMEAN BALCMEAN SSTMEAN PP BY SEX (1,2) FIELD (1,3)
  /METHOD=SSTYPE (UNIQUE)
  /PRINT=PMEANS (TABLES (SEX BY FIELD))
  /DESIGN
```

[11]With releases before 2.2, replace the MANOVA command with the following:

```
MANOVA BALOMEAN BALCMEAN SSTMEAN PP BY SEX (1,2) FIELD (1,3)
  /METHOD=SSTYPE (UNIQUE)
  /PRINT=PMEANS (TABLES (SEX, FIELD))
  /DESIGN SEX FIELD
```

6.28 Some Final Comments

In this chapter, only the most basic aspects of multivariate analysis of variance have been covered. The MANOVA procedure is capable of testing more elaborate models of several types. Chapter 7 considers a special class of designs called repeated measures designs. In such designs, the same variable or variables are measured on several occassions. For further discussion about multivariate analysis of variance, consult Morrison (1967) and Tatsuoka (1971).

6.29 RUNNING PROCEDURE MANOVA

MANOVA is a generalized analysis of variance and covariance program that performs both univariate and multivariate procedures. You can analyze such designs as block, split-plot, nested, and repeated measures designs. (Repeated measures designs and the MANOVA commands needed to analyze them are discussed in Chapter 7.) MANOVA can also be used to obtain multivariate regression coefficients, principal components, discriminant function coefficients, canonical correlations, and other statistics.

A program with so many facilities naturally has a large number of subcommands available. This section concentrates on the most commonly used subcommands and briefly describes the rest. The repeated measures subcommands WSFACTORS, WSDESIGN, RENAME, and ANALYSIS(REPEATED) are discussed in Chapter 7. For further information and examples, see *SPSS^X User's Guide.*

6.30 Specifying Factors and the Structure of the Data

To run MANOVA, you must indicate which variables are dependent variables, which (if any) are factors, and which (if any) are covariates. You also need to specify the design to be used.

The simplest MANOVA specification is a list of variables. If no other subcommands or keywords are used, all variables listed are treated as dependent variables and a one-sample Hotelling's T^2 is calculated. Thus, the output in Figure 6.9d was produced by specifying

```
MANOVA BALOMEAN BALCMEAN SSTMEAN PP
```

6.31 The Dependent Variable List

The first variables specified are the dependent variables in the analysis. By default, MANOVA treats a list of dependent variables as jointly dependent and therefore uses a multivariate design. This default can be changed by using the ANALYSIS subcommand (see Section 6.34).

6.32 The Factor List

If factors are to be used in the analysis, they are specified following the dependent variable list and the keyword BY. Each factor is followed by two integer values enclosed in parentheses and separated by a comma, specifying the lowest and highest values for the factor. For example,

```
MANOVA BALOMEAN BALCMEAN SSTMEAN PP BY SEX(1,2) FIELD(1,3)
```

indicates that there are two factors: SEX with possible values 1 and 2, and FIELD with possible values 1, 2, and 3. Cases with values outside the range specified are excluded from the analysis. Since MANOVA requires factor levels to be integer, you need to recode any noninteger factor values. Factors with a wide range of values and many empty categories should also be recoded to decrease processing time.

If several factors have the same value range, you can specify a list of factors followed by a single value range, in parentheses, as in the command

```
MANOVA SALES BY TVAD RADIOAD MAGAD NEWSPAD(2,5)
```

Certain analyses, such as regression, canonical correlation, and the one-sample Hotelling's T^2, do not require a factor specification. For these analyses, the factor list and the keyword BY should be omitted.

6.33 The Covariate List

The covariate list specifies any covariates to be used in the analysis. It follows the factor list and is separated from it by the keyword WITH, as in

```
MANOVA BALOMEAN BALCMEAN SSTMEAN PP BY SEX(1,2) FIELD(1,3) WITH IQ
```

6.34 The ANALYSIS Subcommand

Use the ANALYSIS subcommand to specify a model based on a subset of variables in the variable list. You can also use ANALYSIS to change the model specified in the variable list by changing dependent variables to covariates or covariates to dependent variables. A repeated measures analysis, as discussed in Chapter 7, is requested with the (REPEATED) specification on the ANALYSIS subcommand. When ANALYSIS is specified, it completely overrides the dependent variable list and covariate list in the MANOVA specification, but it does not affect the factors. Only variables in the original MANOVA variable list can be specified on the ANALYSIS subcommand, as in

```
MANOVA BALOMEAN BALCMEAN SSTMEAN PP BY SEX(1,2) FIELD(1,3) WITH IQ
  /ANALYSIS=BALOMEAN BALCMEAN PP WITH SSTMEAN
```

This command changes SSTMEAN from a dependent variable to a covariate. The command

```
MANOVA BALOMEAN BALCMEAN SSTMEAN BY SEX(1,2) FIELD(1,3) WITH IQ PP
  /ANALYSIS=BALOMEAN BALCMEAN SSTMEAN PP WITH IQ
```

changes PP from a covariate to a dependent variable. The factors SEX and FIELD are still used in the analysis (unless eliminated with a DESIGN subcommand; see Section 6.35).

Dependent variables or covariates can be eliminated from the analysis, as in

```
MANOVA SALES OPINION BY TVAD RADIOAD NEWSPAD(2,5) WITH PCTBUSNS
  /ANALYSIS=OPINION
```

which deletes the variables SALES and PCTBUSNS from the analysis.

Although only one ANALYSIS subcommand can be specified per DESIGN subcommand, a single ANALYSIS subcommand can be used to obtain multiple analyses, as long as the lists of dependent variables do not overlap. For example, the command

```
MANOVA BALOMEAN BALCMEAN SSTMEAN PP BY SEX(1,2) FIELD (1,3) WITH EDUC IQ/
  /ANALYSIS=(BALOMEAN BALCMEAN /SSTMEAN /PP WITH IQ)
```

specifies three analyses. The first has BALOMEAN and BALCMEAN as dependent variables and no covariates, the second has SSTMEAN as the dependent variable and no covariates, and the third has PP as the dependent variable and IQ as a covariate. (Note that none of the variable lists overlap.) Although three separate ANALYSIS and DESIGN subcommands could be used to get the same results, this would increase processing time.

To request three separate analyses with EDUC as the covariate for all of them, specify

```
MANOVA BALOMEAN BALCMEAN SSTMEAN PP BY SEX (1,2) FIELD(1,3) WITH EDUC IQ
  /ANALYSIS=(BALOMEAN BALCMEAN /SSTMEAN /PP WITH IQ) WITH EDUC
  /DESIGN
```

This is equivalent to

```
MANOVA BALOMEAN BALCMEAN SSTMEAN PP BY SEX(1,2) FIELD(1,3) WITH EDUC IQ
  /ANALYSIS=BALOMEAN BALCMEAN WITH EDUC
  /DESIGN
  /ANALYSIS=SSTMEAN WITH EDUC
  /DESIGN
  /ANALYSIS=PP WITH IQ EDUC
  /DESIGN
```

When specifying multiple analyses in this fashion, you may sometimes find the keywords CONDITIONAL and UNCONDITIONAL useful. CONDITIONAL indicates that subsequent variable lists should include as covariates all previous dependent variables on that ANALYSIS subcommand. UNCONDITIONAL (the default) indicates that each list should be used as is, independent of the others. For example, the command

```
MANOVA SALES LEADS OPINIONS CONTRACT BY TVAD RADIOAD MAGAD NEWSPAD(2,5)
       WITH PCTHOMES PCTBUSNS
  /ANALYSIS(CONDITIONAL)=(LEADS OPINIONS CONTRACT/SALES) WITH PCTBUSNS
  /DESIGN
```

is equivalent to

```
MANOVA SALES LEADS OPINIONS CONTRACT BY TVAD RADIOAD MAGAD NEWSPAD(2,5)
       WITH PCTHOMES PCTBUSNS
  /ANALYSIS=LEADS OPINIONS CONTRACT WITH PCTBUSNS
  /DESIGN
  /ANALYSIS=SALES WITH LEADS OPINIONS CONTRACT PCTBUSNS
  /DESIGN
```

6.35 The DESIGN Subcommand

Use the DESIGN subcommand to specify the structure of the model. DESIGN must be the *last* subcommand for any given model, and it can be used more than once to specify different models. The default model (obtained when DESIGN is used without further specification) is the full-factorial model.

Because of its importance the DESIGN subcommand is discussed at this point in the chapter. Remember that the other subcommands discussed later on must *precede* the DESIGN subcommand(s) to which they apply.

6.36 Specifying Effects

When a full-factorial model is not desired, the DESIGN subcommand can be used to specify the effects in the model. The format is simply

```
/DESIGN=list of effects
```

with the effects separated by blanks or commas. For example, a model with only main effects is specified by the command

```
MANOVA BALOMEAN BALCMEAN SSTMEAN PP BY SEX(1,2) FIELD(1,3)
  /DESIGN=SEX FIELD
```

Interaction terms are indicated with the keyword BY, so that the command

```
MANOVA SALES BY TVAD RADIOAD MAGAD NEWSPAD(2,5)
  /DESIGN=TVAD RADIOAD MAGAD NEWSPAD TVAD BY RADIOAD TVAD BY RADIOAD
        BY NEWSPAD
```

specifies a model with all main effects, the two-way interaction between TVAD and RADIOAD, and the three-way interaction between TVAD, RADIOAD, and NEWSPAD.

If single-degree-of-freedom effects are to be included, a PARTITION subcommand should be used before specifying these effects in the DESIGN subcommand, as in

```
MANOVA RELIEF BY DRUG(1,4)
  /CONTRAST(DRUG)=SPECIAL(1 1 1 1, 1 -1 0 0, 4 4 -8 0, 4 4 1 -9)
  /PARTITION(DRUG)
  /DESIGN=DRUG(1) DRUG(2) DRUG(3)
```

For further information about the PARTITION subcommand, see Section 6.46. For the CONTRAST subcommand, see Section 6.47.

The keyword CONTIN is used with DESIGN to incorporate continuous variables into a single effect. The variables to be incorporated must not have been specified in the previous ANALYSIS subcommand as dependent variables or covariates. When you use CONTIN on DESIGN, dependent variables must be defined with an ANALYSIS subcommand. For example, the command

```
MANOVA SALES TEST1 TEST2 TEST3 BY TVAD RADIOAD MAGAD NEWSPAD(2,5)
      WITH PCTBUSNS
  /ANALYSIS=SALES WITH PCTBUSNS
  /DESIGN=CONTIN(TEST1 TEST2 TEST3)
```

incorporates TEST1, TEST2, and TEST3 into a single effect with three degrees of freedom. As of Release 2.2, the keyword POOL is an alias of CONTIN. See *SPSS^X User's Guide* for further information about CONTIN.

To specify interactions between factors and continuous variables, simply list these interaction effects on the DESIGN subcommand using keyword BY. You cannot specify interactions between two continuous variables (including covariates), and you cannot use variables that are included in the model by an ANALYSIS subcommand.

Effects can be lumped together into a single effect by using a plus sign. For example,

```
/DESIGN=TVAD + TVAD BY RADIOAD
```

combines the effects of TVAD and TVAD BY RADIOAD into a single effect. (The BY keyword is evaluated before the plus sign.)

To obtain estimates that consist of the sum of the constant term and the parameter values, use the MUPLUS keyword. (With releases before 2.2, use keyword CONSPLUS instead of MUPLUS.) The constant term μ is then combined with the parameter following the MUPLUS keyword. For example, if the subcommand

```
/DESIGN=MUPLUS SEX
```

is specified, the mean of each dependent variable is added to the SEX parameters for that variable. This produces conditional means or "marginals" for each dependent variable. Since these means are adjusted for any covariates in the model, they are also the usual adjusted means when covariates are present. When the adjusted means cannot be estimated, MUPLUS produces estimates of the constant plus the requested effect. These are no longer the predicted means.

The MUPLUS approach is the only way you can obtain the standard errors of the conditional means. (However, conditional and adjusted means can be obtained by using subcommands OMEANS and PMEANS.) You can obtain unweighted conditional means by specifying the full factorial model and specifying MUPLUS before the effect whose means are to be found. (If this is an interaction effect, the DESIGN should not include the lower-order effects contained in it.) For example, the subcommand

```
/DESIGN=MUPLUS SEX FIELD SEX BY FIELD
```

obtains the unweighted marginal means for SEX in a two-factor design. Only one MUPLUS keyword may be used per DESIGN subcommand.

Although MANOVA automatically includes the constant term (the correction for the mean), it will not be included if you specify NOCONSTANT on a METHOD subcommand. You can override NOCONSTANT by specifying CONSTANT on the DESIGN subcommand. A variable named CONSTANT is not recognized on DESIGN.

6.37 Specifying Nested Designs

The WITHIN keyword, or W, indicates that the term to its left is nested in the term to its right. For example, the subcommand

```
/DESIGN=SEX WITHIN TESTCAT
```

indicates that SEX is nested within TESTCAT, while the subcommand

```
/DESIGN=SEX WITHIN TESTCAT BY EDUC BY MOTIVTN
```

indicates that SEX is nested within the interaction TESTCAT by EDUC by MOTIVTN.

6.38 Specifying Error Terms

Error terms for individual effects are specified on the DESIGN subcommand with the following keywords:

WITHIN *Within-cells error terms.* Alias W.

RESIDUAL *Residual error terms.* Alias R.

WR *Combined within-cells and residual error terms.* Alias RW.

To test a term against one of these error terms, specify the term to be tested, followed by the VS or AGAINST keyword and the error-term keyword. For example, to test the SEX by FIELD term against the residual error term, specify

```
/DESIGN=SEX BY FIELD AGAINST RESIDUAL
```

You can also create up to ten user-defined error terms by declaring any term in the model as an error term. To create such a term, specify the term followed by an equals sign and an integer from 1 to 10 on the DESIGN subcommand, as in

```
/DESIGN=SEX BY FIELD=1 FIELD VS 1 SEX VS 1
```

This command designates the SEX by FIELD term as error term 1, which is then used to test the sex and field main effects. To use a special error term in a test of significance, specify

```
term=n {VS     } error-term keyword
       {AGAINST}
```

or

```
term {VS     } term=n
     {AGAINST}
```

Any term present in the design but not specified on DESIGN is lumped into the residual error term. The default error term for all tests is WITHIN.

6.39 The ERROR Subcommand

To specify the default error term for each between-subjects effect in subsequent designs, use the ERROR subcommand with the following keywords:

WITHIN *Within-cells error term.* Alias W.

RESIDUAL *Residual error term.* Alias R.

WR *Pooled within-class and residual error terms.* Alias WITHIN+RESIDUAL or RW.

n *Model term.*

You can designate a model term *(n)* as the default error term only if you explicitly define error term numbers on the DESIGN subcommand. If the specified error term number is not defined for a particular design, MANOVA does not carry out the significance tests involving that error term, although the parameter estimates and hypothesis sums of squares will be computed. For example, if the command

```
MANOVA BALOMEAN BALCMEAN SSTMEAN PP BY SEX(1,2) FIELD(1,3)
  /ERROR=1
  /DESIGN=SEX FIELD SEX BY FIELD=1
  /DESIGN=SEX FIELD
```

is specified, no significance tests for SEX or FIELD are displayed for the second design, which contains no term defined as error term 1.

6.40 The WSFACTORS Subcommand

The WSFACTORS subcommand is used for repeated measures analysis (see Chapter 7). It provides the names and number of levels for within-subjects factors when you use the multivariate data setup. For example, to supply a within-subjects factor name for DRUG1 to DRUG4, specify

```
MANOVA DRUG1 TO DRUG4
  /WSFACTORS=TRIAL(4)
```

Each name follows the naming conventions of SPSS^X, and each name must be unique. That is, a within-subjects factor name cannot be the same as that of any dependent variable, between-subjects factor, or covariate in the MANOVA job. The within-subjects factors exist only during the MANOVA analysis.

WSFACTORS must be the first subcommand after the MANOVA specification, and it can be specified only once per MANOVA command. You can specify up to 20 within-subjects and grouping factors altogether. See Chapter 7 for a complete discussion of the WSFACTORS subcommand.

6.41 The WSDESIGN Subcommand

The WSDESIGN subcommand specifies a within-subjects model and a within-subjects transformation matrix based on the ordering of the continuous variables and the levels of the within-subjects factors. See Chapter 7 for a complete discussion of the WSDESIGN subcommand.

6.42 The MEASURE Subcommand

You can use SPSS^X MANOVA to analyze doubly multivariate repeated measures designs, in which subjects are measured on two or more responses on two or more occasions. When the data are entered using the multivariate setup, you can use the MEASURE subcommand to name the multivariate pooled results. See Chapter 7 for a discussion of the MEASURE subcommand.

6.43 The TRANSFORM Subcommand

To specify linear transformations of the dependent variables and covariates, use the TRANSFORM subcommand. The first specification on TRANSFORM is the list of variables to be transformed in parentheses. Multiple variable lists can be used if they are separated by slashes and each list contains the same number of variables. MANOVA then applies the indicated transformation to each list. By default, MANOVA transforms all dependent variables and covariates. If a list is specified, however, only variables included in the list are transformed.

Any number of TRANSFORM subcommands may be specified in a MANOVA command. A TRANSFORM subcommand remains in effect until MANOVA encounters another one.

Seven types of transformations are available. These are

DEVIATIONS(refcat) *Compare a dependent variable to the means of the dependent variables in the list.* By default, MANOVA omits the comparison of the last variable to the list of variables. You can omit a variable other than the last by specifying the number of the omitted variable in parentheses.

DIFFERENCE *Compare a dependent variable with the mean of the previous dependent variables in the list.* Also known as reverse Helmert.

HELMERT *Compare a dependent variable to the means of the subsequent dependent variables in the list.*

SIMPLE(refcat) *Compare each dependent variable with the last.* You can specify a variable other than the last as the reference variable by giving the number of the variable in parentheses.

REPEATED *Compare contiguous variable pairs, thereby producing difference scores.*

POLYNOMIAL(metric) *Fit orthogonal polynomials to the variables in the transformation list.* The default metric is equal spacing, but you can specify your own metric.

SPECIAL(matrix) *Fit your own transformation matrix reflecting combinations of interest.* The matrix must be square, with the number of rows and columns equal to the number of variables being transformed.

For example, the subcommand

```
/TRANSFORM(SALES LEADS OPINIONS CONTRACT)=POLYNOMIAL
```

fits orthogonal polynomials to variables SALES, LEADS, OPINIONS, and CONTRACT, with equal spacing assumed.

The type of transformation can be preceded by the keywords CONTRAST, BASIS, or ORTHONORM. CONTRAST and BASIS are alternatives; ORTHONORM may be used with either CONTRAST or BASIS, or alone, which implies CONTRAST.

CONTRAST *Generate the transformation matrix directly from the contrast matrix of the given type.* This is the default.

BASIS *Generate the transformation matrix from the one-way basis corresponding to the specified CONSTRAST.*

ORTHONORM *Orthonormalize the transformation matrix by rows before use.* MANOVA does not, by default, orthonormalize rows.

CONTRAST or BASIS can be used with any of the available methods for defining contrasts on the CONTRAST subcommand (see Section 6.47). On the TRANSFORM subcommand, keywords CONTRAST and BASIS are used to generate the transformed variables for later analysis, rather than simply to specify the contrasts on which significance testing and parameter estimation will be based.

For further information on the TRANSFORM subcommand, see *SPSS^X User's Guide* and Chapter 7.

6.44 The RENAME Subcommand

Use the RENAME subcommand to rename dependent variables and covariates after they have been transformed using TRANSFORM or WSDESIGN. The format is

```
/RENAME=newname1 newname2 ... newnamek
```

The number of new names must be equal to the number of dependent variables and covariates. For further information about RENAME, see the *SPSS^X User's Guide* and Chapter 7.

6.45 The METHOD Subcommand

The METHOD subcommand is used to control some of the computational aspects of MANOVA. The following keywords are available:

MODELTYPE *The model for parameter estimation.*

ESTIMATION *The method for estimating parameters.*

SSTYPE *The method of partitioning sums of squares.*

Each keyword has associated options as listed below. These options are specified in parentheses after the keyword.

The options available on **MODELTYPE** are

MEANS *Use the cell-means model for parameter estimation.*

OBSERVATIONS *Use the observations model for parameter estimation.*

If continuous variables are specified on the DESIGN subcommand, MANOVA automatically uses the observations model. Since the observations model is computationally less efficient than the means model and the same estimates are obtained, the observations model should be used only when it is appropriate.

Up to four keywords, one from each of the following pairs, may be specified on **ESTIMATION.** The first keyword in each pair is the default.

QR/CHOLESKY QR estimates parameters using the Householder transformations to effect an orthogonal decomposition of the design matrix. A less expensive (and sometimes less accurate) procedure is the Cholesky method, selected by specifying the alternative CHOLESKY keyword.

NOBALANCED/BALANCED NOBALANCED assumes that the design is unbalanced. If your design is balanced and orthogonal, request balanced processing by specifying the alternative BALANCED keyword. BALANCED should be specified only when no cell is empty, the cell-means model applies, all cell sizes are equal, and the contrast type for each factor is orthogonal.

NOLASTRES/LASTRES NOLASTRES calculates sums of squares for all effects. The alternative LASTRES keyword computes the last effect in the design by subtracting the between-groups sums of squares and cross-products from the total sums of squares and cross-products. When applicable, LASTRES can significantly decrease processing costs. Parameter estimates will not be available for the effect whose sum of squares was computed by subtraction. If LASTRES is specified, you may not use the CONTIN specification on

DESIGN to include continuous variables in the last effect (see Section 6.36). Do not use LASTRES unless you have specified SEQUENTIAL for the SSTYPE parameter (see below). It should not be used with UNIQUE since component sums of squares do not add up to the total sum of squares in a UNIQUE decomposition.

CONSTANT/NOCONSTANT CONSTANT requests that the model contain a constant term. The alternative keyword NOCONSTANT suppresses the constant term. NOCONSTANT can be overridden on a subsequent DESIGN subcommand (see Section 6.36).

The following options may be specified on **SSTYPE:**

UNIQUE *Requests sums of squares corresponding to unweighted combinations of means* (the regression approach). These sums of squares are not orthogonal unless the design is balanced. As of Release 2.1 of SPSS^X, SSTYPE(UNIQUE) is the default.

SEQUENTIAL *Requests an orthogonal decomposition of the sums of squares.* A term is corrected for all terms to its left in a given DESIGN specification, and confounded with all terms to its right.

For example, the subcommand

```
/METHOD=ESTIMATION(CHOLESKY,LASTRES) SSTYPE(SEQUENTIAL)
```

requests the less-expensive CHOLESKY estimation method, with the sums of squares for the last effect calculated by subtraction. SEQUENTIAL decomposition is requested, as is required for LASTRES. We assume that parameter estimates are not needed for the last effect and that the CONTIN keyword will not appear in the last effect on a DESIGN statement for this METHOD subcommand.

6.46 The PARTITION Subcommand

The degrees of freedom associated with a factor can be subdivided by using a PARTITION subcommand. Specify the factor name in parentheses, an equals sign, and a list of integers in parentheses indicating the degrees of freedom for each partition. For example, if EDUCATN has six values (five degrees of freedom), it can be partitioned into single degrees of freedom by specifying

```
/PARTITION(EDUCATN)=(1,1,1,1,1)
```

or, more briefly, by specifying

```
/PARTITION(EDUCATN)=(5*1)
```

Since the default degrees-of-freedom partition consists of the single degrees-of-freedom partition, these subcommands are equivalent to

```
/PARTITION(EDUCATN)
```

The subcommand

```
/PARTITION(EDUCATN)=(2,2,1)
```

partitions EDUCATN into three subdivisions, the first two with 2 degrees of freedom and the third with 1 degree of freedom. This subcommand can also be specified as

```
/PARTITION(EDUCATN)=(2,2)
```

since MANOVA automatically generates a final partition with the remaining degree(s) of freedom (1 in this case). If you were to then specify ED(1) on the DESIGN subcommand, it would refer to the first partition, which in this case has 2 degrees of freedom.

6.47 The CONTRAST Subcommand

The contrasts desired for a factor are specified by the CONTRAST subcommand. Specify the factor name in parentheses, followed by an equals sign and a contrast keyword. The constrast keyword can be any of the following:

DEVIATION *The deviations from the grand mean.*

DIFFERENCE *Difference or reverse Helmert contrast.* Compare levels of a factor with the mean of the previous levels of the factor.

SIMPLE *Simple contrasts.* Compare each level of a factor to the last level.

HELMERT *Helmert contrasts.* Compare levels of a factor with the mean of the subsequent levels of the factor.

POLYNOMIAL *Orthogonal polynomial contrasts.*

REPEATED *Adjacent levels of a factor.*

SPECIAL *A user-defined contrast.* See the example in Section 6.36.

6.48 The PRINT and NOPRINT Subcommands

The PRINT and NOPRINT subcommands control the output produced by MANOVA. PRINT requests specified output, while NOPRINT suppresses it. On both PRINT and NOPRINT, you specify keywords followed by the keyword options in parentheses. For example, the command

```
MANOVA SALES BY TVAD RADIOAD MAGAD NEWSPAD(2,5)
  /PRINT=CELLINFO(MEANS)
```

requests the display of cell means of SALES for all combinations of values of TVAD, RADIOAD, MAGAD, and NEWSPAD.

The specifications available on PRINT and NOPRINT are listed below, followed by the options available for each.

CELLINFO *Cells information.*

HOMOGENEITY *Homogeneity of variance tests.*

DESIGN *Design information.*

ERROR *Error matrices.*

SIGNIF *Significance tests.*

PARAMETERS *Estimated parameters.*

TRANSFORM *Transformation matrix.*

The options for **CELLINFO** are

MEANS *Cell means, standard deviations, and counts.*

SSCP *Cell sums-of-squares and cross-products matrices.*

COV *Cell variance-covariance matrices.*

COR *Cell correlation matrices.*

The options for **HOMOGENEITY** are

BARTLETT *Bartlett-Box* F *test.*

COCHRAN *Cochran's* C.

BOXM *Box's* M *(multivariate case only).*

The options for **DESIGN** are

ONEWAY *The one-way basis for each factor.*

OVERALL *The overall reduced-model basis (design matrix).*

DECOMP *The QR/CHOLESKY decomposition of the design.*

BIAS *Contamination coefficients displaying the bias present in the design.*

SOLUTION *Coefficients of the linear combination of the cell means being tested.*

The options available for **ERROR** are

SSCP *Error sums-of-squares and cross-product matrix.*

COV *Error variance-covariance matrix.*

COR *Error correlation matrix and standard deviations.*

STDDEV *Error standard deviations (univariate case).*

If ERROR(COR) is specified in the multivariate case, MANOVA automatically displays the determinant and Bartlett's test of sphericity.

The options for **SIGNIF** are

MULTIV *Multivariate* F *tests for group differences* (default display).

EIGEN *Eigenvalues of* $S_h S_e^{-1}$ (default display).

DIMENR *A dimension-reduction analysis* (default display).

UNIV *Univariate* F *tests* (default display).

HYPOTH *The hypothesis SSCP matrix.*

STEPDOWN *Roy-Bargmann step-down* F *tests.*

AVERF *An averaged* F *test.* Use with repeated measures.

BRIEF *A shortened multivariate output.* BRIEF overrides any of the preceding SIGNIF keywords.

AVONLY *Averaged results only.* Use with repeated measures.

SINGLEDF *Single-degree-of-freedom listings of effects.*

When BRIEF is used, the output consists of a table similar in appearance to a univariate ANOVA table, but with the generalized *F* and Wilks' lambda replacing the univariate *F*.

The options available for **PARAMETERS** are

ESTIM *The estimates themselves, along with their standard errors, t tests, and confidence intervals.*

ORTHO *The orthogonal estimates of parameters used to produce the sums of squares.*

COR *Correlations between the parameters.*

NEGSUM *For main effects, the negative sum of the other parameters* (representing the parameter for the omitted category).

As of Release 2.1 of SPSS^X, parameters are not displayed by default.

TRANSFORM produces the transformation matrix, which shows how MANOVA transforms variables when a multivariate repeated measures design and a WSFACTORS subcommand are used (see Chapter 7). There are no subspecifications for PRINT=TRANSFORM.

6.49 The PCOMPS Subcommand

The PCOMPS subcommand requests a principal components analysis of each error SSCP in a multivariate design. COR prints principal components of the error correlation matrix; COV prints principal components of the error variance-covariance matrix. Factors extracted from these matrices are corrected for group differences and covariates. Such factors tend to be more useful than factors extracted from an uncorrected matrix when significant group differences are present or when a significant amount of error variance is accounted for by the covariates.

The keywords for **PCOMPS** are

COR *Principal components analysis of the error correlation matrix.*

COV *Principal components analysis of the error variance-covariance matrix.*

ROTATE(rottype) *Rotation of the principal component loadings.* For rottype, substitute VARIMAX, EQUAMAX, QUARTIMAX, or NOROTATE.

NCOMP(n) *The number of principal components to be rotated.* Specify *n*, or let *n* default to all components extracted.

MINEIGEN(eigcut) *The eigenvalue cutoff value for principal components extraction.*

With releases before 2.2, use the PRINT subcommand with keyword PRINCOMPS, followed by one or more of the above options in parentheses, instead of subcommand PCOMPS.

6.50 The DISCRIM Subcommand

DISCRIM requests a canonical analysis of dependent and independent variables in multivariate analyses. If the independent variables are continuous, MANOVA produces a canonical correlation analysis; if they are categorical, MANOVA produces a canonical discriminant analysis. Available keywords are

RAW *Raw discriminant function coefficients.*

STAN *Standardized discriminant function coefficients.*

ESTIM *Effect estimates in discriminant function space.*

COR *Correlations between the dependent and canonical variables defined by the discriminant functions.*

ROTATE(rottyp) *Rotation of the matrix of correlations between dependent and canonical variates.* For rottype, specify VARIMAX, EQUAMAX, or QUARTIMAX.

ALPHA(alpha) *The significance level for the canonical variate.* The default is 0.15.

MANOVA does not perform rotation unless there are at least two significant canonical variates.

With releases before 2.2, use subcommand PRINT with keyword DISCRIM, followed by one or more of the above options in parentheses, instead of the DISCRIM subcommand.

6.51 The OMEANS Subcommand

OMEANS produces tables of combined observed means. The specification on OMEANS is an open parenthesis, the keyword VARIABLES, another open parenthesis, the names of the dependent variables and covariates for which means are desired, and two closed parentheses, as in

```
MANOVA BALOMEAN BALCMEAN SSTMEAN PP BY SEX(1,2) FIELD(1,3)
  /OMEANS(VARIABLES(BALOMEAN BALCMEAN SSTMEAN PP))
```

If the variable list is omitted, MANOVA displays combined means for all variables. MANOVA also displays both weighted and unweighted means. Tables of observed means are displayed if the keyword TABLES is used, as in

```
  /OMEANS(TABLES(SEX,FIELD,SEX BY FIELD))
```

This subcommand results in three tables, one collapsed over SEX, one collapsed over FIELD, and one showing the observed means themselves.

With releases before 2.2, use subcommand PRINT with keyword OMEANS instead of the OMEANS subcommand.

6.52 The PMEANS Subcommand

PMEANS computes predicted and adjusted (for covariates) means, which are displayed for each error term in each design. VARIABLES and TABLES are two specifications that can be used; the format is the same as that for OMEANS. You can also use keyword **PLOT** on the PMEANS subcommand to obtain a plot of predicted means for each cell. Predicted means are suppressed if the last term is being calculated by subtraction (METHOD=ESTIM(LASTRES)) or if the design contains the MUPLUS keyword (see Section 6.36).

If the WSFACTORS or WSDESIGN subcommand is used to specify a repeated measures design (see Chapter 7), the means of the orthonormalized variables are displayed when PMEANS is used. If a PMEANS subcommand follows a TRANSFORM subcommand, the means of the transformed variables are displayed.

With releases before 2.2, use subcommand PRINT with keyword PMEANS instead of the PMEANS subcommand.

6.53 The RESIDUALS Subcommand

The RESIDUALS subcommand displays and plots casewise values and residuals for your models. The RESIDUALS subcommand has the following keywords:

CASEWISE *A case-by-case listing of the observed, predicted, residual, and standardized residual values for each dependent variable.*

PLOT *A plot of observed values, predicted values, and case numbers vs. the standardized residuals, plus normal and detrended normal probability plots for the standardized residuals* (5 plots in all).

To print predicted values and residuals without plotting them, specify CASEWISE. To plot the values without printing them, specify PLOT. To both print and plot these values, specify

```
RESIDUALS=CASEWISE PLOT
```

Use the ERROR subcommand to specify the error term to be used to standardize the residuals if one other than the default error term is produced.

If a designated error term does not exist for a given design, no predicted values or residuals are calculated. If you specify RESIDUALS without any specifications, CASEWISE output is displayed.

With releases before 2.2, use subcommands PRINT and/or PLOT with the keyword POBS instead of the RESIDUALS subcommand.

6.54 The PLOT Subcommand

Line-printer plots are requested with the PLOT subcommand. The following keywords are available:

CELLPLOTS *Plot cell statistics,* including a plot of cell means vs. cell variances, a plot of cell means vs. cell standard deviations, and a histogram of cell means, for each of the continuous variables (dependent variables and covariates) defined in the MANOVA specification.

BOXPLOTS *Plot a boxplot for each continuous variable.*

NORMAL *Plot a normal plot and a detrended normal plot* for each continuous variable.

STEMLEAF *Plot a stem-and-leaf display* for each continuous variable.

ZCORR *Plot a half-normal plot* of the within-cells correlations between the dependent variables in a multivariate analysis.

If there is not enough memory to produce a plot, MANOVA displays a warning and does not produce the plot.

6.55 The MATRIX Subcommand

MANOVA can write matrix materials built from the raw data it reads. It can also read matrix materials written by previous MANOVA procedures. To read and write matrices in MANOVA, you use the MATRIX subcommand.

The MATRIX subcommand has two keywords, IN and OUT, which specify reading and writing matrix files, respectively. The OUT keyword on MATRIX specifies the file to which the matrix is written. There are two options:

(file) *Write the correlation matrix to a system file.* MANOVA creates a system file containing the matrix materials. The name of the file is specified in parentheses. The system file is stored on disk and can be retrieved at any time.

(*) *Replace the active file with the correlation matrix.* The matrix materials replace the active file. The correlation matrix is *not* stored on disk. It is resident in the active file. For this specification, you can use an empty set of parentheses () in place of the asterisk in parentheses (*).

The matrix materials include the N, mean, and standard deviation. Documents from the original file will not be included in the matrix file and will not be present if the matrix file becomes the active file.

The IN keyword on MATRIX specifies the file from which the matrix is read. There are two options:

(file) *Read the correlation matrix from a matrix system file.*

(*) *Read the correlation matrix from the active file.* The active file must be an appropriate matrix system file. For this specification, you can use an empty set of parentheses () in place of the asterisk in parentheses (*).

MATRIX=IN cannot be used in place of GET or DATA LIST to begin a new SPSS^X command file. MATRIX is a subcommand on MANOVA and MANOVA cannot run before an active file is defined.

With releases before 3.0, use the READ and WRITE subcommands instead of the MATRIX subcommand.

6.56 The MISSING Subcommand

By default, cases with missing values on any of the variables named in the MANOVA specification are not included in the analysis. Use the MISSING subcommand to control missing values. The minimum specification is a single keyword. The default keywords are EXCLUDE and LISTWISE.

LISTWISE *Exclude missing values listwise.* Cases with missing values for any variable named on the MANOVA variable list are excluded from the analysis. This is the default.

INCLUDE *Include user-defined missing values.* User-missing values are treated as valid. For factors, you must include the missing-value codes within the range specified on the MANOVA variable list. It may be necessary to recode these values so they will be adjacent to the other factor values. You must also include the missing values within the range for categorical variables to enter the cases into the analysis. System-missing values cannot be included in the analysis.

EXCLUDE *Exclude both user-missing and system-missing values.*

The INCLUDE and EXCLUDE keywords are mutually exclusive; however, each can be specified with LISTWISE. For example, to include user-missing values in an analysis that excludes system missing values listwise, specify

```
MANOVA Y BY CAT(1,2) DRUG (1,3)/ DESIGN=CAT,DRUG
       /MISSING=INCLUDE LISTWISE
```

With releases before 3.0, specify OPTION 1 to include user-missing values in the analysis.

6.57 The CRITERIA Subcommand

The CRITERIA subcommand sets important constants used in the MANOVA procedure.

ZETA(zeta) *Set the absolute value of zero* used for display purposes and when constructing basis matrices for estimation. The default value of ZETA is 10^{-8}.

EPS(eps) *Set the relative value of zero* used in checking the diagonal elements of matrices when performing the QR reduction or CHOLESKY decompositions. The default value of EPS is 10^{-8}.

With releases before 2.2, use the subcommand SETCONST instead of CRITERIA.

6.58 EXERCISES

Syntax

1. Find the errors in the MANOVA commands below:

a.
```
MANOVA ESTEEM SEX(1,2) ATTRACT(1,5) IQ(1,3)
```

b.
```
MANOVA INCOME PRESTIGE BY AGE(1,4) SEX(1,2) EDUC(1,5)
   /ANALYSIS=INCOME WITH AGE
```

c.
```
MANOVA PRICE SALES PROFITS BY ADS(1,4) QUALITY(1,3)
   /ANALYSIS=PRICE
   /ANALYSIS=SALES
   /ANALYSIS=PROFITS WITH SALES
   /DESIGN
```

d.
```
MANOVA AGGRESSN ALTRUISM BY FILM(1,2) SEX(1,2) RACE(1,3)
   /ANALYSIS=AGGRESSN
   /DESIGN
   /ANALYSIS=ALTRUISM BY FILM SEX
```

c.
```
MANOVA RACISM SEXISM HOMPHBIA BY EDUC(1,5) SEX(1,2) RACE(1,3)
         WITH CONSRVSM
         ANALYSIS RACISM/
         DESIGN/
         ANALYSIS SEXISM/
         DESIGN/
         ANALYSIS HOMPHBIA/
         DESIGN/
```

f.
```
MANOVA ETHNOCNT POLITICS BY INTEGRTN(1,2) BY RACE(1,2) BY SEX(1,2)
   /PRINT=CELLINFO(MEANS) HOMOGENEITY(BARTLETT)
```

g.
```
MANOVA QUALITY ERRORATE DIFFCLTY BY SETTING(1,3) MATERIAL(1,2)
         TRAINING(1,2) WITH EXPERNCE
   /ANALYSIS=(QUALITY DIFFCLTY/ERRORATE WITH DIFFCLTY)
```

2. A researcher wants to obtain a univariate analysis of variance using a full-factorial model and writes the following MANOVA command. Will this produce the analysis she wants?

```
MANOVA ENDURNCE BY SEX(1,2) PROGRAM(1,2) PASTSCOR(1,5)
   /DESIGN=SEX PROGRAM PASTSCOR SEX BY PROGRAM SEX BY PASTSCOR
            PROGRAM BY PASTSCOR
```

3. What sort of nesting is indicated in the following WSDESIGN command?

```
/WSDESIGN=AGE WITHIN RACE BY SEX
```

4. What terms will be included in the residual error term if the MANOVA command below is used?

```
MANOVA TIME BY WEIGHTS(1,2) RUNPROG(1,3) DIET(1,2) WITH PASTTIME
   /DESIGN=WEIGHTS RUNPROG DIET
```

5. Write a MANOVA subcommand that partitions the factor AGGRESSN into four subdivisions, the first with one degree of freedom, the second with two degrees of freedom, and the last two with one degree of freedom.

6. A physician wants to obtain a multivariate analysis of variance, with STRESS, PAIN, and ATTITUDE as the dependent variables, SURGERY (with values 1 and 2), DRUG (with values 1, 2, 3, and 4), and ILLNESS (with values 1, 2, and 3) as the factors, and STAYTIME as the covariate. She wants the design to exclude the three-way interaction term and wants to print the following: the Bartlett-Box *F*-test, cell means and cell sums of squares, boxplots, normal plots, detrended normal plots, the error correlation matrix with varimax rotation, univariate *F*-tests, parameter estimates, and standardized discriminant-function coefficients. Write the MANOVA command that will produce this analysis.

7. Write the subcommand needed to lump the effects ANGER by SEX and TEST by ANGER into a single effect.

8. A market researcher wants three univariate analyses of variance, one with GENRLATT as the dependent variable and INCOME as the covariate, one with PURCHASE as the dependent variable and INTEREST and INCOME as the covariates, and one with NEED as the dependent variable and INCOME as the covariate. A full-factorial design is desired for each analysis, and the factors are SEX (with values 1 and 2), FOLLOWUP (with values 1 and 2), and HOMOWNR (with values 1 and 2). Write the shortest MANOVA command that will produce all three analyses.

Statistical Concepts

1. Indicate whether the following are true or false:
   a. Discriminant coefficients are somewhat more likely than correlations between discriminant scores and variables to be influenced by correlations among the variables.
   b. A canonical variable with small effects contributes substantially to separation between groups.
   c. If we are 95% sure that each of three confidence intervals contains the true mean that it estimates, we can be 95% sure that all of them contain the true means they estimate.
   d. A primary reason for obtaining univariate descriptive statistics in a multivariate analysis is to check on assumptions.
   e. Univariate tests are sufficient for testing the hypothesis that two covariance matrices are equal.
   f. Multivariate procedures should not be used when the dependent variables are correlated.
2. Consider the following output:

```
Estimates for HLTHSCOR
CONSTANT

 Parameter          Coeff.        Std. Err.          T-Value        Sig. of T

         1          73.421            9.511            7.720             .000
UNEMPLOY

 Parameter          Coeff.        Std. Err.          T-Value        Sig. of T

         2          -4.735            2.986           -1.586             .113
- - - - - - - - - - - - - - - - - - - - - - - - - - - - - - - - - - - - - - -

Estimates for FAMILY
CONSTANT

 Parameter          Coeff.        Std. Err.          T-Value        Sig. of T

         1          53.556           10.437            5.131             .000
UNEMPLOY

 Parameter          Coeff.        Std. Err.          T-Value        Sig. of T

         2          -2.158             .837           -2.578             .010
- - - - - - - - - - - - - - - - - - - - - - - - - - - - - - - - - - - - - - -

Estimates for ALCOHOL
CONSTANT

 Parameter          Coeff.        Std. Err.          T-Value        Sig. of T

         1           3.813            1.762            2.164             .031
UNEMPLOY

 Parameter          Coeff.        Std. Err.          T-Value        Sig. of T

         2            .965             .373            2.587             .010
```

Based on this output, fill in the missing entries in the following:

```
EFFECT .. UNEMPLOY
Univariate F-tests with (1,398) D. F.
```

Variable	Hypoth. SS	Error SS	Hypoth. MS	Error MS	F	Sig. of F
HLTHSCOR	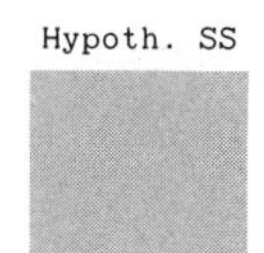		31.963	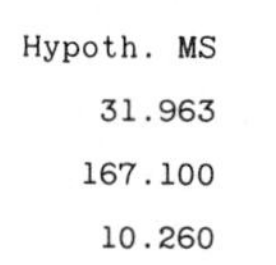		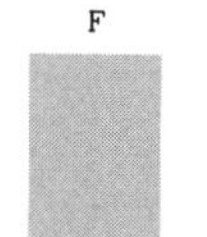 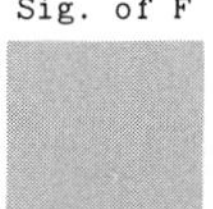
FAMILY			167.100			
ALCOHOL			10.260			

3. Each of the following multivariate procedures is an extension of some nonmultivariate procedure. Indicate what these nonmultivariate procedures are.
   a. Hotelling's T^2 (one sample).
   b. One-way MANOVA.
   c. Hotelling's T^2 (two independent samples).

4. a. Plot the means and variances shown below against each other. Is any relationship evident? If so, how are they related?

Mean	Variance	Mean	Variance
−2.13	0.28	18.83	27.12
−0.56	0.02	9.40	5.02
−11.10	6.51	−5.63	2.08
−1.21	0.09	−4.74	1.47
−6.99	2.65	−15.58	15.8
−3.14	0.65		

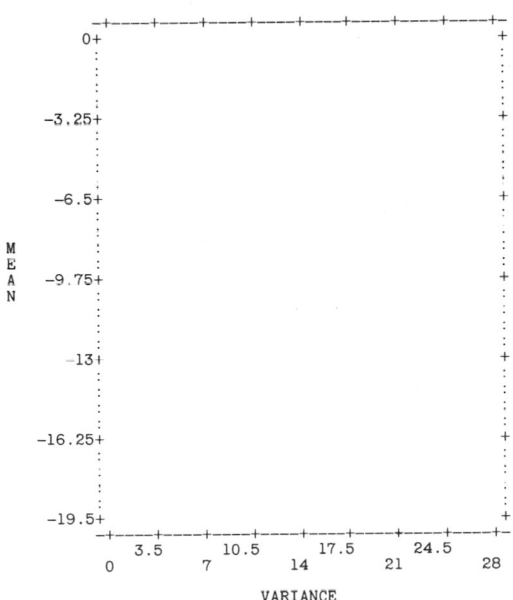

b. Obtain the standard deviations from the variances given in (a) and plot the means shown in (a) against these standard deviations. Is any relationship evident? If so, how are they related?

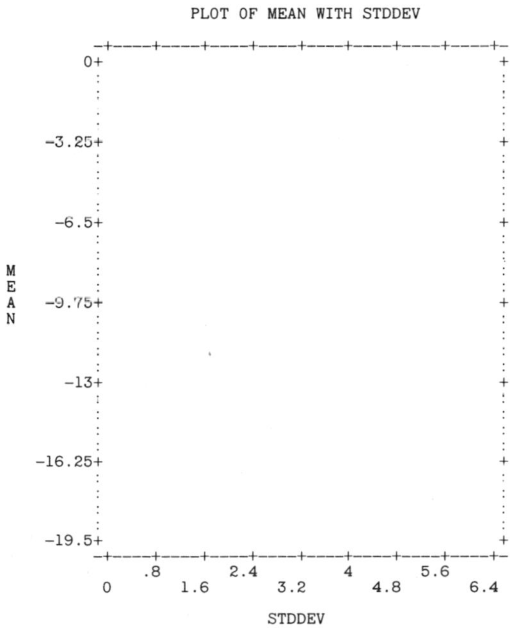

c. Why are plots like the ones done for (a) and (b) an important part of a MANOVA analysis?

5. A two-sample Hotelling's T^2 test resulted in the output below:

Multivariate Tests of Significance (S = 1, M = 1 , N = 48)

Test Name	Value	Approx. F	Hypoth. DF	Error DF	Sig. of F
Hotellings	21.945	6.997	1.00	46.00	.011

A two-group discriminant analysis was also performed on the same data, producing the following. Fill in the missing entries.

Dimension Reduction Analysis

Roots	Wilks Lambda	F	Hypoth. DF	Error DF	Sig. of F
1 TO 1	.868				

6. Construct a stem-and-leaf plot from the following exam scores. Do you think these data were taken from a normal population? Why or why not?

100	53	60
91	61	98
18	61	84
27	61	98
41	99	77
100	93	65
71	57	91
71	94	98
82	63	61
52	58	99
76	65	69

7. A MANOVA analysis produced the within-cells sums of squares and cross-products matrix shown below.

WITHIN CELLS Sum-of-Squares and Cross-Products

	CREATVTY	SAT	POLITICS	PREDJDCE
CREATVTY	49.223			
SAT	508.654	11438.150		
POLITICS	94.428	614.586	3.497	
PREDJDCE	252.441	86.251	105.882	10.895

Univariate *F*-tests were also conducted to determine where the differences between means were. These are given in the table below. Fill in the missing entries.

EFFECT .. INDEPDCE BY BACKGRND

Univariate F-tests with (4,136) D. F.

Variable	Hypoth. SS	Error SS	Hypoth. MS	Error MS	F	Sig. of F
CREATVTY					8.172	.000
SAT					3.815	.004
POLITICS					.804	.501
PREDJDCE					2.131	.093

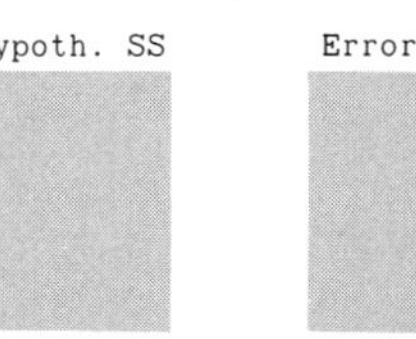

8. a. Use the information below to construct the adjusted hypothesis sums of squares and cross-products matrix for a one-sample Hotelling's T^2.

Variable	**Mean**	μ_0
IQ	112.51	100
ALIENATN	86.83	81
PREDJDCE	42.11	62
NEWSINFO	59.34	35

b. Use the information below to construct the adjusted hypothesis sums of squares and cross-products matrix for a two-sample Hotelling's T^2:

	FEMINIST (n=84)	NOT FEMINIST (n=51)
Variable	**Mean**	**Mean**
DESEGRTN	58.94	51.44
NUKEFREZ	83.50	67.91
GAYRGHTS	41.32	19.85

9. Consider the within-cells sums of squares and cross-products matrix shown below. Would you use the computer program that produced it? Why or why not?

	CHOL	CLOTRISK	SMOKAVG	OBESITY
CHOL	7358.23			
CLOTRISK	75.96	490.11		
SMOKAVG	313.54	79.95	8150.66	
OBESITY	221.92	56.59	230.76	-4083.14

10. Use the box and whisker plots shown below to answer the following questions:

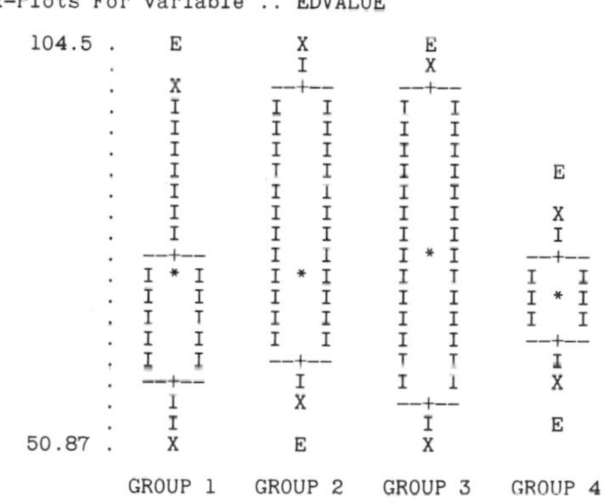

a. Which group has the most extreme outlier (relative to the rest of the observations)?
b. Which group has the largest spread, not counting outliers?
c. Which group has the largest median?
d. Does the assumption of equal group variances seem reasonable for these data? Why or why not?

11. A two-group MANOVA was performed on data with the following means:

	LOW INCOME	HIGH INCOME
Variable	**Mean**	**Mean**
HLTHINFO	30.48	41.63
HLTHCARE	20.89	39.77
HEALTH	19.45	28.31

Use this information to complete the table below:

Estimates for HLTHINFO		Estimates for HLTHCARE		Estimates for HEALTH	
CONSTANT		CONSTANT		CONSTANT	
Parameter	Coeff.	Parameter	Coeff.	Parameter	Coeff.
1		1		1	
INCOME		INCOME		INCOME	
Parameter	Coeff.	Parameter	Coeff.	Parameter	Coeff.
2		2		2	

12. a. Which of the normal probability plots shown below are inconsistent with the assumption of normality?

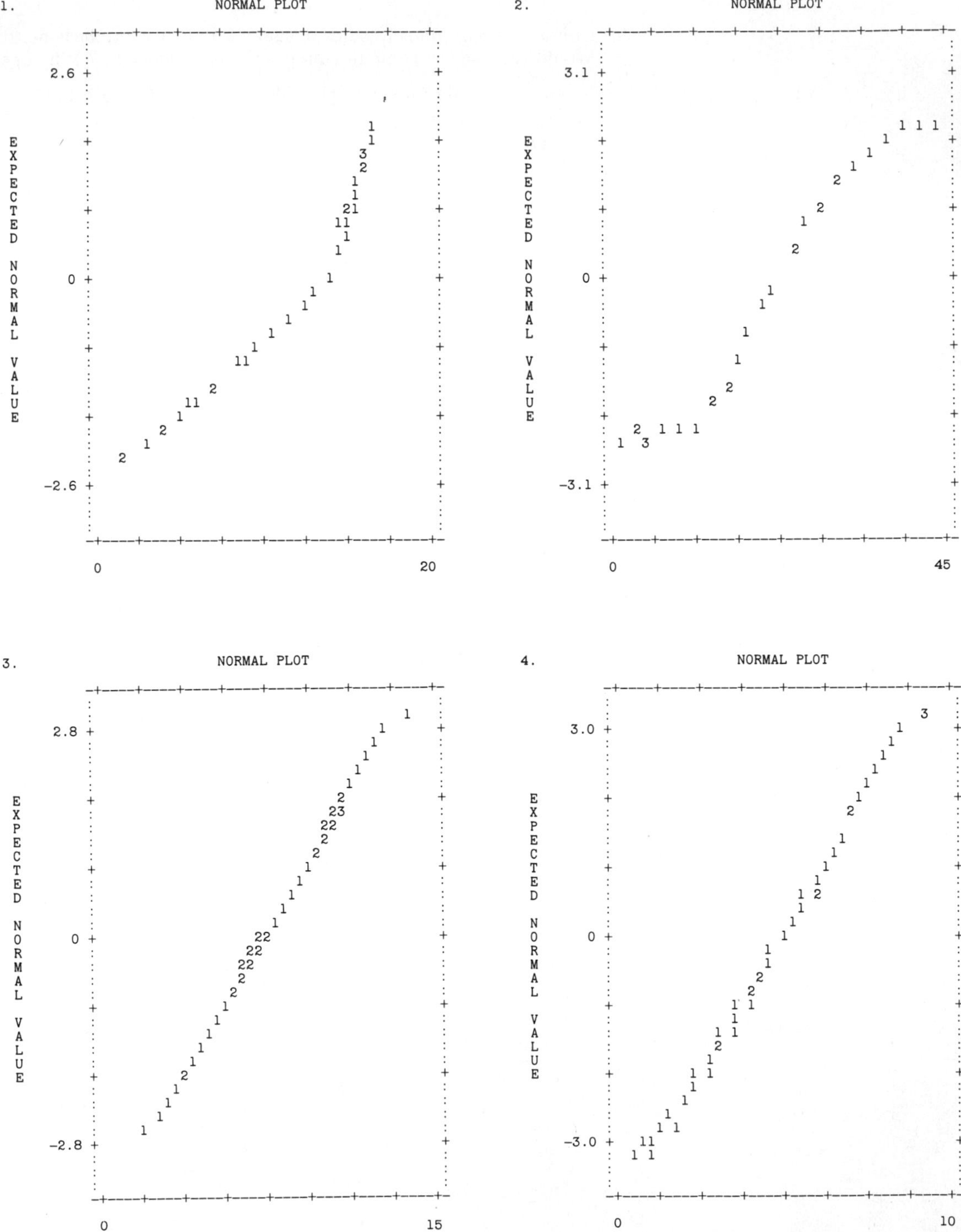

b. Which of the detrended normal probability plots shown below is not consistent with the assumption of normality?

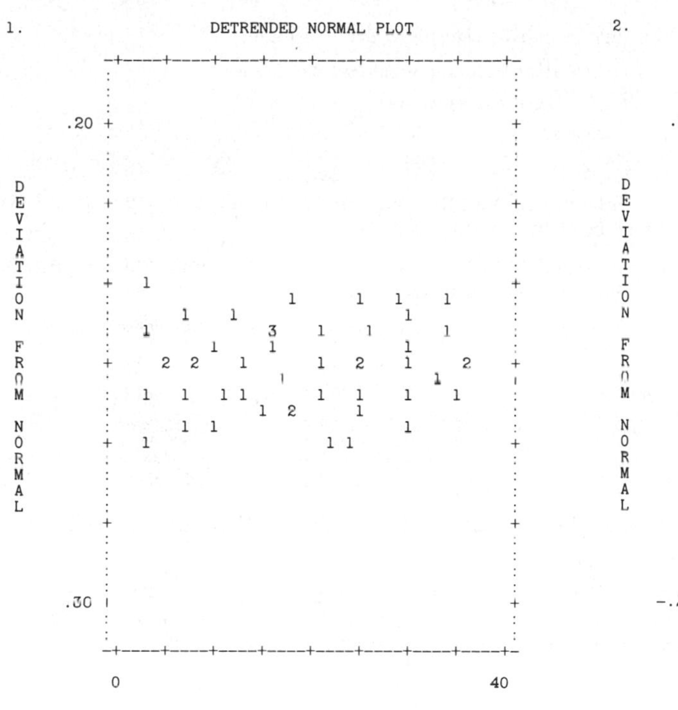

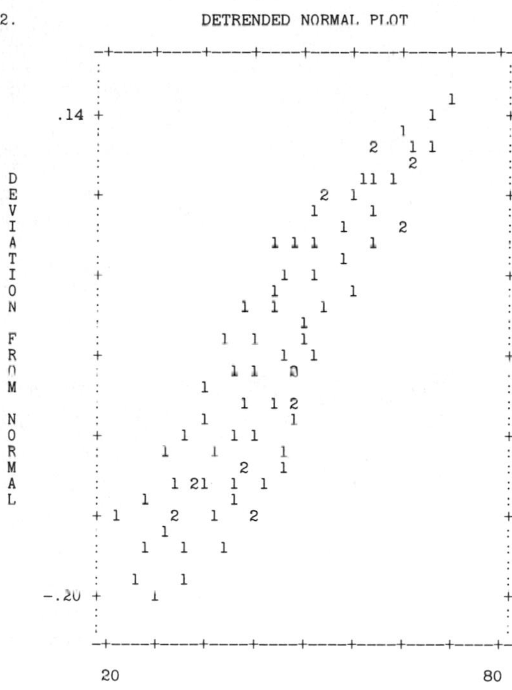

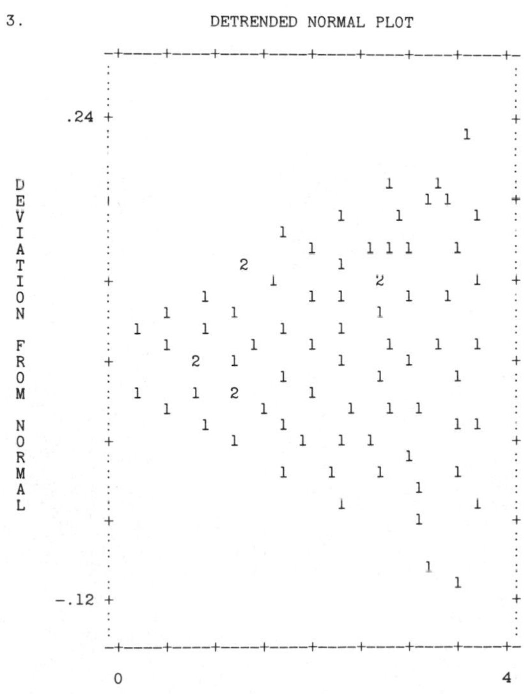

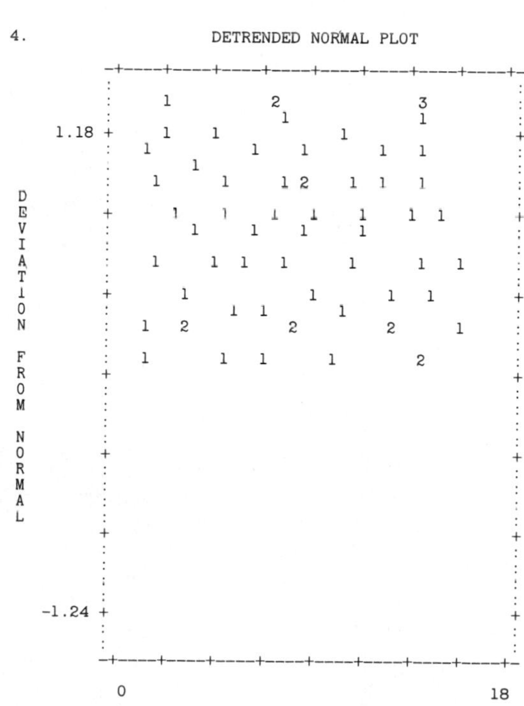

13. a. Consider the following the discriminant output (produced by MANOVA):

```
CANONICAL DISCRIMINANT FUNCTIONS EVALUATED AT GROUP MEANS (GROUP CENTROIDS)

   GROUP        FUNC  A     FUNC  B     FUNC  C     FUNC  D

     1           .203       -.811        .773       -.801
     2          -.415       -.952        .408        .865
```

Use this output to complete the following:

```
 Estimates of effects for canonical variables

          Canonical Variable

 Parameter               A           B           C           D

     2                  ███         ███         ███         ███
```

b. Which canonical variable contributes the most to separation between groups? Which contributes the least?

14. As part of a MANOVA analysis, a researcher obtained a principal components analysis with the results shown below.

```
VARIMAX rotated correlations between components and DEPENDENT variable

         Can. Var.

Dep. Var.            1            2            3            4            5

X1             -.90570       .75812       .15508       .16299       .02234
X2              .87099      -.14708       .68579       .09924      -.07271
X3              .82171      -.06205      -.05483      -.57256       .03735
X4              .80592       .01612       .10517       .03260       .05169
X5              .91298       .15706      -.10635       .04827       .55666
```

Do these loadings indicate any potential problems for a MANOVA analysis? If so, what?

15. If a MANOVA analysis concerns a single dependent variable, is it possible to have a significant Pillais' trace (e.g., with a P value less than 0.01) and an insignificant analysis of variance F statistic (P greater than 0.01)?

7

Repeated Measures Analysis of Variance

In this chapter:

Goals:

- To test hypotheses about the relationship of the dependent variable and the conditions under which it is measured when the same dependent variable is measured on more than one occasion for each subject.
- To identify the variables that contribute to differences between the treatment conditions.

Examples:

- Compare the effect of three physical fitness programs on heart rate. Each subject performs a series of exercises, and after each set pulse rate is measured.
- Compare the length of time required to memorize a list of nonsense syllables under conditions of high and low stress and positive and negative reinforcement. Each subject memorizes lists under all combinations of reinforcement and stress.
- Evaluate the influence of maturation on social adjustment. College students are administered a social adjustment scale twice a year for four years. Possible differences between males and females and science and humanities majors are examined.

How it's done:

Linear combinations of the dependent variables are formed and hypotheses based on them are tested. Several approaches to the analysis are possible, depending on the underlying structure of the data.

Data considerations:

Each case has multiple measurements of the same dependent variable for various within-subject factor combinations. Discrete values of the classification variables for between-subjects factors are also included. The assumptions necessary for hypothesis testing depend on the method of analysis selected.

General references:

Winer (1971)
Timm (1975)
Horton (1978)

Contents

7.1 REPEATED MEASURES
7.2 Describing the Data
7.3 Analyzing Differences
7.4 Transforming the Variables
7.5 Testing for Differences
7.6 Testing the Constant Effect
7.7 The Analysis of Variance Table
7.8 Testing the Digit Effect
7.9 Averaged Univariate Results
7.10 Choosing Multivariate or Univariate Results
7.11 Assumptions Needed for the Univariate Approach
7.12 Selecting Other Contrasts
7.13 Adding Another Factor
7.14 Testing a Two-Factor Model
7.15 The Transformed Variables
7.16 Testing Hypotheses
7.17 The CONDITION Effect
7.18 The Number of Digits
7.19 The Interaction
7.20 Putting it Together
7.21 Within-Subjects and Between-Subjects Factors
7.22 Additional Univariate Assumptions
7.23 Back to Memory
7.24 Summarizing the Results
7.25 Analysis of Covariance with a Constant Covariate
7.26 Doubly Multivariate Repeated Measures Designs
7.27 RUNNING MANOVA FOR REPEATED MEASURES DESIGNS
7.28 The Variable List
7.29 Specifying A Constant Covariate
7.30 The WSFACTORS Subcommand
7.31 The RENAME Subcommand
7.32 The MEASURE Subcommand
7.33 The CONTRAST Subcommand
7.34 THE WSDESIGN Subcommand
7.35 The ANALYSIS(REPEATED) Subcommand
7.36 The DESIGN Subcommand
7.37 The PRINT Subcommand
7.38 EXERCISES

7 Storing Memories: Repeated Measures Analysis of Variance

Anyone who experiences difficulties sorting through piles of output, stacks of bills, or assorted journals must be awed by the brain's ability to organize, update, and maintain the memories of a lifetime. It seems incredible that someone can instantly recall the name of his first-grade teacher. On the other hand, that same person might spend an entire morning searching for a misplaced shoe.

Memory has two components—storage and retrieval. Many different theories explaining its magical operation have been proposed (for example, see Eysenck, 1977). In this chapter, an experiment concerned with latency—the length of time required to search a list of items in memory—is examined.

Bacon (1980) conducted an experiment in which subjects were instructed to memorize a number. They were then given a "probe" digit and told to indicate whether it was included in the memorized number. One hypothesis of interest is the relationship between the number of digits in the memorized number and the latency. Is more time required to search through a longer number than a shorter one? Twenty-four subjects were tested on 60 memorized numbers, 20 each of two, three, and four digits in random order. The average latencies, in milliseconds, were calculated for each subject on the two-, three-, and four-digit numbers. Thus, three scores are recorded for each subject, one for each of the number lengths. The probe digit was included in the memorized number in a random position.

7.1 REPEATED MEASURES

When the same variable is measured on several occasions for each subject, it is a *repeated measures* design. The simplest repeated measures design is one in which two measurements are obtained for each subject—such as pre- and post-test scores. These type of data are usually analyzed with a paired t test.

The advantages of repeated measurements are obvious. Besides requiring fewer experimental units (in this study, human subjects), they provide a control on their differences. That is, variability due to differences between subjects can be eliminated from the experimental error. Less attention has been focused on some of the difficulties that may be encountered with repeated measurements. Broadly, these problems can be classified as the carry-over effect, the latent effect, and the order or learning effect.

The carry-over effect occurs when a new treatment is administered before the effect of a previous treatment has worn off. For example, Drug B is given while Drug A still has an effect. The carry-over effect can usually be controlled by increasing the time between treatments. In addition, special designs that allow one to assess directly the carry-over effects are available (Cochran & Cox, 1957).

The latent effect—when one treatment may activate the dormant effect of the previous treatment, or interact with the previous treatment—is not so easily countered. This effect is especially problematic in drug trials and should be considered before using a repeated measures experimental design. Usually, if a latency effect is suspected, a repeated measures design should not be used.

The learning effect occurs when the response may improve merely by repetition of a task, independent of any treatment. For example, subjects' scores on a test may improve each time they take the test. Thus, treatments that are administered later may appear to improve performance, even though they have no effect. In such situations it is important to pay particular attention to the sequencing of treatments. Learning effects can be assessed by including a control group that performs the same tasks repeatedly without receiving any treatment.

7.2 Describing the Data

In a repeated measures experiment, as well as any other, the first step is to obtain descriptive statistics. These provide some idea of the distributions of the variables as well as their average values and dispersions. Figure 7.2a contains cell means and standard deviations, as well as individual confidence intervals, for the variables P2DIGIT, P3DIGIT, and P4DIGIT. The shortest average latency time (520 milliseconds) was observed for the two-digit numbers (P2DIGIT). The longest (581 milliseconds) was observed for the four-digit numbers. A plot of the mean latency times against the number of digits is shown in Figure 7.2b. Note that there appears to be a linear relationship between the latency time and the number of digits in the memorized number.

Figure 7.2a Means and standard deviations

```
MANOVA P2DIGIT P3DIGIT P4DIGIT
  /PRINT=CELLINFO(MEANS)
  /DESIGN
```

```
Cell Means and Standard Deviations
Variable .. P2DIGIT
                                         Mean      Std. Dev.           N   95 percent Conf. Interval

For entire sample                   520.58333      131.36604          24     465.11232      576.05435
- - - - - - - - - - - - - - - - - - - - - - - - - - - - - - - - - - - - - - - - - - - - - - - - - -
Variable .. P3DIGIT
                                         Mean      Std. Dev.           N   95 percent Conf. Interval

For entire sample                   560.00000      118.77600          24     509.84529      610.15471
- - - - - - - - - - - - - - - - - - - - - - - - - - - - - - - - - - - - - - - - - - - - - - - - - -
Variable .. P4DIGIT
                                         Mean      Std. Dev.           N   95 percent Conf. Interval

For entire sample                   581.25000      117.32461          24     531.70816      630.79184
```

Figure 7.2b Plot of means from procedure PLOT

```
COMPUTE CONS=1
AGGREGATE OUTFILE=*
  /BREAK=CONS
  /MPDIG2 MPDIG3 MPDIG4=MEAN(P2DIGIT P3DIGIT P4DIGIT)
COMPUTE C2=2
COMPUTE C3=3
COMPUTE C4=4
PLOT SYMBOLS='***'/VSIZE=15/HSIZE=30
 /FORMAT=OVERLAY
 /TITLE 'MEAN LATENCY TIMES'
 /HORIZONTAL 'NUMBER OF DIGITS'/VERTICAL 'MEAN LATENCY'
 /PLOT=MPDIG2 WITH C2;MPDIG3 WITH C3;MPDIG4 WITH C4
```

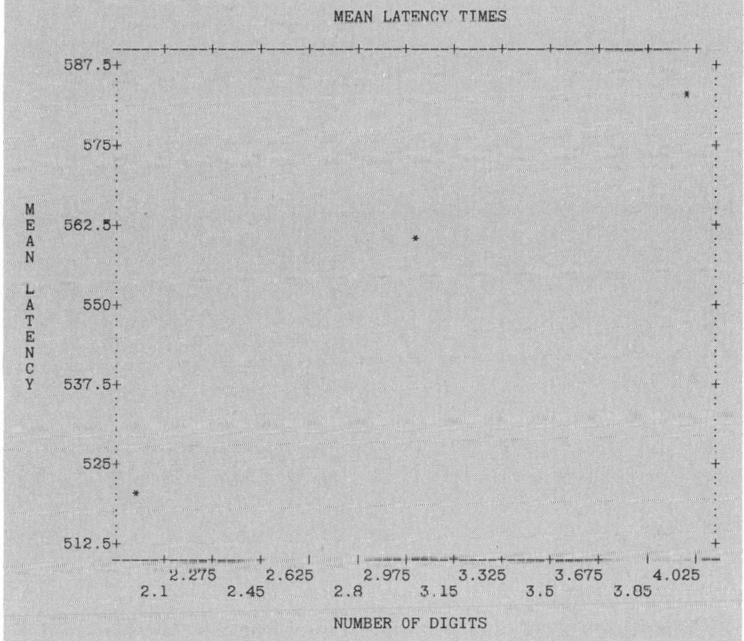

The stem-and-leaf plot of latencies for the P4DIGIT is shown in Figure 7.2c. The corresponding normal probability plot is shown in Figure 7.2d. From this, it appears that the values are somewhat more "bunched" than one would expect if they were normally distributed. The bunching of the data might occur because of limitations in the accuracy of the measurements. Similar plots can be obtained for the other two variables.

Figure 7.2c Stem-and-leaf plot for P4DIGIT

```
MANOVA P2DIGIT P3DIGIT P4DIGIT
  /PLOT=STEMLEAF
  /DESIGN
```

```
Stem-and-leaf display for variable .. P4DIGIT

    3 . 9
    4 . 347
    5 . 01111225558
    6 . 2889
    7 . 0125
    8 . 6
```

Figure 7.2d Normal probability plot for P4DIGIT

```
MANOVA P2DIGIT P3DIGIT P4DIGIT
  /PLOT= NORMAL
  /DESIGN
```

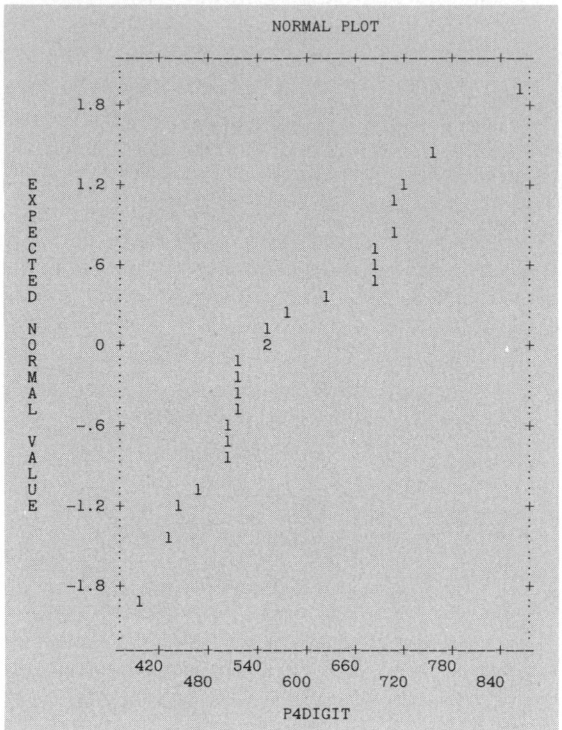

7.3 Analyzing Differences

Since multiple observations are made on the same experimental unit, in a repeated measures design, special procedures that incorporate dependencies within an experimental unit must be used. For example, in the paired *t* test design, instead of analyzing each score separately, we analyze the difference between the two scores. When there are more than two scores for a subject, the analysis becomes somewhat more complicated. For example, if each subject receives three treatments, there are three pairwise differences: the difference between the first two treatments, the difference between the second two treatments, and the difference between the first and third treatments.

Performing three paired *t* tests of the differences may seem to be the simplest analysis, but it is not, for several reasons, the best strategy. First, the three *t* tests are not statistically independent, since they involve the same means in overlapping combinations. Some overall protection against calling too many differences significant is needed, especially as the number of treatments increases. Second, since there are three separate *t* tests, a single test of the hypothesis that there is no difference between the treatments is not available.

There are several approaches for circumventing such problems in the analysis of data from repeated measures experiments. These approaches are described in the remainder of this chapter.

7.4 Transforming the Variables

To test the null hypothesis that the mean latencies are the same for the three digit lengths, the original three variables must be "transformed." That is, instead of analyzing the original three variables, we analyze linear combinations of their differences. (In the paired t-test, the transformation is the difference between the values for each subject or pair.) For certain methods of analysis, these linear combinations, sometimes called *contrasts,* must be chosen so that they are statistically independent (orthogonal) and so that the sum of the squared coefficients is 1 (normalized). Such contrasts are termed *orthonormalized.* The number of statistically independent contrasts that can be formed for a factor is one less than the number of levels of the factor. In addition, a contrast corresponding to the overall mean (the constant term in the model) is always formed. For this example, this contrast is

$$\text{CONTRAST 1} = \text{P2DIGIT} + \text{P3DIGIT} + \text{P4DIGIT} \qquad \textbf{Equation 7.4a}$$

There are many types of transformations available. One is the difference contrast, which compares each level of a factor to the average of the levels that precede it. (Another transformation, orthogonal polynomials, is discussed in Section 7.12.)

The first difference contrast for the DIGIT factor is

$$\text{CONTRAST 2} = \text{P3DIGIT} - \text{P2DIGIT} \qquad \textbf{Equation 7.4b}$$

The second difference contrast is

$$\text{CONTRAST 3} = 2 \times \text{P4DIGIT} - \text{P3DIGIT} - \text{P2DIGIT} \qquad \textbf{Equation 7.4c}$$

The contrasts can be normalized by dividing each contrast by the square root of the sum of the coefficients squared. The contrast for the overall mean is divided by

$$\sqrt{3} \qquad \textbf{Equation 7.4d}$$

and the second difference constrast is divided by

$$\sqrt{2^2 + 1^2 + 1^2} = \sqrt{6} \qquad \textbf{Equation 7.4e}$$

Figure 7.4a shows the orthonormalized transformation matrix from MANOVA for creating new variables from P2DIGIT, P3DIGIT, and P4DIGIT with the difference transformation. A column contains the coefficients for a particular contrast. Each row corresponds to one of the original variables. Thus, the first linear combination is

$$\text{CONSTANT} = 0.57735(\text{P2DIGIT} + \text{P3DIGIT} + \text{P4DIGIT}) \qquad \textbf{Equation 7.4f}$$

This new variable is, for each case, the sum of the values of the three original variables, multiplied by 0.57735. Again, the coefficients are chosen so that the sum of their squared values is 1. The next two variables are the normalized difference contrasts for the DIGIT effect.

Figure 7.4a Orthonormalized transformation matrix for difference contrasts

```
MANOVA P2DIGIT P3DIGIT P4DIGIT
  /WSFACTORS=DIGIT(3)
  /CONTRAST(DIGIT)=DIFFERENCE
  /RENAME=CONS DIF12 DIF12V3
  /PRINT=TRANSFORM
  /METHOD=SSTYPE(UNIQUE)
  /DESIGN 1
```

Orthonormalized Transformation Matrix (Transposed)

	CONS	DIF12	DIF12V3
P2DIGIT	.57735	-.70711	-.40825
P3DIGIT	.57735	.70711	-.40825
P4DIGIT	.57735	.00000	.81650

What do these new variables represent? The first variable, the sum of the original variables, is the average response over all treatments. It measures latency times over all digit lengths. The hypothesis that the average response, the constant, is equal to 0 is based on this variable. The second two contrasts together represent the treatment (DIGIT) effect. These two contrasts are used to test hypotheses about differences in latencies for the three digit lengths.

In releases before 2.2, the rows and columns of the orthonormalized transformation matrix are numbered rather than labeled with variable names. In these releases, a table like the one in Figure 7.4b is printed showing the correspondence between the effects tested and the columns of the transformation matrix. In this case, Column 1 is for the CONSTANT effect and Columns 2 and 3 for the DIGIT effect. It is important to realize that all subsequent analyses are based on these new, transformed variables and not the original variables.

Figure 7.4b Effects tested by transformed variables

Correspondence between Effects and Columns of WITHIN-Subjects Design 1

Starting Column	Ending Column	Effect Name
1	1	CONSTANT
2	3	DIGIT

7.5 Testing for Differences

In Chapter 6, analysis of variance models with more than one dependent variable are described. The same techniques can be used for repeated measures data. For example, we can use the single-sample tests to test whether particular sets of the transformed variables in the Bacon experiment have means of 0. If the number of digits does not affect latency times, the mean values of the two contrasts for the DIGIT effect are expected to be 0. Different hypotheses are tested using different transformed variables.

7.6 Testing the Constant Effect

When a repeated measures design is specified in SPSS^X MANOVA, several hypotheses are automatically tested. The first hypothesis is that the overall mean latency time is 0. It is based on the first transformed variable, which corresponds to the CONSTANT effect.

To help identify results, MANOVA prints the names of the transformed variables used to test a hypothesis. In this example, we assigned new names to the transformed variables within the MANOVA procedure (see Figure 7.4a). These new names will appear on the output. The first transformed variable is renamed to CONS, the second to DIF12, and the third to DIF12V3.

[1]With releases before 2.2, you must use the WSDESIGN and ANALYSIS(REPEATED) subcommands whenever you want to specify a repeated measures design, as in

```
MANOVA P2DIGIT P3DIGIT P4DIGIT
  /WSFACTORS=DIGIT(3)
  /CONTRAST(DIGIT)=DIFFERENCE
  /RENAME=CONS DIF12 DIF12V3
  /WSDESIGN
  /PRINT=TRANSFORM
  /METHOD=SSTYPE(UNIQUE)
  /ANALYSIS(REPEATED)
  /DESIGN
```

As of release 2.2, if new names are not assigned to the transformed variables, MANOVA assigns the names T1, T2, and so on, to the transformed variables. Before Release 2.2, the original variable names are reused. Figure 7.6a shows some MANOVA output when the variables have not been renamed in releases before 2.2. These names are simply the original variable names, prefaced by an asterisk to indicate that they have been transformed. Thus, *P2DIGIT is not the latency time for a two-digit number but is the linear combination of all latency times. This can be very confusing, especially to the novice user. Therefore, it is a good idea to rename the transformed variables, as shown in Figure 7.6b.

Figure 7.6a Effect of not renaming before Release 2.2

```
Order of Variables for Analysis

  Variates      Covariates       Not Used

  *P2DIGIT                       P3DIGIT
                                 P4DIGIT

   1 Dependent Variable
   0 Covariates
   2 Variables not used

- - - - - - - - - - - - - - - - - - - - - - - - - - - - - - - - - -

     Note..  "*" marks TRANSFORMED variables.

             These TRANSFORMED variables correspond to the
             'CONSTANT' WITHIN-SUBJECT effect.
```

Figure 7.6b shows the explanation displayed when the CONSTANT effect is tested. The column labeled "Variates" indicates which transformed variables are involved in the test of a particular effect. Since the test for the constant is based only on variable CONS, its name appears in that column. When there are no covariates in the analysis, the column labeled "Covariates" is empty, as shown. The note below the table is a reminder that analyses are based on the transformed variables, and that the particular analysis is for the CONSTANT effect.

Figure 7.6b Renamed variables used in the analysis

```
MANOVA P2DIGIT P3DIGIT P4DIGIT
  /WSFACTORS=DIGIT(3)
  /CONTRAST(DIGIT)=DIFFERENCE
  /RENAME=CONS DIF12 DIF12V3
  /METHOD=SSTYPE(UNIQUE)
  /DESIGN
```

```
Order of Variables for Analysis

  Variates      Covariates

  CONS

   1 Dependent Variable
   0 Covariates

- - - - - - - - - - - - - - - - - - - - - - - - - - - - - - - - - -

     Note..  TRANSFORMED variables are in the variates column.
             These TRANSFORMED variables correspond to the
             Between-subject effects.
```

7.7 The Analysis of Variance Table

Since the test for the constant is based on a single variable, the results are displayed in the usual univariate analysis of variance table (Figure 7.7a). The large *F* value and the small observed significance level indicate that the hypothesis that the constant is 0 is rejected. This finding is of limited importance here, since we do not expect the time required to search a number to be 0. Tests about the constant might be of interest if the original variables are difference scores—change from baseline for example—since the test of the constant would then correspond to the test that there has been no overall change from baseline.

Figure 7.7a Analysis of variance table

```
MANOVA P2DIGIT P3DIGIT P4DIGIT
  /WSFACTORS=DIGIT(3)
  /CONTRAST(DIGIT)=DIFFERENCE
  /RENAME=CONS DIF12 DIF12V3
  /METHOD=SSTYPE(UNIQUE)
  /PRINT=PARAMETERS(ESTIM)
  /DESIGN
```

Tests of Significance for CONS using UNIQUE Sums of Squares

Source of Variation	Sum of Squares	DF	Mean Square	F	Sig. of F
WITHIN CELLS	995411.11111	23	43278.74396		
CONSTANT	22093520.22222	1	22093520.22222	510.49356	.000

After the ANOVA table, SPSS^{X} MANOVA prints parameter estimates and tests of the hypotheses that the individual transformed variables have means of 0. These are shown in Figure 7.7b. For the CONSTANT effect, the parameter estimate is nothing more than

$$0.57735 \times (520.58 + 560.00 + 581.25) \quad \textbf{Equation 7.7}$$

where the numbers within the parentheses are just the means of the original three variables shown in Figure 7.2a. The 0.57735 is the value used to normalize the contrast from Figure 7.4a. The test of the hypothesis that the true value of the first parameter is 0 is equivalent to the test of the hypothesis that the constant is 0. Therefore, the *t* value printed for the test is the square root of the *F* value from the ANOVA table (the square root of 510.49 = 22.59). (When the *t* statistic is squared it is equal to an *F* statistic with one degree of freedom for the numerator and the same degrees of freedom for the denominator as the *t* statistic.)

Figure 7.7b Parameter estimates

Estimates for CONS

CONSTANT

Parameter	Coeff.	Std. Err.	T-Value	Sig. of T	Lower 95% CL	Upper 95% CL
1	959.4599223483	42.46506	22.59410	.000	871.61426	1047.30558

7.8 Testing the Digit Effect

The hypothesis of interest in this study is whether latency time depends on the number of digits in the memorized number. As shown in Figure 7.8a, this test is based on the two transformed variables, labeled DIF12 and DIF12V3. Figure 7.8b contains the multivariate tests of the hypothesis that the means of these two variables are 0. In this situation, all multivariate criteria are equivalent and lead to rejection of the hypothesis that the number of digits does not affect latency time.

Figure 7.8a Transformed variables used

```
Order of Variables for Analysis

  Variates      Covariates

  DIF12
  DIF12V3

   2 Dependent Variables
   0 Covariates

- - - - - - - - - - - - - - - - - - - - - - - - - - - - - -

   Note..  TRANSFORMED variables are in the variates column.
           These TRANSFORMED variables correspond to the
           'DIGIT' WITHIN-SUBJECT effect.
```

Figure 7.8b Multivariate hypothesis tests

```
EFFECT .. DIGIT
Multivariate Tests of Significance (S = 1, M = 0, N = 10 )

Test Name            Value      Approx. F    Hypoth. DF       Error DF      Sig. of F

Pillais             .60452      16.81439          2.00          22.00           .000
Hotellings         1.52858      16.81439          2.00          22.00           .000
Wilks               .39548      16.81439          2.00          22.00           .000
Roys                .60452
```

Univariate *F* tests for the individual transformed variables are shown in Figure 7.8c. The first row corresponds to a test of the hypothesis that there is no difference in average latency times for numbers consisting of two digits and those consisting of three. (This is equivalent to a one-sample *t* test that the mean of the second transformed variable DIF12 is 0.) The second row of Figure 7.8c provides a test of the hypothesis that there is no difference between the average response to numbers with two and three digits and numbers with four digits. The average value of this contrast is also significantly different from 0, since the observed significance level is less than 0.0005. (See Section 7.12 for an example of a different contrast type.)

Figure 7.8c Univariate hypothesis tests

```
Univariate F-tests with (1,23) D. F.

Variable      Hypoth. SS       Error SS     Hypoth. MS      Error MS            F     Sig. of F

DIF12        18644.08333    19800.91667    18644.08333     860.90942     21.65627          .000
DIF12V3      26841.36111    22774.30556    26841.36111     990.18720     27.10736          .000
```

To estimate the magnitudes of differences among the digit lengths, we can examine the values of each contrast. These are shown in Figure 7.8d. The column labeled COEFF is the average value for the normalized contrast. As shown in Section 7.4, the second contrast is 0.707 times the difference between two- and three-digit numbers, which is $0.707 \times (520.58 - 560.00) = 27.87$, the value shown in Figure 7.8d. To obtain an estimate of the absolute difference between mean response to two and three digits, the parameter estimate must be divided by 0.707. This value is 39.42. Again, the *t* value for the hypothesis that the contrast is 0 is equivalent to the square root of the *F* value from the univariate analysis of variance table.

Figure 7.8d Estimates for contrasts

```
Estimates for DIF12
DIGIT
 Parameter          Coeff.         Std. Err.         T-Value       Sig. of T    Lower 95% CL    Upper 95% CL
        1   27.8717922918           5.98926          4.65363            .000        15.48207        40.26152
- - - - - - - - - - - - - - - - - - - - - - - - - - - - - - - - - - - - - - - - - - - - - - - - - - - - - -
Estimates for DIF12V3
DIGIT
 Parameter          Coeff.         Std. Err.         T-Value       Sig. of T    Lower 95% CL    Upper 95% CL
        1   33.4423391272           6.42322          5.20647            .000        20.15489        46.72979
```

Similarly, the parameter estimate for the third contrast, the normalized difference between the average of two and three digits and four digits, is 33.44. The actual value of the difference is 40.96 (33.44 divided by 0.8165). The *t* value, the ratio of the parameter estimate to its standard error, is 5.206, which when squared equals the *F* value in Figure 7.8c. The t-values are the same for normalized and nonnormalized contrasts.

The parameter estimates and univariate *F* tests help identify which individual contrasts contribute to overall differences. However, the observed significance levels for the individual parameters are not adjusted for the fact that several comparisons are being made (see Miller, 1981; Burns, 1984). Thus, the significance levels should serve only as guides for identifying potentially important differences.

7.9 Averaged Univariate Results

The individual univariate tests can be "pooled" to obtain the averaged *F* test shown in Figure 7.9. The entries in Figure 7.9 are obtained from Figure 7.8c by summing the hypothesis and error sums of squares and the associated degrees of freedom. In this example, the averaged *F* test also leads us to reject the hypothesis that average latency times do not differ for numbers of different lengths. This is the same *F* statistic obtained by specifying a repeated measures design as a "mixed-model" univariate analysis of variance (Winer, 1971).

Figure 7.9 Averaged univariate hypothesis tests

```
MANOVA P2DIGIT P3DIGIT P4DIGIT
  /WSFACTORS=DIGIT(3)
  /CONTRAST(DIGIT)=DIFFERENCE
  /RENAME=CONS DIF12 DIF12V3
  /PRINT=SIGNIF(AVERF)
  /METHOD=SSTYPE(UNIQUE)
  /DESIGN
```

```
AVERAGED Tests of Significance for MEAS.1 using UNIQUE Sums of Squares
Source of Variation                  Sum of Squares      DF   Mean Square            F    Sig. of F
WITHIN CELLS                            42575.22222      46     925.54831
DIGIT                                   45485.44444       2   22742.72222     24.57216         .000
```

7.10 Choosing Multivariate or Univariate Results

In the previous section, we saw that hypothesis tests for the DIGIT effect could be based on multivariate criteria such as Wilks' lambda, or on the averaged univariate *F* tests. When both approaches lead to similar results, choosing between them is not of much importance. However, there are situations in which the multivariate and univariate approaches lead to different results and the question of which is appropriate arises.

The multivariate approach considers the measurements on a subject to be a sample from a multivariate normal distribution, and makes no assumption about the characteristics of the variance-covariance matrix. The univariate (sometimes called *mixed-model*) approach requires certain assumptions about the variance-covariance matrix. If these conditions are met, especially for small sample sizes, the univariate approach is more powerful than the multivariate approach. That is, it is more likely to detect differences when they exist.

Modifications of the univariate results when the assumptions are violated have also been proposed. These corrected results are approximate and are based on the adjustment of the degrees of freedom of the *F* ratio (Greenhouse-Geisser, 1959; Huynh & Feldt, 1976). The significance levels for the corrected tests will always be larger than for the uncorrected. Thus, if the uncorrected test is not significant, there is no need to calculate corrected values.

7.11 Assumptions Needed for the Univariate Approach

Since subjects in the current example are not subdivided by any grouping characteristics, the only assumption required for using the univariate results is that the variances of all the transformed variables for an effect be equal and that their covariances be 0. (Assumptions required for more complicated designs are described in Section 7.22.)

Mauchly's test of sphericity is available in MANOVA for testing the hypothesis that the covariance matrix of the transformed variables has a constant variance on the diagonal and zeroes off the diagonal (Morrison (1976)). For small sample sizes this test is not very powerful. For large sample sizes the test may be significant even when the impact of the departure on the analysis of variance results may be small.

Releases before 2.2 use Bartlett's test of sphericity instead of Mauchley's. The covariance matrix of the transformed variables is converted to a correlation matrix, and the test for an identity matrix is performed. However, this test depends on the transformation. Different transformations may lead to different results, which diminishes the usefulness of the test in this context. The test is also highly sensitive to departures from multivariate normality (Barcikowski & Robey, 1984).

Figure 7.11 contains the correlation matrix with standard deviations on the diagonal for the two transformed variables corresponding to the DIGIT effect, Mauchly's test of sphericity, and the observed significance level based on a chi-square approximation. The observed significance level is 0.149, so the

Figure 7.11 Within-cells correlation

```
MANOVA P2DIGIT P3DIGIT P4DIGIT
  /WSFACTORS=DIGIT(3)
  /CONTRAST(DIGIT)=DIFFERENCE
  /RENAME=CONS DIF12 DIF12V3
  /PRINT=SIGNIF(AVERF) ERROR(COR)
  /METHOD=SSTYPE(UNIQUE)
  /DESIGN
```

```
WITHIN CELLS Correlations with Std. Devs. on Diagonal

                DIF12    DIF12V3

DIF12          29.384
DIF12V3          .394     31.484

- - - - - - - - - - - - - - - - - - - - - - - - - - - - - - - - - -

Tests involving 'DIGIT' Within-Subject Effect.

Mauchly sphericity test, W =      .84103
Chi-square approx. =            3.80873 with 2 D. F.
Significance =                     .149

Greenhouse-Geisser Epsilon =      .86284
Huynh-Feldt Epsilon =             .92638
Lower-bound Epsilon =             .50000
```

hypothesis of sphericity is not rejected. If the observed significance level is small and the sphericity assumption appears to be violated, an adjustment to the numerator and denominator degrees of freedom can be made. Two estimates of this adjustment, called epsilon, are available in MANOVA. These are also shown in Figure 7.11. Both the numerator and denominator degrees of freedom must be multiplied by epsilon, and the significance of the F-ratio evaluated with the new degrees of freedom. The Huynh-Feldt epsilon is an attempt to correct the Greenhouser-Geisser epsilon which tends to be overly conservative, especially for small sample sizes. The lowest value possible for epsilon is also printed. The Huynh-Feldt epsilon sometimes exceeds the value of one. When this occurs MANOVA prints a value of one.

7.12 Selecting Other Contrasts

Based on the orthonormalized transformation matrix shown in Figure 7.4a and the corresponding parameter estimates in Figure 7.8d, hypotheses about particular combinations of the means were tested. Remember, the second contrast compared differences between the two- and three-digit numbers, while the third contrast compared the average of the two- and three-digit number to the 4-digit number. A variety of other hypotheses can be tested by selecting different orthogonal contrasts.

For example, to test the hypothesis that latency time increases linearly with the number of digits in the memorized number, orthogonal polynomial contrasts can be used. (In fact, polynomial contrasts should have been the first choice for data of this type. Difference contrasts were used for illustrative purposes.) When polynomial contrasts are used, the first contrast for the DIGIT effect represents the linear component, and the second contrast represents the quadratic component. Figure 7.12 contains parameter estimates corresponding to the polynomial contrasts. You can see that there is a significant linear trend, but the quadratic trend is not significant. This is also shown in the plot in Figure 7.2b, since the means fall more or less on a straight line, which does not appear to curve upward or downward.

Figure 7.12 Parameter estimates for polynomial contrasts

```
MANOVA P2DIGIT P3DIGIT P4DIGIT
  /WSFACTORS=DIGIT(3)
  /CONTRAST(DIGIT)=POLYNOMIAL
  /RENAME=CONS LIN QUAD
  /PRINT=PARAMETERS(ESTIM)
  /METHOD=SSTYPE(UNIQUE)
  /DESIGN
```

Estimates for LIN

DIGIT

Parameter	Coeff.	Std. Err.	T-Value	Sig. of T	Lower 95% CL	Upper 95% CL
1	42.8683486094	7.28780	5.88221	.000	27.79239	57.94430

Estimates for QUAD

DIGIT

Parameter	Coeff.	Std. Err.	T-Value	Sig. of T	Lower 95% CL	Upper 95% CL
1	-7.3995002647	4.91598	-1.50519	.146	-17.56898	2.76998

The requirement that contrasts be orthonormalized is necessary for the averaged F tests. It is not required for the multivariate approach. The SPSS^{X} MANOVA procedure, however, requires all contrasts for the within-subjects factors to be orthonormal. If nonorthogonal contrasts, such as simple or deviation are requested, they are orthonormalized prior to the actual analysis. The transformation matrix should always be printed so that the parameter estimates and univariate F ratios can be properly interpreted.

7.13 Adding Another Factor

The experimental design discussed so far is a very simple one. Responses to all levels of one factor (number of digits) were measured for all subjects. However, repeated measures designs can be considerably more complicated. Any factorial design can be applied to a single subject. For example, we can administer several different types of medication at varying dosages and times of day. Such a design has three factors (medication, dosage, and time) applied to each subject.

All of the usual analysis of variance hypotheses for factorial designs can be tested when each subject is treated as a complete replicate of the design. However, since observations from the same subject are not independent, the usual ANOVA method is inappropriate. Instead, we need to extend the previously described approach to analyzing repeated measures experiments.

To illustrate the analysis of a two-factor repeated measures design, consider the Bacon data again. The experiment was actually more involved than first described. The single "probe" digit was not always present in the memorized number. Instead, each subject was tested under two conditions—probe digit present and probe digit absent. Presence and absence of the probe digit was randomized. The two conditions were included to test the hypothesis that it takes longer to search through numbers when the probe digit is not present than when it is present. If memory searches are performed sequentially, one would expect that when the probe digit is encountered, searching stops. When the probe digit is not present in a number, searching must continue through all digits of the memorized number.

Thus, each subject has in fact six observations: latency times for the three number lengths when the probe is present, and times for the numbers when the probe is absent. This design has two factors—number of digits, and the probe presence/absence condition. The DIGIT factor has three levels (two, three, and four digits) and the CONDITION factor has two levels (probe present and probe absent).

7.14 Testing a Two-Factor Model

The analysis of this modified experiment proceeds similarly to the analysis described for the single-factor design. However, instead of testing only the DIGIT effect, tests for the DIGIT effect, the CONDITION effect, and the DIGIT by CONDITION interaction are required. Figure 7.14 is the orthonormalized transformation matrix for the two-factor design.

Figure 7.14 Orthonormalized transformation matrix for the two-factor design

```
MANOVA P2DIGIT P3DIGIT P4DIGIT NP2DIGIT NP3DIGIT NP4DIGIT
  /WSFACTORS=COND(2) DIGIT(3)
  /CONTRAST(DIGIT)=DIFFERENCE
  /RENAME=CONS TCONDIF TDIGIT1 TDIGIT2 TINT1 TINT2
  /PRINT=TRANSFORM PARAM(ESTIM)
  /METHOD=SSTYPE(UNIQUE)
  /DESIGN
```

Orthonormalized Transformation Matrix (Transposed)

	CONS	TCONDIF	TDIGIT1	TDIGIT2	TINT1	TINT2
P2DIGIT	.40825	.40825	-.50000	-.28868	-.50000	-.28868
P3DIGIT	.40825	.40825	.50000	-.28868	.50000	-.28868
P4DIGIT	.40825	.40825	.00000	.57735	.00000	.57735
NP2DIGIT	.40825	-.40825	-.50000	-.28868	.50000	.28868
NP3DIGIT	.40825	-.40825	.50000	-.28868	-.50000	.28868
NP4DIGIT	.40825	-.40825	.00000	.57735	.00000	-.57735

7.15 The Transformed Variables

The coefficients of the transformation matrix indicate that the first contrast is an average of all six variables. The second contrast is the average response under the "present" condition compared to the average response under the "absent" condition. The third contrast is the difference between two and three digits averaged over the two conditions. The fourth contrast is the average of two and three digits compared to four digits, averaged over both conditions. As before, these two contrasts jointly provide a test of the DIGIT effect. The last two contrasts are used for the test of interaction. If there is no interaction effect, the difference between the two- and three-digit numbers should be the same for the two probe conditions. Contrast TINT1 is the difference between two and three digits for Condition 1, minus two and three digits for Condition 2. Similarly, if there is no interaction between probe presence and the number of digits, the average of two and three digits compared to four should not differ for the two probe conditions. Contrast TINT2 is used to test this hypothesis.

7.16 Testing Hypotheses

Hypothesis testing for this design proceeds similarly to the single factor design. Each effect is tested individually. Both multivariate and univariate results can be obtained for tests of each effect. (When a factor has only two levels, there is one contrast for the effect and the multivariate and univariate results are identical.) Since the test of the constant is not of interest, we will proceed to the test of the CONDITION effect.

7.17 The CONDITION Effect

The table in Figure 7.17a explains that variable TCONDIF is being used in the analysis of the CONDITION effect. The analysis of variance table in Figure 7.17b indicates that the CONDITION effect is significant. The F value of 52 has an observed significance level of less than 0.0005. The parameter estimate for the difference between the two conditions is −75 as shown in Figure 7.17c. The estimate of the actual difference between mean response under the two conditions is obtained by dividing −75 by 0.408, since the contrast is actually

$$\text{contrast} = 0.408 \times (\text{mean present} - \text{mean absent}) \quad \textbf{Equation 7.17}$$

Since the contrast value is negative, the latency times for the absent condition are larger than the latency times for the present condition. This supports the notion that memory searching may be sequential, terminating when an item is found rather than continuing until all items are examined.

Figure 7.17a Test of the CONDITION effect

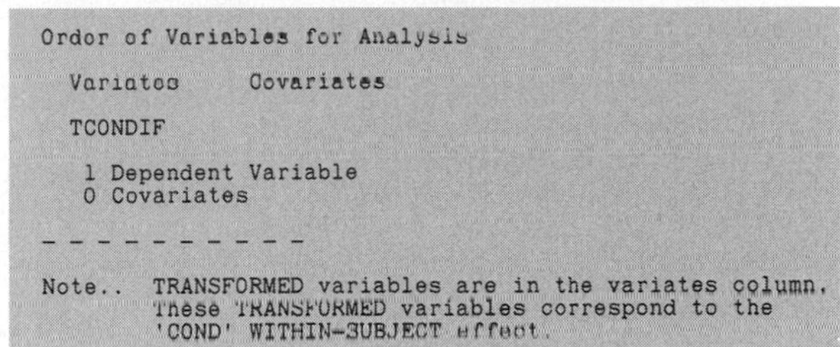

```
Order of Variables for Analysis

  Variates      Covariates

  TCONDIF

   1 Dependent Variable
   0 Covariates

 - - - - - - - - - -

Note..  TRANSFORMED variables are in the variates column.
        These TRANSFORMED variables correspond to the
        'COND' WITHIN-SUBJECT effect.
```

Figure 7.17b Analysis of variance table for the CONDITION effect

```
Tests of Significance for TCONDIF using UNIQUE Sums of Squares

Source of Variation               Sum of Squares     DF   Mean Square          F    Sig. of F

WITHIN CELLS                         58810.08333     23    2556.96014
COND                                134322.25000      1  134322.25000   52.53201        .000
```

Figure 7.17c Parameter estimates for the CONDITION effect

```
Estimates for TCONDIF

COND

 Parameter          Coeff.        Std. Err.      T-Value    Sig. of T   Lower 95% CL   Upper 95% CL

         1  -74.8114992275         10.32182     -7.24790         .000      -96.16381      -53.45918
```

7.18 The Number of Digits

The next effect to be tested is the number of digits in the memorized number. As shown in Figure 7.18a, the test is based on the two contrasts labeled TDIGIT1 and TDIGIT2. To use the univariate approach, the assumption of sphericity is necessary.

Figure 7.18a Test of the DIGIT effect

```
Order of Variables for Analysis

  Variates      Covariates

  TDIGIT1
  TDIGIT2

   2 Dependent Variables
   0 Covariates
 - - - - - - - - - -

Note..  TRANSFORMED variables are in the variates column.
        These TRANSFORMED variables correspond to the
        'DIGIT' WITHIN-SUBJECT effect.
```

Based on the multivariate criteria in Figure 7.18b, the hypothesis that there is no DIGIT effect should be rejected. From Figure 7.18c, we see that both of the contrasts are also individually different from 0. This can also be seen from Figure 7.18d, which contains the parameter estimates for the contrasts. Note that the tests that the parameter values are 0 are identical to the corresponding univariate *F* tests. The averaged tests of significance for the DIGIT effect, as shown in Figure 7.18e, lead to the same conclusion as the multivariate results in Figure 7.18b.

Figure 7.18b Multivariate tests of significance

```
EFFECT .. DIGIT
Multivariate Tests of Significance (S = 1, M = 0, N = 10 )

Test Name          Value     Approx. F    Hypoth. DF     Error DF     Sig. of F

Pillais           .64216      19.73989          2.00        22.00          .000
Hotellings       1.79454      19.73989          2.00        22.00          .000
Wilks             .35784      19.73989          2.00        22.00          .000
Roys              .64216
```

Figure 7.18c Univariate tests of significance

```
Univariate F-tests with (1,23) D. F.

Variable     Hypoth. SS      Error SS     Hypoth. MS      Error MS            F    Sig. of F

TDIGIT1     41002.66667   34710.83333   41002.66667    1509.16667      27.16908         .000
TDIGIT2     53682.72222   30821.44444   53682.72222    1340.06280      40.05986         .000
```

Figure 7.18d Parameter estimates for the DIGIT contrasts

```
Estimates for TDIGIT1
DIGIT

 Parameter        Coeff.        Std. Err.       T-Value     Sig. of T   Lower 95% CL   Upper 95% CL

      1   41.3333333333        7.92981       5.21240          .000       24.92926       57.73740
- - - - - - - - - - - - - - - - - - - - - - - - - - - - - - - - - - - - - - - - - - - - - - - - -
Estimates for TDIGIT2
DIGIT

 Parameter        Coeff.        Std. Err.       T-Value     Sig. of T   Lower 95% CL   Upper 95% CL

      1   47.2946095511        7.47235       6.32929          .000       31.83688       62.75233
```

Figure 7.18e Averaged tests of significance

```
AVERAGED Tests of Significance for MEAS.1 using UNIQUE Sums of Squares
Source of Variation           Sum of Squares     DF   Mean Square          F   Sig. of F

WITHIN CELLS                     65532.27778     46    1424.61473
DIGIT                            94685.38889      2   47342.69444   33.23193        .000
```

7.19 The Interaction

The interaction between the number of digits in the memorized number and the presence or absence of the probe digit is based on the last two contrasts, labeled TINT1 and TINT2, as indicated in Figure 7.19a. Based on the multivariate criteria shown in Figure 7.19b and the averaged univariate results in Figure 7.19c, the hypothesis that there is no interaction is not rejected.

Figure 7.19a Test of the interaction effect

```
Order of Variables for Analysis

  Variates      Covariates

  TINT1
  TINT2

   2 Dependent Variables
   0 Covariates
 - - - - - - - - - - -

Note..  TRANSFORMED variables are in the variates column.
        These TRANSFORMED variables correspond to the
        'COND BY DIGIT' WITHIN-SUBJECT effect.
```

Figure 7.19b Multivariate tests of significance

```
EFFECT .. COND BY DIGIT
Multivariate Tests of Significance (S = 1, M = 0, N = 10 )

Test Name          Value      Approx. F    Hypoth. DF      Error DF      Sig. of F

Pillais           .00890        .09873         2.00          22.00          .906
Hotellings        .00898        .09873         2.00          22.00          .906
Wilks             .99110        .09873         2.00          22.00          .906
Roys              .00890
```

Figure 7.19c Averaged tests of significance

```
AVERAGED Tests of Significance for MEAS.1 using UNIQUE Sums of Squares
Source of Variation                  Sum of Squares      DF   Mean Square          F    Sig. of F

WITHIN CELLS                            20751.50000      46     451.11957
COND BY DIGIT                              88.16667       2      44.08333     .00770        .907
```

7.20 Putting it Together

Consider Figure 7.20a, which contains a plot of the average latencies for each of the three number lengths and conditions. Means and standard deviations are shown in Figure 7.20b. Note that the average latency times for the absent condition are always higher than those for the present condition. The test for the statistical significance of this observation is based on the CONDITION factor. Figure 7.20a shows that as the number of digits in a number increases, so does the average latency time. The test of the hypothesis that latency time is the same regardless of the number of digits is based on the DIGIT factor. Again, the hypothesis that there is no DIGIT effect is rejected. The relationship between latency time and the number of digits appears to be fairly similar for the two probe conditions. This is tested by the CONDITION by DIGIT interaction, which was not found to be statistically significant. If there is a signficant interaction, the relationship between latency time and the number of digits would differ for the two probe conditions.

Figure 7.20a Plot of average latencies from procedure PLOT

```
COMPUTE CONS=1
AGGREGATE OUTFILE=*/BREAK=CONS/MPDIG2 MPDIG3 MPDIG4
 MNPDIG2 MNPDIG3 MNPDIG4=MEAN(P2DIGIT P3DIGIT P4DIGIT
   NP2DIGIT NP3DIGIT NP4DIGIT)
COMPUTE C2=2
COMPUTE C3=3
COMPUTE C4=4
PLOT SYMBOLS='PPPAAA'
   /VSIZE=45
   /HSIZE=45
   /TITLE 'LATENCY TIMES (P=PROBE PRESENT A=PROBE ABSENT)'
   /FORMAT=OVERLAY
   /HORIZONTAL 'NUMBER OF DIGITS' /VERTICAL 'MEAN LATENCY TIME'
   /PLOT=MPDIG2 WITH C2;MPDIG3 WITH C3;MPDIG4 WITH C4;
        MNPDIG2 WITH C2;MNPDIG3 WITH C3;MNPDIG4 WITH C4/
```

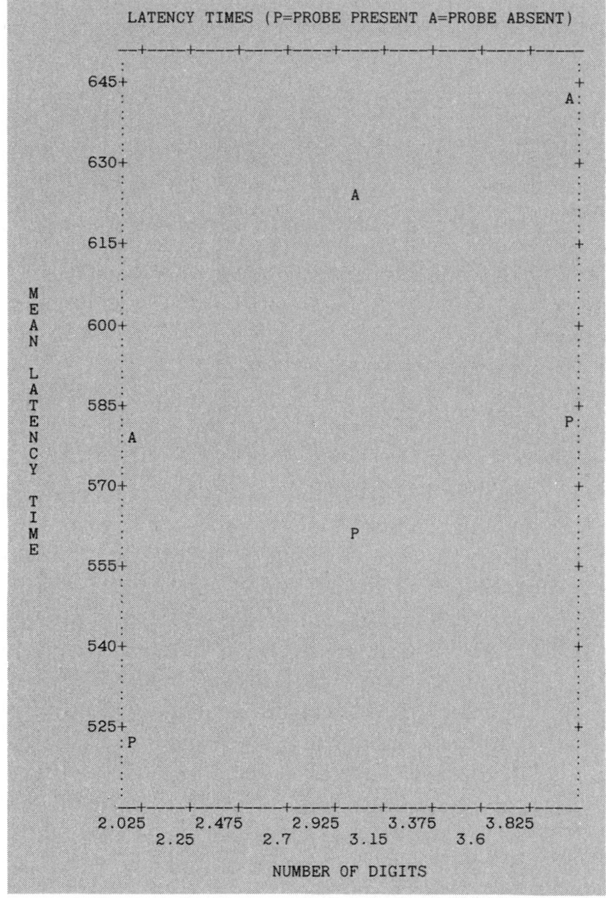

Figure 7.20b Means and standard deviations from TABLES

```
COMPUTE DUMMY1=1
COMPUTE DUMMY2=1
VARIABLE LABEL DUMMY1 'PRESENT'/DUMMY2 'ABSENT'
 /P2DIGIT '2 DIGIT'/P3DIGIT '3 DIGIT' /P4DIGIT '4 DIGIT'
 /NP2DIGIT '2 DIGIT'/NP3DIGIT '3 DIGIT' /NP4DIGIT '4 DIGIT'
VALUE LABEL DUMMY1 DUMMY2 1 ''
TABLES OBSERV=P2DIGIT TO NP4DIGIT
 /TABLE DUMMY1 BY P2DIGIT+P3DIGIT+P4DIGIT
 /STATISTICS MEAN STDDEV
 /TABLE DUMMY2 BY NP2DIGIT+NP3DIGIT+NP4DIGIT
 /STATISTICS MEAN STDDEV
```

	2 DIGIT		3 DIGIT		4 DIGIT	
	Mean	Standard Deviation	Mean	Standard Deviation	Mean	Standard Deviation
PRESENT	520.58	131.37	560.00	118.78	581.25	117.32

	2 DIGIT		3 DIGIT		4 DIGIT	
	Mean	Standard Deviation	Mean	Standard Deviation	Mean	Standard Deviation
ABSENT	579.75	132.17	623.00	135.14	642.33	144.81

7.21 Within-Subjects and Between-Subjects Factors

Both number of digits and probe status are called "within-subjects" factors since all combinations occur within each of the subjects. It is also possible to have "between-subjects" factors in repeated measures designs. Between-subjects factors subdivide the sample into discrete subgroups. Each subject has only one value for a between-subjects factor. For example, if cases in the previously described study are subdivided into males and females, sex is a between-subjects factor. Similarly, if cases are classified as those who received "memory enhancers" and those who did not, the memory enhancement factor is a between-subjects factor. If the same subject is tested with and without memory enhancers, memory enhancement would be a within-subjects factor. Thus, the same factor can be either a within-subjects or between-subjects factor, depending on the experimental design. Some factors, such as sex and race, can only be between-subjects factors since the same subject can be of only one sex or race.

7.22 Additional Univariate Assumptions

In a within-subjects design, a sufficient condition for the univariate model approach to be valid is that, for each effect, the variance-covariance matrix of the transformed variables used to test the effect has covariances of 0 and equal variances. Including between-subjects factors in a design necessitates an additional assumption. The variance-covariance matrices for the transformed variables for a particular effect must be equal for all levels of the between-subjects factors. These two assumptions are often called the "symmetry conditions." If they are not tenable, the F ratios from the averaged univariate results may not be correct.

7.23 Back to Memory

In addition to the two within-subjects factors, Bacon's experiment also included a between-subjects factor—the hand subjects used to press the instrument that signaled the presence or absence of the probe digit. All subjects were right-handed, but half were required to signal with the right hand and half with the left. (If a subject had been tested under both conditions, right hand and left hand, hand would be a within-subjects factor.) The hypothesis of interest was whether latency would increase for subjects using the left hand.

The hypothesis that the variance-covariance matrices are equal across all levels of the between-subjects factor can be examined using the multivariate generalization of Box's *M* test. It is based on the determinants of the variance-covariance matrices for all between-subjects cells in the design. Figure 7.23a contains the multivariate test for equality of the variance-covariance matrices for the two levels of the HAND factor (which hand the subject used). Note that in SPSS^X MANOVA, this test is based on all the original variables for the within-subjects effects.

Figure 7.23a Box's *M*

```
MANOVA P2DIGIT P3DIGIT P4DIGIT NP2DIGIT NP3DIGIT NP4DIGIT BY HAND(1,2)
  /WSFACTORS=COND(2) DIGIT(3)
  /CONTRAST(DIGIT)=DIFFERENCE
  /RENAME=CONS TCONDIF TDIGIT1 TDIGIT2 TINT1 TINT2
  /PRINT=HOMOGENEITY(BOXM) PARAM(ESTIM)
  /METHOD=SSTYPE(UNIQUE)
  /DESIGN
```

```
Multivariate test for Homogeneity of Dispersion matrices

Boxs M =                          25.92434
F with (21,1780) DF =               .86321, P =    .641 (Approx.)
Chi-Square with 21 DF =           18.43322, P =    .621 (Approx.)
```

Adding a between-subjects factor to the experiment introduces more terms into the analysis of variance model. Besides the DIGIT, CONDITION, and CONDITION by DIGIT effects, the model includes the main effect HAND and the interaction terms HAND by DIGIT, HAND by CONDITION, and HAND by DIGIT by CONDITION.

The analysis proceeds as before. Variables corresponding to the within-subjects factors are again transformed using the transformation matrix shown in Figure 7.23b. The between-subjects factors are not transformed.

Figure 7.23b Transformation matrix

```
MANOVA P2DIGIT P3DIGIT P4DIGIT NP2DIGIT NP3DIGIT NP4DIGIT BY HAND(1,2)
  /WSFACTORS=COND(2) DIGIT(3)
  /CONTRAST(DIGIT)=DIFFERENCE
  /RENAME=CONS TCONDIF TDIGIT1 TDIGIT2 TINT1 TINT2
  /PRINT=HOMOGENEITY(BOXM) TRANSFORM
  /METHOD=SSTYPE(UNIQUE)
  /DESIGN
```

Orthonormalized Transformation Matrix (Transposed)

	CONS	TCONDIF	TDIGIT1	TDIGIT2	TINT1	TINT2
P2DIGIT	.40825	.40825	-.50000	-.28868	-.50000	-.28868
P3DIGIT	.40825	.40825	.50000	-.28868	.50000	-.28868
P4DIGIT	.40825	.40825	.00000	.57735	.00000	.57735
NP2DIGIT	.40825	-.40825	-.50000	-.28868	.50000	.28868
NP3DIGIT	.40825	-.40825	.50000	-.28868	-.50000	.28868
NP4DIGIT	.40825	-.40825	.00000	.57735	.00000	-.57735

The within-subjects factors and their interactions are tested as when there were no between-subject factors in the design. Tests of the between-subjects factors and the interactions of the between- and within-subjects factors treat the transformed within-subjects variables as dependent variables. For example, the test of the HAND effect is identical to a two-sample *t* test, with the transformed variable corresponding to the constant as the dependent variable. The test of the CONDITION by HAND interaction treats the transformed variable corresponding to the CONDITION effect as the dependent variable. Similarly, the DIGIT by HAND interaction considers the two transformed variables for the DIGIT effect as dependent variables. The test of the three-way interaction HAND by DIGIT by CONDITION treats the two variables corresponding to the interaction of DIGIT by CONDITION as the dependent variables. HAND is always the grouping variable.

The SPSSˣ output for a design with both within- and between-subjects factors looks much like before. The variables used for each analysis are first identified, as shown for the CONSTANT effect in Figure 7.23c.

Figure 7.23c Test of the HAND effect

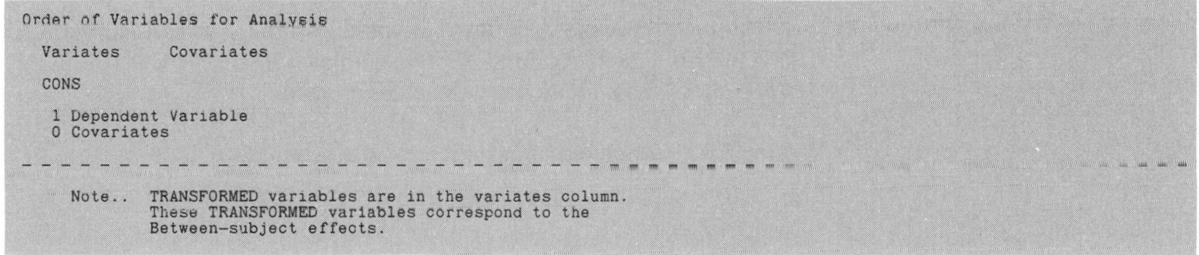

```
Order of Variables for Analysis

  Variates     Covariates

  CONS

   1 Dependent Variable
   0 Covariates

- - - - - - - - - - - - - - - - - - - - - - - - - - - - - - - - - - - - - - - - - - - - - - - - - -

     Note..  TRANSFORMED variables are in the variates column.
             These TRANSFORMED variables correspond to the
             Between-subject effects.
```

All tests based on the same transformed variables are presented together. Since the test of the HAND effect is based on the same variable as the test for the CONSTANT effect, the tests are displayed together, as shown in Figure 7.23d. The table is the usual analysis of variance table since there is only one dependent variable in the analyses. From the ANOVA table, it appears that the CONSTANT is significantly different from 0, an uninteresting finding we have made before. The HAND effect, however, is not statistically significant since its observed significance level is very close to 1. This means that there is not sufficient evidence to reject the null hypothesis that there is no difference in average latency times for subjects who used their right hand and subjects who used their left.

Figure 7.23d Tests of significance using unique sums of squares

Tests of significance for CONS using UNIQUE sums of squares

Source of Variation	Sum of Squares	DF	Mean Square	F	Sig. of F
WITHIN CELLS	2196663.86111	22	99848.35732		
CONSTANT	49193858.02778	1	49193858.02778	492.68570	.000
HAND	300.44444	1	300.44444	.00301	.957

For the transformed variable used to test the HAND effect, the overall mean is 1,432. The mean for the right-hand subjects is 1435 and for the left-hand subjects is 1,428. The parameter estimates in Figure 7.23e are based on these means. The parameter estimate for CONSTANT is the unweighted grand mean, while the parameter estimate for HAND is the deviation of the right-hand group from the overall mean. (For between-subjects variables such as HAND, deviation parameter estimates are the default.)

Figure 7.23e Parameter estimates for the HAND contrasts

```
Estimates for CONS
CONSTANT
 Parameter          Coeff.         Std. Err.          T-Value        Sig. of T    Lower 95% CL    Upper 95% CL
        1   1431.6927339659        64.50076          22.19652            .000      1297.92634      1565.45913
HAND
 Parameter          Coeff.         Std. Err.          T-Value        Sig. of T    Lower 95% CL    Upper 95% CL
        2      3.5381518507        64.50076            .05485            .957      -130.22824       137.30454
```

Figure 7.23f is the ANOVA table based on the transformed variable for the CONDITION effect. Again there is a significant effect for CONDITION, but the HAND by CONDITION effect is not significant.

Figure 7.23f Analysis of variance for the interaction

```
Tests of Significance for TCONDIF using UNIQUE Sums of Squares
Source of Variation                        Sum of Squares      DF   Mean Square            F    Sig. of F

WITHIN CELLS                                  57889.97222      22    2631.36237
COND                                         134322.25000       1  134322.25000     51.04666         .000
HAND BY COND                                    920.11111       1     920.11111       .34967         .560
```

Since the DIGIT effect has two degrees of freedom, its test is based on two transformed variables, and both univariate and multivariate results are printed for hypotheses involving DIGIT. The multivariate results for the HAND by DIGIT interaction are shown in Figure 7.23g. It appears that there is no interaction between number of digits and the hand used to signal the response. The multivariate results for the DIGIT effect are shown in Figure 7.23h. Again, they are highly significant. Figure 7.23i shows the averaged univariate results for terms involving the DIGIT effect.

Figure 7.23g Multivariate tests of significance for the HAND by DIGIT interaction

```
EFFECT .. HAND BY DIGIT
Multivariate Tests of Significance (S = 1, M = 0, N = 9 1/2)
Test Name          Value      Approx. F      Hypoth. DF        Error DF      Sig. of F

Pillais           .08477         .97258            2.00           21.00           .394
Hotellings        .09263         .97258            2.00           21.00           .394
Wilks             .91523         .97258            2.00           21.00           .394
Roys              .08477
```

Figure 7.23h Multivariate tests of significance for DIGIT effect

EFFECT .. DIGIT

Multivariate Tests of Significance (S = 1, M = 0, N = 9 1/2)

Test Name	Value	Approx. F	Hypoth. DF	Error DF	Sig. of F
Pillais	.64219	18.84488	2.00	21.00	.000
Hotellings	1.79475	18.84488	2.00	21.00	.000
Wilks	.35781	18.84488	2.00	21.00	.000
Roys	.64219				

Figure 7.23i Averaged tests of significance

```
MANOVA P2DIGIT P3DIGIT P4DIGIT NP2DIGIT NP3DIGIT NP4DIGIT BY HAND(1,2)
  /WSFACTORS=COND(2) DIGIT(3)
  /CONTRAST(DIGIT)-DIFFERENCE
  /RENAME=CONS TCONDIF TDIGIT1 TDIGIT2 TINT1 TINT2
  /PRINT=HOMOGENEITY(BOXM) TRANSFORM ERROR(COR) SIGNIF(AVERF)
  /METHOD=SSTYPE(UNIQUE)
  /DESIGN
```

AVERAGED Tests of Significance for MEAS.1 using UNIQUE Sums of Squares

Source of Variation	Sum of Squares	DF	Mean Square	F	Sig. of F
WITHIN CELLS	64376.88889	44	1463.11111		
DIGIT	94685.38889	2	47342.69444	32.35755	.000
HAND BY DIGIT	1155.38889	2	577.69444	.39484	.676

Figure 7.23j shows the multivariate results for the HAND by CONDITION by DIGIT effect. Again these are not significant. The univariate tests, shown in Figure 7.23k, agree with the multivariate results.

Figure 7.23j Multivariate tests of significance for the three-way interaction

EFFECT .. HAND BY COND BY DIGIT

Multivariate Tests of Significance (S = 1, M = 0, N = 9 1/2)

Test Name	Value	Approx. F	Hypoth. DF	Error DF	Sig. of F
Pillais	.07632	.86760	2.00	21.00	.434
Hotellings	.08263	.86760	2.00	21.00	.434
Wilks	.92368	.86760	2.00	21.00	.434
Roys	.07632				

Figure 7.23k Averaged tests of significance for the three-way interaction

AVERAGED Tests of Significance for MEAS.1 using UNIQUE Sums of Squares

Source of Variation	Sum of Squares	DF	Mean Square	F	Sig. of F
WITHIN CELLS	20138.11111	44	457.68434		
COND BY DIGIT	88.16667	2	44.08333	.09632	.908
HAND BY COND BY DIGIT	613.38889	2	306.69444	.67010	.517

7.24 Summarizing the Results

The hand used by the subject to signal the response does not seem to affect overall latency times. It also does not appear to interact with the number of digits in the memorized number, nor the presence or absence of the probe digit. This is an interesting finding, since it was conceivable that using a nonpreferred hand would increase the time required to signal. Or, subjects using their right hands might have had shorter latency times because of the way different activities are governed by the hemispheres of the brain. Memory is thought to be a function of the left hemisphere, which also governs the activity of the right hand. Thus, using the right hand would not necessitate a "switch" of hemispheres and might result in shorter latency times.

7.25 Analysis of Covariance with a Constant Covariate

The speed with which a subject signals that the probe digit is or is not present in the memorized number may depend on various characteristics of the subject. For example, some subjects may generally respond more quickly to stimuli than others. The reaction time or "speed" of a subject may influence performance in the memory experiments. To control for differences in responsiveness, we might administer a reaction-time test to each subject. This time can then be used as a covariate in the analysis. If subjects responding with the right hand are generally slower than subjects responding with their left, we may be able to account for the fact that no differences between the two groups were found.

To adjust for differences in covariates, the regression between the dependent variable and the covariate is calculated. For each subject, the response that would have been obtained if they had the same average "speed" is then calculated. Further analyses are based on these corrected values.

In a repeated measures design, the general idea is the same. The between-subjects effects are adjusted for the covariates. There is no need to adjust the within-subjects effects for covariates whose values do not change during the course of an experiment, since within-subjects factor differences are obtained from the same subject. That is, a subject's "quickness" or "slowness" is the same for all within-subjects factors.

To see how this is done, consider a hypothetical extension of Bacon's experiment. Let's assume that prior to the memory tests, each subject was given a series of trials in which he or she pressed a bar as soon as a light appeared. The interval between the time the light appeared and the time the subject pressed the bar will be termed the reaction time. For each subject, the average reaction time over a series of trials is calculated. This reaction time will be considered a covariate in the analysis.

As in the previous examples, all analyses are based on the transformed within-subjects variables. Figure 7.25a shows the orthonormalized transformation matrix. It is similar to the one used before, except that there are now six additional rows and columns that are used to transform the covariates. Although there is only one covariate in this example, the MANOVA procedure requires you to specify a covariate for each within-subjects variable, which is done by repeating the same covariate. The transformation applied to the covariates is the same as the transformation for the within-subjects factors.

Figure 7.25a Transformation matrix with covariates

```
COMPUTE C1=REACT
COMPUTE C2=REACT
COMPUTE C3=REACT
COMPUTE C4=REACT
COMPUTE C5=REACT
COMPUTE C6=REACT
MANOVA P2DIGIT P3DIGIT P4DIGIT NP2DIGIT NP3DIGIT NP4DIGIT BY HAND(1,2)
        WITH C1 C2 C3 C4 C5 C6
  /WSFACTORS=COND(2) DIGIT(3)
  /CONTRAST(DIGIT)=DIFFERENCE
  /RENAME=CONS TCONDIF TDIGIT1 TDIGIT2 TINT1 TINT2
          TC1 TC2 TC3 TC4 TC5 TC6
  /PRINT=TRANSFORM
  /METHOD=SSTYPE(UNIQUE)
  /DESIGN
```

Orthonormalized Transformation Matrix (Transposed)

	CONS	TCONDIF	TDIGIT1	TDIGIT2	TINT1	TINT2	TC1
P2DIGIT	.40825	.40825	-.50000	-.28868	-.50000	-.28868	.00000
P3DIGIT	.40825	.40825	.50000	-.28868	.50000	-.28868	.00000
P4DIGIT	.40825	.40825	.00000	.57735	.00000	.57735	.00000
NP2DIGIT	.40825	-.40825	-.50000	-.28868	.50000	.28868	.00000
NP3DIGIT	.40825	-.40825	.50000	-.28868	-.50000	.28868	.00000
NP4DIGIT	.40825	-.40825	.00000	.57735	.00000	-.57735	.00000
C1	.00000	.00000	.00000	.00000	.00000	.00000	.40825
C2	.00000	.00000	.00000	.00000	.00000	.00000	.40825
C3	.00000	.00000	.00000	.00000	.00000	.00000	.40825
C4	.00000	.00000	.00000	.00000	.00000	.00000	.40825
C5	.00000	.00000	.00000	.00000	.00000	.00000	.40825
C6	.00000	.00000	.00000	.00000	.00000	.00000	.40825

	TC2	TC3	TC4	TC5	TC6
P2DIGIT	.00000	.00000	.00000	.00000	.00000
P3DIGIT	.00000	.00000	.00000	.00000	.00000
P4DIGIT	.00000	.00000	.00000	.00000	.00000
NP2DIGIT	.00000	.00000	.00000	.00000	.00000
NP3DIGIT	.00000	.00000	.00000	.00000	.00000
NP4DIGIT	.00000	.00000	.00000	.00000	.00000
C1	.40825	-.50000	-.28868	-.50000	-.28868
C2	.40825	.50000	-.28868	.50000	-.28868
C3	.40825	.00000	.57735	.00000	.57735
C4	-.40825	-.50000	-.28868	.50000	.28868
C5	-.40825	.50000	-.28868	-.50000	.28868
C6	-.40825	.00000	.57735	.00000	-.57735

Figure 7.25b is a description of the variables used in the analysis of the constant and the between-subjects variable. The dependent variable is CONSTANT, the covariate TC1. All of the other variables, including the five transformed replicates of the same covariate labeled TC2 to TC6, are not used for this analysis.

Figure 7.25b Test of the constant effect

```
Order of Variables for Analysis

  Variates    Covariates

  CONS        TC1

   1 Dependent Variable
   1 Covariate

- - - - - - - - - - - - - - - - - - - - - - - - - - - - - - - - - - - - - - - -

      Note.. TRANSFORMED variables are in the variates column.
             These TRANSFORMED variables correspond to the
             Between-subject effects.
```

The analysis of variance table for the HAND and CONSTANT effects is shown in Figure 7.25c. Note how the table has changed from Figure 7.23e, the corresponding table without the reaction-time covariate. In Figure 7.25c, the within-cells error term is subdivided into two components—error sums of squares and sums of squares due to the regression. In an analysis of covariance model, we are able to explain some of the variability within a cell of the design by the fact that cases have different values for the covariates. The regression sum of squares is the variability attributable to the covariate. If one were to calculate a regression between the transformed constant term and the transformed covariate, the regression sums of squares would be identical to those in Figure 7.25c. The test for the HAND effect is thus no longer based on the CONSTANT, but on the CONSTANT adjusted for the covariate. Thus, differences between the groups in overall reaction time are eliminated. The HAND effect is still not significant, however. The sums of squares attributable to the CONSTANT have also changed. This is because the hypothesis tested is no longer that the overall mean is 0, but that the intercept in the regression equation for the constant and the reaction time is 0.

Figure 7.25c Analysis of covariance

Tests of Significance for CONS using UNIQUE Sums of Squares

Source of Variation	Sum of Squares	DF	Mean Square	F	Sig. of F
WITHIN CELLS	656243.80460	21	31249.70498		
Regression	1540420.05651	1	1540420.05651	49.29391	.000
CONSTANT	126.80817	1	126.80817	.00406	.950
HAND	3745.90085	1	3745.90085	.11987	.733

Figure 7.25d shows that the regression coefficient for the transformed reaction time is 97.5746. The test of the hypothesis that the coefficient is 0 is identical to the test of the regression effect in the ANOVA table.

Figure 7.25d Regression coefficient for reaction time

Regression analysis for WITHIN CELLS error term

Dependent variable .. CONS

Covariate	B	Beta	Std. Err.	T-Value	Sig. of T	Lower 95% CL	Upper 95% CL
TC1	97.5746661658	.8374092999	13.89762	7.02096	.000	68.67298	126.47635

When constant covariates are specified, messages such as that shown in Figure 7.25e are displayed. All the message says is that since all the covariates are identical, they are linearly dependent. You can simply ignore this message.

Figure 7.25e Linear dependency warning message

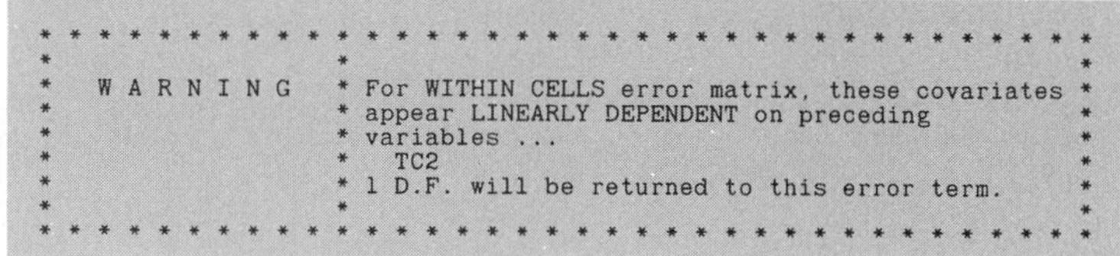

```
* * * * * * * * * * * * * * * * * * * * * * * * * * * * * * * * * * * * *
*                *                                                        *
*  W A R N I N G  * For WITHIN CELLS error matrix, these covariates       *
*                * appear LINEARLY DEPENDENT on preceding                 *
*                * variables ...                                          *
*                *   TC2                                                  *
*                * 1 D.F. will be returned to this error term.            *
*                *                                                        *
* * * * * * * * * * * * * * * * * * * * * * * * * * * * * * * * * * * * *
```

7.26 Doubly Multivariate Repeated Measures Designs

There is only one dependent variable in Bacon's experiment, latency time, which was measured for all subjects. In some situations, more than one dependent variable may be measured for each factor combination. For example, to test the effect of different medications on blood pressure, both systolic and diastolic blood pressures may be recorded for each treatment. This is sometimes called a doubly multivariate repeated measures design, since each subject has multiple variables measured at multiple times.

Analysis of doubly multivariate repeated measures data is similar to the analyses above. Each dependent variable is transformed using the same orthonormalized transformation. All subsequent analyses are based on these transformed variables. The tests for each effect are based on the appropriate variables for all dependent variables. For example, in the memory experiment, if two dependent variables had been measured for the three number lengths, the test of the DIGIT effect would be based on four transformed variables, two for the first dependent variable and two for the second. Similarly, the test for CONSTANT would have been based on two variables corresponding to averages for each dependent variable.

7.27 RUNNING MANOVA FOR REPEATED MEASURES DESIGNS

The operation of the MANOVA procedure is more fully documented in Chapter 6. Most of the subcommands described there can be used with repeated measures designs as well. This chapter covers only the subcommands needed to specify repeated measures designs.

7.28 The Variable List

The first MANOVA specification is the list of variables to be used in the analyses. Dependent variables are named first, followed by the keyword BY and factor names and ranges. If there are covariates, list them last following keyword WITH. In a repeated measures design, list all variables that correspond to within-subjects factors as dependent variables. between-subjects variables are considered factors.

For example, the command

```
MANOVA P2DIGIT P3DIGIT P4DIGIT
```

specifies the three variables corresponding to number length when the probe digit is present as the dependent variable. To include the present/absent condition in the analysis as well, specify

```
MANOVA P2DIGIT P3DIGIT P4DIGIT NP2DIGIT NP3DIGIT NP4DIGIT
```

To include the between-groups factor HAND with two levels coded as 1 and 2, specify

```
MANOVA P2DIGIT P3DIGIT P4DIGIT NP2DIGIT NP3DIGIT NP4DIGIT BY HAND(1,2)
```

When there are additional between-subjects factors, list them all after the BY keyword. Additional rules for specifying variables are given in Chapter 6.

7.29 Specifying A Constant Covariate

In a repeated measures design, you must specify as many covariate names as there are dependent variables on the MANOVA command. If there is a single covariate that is measured only once, for example before the experiment was conducted, use the COMPUTE command to replicate the covariate values. (A covariate that is measured once is called a *constant covariate.*) For example, the analysis of covariance described in Section 7.25, where REACT is the value of the reaction time can be specified as

```
COMPUTE C1=REACT
COMPUTE C2=REACT
COMPUTE C3=REACT
COMPUTE C4=REACT
COMPUTE C5=REACT
COMPUTE C6=REACT
MANOVA P2DIGIT P3DIGIT P4DIGIT NP2DIGIT NP3DIGIT NP4DIGIT BY HAND(1,2)
       WITH C1 C2 C3 C4 C5 C6
```

7.30 The WSFACTORS Subcommand

For a repeated measures design, you must also specify the structure of the design. For example, if there are six variables in the dependent variable list, they may have originated from a variety of repeated measures designs. There may be one within-subjects factor, say TREATMENT, which has six values representing six different agents administered to the same subject. Or there may be two within-subjects factors such as TREATMENT and DOSE, one having three levels and the other having two, e.g., each subject receives three different treatments at two dosage levels. Or, perhaps two treatments at each of three dosage levels are given.

The WSFACTORS subcommand identifies the correspondence between the variables list and the within-subjects factors. WSFACTORS supplies the name of each factor, followed by the number of levels in parentheses. The product of the number of levels of the factors must equal the number of dependent variables (except in doubly multivariate repeated measures; see Section 7.32). WSFACTOR must be the first subcommand after the variable list.

For example, to indicate that the three variables P2DIGIT, P3DIGIT, and P4DIGIT correspond to three levels of a within-subjects factor, which is to be assigned the name DIGIT, specify

```
MANOVA P2DIGIT P3DIGIT P4DIGIT
  /WSFACTORS=DIGIT(3)
```

The names assigned to the within-subjects factors must follow the SPSS^X variable-naming conventions. Each within-subjects factor name must be unique. The within-subjects factor names exist only during the MANOVA analysis in which they are defined.

A name must be assigned to each within-subjects factor. For example, to define the two within-subjects factors for number length and presence/absence condition, specify

```
MANOVA P2DIGIT P3DIGIT P4DIGIT NP2DIGIT NP3DIGIT NP4DIGIT
  /WSFACTORS=COND(2) DIGIT(3)
```

Each variable named on the variables list corresponds to a particular combination of within-subjects factor levels. For example, variable P2DIGIT is the latency time for a two-digit number when the probe digit is present.

The order in which factors are named on WSFACTORS must correspond to the sequence of variables on the variable list. The first factor named on WSFACTORS changes most slowly. Thus, in the example above, values of the DIGIT factor change faster than values of the COND factor. For example, P2DIGIT is the response at the first level of CONDITION and the first level of DIGIT, and P3DIGIT is the response at the first level of CONDITION and the second level of DIGIT. If the order of the variables on the MANOVA command is changed, the order of factor names on the WSFACTORS subcommand must also be changed, as in

```
MANOVA P2DIGIT NP2DIGIT P3DIGIT NP3DIGIT P4DIGIT NP4DIGIT
  /WSFACTORS=DIGIT(3) COND(2)
```

In general, the variables must be arranged in the variable list in such a way that their structure can be represented on a WSFACTORS subcommand. For example, it is not possible to represent the following list of variables on a WSFACTORS subcommand, since the variables are not arranged in a predictable sequence:

```
MANOVA P2DIGIT P3DIGIT NP2DIGIT NP3DIGIT P4DIGIT NP4DIGIT
```

7.31 The RENAME Subcommand

When a repeated measures design is specified, the original variables are transformed using an orthonormal transformation matrix, and the transformed variables are then analyzed. To make the SPSS^X MANOVA output easier to interpret, it is a good idea to assign names to the new variables. This is done with the RENAME subcommand.

For example, the following command created the output shown in Figure 7.23d:

```
MANOVA P2DIGIT P3DIGIT P4DIGIT NP2DIGIT NP3DIGIT NP4DIGIT BY HAND(1,2)
  /WSFACTORS=COND(2) DIGIT(3)
  /RENAME=CONS TCONDIF TDIGIT1 TDIGIT2 TINT1 TINT2
```

The name CONS is assigned to the CONSTANT effect, the name TCONDIF to the CONDITION effect, the names TDIGIT1 and TDIGIT2 to the two transformed variables for the DIGIT effect, and TINT1 and TINT2 to the two transformed variables that represent the interaction of condition and digit length.

The number of names listed on the RENAME subcommand must equal the number of dependent variables and covariates on the variables list. To retain a variable's original name, specify either the original name or an asterisk. For example, to retain the names of the covariates in the following command, specify:

```
MANOVA P2DIGIT P3DIGIT P4DIGIT NP2DIGIT NP3DIGIT NP4DIGIT BY HAND(1,2)
       WITH C1 C2 C3 C4 C5 C6
  /WSFACTORS=COND(2) DIGIT(3)
  /RENAME=CONS TCONDIF TDIGIT1 TDIGIT2 TINT1 TINT2 * * * * * *
```

7.32 The MEASURE Subcommand

In a doubly multivariate repeated measures design (when more than one variable is measured at each combination of the factor levels), you can use the MEASURE subcommand to differentiate sets of dependent variables. In a doubly multivariate design, the arrangement of the within-subjects factors must be the same for all sets of variables. For example, if both systolic and diastolic blood pressure are measured at three points in time, you could specify

```
MANOVA SYS1 SYS2 SYS3 DIAS1 DIAS2 DIAS3
  /WSFACTORS=TIME(3)
  /MEASURE=SYSTOL DIASTOL
```

This command names one factor, TIME, which has three levels for two sets of dependent variables. Variables SYS1, SYS2, and SYS3 are in the SYSTOL set, and DIAS1, DIAS2, and DIAS3 are DIASTOL. Note that the product of the number of variables named on MEASURE times the product of the levels of factors named on WSFACTORS equals the number of dependent variables on the variables list.

If you omit MEASURE from the above command, SPSS^X MANOVA will automatically generate a doubly multivariate design based on the three levels of the TIME factor. The advantage of using MEASURE is that the display of averaged results (produced by SIGNIF(AVERF) on the PRINT subcommand) will be labeled with the names you specify on MEASURE. If you do not use MEASURE, MANOVA prints the results but uses its own labeling. Thus, the MEASURE subcommand is optional but is recommended for clarity.

7.33 The CONTRAST Subcommand

All of the CONTRASTS described in Chapter 6 can also be used for between-subjects factors in repeated measures designs. In the case of within-subjects factors, nonorthogonal contrasts such as deviation and simple are orthonormalized prior to the repeated measures analysis. Thus, if the contrast requested is not orthogonal, the parameter estimates obtained for terms involving the within-subjects factors will not correspond to the contrast requested. Therefore, it is recommended that only orthogonal contrasts be specified on the CONTRAST subcommand for within-subjects factors.

If nonorthogonal contrasts are requested, the transformation matrix should always be printed to ascertain what orthonormalized contrasts are used. Since the default contrasts are deviation, they produce parameter estimates that are not easily interpreted.

7.34 The WSDESIGN Subcommand

The WSDESIGN subcommand specifies the design for the within-subjects factors. Its specification is similar to the DESIGN subcommand discussed in Chapter 6. For example, to specify a complete factorial design for the DIGIT and COND within-subjects factors, specify

```
MANOVA P2DIGIT P3DIGIT P4DIGIT NP2DIGIT NP3DIGIT NP4DIGIT
  /WSFACTORS=COND(2) DIGIT(3)
  /WSDESIGN=COND DIGIT COND BY DIGIT
```

To suppress estimation of the CONDITION by DIGIT interaction and specify a main-effects model, specify

```
MANOVA P2DIGIT P3DIGIT P4DIGIT NP2DIGIT NP3DIGIT NP4DIGIT
  /WSFACTORS=COND(2) DIGIT(3)
  /WSDESIGN=COND DIGIT
```

The following specifications, which can be used on the DESIGN subcommand, are not permitted on the WSDESIGN subcommand:

- Error term references and definitions.
- The MUPLUS and CONSTANT keywords.
- Interval-level variables.
- Between-subjects factors.

The WSDESIGN subcommand is required for all repeated measures designs in releases prior to 2.2. As of Release 2.2, a full-factorial design is assumed by default if the subcommand is omitted or is used without any further specifications. For example, the following command is equivalent to the full-factorial within-subjects design specification.

```
MANOVA P2DIGIT P3DIGIT P4DIGIT NP2DIGIT NP3DIGIT NP4DIGIT
  /WSFACTORS=COND(2) DIGIT(3)
```

The WSDESIGN specification signals the beginning of within-subjects design processing so, if it is specified, all subcommands that affect the within-subjects design must appear before it. For example, if a POLYNOMIAL contrast is to be used for the DIGIT effect, this must be indicated prior to a WSDESIGN subcommand, as in

```
MANOVA P2DIGIT P3DIGIT P4DIGIT NP2DIGIT NP3DIGIT NP4DIGIT
  /WSFACTORS=COND(2) DIGIT(3)
  /CONTRAST(DIGIT)=POLY(1,2)
  /WSDESIGN
```

7.35 The ANALYSIS(REPEATED) Subcommand

In a repeated measures analysis of variance, all dependent variables are not tested together as is usually done in MANOVA. Instead, sets of transformed variables that correspond to particular effects are tested. For example, in the memory experiment, the constant is tested first, then the variable that represents the CONDITION effect, then the two variables that represent the DIGIT effect, and finally the two variables that represent the DIGIT by CONDITION interaction. With releases before 2.2, the cycling through the dependent variables is accomplished with the ANALYSIS(REPEATED) subcommand. The WSFACTORS and WSDESIGN subcommands must be specified before ANALYSIS(REPEATED). In these earlier releases, if you do not specify ANALYSIS(REPEATED) for a repeated measures design, the format of the output will not be easily understood. As of Release 2.2, a repeated measures analysis is assumed whenever WSFACTORS is specified and the ANALYSIS(REPEATED) command is obsolete.

7.36 The DESIGN Subcommand

Use the DESIGN subcommand according to the rules defined in Chapter 6 to list between-subjects effects to be tested. If no effects are listed on the DESIGN subcommand, the default is a full-factorial design. Thus, the complete memory experiment can be analyzed with the commands

```
MANOVA P2DIGIT P3DIGIT P4DIGIT NP2DIGIT NP3DIGIT NP4DIGIT BY HAND(1,2)
  /WSFACTORS=COND(2) DIGIT(3)
  /RENAME=CONS TCONDIF TDIGIT1 TDIGIT2 TINT1 TINT2
  /WSDESIGN=COND DIGIT COND BY DIGIT
  /DESIGN=HAND
```

7.37 The PRINT Subcommand

All statistics and plots described in Chapter 6 are also available for repeated measures designs. However, some output is particularly useful for repeated measures designs. The orthonormalized transformation matrix used to generate the transformed variables is requested with the keyword TRANSFORM. The averaged univariate *F* tests are requested with the keywords SIGNIF(AVERF).

For example, to print the transformation matrix and averaged *F* values, specify

```
/PRINT=TRANSFORM SIGNIF(AVERF)
```

As of Release 2.2, Mauchley's test of sphericity and related statistics are automatically output for repeated measures designs. In earlier releases, homogeneity of variance tests and Bartlett's test of sphericity may be used to analyze departures from the symmetry assumptions necessary for a univariate analysis. To obtain these, use keywords HOMOGENEITY (BARTLETT, COCHRAN, and/or BOXM) and ERROR(COR) to request the tests as in

```
/PRINT=TRANSFORM SIGNIF(AVERF) HOMOGENEITY(BARTLETT BOXM) ERROR(COR)
```

7.38 EXERCISES

Syntax

1. For the MANOVA command below, what are the within-subjects factors, the between-subjects factors, and the covariates.

```
MANOVA ENTHUS1 TO ENTHUS12 BY PROGRAM(1,5) WITH GNENTH1 TO GNENTH12
  /WSFACTORS=EXAMTIME(1,4) SEASON(1,3)
```

2. A drug study has the following repeated measures design. There are 18 measurements for each subject.

			Variables
IM Injection	Dose 1	a.m.	RELIEF1
		noon	RELIEF2
		p.m.	RELIEF3
	Dose 2	a.m.	RELIEF4
		noon	RELIEF5
		p.m.	RELIEF6
	Dose 3	a.m.	RELIEF7
		noon	RELIEF8
		p.m.	RELIEF9
SC Injection	Dose 1	A.M.	RELIEF10
		noon	RELIEF11
		p.m.	RELIEF12
	Dose 2	a.m.	RELIEF13
		noon	RELIEF14
		p.m.	RELIEF15
	Dose 3	a.m.	RELIEF16
		noon	RELIEF17
		p.m.	RELIEF18

The researcher wants to examine the effects of sex (SEX) and ethnic group (ETHNIC, with four levels) and to eliminate variability due to age (AGE). Write the MANOVA command needed for the analysis that eliminates the three-way interaction for within-subjects factors and the two-way interaction for between-subjects factors.

3. Some of the following MANOVA commands contain errors, and some are correct. Indicate which commands are correct, and list the errors in the incorrect commands.

a.
```
MANOVA RATING1 TO RATING12 BY SEX(1,2) EDUC(1,4) WITH HUMOR
  /WSFACTORS=CONTENT(4) LENGTH(3)
  /CONTRAST(LENGTH)=POLY(1,2,3)
```

b.
```
MANOVA C2AD1BUY C2AD2BUY C2AD3BUY C1AD1BUY C1AD2BUY
        BY VEGPREF(1,4) EMPLOY(1,3) GOURMET(1,3)
  /WSFACTORS=AD(3) PKGCOLOR(2)
  /WSDESIGN
```

c.
```
MANOVA TEMPMNT1 TO TEMPMNT3 BY BREED(1,3) SOCIALZN(1,4) WITH
        DAMTEMP1 TO DAMTEMP3 SIRTEMP1 TO SIRTEMP3
  /WSFACTORS=AGE(3)
  /RENAME=CONSTANT AGE1V2 AGE12V3 * * * * * *
  /WSDESIGN
```

d.
```
MANOVA SOLTIME1 TO SOLTIME5 BY TRAINING(1,2) EMOTION(1,3) WITH
        PRESCOR1 TO PRESCOR5
  /WSFACTORS=ROOM TRAINING EMOTION
```

e.
```
MANOVA AGGRSSN1 TO AGGRSSN6 BY SEX MENACE WITH SEXISM1 TO SEXISM6
  /WSFACTORS=FILM(1,3) CONFED(1,2)
  /ANALYSIS(REPEATED)
  /WSDESIGN=FILM CONFED
  /CONTRAST(FILM)=POLY(1,2,3)
```

4. Correct the following MANOVA command:

```
MANOVA FUNNY1 TO FUNNY4 BY SEX
  /WSFACTORS=OBSCENE(1,2) SEXIST(1,2) RACE(1,2)
  /RENAME=CONSTANT TOBSDIFF
  /WSDESIGN=OBSCENE SEXIST SEX RACE
```

5. An outdoor-equipment mail-order company conducted a study to determine the effect of various factors on sales and customer satisfaction. A random sample of customers was taken, and the amount of merchandise each customer purchased was determined for the first and second half of each season. Extra advertising was sent to each customer at the beginning of each season. Customers were also asked to fill out a questionnaire about customer satisfaction during each of these time periods. Each customer therefore had eight repeated sales measurements (ADWINS, NOADWINS, ADSPRS, NOADPRS, ADSUMS, NOADSUMS, ADFALS, NOADFALS) and eight repeated satisfaction measurements (ADWINC, NOADWINC, ADSPRC, NOADSPRC, ADSUMC, NOADSUMC, ADFALC, NOADFALC).

   The company wants to investigate the effects of season, advertising, sex, and race (with three levels) on sales and satisfaction. They also want to adjust for income. They want averaged *F*-tests for the full-factorial model and Box's *M* test, and they are not interested in the parameter estimates. Write the MANOVA command necessary to obtain this doubly multivariate analysis.

Statistical Concepts

1. For each study described below, indicate whether a repeated measures analysis of variance, an independent-samples analysis of variance, or neither is appropriate.
   a. A psychologist wants to investigate the effects of three over-the-counter drugs on performance on a logical reasoning test. Ninety students are randomly assigned to three groups of thirty students each, with each group getting one of the drugs. One hour after taking the drug, the students are tested and their scores determined.
   b. A dog food manufacturer is testing the palatability of four new canned dog foods: A, B, C, and D. Twenty-five dogs who haven't eaten in 24 hours are first offered Dog Food A. The amount eaten in two minutes is recorded for each dog. One week later, Dog Food B is given in the same manner to the twenty-five dogs and the amount eaten in two minutes recorded. Dog Foods C and D are given to the same dogs in the same manner in the third and fourth weeks of the study. The manufacturer wants to compare the average amounts of the four foods consumed in two minutes.
   c. A group of 50 patients with arthritis is used to test five new anti-inflammatory drugs. For one month, patients are drug free. During the second month, the patients are given Drug 1. For the next month, no drugs are administered. Then Drug 2 is given during the fourth month. No drugs are administered in the fifth month and then Drug 3 is given during the sixth month, and so forth. For each month in which a drug is administered, the patient is assigned the value 1 if arthritis symptoms are less severe than during the previous drug-free month. If there is no improvement, the patient is assigned the value 0. Based on these 0 and 1 scores, a physician wants to compare the effectiveness of these five drugs.

d. A professor conducts a study to determine whether memory is affected by changes in environment. Sixty students are given an exam, with students randomly assigned to one of three rooms (20 students per room). One week later, the first group of students retakes the exam in the same room as before, the second group retakes the exam in a room similar to the room in which they originally took the exam, and the third group retakes the exam in a room totally unlike their original room. The differences between the second and first exam scores are obtained. The professor wants to examine the average differences for the three groups.

2. Fill in the missing entries in the following output:

Univariate F-tests with (1,41) D. F.

Variable	Hypoth. SS	Error SS	Hypoth. MS	Error MS	F	Sig. of F
DIF12	34186	23857	34186	582	59	.000
DIF12V3	13222	17921	13222	437	30	.000

AVERAGED Tests of Significance for MEAS.1 using UNIQUE Sums of Squares

Source of Variation	Sum of Squares	DF	Mean Square	F	Sig. of F
WITHIN CELLS					
CLASS					.000

3. Let $\bar{X}_{DIGIT=i,COND=PRES}$ and $\bar{X}_{DIGIT=i,COND=ABS}$ (where i=1,2,3) represent the six means involved in the two-factor memory example described in this chapter. Using the orthonormalized transformation matrix shown below, write the six transformed variables in terms of these means. For example,

$$CONS=0.40825 \times (\bar{X}_{DIGIT=1,COND=PRES} + \bar{X}_{DIGIT=2,COND=PRES} + \bar{X}_{DIGIT=3,COND=PRES} + \bar{X}_{DIGIT=1,COND=ABS} + \bar{X}_{DIGIT=2,COND=ABS} + \bar{X}_{DIGIT=3,COND=ABS})$$

Orthonormalized Transformation Matrix (Transposed)

	1	2	3	4	5	6
1	.40825	.40825	-.50000	-.28868	-.50000	-.28868
2	.40825	.40825	.50000	-.28868	.50000	-.28868
3	.40825	.40825	.00000	.57735	.00000	.57735
4	.40825	-.40825	-.50000	-.28868	.50000	.28868
5	.40825	-.40825	.50000	-.28868	-.50000	.28868
6	.40825	-.40825	.00000	.57735	.00000	-.57735

4. a. Show that the coefficients in the orthonormalized transformation matrix below have been normalized.

Orthonormalized Transformation Matrix (Transposed)

	1	2	3
1	.57735	-.70711	-.40825
2	.57735	.70711	-.40825
3	.57735	.00000	.81650

b. The columns of a transformation matrix are made orthogonal by ensuring that, for any two columns, the sum of the cross-products between corresponding column entries is 0. For example, Columns 1 and 2 in the orthonormalized transformation matrix above are orthogonal because

$(0.57735 \times -0.70711) + (0.57735 \times 0.70711) + (0.57735 \times 0) = -0.40825 + 0.40825 + 0 = 0$

Show that columns 1 and 2 of this matrix are orthogonal to column 3.

5. Fill in the missing information in the following output:

```
Tests of Significance for CONS using UNIQUE Sums of Squares

Source of Variation          Sum of Squares      DF   Mean Square        F   Sig. of F

WITHIN CELLS                 [      ]            45        58714
CONSTANT                     [      ]             1   [      ]        322        .000
------------------------------------------------------------------------------------

Estimates for CONS

CONSTANT

 Parameter       Coeff.     Std. Err.      T-Value     Sig. of T   Lower 95% CL   Upper 95% CL

     1          [    ]        43          [    ]         .000          686          [      ]
```

6. Based on the output shown below, would you recommend a univariate or a multivariate approach to the repeated measures analysis? Why?

```
WITHIN CELLS Correlations with Std. Devs. on Diagonal

              TDIGIT1        TDIGIT2

TDIGIT1         21.78
TDIGIT2           .35          20.99

----------------------------------------

Tests involving 'DIGIT' Within-Subject Effect.

 Mauchly sphericity test, W =      .87321
 Chi-square approx. =             2.84712 with 2 D. F.
 Significance =                     .241

 Greenhouse-Geisser Epsilon =      .88748
 Huynh-Feldt Epsilon =            1.00000
 Lower-bound Epsilon =             .50000
```

7. In a repeated measures analysis with the between-subjects factor HOSPITAL, the following (transformed) pain scores were obtained.

Hospital A	42
Hospital B	65
Grand mean	54

Use these means to complete the output shown below. From the results, do you think there is a HOSPITAL effect?

```
Estimates for CONS

CONSTANT

 Parameter     Coeff.    Std. Err.      T-Value     Sig. of T   Lower 95% CL   Upper 95% CL

     1        [    ]        20          [    ]         .007        [      ]            93

HOSPITAL

 Parameter     Coeff.    Std. Err.      T-Value     Sig. of T   Lower 95% CL   Upper 95% CL

     2        [    ]      [    ]          1.4          .162          -29          [      ]
```

8. If you got the following output, you should be certain that the program is not working properly. Why?

```
Tests of Significance for CONS using UNIQUE Sums of Squares

Source of Variation          Sum of Squares      DF   Mean Square        F   Sig. of F

WITHIN CELLS                       518371       149         3479
Regression                         129071         1       129071      37.1        .000
CONSTANT                              174         1          174       .05        .961
SEX                                   383         1          383       .11        .842
------------------------------------------------------------------------------------

Regression analysis for WITHIN CELLS error term

Dependent variable .. CONS

Covariate          B        Beta    Std. Err.     T-Value    Sig. of T  Lower 95% CL  Upper 95% CL

TC1             -7.7         .25          3.3        -2.3         .021         -14.2          -1.2
```

9. A psychologist examined the effect of caffeine on students' performances in videotaped interviews. Thirty students were interviewed one hour after they had taken a placebo. One month later, the same students were interviewed one hour after they had taken 100 mg of caffeine. One month after the second interview, the students were again interviewed one hour after they had taken 350 mg of caffeine. The following average performance ratings were obtained (the higher the score, the better the interview performance.)

Placebo	**100 mg**	**250 mg**
20.7	34.5	41.9

   a. If the repeated measures analysis of variance indicates a significant within-subjects drug effect, does this indicate that interview performance is improved by caffeine?
   b. Was there a better way to design the study?

10. Indicate whether the following statements are true or false.
   a. Using several paired *t* tests always leads to the same conclusions as a repeated measures analysis.
   b. In a repeated measures analysis, the hypothesis of greatest interest is usually the hypothesis that the overall mean is 0.
   c. It is possible for the univariate and multivariate approaches to repeated measures analysis to produce different results.
   d. The univariate approach to repeated measures is less powerful than the multivariate approach.
   e. Within-subjects effects must be adjusted for a covariate whenever the between-subjects effects are adjusted for the covariate.

11. Identify the within-subjects factors, the between-subjects factors, and the covariates in the following study: To determine the effect of various factors on the amount of weight a person can bench press, eighty people were examined. Twenty did warm-up exercises and saw a film explaining bench-press techniques, twenty warmed up but did not see the film, twenty did not warm up but saw the film, and twenty neither warmed up nor saw the film. At the beginning of the study, a measure of overall strength was obtained for each subject, since the researchers wanted to eliminate variability due to overall strength.

    Each subject performed the bench-press activity under each of four conditions: weightlifters present in the background and coach present to give encouragement to subjects; weightlifters present but coach not present; weightlifters not present but coach present; and neither weightlifters nor coach present. The maximum amount of weight lifted after five attempts was recorded at each bench-press session, with two weeks elapsing between each session.

12. A humane society investigated the effect of several educational programs on the willingness of pet owners to support spay and neuter programs for pets. Thirty-six pet owners were randomly assigned to see one of three films: twelve saw a film about pet care that briefly described the health advantages of neutering (Film 1), another twelve saw a film focusing entirely on the health and behavioral advantages of neutering (Film 2), and the remaining twelve saw a film that graphically depicted the problems caused by the surplus of pets (Film 3).

    A week after seeing the film, subjects filled out a questionnaire measuring the intensity of their support for spay and neuter programs. Subjects then toured an animal shelter, visiting stray wards and a clinic where they watched the euthanasia of several animals. One week following the tour, the same questionnaire was adminstered again. The means obtained are shown in the overlay plot below. (The higher the score, the stronger the support for spay and neuter programs.)

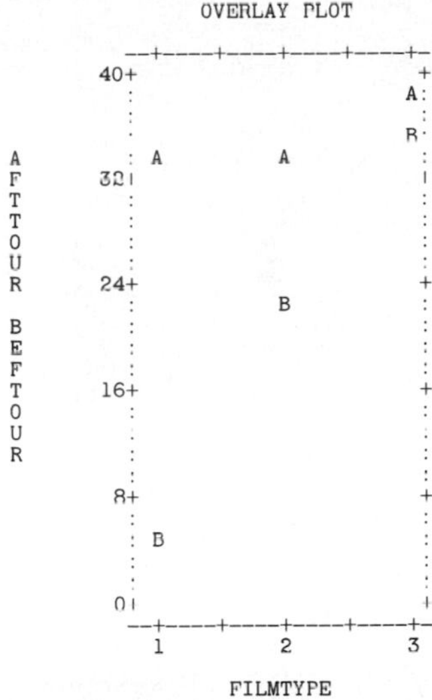

A:AFTTOUR WITH FILMTYPE B:BEFTOUR WITH FILMTYPE

a. Is an interaction between the film and tour factors evident from this plot?

b. Describe substantively the effects of these factors.

c. What type of educational program is the humane society likely to recommend?

13. A researcher performed a repeated measures analysis with a covariate, obtaining a regression sum of squares of 47813 and an F statistic of 25.3 (significance less than 0.0005) for this regression. The regression coefficient was −3.7. Is this information sufficient to complete the missing entries in the output shown below? If so, complete the output. If not, explain what other information is needed.

Regression analysis for WITHIN CELLS error term

Dependent variable .. CON3

Covariate	B	Beta	Std. Err.	T-Value	Sig. of T	Lower 95% CL	Upper 95% CL
TC1		-.62				-5.15	-2.25

8

Hierarchical Log-Linear Models

In this chapter:

Goals:

- To identify the relationships among categorical variables.
- To build a model that predicts the number of cases in a cell of a multidimensional contingency table.

Examples:

- Study the relationships among the incidence of blood clots, smoking, and contraceptive use.
- Study the relationships among self-esteem, religious preference, and father's education.
- Study the relationships among political party membership, education, and income.
- Examine consumer buying habits and their relationship to home ownership, family size, and region of residence.

How it's done:

The starting point for estimation of log-linear models is a multidimensional cross-classification table. A linear model that represents the log of the frequencies in each cell as a function of the values of the various combinations of the classification variables is developed. Based on this model, predicted frequencies are calculated and compared to those actually observed. If the model fits well, the differences between the observed and expected frequencies should not be large.

Data considerations:

The classification variables must be discrete, though they may represent an underlying continuum. For example, income may be grouped into four mutually exclusive categories. The observations may have resulted from one of several sampling schemes. When the cross-classification table has many empty cells, the classification variables should be grouped into fewer categories, if possible.

General references:

Fienberg (1980)
Haberman (1978)
Bishop, Fienberg, & Holland (1975)
Everitt (1977)

Contents

8.1 LOG-LINEAR MODELS
8.2 A Fully Saturated Model
8.3 Output for the Cells
8.4 Parameter Estimates
8.5 The Independence Model
8.6 Chi-square Goodness-of-Fit Tests
8.7 Residuals
8.8 Hierarchical Models
8.9 Model Selection
8.10 Partitioning the Chi-Square Statistic
8.11 Testing Individual Terms in the Model
8.12 Model Selection Using Backward Elimination
8.13 RUNNING PROCEDURE HILOGLINEAR
8.14 Specifying the Variables
8.15 The DESIGN Subcommand
8.16 Building a Model
8.17 The MAXORDER Subcommand
8.18 The CRITERIA Subcommand
8.19 The METHOD Subcommand
8.20 The CWEIGHT Subcommand
8.21 The PRINT Subcommand
8.22 The PLOT Subcommand
8.23 The MISSING Subcommand
8.24 EXERCISES

8 Pursuing Happiness: Hierarchical Log-Linear Models

There is only one way to achieve
happiness on this terrestrial ball,
And that is to have either a clear
conscience or, none at all.

Ogden Nash

Ignoring Nash's warning, many of us continue to search for happiness in terrestrial institutions and possessions. Marriage, wealth, and health are all hypothesized to contribute to happiness. But do they really? And how would one investigate possible associations?

Consider Figure 8.0, which is a two-way classification of marital status and score on a happiness scale. The data are from the 1982 General Social Survey conducted by the National Opinion Research Center. Of the 854 currently married respondents, 92% indicated that they were very happy or pretty happy, while only 79% of the 383 divorced, separated, or widowed people classified themselves as happy.

Figure 8.0 Output from procedure CROSSTABS

```
CROSSTABS TABLES=HAPPY BY MARITAL
  /CELLS=COLUMN
```
[1]

	COUNT / COL PCT	MARITAL: MARRIED 1	SINGLE 2	SPLIT 3	ROW TOTAL
HAPPY YES	1	787 92.2	221 82.5	301 78.6	1309 87.0
NO	2	67 7.8	47 17.5	82 21.4	196 13.0
	COLUMN TOTAL	854 56.7	268 17.8	383 25.4	1505 100.0

Although the results in Figure 8.0 are interesting, they suggest many new questions. What role does income play in happiness? Are poor married couples happier than affluent singles? What about health? Determining the relationship among such variables is potentially complicated. If family income is recorded in three categories and condition of health in two, a separate two-way table of happiness score and marital status is obtained for each of the six possible combinations of health and income. As additional variables are included in the cross-classification tables, the number of cells rapidly increases and it is difficult, if not impossible, to unravel the associations among the variables by examining only the cell entries.

[1]With releases before 3.0, replace the CROSSTABS command with the following:

```
CROSSTABS TABLES=HAPPY BY MARITAL
OPTIONS 4
```

The usual response of researchers faced with crosstabulated data is to compute a chi-square test of independence for each subtable. This strategy is fraught with problems and usually does not result in a systematic evaluation of the relationship among the variables. The classical chi-square approach also does not provide estimates of the effects of the variables on each other, and its application to tables with more than two variables is complicated.

8.1 LOG-LINEAR MODELS

The advantages of statistical models that summarize data and test hypotheses are well recognized. Regression analysis, for example, examines the relationship between a dependent variable and a set of independent variables. Analysis of variance techniques provide tests for the effects of various factors on a dependent variable. But neither technique is appropriate for categorical data, where the observations are not from populations that are normally distributed with constant variance.

A special class of statistical techniques, called log-linear models, has been formulated for the analysis of categorical data (Haberman, 1978; Bishop, Feinberg, & Holland, 1975). These models are useful for uncovering the potentially complex relationships among the variables in a multiway crosstabulation. Log-linear models are similar to multiple regression models. In log-linear models, all variables that are used for classification are independent variables, and the dependent variable is the number of cases in a cell of the crosstabulation.

8.2 A Fully Saturated Model

Consider Figure 8.0 again. Using a log-linear model, the number of cases in each cell can be expressed as a function of marital status, degree of happiness, and the interaction between degree of happiness and marital status. To obtain a linear model, the natural logs of the cell frequencies, rather than the actual counts, are used. The natural logs of the cell frequencies in Figure 8.0 are shown in Table 8.2a. (Recall that the natural log of a number is the power to which the number e (2.718) is raised to give that number. For example, the natural log of the first cell entry in Figure 8.0 is 6.668, since $e^{6.668}=787$.)

Table 8.2a Natural logs

Happy	Married	Single	Split	Average
Yes	6.668	5.398	5.707	5.924
No	4.205	3.850	4.407	4.154
Average	5.436	4.624	5.057	5.039

The log-linear model for the first cell in Figure 8.0 is

$$\log(787)=\mu+\lambda_{\text{yes}}^{\text{happy}}+\lambda_{\text{married}}^{\text{marital}}+\lambda_{\text{yes}\ \text{married}}^{\text{happy}\ \text{marital}}$$ **Equation 8.2a**

The term denoted as μ is comparable to the grand mean in the analysis of variance. It is the average of the logs of the frequencies in all table cells. The lambda parameters represent the increments or decrements from the base value (μ) for particular combinations of values of the row and column variables.

Each individual category of the row and column variables has an associated lambda. The term $\lambda_{\text{married}}^{\text{marital}}$ indicates the effect of being in the married category of the marital-status variable, and similarly $\lambda_{\text{yes}}^{\text{happy}}$ is the effect of being in the very happy category. The term $\lambda_{\text{yes}\ \text{married}}^{\text{happy}\ \text{marital}}$ represents the interaction of being very happy and married. Thus, the number of cases in a cell is a function of the values of the row and column variables and their interactions.

In general the model for the log of the observed frequency in the *i*th row and the *j*th column is given by

$$\ln F_{ij} = \mu + \lambda_i^H + \lambda_j^S + \lambda_{ij}^{HS}$$ **Equation 8.2b**

where F_{ij} is the observed frequency in the cell, λ_i^H is the effect of the *i*th happiness category, λ_j^S is the effect of the *j*th marital-status category, and λ_{ij}^{HS} is the interaction effect for the *i*th value of the happiness category, and the *j*th value of the marital status variable.

The lambda parameters and μ are estimated from the data. The estimate for μ is simply the average of the logs of the frequencies in all table cells. From Table 8.2a, the estimated value of μ is 5.039. Estimates for the lambda parameters are obtained in a manner similar to analysis of variance. For example, the effect of the very-happy category is estimated as

$$\lambda_{yes}^{happy} = 5.924 - 5.039 = 0.885$$ **Equation 8.2c**

where 5.924 is the average of the logs of the observed counts in the happy cells. The lambda parameter is just the average log of the frequencies in a particular category minus the grand mean. In general, the effect of the *i*th category of a variable, called a main effect, is estimated as

$$\lambda_i^{VAR} = \mu_i - \mu$$ **Equation 8.2d**

where μ_i is the mean of the logs in the *i*th category and μ is the grand mean. Positive values of lambda occur when the average number of cases in a row or a column is larger than the overall average. For example, since there are more married people in the sample than single or separated, the lambda for married is positive. Similarly, since there are fewer unhappy people than happy people, the lambda for not happy is negative.

The interaction parameters indicate how much difference there is between the sums of the effects of the variables taken individually and collectively. They represent the "boost" or "interference" associated with particular combinations of the values. For example, if marriage does result in bliss, the number of cases in the happy and married cell would be larger than the number expected based only on the frequency of married people ($\lambda_{married}^{marital}$) and the frequency of happy people (λ_{yes}^{happy}). This excess would be represented by a positive value for $\lambda_{yes\ married}^{happy\ marital}$. If marriage decreases happiness, the value for the interaction parameter would be negative. If marriage neither increases nor decreases happiness, the interaction parameter would be zero.

The estimate for the interaction parameter is the difference between the log of the observed frequency in a particular cell and the log of the predicted frequency using only the lambda parameters for the row and column variables. For example,

$$\lambda_{yes\ married}^{happy\ marital} = \ln F_{11} - (\mu + \lambda_{yes}^{happy} + \lambda_{married}^{marital}) = 6.668 - (5.039 + 0.885 + 0.397) = 0.347$$ **Equation 8.2e**

where F_{11} is the observed frequency in the married and happy cell. Table 8.2b contains the estimates of the λ parameters for the main effects (marital status and happiness) and their interactions.

Table 8.2b Estimates of lambda parameters

$\lambda_{yes}^{happy}=5.924-5.039=0.885$
$\lambda_{no}^{happy}=4.154-5.039=-0.885$
$\lambda_{married}^{marital}=5.436-5.039=0.397$
$\lambda_{single}^{marital}=4.624-5.039=-0.415$
$\lambda_{split}^{marital}=5.057-5.039=0.018$
$\lambda_{YM}^{HM}=6.668-(5.039+0.885+0.397)=0.346$
$\lambda_{NM}^{HM}=4.205-(5.039-0.885+0.397)=-0.346$
$\lambda_{YSi}^{HM}=5.398-(5.039+0.885-0.415)=-0.111$
$\lambda_{NSi}^{HM}=3.850-(5.039-0.885-0.415)=0.111$
$\lambda_{YSp}^{HM}=5.707-(5.039+0.885+0.018)=-0.235$
$\lambda_{NSp}^{HM}=4.407-(5.039-0.885+0.018)=0.235$

To uniquely estimate the lambda parameters, we need to impose certain constraints on them. The lambdas must sum to zero across the categories of a variable. For example, the sum of the lambdas for marital status is 0.397 + (−0.415) +0.018 =0. Similar constraints are imposed on the interaction terms. They must sum to zero over all categories of a variable.

Each of the observed cell frequencies is reproduced exactly by a model that contains all main-effect and interaction terms. This type of model is called a *saturated* model. For example, the observed log frequency in Cell 1 of Figure 8.0 is given by

$$\ln F_{11}=\mu+\lambda_{yes}^{happy}+\lambda_{married}^{marital}+\lambda_{yes\ married}^{happy\ marital} = 5.039+0.885+0.397+0.346=6.67$$ **Equation 8.2f**

All other observed cell frequencies can be similarly expressed as a function of the lambdas and the grand mean.

8.3 Output for the Cells

Consider Figure 8.3, which contains the observed and expected (predicted from the model) counts for the data shown in Figure 8.0. The first column gives the names of the variables used in the analysis, and the second contains the value labels for the cells in the table. The next column indicates the number of cases in each of the cells. For example, 787 people who classify themselves as happy are married, which is 52.29% of all respondents in the survey (787 out of 1505). This percentage is listed in the next column. Since the number of cases in each cell is expressed as a percentage of the total cases, the sum of all the percentages is 100. The saturated model reproduces the observed cell frequencies exactly, so the expected and observed cell counts and percentages are equal. For the same reason the next two columns, which compare the observed and expected counts, are all zeros. (Models that do not exactly reproduce the observed cells counts are examined later.)

Figure 8.3 Observed and expected frequencies for saturated model

```
HILOGLINEAR HAPPY(1,2) MARITAL(1,3)
  /DESIGN=HAPPY*MARITAL
```

```
Observed, Expected Frequencies and Residuals.

    Factor           Code          OBS. count  & PCT.    EXP. count  & PCT.      Residual    Std. Resid.

HAPPY              YES
 MARITAL            MARRIED         787.00 (52.29)        787.00 (52.29)          .000           .000
 MARITAL            SINGLE          221.00 (14.68)        221.00 (14.68)          .000           .000
 MARITAL            SPLIT           301.00 (20.00)        301.00 (20.00)          .000           .000

HAPPY              NO
 MARITAL            MARRIED          67.00 ( 4.45)         67.00 ( 4.45)          .000           .000
 MARITAL            SINGLE           47.00 ( 3.12)         47.00 ( 3.12)          .000           .000
 MARITAL            SPLIT            82.00 ( 5.45)         82.00 ( 5.45)          .000           .000
```

8.4 Parameter Estimates

The estimates of the log-linear model parameters are also displayed as part of the HILOGLINEAR output. Figure 8.4 contains parameter estimates for the data in Figure 8.0. The parameter estimates are displayed in blocks for each effect.

Parameter estimates for the interaction effects are displayed first. Because estimates must sum to zero across the categories of each variable, only two parameter estimates need to be displayed for the interaction effects: those for $\lambda^{happy\ marital}_{yes\ \ married}$ and for $\lambda^{happy\ marital}_{yes\ \ single}$. All other interaction parameter estimates can be derived from these.

After the interaction terms, parameter estimates for the main effects of the variables are displayed. The first estimate is for λ^{happy}_{yes} and is identical to the value given in Table 8.2b (0.885). Again, only one parameter estimate is displayed, since we can infer that the parameter estimate for λ^{happy}_{no} is −0.885 (the two estimates must sum to zero). Two parameter estimates and associated statistics are displayed for the marital variable, since it has three categories. The estimate for the third parameter $\lambda^{marital}_{split}$ is the negative of the sum of the estimates for $\lambda^{marital}_{married}$ and $\lambda^{marital}_{single}$. Thus $\lambda^{marital}_{split}$ is estimated to be 0.0178, as shown in Figure 8.2b.

Since the individual parameter estimates in Figure 8.4 are not labeled, the following rules for identifying the categories to which they correspond may be helpful. For main effects, the parameter estimates correspond to the first $K-1$ categories of the variable, where K is the total number of categories. For interaction parameters, the number of estimates displayed is the product of the number of categories, minus one, of each variable in the interaction, multiplied together. For example, marital status has three categories and happiness has two, so the number of estimates displayed is $(3-1) \times (2-1) = 2$.

To identify individual parameters, first look at the order in which the variable labels are listed in the heading. In this case the heading is HAPPY*MARITAL. The first estimate corresponds to the first category of both variables, which is happy-yes and marital-married. The next estimate corresponds to the first category of the first variable (HAPPY) and the second category of the second variable (MARITAL). In general, the categories of the last variable rotate most quickly and those of the first variable most slowly. Terms involving the last categories of the variables are omitted.

Figure 8.4 also displays the standard error for each estimate. For the λ^{happy}_{yes} parameter, the standard error is 0.03997. The ratio of the parameter estimate to its standard error is given in the column labeled Z-Value. For sufficiently large sample sizes, the test of the null hypothesis that lambda is zero can be based on this Z value, since the standardized lambda is approximately normally distributed with a mean of zero and a standard deviation of 1 if the model fits the data. Lambdas with Z values greater than 1.96 in absolute value can be considered significant at the 0.05 level. When tests for many lambdas are calculated, however, the usual problem of multiple comparisons arises. That is, when many comparisons are made, the probability that some are found to be significant when there is no effect increases rapidly. Special multiple-comparison procedures for testing the lambdas are discussed in Goodman (1964).

Figure 8.4 Estimates for parameters

```
HILOGLINEAR HAPPY(1,2) MARITAL(1,3)
  /DESIGN=HAPPY*MARITAL /PRINT=ESTIM
```

```
Estimates for Parameters.

HAPPY*MARITAL

 Parameter        Coeff.      Std. Err.      Z-Value Lower 95 CI Upper 95 CI

        1   .3464441901         .05429      6.38147       .24004      .45285
        2  -.1113160745         .06122     -1.81833      -.23131      .00867

HAPPY

 Parameter        Coeff.      Std. Err.      Z-Value Lower 95 CI Upper 95 CI

        1   .8853236244         .03997     22.14946       .80698      .96367

MARITAL

 Parameter        Coeff.      Std. Err.      Z-Value Lower 95 CI Upper 95 CI

        1   .3972836534         .05429      7.31793       .29088      .50369
        2  -.4150216289         .06122     -6.77930      -.53501     -.29503
```

Individual confidence intervals can be constructed for each lambda. The 95% confidence interval for λ^{happy}_{yes} is $0.885 \pm (1.96 \times 0.03997)$, which results in a lower limit of 0.80698 and an upper limit of 0.96367. Since the confidence interval does not include zero, the hypothesis that the population value is zero can be rejected. These values are displayed in the last two columns of Figure 8.4.

8.5 The Independence Model

Representing an observed-frequency table with a log-linear model that contains as many parameters as there are cells (a saturated model) does not result in a parsimonious description of the relationship between the variables. It may, however, serve as a good starting point for exploring other models that could be used to represent the data. Parameters that have small values can be excluded from subsequent models.

To illustrate the general procedure for fitting a model that does not contain all possible parameters (an unsaturated model), consider the familiar independence hypothesis for a two-way table. If variables are independent they can be represented by a log-linear model that does not have any interaction terms. For example, if happiness and marital status are independent

$$\log \hat{F}_{ij} = \mu + \lambda_i^{happy} + \lambda_j^{marital}$$ **Equation 8.5a**

Note that $\hat{F}_{ij}$ is no longer the observed frequency in the (i,j)th cell, but is now the expected frequency based on the model. The estimates of the lambda parameters are obtained using an iterative algorithm (the previously described formulas, which provide direct estimates, apply only to saturated models). That is, the λ's are repeatedly estimated until successive estimates do not differ from each other by more than a preset amount. Each time an estimate is obtained it is called an iteration, while the preset amount is called the convergence criterion.

The message in Figure 8.5a gives the number of iterations required for convergence. For this example, two iterations were required for convergence. The observed and expected counts in each of the cells of the table are shown in Figure 8.5b.

Figure 8.5a HILOGLINEAR message: iterations required for convergence

```
HILOGLINEAR HAPPY(1,2) MARITAL(1,3)
  /DESIGN=MARITAL HAPPY
```

```
DESIGN 1 has generating class

   MARITAL
   HAPPY

The Iterative Proportional Fit algorithm converged at iteration 2.
The maximum difference between observed and fitted marginal totals is      .000
and the convergence criterion is      .250
```

Figure 8.5b Observed and expected frequencies for unsaturated model

Observed, Expected Frequencies and Residuals.

Factor	Code	OBS count	EXP count	Residual	Std Resid
HAPPY	HAPPY				
MARITAL	MARRIED	787.0	742.8	44.22	1.62
MARITAL	SINGLE	221.0	233.1	-12.10	-.79
MARITAL	SPLIT	301.0	333.1	-32.12	-1.76
HAPPY	NHAPPY				
MARITAL	MARRIED	67.0	111.2	-44.22	-4.19
MARITAL	SINGLE	47.0	34.9	12.10	2.05
MARITAL	SPLIT	82.0	49.9	32.12	4.55

The expected values are identical to those obtained from the usual formulas for expected values in a two-way crosstabulation, as shown in Figure 8.5c. For example, from Figure 8.0, the estimated probability of an individual being happy is 1309/1505, and the estimated probability of an individual being married is

854/1505. If marital status and happiness are independent, the probability of a happy, married person is estimated to be

$$1309/1505 \times 854/1505 = 0.4935$$ **Equation 8.5b**

The expected number of happy, married people in a sample of 1505 is then

$$0.4935 \times 1505 = 742.78$$ **Equation 8.5c**

This is the value displayed in the expected-count column in Figure 8.5b. Since the independence model is not saturated, the observed and expected counts are no longer equal, as was the case in Figure 8.3.

Figure 8.5c Crosstabulation of happiness by marital status

```
CROSSTABS TABLE=HAPPY BY MARITAL
  /CELLS=EXPECTED
  /STATISTICS=CHISQ 2
```

```
                  MARITAL
           COUNT |
         EXP VAL |MARRIED  SINGLE   SPLIT         ROW
                 |                                TOTAL
                 |       1|       2|       3|
HAPPY            +--------+--------+--------+
               1 |   787  |   221  |   301  |    1309
  YES            | 742.8  | 233.1  | 333.1  |    87.0%
                 +--------+--------+--------+
               2 |    67  |    47  |    82  |     196
  NO             | 111.2  |  34.9  |  49.9  |    13.0%
                 +--------+--------+--------+
          COLUMN     854      268      383        1505
           TOTAL    56.7%    17.8%    25.4%     100.0%

 CHI-SQUARE    D.F.      SIGNIFICANCE        MIN E.F.       CELLS WITH E.F.| 5
 ----------    ----      ------------        --------       -----------------

   48.81639      2          0.0000            34.902          NONE
```

8.6 Chi-square Goodness-of-Fit Tests

The test of the hypothesis that a particular model fits the observed data can be based on the familiar Pearson chi-square statistic, which is calculated as

$$\chi^2 = \sum_i \sum_j \frac{(F_{ij} - \hat{F}_{ij})^2}{\hat{F}_{ij}}$$ **Equation 8.6a**

where the subscripts i and j include all cells in the table. An alternative statistic is the likelihood-ratio chi-square, which is calculated as

$$L^2 = 2 \sum_i \sum_j F_{ij} \, ln \frac{F_{ij}}{\hat{F}_{ij}}$$ **Equation 8.6b**

For large sample sizes these statistics are equivalent. The advantage of the likelihood-ratio chi-square statistic is that it, like the total sums of squares in analysis of variance, can be subdivided into interpretable parts that add up to the total (see Section 8.10).

---

[2]With releases before 3.0, replace the CROSSTABS command with the following:

```
CROSSTABS TABLES=HAPPY BY MARITAL
OPTIONS 14
STATISTICS 1
```

Figure 8.6 shows that the value of the Pearson chi-square statistic is 48.82 and the likelihood-ratio chi-square is 48.01. The degrees of freedom associated with a particular model are the number of cells in the table minus the number of independent parameters in the model. In this example, there are six cells and four independent parameters to be estimated (the grand mean, λ_{yes}^{happy}, $\lambda^{married}$, λ^{split}), so there are two degrees of freedom. (There are only four independent parameters because of the constraint that parameter estimates must sum to zero over the categories of a variable. Therefore, the value for one of the categories is determined by the values of the others and is not, in a statistical sense, independent.)

The observed significance level associated with both chi-square statistics is very small (less than 0.0005), and the independence model is rejected. Note that the Pearson chi-square statistic displayed for independence model is identical to the chi-square value displayed by procedure CROSSTABS, as shown in Figure 8.5c.

Figure 8.6 Chi-square goodness-of-fit test

```
Goodness-of-fit test statistics

  Likelihood ratio chi square =    48.01198    DF = 2  P =  .000
             Pearson chi square =    48.81638    DF = 2  P =  .000
```

8.7 Residuals

Another way to assess how well a model fits the data is to examine the differences between the observed and expected cell counts based on the model. If the model fits the observed data well, these differences, called residuals, should be fairly small in value and not have any discernible pattern. The column labeled Residual in Figure 8.5b shows the differences between the observed and expected counts in each cell. For example, since 787 individuals were found to be very happy and married, while 742.78 are expected to fall into this category if the independence model is correct, the residual is 787 − 742.78 = 44.22.

As in regression analysis, it is useful to standardize the residuals by dividing them by their standard error, in this case the square root of the expected cell count. For example, the standardized residual for the first cell in Figure 8.5b is

$$\text{Standardized Residual} = \frac{\text{Observed Count} - \text{Expected Count}}{\sqrt{\text{Expected Count}}} = 1.622 \quad \textbf{Equation 8.7}$$

This value is displayed in the column labeled Std. Resid. in Figure 8.5b. If the model is adequate, the standardized residuals are approximately normally distributed with a mean of zero and standard deviation of one. Standardized residuals greater than 1.96 or less than −1.96 suggest important discrepancies, since they are unlikely to occur if the model is adequate. Particular combinations of cells with large standardized residuals may suggest which other models might be more appropriate.

Figures 8.7a and 8.7b Plot of standardized residuals vs. observed (left) and expected (right) cell frequencies

```
HILOGLINEAR HAPPY(1,2) MARITAL(1,3)
  /PLOT=RESID
  /DESIGN=MARITAL HAPPY
```

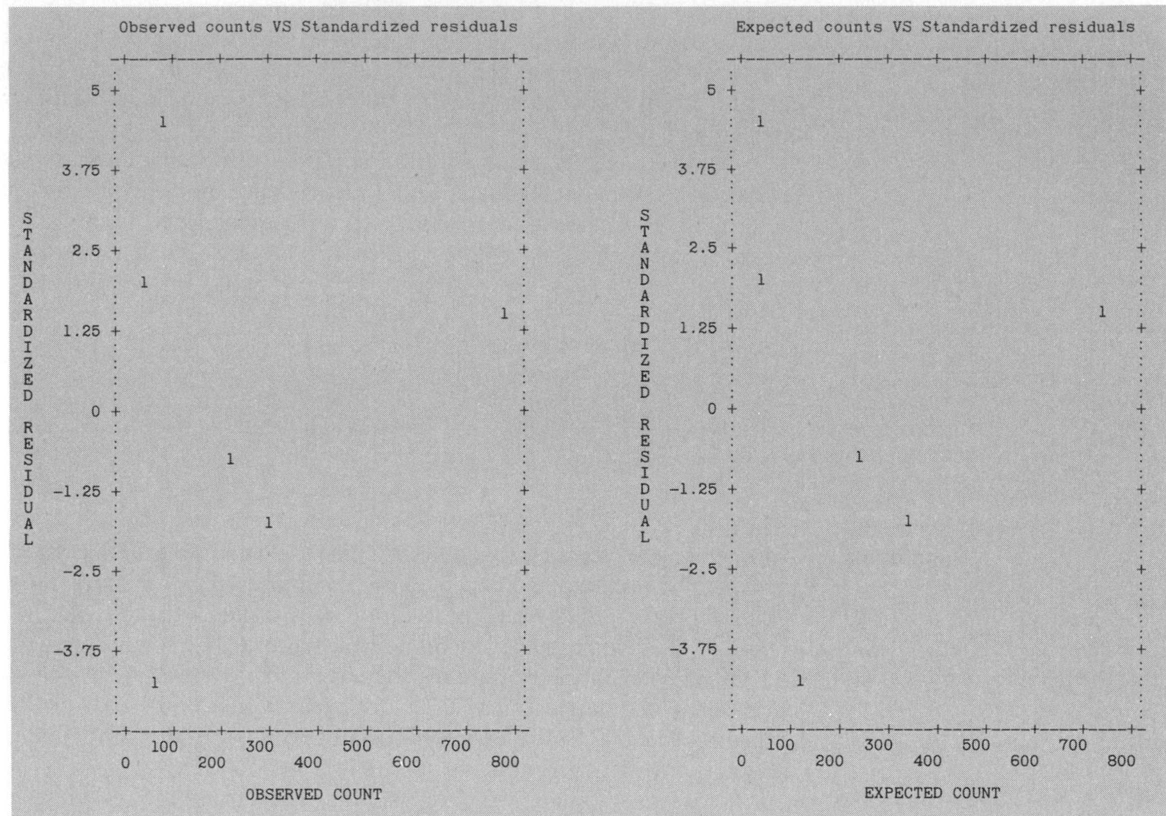

The same types of diagnostics for residuals used in regression analysis can be used in log-linear models (see Chapter 2). Figures 8.7a and 8.7b are plots of the standardized residuals against the observed and expected cell frequencies, respectively. If the model is adequate, there should be no discernible pattern in the plots. Patterns suggest that the chosen log-linear model, or the log-linear representation in general, may not be appropriate for the data.

If the standardized residuals are normally distributed, the normal probability plot (Figure 8.7c) should be approximately linear. In this plot, the standardized residuals are plotted against "expected" residuals from a normal distribution.

Figure 8.7c Plot of standardized residuals against expected residuals

```
HILOGLINEAR HAPPY(1,2) MARITAL(1,3)
  /PLOT=NORMPROB
  /DESIGN=MARITAL HAPPY
```

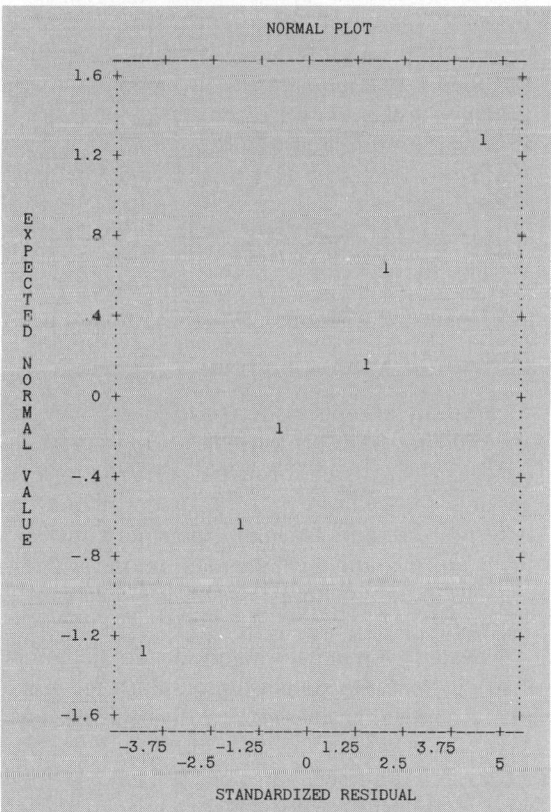

8.8 Hierarchical Models

A saturated log-linear model contains all possible effects. For example, a saturated model for a two-way table contains terms for the row main effects, the column main effects, and their interaction. Different models can be obtained by deleting terms from a saturated model. The independence model is derived by deleting the interaction effect. Although it is possible to delete any particular term from a model, in log-linear analysis attention is often focused on a special class of models which are termed *hierarchical*.

In a hierarchical model, if a term exists for the interaction of a set of variables, then there must be lower-order terms for all possible combinations of these variables. For a two-variable model, this means that the interaction term can only be included if both main effects are present. For a three-variable model, if the term λ^{ABC} is included in a model, then the terms λ^{A}, λ^{B}, λ^{C}, λ^{AB}, λ^{BC}, and λ^{AC} must also be included.

To describe a hierarchical model, it is sufficient to list the highest-order terms in which variables appear. This is called the *generating class* of a model. For example, the specification *ABC* indicates that a model contains the term λ^{ABC} and all its lower-order relations. (Terms are "relatives" if all variables that are included in one term are also included in the other. For example, the term λ^{ABCD} is a higher-order relative of the terms λ^{ABC}, λ^{BCD}, λ^{ACD}, λ^{BAD}, as well as all other lower-order terms involving variables *A, B, C,* or *D*. Similarly, λ^{AB} is a lower-order relative of both λ^{ABC} and λ^{ABD}.) The model

$$\ln F_{ijk} = \mu + \lambda_i^A + \lambda_j^B + \lambda_k^C + \lambda_{ij}^{AB} \qquad \textbf{Equation 8.8}$$

can be represented by the generating class $(AB)(C)$, since AB is the highest-order term in which A and B occur, and C is included in the model only as a main effect.

8.9 Model Selection

Even if attention is restricted to hierarchical models, many different models are possible for a set of variables. How do you choose among them? The same guidelines discussed for model selection in regression analysis apply to log-linear models (see Chapter 2). A model should fit the data and be substantively interpretable and as simple (parsimonious) as possible. For example, if models with and without higher-order interaction terms fit the data well, the simpler models are usually preferable since higher-order interaction terms are difficult to interpret.

A first step in determining a suitable model might be to fit a saturated model and examine the standardized values for the parameter estimates. Effects with small estimated values can usually be deleted from a model. Another strategy is to systematically test the contribution to a model made by terms of a particular order. For example, you might fit a model with interaction terms and then a model with main effects only. The change in the chi-square value between the two models is attributable to the interaction effects.

8.10 Partitioning the Chi-Square Statistic

In regression analysis, the change in multiple R^2 when a variable is added to a model indicates the additional "information" conveyed by the variable. Similarly, in log-linear analysis the decrease in the value of the likelihood-ratio chi-square statistic when terms are added to the model signals their contribution to the model. (Remember R^2 increases when additional variables are added to a model, since large values of R^2 are associated with good models. Chi-square decreases when terms are added, since small values of chi-square are associated with good models.)

As an example, consider the happiness and marital-status data when two additional variables, total income in 1982 and the condition of one's health, are included. Figure 8.10a contains goodness-of-fit statistics for three different models. Design 3 contains all terms except the four-way interaction of HAPPY, MARITAL, INCOME82, and HEALTH. Design 2 contains main effects and second-order interactions only, and Design 1 is a main-effects-only model.

Design 1 has a large chi-square value and an observed significance level less than 0.0005, so it definitely does not fit well. To judge the adequacy of Designs 2 and 3, consider the changes in the chi-square goodness-of-fit statistic as terms are removed from the model.

Figure 8.10a Goodness-of-fit statistics for three models

```
HILOGLINEAR HAPPY(1,2) MARITAL(1,3) INCOME82(1,3) HEALTH(1,2)
  /PRINT=ESTIM
  /DESIGN=HAPPY MARITAL INCOME82 HEALTH
  /PRINT=ESTIM
  /DESIGN=HAPPY*MARITAL  HAPPY*INCOME82  HAPPY*HEALTH  MARITAL*INCOME82
       MARITAL*HEALTH  INCOME82*HEALTH
  /PRINT=ESTIM
  /DESIGN=HAPPY*MARITAL*INCOME82  HAPPY*MARITAL*HEALTH
       MARITAL*INCOME82*HEALTH  HAPPY*INCOME82*HEALTH
```

```
* * * * * * * *  H I E R A R C H I C A L   L O G   L I N E A R  * * * * * * * *

DESIGN 1 has generating class

    HAPPY
    MARITAL
    INCOME82
    HEALTH

The Iterative Proportional Fitting converged at iteration 2.

- - - - - - - - - - - - - - - - - - - - - - - - - - - - - - - - - - - - - - - -

 Goodness-of-fit test statistics

    Likelihood ratio chi square =   404.06381     DF = 29  P =  .000
             Pearson chi square =   592.88247     DF = 29  P =  .000

* * * * * * * *  H I E R A R C H I C A L   L O G   L I N E A R  * * * * * * * *

DESIGN 2 has generating class

    HAPPY*MARITAL
    HAPPY*INCOME82
    HAPPY*HEALTH
    MARITAL*INCOME82
    MARITAL*HEALTH
    INCOME82*HEALTH

The Iterative Proportional Fitting converged at iteration 6.

- - - - - - - - - - - - - - - - - - - - - - - - - - - - - - - - - - - - - - - -

 Goodness-of-fit test statistics

    Likelihood ratio chi square =    12.60130     DF = 16  P =  .702
             Pearson chi square =    12.31572     DF = 16  P =  .722

* * * * * * * *  H I E R A R C H I C A L   L O G   L I N E A R  * * * * * * * *

DESIGN 3 has generating class

    HAPPY*MARITAL*INCOME82
    HAPPY*MARITAL*HEALTH
    MARITAL*INCOME82*HEALTH
    HAPPY*INCOME82*HEALTH

The Iterative Proportional Fitting converged at iteration 3.

- - - - - - - - - - - - - - - - - - - - - - - - - - - - - - - - - - - - - - - -

 Goodness-of-fit test statistics

    Likelihood ratio chi square =     3.99256     DF = 4  P =  .407
             Pearson chi square =     3.97332     DF = 4  P =  .410
```

For a saturated model, the value of the chi-square statistic is always zero. Eliminating the fourth-order interaction (Design 3) results in a likelihood-ratio chi-square value of 3.99. The change in chi-square from zero to 3.99 is attributable to the fourth-order interaction. The change in the degrees of freedom between the two models equals 4, since a saturated model has zero degrees of freedom and the third-order interaction model has four. The change in the chi-square value can be used to test the hypothesis that the fourth-order interaction term is zero. If the observed significance level for the change is small, the hypothesis that the fourth-order term is zero is rejected, since this indicates that the model without the fourth-order term does not fit well. A chi-square value of 3.99 has an observed significance of 0.41, so the hypothesis that the fourth-order term is zero is not rejected.

The likelihood-ratio chi-square value for Design 2, the second-order interaction model, is 12.60. This value provides a test of the hypothesis that all third- and fourth-order interaction terms are zero. The difference between 12.60 and 3.99 (8.61) provides a test of the hypothesis that all third-order terms are zero. In general, the test of the hypothesis that the *k*th order terms are zero is based on

$$\chi^2 = \chi^2_{k-1} - \chi^2_k$$ **Equation 8.10**

where χ^2_k is the value for the model that includes the *k*th-order effect or effects, and χ^2_{k-1} is the chi-squared value for the model without the *k*th-order effects.

The SPSS^X HILOGLINEAR (hierarchical log-linear) procedure automatically calculates tests of two types of hypotheses: the hypothesis that all *k*th- and higher-order effects are zero and the hypothesis that the *k*th-order effects are zero. Figure 8.10b contains the test for the hypothesis that *k*- and higher-order effects are zero.

Figure 8.10b Tests that *k*-way and higher-order effects are zero

```
HILOGLINEAR HAPPY(1,2) MARITAL(1,3) INCOME82(1,3) HEALTH(1,2)
  /DESIGN /PRINT ASSOCIATION
```

Tests that K-way and higher order effects are zero.

K	DF	L.R. Chisq	Prob	Pearson Chisq	Prob	Iteration
4	4	3.994	.4069	3.973	.4097	3
3	16	12.602	.7016	12.316	.7220	6
2	29	404.064	.0000	592.882	.0000	2
1	35	2037.779	.0000	2938.738	.0000	0

The first line of Figure 8.10b is a test of the hypothesis that the fourth-order interaction is zero. Note that the likelihood-ratio chi-square value of 3.99 is identical to the value displayed for Design 3 in Figure 8.10a. This is the goodness-of-fit statistic for a model without the fourth-order interaction. Similarly, the entry for the *k* of 3 is the goodness-of-fit test for a model without third- and fourth-order effects, like Design 2 in Figure 8.11. The last line, $k=1$, corresponds to a model that has no effects except the grand mean. That is, the expected value for all cells is the same—the average of the logs of the observed frequencies in all cells.

The column labeled Prob in Figure 8.10b gives the observed significance levels for the tests that *k*- and higher-order effects are zero. Small observed significance levels indicate that the hypothesis that terms of particular orders are zero should be rejected. Note in Figure 8.10b that the hypotheses that all effects are zero and that second-order and higher effects are zero should be rejected. Since the observed significance level for the test that third- and higher-order terms are zero is large (0.72), the hypothesis that third- and fourth-order interactions are zero should not be rejected. Thus, it appears that a model with first- and second-order effects is adequate to represent the data.

It is sometimes also of interest to test whether interaction terms of a *particular* order are zero. For example, rather than asking if all effects greater than two-way are zero, the question is whether two-way effects are zero. Figure 8.10c gives the tests for the hypothesis that *k*-way effects are zero.

Figure 8.10c Tests that *k*-way effects are zero

Tests that K-way effects are zero.

K	DF	L.R. Chisq	Prob	Pearson Chisq	Prob	Iteration
1	6	1633.715	.0000	2345.856	.0000	0
2	13	391.462	.0000	580.567	.0000	0
3	12	8.608	.7360	8.343	.7578	0
4	4	3.994	.4069	3.973	.4097	0

From Figure 8.10b the likelihood-ratio chi-square for a model with only the mean is 2037.779. The value for a model with first-order effects is 404.064. The difference between these two values, 1633.715, is displayed on the first line of Figure 8.10c. The difference is an indication of how much the model improves when first-order effects are included. The observed significance level for a chi-square value of 1634 with six degrees of freedom (35−29) is small, less than 0.00005, so the hypothesis that first-order effects are zero is rejected. The remaining entries in Figure 8.10c are obtained in a similar fashion. The test that third-order effects are zero is the difference between a model without third-order terms (χ^2_{LR}=12.602) and a model with third-order terms (χ^2_{LR}=3.994). The resulting chi-square value of 8.608 with 12 degrees of freedom has a large observed significance level (0.736), so the hypothesis that third-order terms are zero is not rejected.

8.11 Testing Individual Terms in the Model

The two tests described in Section 8.10 provide an indication of the collective importance of effects of various orders. They do not, however, test the individual terms. That is, although the overall hypothesis that second-order terms are zero may be rejected, that does not mean that every second-order effect is present.

One strategy for testing individual terms is to fit two models differing only in the presence of the effect to be tested. The difference between the two likelihood-ratio chi-square values, sometimes called the partial chi-square, also has a chi-square distribution and can be used to test the hypothesis that the effect is zero. For example, to test that the HAPPY by MARITAL by INCOME effect is zero, a model with all three-way interactions can be fit. From Figure 8.10a, the likelihood-ratio chi-square value for this model is 3.99. When a model without the HAPPY by MARITAL by INCOME effect is fit (Figure 8.11a), the likelihood-ratio is 7.363. Thus the partial chi-square value with four (8−4) degrees of freedom is 3.37 (7.36−3.99).

Figure 8.11a Model without HAPPY by MARITAL by INCOME

```
HILOGLINEAR HAPPY(1,2) MARITAL(1,3) INCOME82(1,3) HEALTH(1,2)
  /PRINT=ESTIM
  /DESIGN=HAPPY*MARITAL*HEALTH
          MARITAL*INCOME82*HEALTH
          HAPPY*INCOME82*HEALTH
```

```
DESIGN 1 has generating class

    HAPPY*MARITAL*HEALTH
    MARITAL*INCOME82*HEALTH
    HAPPY*INCOME82*HEALTH

The Iterative Proportional Fitting converged at iteration 4.

- - - - - - - - - - - - - - - - - - - - - - - - - - - - - - - - - - - - -

 Goodness-of-fit test statistics

    Likelihood ratio chi square =    7.36257    DF = 8  P =  .498
             Pearson chi square =    7.50541    DF = 8  P =  .483
```

Figure 8.11b contains the partial chi-square values and their observed significance levels for all effects in the HAPPY by MARITAL by HEALTH by INCOME table. Note that the observed significance levels are large for all three-way effects, confirming that first- and second-order effects are sufficient to represent the data. The last column indicates the number of iterations required to achieve convergence.

Figure 8.11b Partial chi-squares for HAPPY by MARITAL by HEALTH by INCOME

```
HILOGLINEAR HAPPY(1,2) MARITAL(1,3) INCOME82(1,3) HEALTH(1,2)
  /PRINT=ASSOCIATION
  /DESIGN=HAPPY*MARITAL*HEALTH*INCOME82
```

Tests of PARTIAL associations.

Effect Name	DF	Partial Chisq	Prob	Iter
HAPPY*MARITAL*INCOME82	4	3.370	.4979	4
HAPPY*MARITAL*HEALTH	2	.458	.7954	4
HAPPY*INCOME82*HEALTH	2	.955	.6203	3
MARITAL*INCOME82*HEALTH	4	3.652	.4552	5
HAPPY*MARITAL	2	15.050	.0005	5
HAPPY*INCOME82	2	16.120	.0003	5
MARITAL*INCOME82	4	160.739	.0000	4
HAPPY*HEALTH	1	55.696	.0000	5
MARITAL*HEALTH	2	8.391	.0151	5
INCOME82*HEALTH	2	35.602	.0000	5
HAPPY	1	849.539	.0000	2
MARITAL	2	343.394	.0000	2
INCOME82	2	86.114	.0000	2
HEALTH	1	354.661	.0000	2

8.12 Model Selection Using Backward Elimination

As in regression analysis, another way to arrive at a "best" model is by using variable-selection algorithms. Forward selection adds effects to a model, while backward elimination starts with all effects in a model and then removes those that do not satisfy the criterion for remaining in the model. Since backward elimination appears to be the better procedure for model selection (Benedetti & Brown 1978), it is the only procedure described here.

The initial model for backward elimination need not be saturated but can be any hierarchical model. At the first step, the effect whose removal results in the least-significant change in the likelihood-ratio chi-square is eligible for elimination, provided that the observed significance level is larger than the criterion for remaining in the model. To ensure a hierarchical model, only effects corresponding to the generating class are examined at each step. For example, if the generating class is MARITAL*HAPPY*INCOME*HEALTH, the first step examines only the fourth-order interaction.

Figure 8.12a shows output at the first step. Elimination of the fourth-order interaction results in a chi-square change of 3.994, which has an associated significance level of 0.4069. Since this significance level is not less than 0.05 (the default HILOGLINEAR criterion for remaining in the model), the effect is removed. The new model has all three-way interactions as its generating class.

Figure 8.12a First step in backward elimination

```
HILOGLINEAR HAPPY(1,2) MARITAL(1,3) INCOME82(1,3) HEALTH(1,2)
   /METHOD=BACKWARD
   /MAXSTEPS=6
   /DESIGN=HAPPY*MARITAL*INCOME82*HEALTH
```

```
Backward Elimination for DESIGN 1 with generating class

  HAPPY*MARITAL*INCOME82*HEALTH

 Likelihood ratio chi square =      .00000    DF = 0  P = 1.000

- - - - - - - - - - - - - - - - - - - - - - - - - - - - - - - - - - - - -

If Deleted Simple Effect is                 DF   L.R. Chisq Change    Prob  Iter

 HAPPY*MARITAL*INCOME82*HEALTH               4              3.994   .4069     3

Step 1

  The best model has generating class

      HAPPY*MARITAL*INCOME82
      HAPPY*MARITAL*HEALTH
      HAPPY*INCOME82*HEALTH
      MARITAL*INCOME82*HEALTH

  Likelihood ratio chi square =    3.99354    DF = 4  P =  .407
```

Figure 8.12b contains the statistics for the second step. The effects eligible for removal are all three-way interactions. The HAPPY*MARITAL*HEALTH interaction has the largest observed significance level for the change in the chi-square if it is removed, so it is eliminated from the model. The likelihood-ratio chi-square for the resulting model is 4.45.

Figure 8.12b Statistics used to eliminate second effect

```
If Deleted Simple Effect is                                        DF   L.R. Chisq Changed     Prob  Iter

 HAPPY*MARITAL*INCOME82                                              4              3.370    .4979     4
 HAPPY*MARITAL*HEALTH                                                2               .458    .7954     4
 HAPPY*INCOME82*HEALTH                                               2               .955    .6203     3
 MARITAL*INCOME82*HEALTH                                             4              3.652    .4552     5

Step 2

  The best model has generating class

      HAPPY*MARITAL*INCOME82
      HAPPY*INCOME82*HEALTH
      MARITAL*INCOME82*HEALTH

  Likelihood ratio chi square =     4.45127     DF = 6  P =  .616
```

At the next three steps the remaining third-order interactions are removed from the model. The sixth step begins with all second-order items in the model, as shown in Figure 8.12c.

Figure 8.12c Sixth step in backward elimination

```
If Deleted Simple Effect is                                  DF  L.R. Chisq Changed    Prob  Iter

 HAPPY*HEALTH                                                 1             55.697    .0000     5
 HAPPY*MARITAL                                                2             15.052    .0005     5
 HAPPY*INCOME82                                               2             16.121    .0003     5
 MARITAL*INCOME82                                             4            160.739    .0000     5
 MARITAL*HEALTH                                               2              8.392    .0151     5
 INCOME82*HEALTH                                              2             35.603    .0000     4

Step 6

  The best model has generating class

      HAPPY*HEALTH
      HAPPY*MARITAL
      HAPPY*INCOME82
      MARITAL*INCOME82
      MARITAL*HEALTH
      INCOME82*HEALTH

  Likelihood ratio chi square =     12.60116    DF = 16  P =  .702

- - - - - - - - - - - - - - - - - - - - - - - - - - - - - - - - - - - - - - - - - - - - - - - -

The final model has generating class

    HAPPY*HEALTH
    HAPPY*MARITAL
    HAPPY*INCOME82
    MARITAL*INCOME82
    MARITAL*HEALTH
    INCOME82*HEALTH

The Iterative Proportional Fitting converged at iteration 0.
```

Since the observed significance level for removal of any of the two-way interactions is smaller than 0.05, no more effects are removed from the model. The final model contains all second-order interactions, and has a chi-square value of 12.60. This is the same model suggested by the partial-association table.

At this point it is a good idea to examine the residuals to see if any anomalies are apparent. The largest standardized residual is 1.34, which suggests that the model fits well. The residual plots also show nothing suspicious.

8.13 RUNNING PROCEDURE HILOGLINEAR

The SPSS^X HILOGLINEAR procedure allows you to fit, test, and estimate parameters of hierarchical log-linear models. Using HILOGLINEAR, you can examine and compare a variety of hierarchical models, either by specifying tests of partial association or by requesting backward elimination. HILOGLINEAR also provides estimates of the parameters for saturated models.

HILOGLINEAR operates via a variables list and subcommands. None of the subcommands are required; the minimum specification on HILOGLINEAR is simply the variable list. The output for the minimum specification includes observed and expected frequencies for a *k*-way table and parameter estimates for the saturated model.

8.14 Specifying the Variables

The variables list identifies the categorical variables used in the model or models you fit. Variables must be numeric and integer. Each variable in the list must be accompanied by minimum and maximum values in parentheses, as in the command

```
HILOGLINEAR SEX(1,2) RACE(1,2) HAPPY(1,2) MARITAL(1,3) INCOME82(1,3)
```

If several consecutive variables in the variables list have the same ranges, the minimum and maximum values can be listed after the last variable with these values. Thus, the command

```
HILOGLINEAR SEX RACE HAPPY(1,2) MARITAL INCOME82(1,3)
```

is equivalent to the previous command.

The values of the variables should be consecutive positive integers because HILOGLINEAR assumes there is a category for every value in the specified range. For example, the values 1, 2, and 3 are preferable to the values 5, 10, and 15. If necessary, you can recode variables using the RECODE command prior to the HILOGLINEAR command.

8.15 The DESIGN Subcommand

Use the DESIGN subcommand to specify the generating class for the terms in a model. Asterisks are used to specify the highest-order interactions in a generating class. For example, the command

```
HILOGLINEAR SEX RACE HAPPY(1,2) MARITAL INCOME82(1,3)
  /DESIGN=HAPPY*MARITAL*INCOME82 SEX
```

specifies a hierarchical model with the main effects HAPPY, MARITAL, INCOME82, and SEX; all second-order effects involving HAPPY, MARITAL, and INCOME82; and the third-order interaction term HAPPY *MARITAL*INCOME82. The command

```
HILOGLINEAR HAPPY(1,2) MARITAL(1,3)
  /DESIGN HAPPY*MARITAL
```

specifies a hierarchical model with the main effects HAPPY and MARITAL and the second-order interaction of HAPPY and MARITAL, producing the output in Figures 8.3 and 8.4.

You can use multiple DESIGN subcommands on a HILOGLINEAR command. If you omit the DESIGN subcommand or use it without specifications, a default model is fit. SPSS^X produces parameter estimates only if the saturated model is specified. If you request an unsaturated model, the output will contain only the goodness-of-fit test for the model, the observed and expected frequencies, and the residuals and standardized residuals.

8.16 Building a Model

Use the MAXORDER, CRITERIA, METHOD, and CWEIGHT subcommands to control computational and design aspects of a model and to perform model selection. Each of these subcommands remains in effect for any subsequent DESIGN subcommands unless overridden by new subcommand specifications.

8.17 The MAXORDER Subcommand

The MAXORDER subcommand specifies the maximum order of terms in a model. If you specify MAXORDER=k, HILOGLINEAR fits a model with all terms of order k or less. Thus, MAXORDER provides an abbreviated way of specifying models. For example, the command

```
HILOGLINEAR MARITAL(1,3) HAPPY RACE SEX(1,2)
  /MAXORDER=2
```

is equivalent to

```
HILOGLINEAR MARITAL(1,3) HAPPY RACE SEX(1,2)
  /DESIGN=MARITAL*HAPPY
          MARITAL*RACE
          MARITAL*SEX
          HAPPY*RACE
          HAPPY*SEX
          RACE*SEX
```

If both MAXORDER and DESIGN are used, the MAXORDER subcommand restricts the model stated on the DESIGN subcommand. If MAXORDER specifies an order less than the total number of variables (i.e., if an unsaturated model is fit), HILOGLINEAR does not display parameter estimates but does produce a goodness-of-fit test and the observed and expected frequencies for the model.

8.18 The CRITERIA Subcommand

HILOGLINEAR uses an iterative procedure to fit models. Use the CRITERIA subcommand to specify the values of constants in the iterative proportional-fitting and model-selection routines. The keywords available for CRITERIA are

CONVERGE(n) *Convergence criterion.* The default is 10^{-3} * the largest cell size, or .25, whichever is larger. Iterations stop when the change in fitted frequencies is less than the specified value.

ITERATE(n) *Maximum number of iterations.* The default is 20.

P(p) *Probability of chi-square for removal.* The default value is 0.05.

MAXSTEPS(n) *Maximum number of steps.* The default is 10.

DELTA(d) *Cell delta value.* The value of delta is added to each cell frequency for the first iteration. It is left in the cells for saturated models only. The default value is 0.5. You can specify any decimal value between 0 and 1 for d. HILOGLINEAR does not print parameter estimates or the covariance matrix of parameter estimates if any zero cells (either structural or sampling) exist in the expected table after DELTA is added. (Not available before Release 2.2.)

DEFAULT *Default values.* Use DEFAULT to restore defaults altered by a previous CRITERIA subcommand.

The value for each keyword must be enclosed in parentheses. You can specify more than one keyword on a CRITERIA subcommand. Only those criteria specifically altered are changed. The keywords P and MAXSTEPS apply only to model selection and, therefore, must be used with an accompanying METHOD subcommand.

8.19 The METHOD Subcommand

The METHOD subcommand requests a search for the "best" model through backward elimination of terms from the model. Use the subcommand METHOD alone or with the BACKWARD keyword.

If you omit the METHOD subcommand, HILOGLINEAR tests the model requested on the DESIGN subcommand but does not perform any model selection.

You can use the METHOD subcommand with DESIGN specifications (Section 8.15) or MAXORDER (Section 8.16) to obtain backward elimination that begins with the specified hierarchical model. For example, the command

```
HILOGLINEAR RACE SEX HAPPY(1,2) MARITAL INCOME82(1,3)
  /MAXORDER=3
  /METHOD=BACKWARD
```

requests backward elimination beginning with a hierarchical model that contains all three-way interactions and excludes all four- and five-way interactions.

You can use the CRITERIA subcommand with METHOD to specify the removal criterion and maximum number of steps for a backward-elimination analysis. Thus, the command

```
HILOGLINEAR MARITAL INCOME(1,3) SEX HAPPY(1,2)
  /METHOD=BACKWARD
  /CRITERIA=P(.01) MAXSTEPS(25)
```

specifies a removal probability criterion of 0.01 and a maximum of 25 steps. The command

```
HILOGLINEAR HAPPY(1,2) MARITAL (1,3) INCOME82 (1,3) HEALTH (1,2)
  /METHOD=BACK
  /CRITERIA=MAXSTEPS(6)
  /DESIGN HAPPY*MARITAL*INCOME82*HEALTH
```

requests a backward elimination of terms with a maximum of six steps. These commands produce the output in Figures 8.12a, 8.12b, and 8.12c.

8.20 The CWEIGHT Subcommand

Use the CWEIGHT subcommand to specify cell weights for a model. Do not use CWEIGHT to weight aggregated input data (use the SPSS^X WEIGHT command instead). CWEIGHT allows you to impose structural zeros on a model. HILOGLINEAR ignores the CWEIGHT subcommand with a saturated model.

There are two ways to specify cell weights. First, you can specify a numeric variable whose values are the cell weights. The command

```
HILOGLINEAR MARITAL(1,3) SEX HAPPY(1,2)
  /CWEIGHT CELLWGT
  /DESIGN=MARITAL*SEX SEX*HAPPY MARITAL*HAPPY
```

weights a cell by the value of the variable CELLWGT when a case containing the frequency for that cell is read. Alternatively, you can specify a matrix of weights enclosed in parentheses on the CWEIGHT subcommand. You can use the prefix *n∗* to indicate that a cell weight is repeated *n* times in the matrix. The command

```
HILOGLINEAR MARITAL(1,3) INCOME(1,3)
  /CWEIGHT=(0 1 1 1 0 1 1 1 0)
  /DESIGN=MARITAL INCOME
```

is equivalent to

```
HILOGLINEAR MARITAL(1,3) INCOME(1,3)
  /CWEIGHT (0 3*1 0 3*1 0)
  /DESIGN=MARITAL INCOME
```

You must specify a weight for every cell in the table. Cell weights are indexed by the levels of the variables in the order they are specified in the variables list. The index values of the rightmost variable change the most quickly.

8.21 The PRINT Subcommand

By default, HILOGLINEAR displays observed and expected cell frequencies, residuals and standardized residuals, and, for saturated models, parameter estimates. Use the following keywords on the PRINT command to obtain additional output:

FREQ *Observed and expected cell frequencies.*

RESID *Residuals and standardized residuals.*

ESTIM *Parameter estimates, standard errors of estimates, and confidence intervals for parameters.* These are calculated only for saturated models.

ASSOCIATION *Tests of partial association.* These are calculated only for saturated models.

DEFAULT *Default display.* FREQ and RESID for all models plus ESTIM for saturated models.

ALL *All available output.*

If you specify PRINT, only output explicitly requested is displayed. The PRINT subcommand affects all subsequent DESIGN subcommands unless a new PRINT subcommand is specified.

For example, the command

```
HILOGLINEAR HAPPY(1,2) MARITAL (1,3)
  /PRINT=ESTIM
  /DESIGN HAPPY*MARITAL
```

limits the display to parameter estimates, standard errors of estimates, and confidence intervals for the saturated model. This command produces the output in Figure 8.4.

8.22 The PLOT Subcommand

To obtain plots of residuals, you must specify the PLOT subcommand. The following keywords are available on PLOT:

RESID *Plot of standardized residuals against observed and expected counts.*

NORMPLOT *Normal and detrended normal probability plots of the standardized residuals.*

NONE *No plots.* Suppresses any plots requested on a previous PLOT subcommand. This is the default if the subcommand is omitted.

DEFAULT *Default plots.* RESID and NORMPLOT are plotted when PLOT is used without keyword specifications or with keyword DEFAULT. No plots are produced if the subcommand is omitted entirely.

The PLOT subcommand affects all subsequent DESIGN subcommands unless a new PLOT subcommand is specified.

8.23 The MISSING Subcommand

By default, HILOGLINEAR deletes cases with missing values for any variable named on the variables list from the analysis. Use the MISSING subcommand to include cases with user-missing values or to specify the default explicitly. The keywords are

LISTWISE *Delete cases with missing values listwise.* This is the default.

INCLUDE *Include cases with user-missing values.*

The MISSING subcommand can be specified only once on each HILOGLINEAR command and applies to all the designs specified on that command.

8.24 EXERCISES

Syntax

1. Find the syntax errors in the HILOGLINEAR commands below, and, if possible, write the correct commands:

   a.
   ```
   HILOGLINEAR VARIABLES=JOY(1,2) DAY(1,7) SEASON
         /DESIGN MAXORDER=5
   ```
   b.
   ```
   HILOGLINEAR A B(1,2)
         /DESIGN A B A*B
   ```
   c.
   ```
   HILOGLINEAR A B(1,2)
         /CWEIGHT = (0 1 1)
   ```
   d.
   ```
   HILOGLINEAR A B C(1,3)
         /METHOD STEP
         /DESIGN A*C B
   ```

2. Indicate whether the following statements are true or false:

   a. In HILOGLINEAR, parameter estimates can be obtained for any model specified
   b. Forward selection, backward elimination, and stepwise selection are all available in HILOGLINEAR for model building.
   c. A model including only the main effects A B C and the three-way interaction A by B by C cannot be estimated in HILOGLINEAR.
   d. In HILOGLINEAR the term A*B*C on a DESIGN subcommand refers to the three-way interaction of A by B by C.

3. If possible, complete the following HILOGLINEAR specification

   ```
   HILOGLINEAR A B C (1,3)
   ```

   by writing the necessary DESIGN subcommands for the models listed below:

   a. The main-effects model.
   b. The model including only main effects and second-order interactions.

c. The model including only main effects and the A-by-B interaction.
d. The model including only the second-order interactions.
e. The model including only the A and B main effects, and the B-by-C interaction.

4. For the HILOGLINEAR command

```
HILOGLINEAR A B C D(1,2)
```

write the DESIGN subcommand that will specify the same model as the following MAXORDER subcommands:

a. `/MAXORDER = 2`
b. `/MAXORDER = 1`
c. `/MAXORDER = 3`
d. `/MAXORDER = 4`

5. A market researcher is investigating the relationship between consumer satisfaction (SAT, coded on a scale of 1 to 3), sex (SEX, coded 0=male and 1=female), and marital status (MARITAL, coded 0=not married and 1=currently married). Write the HILOGLINEAR commands that

a. Fit a saturated model and obtain parameter estimates, tests of partial association, and observed frequencies.
b. Fit a hierarchical model that includes only second order interaction terms involving the satisfaction variable. Request cell frequencies and residuals and a normal probability plot of the residuals.

Statistical Concepts

1. For each model shown below, indicate whether or not it is a hierarchical model. If it is not hierarchical, list the effect(s) needed to make it hierarchical.

a. The simple effects included are

```
OVERWT, HIGHBP, SEX, CORONARY, OVERWT*HIGHBP, OVERWT*CORONARY,
HIGHBP*CORONARY, HIGHBP*AGE, CORONARY*AGE
```

b. The simple effects included are

```
NUMBSIBS, CHILDREN, MARITAL, SEX, EDUC, ABORTION, NUMBSIBS*EDUC,
NUMBSIBS*ABORTION, CHILDREN*MARITAL, CHILDREN*EDUC, CHILDREN*A-
BORTION,
MARITAL*ABORTION, SEX*EDUC, EDUC*ABORTION, NUMBSIBS*EDUC*ABOR-
TION,
CHILDREN*SEX*EDUC, SEX*EDUC*ABORTION
```

c. The simple effects included are

```
ALIVE1, MARITAL, PETS, RELATIVES, SOCIALFE, ALIVE1*MARITAL,
ALIVE1*PETS, ALIVE1*RELATIVES, ALIVE1*SOCIALFE, MAR-
ITAL*SOCIALFE,
PETS*SOCIALFE, RELATIVES*SOCIALFE, ALIVE1*MARITAL*SOCIALFE,
ALIVE1*MARITAL*RELATIVES*SOCIALFE
```

d. The simple effects included are

```
ESTEEM, SEX, MARITAL, RACE, FAMILY, ESTEEM*SEX, ESTEEM*MARITAL,
ESTEEM*FAMILY, SEX*FAMILY, MARITAL*FAMILY, ESTEEM*FAMILY*SEX
```

2. Write out the hierarchical models specified by the following generating classes:

a. `A*B*C, A*D*E`
b. `A*B*C*D`
c. `A*B*C*D, A*E, D*E`
d. `A*B*C*D, A*E, B*E, C*E, D*E`

3. Write the generating classes that specify the following hierarchical models:

a. The simple effects included are

```
CRIMETYP, GANGMEMB, AGE, RACE, SEX, CRIMETYP*GANGMEMB,
CRIMETYP*AGE,
CRIMETYP*RACE, CRIMETYP*SEX, GANGMEMB*AGE, CRIMETYP*GANGMEMB*AGE
```

b. The simple effects included are

DIVNLABR, LAWTYPE, SOLIDRTY, DEVIANCE, RITUALS, DIVNLABR*LAWTYPE, DIVNLABR*SOLIDRTY, DIVNLABR*DEVIANCE, DIVNLABR*RITUALS, LAW-TYPE*SOLIDRTY, LAWTYPE*DEVIANCE, LAWTYPE*RITUALS, SOLIDRTY*DEVIANCE, SOLIDRTY*RITUALS, DEVIANCE*RITUALS, DIVNLABR*LAWTYPE*SOLIDRTY, DIVNLABR*DEVIANCE*RITUALS, LAWTYPE*SOLIDRTY*DEVIANCE, SOLIDRTY*DEVIANCE*RITUALS

c. The simple effects included are

HEALTH, MARITAL, PETS, INCOME, HEALTH*MARITAL, HEALTH*PETS, HEALTH*INCOME, PETS*INCOME

d. The simple effects included are

HIGHBP, SALT, SUGAR, AGE, SEX, STRESS, HIGHBP*SALT, HIGHBP*SUGAR, HIGHBP*AGE, HIGHBP*SEX, HIGHBP*STRESS, SALT*SUGAR, SEX*STRESS, HIGHBP*SALT*SUGAR, HIGHBP*SEX*STRESS

4. Consider the output below:

If Deleted Simple Effect is	DF	L.R. Chisq Changed	Prob
BRSTCANC*AGE	2	16.200	.0003
BRSTCANC*MOTHERBC	1	10.901	.0010
BRSTCANC*XRAYS	2	5.389	.0676
BRSTCANC*DIETFAT	1	11.199	.0008
AGE*XRAYS	4	10.387	.0344
AGE*DIETFAT	2	3.203	.2016

a. If the probability removal criterion is 0.02, which effect will be deleted next?

b. Suppose the likelihood chi-square for the model with the generating class shown above is 37.914 with 54 DF. If the effect you named in (a) is dropped, what is the chi-square and DF for the model with the resulting generating class?

5. Use the chi-square values and DF shown below to complete Tables A and B.

Generating class	DF	L.R. Chisq	Prob
MLTRYAID*RACE*EDUC*AGE	0	0.000	—
MLTRYAID*RACE*EDUC, MLTRYAID*RACE*AGE, MLTRYAID*EDUC*AGE, RACE*EDUC*AGE	4	2.290	0.683
MLTRYAID*RACE, MLTRYAID*EDUC, MLTRYAID*AGE, RACE*EDUC, RACE*AGE, EDUC*AGE	16	33.746	0.006
MLTRYAID, RACE, EDUC, AGE	29	167.442	0.000
GRAND MEAN ONLY	35	234.101	0.000

Table A

Tests that K-way and higher-order effects are zero.

K	DF	L.R. Chisq	Prob
4			.683
3			.006
2			.000
1			.000

Table B

Tests that K-way effects are zero.

K	DF	L.R. Chisq	Prob
1			.000
2			.000
3			.002
4			.683

6. Consider the following:

Generating class	DF	L.R. Chisq	Prob
TEST*STRESS, TEST*PASSFAIL, STRESS*PASSFAIL	4	5.137	0.273
TEST*PASSFAIL, STRESS*PASSFAIL	8	20.902	0.007
TEST*STRESS, STRESS*PASSFAIL	6	68.961	0.000
TEST*STRESS, TEST*PASSFAIL	6	10.095	0.121
TEST, STRESS, PASSFAIL	12	93.075	0.000
STRESS, PASSFAIL	14	364.332	0.000
TEST, PASSFAIL	14	232.985	0.000
TEST, STRESS	13	111.055	0.000

Use the chi-square values and DF to complete the table below:

Tests of PARTIAL associations.

Effect Name	DF	Partial Chisq	Prob
STRESS*TEST			.0034
TEST*PASSFAIL			.0000
STRESS*PASSFAIL			.0838
TEST			.0000
STRESS			.0000
PASSFAIL			.0000

7. Indicate whether the following statements are true or false:
   a. If the Pearson chi-square value for the hierarchical model with the generating class FOODPOIS*EGGSALAD, FOODPOIS*CHICKEN, EGGSALAD*CHICKEN is 87.312, and the Pearson chi-square value for the model with the generating class FOODPOIS*EGGSALAD, FOODPOIS*CHICKEN is 93.558, then the partial chi-square value for the effect EGGSALAD*CHICKEN is 6.246.
   b. Effects with small standardized estimated values should usually be deleted from a model.
   c. A saturated model always has a chi-square value of zero.
   d. The larger the likelihood-ratio chi-square value for a model, the better the model.
   e. An effect with a small observed significance level should usually be dropped from a model.
   f. A large increase in the chi-square value for a model when an additional effect is added indicates that the effect contributes substantially to the model.

8. Consider the parameter estimates shown below.

Parameter	Coeff.	Std. Err.	Z Value
$\lambda^{HAPPY\ PRESTIGE}_{YES\ LOW}$	-0.356	0.136	-2.618
$\lambda^{HAPPY\ EDUC}_{YES\ LESSHIGH}$	-0.252	0.195	-1.292
$\lambda^{PRESTIGE\ EDUC}_{LOW\ LESSHIGH}$	0.915	0.204	4.485

   a. What is the effect (if any) of low prestige on happiness?
   b. What is the effect (if any) of a lack of a high school education on happiness?
   c. What is the effect (if any) of a lack of a high school education on prestige?

9. Use the variables and parameter estimates shown below to fill in the missing parameter estimates.

   a.

Variable	Coding
SALE	1=Yes, 0=No
DISTRICT	1, 2, 3

Parameter	Coefficient
λ^{SALE}_{YES}	0.682
$\lambda^{DISTRICT}_{1}$	0.255
$\lambda^{DISTRICT}_{2}$	−0.752
$\lambda^{DISTRICT-SALE}_{2-YES}$	0.486
$\lambda^{DISTRICT-SALE}_{3-NO}$	0.205
λ^{SALE}_{NO}	
$\lambda^{DISTRICT}_{3}$	
$\lambda^{DISTRICT-SALE}_{2-NO}$	
$\lambda^{DISTRICT-SALE}_{1-NO}$	

   b. If you were a salesperson, which district would you want to go to?

10. A personnel manager, in order to determine the effect of certain procedures on employee morale, crosstabulates variables MORALE, BREAKTYP, INPUT, and OFFICE and then obtains a log-linear model. He considers MORALE to be the dependent variable in his log-linear model. Is this correct? Why or why not?

11. Fill in the missing entries in the output below:

```
Estimates for Parameters

SEX*AUTOPREF

 Parameter           Coeff.        Std. Err.       Z-Value     Lower 95 CI     Upper 95 CI

         1            -1.06              .26
         2              .09              .28

SEX

 Parameter           Coeff.        Std. Err.       Z-Value     Lower 95 CI     Upper 95 CI

         1             1.11              .25

AUTOPREF

 Parameter           Coeff.        Std. Err.       Z-Value     Lower 95 CI     Upper 95 CI

         1              .79              .26
         2              .40              .28
```

12. Consider the model whose parameter estimates are shown below (only estimates for independent parameters are given):

Estimates for Parameters

POSTNTYP

Parameter	Coeff.	Std. Err.	Z-Value	Lower 95 CI	Upper 95 CI
1	.2475960090	.07292	3.39560	.10468	.39051

PAYLEVEL

Parameter	Coeff.	Std. Err.	Z-Value	Lower 95 CI	Upper 95 CI
2	.9309710962	.12147	7.66396	.69288	1.16906
3	.6442332437	.12959	4.97121	.39023	.89824
4	-.7167099619	.20248	-3.53964	-1.11357	-.31985

PRDCTVTY

Parameter	Coeff.	Std. Err.	Z-Value	Lower 95 CI	Upper 95 CI
5	.1170305420	.15555	-.75820	-.42282	.18694
6	.2383889874	.12888	1.84976	-.01421	.49098

POSTNTYP BY PAYLEVEL

Parameter	Coeff.	Std. Err.	Z-Value	Lower 95 CI	Upper 95 CI
7	-.0296006786	.10125	-.29235	-.22805	.16885
8	.0448127969	.10763	.41636	-.16614	.25577
9	.3328998204	.15715	2.11838	.02489	.64091

POSTNTYP BY PRDCTVTY

Parameter	Coeff.	Std. Err.	Z-Value	Lower 95 CI	Upper 95 CI
10	-.0473822493	.08838	-.53615	-.22060	.12583
11	-.1981810518	.08949	-2.21461	-.37358	-.02278

PAYLEVEL BY PRDCTVTY

Parameter	Coeff.	Std. Err.	Z-Value	Lower 95 CI	Upper 95 CI
12	.7652410877	.17494	4.37439	.42237	1.10812
13	-.0573833262	.15769	-.36390	-.36646	.25169
14	.8491421214	.18142	4.68064	.49357	1.20472
15	-.0141117536	.16648	-.08476	-.34042	.31219
16	-.9405573695	.32578	-2.88706	-1.57909	-.30202
17	.8470318438	.22604	3.74726	.40399	1.29007

How many degrees of freedom does this model have? (Note that POSNTYP has two values, PAYLEVEL has four values, and PRDCTVTY has three values.)

13. Suppose the log-linear model

$$\log F_{ij} = \mu + \lambda^{DIET} + \lambda^{BP}$$

is fitted to the table below:

	DIET TYPE		
	HIGH SALT	MODERATE SALT	LOW SALT
BLOOD PRESSURE			
HIGH	10	6	3
NORMAL	8	16	11

What are the degrees of freedom for this model? What is its Pearson chi-square value and observed significance level?

14. a. Fill in the missing entries in the output shown below.

```
Observed, Expected Frequencies and Residuals

     Factor            Code              OBS. count & PCT.   EXP. count & PCT.      Residual     Std. Resid.

BREED                   1
 TRNABLTY               1
  SOCLZATN              1                  4.00 ( 9.76)        3.12 ( 7.62)
  SOCLZATN              2                  1.00 ( 2.44)        1.87 ( 4.57)
 TRNABLTY               2
  SOCLZATN              1                  7.00 (17.07)        6.18 (15.06)
  SOCLZATN              2                  8.00 (19.51)        8.82 (21.52)

BREED                   2
 TRNABLTY               1
  SOCLZATN              1                 11.00 (26.83)       11.87 (28.96)
  SOCLZATN              2                  8.00 (19.51)        7.12 (17.38)
 TRNABLTY               2
  SOCLZATN              1                   .00 (   .00)        .82 ( 2.01)
  SOCLZATN              2                  2.00 ( 4.88)        1.18 ( 2.87)
```

b. Construct (by hand) a plot of the standardized residuals against the observed values. Does this plot appear to be satisfactory?

15. a. The following table shows the standardized residuals for a log-linear model. Would you recommend using this model? Why or why not?

	Textbook					
	A		B		C	
	A in course		B in course		C in course	
Instructor	Yes	No	Yes	No	Yes	No
Jackson	0.312	0.115	0.623	0.440	0.811	0.229
Maxwell	−0.714	−0.538	−0.542	−0.389	−0.106	−0.651

b. What do the following residual plots shown below indicate about the adequacy of the log-linear models from which they were obtained?

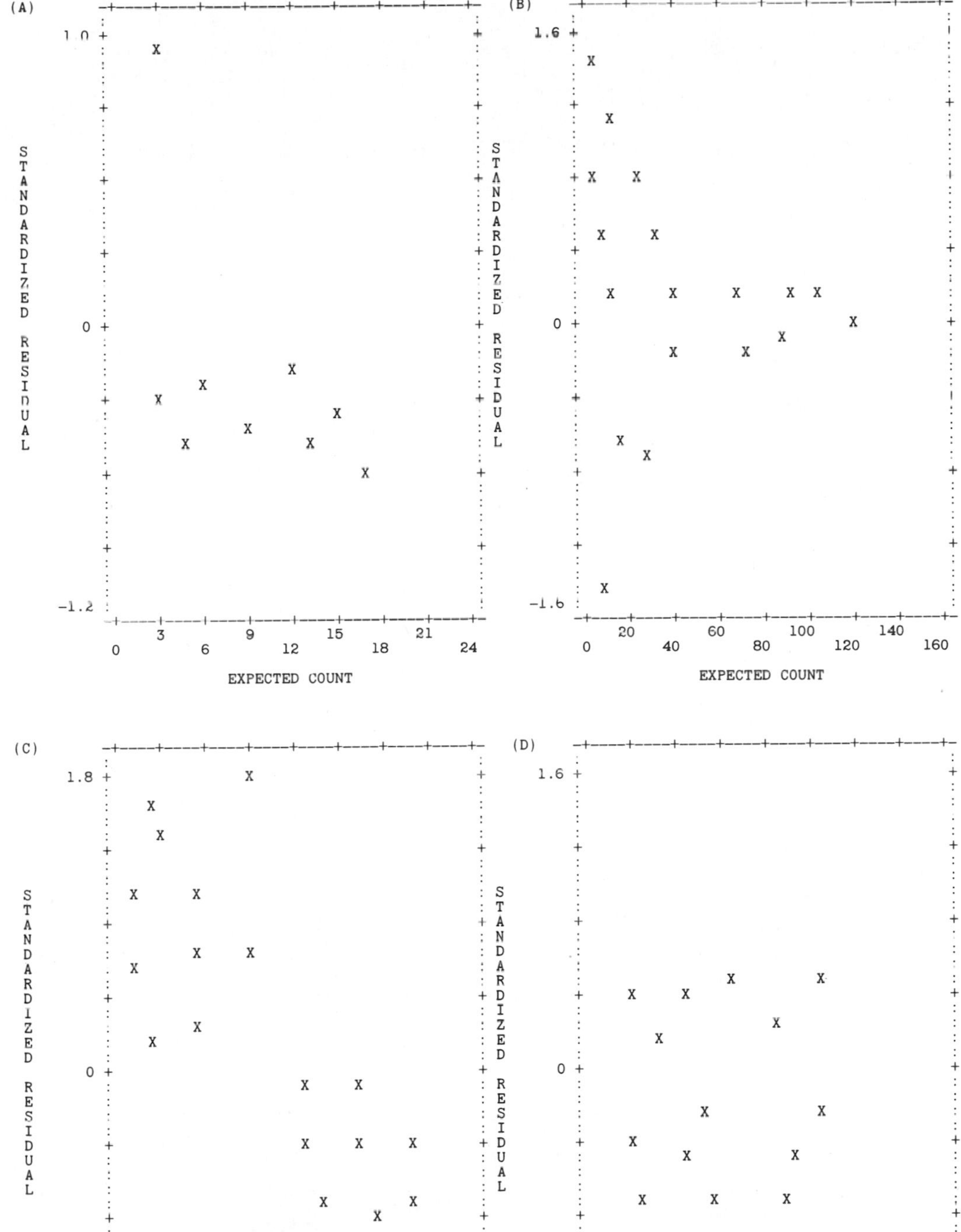

9

Further Topics in Log-Linear Models

In this chapter:

Goals:

- To examine the relationships among a set of ordinal categorical variables.
- To explore the relationship between a dichotomous dependent variable and one or more independent variables.
- To test hypotheses about tables that contain cells that are to be ignored.

Examples:

- Predict attitudes toward women staying at home from the sex and education of the respondent.
- Examine the relationship between husband's and wife's educational level.
- Model social mobility by comparing respondents' social status to that of their parents.

How it's done:

The starting point for the analysis is a multidimensional crosstabulation table. For certain analyses, some of the cells are excluded from the model. Based on the table, a model is formulated and parameter estimates obtained. Observed cell frequencies and those predicted from a model are compared. If the model does not fit well, an alternative model is selected and tested.

Data considerations:

The classification variables must be discrete, though they may represent an underlying continuum. For example, income may be grouped into four mutually exclusive categories. The observations may have resulted from one of several sampling schemes. When the cross-classification table has many empty cells, the classification variables should, if possible, be grouped into fewer categories.

General references:

Fienberg (1980)
Haberman (1978)
Bishop, Fienberg, & Holland (1975)
Agresti (1984)
Goodman (1984)

Contents

9.1 LOG-LINEAR MODELS
9.2 Frequency Table Models
9.3 Generalized Residuals
9.4 Fitting A Quadratic Function
9.5 The Zodiac and Job Satisfaction
9.6 Fitting A Logit Model
9.7 Parameter Estimates
9.8 Measures of Dispersion and Association
9.9 Fitting an Unsaturated Logit Model
9.10 Fitting a More Complicated Logit Model
9.11 The Equivalent Log-Linear Model
9.12 MODELS FOR ORDINAL DATA
9.13 The Linear-by-Linear Association Model
9.14 Row- and Column-Effects Models
9.15 INCOMPLETE TABLES
9.16 Testing Real Against Ideal
9.17 Quasi-Independence
9.18 Symmetry Models
9.19 Adjusted Quasi-Symmetry
9.20 AN ORDINAL MODEL FOR REAL VERSUS IDEAL
9.21 Parameter Estimates
9.22 The Design Matrix
9.23 RUNNING PROCEDURE LOGLINEAR
9.24 The Variable List
9.25 The DESIGN Subcommand
9.26 The CWEIGHT Subcommand
9.27 The GRESID Subcommand
9.28 The PRINT and NOPRINT Subcommands
9.29 The PLOT Subcommand
9.30 The CONTRAST Subcommand
9.31 The CRITERIA Subcommand
9.32 The WIDTH Subcommand
9.33 The MISSING Subcommand
9.34 EXERCISES

9 Reading the Stars: Further Topics in Log-Linear Models

Why do some people slip on banana peels while others glide through life unscathed? Why are some people Pollyannas while others are Ebenezer Scrooges? Throughout history, many theories have been proposed to explain such differences. The ancient Greeks believed that the human body was composed of four humors: phlegm, blood, yellow bile, and black bile. The predominant humor determined the personality. For example, black bile is associated with melancholia, and phlegm with a phlegmatic disposition.

The Babylonians and Egyptians looked to the positions of the stars and planets to explain differences among people. The position of the sun and planets at the time of one's birth determined destiny. Though the four-humors theory has few followers today, astrology continues to intrigue many. Even the most serious scientist may on occasion sneak a look at the horoscope page, just for fun, of course...

The ultimate test of any theory is how well it withstands the rigors of scientific testing. The General Social Survey in 1984 recorded the zodiac signs of 1,462 persons, along with a variety of other information, ranging from views on the after-life to mother's employment status when the respondent was 16 years old. In this chapter, the LOGLINEAR procedure is used to test a variety of hypotheses about zodiac signs and their relationships to other variables.

9.1 LOG-LINEAR MODELS

Chapter 8 described the HILOGLINEAR procedure for testing hypotheses about hierarchical log-linear models. In this chapter, additional types of models, including nonhierarchical models, produced by the LOGLINEAR procedure are examined. Section 9.23 describes additional differences between HILOGLINEAR and LOGLINEAR. This chapter assumes familiarity with the hierarchical log-linear models described in Chapter 8.

9.2 Frequency Table Models

One of the first hypotheses you might want to test is whether all twelve zodiac signs appear to be equally likely in the population from which the General Social Survey draws its sample. Figure 9.2 contains the observed and expected cell counts under the model of *equiprobability*. For example, there are 113 Ariens, which is (113/1462) or 7.73% of the sample. These values are shown in the column labeled OBS. count & PCT. If all zodiac signs are equally likely, 8.33% of the sample (1/12), or 121.83 (1,462/12) respondents, are expected in each cell. These values are shown in the column labeled EXP. count & PCT. The differences between the observed and expected counts are in the column labeled Residual.

Figure 9.2 Frequencies and residuals for the equiprobability model

```
COMPUTE X=1
LOGLINEAR ZODIAC(1,12) WITH X
  /DESIGN=X
```

Observed, Expected Frequencies and Residuals

Factor	Code	OBS. count & PCT.	EXP. count & PCT.	Residual	Std. Resid.	Adj. Resid.
ZODIAC	ARIES	113.00 (7.73)	121.83 (8.33)	-8.8333	-.8003	-.8359
ZODIAC	TAURUS	115.00 (7.87)	121.83 (8.33)	-6.8333	-.6191	-.6466
ZODIAC	GEMINI	137.00 (9.37)	121.83 (8.33)	15.1667	1.3741	1.4352
ZODIAC	CANCER	121.00 (8.28)	121.83 (8.33)	-.8333	-.0755	-.0789
ZODIAC	LEO	122.00 (8.34)	121.83 (8.33)	.1667	.0151	.0158
ZODIAC	VIRGO	133.00 (9.10)	121.83 (8.33)	11.1667	1.0117	1.0567
ZODIAC	LIBRA	144.00 (9.85)	121.83 (8.33)	22.1667	2.0082	2.0975
ZODIAC	SCORPIO	114.00 (7.80)	121.83 (8.33)	-7.8333	-.7097	-.7412
ZODIAC	SAGITTAR	116.00 (7.93)	121.83 (8.33)	-5.8333	-.5285	-.5520
ZODIAC	CAPRICOR	131.00 (8.96)	121.83 (8.33)	9.1667	.8305	.8674
ZODIAC	AQUARIUS	93.00 (6.36)	121.83 (8.33)	-28.8333	-2.6122	-2.7284
ZODIAC	PISCES	123.00 (8.41)	121.83 (8.33)	1.1667	.1057	.1104

Goodness-of-Fit test statistics

```
Likelihood Ratio Chi Square =   16.58881    DF = 11  P =  .121
        Pearson Chi Square =   16.28181    DF = 11  P =  .131
```

As in regression analysis, it is useful to normalize the residuals by dividing them by their standard deviations. Both standardized and adjusted residuals are calculated by LOGLINEAR. Standardized residuals are obtained by dividing each residual by the square root of the expected count. Adjusted residuals are calculated by dividing each standardized residual by an estimate of its standard error. If the number of cells in the table is large when compared to the number of estimated parameters for a model, the adjusted and standardized residuals should be similar. For large sample sizes, the distribution of both standardized and adjusted residuals is approximately standard normal.

By examining residuals we can identify patterns of deviation from the model. In this example, the standardized and adjusted residuals are fairly comparable. The only noticeable deviations from the equiprobability model occur for the Librans and Aquarians. Both of these zodiac signs have adjusted residuals greater than 2 in absolute value. The value 2 is a rule of thumb for "suspiciousness" since, in a standard normal distribution, only 5% of the absolute values exceed 1.96.

From the chi-square goodness-of-fit statistics shown in Figure 9.2, it appears that there is not sufficient evidence to reject the hypothesis that all zodiac signs are equally likely. The likelihood ratio chi-square value is 16.59 with 11 degrees of freedom. The observed significance level is 0.12.

9.3 Generalized Residuals

Figure 9.2 shows the results for each zodiac sign individually. It might be interesting to collapse the signs into four categories based on seasons of the year and see whether a seasonal effect may be present. This can be done by forming a linear combination of observed and expected values corresponding to each season. The goodness of fit of the equiprobability model does not change since the model remains the same.

Figure 9.3 contains results for the four seasons of the year. The first contrast corresponds to the Spring zodiac signs (Aries, Taurus and Gemini), the second to the Summer signs, the third to the Fall signs, and the fourth to the Winter signs.

Spring comes very close to the expected number of births, Summer and Fall have a few more births than expected, while Winter has the fewest number of births. Residuals corresponding to linear combinations of the cells are called *generalized residuals* (Haberman, 1979).

Figure 9.3 Generalized residuals

```
COMPUTE X=1
LOGLINEAR ZODIAC(1,12) WITH X
  /GRESID=(3*1 9*0) /GRESID=(3*0 3*1 6*0)
  /GRESID=(6*0 3*1 3*0) /GRESID=(9*0 3*1)
  /DESIGN=X
```

```
Goodness-of-Fit test statistics

   Likelihood Ratio Chi Square =   16.58881   DF = 11  P =  .121
            Pearson Chi Square =   16.28181   DF = 11  P =  .131

- - - - - - - - - - - - - - - - - - - - - - - - - - - - - - - - - - - -

Generalized Residual

Contrast      OBS count   EXP count    Residual  Std Resid.  Adj Resid.

     1          365.0      365.50       -.500      -.026       -.030
     2          376.0      365.50      10.500       .549        .634
     3          374.0      365.50       8.500       .445        .513
     4          347.0      365.50     -18.500       .968      -1.117
```

9.4 Fitting A Quadratic Function

Instead of assuming an equiprobability model, let's see if some other relationship exists between seasons and number of births. For example, if the number of births steadily increases from Spring to Winter, we might consider a linear relationship. From Figure 9.3, one can see the relationship between the number of births and the seasons does not appear linear. Instead a function that "peaks" and then decreases again is needed. (Note: in the previous analysis, the original twelve zodiac signs are analyzed and the results of this analysis grouped into seasons for display. In this analysis, the data are the number of births in each season.)

Let's consider a quadratic function. Figure 9.4a contains the observed and expected frequencies for each of the seasons when the expected number of cases for a season is expressed as a quadratic function.

Figure 9.4a Frequencies and residuals for the quadratic model

```
RECODE ZODIAC(1,2,3=1) (4,5,6=2) (7,8,9=3) (10,11,12=4) INTO SEASON
VALUE LABELS SEASON 1'SPRING' 2'SUMMER' 3'FALL' 4'WINTER'
COMPUTE LIN=SEASON
COMPUTE LIN2=SEASON*SEASON
LOGLINEAR SEASON(1,4) WITH LIN LIN2
  /DESIGN=LIN LIN2
```

```
Observed, Expected Frequencies and Residuals

    Factor          Code            OBS. count & PCT.   EXP. count & PCT.     Residual   Std. Resid.   Adj. Resid.

SEASON          SPRING                365.00 (24.97)     364.36 (24.92)         .6447        .0338        .1493
SEASON          SUMMER                376.00 (25.72)     377.93 (25.85)       -1.9342       -.0995       -.1493
SEASON          FALL                  374.00 (25.58)     372.07 (25.45)        1.9342        .1003        .1493
SEASON          WINTER                347.00 (23.73)     347.64 (23.78)        -.6447       -.0346       -.1493
```

Note that the expected values are no longer equal for each season. Summer has the largest expected frequency, 377.93, while Winter has the smallest. This is true for the observed frequencies as well. The observed and expected values are closer than in an equiprobability model. The statistics for the overall fit of the quadratic model are shown in Figure 9.4b. Note that the chi-squared value is very small (0.02229), indicating that the model fits quite well. Figure 9.4c shows that the coefficients for the linear and quadratic terms for the log frequencies are small. In addition, both 95% confidence intervals include zero.

Figure 9.4b Goodness of fit for the quadratic model

```
Goodness-of-Fit test statistics

  Likelihood Ratio Chi Square =     .02229    DF = 1  P =  .881
          Pearson Chi Square =     .02229    DF = 1  P =  .881
```

Figure 9.4c Parameter estimates for the linear and quadratic terms

```
RECODE ZODIAC(1,2,3=1) (4,5,6=2) (7,8,9=3) (10,11,12=4) INTO SEASON
COMPUTE LIN=SEASON
COMPUTE LIN2=SEASON*SEASON
LOGLINEAR SEASON(1,4) WITH LIN LIN2
  /PRINT=ESTIM
  /DESIGN=LIN LIN2
```

```
Estimates for Parameters
LIN

 Parameter        Coeff.       Std. Err.      Z-Value    Lower 95 CI   Upper 95 CI

      1      .1149510016         .13261        .86681       -.14497        .37487
LIN2

 Parameter        Coeff.       Std. Err.      Z-Value    Lower 95 CI   Upper 95 CI

      2     -.0261200872         .02616       -.99829       -.07740        .02516
```

An equiprobability model also fits the data reasonably well, as shown in Figure 9.4d. It has an observed significance level for goodness of fit of 0.694. Note that the goodness-of-fit statistics for this are not the same as for the individual zodiac signs. However, the generalized residuals for the seasons (Figure 9.3) are equal to the residuals in Figure 9.4d.

Including additional terms in the model improves the fit, but not by much. The additional parameters decrease the degrees of freedom and should only be used if they substantially improve the fit. In other words, a good model should fit the data well and be as simple as possible.

Figure 9.4d Statistics for the equiprobability model

```
RECODE ZODIAC(1,2,3=1) (4,5,6=2) (7,8,9=3) (10,11,12=4) INTO SEASON
VALUE LABELS SEASON 1'SPRING' 2'SUMMER' 3'FALL' 4'WINTER'
COMPUTE X=1
LOGLINEAR SEASON(1,4) WITH X
  /DESIGN=X
```

```
Observed, Expected Frequencies and Residuals

    Factor          Code              OBS. count & PCT.  EXP. count & PCT.    Residual  Std. Resid.  Adj. Resid.

SEASON          SPRING                  365.00 (24.97)    365.50 (25.00)      -.5000      -.0262      -.0302
SEASON          SUMMER                  376.00 (25.72)    365.50 (25.00)     10.5000       .5492       .6342
SEASON          FALL                    374.00 (25.58)    365.50 (25.00)      8.5000       .4446       .5134
SEASON          WINTER                  347.00 (23.73)    365.50 (25.00)    -18.5000      -.9677     -1.1174

- - - - - - - - - - - - - - - - - - - - - - - - - - - - - - - - - - - - - - - - - - - - - - - - -

Goodness-of-Fit test statistics

  Likelihood Ratio Chi Square =     1.44824    DF = 3  P =  .694
          Pearson Chi Square =     1.43639    DF = 3  P =  .697
```

9.5 The Zodiac and Job Satisfaction

Now that we've established that there is no reason to disbelieve that all zodiac signs are equally likely (Figure 9.2), let's consider the possible relationship of zodiac sign to various aspects of life. Since zodiac sign is thought to influence everything from love to numerical aptitude, it might be associated with characteristics such as income, education, happiness, and job satisfaction.

Consider Figure 9.5, which is a crosstabulation of zodiac sign and response to a question about job satisfaction. Respondents are grouped into two categories: those who are very satisfied with their jobs and those who are less enthusiastic. The row percentages show quite a bit of variability among the signs. The irrepressible Aquarians are most likely to be satisfied with their jobs, while Virgos are the least likely to be content.

Figure 9.5 Zodiac sign by job satisfaction from CROSSTABS

```
RECODE SATJOB(1=1) (2,3,4=2) (ELSE=SYSMIS)
VALUE LABELS SATJOB 1 'VERY SAT' 2 'NOT VERY SAT'
CROSSTABS ZODIAC BY SATJOB
 /CELLS=ROW ¹
```

```
- - - - - - - -   C R O S S T A B U L A T I O N   O F   - - - -
   ZODIAC      RESPONDENT'S ASTROLOGICAL SIGN
BY  SATJOB     JOB OR HOUSEWORK
- - - - - - - - - - - - - - - - - - - - - - - - - - - - - - - - -
```

ZODIAC		SATJOB VERY SAT 1	NOT VERY SAT 2	ROW TOTAL
	COUNT / ROW PCT			
ARIES	1	45 / 49.5	46 / 50.5	91 / 7.6
TAURUS	2	42 / 43.3	55 / 56.7	97 / 8.1
GEMINI	3	61 / 53.0	54 / 47.0	115 / 9.6
CANCER	4	48 / 48.5	51 / 51.5	99 / 8.2
LEO	5	48 / 48.0	52 / 52.0	100 / 8.3
VIRGO	6	41 / 38.0	67 / 62.0	108 / 9.0
LIBRA	7	51 / 42.5	69 / 57.5	120 / 10.0
SCORPIO	8	37 / 38.9	58 / 61.1	95 / 7.9
SAGITTARIUS	9	46 / 47.9	50 / 52.1	96 / 8.0
CAPRICORN	10	46 / 42.2	63 / 57.8	109 / 9.1
AQUARIUS	11	49 / 63.6	28 / 36.4	77 / 6.4
PISCES	12	37 / 38.9	58 / 61.1	95 / 7.9
	COLUMN TOTAL	551 / 45.8	651 / 54.2	1202 / 100.0

NUMBER OF MISSING OBSERVATIONS = 271

[1]With releases before 3.0, replace the CROSSTABS command with the following:

```
CROSSTABS ZODIAC BY SATJOB
OPTIONS 3
```

9.6 Fitting A Logit Model

To test whether zodiac sign and job satisfaction are independent, a log-linear model can be fit to the data in Figure 9.5. If the two variables are independent, a model without the interaction term should be sufficient. In such models, no distinction is made between independent and dependent variables. Zodiac sign and job satisfaction are both used to estimate the expected number of cases in each cell.

When one variable is thought to depend on the others, a special class of log-linear models, called *logit models*, can be used to examine the relationship between the dichotomous dependent variable, such as job satisfaction, and one or more independent variables. Let's examine the relationship between job satisfaction and zodiac sign, considering job satisfaction as the dependent variable and zodiac sign as independent.

In many statistical procedures, a dichotomous dependent variable is coded as having values of 0 or 1, and subsequent calculations are based on these values. In a logit model, the dependent variable is not the actual value of the variable but the log odds. An odds is the ratio of the frequency that an event occurs and the frequency that it does not occur. For example, from Figure 9.5 the observed frequency of an Arien's being very satisfied with his job is 45, while the observed frequency of an Arien's being not very satisfied with his job is 46. The estimated odds that an Arien is very satisfied are 45 to 46, or 0.98. This means that an Arien is about equally likely to be very satisfied or not very satisfied. Similarly, the odds for an Aquarian of being very satisfied are 1.25 (49/28), indicating that Aquarians are somewhat more likely to be very satisfied than unsatisfied. The odds can also be interpreted as the ratio of two probabilities—the probability that an Arien is very satisfied and the probability that an Arien is not very satisfied.

Let's consider how a logit model can be derived from the usual log-linear model. In a saturated log-linear model, the log of the number of very satisfied Ariens can be expressed as

$$\ln F_{11} = \mu + \lambda^{\text{very satisfied}} + \lambda^{\text{Ariens}} + \lambda^{\text{very satisfied|Ariens}} \qquad \textbf{Equation 9.6a}$$

Similarly, the log of the number of unsatisfied Ariens is

$$\ln F_{12} = \mu + \lambda^{\text{unsatisfied}} + \lambda^{\text{Ariens}} + \lambda^{\text{unsatisfied|Arien}} \qquad \textbf{Equation 9.6b}$$

The log of the ratio of the two frequencies is called a "logit." Recalling that the log of the ratio is

$$\ln (F_{11}/F_{12}) = \ln F_{11} - \ln F_{12} \qquad \textbf{Equation 9.6c}$$

we can compute the logit for Ariens as

$$\ln (F_{11}/F_{12}) = (\mu\text{-}\mu) + (\lambda^{\text{satisfied}} - \lambda^{\text{unsatisfied}}) + (\lambda^{\text{Ariens}} - \lambda^{\text{Ariens}}) + (\lambda^{\text{very satisfied|Arien}} - \lambda^{\text{unsatisfied|Arien}}) \qquad \textbf{Equation 9.6d}$$

Equation 9.6d can be considerably simplified. Note first that all the μ and λ^{Arien} terms cancel. Next, remember that the lambda terms must sum to 0 over all categories of a variable. For a variable that has two categories, this means that the values of the lambda parameters are equal in absolute value but opposite in sign. Thus, $\lambda^{very\ satisfied} = -\lambda^{unsatisfied}$, and $\lambda^{very\ satisfied—Arien} = -\ \lambda^{unsatisfied—Arien}$. Using these observations, the previous equation can be expressed as

$$\ln\,(F_{11}/F_{12}) = 2\ (\lambda^{satisfied} + \lambda^{satisfied—Arien}) \quad \textbf{Equation 9.6e}$$

Thus, the logit is a function of the same lambda parameters that appear in the general log-linear model.

The the output for a logit model differs somewhat from the usual log-linear model. As shown in Figure 9.6, the percentages are not based on the total table count but on the counts in each category of the independent variable. Thus, the percentages sum to 100 for each zodiac sign. For example, 49.5% of all Ariens are very satisfied with their jobs, while 50.5% are not. Since the logit model is saturated, the observed and expected frequencies are equal and all of the residuals are 0.

Figure 9.6 Observed and expected frequencies for the saturated logit model

```
LOGLINEAR SATJOB(1,2) BY ZODIAC(1,12)
  /DESIGN SATJOB SATJOB BY ZODIAC
```

Observed, Expected Frequencies and Residuals

Factor	Code	OBS. count & PCT.	EXP. count & PCT.	Residual	Std. Resid.	Adj. Resid.
SATJOB	VERY SAT					
ZODIAC	ARIES	45.00 (49.45)	45.00 (49.45)	.0000	.0000	.0000
ZODIAC	TAURUS	42.00 (43.30)	42.00 (43.30)	.0000	.0000	.0000
ZODIAC	GEMINI	61.00 (53.04)	61.00 (53.04)	.0000	.0000	.0000
ZODIAC	CANCER	48.00 (48.48)	48.00 (48.48)	.0000	.0000	.0000
ZODIAC	LEO	48.00 (48.00)	48.00 (48.00)	.0000	.0000	.0000
ZODIAC	VIRGO	41.00 (37.96)	41.00 (37.96)	.0000	.0000	.0000
ZODIAC	LIBRA	51.00 (42.50)	51.00 (42.50)	.0000	.0000	.0000
ZODIAC	SCORPIO	37.00 (38.95)	37.00 (38.95)	.0000	.0000	.0000
ZODIAC	SAGITTAR	46.00 (47.92)	46.00 (47.92)	.0000	.0000	.0000
ZODIAC	CAPRICOR	46.00 (42.20)	46.00 (42.20)	.0000	.0000	.0000
ZODIAC	AQUARIUS	49.00 (63.64)	49.00 (63.64)	.0000	.0000	.0000
ZODIAC	PISCES	37.00 (38.95)	37.00 (38.95)	.0000	.0000	.0000
SATJOB	NOT VERY					
ZODIAC	ARIES	46.00 (50.55)	46.00 (50.55)	.0000	.0000	.0000
ZODIAC	TAURUS	55.00 (56.70)	55.00 (56.70)	.0000	.0000	.0000
ZODIAC	GEMINI	54.00 (46.96)	54.00 (46.96)	.0000	.0000	.0000
ZODIAC	CANCER	51.00 (51.52)	51.00 (51.52)	.0000	.0000	.0000
ZODIAC	LEO	52.00 (52.00)	52.00 (52.00)	.0000	.0000	.0000
ZODIAC	VIRGO	67.00 (62.04)	67.00 (62.04)	.0000	.0000	.0000
ZODIAC	LIBRA	69.00 (57.50)	69.00 (57.50)	.0000	.0000	.0000
ZODIAC	SCORPIO	58.00 (61.05)	58.00 (61.05)	.0000	.0000	.0000
ZODIAC	SAGITTAR	50.00 (52.08)	50.00 (52.08)	.0000	.0000	.0000
ZODIAC	CAPRICOR	63.00 (57.80)	63.00 (57.80)	.0000	.0000	.0000
ZODIAC	AQUARIUS	28.00 (36.36)	28.00 (36.36)	.0000	.0000	.0000
ZODIAC	PISCES	58.00 (61.05)	58.00 (61.05)	.0000	.0000	.0000

9.7 Parameter Estimates

In the logit model, the parameter estimates displayed (Figure 9.7) are the actual lambdas, not twice lambda. Thus, the values are identical to those obtained in the log-linear model. No coefficient is printed for the zodiac variable since it does not directly appear in the logit model (see Equation 9.6e).

Figure 9.7 Parameter estimates for the logit model

```
LOGLINEAR SATJOB(1,2) BY ZODIAC(1,12)
  /PRINT=ESTIM
  /DESIGN
```

Estimates for Parameters

SATJOB

Parameter	Coeff.	Std. Err.	Z-Value	Lower 95 CI	Upper 95 CI
1	-.0767137815	.02943	-2.60689	-.13439	-.01904

SATJOB BY ZODIAC

Parameter	Coeff.	Std. Err.	Z-Value	Lower 95 CI	Upper 95 CI
13	.0657243282	.10012	.65644	-.13052	.26197
14	-.0581180019	.09805	-.59273	-.25030	.13406
15	.1376586903	.09022	1.52584	-.03917	.31449
16	.0464014706	.09639	.48139	-.14252	.23533
17	.0366924277	.09598	.38228	-.15143	.22482
18	-.1688464948	.09517	-1.77422	-.35537	.01768
19	-.0744266544	.08928	-.83367	-.24941	.10055
20	-.1480487674	.10044	-1.47398	-.34491	.04882
21	.0350229771	.09778	.35817	-.15663	.22668
22	-.0805328834	.09328	-.86331	-.26337	.10230
23	.3565216755	.11206	3.18144	.13688	.57617

As in the general log-linear model, the deviation parameter estimates (the default) can be used to predict the expected cell frequencies. However, in a logit model, instead of predicting individual cell frequencies, the log odds are predicted. For example, the predicted log odds for the Ariens is

$$\begin{aligned} \ln(F_{11}/F_{12}) &= 2 \times (\lambda^{satjob} + \lambda^{satjob|Arien}) \\ &= 2\,(-0.0767 + 0.0657) = -0.022 \\ F_{11}/F_{12} &= e^{-0.022} = 0.98 \end{aligned}$$ **Equation 9.7**

Since this is a saturated model, the predicted odds equal the observed odds, the ratio of satisfied to dissatisfied Ariens (45/46).

9.8 Measures of Dispersion and Association

When a model is formulated with one classification variable considered as dependent, it is possible to analyze the dispersion or spread in the dependent variable. Two statistics that are used to measure the spread of a nominal variable are Shannon's entropy measure

$$H = -\sum p_j \log p_j$$ **Equation 9.8a**

and Gini's concentration measure:

$$C = 1 - \sum p_j^2$$ **Equation 9.8b**

Using either of these measures, it is possible to subdivide the total dispersion of the dependent variable into that explained by the model and the residual, or unexplained, variance. Figure 9.8 contains the analysis of dispersion for the satisfaction and zodiac sign when a saturated logit model is fit.

Based on the analysis of dispersion, it is possible to calculate statistics similar to R^2 in regression that indicate what proportion of the total dispersion in the dependent variable is attributable to the model. In Figure 9.8, when dispersion is measured by the entropy criterion, the ratio of the dispersion "explained" by the

Figure 9.8 Analysis of dispersion

Analysis of Dispersion

Source of Variation	Dispersion Entropy	Dispersion Concentration	DF
Due to Model	10.564	10.450	
Due to Residual	818.434	586.390	
Total	828.998	596.840	1201

Measures of Association

Entropy = .012744
Concentration = .017509

model to the total dispersion is 0.013. When measured by the concentration criterion it is 0.0175. These values can be interpreted as measures of association. Although it is tempting to interpret the magnitudes of these measures similarly to R^2 in regression, this may be misleading since the coefficients may be small even when the variables are strongly related (Haberman, 1982). It appears that the coefficients are best interpreted in the light of experience.

9.9 Fitting an Unsaturated Logit Model

As discussed in Chapter 8, a saturated model exactly fits the data. This is also true for a logit model, which contains all interaction terms between the dependent variable and all combinations of the independent variables. Alternative models can be formed by deleting some terms from the saturated logit model. For example, to ascertain whether job satisfaction and zodiac sign are independent, we need to fit a logit model without the interaction term between job satisfaction and zodiac sign. Figure 9.9a contains the statistics for the cells and the chi-square values when the interaction term is eliminated.

Figure 9.9a Statistics for the unsaturated model

```
LOGLINEAR SATJOB(1,2) BY ZODIAC(1,12)
  /DESIGN=SATJOB
```

Observed, Expected Frequencies and Residuals

Factor	Code	OBS. count & PCT.	EXP. count & PCT.	Residual	Std. Resid.	Adj. Resid.
SATJOB	VERY SAT					
ZODIAC	ARIES	45.00 (49.45)	41.71 (45.84)	3.2854	.5087	.7189
ZODIAC	TAURUS	42.00 (43.30)	44.47 (45.84)	-2.4651	-.3697	-.5239
ZODIAC	GEMINI	61.00 (53.04)	52.72 (45.84)	8.2837	1.1409	1.6302
ZODIAC	CANCER	48.00 (48.48)	45.38 (45.84)	2.6181	.3886	.5513
ZODIAC	LEO	48.00 (48.00)	45.84 (45.84)	2.1597	.3190	.4527
ZODIAC	VIRGO	41.00 (37.96)	49.51 (45.84)	-8.5075	-1.2091	-1.7222
ZODIAC	LIBRA	51.00 (42.50)	55.01 (45.84)	-4.0083	-.5404	-.7740
ZODIAC	SCORPIO	37.00 (38.95)	43.55 (45.84)	-6.5483	-.9923	-1.4050
ZODIAC	SAGITTAR	46.00 (47.92)	44.01 (45.84)	1.9933	.3005	.4257
ZODIAC	CAPRICOR	46.00 (42.20)	49.97 (45.84)	-3.9659	-.5611	-.7995
ZODIAC	AQUARIUS	49.00 (63.64)	35.30 (45.84)	13.7030	2.3065	3.2395
ZODIAC	PISCES	37.00 (38.95)	43.55 (45.84)	-6.5483	-.9923	-1.4050
SATJOB	NOT VERY					
ZODIAC	ARIES	46.00 (50.55)	49.29 (54.16)	-3.2854	-.4680	-.7189
ZODIAC	TAURUS	55.00 (56.70)	52.53 (54.16)	2.4651	.3401	.5239
ZODIAC	GEMINI	54.00 (46.96)	62.28 (54.16)	-8.2837	-1.0496	-1.6302
ZODIAC	CANCER	51.00 (51.52)	53.62 (54.16)	-2.6181	-.3575	-.5513
ZODIAC	LEO	52.00 (52.00)	54.16 (54.16)	-2.1597	-.2935	-.4527
ZODIAC	VIRGO	67.00 (62.04)	58.49 (54.16)	8.5075	1.1124	1.7222
ZODIAC	LIBRA	69.00 (57.50)	64.99 (54.16)	4.0083	.4972	.7740
ZODIAC	SCORPIO	58.00 (61.05)	51.45 (54.16)	6.5483	.9129	1.4050
ZODIAC	SAGITTAR	50.00 (52.08)	51.99 (54.16)	-1.9933	-.2764	-.4257
ZODIAC	CAPRICOR	63.00 (57.80)	59.03 (54.16)	3.9659	.5162	.7995
ZODIAC	AQUARIUS	28.00 (36.36)	41.70 (54.16)	13.7030	2.1210	-3.2395
ZODIAC	PISCES	58.00 (61.05)	51.45 (54.16)	6.5483	.9129	1.4050

Goodness-of-Fit test statistics

Likelihood Ratio Chi Square = 21.12888 DF = 11 P = .032
Pearson Chi Square = 21.04523 DF = 11 P = .033

The chi-square values indicate that an independence model does not fit the data well. The observed significance level is about 0.03. The adjusted residuals for the Aquarians are particularly large, so the model fits very poorly for this zodiac sign. The proportion of very satisfied Aquarians is substantially larger than expected.

Figure 9.9b is a plot of the observed values against the adjusted residuals. Two residuals are large in absolute value, and there may be a linear trend.

Figure 9.9b Plot of observed counts and adjusted residuals

```
LOGLINEAR SATJOB(1,2) BY ZODIAC(1,12)
  /PLOT=RESID
  /DESIGN=SATJOB
```

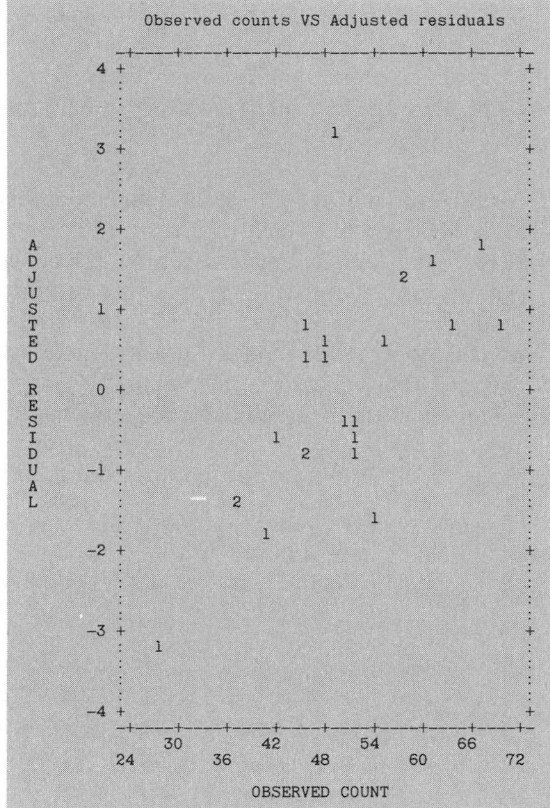

The results obtained from fitting a logit model without the interaction term are exactly identical to those that would be obtained if the usual log-linear model of independence were fit. The only difference is that, in the logit model, the parameter estimates for the zodiac values are not printed, since they do not appear directly in the model. (The LOGLINEAR procedure, unlike HILOGLINEAR, produces parameter estimates for unsaturated models.)

9.10 Fitting a More Complicated Logit Model

Since earning money is usually an important reason for working, it is interesting to see what happens when income is included in the logit model of job satisfaction.

For the analysis, respondents' income is grouped into four categories, each containing roughly the same number of cases. Figure 9.10a contains the observed frequencies for the crosstabulation of job satisfaction with zodiac sign and income level.

Figure 9.10a Three-way crosstabulation from TABLES

```
TABLES /FORMAT=CWIDTH(15,7)
  /FTOTAL=T1'COLUMN TOTAL' T2'ROW TOTAL'
  /TABLE=ZODIAC + T1 BY SATJOB > (RINCOME+ T2)
  /STATISTICS=COUNT(ZODIAC'') CPCT(ZODIAC' ':ZODIAC SATJOB)
```

	JOB OR HOUSEWORK									
	VERY SATISFIED					NOT VERY SATISFIED				
	RESPONDENT'S INCOME				ROW TOTAL	RESPONDENT'S INCOME				ROW TOTAL
	LESS THAN $6000	$6000 TO $14,999	$15,000 TO $24,999	$25,000 AND UP		LESS THAN $6000	$6000 TO $14,999	$15,000 TO $24,999	$25,000 AND UP	
RESPONDENT'S ASTROLOGICAL SIGN										
ARIES	8 29.6%	9 33.3%	2 7.4%	8 29.6%	27 100.0%	9 31.0%	10 34.5%	5 17.2%	5 17.2%	29 100.0%
TAURUS	7 25.0%	10 35.7%	10 35.7%	1 3.6%	28 100.0%	9 20.5%	21 47.7%	6 13.6%	8 18.2%	44 100.0%
GEMINI	8 17.4%	17 37.0%	9 19.6%	12 26.1%	46 100.0%	16 36.4%	14 31.8%	9 20.5%	5 11.4%	44 100.0%
CANCER	8 20.0%	11 27.5%	14 35.0%	7 17.5%	40 100.0%	11 28.9%	14 36.8%	10 26.3%	3 7.9%	38 100.0%
LEO	7 20.6%	13 38.2%	8 23.5%	6 17.6%	34 100.0%	12 33.3%	11 30.6%	9 25.0%	4 11.1%	36 100.0%
VIRGO	6 16.7%	9 25.0%	12 33.3%	9 25.0%	36 100.0%	5 10.4%	16 33.3%	23 47.9%	4 8.3%	48 100.0%
LIBRA	4 12.5%	10 31.3%	9 28.1%	9 28.1%	32 100.0%	15 26.8%	19 33.9%	11 19.6%	11 19.6%	56 100.0%
SCORPIO	7 25.9%	10 37.0%	6 22.2%	4 14.8%	27 100.0%	10 23.3%	11 25.6%	15 34.9%	7 16.3%	43 100.0%
SAGITTARIUS	7 18.9%	9 24.3%	12 32.4%	9 24.3%	37 100.0%	7 18.9%	13 35.1%	10 27.0%	7 18.9%	37 100.0%
CAPRICORN	3 8.6%	8 22.9%	12 34.3%	12 34.3%	35 100.0%	10 22.7%	14 31.8%	9 20.5%	11 25.0%	44 100.0%
AQUARIUS	12 30.8%	10 25.6%	11 28.2%	6 15.4%	39 100.0%	5 22.7%	9 40.9%	5 22.7%	3 13.6%	22 100.0%
PISCES	5 17.2%	8 27.6%	8 27.6%	8 27.6%	29 100.0%	15 31.3%	12 25.0%	10 20.8%	11 22.9%	48 100.0%
COLUMN TOTAL	82 20.0%	124 30.2%	113 27.6%	91 22.2%	410 100.0%	124 25.4%	164 33.5%	122 24.9%	79 16.2%	489 100.0%

Consider a logit model that includes only the effects of job satisfaction, job satisfaction by income, and job satisfaction by zodiac. Based on the statistics displayed in Figure 9.10b, it appears that the logit model without the three-way interaction of job satisfaction, income, and zodiac sign fits the data well. The observed significance level for the goodness-of-fit statistic is about 0.5. The diagnostic plots of adjusted residuals give no indication that there are suspicious departures from the model.

Figure 9.10b Goodness of fit for the expanded logit model

```
LOGLINEAR SATJOB(1,2) BY ZODIAC(1,12) RINCOME(1,4)
  /DESIGN=SATJOB, SATJOB BY ZODIAC, SATJOB BY RINCOME
```

```
Goodness-of-Fit test statistics

  Likelihood Ratio Chi Square =    31.62898    DF = 33  P =  .535
            Pearson Chi Square =    30.67426    DF = 33  P =  .583
```

Deviation parameter estimates for the logit model are shown in Figure 9.10c. The SATJOB parameter estimate is negative, indicating that overall the proportion of people highly satisfied with their jobs is less than the proportion that are dissatisfied. The coefficients corresponding to the RINCOME by SATJOB effect show the increase or decrease in the log-odds ratio associated with each income category. The parameter estimate shows that there is a progression from a fairly large negative value, −0.145, to a fairly large positive value, 0.166. (The estimate for the last income category is not printed. It is obtained as the negative of the sum of the previous estimates.) Thus, it appears that lower income categories are associated with less job satisfaction than higher income categories. The parameter estimates for the ZODIAC by SATJOB interaction give the contribution of each zodiac sign to job satisfaction. Again, negative values are associated with dissatisfied zodiac signs while positive values are associated with more content signs. The largest positive parameter estimate (parameter 12) is for the Aquarians, who as a group are the most satisfied.

Figure 9.10c Parameter estimates for the expanded logit model

```
LOGLINEAR SATJOB(1,2) BY ZODIAC(1,12) RINCOME(1,4)
  /PRINT=ESTIM
  /DESIGN=SATJOB, SATJOB BY ZODIAC, SATJOB BY RINCOME
```

Estimates for Parameters

SATJOB

Parameter	Coeff.	Std. Err.	Z-Value	Lower 95 CI	Upper 95 CI
1	-.0704541613	.03499	-2.01344	-.13904	-.00187

SATJOB BY ZODIAC

Parameter	Coeff.	Std. Err.	Z-Value	Lower 95 CI	Upper 95 CI
2	.0564737768	.12811	.44083	-.19462	.30757
3	-.1279033527	.11635	-1.09932	-.35594	.10014
4	.1140066820	.10289	1.10807	-.08765	.31567
5	.1178086027	.10963	1.07465	-.09706	.33267
6	.0689561722	.11512	.59900	-.15667	.29459
7	-.0802959724	.10761	-.74615	-.29122	.13063
8	-.2077153468	.10751	-1.93201	-.41844	.00301
9	-.1492020965	.11786	-1.26593	-.38021	.08180
10	.0683122274	.11222	.60873	-.15164	.28826
11	-.0634811554	.11004	-.57688	-.27916	.15220
12	.3845323775	.12723	3.02224	.13515	.63391

SATJOB BY RINCOME

Parameter	Coeff.	Std. Err.	Z-Value	Lower 95 CI	Upper 95 CI
13	-.1451090801	.06216	-2.33441	-.26694	-.02327
14	-.0643412033	.05513	-1.16708	-.17240	.04371
15	.0435190304	.05889	.73898	-.07191	.15894

Note that the logit is calculated as the ratio of the number of cases in the first category to the number of cases in the second category. If SATJOB had been coded so that the first value was for the dissatisfied category, positive parameter estimates would occur for dissatisfied signs.

The expected log odds for each combination of income and zodiac sign can be obtained from the coefficients in Figure 9.10c. For example, the predicted log odds for Ariens with incomes of less than $6,000 is

$$2(-0.0704 - 0.145 + 0.0565) = - .318$$ **Equation 9.10**

The expected odds are $e^{-0.318}$, or 0.728. Thus, Ariens in low income categories are less likely to be highly satisfied than dissatisfied. Predicted odds values for the other cells are found in a similar fashion.

9.11 The Equivalent Log-Linear Model

As previously discussed, logit models can also be formulated as log-linear models. However, not all terms that are in the log-linear model appear in the logit model, since logit models do not include relationships among the independent variables. When the odds ratios are formed, terms involving only the independent variables cancel, since for a particular combination of values of the independent variables, the effects are the same for both categories of the dependent variable.

Thus, the log-linear representation of a logit model contains additional terms for the independent variables. For example, the log-linear model that corresponds to the logit model described above has three additional terms: the main effect for zodiac, the main effect for income category, and the interaction between zodiac sign and income category (see Figure 9.11).

Figure 9.11 Goodness-of-fit statistics for the equivalent log linear model

```
LOGLINEAR SATJOB(1,2) ZODIAC(1,12) RINCOME(1,4)
 /DESIGN SATJOB ZODIAC RINCOME SATJOB BY ZODIAC
        SATJOB BY RINCOME ZODIAC BY RINCOME
```

```
Goodness-of-Fit test statistics

   Likelihood Ratio Chi Square =    31.62898    DF = 33   P =  .535
            Pearson Chi Square =    30.67426    DF = 33   P =  .583
```

9.12 MODELS FOR ORDINAL DATA

In many situations, the categorical variables used in log-linear models are ordinal in nature. For example, income levels range from low to high, as does interest in a product, or severity of a disease. Ordinal variables may result from grouping values of interval variables such as income or education, or they may arise when ordering, but not distance, between categories can be established. Happiness, interest, and opinions on various issues are measured on ordinal scales. Although "a lot" is more than "some," the actual distance between the two response categories cannot be determined. The additional information contained in the ordering of the categories can be incorporated into log-linear models, which may result in a more parsimonious representation of the data (see Agresti, 1984).

Let's consider some common models for ordinal data using the job satisfaction and income variables. Although only two categories of job satisfaction were used to illustrate logit models, there were actually four possible responses to the question: very satisfied, moderately satisfied, a little dissatisfied, and very dissatisfied. Figure 9.12 is the crosstabulation of job satisfaction and income categories. You can see that as salary increases so does job satisfaction, especially at the ends of the salary scale. Almost 10% of people earning less than $6,000 are very dissatisfied with their jobs, while only 4% of those earning $25,000 or more are very dissatisfied with theirs. Similarly, almost 54% of those earning over $25,000 are very satisfied with their jobs, while only 40% of those earning less than $6,000 are very satisfied.

Figure 9.12 Job satisfaction by income level from CROSSTABS

```
RECODE SATJOB (1=4) (2=3) (3=2) (4=1) (ELSE=SYSMIS)
VALUE LABELS SATJOB 1 'VERY DIS' 2 'A LITTLE' 3 'MOD SAT' 4 'VER SAT'/
             RINCOME 1 'LT 6000' 2 '6-15' 3 '15-25' '4 '25+'
CROSSTABS SATJOB BY RINCOME
  /CELLS=COLUMN
  /STATISTICS=CHISQ 2
```

```
- - - - - - - - - -  C R O S S T A B U L A T I O N   O F  - - - - - - - - - -
   SATJOB     JOB OR HOUSEWORK
BY  RINCOME    RESPONDENT'S INCOME
- - - - - - - - - - - - - - - - - - - - - - - - - - - - - - - - - -   PAGE  1 OF  1
```

SATJOB	COUNT / COL PCT	RINCOME LT 6000 1	6-15 2	15-25 3	25+ 4	ROW TOTAL
VERY DIS	1	20 9.7	22 7.6	13 5.5	7 4.1	62 6.9
A LITTLE	2	24 11.7	38 13.1	28 11.9	18 10.5	108 12.0
MOD SAT	3	80 38.8	104 36.0	81 34.5	54 31.6	319 35.4
VER SAT	4	82 39.8	125 43.3	113 48.1	92 53.8	412 45.7
	COLUMN TOTAL	206 22.9	289 32.1	235 26.1	171 19.0	901 100.0

CHI-SQUARE	D.F.	SIGNIFICANCE	MIN E.F.	CELLS WITH E.F.| 5
11.98857	9	0.2140	11.767	NONE

NUMBER OF MISSING OBSERVATIONS = 572

A variety of log-linear models that use the ordering of the job satisfaction and income variables can be entertained. Some of the models depend on the "scores" assigned to each category of response. Sometimes these may be arbitrary, since the actual distances between the categories are unknown. In this example, scores from 1 to 4 are assigned to both the income and job satisfaction categories. Other scores, such as the midpoints of the salary categories, might also be considered.

Three types of models will be considered for these data. One is the linear-by-linear association model, which uses the ordering of both variables. Another is the row effects model, which uses only the ordering of the column variable. The third is the column-effects model, which uses the ordering of the row variable.

9.13 The Linear-by-Linear Association Model

The linear-by-linear association model for two variables can be expressed as

$$\ln \hat{F}_{ij} = \mu + \lambda_i^X + \lambda_j^Y + B(U_i - \overline{U})(V_j - \overline{V}) \qquad \textbf{Equation 9.13}$$

---

[2]With releases before 3.0, replace the CROSSTABS command with the following:

```
CROSSTABS SATJOB BY RINCOME
OPTIONS 4
STATISTICS 1
```

In this model, μ and the two lambda parameters are the usual log-linear terms for the overall mean and the main effects of income and job satisfaction. What differs is the inclusion of the term involving B. The coefficient B is essentially a regression coefficient that, for a particular cell, is multiplied by the scores assigned to that cell for income and job satisfaction. If the two variables are independent, the coefficient should be close to 0. (However, a coefficient of 0 does not necessarily imply independence since the association between the two variables may be non-linear.) If the coefficient is positive, more cases are expected to fall in cells with large scores or small scores for both variables than would be expected if the two variables are independent. If the coefficient is negative, an excess of cases are expected in cells that have small values for one variable and large for the other.

Consider Figure 9.13a, which contains the deviation parameter estimates for the linear-by-linear association model for job satisfaction and income. The coefficient labeled B is the regression coefficient. It is positive and large when compared to its standard error, indicating that there is a positive association between income and job satisfaction. That is, as income increases or decreases, so does job satisfaction. The goodness-of-fit statistics displayed in Figure 9.13b indicate that the linear-by-linear interaction model fits the data very well. Inclusion of one additional parameter in the model has changed the observed significance level from 0.21 for the independence model (see Figure 9.12) to 0.97 for the linear-by-linear interaction model (see Figure 9.13b).

Figure 9.13a Parameter estimates for the linear-by-linear model

```
COMPUTE B=RINCOME*SATJOB
LOGLINEAR SATJOB(1,4) RINCOME(1,4) WITH B
  /PRINT=ESTIM
  /DESIGN=SATJOB RINCOME B
```

```
Estimates for Parameters

SATJOB

 Parameter        Coeff.     Std. Err.      Z-Value Lower 95 CI Upper 95 CI

        1  -.6373902979       .15514     -4.10855     -.94146     -.33332
        2  -.3298650538       .09273     -3.55723     -.51162     -.14811
        3   .4926713610       .06961      7.07754      .35623      .62911

RINCOME

 Parameter        Coeff.     Std. Err.      Z-Value Lower 95 CI Upper 95 CI

        4   .4628350833       .18277      2.53232      .10460      .82107
        5   .4523050202       .08199      5.51637      .29160      .61301
        6  -.1140864252       .07981     -1.42945     -.27052      .04234

B

 Parameter        Coeff.     Std. Err.      Z-Value Lower 95 CI Upper 95 CI

        7   .1119394092       .03641      3.07462      .04058      .18330
```

Figure 9.13b Goodness of fit for the linear-by-linear model

```
Goodness-of-Fit test statistics

  Likelihood Ratio Chi Square =    2.38592    DF = 8  P =  .967
          Pearson Chi Square =    2.32965    DF = 8  P =  .969
```

9.14 Row- and Column-Effects Models

In a row-effects model, only the ordinal nature of the column variable is used. For each row, a separate slope based on the values of the column variables is estimated. The magnitude and sign of the coefficient indicates whether cases are more or less likely to fall in a column with a high or low score, as compared to the independence model.

Consider the row-effects model when job satisfaction is the row variable. The coefficients for each row are displayed in Figure 9.14a under the heading SATJOB BY COV. The first coefficient is negative, indicating that very dissatisfied people are less likely to be in high income categories than the independence model would predict. The next two coefficients are positive but small, indicating that there is not much difference from the independence model in these rows. The fourth coefficient, which is not displayed, is the negative of the sum of the previous three coefficients (see Section 9.21). Its value is 0.17, indicating that there is an excess of respondents in the high income category who classify themselves as very satisfied. Overall, the row-effects model fits quite well, as shown in the goodness-of-fit statistics in Figure 9.14b. The observed significance level, 0.998, is quite large.

Figure 9.14a Parameter estimates for the row-effects model

```
COMPUTE COV=RINCOME
LOGLINEAR SATJOB(1,4) RINCOME(1,4) WITH COV
  /PRINT=ESTIM
  /DESIGN=SATJOB, RINCOME, SATJOB BY COV
```

```
Estimates for Parameters

SATJOB

 Parameter        Coeff.     Std. Err.      Z-Value  Lower 95 CI  Upper 95 CI

         1  -.5315173884       .23757      -2.23727      -.99716      -.06587
         2  -.5365551858       .20123      -2.66635      -.93097      -.14214
         3   .6100166132       .14540       4.19540       .32503       .89500

RINCOME

 Parameter        Coeff.     Std. Err.      Z-Value  Lower 95 CI  Upper 95 CI

         4   .0324159194       .07298        .44420      -.11062       .17545
         5   .3101582155       .05654       5.48563       .19934       .42098
         6   .0299955391       .05864        .51154      -.08493       .14493

SATJOB BY COV

 Parameter        Coeff.     Std. Err.      Z-Value  Lower 95 CI  Upper 95 CI

         7  -.2159732482       .10077      -2.14329      -.41348      -.01847
         8   .0340580646       .07897        .43129      -.12072       .18884
         9   .0071007552       .05807        .12228      -.10671       .12092
```

Figure 9.14b Goodness of fit for the row-effects model

```
Goodness-of-Fit test statistics

   Likelihood Ratio Chi Square =      .52562     DF = 6   P =   .998
            Pearson Chi Square =      .52573     DF = 6   P =   .998
```

The column-effects model, which treats job satisfaction as an ordinal variable and ignores the ranking of the income categories, also fits the data reasonably well, as shown in Figure 9.14c. The observed significance level is 0.91. In fact, all three models that incorporate the ordinal nature of the classification variables result in good fit. Of the three, the linear-by-linear model is the most parsimonious since, when compared to the independence model, it estimates only one additional parameter. The row- and column-effects models are particular useful when only one classification variable is ordinal or when both variables are ordinal but a linear trend across categories exists only for one.

Figure 9.14c Goodness of fit for the column-effects model

```
COMPUTE COV=SATJOB
LOGLINEAR SATJOB(1,4) RINCOME(1,4) WITH COV
  /DESIGN=SATJOB, RINCOME, COV BY RINCOME
```

```
Goodness-of-Fit test statistics

  Likelihood Ratio Chi Square =     2.13725     DF = 6  P =  .907
            Pearson Chi Square =     2.11052     DF = 6  P =  .909
```

9.15 INCOMPLETE TABLES

All models examined so far have been based on complete tables. That is, all cells of the crosstabulation tables can have nonzero observed frequencies. This is not necessarily the case. For example, if you are studying the association between types of surgery and sex of the patient, the cell corresponding to cesarian sections for males must be 0. This is termed a *fixed zero cell,* since no cases can ever fall into it. Also, certain types of models "ignore" cells by treating them as if they were fixed zeroes. Fixed-zero cells lead to incomplete tables, and special provisions must be made during analysis.

Cells in which the observed frequency is zero but in which it is *possible* to have cases are sometimes called *random zeroes.* For example, in a cross-classification of occupation and ethnic origin, the cell corresponding to Lithuanian sword-swallowers would probably be a random zero.

If a table has many cells with small expected values (say, less than 5), the chi-squared approximation for the goodness-of-fit statistics may be inadequate. In this case, pooling of categories should be considered.

There are many types of models for analyzing incomplete tables. In the next section, we will consider one of the simplest, the quasi-independence model, which considers the diagonal entries of a square table to be fixed zeroes.

9.16 Testing Real Against Ideal

What is the "ideal" number of children? The answer to the question is obviously influenced by various factors, including the size of the family in which one was raised. The 1982 General Social Survey asked respondents how many siblings they have as well as how many children should be in the "ideal" family. Figure 9.16

contains the crosstabulation of the number of children in the respondent's family and the number of children perceived as "ideal."

Figure 9.16 Actual children by ideal number of children from CROSSTABS

```
CROSSTABS IDEAL BY REAL
  /CELLS=COLUMN
  /STATISTICS=CHISQ³
```

```
- - - - - - - - - -  C R O S S T A B U L A T I O N   O F  - -
   IDEAL     IDEAL NUMBER OF CHILDREN
BY  REAL      ACTUAL NUMBER OF CHILDREN
- - - - - - - - - - - - - - - - - - - - - - - - - - - - - - - -

                   REAL
          COUNT  |
         COL PCT |0-1       2         3-4       5 +        ROW
                 |                                         TOTAL
                 |    1.00|     2.00|     3.00|     4.00|
IDEAL    --------+--------+---------+---------+---------+
               1 |     2  |     6   |    20   |    26   |     54
  0-1            |   2.7  |   3.0   |   4.5   |   3.9   |    3.9
                 +--------+---------+---------+---------+
               2 |    55  |   138   |   278   |   335   |    806
  2              |  74.3  |  68.7   |  62.3   |  49.7   |   57.8
                 +--------+---------+---------+---------+
               3 |    16  |    48   |   139   |   287   |    490
  3-4            |  21.6  |  23.9   |  31.2   |  42.6   |   35.1
                 +--------+---------+---------+---------+
               4 |     1  |     9   |     9   |    26   |     45
  5 +            |   1.4  |   4.5   |   2.0   |   3.9   |    3.2
                 +--------+---------+---------+---------+
          COLUMN      74       201       446       674      1395
           TOTAL     5.3      14.4      32.0      48.3     100.0

 CHI-SQUARE    D.F.       SIGNIFICANCE        MIN E.F.       CELLS WITH E.F.| 5
 ----------    ----       ------------        --------       -----------------

  46.30171       9           0.0000             2.387        2 OF    16 ( 12.5%)

NUMBER OF MISSING OBSERVATIONS =      111
```

To test the hypothesis that the "real" number of children and the "ideal" number are independent, the chi-squared test of independence can be used. From Figure 9.16, the chi-squared value is 46 with 9 degrees of freedom. The observed significance level is very small, indicating that it is unlikely that the numbers of real children and ideal children are independent.

9.17 Quasi-Independence

There are many reasons why the independence model may not fit the data. One possible explanation is that, in fact, the real and ideal sizes are fairly close to one another. However, if we ignore the diagonal entries of the table, we may find that the remaining cells are independent, in other words, that there is no tendency for children from small families to want large families or children from large families to want small families.

This hypothesis may be tested by ignoring the diagonal entries of the table and testing independence for the remaining cells, using the test of *quasi-independence*. Figure 9.17 contains the observed and expected cell frequencies for this model. Note that all diagonal entries have values of zero for observed and expected cell frequencies. However, the residuals and goodness-of-fit statistics indicate that the quasi-independence model does not fit well either.

---

[3]With releases before 3.0, replace the CROSSTABS command with the following:

```
CROSSTABS IDEAL BY REAL
OPTIONS 4
STATISTICS 1
```

Figure 9.17 Statistics for the quasi-independence model

```
COMPUTE WEIGHT=1
IF (IDEAL EQ REAL) WEIGHT=0
LOGLINEAR REAL IDEAL(1,4)
  /CWEIGHT=WEIGHT
  /DESIGN=REAL IDEAL
```

```
Observed, Expected Frequencies and Residuals

   Factor          Code         OBS. count & PCT.   EXP. count & PCT.    Residual   Std. Resid.   Adj. Resid.

REAL             0-1
 IDEAL            0-1               .00 (  .00)         .00 (  .00)       .0000        .0000        .0000
 IDEAL            2               55.00 ( 5.05)       39.97 ( 3.67)     15.0308       2.3775       3.7476
 IDEAL            3-4             16.00 ( 1.47)       30.06 ( 2.76)    -14.0590      -2.5643      -3.5402
 IDEAL            5 +              1.00 (  .09)        1.97 (  .18)      -.9718       -.6921       -.7423

REAL             2
 IDEAL            0-1              6.00 (  .55)        5.34 (  .49)       .6554        .2835        .3143
 IDEAL            2                 .00 (  .00)         .00 (  .00)       .0000        .0000        .0000
 IDEAL            3-4             48.00 ( 4.40)       54.11 ( 4.96)     -6.1061       -.8301      -2.3969
 IDEAL            5 +              9.00 (  .83)        3.55 (  .33)      5.4508       2.8933       3.3175

REAL             3-4
 IDEAL            0-1             20.00 ( 1.83)       20.30 ( 1.86)      -.2973       -.0660        .0879
 IDEAL            2              278.00 (25.50)      273.22 (25.07)      4.7763        .2890       1.2556
 IDEAL            3-4               .00 (  .00)         .00 (  .00)       .0000        .0000        .0000
 IDEAL            5 +              9.00 (  .83)       13.48 ( 1.24)     -4.4790      -1.2200      -2.3296

REAL             5 +
 IDEAL            0-1             26.00 ( 2.39)       26.36 ( 2.42)      -.3580       -.0697       -.1025
 IDEAL            2              335.00 (30.73)      354.81 (32.55)    -19.8071      -1.0515      -3.7838
 IDEAL            3-4            287.00 (26.33)      266.83 (24.48)     20.1652       1.2345       4.4107
 IDEAL            5 +               .00 (  .00)         .00 (  .00)       .0000        .0000        .0000
- - - - - - - - - - - - - - - - - - - - - - - - - - - - - - - - - - - - - - - - - - - - - - - - - - - -

Goodness-of-Fit test statistics

   Likelihood Ratio Chi Square =   24.61341    DF = 5  P =  .000
            Pearson Chi Square =   26.05831    DF = 5  P =  .000
```

9.18 Symmetry Models

If the diagonal terms of Figure 9.16 are ignored, the table can be viewed as consisting of two triangles. The lower triangle consists of cells in which the ideal number of children is larger than the actual number of children. The upper triangle consists of cells in which the ideal number is smaller than the actual number. A three-variable representation of the data using the two lower triangles (the upper triangle is rotated around the diagonal) and the triangle number as a third variable is shown in Table 9.18.

Table 9.18 Two triangles for the symmetry model

Lower-left Triangle 1 (real > ideal)

	1	2	3	4
1				
2	55			
3	16	48		
4	1	9	9	

Upper-right (rotated) Triangle 2 (real < ideal)

	1	2	3	4
1				
2	6			
3	20	278		
4	26	335	287	

Several hypotheses about the two triangles may be of interest. One is the symmetry hypothesis. That is, are the corresponding entries of the two triangles equal? In a log-linear model framework, this implies that the main effects for the row and column variables, as well as their interaction, are the same for the two triangles. The log-linear representation of this model is

$$\ln(\hat{F}_{ijk}) = \mu + \lambda_i^{Real} + \lambda_j^{Ideal} + \lambda_i^{Real}{}_j^{Ideal} \qquad \text{Equation 9.18a}$$

Figure 9.18a contains the LOGLINEAR output for this hypothesis. The expected values are simply the average of the observed frequencies for the two cells. Thus, the expected values for corresponding cells are are always equal. For example, the first expected frequency, 30.5, is the average of 55 and 6. Note also that the second triangle has been "rotated" into lower-triangular form without changing the variable names, so that the variables are mislabeled in Triangle 2. For example, the entry labeled TRIANGLE 2, IDEAL 2, SIBS 1 is really the entry for an ideal number of children of 0 or 1 and an actual number of 2.

Figure 9.18a Statistics for the symmetry model

```
NUMERIC TRIANGLE
DO IF IDEAL GE REAL        /*When IDEAL greater than or same as REAL
COMPUTE TRIANGLE=1
ELSE                       /*When IDEAL less than REAL
COMPUTE TRIANGLE=2
COMPUTE #TEMP=IDEAL        /*Flip variables
COMPUTE IDEAL=REAL
COMPUTE REAL=#TEMP
END IF
LOGLINEAR TRIANGLE(1,2) IDEAL(2,4) REAL(1,3)
  /CWEIGHT=(1 0 0
            1 1 0
            1 1 1
            1 0 0
            1 1 0
            1 1 1)
  /DESIGN=REAL, IDEAL, REAL BY IDEAL
```

Observed, Expected Frequencies and Residuals

Factor	Code	OBS. count & PCT.	EXP. count & PCT.	Residual	Std. Resid.	Adj. Resid.
TRIANGLE	1					
IDEAL	2					
REAL	0-1	55.00 (5.05)	30.50 (2.80)	24.5000	4.4363	6.2738
REAL	2	.00 (.00)	.00 (.00)	.0000	.0000	.0000
REAL	3-4	.00 (.00)	.00 (.00)	.0000	.0000	.0000
IDEAL	3-4					
REAL	0-1	16.00 (1.47)	18.00 (1.65)	-2.0000	-.4714	-.6667
REAL	2	48.00 (4.40)	163.00 (14.95)	-115.0000	-9.0075	-12.7385
REAL	3-4	.00 (.00)	.00 (.00)	.0000	.0000	.0000
IDEAL	5 +					
REAL	0-1	1.00 (.09)	13.50 (1.24)	-12.5000	-3.4021	-4.8113
REAL	2	9.00 (.83)	172.00 (15.78)	-163.0000	-12.4286	-17.5767
REAL	3-4	9.00 (.83)	148.00 (13.58)	-139.0000	-11.4257	-16.1584
TRIANGLE	2					
IDEAL	2					
REAL	0-1	6.00 (.55)	30.50 (2.80)	-24.5000	-4.4363	-6.2738
REAL	2	.00 (.00)	.00 (.00)	.0000	.0000	.0000
REAL	3-4	.00 (.00)	.00 (.00)	.0000	.0000	.0000
IDEAL	3-4					
REAL	0-1	20.00 (1.83)	18.00 (1.65)	2.0000	.4714	.6667
REAL	2	278.00 (25.50)	163.00 (14.95)	115.0000	9.0075	12.7385
REAL	3-4	.00 (.00)	.00 (.00)	.0000	.0000	.0000
IDEAL	5 +					
REAL	0-1	26.00 (2.39)	13.50 (1.24)	12.5000	3.4021	4.8113
REAL	2	335.00 (30.73)	172.00 (15.78)	163.0000	12.4286	17.5767
REAL	3-4	287.00 (26.33)	148.00 (13.58)	139.0000	11.4257	16.1584

Goodness-of-Fit test statistics

Likelihood Ratio Chi Square = 977.41822 DF = 6 P = .000
Pearson Chi Square = 795.25964 DF = 6 P = .000

The goodness-of-fit statistics, as well as the large residuals, indicate that the symmetry model fits poorly. This is not very surprising, since examination of Table 9.18 shows that the number of cases in each triangle is quite disparate.

The symmetry model provides a test of whether the probability of falling into cell (i,j) of Triangle 1 is the same as the probability of falling into cell (i,j) of Triangle 2. It does not take into account the fact that the overall observed probability of membership in Triangle 2 is much greater than the probability of membership in Triangle 1.

Since the triangle totals are so disparate, a more reasonable hypothesis to test is whether the probability of falling into corresponding cells in the two triangles is equal, adjusting for the observed totals in the two triangles. In other words, we test whether the probability of falling in cell (i,j) is the same for Triangle 1 and Triangle 2, assuming that the probability of membership in the two triangles is equal. The expected value for each cell is no longer the average of the observed frequencies for the two triangles but is a weighted average. The weights are the proportion of cases in each triangles. The expected value is the product of the expected probability and the sample size in the triangle.

The symmetry model that preserves triangle totals is represented by the following log-linear model:

$$\ln \hat{F}_{ijk} = \mu + \lambda_i^{Real} + \lambda_j^{Ideal} + \lambda_k^{Triangle} + \lambda_{ij}^{Real\,Ideal} \qquad \textbf{Equation 9.18b}$$

This differs from the previous symmetry model in that the term $\lambda_k^{Triangle}$, which preserves triangle totals, is included.

Figure 9.18b shows part of the LOGLINEAR output a symmetry model that preserves triangle totals. Note that the expected number of cases in the first cell is 7.72. This is 5.59% of the total number of cases in Triangle 1. Similarly for Triangle 2, the expected number of cases in the first cell is 53.28. This is 5.59% of the cases in Triangle 2. Thus, the estimated probabilities are the same for the two triangles, although the actual numbers differ. The residuals and goodness-of-fit tests, however, suggest that a symmetry model preserving the observed totals in the two triangles does not fit the data well either.

Figure 9.18b Statistics for the symmetry model preserving observed totals

```
LOGLINEAR TRIANGLE(1,2) IDEAL(2,4) REAL(1,3)
   /CWEIGHT=(1 0 0
             1 1 0
             1 1 1
             1 0 0
             1 1 0
             1 1 1)
   /DESIGN=TRIANGLE, IDEAL, REAL, IDEAL BY REAL
```

Observed, Expected Frequencies and Residuals

Factor	Code	OBS. count & PCT.	EXP. count & PCT.	Residual	Std. Resid.	Adj. Resid.
TRIANGLE	1					
IDEAL	2					
REAL	0-1	55.00 (5.05)	7.72 (.71)	47.2771	17.0122	18.7353
REAL	2	.00 (.00)	.00 (.00)	.0000	.0000	.0000
REAL	3-4	.00 (.00)	.00 (.00)	.0000	.0000	.0000
IDEAL	3-4					
REAL	0-1	16.00 (1.47)	4.56 (.42)	11.4422	5.3596	5.8320
REAL	2	48.00 (4.40)	41.27 (3.79)	6.7266	1.0470	1.3382
REAL	3-4	.00 (.00)	.00 (.00)	.0000	.0000	.0000
IDEAL	5 +					
REAL	0-1	1.00 (.09)	3.42 (.31)	-2.4183	-1.3080	-1.4173
REAL	2	9.00 (.83)	43.55 (4.00)	-34.5523	-5.2357	-6.7719
REAL	3-4	9.00 (.83)	37.48 (3.44)	-28.4752	-4.6515	-5.8317
TRIANGLE	2					
IDEAL	2					
REAL	0-1	6.00 (.55)	53.28 (4.89)	-47.2771	-6.4771	-18.7353
REAL	2	.00 (.00)	.00 (.00)	.0000	.0000	.0000
REAL	3-4	.00 (.00)	.00 (.00)	.0000	.0000	.0000
IDEAL	3-4					
REAL	0-1	20.00 (1.83)	31.44 (2.88)	-11.4422	-2.0406	-5.8320
REAL	2	278.00 (25.50)	284.73 (26.12)	-6.7266	-.3986	-1.3382
REAL	3-4	.00 (.00)	.00 (.00)	.0000	.0000	.0000
IDEAL	5 +					
REAL	0-1	26.00 (2.39)	23.58 (2.16)	2.4183	.4980	1.4173
REAL	2	335.00 (30.73)	300.45 (27.56)	34.5523	1.9934	6.7719
REAL	3-4	287.00 (26.33)	258.52 (23.72)	28.4752	1.7710	5.8317

Goodness-of-Fit test statistics

```
Likelihood Ratio Chi Square =  294.50141   DF = 5  P =  .000
         Pearson Chi Square =  423.62825   DF = 5  P =  .000
```

9.19 Adjusted Quasi-Symmetry

The previously described symmetry model preserves only totals in each triangle. It does not require that the row and column sums for the expected values equal the observed row and column sums. The original crosstabulation table shows that the marginal distributions of real and ideal children are quite different. The *adjusted quasi-symmetry model* can be used to test whether the pattern of association in the two triangles is similar when row and column totals are preserved in each triangle.

The log-linear model for adjusted quasi-symmetry is

$$\ln \hat{F}_{ijk} = \mu + \lambda_i^{Real} + \lambda_j^{Ideal} + \lambda_k^{Triangle} + \lambda_{ij}^{RealIdeal} + \lambda_{ik}^{RealTriangle} + \lambda_{jk}^{IdealTriangle} \quad \textbf{Equation 9.19}$$

This model differs from the completely saturated model for the three variables only in that it does not contain the three-way interaction among number of real children, number of ideal children, and triangle number. Thus, the adjusted quasi-symmetry model tests whether the three-way interaction is significantly different from 0.

Figure 9.19 contains the goodness-of-fit statistics for the quasi-symmetry model. The small chi-squared value suggests that there is no reason to believe that the model does not fit well. However, there is only one degree of freedom for the model, since many parameters have been estimated.

Figure 9.19 Statistics for the adjusted quasi-symmetry model

```
LOGLINEAR TRIANGLE(1,2) IDEAL(2,4) REAL(1,3)
  /CWEIGHT=(1 0 0
            1 1 0
            1 1 1
            1 0 0
            1 1 0
            1 1 1)
  /DESIGN=IDEAL, REAL, TRIANGLE, IDEAL BY REAL,
          TRIANGLE BY REAL, TRIANGLE BY IDEAL
```

```
Observed, Expected Frequencies and Residuals

    Factor          Code            OBS. count & PCT.   EXP. count & PCT.      Residual   Std. Resid.   Adj. Resid.

TRIANGLE              1
 IDEAL          2
  REAL          0-1                   55.00 ( 5.05)      55.00 ( 5.05)          .0000        .0000         .0000
  REAL          2                       .00 (  .00)        .00 (  .00)          .0000        .0000         .0000
  REAL          3-4                     .00 (  .00)        .00 (  .00)          .0000        .0000         .0000
 IDEAL          3-4
  REAL          0-1                   16.00 ( 1.47)      14.76 ( 1.35)         1.2352        .3215        1.0756
  REAL          2                     48.00 ( 4.40)      49.24 ( 4.52)        -1.2352      -.1760       -1.0756
  REAL          3-4                     .00 (  .00)        .00 (  .00)          .0000        .0000         .0000
 IDEAL          5 +
  REAL          0-1                    1.00 (  .09)       2.24 (  .21)        -1.2352      -.8262       -1.0756
  REAL          2                      9.00 (  .83)       7.76 (  .71)         1.2352       .4433        1.0756
  REAL          3-4                    9.00 (  .83)       9.00 (  .83)          .0000        .0000         .0000

TRIANGLE              2
 IDEAL          2
  REAL          0-1                    6.00 (  .55)       6.00 (  .55)          .0000        .0000         .0000
  REAL          2                       .00 (  .00)        .00 (  .00)          .0000        .0000         .0000
  REAL          3-4                     .00 (  .00)        .00 (  .00)          .0000        .0000         .0000
 IDEAL          3-4
  REAL          0-1                   20.00 ( 1.83)      21.24 ( 1.95)        -1.2352      -.2681       -1.0756
  REAL          2                    278.00 (25.50)     276.76 (25.39)         1.2352       .0742        1.0756
  REAL          3-4                     .00 (  .00)        .00 (  .00)          .0000        .0000         .0000
 IDEAL          5 +
  REAL          0-1                   26.00 ( 2.39)      24.76 ( 2.27)         1.2352       .2482        1.0756
  REAL          2                    335.00 (30.73)     336.24 (30.85)        -1.2352      -.0674       -1.0756
  REAL          3-4                  287.00 (26.33)     287.00 (26.33)          .0000        .0000         .0000
- - - - - - - - - - - - - - - - - - - - - - - - - - - - - - - - - - - - - - - - - - - - - - - - - - - -

Goodness-of-Fit test statistics

  Likelihood Ratio Chi Square =    1.32440    DF = 1  P =  .250
           Pearson Chi Square =    1.15697    DF = 1  P =  .282
```

9.20 AN ORDINAL MODEL FOR REAL VERSUS IDEAL

Although the various symmetry models provide information about the relationship between the two triangles of a square table, we might wish to develop a more general model for the association between number of siblings in a family and one's view on the ideal number of children. The ordinal models considered in Sections 9.12 through 9.19 might be a good place to start.

Figure 9.16 reveals that two children seems to be the most popular number. However, as the number of real children in a family increases, so does the tendency toward a larger family size. For example, only 21.6% of only children consider 3 to 4 children to be ideal. Almost 43% of those from families of 5 or more children consider 3 or 4 children to be optimal. Thus, we might consider a row-effects model that incorporates the ordinal nature of the real number of children. Figure 9.20 contains the statistics for the row-effects model. The large observed significance level and small residuals indicate that the model fits reasonably well.

Figure 9.20 Statistics for the row-effects ordinal model

```
COMPUTE COV=REAL
LOGLINEAR IDEAL REAL(1,4) WITH COV
  /DESIGN=IDEAL, REAL, COV BY IDEAL
```

```
Observed, Expected Frequencies and Residuals

    Factor          Code              OBS. count & PCT.    EXP. count & PCT.       Residual   Std. Resid.   Adj. Resid.

IDEAL             0-1
 REAL              0-1                    2.00 (   .14)       2.26 (   .16)         -.2621       -.1742        -.2196
 REAL              2                      6.00 (   .43)       7.02 (   .50)        -1.0160       -.3838        -.5189
 REAL              3-4                   20.00 ( 1.43)       17.18 ( 1.23)         2.8197        .6803         .8651
 REAL              5 +                   26.00 ( 1.86)       27.54 ( 1.97)        -1.5409       -.2936        -.8027

IDEAL             2
 REAL              0-1                   55.00 ( 3.94)       56.98 ( 4.08)        -1.9848       -.2629        -.6737
 REAL              2                    138.00 ( 9.89)      139.41 ( 9.99)        -1.4129        .1107        -.2880
 REAL              3-4                  278.00 (19.93)      269.22 (19.30)         8.7801        .5351        1.0663
 REAL              5 +                  335.00 (24.01)      340.38 (24.40)        -5.3824       -.2917       -1.1155

IDEAL             3-4
 REAL              0-1                   16.00 ( 1.15)       13.08 (   .94)         2.9156        .8060        1.0759
 REAL              2                     48.00 ( 3.44)       49.11 ( 3.52)        -1.1141       -.1590        -.2443
 REAL              3-4                  139.00 ( 9.96)      145.52 (10.43)        -6.5184       -.5404        -.8302
 REAL              5 +                  287.00 (20.57)      282.28 (20.24)         4.7170        .2808        1.0304

IDEAL             5 +
 REAL              0-1                    1.00 (   .07)       1.67 (   .12)         -.6687       -.5177        -.6410
 REAL              2                      9.00 (   .65)       5.46 (   .39)         3.5438       1.5172        2.0459
 REAL              3-4                    9.00 (   .65)      14.08 ( 1.01)        -5.0814      -1.3541       -1.7244
 REAL              5 +                   26.00 ( 1.86)      23.79 ( 1.71)         2.2063        .4523        1.2775

- - - - - - - - - - - - - - - - - - - - - - - - - - - - - - - - - - - - - - - - - - - - - - - - - - - - - - - - - -

Goodness-of-Fit test statistics

  Likelihood Ratio Chi Square =    6.71177    DF = 6  P =  .348
           Pearson Chi Square =    6.83537    DF = 6  P =  .336
```

9.21 Parameter Estimates

Once an adequate model has been identified, you can examine the parameter estimates to assess the effects of the individual categories of the variables. Several different types of parameter estimates, corresponding to different types of contrasts, can be obtained. Consider Table 9.21a, which contains the expected cell frequencies for the row-effects model previously described. The natural logs of the expected cell frequencies are in Table 9.21b.

Table 9.21a Expected cell frequencies for the row-effect model

	Real			
Ideal	1	2	3	4
1	2.26	7.02	17.18	27.54
2	56.98	139.41	269.22	340.38
3	13.08	49.11	145.52	282.28
4	1.67	5.46	14.08	23.79

Table 9.21b Natural logs of the expected cell frequencies

	1	2	3	4	Average
1	0.815	1.949	2.844	3.316	
2	4.043	4.937	5.595	5.830	
3	2.571	3.894	4.980	5.643	
4	0.513	1.697	2.645	3.169	
Average	1.986	3.119	4.016	4.489	3.403

From Table 9.21b, parameter estimates can be obtained for both variables. We will restrict our attention to estimates for the REAL variable, since they can be obtained from the column averages and the grand mean. Estimates for the IDEAL variable are a little more complicated to obtain, since the covariate effect must be eliminated from the row entries.

Often it is desirable to compare each effect to the grand mean. The parameter estimate for a category is its difference from the overall mean. These types of estimates are called deviation parameter estimates. (They are included in the default LOGLINEAR output if parameter estimates are requested.) For the first category of the REAL variable the value of the deviation parameter estimate is $1.986 - 3.403 = -1.417$. Similarly, for the second category it is $3.119 - 3.403 = -0.284$. These values are shown in the output displayed in Figure 9.21a. The value for the last category is not printed and must be estimated as the negative of the sum of the previous values, since the sum of deviations about the mean is zero.

Figure 9.21a Deviation parameter estimates

```
COMPUTE COV=REAL
LOGLINEAR IDEAL REAL(1,4) WITH COV/
  CONTRAST(REAL)=DEV/PRINT=ESTIM/DESIGN=IDEAL REAL COV BY IDEAL
```

Parameter	Coeff.	Std. Err.	Z-Value	Lower 95 CI	Upper 95 CI
4	-1.4169683119	.12503	-11.33288	-1.66203	-1.17191
5	-.2834476028	.06767	-4.18893	-.41607	-.15082
6	.6135052404	.05876	10.44092	.49834	.72867

Difference contrasts are obtained by comparing the levels of a factor with the average effects of the previous levels of the factor. For example, the first parameter estimate in Figure 9.21b is just the difference between the mean of the second category and the mean of the first category, or $3.119 - 1.986 = 1.133$. Similarly, the second parameter estimate is obtained by comparing the third category of the REAL variable to the average of the first two categories. Thus the difference parameter estimate for the third level of the REAL variable is calculated as

$$-0.5 \times 1.986 - 0.5 \times 3.119 + 4.016 = 1.463 \qquad \textbf{Equation 9.21a}$$

This value is displayed in Figure 9.21b as the fifth parameter estimate. For the fourth category, the value is

$$-0.33 \times 1.986 - 0.33 \times 3.119 - 0.33 \times 4.016 + 4.489 = 1.449 \quad \textbf{Equation 9.21b}$$

Note that difference parameter estimates, unlike deviation parameter estimates, do not sum to 0 over all categories of a variable.

Figure 9.21b Difference parameter estimates

```
LOGLINEAR IDEAL REAL(1,4) WITH COV/
  CONTRAST(REAL)=DIFF/PRINT=ESTIM/DESIGN=IDEAL REAL COV BY IDEAL
```

Parameter	Coeff.	Std. Err.	Z-Value	Lower 95 CI	Upper 95 CI
4	1.1335207090	.14907	7.60383	.84134	1.42570
5	1.4637131978	.11986	12.21180	1.22879	1.69864
6	1.4492142324	.12597	11.50452	1.20231	1.69611

When the last category of a variable is considered a reference category, for example, when it corresponds to a control group, all parameter estimates can be expressed as deviations from it. These are called simple contrasts. For example, for the first category of the REAL variable, the parameter estimate corresponding to a simple contrast is $1.986 - 4.490 = -2.504$. Similarly, for the second category it is $3.119 - 4.490 = -1.370$. The value for the fourth category, which is not printed, is zero, since this category is the comparison category (see Figure 9.21c).

Figure 9.21c Simple parameter estimates

```
LOGLINEAR IDEAL REAL(1,4) WITH COV/
  CONTRAST(REAL)=SIMPLE/PRINT=ESTIM/DESIGN=IDEAL REAL COV BY IDEAL
```

Parameter	Coeff.	Std. Err.	Z-Value	Lower 95 CI	Upper 95 CI
4	-2.5038789861	.20842	-12.01359	-2.91238	-2.09537
5	-1.3703582771	.13527	-10.13055	-1.63549	-1.10523
6	-.4734054338	.08097	-5.84648	-.63211	-.31470

When the categories of a variable are ordered, parameter estimates corresponding to linear, quadratic, and higher-order polynomial effects can be obtained, as shown in Figure 9.21d. The first coefficient is for the linear effect, the second for the quadratic, and the third for the cubic. From the large Z values it appears that there is a significant linear and quadratic component.

Figure 9.21d Polynomial parameter estimates

```
LOGLINEAR IDEAL REAL(1,4) WITH COV/
  CONTRAST(REAL)=POLY/PRINT=ESTIM/DESIGN=IDEAL REAL COV BY IDEAL/
```

Parameter	Coeff.	Std. Err.	Z-Value	Lower 95 CI	Upper 95 CI
4	1.8802178391	.15137	12.42113	1.58353	2.17691
5	-.3300576376	.07536	-4.38000	-.47775	.18236
6	-.0418098970	.06323	-.66123	-.16574	.08212

9.22 The Design Matrix

LOGLINEAR also prints a "design" matrix, as shown in Figure 9.22. The columns of the matrix correspond to the parameter estimates for an effect. The number of columns for an effect is equal to its degrees of freedom. As indicated in the table labeled "Correspondence between effects and columns of design," the first three columns of Figure 9.22 are for the IDEAL variable, the next three are for the REAL variable, and the last three are for the IDEAL-by-cell covariate effect.

Figure 9.22 Design matrix

```
COMPUTE COV=REAL
LOGLINEAR CHLDIDEL REAL(1,4) WITH COV/
  CONTRAST(REAL)=POLY/PRINT=ALL/DESIGN=CHLDIDEL REAL COV BY CHLDIDEL/
```

Correspondence Between Effects and Columns of Design/Model 1

Starting Column	Ending Column	Effect Name
1	3	CHLDIDEL
4	6	REAL
7	9	COV BY CHLDIDEL

- -

Design Matrix

1-CHLDIDEL 2-REAL

Factor		Parameter								
1	2	1	2	3	4	5	6	7	8	9
1	1	.75000	-.25000	-.25000	-.67082	.50000	-.22361	.75000	-.25000	-.25000
1	2	.75000	-.25000	-.25000	-.22361	-.50000	.67082	1.50000	-.50000	-.50000
1	3	.75000	-.25000	-.25000	.22361	-.50000	-.67082	2.25000	-.75000	-.75000
1	4	.75000	-.25000	-.25000	.67082	.50000	.22361	3.00000	-1.00000	-1.00000
2	1	-.25000	.75000	-.25000	-.67082	.50000	-.22361	-.25000	.75000	-.25000
2	2	-.25000	.75000	-.25000	-.22361	-.50000	.67082	-.50000	1.50000	-.50000
2	3	-.25000	.75000	-.25000	.22361	-.50000	-.67082	-.75000	2.25000	-.75000
2	4	-.25000	.75000	-.25000	.67082	.50000	.22361	-1.00000	3.00000	-1.00000
3	1	-.25000	-.25000	.75000	-.67082	.50000	-.22361	-.25000	-.25000	.75000
3	2	-.25000	-.25000	.75000	-.22361	-.50000	.67082	-.50000	-.50000	1.50000
3	3	-.25000	-.25000	.75000	.22361	-.50000	-.67082	-.75000	-.75000	2.25000
3	4	-.25000	-.25000	.75000	.67082	.50000	.22361	-1.00000	-1.00000	3.00000
4	1	-.25000	-.25000	-.25000	-.67082	.50000	-.22361	-.25000	-.25000	-.25000
4	2	-.25000	-.25000	-.25000	-.22361	-.50000	.67082	-.50000	-.50000	-.50000
4	3	-.25000	-.25000	-.25000	.22361	-.50000	-.67082	-.75000	-.75000	-.75000
4	4	-.25000	-.25000	-.25000	.67082	.50000	.22361	-1.00000	-1.00000	-1.00000

When orthogonal contrasts are requested for a variable (when the sum of the product of corresponding coefficients for any two contrasts is zero), the numbers in the columns are the coefficients of the linear combinations of the logs of the predicted cell frequencies. For example, since polynomial contrasts are requested in Figure 9.22 for the REAL variable and they are orthogonal, Column 4 contains the coefficients for the linear effect, Column 5 for the quadratic effect, and Column 6 for the cubic effect. The parameter estimate for the quadratic effect is calculated as

$$\begin{aligned} &0.5(.815 + 3.316 + 4.043 + 5.830 + 2.571 + 5.643 + 0.513 + 3.169) \\ &- 0.5(1.949 + 2.844 + 4.937 + 5.595 + 3.894 + 4.980 + 1.697 + 2.645)/4 \\ &= -0.33. \end{aligned} \quad \textbf{Equation 9.22}$$

The linear combination of the cell means is divided by the sum of all of the coefficients squared. In this example, that sum is $16 \times 0.5^2 = 4$. The value of -0.33 corresponds to the parameter estimate for the quadratic effect printed in Figure 9.21d. The estimates for the linear and cubic effects can be obtained in a similar fashion using the coefficients in Columns 4 and 6.

LOGLINEAR uses a "reparameterized" model. When nonorthogonal contrasts, such as deviation and simple are requested for an effect, the columns of the "design" matrix for that effect are not the contrast coefficients. Instead they are the "basis" for the requested contrasts (see Bock, 1975; Finn, 1974). For example, in Figure 9.22, the default deviation contrasts are used for the IDEAL variable.

The three columns for the IDEAL effect, however, contain coefficients for simple contrasts, the basis for deviation contrasts. The parameter estimates printed correspond to those requested in the LOGLINEAR CONTRAST specification, in this case, DEVIATION for the IDEAL variable and POLYNOMIAL for the REAL variable.

When covariates are included in a model, they also occur in the design matrix. In this example the covariate values are just the scores from 1 to 4. For each cell these scores are multiplied by the corresponding entries of the first three columns to obtain the entries for the covariate by IDEAL interaction effects in Figure 9.22. Covariates in LOGLINEAR are treated as cell covariates. That is, all cases in the cell are assumed to have the same value for the covariate. If all cases in the cell do not have the same covariate value the cell average is used to represent all cases in that cell. This will, in general, give different results from models that adjust for covariates on a case-by-case basis.

9.23 RUNNING PROCEDURE LOGLINEAR

The LOGLINEAR procedure can be used to fit many different types of models, including logit models and non-hierarchical log-linear models. Parameter estimates can be obtained for all types of models. For hierarchical models, the HILOGLINEAR procedure, which uses an iterative proportional fitting algorithm, may require less computing time. However, parameter estimates for unsaturated models cannot be obtained in HILOGLINEAR.

The LOGLINEAR command must begin with a list of variables, optionally followed by one or more subcommands. One model is produced for each DESIGN subcommand. All subcommands can be used more than once and, with the exception of the DESIGN subcommand, are carried from model to model unless explicitly overridden. The subcommands that affect a DESIGN subcommand should be placed before that DESIGN subcommand. If subcommands are placed after the last DESIGN subcommand, LOGLINEAR generates a saturated model as the last design.

9.24 The Variable List

The only required specification for LOGLINEAR is a list of all variables used in the models specified on the command. LOGLINEAR analyzes two classes of variables: categorical and continuous. Categorical variables are used to define the cells of the table. Continuous variables can be used as covariates.

Categorical variables must be numeric and integer. Specify a range in parentheses indicating the minimum and maximum values, as in

```
LOGLINEAR ZODIAC(1,12) RINCOME(1,4)
```

This command builds a 12 × 4 frequency table for analysis. The model produced is a general log-linear model since no BY keyword appears. The design defaults to a saturated model in which all main effects and interaction effects are fitted.

Cases with values outside the specified range are excluded from the analysis, and noninteger values within the range are truncated for purposes of building the table. The value range specified must match the values in the data. That is, if the range specified for a variable is 1 and 4, there should be cases for values 1, 2, 3, and 4. Empty categories are not allowed. Use the RECODE command to assign successive integer values to factor levels.

If several variables have the same range, you can specify the range following the last variable in the list, as in

```
LOGLINEAR ZODIAC(1,12) REAL IDEAL(1,4)
```

ZODIAC has twelve values ranging from 1 to 12, and both REAL and IDEAL have four values ranging from 1 to 4.

The BY Keyword. Use the BY keyword to segregate the independent variables from the dependent variables in a logit model, as in

```
LOGLINEAR SATJOB(1,12) BY ZODIAC(1,2)
```

Categorical variables preceding the keyword BY are the dependent variables; categorical variables following the keyword BY are the independent variables. Usually you also specify a DESIGN subcommand to request the desired logit model (see Section 9.25).

The WITH Keyword. Specify cell covariates at the end of the variables specification following the keyword WITH, as in

```
LOGLINEAR ZODIAC(1,12) SATJOB(1,2) WITH B
```

To enter cell covariates into the model, you must specify them on the DESIGN subcommand (see Section 9.25). Section 9.22 discusses computations involving covariates in LOGLINEAR.

9.25 The DESIGN Subcommand

The DESIGN subcommand specifies the model or models to be fit. If you do not specify the DESIGN subcommand or if you specify it without naming any variables on it, the default is a saturated model, in which all interaction effects are fit.

You can use multiple DESIGN subcommands, each specifying one model. Variables named on DESIGN must have been specified on the initial list of variables (see Section 9.24).

Main-Effects Models. To test for independence, a model with only main effects is fit. For example, to test that ZODIAC and SATJOB are independent, specify

```
LOGLINEAR ZODIAC(1,12) SATJOB(1,2)
  /DESIGN=ZODIAC SATJOB
```

Interactions. Use the BY keyword to specify interaction terms. For example, to fit the saturated model that consists of the ZODIAC main effect, the SATJOB main effect, and the interaction of ZODIAC and SATJOB, specify

```
LOGLINEAR ZODIAC(1,12) SATJOB(1,2)
  /DESIGN=ZODIAC, SATJOB, ZODIAC BY SATJOB
```

For the general log-linear model, this DESIGN specification is the same as the default model. Thus, the specification

```
LOGLINEAR ZODIAC(1,12) SATJOB(1,2)
  /DESIGN
```

is equivalent to the preceding one.

Covariates. To include covariates, you must first identify them on the LOGLINEAR variables list by naming them after the keyword WITH. Then, simply specify the covariate on the DESIGN subcommand, as in

```
LOGLINEAR ZODIAC(1,12) SATJOB(1,2) WITH COV
  /DESIGN=ZODIAC SATJOB COV
```

You can specify an interaction of a covariate and an independent variable. However, a covariate-by-covariate interaction is not allowed. Instead, use the COMPUTE command to create interaction variables (see Section 9.13). For example, for a linear-by-linear association model, specify

```
COMPUTE B=SATJOB*RINCOME
LOGLINEAR SATJOB(1,2) RINCOME(1,4) WITH B
  /DESIGN=SATJOB RINCOME B
```

To specify an equiprobability model, use a covariate that is actually a constant of 1 on the DESIGN subcommand, as in

```
COMPUTE X=1
LOGLINEAR ZODIAC(1,12) WITH X
  /DESIGN=X
```

This model tests whether the frequencies in the 12-cell table are equal (see Section 9.3).

Single-Degree-of-Freedom Partitions. A variable followed by an integer in parentheses refers to a single-degree-of-freedom partition of a specified contrast. For example, you can specify the row-effects model described in Section 9.14 as

```
LOGLINEAR SATJOB(1,4) RINCOME(1,4)
  /CONTRAST(RINCOME)=POLYNOMIAL
  /DESIGN=SATJOB, RINCOME, SATJOB BY RINCOME(1)
```

RINCOME(1) refers to the first partition of RINCOME, which is the linear effect of RINCOME since a polynomial contrast is specified.

Similarly, to fit the quadratic model for the season data (Section 9.4), specify

```
LOGLINEAR SEASON(1,4)
  /CONTRAST(SEASON)=POLYNOMIAL
  /DESIGN=SEASON(1) SEASON(2)
```

The actual parameter estimates for SEASON(1) and SEASON(2) will differ from those displayed in Figure 9.4c since the polynomial contrasts are orthonormalized. The ratio of the estimate to the standard error and other statistics will be the same for the two specifications.

9.26 The CWEIGHT Subcommand

Use the CWEIGHT subcommand to specify cell weights for the model. By default, cell weights are equal to 1. You can specify either a matrix of weights or a numeric variable, as in

```
LOGLINEAR REAL, IDEAL(1,4)
  /CWEIGHT=CWT
```

This is useful for specifying structural zeros. Only one variable can be named as a weight variable. You can specify multiple CWEIGHT subcommands per LOGLINEAR command, but only one of these subcommands can name a weight variable. The rest must use matrices of weights.

If you specify a matrix of weights, the matrix is enclosed in parentheses and its elements are separated by blanks and/or commas. The matrix must contain the same number of elements as the product of the levels of the categorical variables. If you specify weights for a multiple-variable model, the index value of the rightmost variable increases most rapidly. For example, the CWEIGHT subcommand

```
LOGLINEAR TRIANGLE(1,2) IDEAL(2,4) REAL(1,3)
  /CWEIGHT=(1 0 0
            1 1 0
            1 1 1
            1 0 0
            1 1 0
            1 1 1)
```

assigns cell weights as follows:

TRIANGLE	IDEAL	REAL	Weight	TRIANGLE	IDEAL	REAL	Weight
1	2	1	1	2	2	1	1
1	2	2	0	2	2	2	0
1	2	3	0	2	2	3	0
1	3	1	1	2	3	1	1
1	3	2	1	2	3	2	1
1	3	3	0	2	3	3	0
1	4	1	1	2	4	1	1
1	4	2	1	2	4	2	1
1	4	3	1	2	4	3	1

You can use the notation $n*c$ to indicate that value c is repeated n times, as in

```
LOGLINEAR TRIANGLE(1,2) IDEAL(2,4) REAL(1,3)
  /CWEIGHT=(1 0 0 1 1 0 3*1 1 0 0 1 1 0 3*1)
```

The CWEIGHT specification remains in effect until explicitly overridden with another CWEIGHT subcommand. For example,

```
LOGLINEAR A B (1,4)
  /CWEIGHT=(0 4*1 0 4*1 0 4*1 0)
  /DESIGN=A B
  /CWEIGHT=(16*1)
  /DESIGN=A B
```

uses a second CWEIGHT subcommand to return to the default cell weights.

You can use CWEIGHT to impose fixed zeros on the model (see Section 9.15). This feature is useful in the analysis of incomplete tables. For example, to impose fixed zeros on the diagonal of a symmetric crosstabulation table, specify

```
COMPUTE CWT=1
IF (REAL EQ IDEAL) CWT=0
LOGLINEAR REAL IDEAL(1,4)
  /CWEIGHT=CWT
```

CWT equals 0 when REAL equals IDEAL. Alternatively, you can specify a CWEIGHT matrix, as in

```
  /CWEIGHT=(0 4*1 0 4*1 0 4*1 0)
```

9.27 The GRESID Subcommand

The GRESID subcommand calculates linear combinations of observed cell frequencies, expected cell frequencies, and adjusted residuals. Specify a variable or variables, or a matrix whose contents are the coefficients of the desired linear combinations. The matrix specification for GRESID is the same as for CWEIGHT (see Section 9.26). You can specify multiple GRESID subcommands, only one of which can specify a variable name. If you specify a matrix, it must contain as many elements as the number of cells implied by the variables specification, as in

```
LOGLINEAR ZODIAC(1;12)
  /GRESID=(3*1 9*0)
  /GRESID=(3*0 3*1 6*0)
  /GRESID=(6*0 3*1 3*0)
  /GRESID=(9*0 3*1)
```

The first GRESID subcommand combines the first three signs into a Spring effect, the second subcommand combines the second three signs into a Summer effect, and the last two subcommands form the Fall and Winter effects. For each effect, LOGLINEAR prints out the observed and expected count, the residual, the standardized residual, and the adjusted residual (see Section 9.3).

9.28 The PRINT and NOPRINT Subcommands

Use the PRINT and NOPRINT subcommands to control the statistical output. PRINT will display the named statistics, and NOPRINT suppresses statistics. You can use the following keywords on both the PRINT and NOPRINT subcommands:

FREQ *Observed and expected cell frequencies and percentages.* This is produced by default.

RESID *Raw, standardized, and adjusted residuals.* This is produced by default.

DESIGN *The design matrix of the model.*

ESTIM *The parameter estimates of the model.* If you do not specify a design on the DESIGN subcommand, LOGLINEAR generates a saturated model and prints the parameter estimates for the saturated model by default

COR *The correlation matrix of the parameter estimates.*

ALL *All available output.*

DEFAULT *FREQ and RESID.* ESTIM is also printed by default if the DESIGN subcommand is not used.

NONE *PRINT=NONE suppresses all statistics except goodness of fit.* NOPRINT=NONE is the same as PRINT=ALL.

You can specify multiple PRINT and NOPRINT subcommands. Specifications are cumulative. For example,

```
LOGLINEAR SATJOB(1,2) RINCOME(1,4)
  /PRINT=ESTIM
  /DESIGN=SATJOB, RINCOME, SATJOB BY RINCOME
  /PRINT=ALL
  /DESIGN=SATJOB RINCOME
```

specifies two designs. The first design is the saturated model. Since it fits the data exactly, you do not want to see the frequencies and residuals. Instead, you want to see parameter estimates, as specified by PRINT=ESTIM. The second design is the main-effects model, which implicitly tests the hypothesis of no association. The PRINT subcommand prints all available display output for this model.

9.29 The PLOT Subcommand

The PLOT subcommand produces optional plots. No plots are displayed if PLOT is not specified.

RESID *Plots of adjusted residuals against observed and expected counts.*

NORMPROB *Normal and detrended normal plots of the adjusted residuals.*

NONE *No plots.* This is the default if the PLOT subcommand is omitted.

DEFAULT *RESID and NORMPROB.* These are the defaults if you specify PLOT without keywords.

You can use multiple PLOT subcommands on one LOGLINEAR command. The specifications are cumulative. For example,

```
LOGLINEAR RESPONSE(1,2) BY TIME(1,4)
  /CONTRAST(TIME)=SPECIAL(4*1 7 14 27 51 8*1)
  /PLOT=RESID NORMPROB
  /DESIGN=RESPONSE TIME(1) BY RESPONSE
  /PLOT=NONE
  /DESIGN
```

prints RESID and NORMPROB plots for the first design and no plots for the second design.

9.30 The CONTRAST Subcommand

The CONTRAST subcommand indicates the type of contrast for a categorical variable. Specify the variable name in parentheses after the CONTRAST subcommand, followed by the name of the contrast. For example,

```
LOGLINEAR SATJOB(1,2) RINCOME(1,4)
  /CONTRAST(RINCOME)=POLYNOMIAL
```

applies a polynomial contrast to RINCOME.

In LOGLINEAR, contrasts do not have to sum to zero or be orthogonal. The following contrasts are available:

DEVIATION(refcat) *Deviations from the overall effect.* These are the default parameter estimates in LOGLINEAR. Refcat is the category for which parameter estimates are not displayed (they must be obtained as the negative of the sum of the others). By default, refcat is the last category of the variable.

DIFFERENCE *Levels of a variable with the average effect of previous levels of a variable.* Also known as *reverse Helmert* contrasts.

HELMERT *Levels of a variable with the average effect of subsequent levels of a variable.*

SIMPLE(refcat) *Each level of a variable to the last level.* You can specify a value for refcat enclosed in parentheses after the keyword SIMPLE. By default, refcat is the last category of the variable as the reference category.

REPEATED *Adjacent comparisons across levels of a variable.*

POLYNOMIAL(metric) *Orthogonal polynomial contrasts.* The default metric is equal spacing (see Sections 9.21 and 9.22). Optionally, you can specify the coefficients of the linear polynomial in parentheses, indicating the spacing between levels of the treatment measured by the given variable.

(BASIS)SPECIAL(matrix) *User-defined contrast.* You must specify as many elements as the number of categories squared. If BASIS is specified, a basis matrix is generated for the special contrast. Otherwise, the matrix specified is the basis matrix.

Only one contrast is in effect for each variable for a DESIGN subcommand. If you do not use the CONTRAST subcommand, the contrast defaults to DEVIATION. You must use separate CONTRAST subcommands for each variable for which you specify contrasts. A contrast specification remains in effect for subsequent designs until explicitly overridden with another CONTRAST subcommand, as in

```
LOGLINEAR SATJOB(1,2) RINCOME(1,4)
  /CONTRAST(RINCOME)=POLYNOMIAL
  /DESIGN=SATJOB, RINCOME, SATJOB BY RINCOME(1)
  /CONTRAST(RINCOME)=SIMPLE
  /DESIGN=SATJOB, RINCOME
```

The first CONTRAST subcommand requests polynomial contrasts of RINCOME for the first design. The second CONTRAST subcommand requests SIMPLE contrasts of RINCOME, with the last category (value 4) used as the reference category for the second DESIGN subcommand.

You can print the design matrix used for the contrasts by specifying the DESIGN keyword on the PRINT subcommand (see Section 9.22).

9.31 The CRITERIA Subcommand

The CRITERIA subcommand specifies the values of some constants in the Newton-Raphson algorithm, the estimation algorithm in LOGLINEAR.

CONVERGE(eps) *Convergence criterion.* Specify *eps* as the convergence criterion. The default is 0.001.

ITERATION(n) *Maximum number of iterations.* Specify *n* as the maximum number of iterations for the algorithm. The default is 20.

DELTA(d) *Cell delta value.* The value *d is added to each cell frequency before analysis.* The default value is 0.5.

DEFAULT *Default values.* Use DEFAULT to reset the parameters to the default.

For example, to increase the maximum number of iterations to 50, specify

```
LOGLINEAR DPREF(2,3) BY RACE ORIGIN CAMP(1,2)
  /CRITERIA=ITERATION(50)
```

Defaults or specifications remain in effect until overridden with another CRITERIA subcommand.

9.32 The WIDTH Subcommand

By default, the display width is 132 or the width specified on the SET command. Use the WIDTH subcommand to specify a different display width. For example, you can specify a width of 72 to avoid wrapping on short-carriage terminals. Only one width can be in effect at a time and it controls all display. The WIDTH subcommand can be placed anywhere after the variables specification, as in

```
LOGLINEAR ZODIAC(1,12) SATJOB(1,2)
  /WIDTH=72
```

A narrow format suppresses the display of variable names and values in frequencies tables.

9.33 The MISSING Subcommand

By default, LOGLINEAR deletes cases with missing values on any variable listed on the variables specification. To include cases with user-defined missing values, specify INCLUDE on the MISSING subcommand. Cases with system-missing values are always deleted from the analysis. If you specify MISSING= INCLUDE, you must also include the missing values in the value range specification for the variables.

INCLUDE *Include missing values.*

9.34 EXERCISES

Syntax

1. Find the syntax errors in the following LOGLINEAR commands:

   a.
   ```
   LOGLINEAR A(1,2) B(1,3) WITH C(1,4)
       /DESIGN
   ```
   b.
   ```
   LOGLINEAR A(1,3) B C (1,2)
       /DESIGN A*B*C
   ```
   c.
   ```
   LOGLINEAR A(1,3) BY B(1,2) BY C(1,2)
       /DESIGN
   ```
   d.
   ```
   LOGLINEAR A(1,3) B C (1,2)
      /DESIGN A B B BY C D by C
   ```

2. For the following LOGLINEAR command

   ```
   LOGLINEAR A B(1,3)
   ```

   write the subcommands that

   a. Set the diagonal of the table to structural zeroes.
   b. Obtain polynomial contrasts for variable A.
   c. Obtain a linear combination of residuals for each level of variable A.
   d. Specify a main-effects model.
   e. Specify a saturated model.

3. Write the DESIGN specification for the log-linear models corresponding to the following logit models:

   a.
   ```
   LOGLINEAR A(1,3) BY B C (1,5)
         /DESIGN A A BY B A BY C A BY B BY C
   ```
   b.
   ```
   LOGLINEAR A(1,3) BY B C (1,5)
         /DESIGN A A BY B A BY C
   ```
   c.
   ```
   LOGLINEAR A(1,3) BY B C (1,5)
         /DESIGN A
   ```

4. An investigator collected data to test hypotheses about how happy (variable JOY, where 0=none, 1=much) people are on each day of the week (DAY, where 1=Sunday, 2=Monday, 3=Tuesday, etc.) and during each season (SEASONS, where 1=Spring, 2=Summer, 3=Fall, 4=Winter). Write the LOGLINEAR commands to test the hypotheses that

   a. JOY, SEASON, and DAY of the week are independent.
   b. The three-way interaction among the variables is 0.
   c. The three-way interaction and the season-by-day interaction are 0.
   d. There are no season and day effects.
   e. People are equally likely to be happy or unhappy.

5. For the following table from Hedlund (1978), using scores of 1–3 for both variables, write the syntax to obtain

   a. A test of independence.
   b. A row-effects model.
   c. A column-effects model.
   d. A linear-by-linear association model.

Party Affiliation	Political Ideology		
	Liberal 1	Moderate 2	Conservative 3
Democrat (1)	143	156	100
Independent (2)	119	210	141
Republican (3)	15	72	127

Statistical Concepts

1. The output below shows the distribution of the number of cars for families with two or more cars, as discovered in a recent survey of households.

Observed, Expected Frequencies and Residuals

Factor	Code	OBS. count & PCT.	EXP. count & PCT.	Residual	Std. Resid.	Adj. Resid.
CARS	2	40.00			4.4721	5.0000
CARS	3	25.00			1.1180	1.2500
CARS	4	20.00			.0000	.0000
CARS	5	10.00			-2.2361	2.5000
CARS	6	5.00			-3.3541	-3.7500

Goodness-of-Fit test statistics

Likelihood Ratio Chi Square = 38.88306 DF = 4 P = .000

Pearson Chi Square = DF = P = .000

a. Write the LOGLINEAR subcommands that test the equiprobability hypothesis.

b. For the test of the equiprobability hypothesis, fill in the missing entries in the output and calculate the value of the Pearson chi-square statistic.

c. Based on the Pearson chi-square value, would you reject the hypothesis that all numbers of cars are equally probable?

d. Write the LOGLINEAR commands to test the hypothesis that there is a linear relationship between the log of the number of cars and the number of cars.

e. The output below tests the hypothesis that there is a linear relationship between the log of the number of cars and the number of cars. Fill in the missing entries:

Observed, Expected Frequencies and Residuals

Facctor	Code	OBS. count & PCT.	EXP. count & PCT.	Residual	Std. Resid.	Adj. Resid.
CARS	2	40.00 (40.00)	41.13		-.1765	-.3634
CARS	3	25.00 (25.00)		-.8828	-.1735	-.2021
CARS	4	20.00 (20.00)	16.29 (16.29)	3.7129	.9200	1.0548
CARS	5	10.00 (10.00)	(10.25)		-.0777	-.0949
CARS	6	5.00 (5.00)	6.45 (6.45)		-.5706	-.7393

f. Based on the goodness-of-fit test statistics shown below, would you reject the null hypothesis that there is a linear association between number of cars and the log frequency?

Goodness-of-Fit test statistics

Likelihood Ratio Chi Square = 1.20978 DF = 3 P = .751
Pearson Chi Square = 1.23939 DF = 3 P = .744

2. In Chapter 8 the relationship between happiness and several other variables is considered. In this exercise we will reexamine some of the data. The output below contains cell statistics from the test of independence of the happiness and health variables.

Observed, Expected Frequencies and Residuals

Factor	Code	OBS. count & PCT.	EXP. count & PCT.	Residual	Std. Resid.	Adj. Resid.
HAPPY	YES					
HEALTH	EXCELLEN	469.00 (31.18)	422.66 (28.10)	46.3351	2.2538	7.5885
HEALTH	GOOD	559.00 (37.17)	546.16 (36.31)	12.8404	.5494	1.9943
HEALTH	FAIR	217.00 (14.43)	246.12 (16.36)	-29.1197	-1.8562	-5.7066
HEALTH	POOR	63.00 (4.19)	93.06 (6.19)	-30.0559	-3.1157	-8.9553
HAPPY	NO					
HEALTH	EXCELLEN	17.00 (1.13)	63.34 (4.21)	-46.3351	-5.8222	-7.5885
HEALTH	GOOD	69.00 (4.59)	81.84 (5.44)	-12.8404	-1.4194	-1.9943
HEALTH	FAIR	66.00 (4.39)	36.88 (2.45)	29.1197	4.7950	5.7066
HEALTH	POOR	44.00 (2.93)	13.94 (.93)	30.0559	8.0488	8.9553

a. Write the LOGLINEAR commands to fit the independence model. (HEALTH is coded from 1 to 4.)

b. From the above output, without computing the chi-squared test, would you or would you not reject the null hypothesis that health and happiness are independent?

c. The output below contains excerpts from the output for another model of the relationship between happiness and health. Write the commands used to produce these results. (HEALTH(1) is the linear component of the HEALTH variable.)

```
Correspondence Between Effects and Columns of Design

Starting  Ending
 Column   Column   Effect Name

   1        1      HAPPY
   2        4      HEALTH
   5        5      HEALTH(1) BY HAPPY
```

d. On the basis of the following statistics, what would you conclude about the goodness of fit of this model?

```
Goodness-of-Fit test statistics

   Likelihood Ratio Chi Square =     1.29534    DF = 2  P =  .523
            Pearson Chi Square =     1.26407    DF = 2  P =  .532
```

3. The output below contains the observed and expected frequencies for the row-effects model for happiness and health. On the basis of the table entries, fill in the missing parameter estimates.

Observed, Expected Frequencies and Residuals

Factor	Code	OBS. count & PCT.	EXP. count & PCT.	Residual	Std. Resid.	Adj. Resid.
HAPPY	YES					
HEALTH	EXCELLEN	469.00 (31.18)	465.47 (30.95)	3.5257	.1634	1.1091
HEALTH	GOOD	559.00 (37.17)	563.61 (37.47)	-4.6076	-.1941	-.8617
HEALTH	FAIR	217.00 (14.43)	218.36 (14.52)	-1.3618	-.0922	-.2502
HEALTH	POOR	63.00 (4.19)	60.56 (4.03)	2.4437	.3140	.7561
HAPPY	NO					
HEALTH	EXCELLEN	17.00 (1.13)	20.53 (1.36)	-3.5257	-.7782	-1.1091
HEALTH	GOOD	69.00 (4.59)	64.39 (4.28)	4.6076	.5742	.8617
HEALTH	FAIR	66.00 (4.39)	64.64 (4.30)	1.3618	.1694	.2502
HEALTH	POOR	44.00 (2.93)	46.44 (3.09)	-2.4437	-.3586	-.7561

HEALTH (DEVIATION PARAMETER ESTIMATES)

Parameter	Coeff.	Std. Err.	Z-Value	Lower 95 CI	Upper 95 CI
2		.06625		-.19259	.06711
3		.04365		.51901	.69013
4		.05911		.01651	.24823

HEALTH (SIMPLE PARAMETER ESTIMATES)

Parameter	Coeff.	Std. Err.	Z-Value	Lower 95 CI	Upper 95 CI
2			4.64429	.35341	.86951
3			11.48590	1.06056	1.49698
4			7.03068	.58172	1.03143

HEALTH (DIFFERENCE PARAMETER ESTIMATES)

Parameter	Coeff.	Std. Err.	Z-Value	Lower 95 CI	Upper 95 CI
2		.07431		.52166	.81295
3		.08504		-.30522	.02814
4		.10849		-1.11157	-.68630

4. An investigator wishes to develop a logit model for happiness, income, and health.

a. Write the LOGLINEAR subcommands to fit a saturated logit model with HAPPY as the dependent variable. (INCOME has three levels: 1=low, 2=middle, and 3=high.)

b. Write the command for the equivalent log-linear model for the saturated logit model specified in (a).

c. For the saturated logit model, fill in the entries for the goodness-of-fit tests.

```
Goodness-of-Fit test statistics

  Likelihood Ratio Chi Square =         DF =    P =

            Pearson Chi Square =         DF =    P =
```

d. How would the goodness-of-fit statistics in (c) differ for the equivalent log-linear model?

e. Write the LOGLINEAR commands for the logit model without the three-way interactions.

f. Write the commands for the equivalent log-linear representation of the model described in (e).

Another Nearly Deleted Residual

Hips swaying gently in the saddle, Svetlana Manova rode into the dude ranch at Jenkin's Box, Arizona. She anticipated a quiet vacation to recover from the effort of publishing an advanced statistical text. In fact, her analysis (at least the principal components) should have been published long ago. Her immediate desires ran more toward the sort of exploratory data analysis for which the ranch was famous. She was too keyed up to concentrate, for it was May, the mythical-man month, and like most of the young women on the ranch, she was dreaming of a mythical man and trying to design May tricks that would make the men she observed agree with her expected values. Meanwhile, the less-than-mythical men at the ranch tried to invert the May tricks. She reflected that they could do so only because their determinant values stubbornly refused to vanish.

Dismounting and handing the reins of her stallion to the stable man Whitney, who hitched it among the tied ranks, Svetlana went inside. The social director had asked her to give a statistical appraisal of astrology the next morning, between two of the regularly scheduled subjects, but she could not concentrate. Memories of "Log" Linear, her aerobics instructor back home, were always with her. She had fabricated an excuse, something about not being able to spare enough degrees of freedom for even a between-subjects analysis. There were more BS factors here than people around her realized.

Manova took a seat at the bar. She tried to calm her emotions with mental calculations, going so far as to compute tests for the equality of the very ants under the rustic log tables. "Got a sis, miss?" As this clever opening line propagated relentlessly (and unexpectedly) through her computations, she became aware of a handsome, if plump, man who had taken the next stool. "Name's Lothario Jit," avowed the stranger, "but you can call me Lo. I'd like you to be my dependent this evening." She started to analyze this Lo Jit, but decided it wouldn't be worth the effort to probe it. "I lost the last cat I owned, my good ol' Anubis," he continued, in a plaintive tone. "I travel, you see, and our separation was too much for him. Had to throw him out. Damned urban environment."

The bartender glanced up. "Damned urban what, son?" he asked sharply, but they excluded him. Svetlana's heart pounded. This overfed but strangely attractive stranger looked more concerned with the cook's distance than with "my ol' Anubis's" distance, but in his out-of-line attempt to gain leverage on her heart, he had unerringly analyzed her residual discontent. A few short weeks ago Log Linear had changed her life astronomically (like a nova, she thought). Unlike Lo Jit, Log Linear never singled out either of them as more dependent than the other. Svetlana hesitated, fascinated by the thought of triangular May tricks.

Contents

A.1 PREPARING DATA FOR ANALYSIS
A.2 Cases, Variables, and Values
A.3 Coding the Variables
A.4 An Example
A.5 Freefield Format
A.6 RUNNING SPSS^X
A.7 The SPSS^X Job
A.8 SPSS^X Syntax
A.9 Commands and Specifications
A.10 A Sample Job
A.11 Files Used in SPSS^X
A.12 DEFINING DATA
A.13 Describing the Data File
A.14 Locating the Data
A.15 Choosing Variable Names
A.16 Indicating Column Locations
A.17 Specifying Data Recorded on Multiple Lines
A.18 Types of Variables
A.19 Indicating Decimal Places
A.20 Establishing Display Formats
A.21 Freefield Data Input
A.22 Variable and Value Labels
A.23 Identifying Missing Values
A.24 Inline Data
A.25 Reading Matrices
A.26 Using an SPSS^X System File
A.27 DATA TRANSFORMATIONS
A.28 Recoding Values of Variables
A.29 Recoding Numeric Variables
A.30 Recoding String Variables
A.31 Recoding Missing Values
A.32 Recoding Continuous Value Ranges
A.33 Recoding into a New Variable
A.34 Computing New Variables
A.35 Establishing the Print and Write Formats
A.36 Specifying Arithmetic Operations
A.37 Specifying Numeric Functions
A.38 Using Functions in Complex Expressions
A.39 Missing Values and Expressions
A.40 Counting Values Across Variables
A.41 Specifying Conditional Transformations
A.42 The DO IF/END IF Structure
A.43 The IF Command
A.44 Logical Expressions
A.45 Temporary Transformations
A.46 SELECTING AND SAMPLING CASES
A.47 Selecting Cases
A.48 Specifying the Logical Expression
A.49 Drawing a Sample
A.50 Selecting the First n Cases
A.51 WEIGHTING CASES
A.52 SORTING CASES

Appendix A

Data Definition and Management

To perform the statistical analyses described in this book, you must, of course, know how to use the SPSS^X system. This appendix is a brief guide to getting data into SPSS^X and performing the transformations that might be necessary to get that data into the form needed for analysis. Sections A.1–A5 discuss techniques of coding data and entering them into a computer file. Sections A.6–A.11 present the fundamental components of an SPSS job, with an annotated example. Sections A.12–A.26 present the commands available for defining basic data files for use in SPSS^X. Sections A.27–A.45 present the commands available for revising the coding structure of variables and creating new variables based on combinations of existing variables and constants. The remaining sections, A.46–A.52, show how to select and sample cases from your data file, weight cases, and sort the file.

This discussion, in conjunction with the syntax guide in Appendix B, should provide enough information for a large number of SPSS^X operations. However, if you use the system extensively, and particularly if you deal with complex data structures, you should have access to the most current edition of *SPSS^X User's Guide.*

A.1 PREPARING DATA FOR ANALYSIS

Before information can be analyzed by SPSS^X, the information must be entered into a disk or tape file. This entails two steps—arranging the data into a suitable format and entering the data into the computer. Entering the data into the computer usually involves using a text editor available at your installation. Other ways may be available, so consult your local computer-center service personnel for assistance. In Sections A.2 to A5, we consider only the first step—preparing information for analysis. The information may be stored in file folders in personnel offices, in patient medical charts, or in some other form that a computer cannot read.

A.2 Cases, Variables, and Values

Consider Figure A.4a, which contains an excerpt from a *Consumer Reports* evaluation of 35 beers (see Chapter 5). The beers were rated on overall quality and a variety of other attributes, such as price, calories, sodium, and alcohol content. Each line in the table represents a *case*, or observation, for which *values* are available for a set of *variables*.

For the first case, Miller High Life, the value of the cost variable is 42 cents, and the value of the alcohol variable is 4.7%. For each beer, the same variables—rating, origin, availability, price, cost, calories, sodium, alcohol content, class, and type (light or regular)—are recorded. What differs are the actual values of the variables. Each case has one and only one value for each variable. "Unknown" and "missing" are acceptable values for a variable, although these values require special treatment during analysis.

The case is the basic unit for which measurements are taken. In this analysis, the case is a brand of beer. In studies of political opinion or brand preference, the case is most likely the individual respondent to a questionnaire. A case may be a larger unit, such as a school, county, or nation; it may be a time period, such as a year or month in which measurements are obtained; or it may be an event, such as an auto accident.

For any single analysis, the cases must be of the same kind. If the unit of analysis is a county, all cases are counties, and the values of each variable are for those individual counties. If the unit is a state, then all cases are states and the values for each variable are for states.

A.3 Coding the Variables

One way to simplify data entry is to assign numbers or symbols to represent responses. This is known as *coding* the data. For example, instead of typing "light" or "regular" as the values for the type-of-beer variable, the codes *1* and *0* can be used. If only numbers are included in a coding scheme, it is called *numeric*. If letters or a mixture of numbers, letters, and special symbols are chosen, the code is termed *alphanumeric*, or *string*. By coding, you substantially decrease the number of symbols that you need to type, especially for variables whose values are originally recorded as words (such as type-of-beer). If you want the coded values to be labeled on the output, a few instructions in SPSSX will take care of it.

Coding schemes are arbitrary by their very nature. The type-of-beer variable could also be coded *R* for regular and *L* for light. All that is necessary is that each possible value has a distinct code. For example, coding the states by their first letters is unacceptable since there are many states that begin with the same letter. Maine, Massachusetts, Michigan, Maryland, Minnesota, Mississippi, Missouri, and Montana would be indistinguishable.

It is usually helpful to have one variable that uniquely identifies each case. For the beer data, that variable is the name of the beer. Sometimes it is useful to identify cases with an ID number. This identifier can help you easily locate the data lines for cases with unusual values or missing information.

A.4 An Example

Figure A.4a shows a portion of the uncoded data from the beer study. A possible coding scheme for these data is shown in Figure A.4b.

Figure A.4a Excerpt from uncoded data for the beer study

Rating	Beer	Origin	Avail	Price	Cost
Very good	MILLER HIGH LIFE	USA	National	2.49	0.42
Very good	BUDWEISER	USA	National	2.59	0.43
Very good	SCHLITZ	USA	National	2.59	0.43
Very good	LOWENBRAU	USA	National	2.89	0.48
Good	OLD MILWAUKEE	USA	Regional	1.69	0.28
Good	DOS EQUIS	Mexico	Regional	4.22	0.70
Fair	PABST EXTRA LIGHT	USA	National	2.29	0.38

Calories	Sodium	Alcohol	Class	Type
149	17	4.7	Premium	Regular
144	15	4.7	Premium	Regular
151	19	4.9	Premium	Regular
157	15	4.9	Super-premium	Regular
145	23	4.6	Popular	Regular
145	14	4.5	Not given	Regular
68	15	2.3	Not given	Light

Figure A.4b Coding scheme for beer data form

Variable	Coding scheme
RATING	1=Very good 2=Good 3=Fair
BEER	Actual name of the beer
ORIGIN	1=USA 2=Canada 3=France 4=Holland 5=Mexico 6=Germany 7=Japan
AVAIL	1=National 2=Regional
PRICE	price per six-pack of 12-ounce containers
COST	cost per 12 fluid ounces
CALORIES	calories per 12 fluid ounces
SODIUM	sodium per 12 fluid ounces in mg
ALCOHOL	alcohol by volume (in %)
CLASS	0=Not given 1=Super-premium 2=Premium 3=Popular
TYPE	0=Regular 1=Light

Figure A.4c contains data for the first three beers coded according to this scheme. Once the data are coded, a format for arranging the data in a computer file must be determined. Each data line (usually entered from a terminal) is also known as a *record*. Each line is composed of columns in which the numbers or characters are stored. Two decisions that must be made are how many lines will be needed for each case and in what column locations each variable will be stored.

Figure A.4c Coded data

RATING	BEER	ORIGIN	AVAIL	PRICE	COST	CALORIES	SODIUM	ALCOHOL	CLASS	TYPE
1	MILLER HIGH LIFE	1	1	249	42	149	17	47	2	0
1	BUDWEISER	1	1	259	43	144	15	47	2	0
1	SCHLITZ	1	1	259	43	151	10	49	2	0

Figure A.4d shows a listing of a file in which one line is used for each case. The column locations for the variables are also indicated. The rating is in column 1; the name of the beer, in columns 3–22; the origin, in column 25; the availability of the beer, in column 27; the price, in columns 29–31; the cost, in columns 33–35; calories, in columns 37–39; the sodium content, in columns 41–42; the alcohol content, in columns 44–45; the class, in column 47; and the type, in column 49. The numbers are positioned in each field so that the last digit is in the last column of the field for the variable. For example, a calorie count of 72 would have the number 7 in column 38; leading blanks or zeros occupy the beginning columns. This is known as *fixed-column format.* (Freefield input is discussed in Section A.5.) The decimal points for the price, cost, and alcohol variables are not included in the file. The decimal points do not need to be included since SPSS^{X} commands can be used to indicate their locations. If a decimal point is included, it occupies a column as any other symbol does.

Figure A.4d Beer data recorded on one record per case

```
         1         2         3         4         5
12345678901234567890123456789012345678901234567890  Columns

1 MILLER HIGH LIFE        1 1 249  42 149 17 47 2 0
1 BUDWEISER               1 1 259  43 144 15 47 2 0
1 SCHLITZ                 1 1 259  43 151 19 49 2 0
```

When there are many variables for each case, more than one line may be necessary to store the information. For example, if your screen width is 80, you may prefer to enter information that requires more than 80 columns on two or more lines. It is usually recommended that you enter an identification number for each case and a record number onto each line if it takes more than one line to record the data for a case. You can then easily locate missing or out-of-order data lines.

It is important to allocate a sufficient number of columns for each variable. For example, if only two columns are used to record a weight variable, only weights less than 100 pounds will fit. Always allocate the maximum number of columns that you might need. Don't worry if your observed data do not actually require that many columns.

All data files considered in this manual are *rectangular*. That is, all cases have the same variables in the same order and the same number of lines per case. Some data files are not rectangular. For instance, every case may not have the same variables recorded. For example, in a study of adverse drug reactions, cases for people who are alive will not have data lines detailing autopsy findings. Another nonrectangular file might not define all cases as the same type of unit, as in a file containing some lines with data about families and some lines with data about individual members within families. SPSS^X also contains facilities for handling these kinds of files. See the FILE TYPE command in the *SPSS^X User's Guide*.

A.5 Freefield Format

Sometimes it is convenient not to have to worry about arranging variables in particular column locations. Instead, for all cases, variables are entered in the same order with at least one blank separating values. Figure A.5 shows how a freefield data file for the first three cases of the beer data might look.

Figure A.5 Beer data in freefield format

```
1 'MILLER HIGH LIFE' 1 1 2.49 .42 149 17 4.7 2 0
1 BUDWEISER 1 1 2.59 .43 144 15 4.7 2 0
1 SCHLITZ 1 1 2.59 .43 151 19 4.9 2 0
```

Whenever there is a blank within the name, the name of the beer is enclosed in apostrophes (or quotation marks). This indicates that the blanks are part of the value. Decimal points must be included in the data. Freefield data are discussed in Section A.21.

A.6 RUNNING SPSS^X

Once your data are in a form that can be read by SPSS^X, you are ready to construct an SPSS^X job. In order to do this, you need to understand how to access SPSS^X and how to build commands.

Getting access to SPSS^X and the handling of files are very specific to your installation and type of computer. Information specific to the computer, operating system, and installation at which you use SPSS^X is not described in this manual. If you don't know how to gain access to SPSS^X, ask your computer-center service personnel. If you do know how to run an SPSS^X job, then you can use the SPSS^X

INFO command to get machine-specific instructions and information about new features and changes to SPSS^X since publication of the *SPSS^X User's Guide*. The INFO command is both an integral part of SPSS^X documentation and a guide to the most recent developments available on your computer. See Appendix B for details.

A.7 The SPSS^X Job

The usual SPSS^X job consists of three main parts: data definitions, optional data transformations, and procedure specifications. The data definition commands provide information about the variables and their location in the data file. The data transformation commands are used to restrict analyses to a subset of cases, create new variables, and modify existing variables. The procedure commands indicate what statistics, reports, or tables are to be produced.

Before learning about individual SPSS^X commands, you should have some general information about the SPSS^X language. The rules, or *syntax*, of this language are easy to learn and follow in writing your own commands.

A.8 SPSS^X Syntax

When processing in batch mode, commands begin in the first column of a new line and continue for as many lines as needed. All continuation lines are indented at least one column. When processing in interactive mode, commands begin in any column, as do continuation lines, but each command terminates with a period. In both batch and interactive modes, you can add spaces or break lines at any point where a single blank is allowed, such as around slashes, parentheses, or equals signs between variable names (the most common use of spaces of break lines), except for text included within apostrophes.

A.9 Commands and Specifications

Each command begins with a *command keyword* (which may contain more than one word). The command keyword is followed by at least one blank space and then any *specifications* required to complete the command, as in

```
LIST VARIABLES=ALL
```

The command keyword is LIST, and VARIABLES=ALL is a specification. Specifications are made up of names, keywords, numbers, literals, arithmetic operators, and special delimiters.

Many specifications include *subcommands*. For example, the LIST command above has a VARIABLES subcommand to tell the system which variables to list. The LIST command can also include a CASES subcommand to specify how many cases to list, as in

```
LIST VARIABLES=ALL/CASES=10
```

Keywords that make up a command can be truncated to the least number of characters needed for identification, down to a minimum of three characters. Exceptions are the reserved keyword WITH, the END DATA command, and all specifications to the INFO command. For example, the following LIST command is identical to the command just above:

```
LIST VAR=ALL/CAS=10
```

A.10 A Sample Job

The SPSS^X job shown in Figure A.10a analyzes data stored in a file named BEER. The SPSS^X commands, each of which is discussed briefly in the following list, accomplish a set of tasks typical in analyzing data: naming and locating a data file;

naming, locating, and labeling variables; and obtaining graphs and statistics describing certain variables.

Figure A.10a Sample SPSS^X job with data in a separate file

```
TITLE 'BEER DATA STUDY'

DATA LIST FILE=BEERDATA
  /RATING 1 BEER 3-22(A) ORIGIN 25 AVAIL 27
  PRICE 29-31(2) COST 33-35(2) CALORIES 37-39
  SODIUM 41-42 ALCOHOL 44-45(1) CLASS 47 TYPE 49

VARIABLE LABELS AVAIL 'AVAILABILITY IN THE U.S.'
  /PRICE 'PRICE PER 6-PACK'
  /COST 'COST PER 12 FLUID OUNCES'
  /CALORIES 'CALORIES PER 12 FLUID OUNCES'
  /SODIUM 'SODIUM PER 12 FLUID OUNCES IN MG'
  /ALCOHOL 'ALCOHOL BY VOLUME (IN %)'
  /CLASS 'PRICE CLASS'

VALUE LABELS RATING 1 'VERY GOOD' 2 'GOOD' 3 'FAIR'
  /ORIGIN 1 'USA' 2 'CANADA' 3 'FRANCE' 4 'HOLLAND'
          5 'MEXICO' 6 'GERMANY'  7 'JAPAN'
  /AVAIL 1 'NATIONAL' 2 'REGIONAL'
  /CLASS 0 'NOT GIVEN' 1 'SUPER-PREMIUM' 2 'PREMIUM' 3 'POPULAR'
  /TYPE 0 'REGULAR' 1 'LIGHT'

MISSING VALUES CLASS(0)

LIST VARIABLES=RATING TO PRICE CALORIES TO ALCOHOL /CASES=10

FREQUENCIES VARIABLES=CALORIES SODIUM ALCOHOL
  /FORMAT=NOTABLE /STATISTICS /HISTOGRAM
```

TITLE assigns the title "BEER DATA STUDY," which will appear at the top of each page of printed output.

DATA LIST tells SPSS^X how to read file BEERDATA. It assigns a name to each variable to be read and specifies the column or range of columns in which the data for each variable are located. The (A) following variable BEER indicates that BEER is an alphanumeric variable (containing characters other than numbers). The numbers in parentheses following PRICE, COST, and ALCOHOL indicate that PRICE and COST should be read with two places to the right of an implied decimal point, ALCOHOL with one place. (See Sections A.12–A.19.)

VARIABLE LABELS assigns labels to the variables. These optional labels appear in printed output to further identify each variable. (See Section A.22.)

VALUE LABELS assigns labels to the specific values of the variables RATING, ORIGIN, AVAIL, CLASS, and LIGHT. For example, the values 1 through 3 for RATING will be labeled "VERY GOOD," "GOOD," and "FAIR" on output. (See Section A.22.)

MISSING VALUES declares that the value 0 for variable CLASS represents missing information and should be treated differently from other values in data transformations and analyses. (See Section A.23.)

LIST requests a listing of the variables named on the VARIABLES subcommand. RATING TO PRICE refers to RATING, PRICE, and all variables between RATING and PRICE in the order the variables are defined on the DATA LIST command. CASES=10 requests that only the first ten cases be listed.

FREQUENCIES is generally used to print tables showing the frequencies and percentages of individual values for selected variables. Here, since the variables can have many different values, the NOTABLE keyword on the FORMAT subcommand suppresses the table, and only descriptive statistics and histograms are requested (see Appendix B).

Figures A.10b–A.10d show printed output generated by the sample job. As shown in Figure A.10b, the first printed page gives you information about the installation where you are running SPSS^{X} and a synopsis of the newest features available in the release you are running, Release 2.1 in this example.

Commands are printed back with two columns of numbers to their left. These numbers are generated by SPSS^{X}. The first column gives the sequence numbers of the command lines, and the second column gives level-of-control numbers. The level-of-control numbers indicate when a set of commands is under the control of another command. While most commands are at the first level, indicated by a 0, some might be under the control of a DO IF stucture that conditionally executes other commands.

Figure A.10b Printback of SPSS^{X} commands with DATA LIST correspondence table

```
26-May-88   SPSS-X RELEASE 3.0 FOR IBM VM/CMS
10:56:05    SPSS Inc Developmental System       IBM 4381-2    VM/CMS 4.2

For   VM/CMS 4.2          SPSS Inc Developmental System       License Number 8807
This software is functional through December 31, 2019.

Try the new SPSS-X Release 3.0 features:

* Interactive SPSS-X command execution          * Improvements in:
* Online Help                                    *   REPORT
* Nonlinear Regression                           *   TABLES
* Time Series and Forecasting (TRENDS)           *   Simplified Syntax
* Macro Facility                                 *   Matrix I/O

See SPSS-X User's Guide, Third Edition, for more information on these features.

   1 0          TITLE 'BEER DATA STUDY'
   2 0
   3 0          DATA LIST FILE=BEER
   4 0            /RATING 1 BEER 3-22(A) ORIGIN 25 AVAIL 27
   5 0             PRICE 29-31(2) COST 33-35(2) CALORIES 37-39
   6 0             SODIUM 41-42 ALCOHOL 44-45(1) CLASS 47 TYPE 49
   7 0

This command will read 1 records from BEER DATA A1

Variable    Rec    Start      End          Format

RATING       1        1         1          F1.0
BEER         1        3        22          A20
ORIGIN       1       25        25          F1.0
AVAIL        1       27        27          F1.0
PRICE        1       29        31          F3.2
COST         1       33        35          F3.2
CALORIES     1       37        39          F3.0
SODIUM       1       41        42          F2.0
ALCOHOL      1       44        45          F2.1
CLASS        1       47        47          F1.0
TYPE         1       49        49          F1.0
```

Figure A.10b also includes a DATA LIST table showing the variables defined, their formats, and their locations in the data file.

Figure A.10c shows the output from the LIST command. A quick look at the listing indicates that the variables have been properly defined. PRICE is properly displayed with two decimal places, ALCOHOL with one. Listing variables is one of the simplest ways to ensure correct coding and definition of the data.

Figure A.10c A listing of the first ten cases from the sample job

```
27 FEB 85    BEER DATA STUDY
17:38:20     SPSS Inc Developmental System          IBM 4381-2   VM/CMS 3.1

RATING BEER                  ORIGIN AVAIL PRICE CALORIES SODIUM ALCOHOL

    1    MILLER HIGH LIFE       1     1    2.49    149      17     4.7
    1    BUDWEISER              1     1    2.59    144      15     4.7
    1    SCHLITZ                1     1    2.59    151      19     4.9
    1    LOWENBRAU              1     1    2.89    157      15     4.9
    1    MICHELOB               1     1    2.99    162      10     5.0
    1    LABATTS                2     2    3.15    147      17     5.0
    1    MOLSON                 2     2    3.35    154      17     5.1
    1    HENRY WEINHARD         1     2    3.65    149       7     4.7
    1    KRONENBOURG            3     2    4.39    170       7     5.2
    1    HEINEKEN               4     1    4.59    152      11     5.0

NUMBER OF CASES READ =       10    NUMBER OF CASES LISTED =       10
```

Figure A.10d shows the histogram and statistics for ALCOHOL produced by the FREQUENCIES procedure.

Figure A.10d A histogram and statistics from the sample job

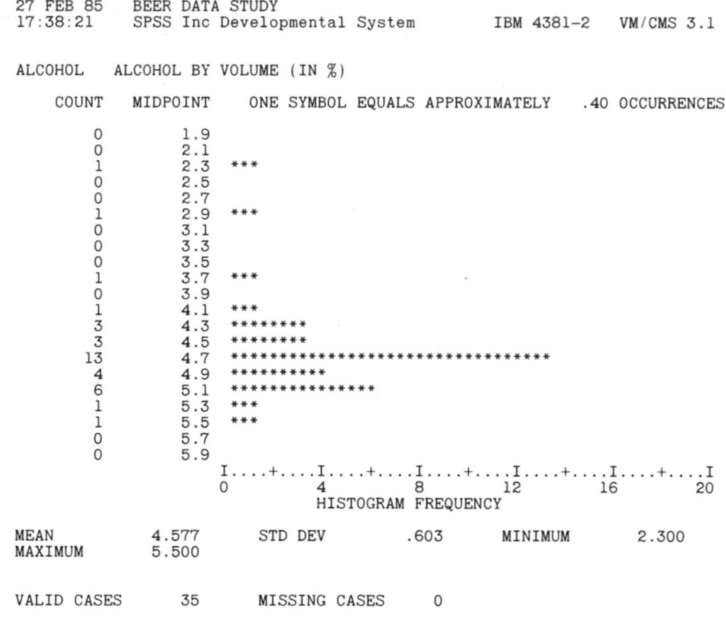

```
27 FEB 85    BEER DATA STUDY
17:38:21     SPSS Inc Developmental System          IBM 4381-2   VM/CMS 3.1

ALCOHOL    ALCOHOL BY VOLUME (IN %)

     COUNT   MIDPOINT    ONE SYMBOL EQUALS APPROXIMATELY    .40 OCCURRENCES

        0        1.9
        0        2.1
        1        2.3    ***
        0        2.5
        0        2.7
        1        2.9    ***
        0        3.1
        0        3.3
        0        3.5
        1        3.7    ***
        0        3.9
        1        4.1    ***
        3        4.3    ********
        3        4.5    ********
       13        4.7    *********************************
        4        4.9    **********
        6        5.1    ***************
        1        5.3    ***
        1        5.5    ***
        0        5.7
        0        5.9
                        I....+....I....+....I....+....I....+....I....+....I
                        0         4         8         12        16        20
                                  HISTOGRAM FREQUENCY

MEAN          4.577      STD DEV         .603       MINIMUM        2.300
MAXIMUM       5.500

VALID CASES       35     MISSING CASES      0
```

Had the job contained errors, error messages would have been included in the printed output.

A.11 Files Used in SPSS[X]

Operating SPSS[X] means dealing with files. Depending on the complexity of your job, you may have one or more of each of the following types of files:

- *Command file* (one per job): Contains your SPSS[X] commands.
- *Input data file:* Contains your data in almost any format. This file can be included within your SPSS[X] command file, or it can be a separate file on tape or disk. The facilities for defining input data are summarized in Sections A.12–A.26.
- *Display file:* Contains the tabular output from the SPSS[X] procedures you have requested and diagnostic information about your job. This file is formatted for listing at a terminal or on a line printer.

- *Output file:* Contains data formatted to be read by a computer. Some procedures create output files containing matrix or other materials.
- *SPSS^{X} system file:* A file specifically formatted for use by SPSS^{X}, containing both data and the *dictionary* that defines the data to the system. System files speed processing.

Conventions for naming, printing, deleting, or permanently saving files, and for submitting command files for processing differ considerably from one computer and operating system to another. Use the INFO command and look for other documentation at your site for information about handling files outside SPSS^{X}.

A.12 DEFINING DATA

The data definition commands in SPSS^{X} answer the following questions:

- Where is the collection of data stored on your machine?
- How many lines are there for each case?
- What are the names of the variables, and where are they located on the data file?
- What labels should be attached to variables and values?
- What values are used to represent missing information?

A.13 Describing the Data File

Data for analysis with SPSS^{X} can reside in an external data file or in the same file as the SPSS^{X} commands. For data included with commands (*inline* data), BEGIN DATA and END DATA commands are required to differentiate data lines from command lines (see Section A.24).

The variables to be analyzed must be identified on a DATA LIST command (Sections A.14–A.21). If the data are in fixed format, as described in Section A.4, their locations are also given on the DATA LIST command, as shown in Sections A.16–A.17. Freefield data, as introduced in Section A.5, are further described in Section A.21.

Besides the name and location of each variable, the DATA LIST command allows you to specify the type of variable (Section A.18) and the number of decimal places (Section A.19).

A.14 Locating the Data

You can enter data along with your SPSS^{X} commands, or you can read data from a separate file. If the data are in a file other than the SPSS^{X} command file, name the file on the FILE subcommand of the DATA LIST command, as in

```
DATA LIST FILE=BEERDATA
```

With releases before 3.0, use the FILE HANDLE command to name the file in which the data are stored, and then use the associated file handle in the DATA LIST command, as in

```
FILE HANDLE BEERDATA /NAME='BEER DATA'
DATA LIST FILE=BEERDATA
```

A.15 Choosing Variable Names

After having identified the data file, you assign names to each of the variables and give their location on the file. You use the assigned variable name to refer to a variable throughout the SPSS^{X} job. For example, a variable that describes father's occupation might be named PAOCCUP. Keep in mind the following rules when you name variables:

- The name must begin with a letter. The remaining characters in the name can be any letter, any digit, a period, or the symbols @, #, _, or $.
- The length of the name cannot exceed eight characters.
- Blanks and special symbols such as &, !, ?, /, ', and * cannot occur in a variable name.
- Each variable must have a unique name—duplication is not allowed.
- The reserved keywords in Table A.15 cannot be used as variable names since they have special meaning in SPSS^X.

The following are all valid variable names: LOCATION, LOC#5, X.1, and OVER$500.

You can create a set of variable names by using the keyword TO. When you are assigning new names, as in DATA LIST specifications, ITEM1 TO ITEM5 is equivalent to five names: ITEM1, ITEM2, ITEM3, ITEM4, and ITEM5. The prefix can be any valid name and the numbers can be any integers, so long as the first number is smaller than the second, and the full variable name, including the number, does not exceed eight characters.

Table A.15 SPSS^X reserved keywords

ALL	AND	BY	EQ	GE	GT	LE
LT	NE	NOT	OR	TO	WITH	

It is a good idea to assign names that help you identify the variables. You could give the names X and Z to variables for age and sex, but the names AGE and SEX give you a much better idea of the nature of each variable. The variable names assigned to the beer data include RATING for the rating of the beer, ALCOHOL for the alcohol content, PRICE for the price of a six-pack, and CALORIES for caloric content.

A.16 Indicating Column Locations

Along with a variable's name, you specify its column location on the data file. All variables on the same line are identified at the same time. For example, the command

```
DATA LIST FILE=BEERDATA
  /RATING 1 BEER 3-22(A) ORIGIN 25 AVAIL 27
```

describes four variables. Variable definition begins with the first slash. The numbers after the variable names give their column locations. For example, RATING is in column 1, and BEER is in columns 3 through 22 (and is alphanumeric, see Section A.18).

Although variables from the same data line must be defined together, they do not need to be defined in any particular sequence within that line. That is, variables at the end of a line can be defined before those at the beginning of the same line. It is the order in which you define variables that determines their order on your SPSS^X active file, not necessarily their original order on your file.

If several variables are recorded in adjacent columns of the same line and have the same width and format type (numeric or string), you can use an abbreviated format to define them on DATA LIST. List all of the variable names followed by the beginning column location of the first variable in the list, a dash, and the ending column location of the last variable in the list. For example, in the following data list,

```
DATA LIST FILE=HUBDATA
  /DEPT82 19 SEX 20 MOHIRED YRHIRED 12-15
```

MOHIRED and YRHIRED form a list of variables, and 12–15 is the column specification for both. The DATA LIST command divides the total number of specified columns equally among the variables in the list. Thus, MOHIRED is in columns 12–13 and YRHIRED is in columns 14–15. Be careful to use variables of equal width when defining data this way. If you use variables of different widths, and SPSS^X can divide the number of columns by the number of variables equally, your data will be read incorrectly. If the total number of columns is not an even multiple of the number of variables listed, SPSS^X displays an error message and does not read the data.

A.17 Specifying Data Recorded on Multiple Lines

Sometimes your data are located on more than one line or record for each case. To read more than one line for each case, use the following procedure. Enter a slash and define the variables recorded on the first line, and then enter a slash followed by the variable definitions for the next line. Repeat this procedure until you have defined all lines for the cases in your data file, as in

```
DATA LIST FILE=HUBDATA
  /DEPT82 19 SEX 20 MOHIRED YRHIRED 12-15
  /SALARY82 21-25
```

This DATA LIST reads variables DEPT82, SEX, MOHIRED, and YRHIRED from the first line and SALARY82 from the second line.

A.18 Types of Variables

You can define two types of variables with SPSS^X—numeric and string (alphanumeric). A numeric variable contains only numbers. Numeric variables can be either decimals (such as 12.345) or integers (such as 1234). A string variable can contain a combination of letters, numbers, and special characters. There are two types of string variables—short strings and long strings. On most computers, a string variable whose values contain eight characters or less is considered a short string (see the LOCAL keyword on the INFO command for the length of a short string on your computer). The variable TYPE, coded as A or B, is a short string on all computers. In the beer data example, the name of the beer is a long string. The difference is that short strings can be used in some data transformation and procedure commands where long strings cannot. String variables are identified with the letter A in parentheses following the column specification on the DATA LIST command, as in

```
DATA LIST FILE=BEERDATA /BEER 3-22(A)
```

where variable BEER is defined as a string variable.

When using freefield format, you should also indicate the width of the string variable, as in BEER (A20). Use the maximum string-value length for a variable as the width. Count all characters and blanks in calculating the width. For example, MILLER HIGH LIFE has a width of 16 with blanks included.

A.19 Indicating Decimal Places

By default, DATA LIST assumes that the data format type is numeric and that the numbers are integers, or that any decimal points are explicitly coded in the data file. To indicate noninteger values when the decimal point is not actually coded in the data, specify the number of *implied* decimal places by enclosing the intended number in parentheses following the column specification. The specification

```
DATA LIST FILE=BEERDATA /ALCOHOL 44-45(1)
```

locates the variable that measures alcohol content in columns 44 through 45. The last digit of ALCOHOL is stored as a decimal position.

For example, if the number 47 is stored in columns 44–45, the specification ALCOHOL 44–45 (1) results in the number 4.7. The specification ALCOHOL 44–45 (2) results in the number 0.47. The dictionary format is also affected by the implied decimal. The two-column designation 44–45 (1) results in a three-column dictionary format in order to accommodate the decimal point. If the number is stored in the data file with the decimal point, the decimal point overrides the DATA LIST format specification (but the dictionary format might have to be adjusted). Implied decimals can only be used with fixed-format data.

A.20 Establishing Display Formats

Whenever you see the values of a variable displayed, SPSS^X knows what format to use because it knows the variable's width and type from the DATA LIST specifications. This information, along with the variable name, labels, and missing values (see Sections A.22 and A.23) form the *dictionary* portion of your SPSS^X active file. Any time that you want to change the format of a numeric variable (string variable formats cannot be changed), use the FORMATS or PRINT FORMATS commands described in Section A.34.

A.21 Freefield Data Input

With freefield format, successive data values are simply separated by one or more blanks or one comma. Variables must be in the same order for each of the cases, but they need not be in the same columns. If you choose this manner of entering data, specify the keyword FREE or LIST after the DATA LIST command. Column locations are not specified after the variable names. However, you must indicate the length of string variables by using the A notation (see Section A.18). For example,

```
DATA LIST FREE
  /RATING BEER (A20) ORIGIN AVAIL PRICE COST CALORIES
   SODIUM ALCOHOL CLASS LIGHT
```

can be used to define the variables for the beer example shown in Figure A.5. Note that if values of string variables include blanks (such as MILLER HIGH LIFE for the BEER variable), they must be enclosed within apostrophes in the data file. Otherwise, the blanks are read as indicating new variables.

The advantage of freefield format is obvious: data entry is much simpler since variables do not have to be put in particular locations. The major disadvantage of freefield data entry is that if you inadvertently omit a data value, all values for subsequent variables and cases are incorrect. For example, if the rating variable is omitted for the second case, the value for the name of beer is taken as the rating (causing an error because the beer name has a string value), and everything that follows is wrong. A similar problem can arise if you mistakenly enter an extra value. Therefore, it is particularly important to list and check the data values after input with freefield format.

These data can actually be defined using the LIST version of freefield data. In this version, each case is expected to be recorded entirely on a single line. With

LIST, one value more or less than the number of variables only adversely affects a single case.

Another disadvantage of freefield input is that all numeric variables are assigned dictionary formats of width eight and two decimal places. However, you can use the FORMAT command to assign proper formats following the DATA LIST command.

A.22 Variable and Value Labels

The VARIABLE LABELS and VALUE LABELS commands supply information that is used for labeling the display output of SPSS^X jobs. These labels are optional, but using them often makes the output more readable. Some variables, such as age and weight, have many values, and do not need value labels since the values themselves are meaningful.

The VARIABLE LABELS command assigns variables extended descriptive labels. Specify the variable name, followed by at least one comma or blank, and the label enclosed in apostrophes or quotation marks. Multiple label specifications are optionally separated by slashes, as in

```
VARIABLE LABELS AVAIL 'AVAILABILITY IN THE U.S.'
  /PRICE 'PRICE PER 6-PACK'
  /COST 'COST PER 12 FLUID OUNCES'
  /CALORIES 'CALORIES PER 12 FLUID OUNCES'
  /SODIUM 'SODIUM PER 12 FLUID OUNCES IN MG'
  /ALCOHOL 'ALCOHOL BY VOLUME (IN %)'
  /CLASS 'PRICE CLASS'
```

This command assigns variable labels to the variables AVAIL through CLASS. A variable label applies to only one variable. The variable must have been previously defined in a DATA LIST (or GET or IMPORT) command, or in one of the transformation commands that create new variables. The label can include blanks and any other characters. SPSS^X prints up to 40 characters for a variable label, but the TABLES procedure available as of Release 2.1 prints up to 120 characters.

To use an apostrophe as part of a label, enclose the label in quotation marks, as in

```
VARIABLE LABELS SALARY82 "EMPLOYEE'S 1982 SALARY"
```

Quotation marks are entered in a label by enclosing the label in apostrophes.

The VALUE LABELS command assigns descriptive labels to values. The VALUE LABELS command is followed by a variable name, or variable list, and a list of values with associated labels. The command

```
VALUE LABELS RATING 1 'VERY GOOD' 2 'GOOD' 3 'FAIR'
  /ORIGIN 1 'USA' 2 'CANADA' 3 'FRANCE' 4 'HOLLAND' 5 'MEXICO'
          6 'GERMANY'  7 'JAPAN'
  /AVAIL 1 'NATIONAL' 2 'REGIONAL'
  /CLASS 0 'NOT GIVEN' 1 'SUPER-PREMIUM' 2 'PREMIUM' 3 'POPULAR'
  /TYPE  0 'REGULAR' 1 'LIGHT'
```

assigns labels to the values for the variables RATING, ORIGIN, AVAIL, CLASS, and TYPE. The labels for each variable are separated from the labels for the preceding variable by a slash. You can assign labels for values of any variable already defined. If the variable is a string, the value must be enclosed in apostrophes. Value labels can contain any characters, including blanks. The slashes between variables are required.

Most SPSS^X procedures print up to 20 characters of a value label. Procedures CROSSTABS and MEANS print 16 characters for column variables. Procedure TABLES, available with Release 2.1 of SPSS^X, prints up to 60 characters.

A.23 Identifying Missing Values

Sometimes information for a particular variable is not available for a case. When information for a variable is unknown, a special code is used to indicate that the value is missing. For example, if a patient's age cannot be determined, this can be indicated by a code such as -1 to indicate that the information is missing. Another code, such as -2, might be entered if a patient refuses to reveal his or her age. These different codes might be used if it is important to distinguish information that is missing for different reasons.

The MISSING VALUE command identifies the value or values that represent missing information. Specify the variable name or variable list and the specified missing value or values in parentheses, as in

```
MISSING VALUE CLASS(0)
```

This command assigns the value 0 as missing for variable CLASS.

Up to three missing values can be indicated per variable. Two of those values can be the end points of a range using keyword THRU, as in

```
MISSING VALUES Q1 TO Q10 (0,7 THRU 9)
```

This command assigns the value 0 and all values from 7 through 9 as missing. Keywords LOWEST (LO) and HIGHEST (HI) can be used for either end of a range.

User-defined missing values specified with the MISSING VALUE command are distinguished from the *system-missing* value (which is indicated on output by a period). SPSS^X assigns the system-missing value when it encounters a value other than a number for a variable declared as numeric on the DATA LIST command. For example, blanks are set to system-missing for numeric variables. An alternative to entering a special value, then, is to leave a field blank. However, you will find that assigning a user-defined missing value gives you more control in tables and other results from SPSS^X.

System-missing values are also assigned when new variables created with data transformation commands are undefined, such as in an attempt to divide by 0 or when a case is missing a value for a variable used in computing the new variable.

A.24 Inline Data

Sometimes, instead of keeping your data in an external file you may prefer to enter your data along with your SPSS^X commands. When this is the case, omit the FILE subcommand on the DATA LIST command, and separate the inline data from the other lines in the command file with the BEGIN DATA and END DATA commands. The BEGIN DATA command follows the command for the first procedure and precedes the data, and the END DATA command follows the last line of the data. Additional transformation and procedure commands can follow the END DATA command. Figure A.24 shows the sample job from Figure A.10b set up with data inline.

Figure A.24 Sample job with inline data

```
TITLE 'BEER DATA STUDY'

DATA LIST /RATING 1 BEER 3-22(A) ORIGIN 25 AVAIL 27
  PRICE 29-31(2) COST 33-35(2) CALORIES 37-39
  SODIUM 41-42 ALCOHOL 44-45(1) CLASS 47 TYPE 49

VARIABLE LABELS AVAIL 'AVAILABILITY IN THE U.S.'
  /PRICE 'PRICE PER 6-PACK'
  /COST 'COST PER 12 FLUID OUNCES'
  /CALORIES 'CALORIES PER 12 FLUID OUNCES'
  /SODIUM 'SODIUM PER 12 FLUID OUNCES IN MG'
  /ALCOHOL 'ALCOHOL BY VOLUME (IN %)'
  /CLASS 'PRICE CLASS'

VALUE LABELS RATING 1 'VERY GOOD' 2 'GOOD' 3 'FAIR'
  /ORIGIN 1 'USA' 2 'CANADA' 3 'FRANCE' 4 'HOLLAND'
          5 'MEXICO' 6 'GERMANY'  7 'JAPAN'
  /AVAIL 1 'NATIONAL' 2 'REGIONAL'
  /CLASS 0 'NOT GIVEN' 1 'SUPER-PREMIUM' 2 'PREMIUM' 3 'POPULAR'
  /TYPE 0 'REGULAR' 1 'LIGHT'

MISSING VALUES CLASS(0)

LIST VARIABLES=RATING TO PRICE CALORIES TO ALCOHOL /CASES=10

BEGIN DATA
1  MILLER HIGH LIFE     1 1 249  42 149 17 47 2 0
1  BUDWEISER            1 1 259  43 144 15 47 2 0
1  SCHLITZ              1 1 259  43 151 19 49 2 0
  .....     Remainder of cases not shown
END DATA

FREQUENCIES VARIABLES=CALORIES SODIUM ALCOHOL
  /FORMAT=NOTABLE /STATISTICS /HISTOGRAM
```

A.25 Reading Matrices

Some SPSS^X procedures such as FACTOR, REGRESSION, ONEWAY, DISCRIMINANT, and CLUSTER allow you to enter certain summary statistics such as means, sample sizes, correlations, covariances, or distance coefficients instead of reading the original cases. This results in a considerable decrease in processing time. All statistical computations are based on the summary statistics. (The results you get are the same as if you had entered the original cases, since all of the necessary information is contained in the summary statistics.)

Reading intermediate values instead of the actual cases is useful when you have used SPSS^X procedures to write a file with summary results or when the summary results are available from some other source, such as a journal.

When you enter summary statistics, special specifications are required. See the *SPSS^X User's Guide* for a complete explanation.

A.26 Using an SPSS^X System File

Once you have defined your data file in SPSS^X, you do not need to repeat the data definition process. Information from the data definition commands described in Sections A.12 through A.23 can be permanently saved along with the data on specially formatted files called the SPSS^X *system file* and the *portable file*. Variables created or altered by data transformations and the descriptive information for these variables can also be saved on these files.

The system file is used in subsequent SPSS^X jobs without requiring respecification of variable locations, formats, missing values, or variable and value labels. You can update the system file, altering the descriptive information or modifying the data, and you can save the updated version in a new system file. See the SAVE, XSAVE, and GET commands in Appendix B.

The portable file is used to transport your data plus definitions between SPSS^X and SPSS/PC+ on a microcomputer or between versions of SPSS^X on different types of computers without having to redefine the data and definitions each time. See the EXPORT and IMPORT commands in the *SPSS^X User's Guide*.

A.27 DATA TRANSFORMATIONS

In the beer data, 35 brands of beer are rated on a three-point scale with the categories "very good,' "good," and "fair." Suppose you want to compare the beers on their ratings, but you are only interested in making a dichotomous distinction between ratings of "good" and "fair." To do this, you would want to collapse the rating categories of "very good" and "good" into a single category.

Or suppose you have done a survey of political attitudes, and you have five yes-or-no questions on the topic of women's rights. You might want to create a new variable that counts the total number of "yes" responses to the five items.

Operations such as these, where you take existing variables and alter their values or use them to create new variables, are called *data transformations*.

There are several commands in SPSS^X that allow you to perform a wide variety of data transformations. Use the RECODE command to alter the values of an existing variable. Typical reasons for recoding variables include combining several values into one, rearranging the order of categories, and carrying out simple data checks. You would use RECODE to collapse the rating categories in the beer data.

The COMPUTE command creates new variables through numeric transformations of existing ones. For instance, the beer data contains a variable that is the number of calories in 12 ounces of beer. You might want to use COMPUTE to figure out how many calories there would be in an 8-ounce glass of each brand.

The COUNT command creates a new variable that, for each case, counts the occurrences of certain values across a list of variables. You would use COUNT to add the "yes" responses to the women's rights questions on the political survey.

You can use the DO IF command structure to transform data differently for subsets of cases. For example, a company may award vacation time on the basis of length of employment and job level. The DO IF command structure could be used to calculate vacation time for employees who have been with the company for varying lengths of time and who are classified at various job levels.

The TEMPORARY command makes all of the transformations work only for the procedure that follows the command. See Section A.45 for a discussion of TEMPORARY.

A.28 Recoding Values of Variables

The RECODE command tells SPSS^X to make specified changes in a variable's values as the data are being read. The command

```
RECODE AVAIL (1=2)(2=1)
```

reverses values 1 and 2 for variable AVAIL (i.e., if a case has value 1, it is changed to 2, and vice versa).

To be recoded, a variable must already exist in your data file. The variable's name precedes the list of value specifications on the RECODE command. You can create as many new values for a variable as you wish, as long as each specification is enclosed in parentheses. A single specification can be used to recode several values as one new value. Thus, the command

```
RECODE RATING (1,2=1)(3,4=2)
```

changes RATING variable values to 1 for cases with original ratings of 1 or 2, and to 2 for cases originally rated as 3 or 4.

You cannot list more than one *new* value in a single value specification. Thus, specifications like (2,3=0,1) or (1=5,6) are not valid.

The value specifications on a RECODE command are evaluated from left to right, and the value of a case is recoded only once in a single RECODE command. For example, if a case has the value 0 for the variable SEX, the command

```
RECODE SEX (0=1)(1=0)(3=99)
```

recodes SEX as 1 for that case. This value is not recoded back to 0 by the second value specification. Variable values that you do not mention on a RECODE command are left unchanged.

If you want to recode several variables in the same way, you can use a single RECODE command to do so, as in the command

```
RECODE SEX RACE SURGERY (0=1)(1=0)(3=99)
```

In addition, you can use one RECODE command to perform different recodes for different variables by separating the variable names and their specifications with a slash, as in the command

```
RECODE SODIUM (6 THRU 10=1)(11 THRU 17=2) (18 THRU 27=3)
  /COST (.27 THRU .42=1)(.43 THRU .48=2)(.50 THRU 1.20=3)
```

You can use the TO keyword to refer to several consecutive variables in the file. For example, the command

```
RECODE SCORE1 TO SCORE5 (5=1)(6=2)(7=3)
```

recodes SCORE1, SCORE5, and all the variables between them in the file.

A.29 Recoding Numeric Variables

Several keywords are available to facilitate recoding of numeric variables. Use the keywords THRU, LOWEST, and HIGHEST to recode a range of variables. Thus, the command

```
RECODE CALORIES (68 THRU 100=1)(101 THRU 170=2)
```

recodes all the values between 68 and 100 (inclusive) as 1 and all the values between 101 and 170 (inclusive) as 2 for the CALORIES variable. The LOWEST (or LO) keyword specifies the lowest value of a variable, while HIGHEST (or HI) specifies the highest value. The command

```
RECODE CALORIES (LO THRU 100=1)(101 THRU HI=2)
```

is equivalent to the previous command if the lowest data value is 68 and the highest value is 170. When you use LOWEST or HIGHEST to specify a range, user-missing values in the range are recoded, but system-missing values are not changed.

You can use the ELSE keyword to recode all values not previously mentioned into a single category. Thus, the command

```
RECODE CALORIES (LO THRU 100=1)(ELSE=2)
```

is equivalent to the previous two commands. ELSE should be the last specification for a variable, since RECODE will ignore subsequent specifications for that variable. ELSE includes system-missing values.

You can also use ELSE as a data-cleaning device. For example, if the variables SCORE1 to SCORE5 have only 5, 6, and 7 as legitimate values, you might use the command

```
RECODE SCORE1 TO SCORE5 (5,6,7=COPY)(ELSE=SYSMIS)
```

to retain the valid values (copy them unchanged) and recode the nonvalid values to the system-missing value.

A.30 Recoding String Variables

You can use the RECODE command to recode string variables. The keywords LOWEST or LO, HIGHEST or HI, THRU, SYSMIS and MISSING do not apply to recoding string variables.

When recoding string variables, enclose all values in apostrophes (or quotation marks). For example, the command

```
RECODE LIGHT ('Y'='A')('N'='B')
```

recodes *Y* into *A* and *N* into *B* for the string variable LIGHT.

A.31 Recoding Missing Values

The MISSING keyword is useful for recoding all missing values (user- or system-missing) to a single value. For example, if −99 is the missing value you have declared for the AGE variable, the command

```
RECODE AGE (MISSING=-1)
```

recodes −99 and any system-missing values for AGE to −1 while leaving the other AGE values unchanged. The output value of a missing-value recode is not considered missing automatically. Use the MISSING VALUE command to declare any new value you want to have treated as a missing value.

You can use the SYSMIS keyword as either an input or output specification. The command

```
RECODE AGE (SYSMIS=-1)
```

recodes the system-missing value to −1.

The SYSMIS keyword as an output specification recodes specified values to system-missing, as in the command

```
RECODE AGE (MISSING,-99=SYSMIS)
```

You *cannot* use the MISSING keyword as an output specification on RECODE to recode values as user-missing.

A.32 Recoding Continuous Value Ranges

If a variable has noninteger values, some values may escape recoding unless you make certain they are included in a value range. For example, the command

```
RECODE AGE (0 THRU 17=1)(18 THRU 65=2)(66 THRU 99=3)
```

does not recode values between 17 and 18 and between 65 and 66. Thus, values like 17.2 and 65.8 would be left unchanged. You can avoid this problem by using overlapping endpoint values in the specifications, as in the command

```
RECODE AGE (66 THRU 99=3)(18 THRU 66=2)(0 THRU 18=1)
```

Note that the order of the recode specifications has been reversed, since a value is recoded only once into the first specification it meets. Thus, the value 66 is coded as a 3 and is not altered further, even though it serves as an endpoint on the following specification.

A.33 Recoding into a New Variable

To recode the values of one variable and store them in another variable, use the keyword INTO, as in

```
RECODE AGE (MISSING=9) (18 THRU HI=1) (0 THRU 18=0) INTO VOTER
```

The recoded AGE values are stored in *target variable* VOTER, leaving AGE unchanged.

You can store values for several input variables in one command, as in

```
RECODE ITEM1 TO ITEM3 (0=1) (1=0) (2=-1) INTO DEFENSE WELFARE HEALTH
```

The number of target variables must equal the number of input variables. Target variables can be existing or new variables. If you use an existing variable, cases with values not mentioned in the recode specification are not changed. If you use a new variable, cases with values not specified for recoding are assigned the system-missing value for that variable. For example, if a case in the example above has a value less than 0 for variable AGE, new variable VOTER is system missing for that case. You can recode all such wild values using keyword ELSE. The command

```
RECODE AGE (MISSING=9) (18 THRU 110=1) (0 THRU 18=0) (ELSE=8) INTO VOTER
```

recodes any case with an AGE value below zero and over 110 to value 8 for variable VOTER.

New numeric variables are assigned print and write formats of F8.2 (see Section A.35).

Keyword COPY. To recode a variable into a new variable or to use keyword ELSE as a cleanup category, you may want to retain a set of input values. The command

```
RECODE ITEM1 TO ITEM3 (0=1) (1=0) (2=-1) (ELSE=COPY)
                          INTO DEFENSE WELFARE HEALTH
```

creates three new variables with values 1, 0, and −1. Input values other than 0, 1, or 2 are retained. In other words, if a case has value 9 for variable ITEM1, it will have value 9 for variable DEFENSE, and so forth.

Keyword COPY is an output specification only. Input values to be copied can be a range of values, keywords SYSMIS or MISSING, or keyword ELSE. User-missing values are copied, but their missing-value status is not. In the example above, value 9 should be redeclared missing for new variables DEFENSE, WELFARE, and HEALTH. System-missing is copied as system-missing.

A.34 Computing New Variables

The COMPUTE command creates new variables through numeric transformations of already existing variables. COMPUTE names the variable you want to create (the *target variable*) followed by an *expression* defining the variable. For example, the command

```
COMPUTE TOTSCORE=MIDTERM+FINAL+HOMEWORK
```

defines the new variable TOTSCORE as the sum of values of the variables MIDTERM, FINAL, and HOMEWORK.

The target variable can be a variable that already exists or a new variable. If the target variable already exists, its values are replaced with those produced by the specified transformation. If it is a new variable, it is added to the end of the dictionary in your active file.

The expression on the COMPUTE command can use existing numeric variables, constants, arithmetic operators (such as + and −), numeric functions such as SQRT (square root) and TRUNC (truncate), the missing-value function (VALUE), the cross-case function (LAG), random-number functions, and the date function (YRMODA). For example, the command

```
COMPUTE GRADESCR=.35*MIDTERM+.45*FINAL+.2*HOMEWORK
```

creates a new variable, GRADESCR, that is the weighted average of the variables MIDTERM, FINAL, and HOMEWORK.

A.35 Establishing the Print and Write Formats

SPSS^X stores numeric data in binary format. However, for most applications you do not want variable values that appear in the results of your SPSS^X job to be displayed or written in this form. So, for each variable defined by using SPSS^X, there are print and write formats stored on the dictionary associated with your data file. These formats control the form in which values are displayed or written to a separate file.

If you define your variables using a DATA LIST command, the dictionary print and write formats are generally those specified on the variable definition portion of the DATA LIST command. However, when you use the transformation language to create a new numeric variable, the dictionary print and write formats are both F8.2 by default.

The FORMATS command changes the print and write formats. The PRINT FORMATS command, which has identical syntax, changes only the print format. To change formats, specify the variable name or variable list followed by the new format specification in parentheses and separate the specifications for variables or variable lists with a slash, as in

```
FORMATS SALARY79 TO SALARY82 (DOLLAR8)
  /HOURLY82 (DOLLAR6.2)
```

This specification sets a dollar print format with eight positions for the first list of variables. The positions include those for the dollar sign and, when appropriate, for a comma. For example, the number 11550 is printed as $11,550. The specification also sets a dollar format with six positions including a decimal point and two decimal digits for variable HOURLY82 (to print $10.56, for example).

The most common formats include F, COMMA, and DOLLAR. F is the simple numeric format, specified as Fw.d, where *w* is the width (including the decimal point) and *d* is the number of places to the right of the decimal point. COMMA is the same as DOLLAR without the dollar sign.

A.36 Specifying Arithmetic Operations

The following arithmetic operators are available for transforming numeric variables with COMPUTE:

+ *Addition.*
– *Subtraction.*
* *Multiplication.*
/ *Division.*
** *Exponentiation.*

Arithmetic operators must be explicitly specified. You cannot, for example, write (PROPTAX)(100) instead of (PROPTAX)*100.

You can include blanks in an arithmetic expression to improve readability, as in the command

```
COMPUTE TAXTOTAL = PROPTAX + FICA + STATETAX + FEDTAX
```

Since fairly complex expressions are possible, it is important to keep in mind the order in which operations are performed. Functions (see Section A.37) are evaluated first, then exponentiation, then multiplication and division, and, finally, addition and subtraction. Thus, if you specify

```
COMPUTE NEWRATE=SQRT(RATE1)/SQRT(RATE1)+SQRT(RATE3)
```

the square roots (SQRT) are calculated first, then the division is performed, and the addition is performed last.

You can control the order in which operations are performed by enclosing the operation you want executed first in parentheses. Thus, the command

```
COMPUTE NEWRATE=SQRT(RATE1)/(SQRT(RATE1)+SQRT(RATE3))
```

produces different results than the previous command, since addition is performed before division.

Operations at the same level, as far as order of execution is concerned, are evaluated from left to right. For example, the command

```
COMPUTE SCORE=( A/B * C )
```

results in a different value than the command

```
COMPUTE SCORE=( A/ (B * C) )
```

since in the first command, A is divided by B and the resulting quantity multiplied by C, while the second command first multiplies B times C and then divides A by the resulting quantity.

If you are uncertain about the order of execution, you should use parentheses to make the order you want explicit.

A.37 Specifying Numeric Functions

You can specify numeric functions such as square roots, logarithms, and trigonometric functions in a COMPUTE expression. The quantity to be transformed by such a function is called the *argument* and is specified in parentheses after the function keyword. For example, in the command

```
COMPUTE TOTLCOST=RND(COST * 6)
```

the function RND (round to the nearest integer) acts on the argument COST * 6 to create the new variable TOTLCOST.

The argument can be a variable name, a number, or an expression involving several variables.

Arithmetic Functions.

ABS(arg) *Absolute value*. ABS(–4.7) is 4.7; ABS(4.7) is 4.7.

RND(arg) *Round the absolute value to an integer (and reaffix the sign).* RND(−4.7) is −5.

TRUNC(arg) *Truncate to an integer.* TRUNC(−4.7) is −4.

MOD(arg,arg) *Remainder (modulo) of the first argument divided by the second.* MOD(1983,100) is 83.

SQRT(arg) *Square root.*

EXP(arg) *Exponential. e* is raised to the power of the argument.

LG10(arg) *Base 10 logarithm.*

LN(arg) *Natural or Naperian logarithm (base* e*).*

ARSIN(arg) *Arcsine.* The result is given in radians (alias ASIN).

ARTAN(arg) *Arctangent.* The result is given in radians (alias ATAN).

SIN(arg) *Sine.* The argument must be specified in radians.

COS(arg) *Cosine.* The argument must be specified in radians.

All arithmetic functions except MOD have single arguments; MOD has two. Arguments can be numeric expressions as in RND(A**2/B).

Statistical Functions.

SUM(arg list) *Sum of the values across the argument list.*

MEAN(arg list) *Mean of the values across the argument list.*

SD(arg list) *Standard deviation of the values across the argument list.*

VARIANCE(arg list) *Variance of the values across the argument list.*

CFVAR(arg list) *Coefficient of variation of the values across the argument list.* The coefficient of variation is the standard deviation divided by the mean.

MIN(arg list) *Minimum value across the argument list.*

MAX(arg list) *Maximum value across the argument list.*

You can use the *.n* suffix with all statistical functions to specify the number of valid arguments you consider acceptable (see Table A.39b). For example, MEAN.2(A,B,C,D) returns the mean of the valid values for variables A, B, C, and D only if at least two of the variables have valid values. You can also use the TO keyword to reference a set of variables in the argument list.

Missing-Value Functions.

VALUE(arg) *Ignore user-defined missing values.* The argument must be a variable name.

MISSING(arg) *Return true if the value is missing and false otherwise.*

SYSMIS(arg) *Return true if the value is system-missing and false otherwise.*

NMISS(arg list) *Count of the number of missing values in the argument list.*

NVALID(arg list) *Count of the number of valid values in the argument list.*

The MISSING and SYSMIS functions are logical functions and not available for use in numeric expressions. See "logical functions" below.

You can use the keyword TO to reference a set of variables in the argument list for functions NMISS and NVALID. For example, NMISS(A TO D) returns a count of the number of variables with missing values in the list from A through D.

The Across-Case LAG Function.

LAG(arg,n) *The value of the variable n cases before.* The argument must be a numeric variable. LAG(GNP,4) returns the value of GNP for the fourth case before the current one.

If you are selecting cases from a file, LAG returns the value for the *n*th case previously selected.

Logical Functions.

RANGE(arg,arg list) *Return true if the value of the first argument is in the inclusive range(s) otherwise false.* The first argument is usually a variable, and the list usually contains pairs of values. RANGE(AGE,1,17,62,99) returns true for ages 1 through 17 and 62 through 99 inclusive.

ANY(arg,arg list) *Return true if the value of the first argument matches one of the arguments in the list, otherwise false.* The first argument is usually a variable. ANY(PROJECT,3,4,7,9) returns true if the value for variable PROJECT is 3, 4, 7, or 9.

The logical functions, including SYSMIS and MISSING, represent true with the value 1 and false with the value 0. They cannot, however, be used in numeric expressions such as SYSMIS(VARA) + 1. Their principal use is in logical expressions, as described in Section A.44.

Other Functions.

UNIFORM(arg) *A uniform pseudo-random number.* The random number is uniformly distributed with values varying between 0 and the value of the argument.

NORMAL(arg) *A normal pseudo random number.* The random number is randomly distributed with a mean of 0 and a standard deviation equal to the argument.

CDFNORM(arg) *Standard normal cumulative distribution.* This function returns the probability that a random variable with a normal distribution falls below the value of the argument.

PROBIT(arg) *Inverse of the standard normal cumulative distribution.* The value of the argument must be greater than 0 and less than 1. The argument is the probability that a normally distributed random variable will be less than the value returned.

YRMODA(arg list) *Convert year, month, and day to a day number.* With this function you must specify the year, month, and day, in that order. The number returned is the day number counting from October 15, 1582 (day 1 of the Gregorian calendar). (See "The YRMODA Function" below.)

The YRMODA Function. The YRMODA function converts a given date into a day count beginning with October 15, 1582. For example the expression YRMODA(1582,10,15) returns a value of 1. YRMODA(1800,1,1) returns 79337, indicating that January 1, 1800 is 79,336 days after the beginning of the Gregorian calendar.

The time interval between two dates can be calculated by converting each of the dates to day numbers and then subtracting the earlier day from the later one. For example, to calculate an individual's age in years on July 4, 1982, specify

```
AGE=(YRMODA(1982,7,4) - YRMODA(BYR,BMO,BDAY)) /365.25
```

where BYR is the year, BMO the month, and BDAY the day of birth.

The YRMODA function has three arguments, which can be variables, constants, or expressions that result in integer values. The following restrictions apply:

- The first argument can be any year from 1582 to 47516. If you specify a number between 00 and 99, SPSS^X will interpret it to mean 1900 to 1999.
- The second argument is the month, coded from 1 to 13. Month 13 refers to the first month of the subsequent year. For example, YRMODA(84,13,1) specifies January 1, 1985.
- The third argument is a day from 0 through 31. Day 0 specifies the last day of the previous month, regardless of whether it was 28, 29, 30, or 31. Thus, (84,2,0) refers to the last day of January in 1984. This is equivalent to (84,1,31) since January has 31 days.

A.38 Using Functions in Complex Expressions

You can specify more than one function in an argument as well as combine functions with arithmetic operators. Such arguments will be evaluated in the order described in Section A.36 or in the order specified by parentheses. For example, if the command

```
COMPUTE PCTTAXES=RND((TAXES/INCOME)*100)
```

is specified, TAXES is first divided by INCOME, then the result is multiplied by 100, and this result is rounded off to the nearest integer to get the new variable PCTTAXES.

A.39 Missing Values and Expressions

If a case has missing values for any of the variables used in a COMPUTE expression, the case is assigned the system-missing value for the computed variable. For example, if the command

```
COMPUTE AGECUBE=AGE**3
```

is specified, the AGECUBE variable will not be computed for any case with a missing value for AGE.

A case is also assigned the system-missing value for a computed variable when the specified operation is not defined for that case. For example, if the command

```
COMPUTE PCTTAXES=(TAXES/INCOME)*100
```

is specified, a case with the value 0 for INCOME is assigned the system-missing value for PCTTAXES because division by 0 is not defined. If the result of an expression cannot be represented on the computer (even when valid values are specified in the expression itself), the system-missing value is assigned to the new variable. The system-missing value is assigned when the following operations and functions are used incorrectly as described:

**	A negative number to a noninteger power.
/	A divisor of 0.
MOD	A divisor of 0.
SQRT	A negative argument.
EXP	An argument that produces a result too large to be represented on the computer.
LG10	A negative or 0 argument.
LN	A negative or 0 argument.
ARSIN	An argument whose absolute value exceeds 1.
ARTAN	An argument whose absolute value exceeds 1.
NORMAL	A negative or 0 argument.
YRMODA	Arguments that do not form a valid date (see "The YRMODA Function" above).
PROBIT	A negative or 0 argument, or an argument of 1 or greater.

Some arithmetic operations involving 0 produce the same result whether any of the arguments have missing values or not. These operations are shown in Table A.39a.

Table A.39a Missing-value exceptions in numeric expressions

Expression	Computed value
0 * missing	= 0
0 / missing	= 0
missing ** 0	= 1
0 ** missing	= 0

SPSS^X tries to evaluate a function using all the information it has, assigning the system-missing value only when there is insufficient information to compute the new variable. Table A.39b summarizes the ways in which the system-missing value is assigned.

Table A.39b Missing values in arguments to functions

Function	Returns system-missing if
ABS (x)	x is missing
ARSIN (x)	
ARTAN (x)	
CDFNORM (x)	
COS (x)	
EXP (x)	
LG10 (x)	
LN (x)	
NORMAL (x)	
PROBIT (x)	
RND (x)	
SIN (x)	
SQRT (x)	
TRUNC (x)	
UNIFORM (x)	
VALUE (x)	x is system-missing
YRMODA (x1,x2,x3)	any x is missing
MOD (x1,x2)	x1 is missing, or x2 is missing and x1 is not 0
MAX.n (x1,x2,...xk)	fewer than n arguments are valid (NVALID (x1,x2,...xk) < n) default n is 1
MEAN.n (x1,x2,...xk)	
MIN.n (x1,x2,...x1)	
SUM.n (x1,x2,...xk)	
CFVAR.n (x1,x2,...xk)	fewer than n arguments are valid (NVALID (x1,x2,...xk) < n) default n is 2
SD.n (x1,x2,...xk)	
VARIANCE.n (x1,x2,...xk)	
LAG (x,n)	x is missing n cases previously (and always for the first n cases)
ANY (x,x1,x2,...xk)	x or all of x1,x2,...xk are missing
RANGE (x,x1,x2,...xk)	x or all of pairs x1,x2, etc. are missing
MISSING (x)	never
NMISS (x1,x2,...xk)	
NVALID (x1,x2,...xk)	
SYSMIS (x)	

A.40 Counting Values Across Variables

Use the COUNT command to create a variable that records, for each case, the number of times some value or list of values occurs in a list of variables (*criterion* variable list). For example, the command

```
COUNT FEMINISM=ERA JOBEQUAL POLEQUAL (1)
```

creates the variable FEMINISM, which indicates the number of times in a case the value 1 occurs for ERA, JOBEQUAL, and POLEQUAL. Thus, the value of FEMINISM is 0, 1, 2, or 3. You can count across more than one variable list and more than one value as in the command

```
COUNT FEMINISM=ERA JOBEQUAL POLEQUAL(1) VOTE CAMPAIGN(3,4)
```

which counts the number of times the value 1 occurs in the variables ERA, JOBEQUAL, and POLEQUAL, and the value 3 or 4 occurs in VOTE and CAMPAIGN.

The criterion variable list can include both string and numeric variables, provided they have separate value specifications. String values must be enclosed in apostrophes.

You can specify adjacent variables with the TO keyword and ranges of numeric values with the LOWEST, HIGHEST, and THRU keywords. (You cannot use keyword names to specify string variables.) More than one variable can be created with a single COUNT command by separating the specifications with a slash, as in the command

```
COUNT PSYCHTIC=PTEST1 TO PTEST10(51 THRU HIGHEST)
  /SCHIZPHR=STEST1 TO STEST10(LOWEST THRU 20)
```

The COUNT command counts user-missing values. For example, the command

```
COUNT RACISM=SCALE1 TO SCALE12(LOWEST THRU 5)
```

counts the value of −99 even though it has been defined by the user as missing.

If you want to count missing values, specify the SYSMIS or MISSING keyword in parentheses after the numeric variable list. For example, the command

```
COUNT PHYSMISS=AGE WEIGHT HEIGHT(SYSMIS)
```

creates the new variable PHYSMISS, which records the number of system-missing values each case has for these variables. The MISSING keyword stands for both user- and system-missing values.

A.41 Specifying Conditional Transformations

You can instruct SPSS[X] to execute data transformations conditionally via the DO IF—END IF structure or the special IF command. The DO IF—END IF structure conditionally executes one or more transformations based on one or more logical expressions (see Section A.44). The IF command executes a single COMPUTE-like assignment based on the truth of a single logical expression.

A.42 The DO IF—END IF Structure

The DO IF—END IF structure begins with the DO IF command and ends with the END IF command. The DO IF and END IF commands by themselves (without ELSE IF or ELSE) are most frequently used to execute RECODE, COUNT, and multiple COMPUTE transformations conditionally. For example, to reverse the coding order of variable RACE for those individuals hired before 1980, specify

```
DO IF (YRHIRED LT 80)
RECODE RACE(1=5)(2=4)(4=2)(5=1)
END IF
```

The logical expression on the DO IF command specifies individuals hired before 1980. Thus, the RACE variable for individuals hired in 1980 or later is not recoded. Parentheses enclosing the logical expression are optional. See Section A.44 for a discussion of logical expressions.

Use the ELSE command to execute one or more transformations when the logical expression on the DO IF command is not true, as in

```
DO IF (X EQ 0)
COMPUTE Y=1
ELSE
COMPUTE Y=2
END IF
```

In this structure, Y is set to 1 for all cases with value 0 for X, and Y is set to 2 for cases with any other valid value for X. The value of Y is not set to anything by this structure if X is missing (see below).

If the logical expression on the DO IF command is true, SPSS[X] executes the transformation command or commands immediately following the DO IF up to the next ELSE (or ELSE IF). Then control passes to the command following the

END IF command. If the result of the logical expression is false, then control passes to ELSE (or ELSE IF).

You can further control the flow of execution by using one or more ELSE IF commands. The structure

```
DO IF (X EQ 0)
COMPUTE Y=1
ELSE IF (X LT 9)
COMPUTE Y=8
ELSE IF (X EQ 9)
COMPUTE Y=9
ELSE
COMPUTE Y=2
END IF
```

sets Y equal to 1 when X equals 0, sets Y equal to 8 when X is less than 9 but not equal to 0, sets Y equal to 9 when X equals 9, and sets Y to 2 for all valid values of X greater than 9. The value of Y is not set at all by this structure if X is missing (see below).

Missing Values. If SPSS^X encounters a case with a missing value for the logical expression on the DO IF, ELSE IF, or ELSE commands, the entire logical structure from that point on is skipped, and control passes to the first command following END IF.

A.43 The IF Command

The IF command allows you to make a single COMPUTE-like transformation in your data contingent on a logical condition. IF consists of a logical expression in parentheses followed by a target variable and an assignment expression exactly as described for the COMPUTE command. For example, the command

```
IF (AGE GE 18) VOTER=1
```

uses the logical expression (AGE GE 18) and the assignment expression VOTER =1 to assign the value 1 to the target variable VOTER for all cases with AGE values greater than or equal to 18. You construct the assignment expression in the same way as the expression in a COMPUTE statement. This command is exactly the same as the structure

```
DO IF (AGE GE 18)
COMPUTE VOTER=1
END IF
```

SPSS^X evaluates logical expressions as true or false and executes the specified assignment only when the expression is true; otherwise, the system-missing value is assigned.

A.44 Logical Expressions

The logical expression on a DO IF, ELSE IF, or IF command (and the SELECT IF command discussed in Section A.47) can be a complex statement involving variables, constants, functions, arithmetic expressions, nested parentheses, and so on. You must include either a relational operator (such as EQ or GE) or one of the logical functions ANY, RANGE, MISSING, or SYSMIS in the logical expression. Other operations and functions are optional. (See Sections A.36 through A.38 for a description of other available operators and functions.)

Comparing Values. A *relation* is a logical expression that compares two values using a *relational operator*. For example, the command

```
IF (COST EQ .43) NEWCOST=2
```

compares the equivalence of the variable COST and the value .43. The following relational operators are available:

EQ *Equal to.* The logical expression is true if the expression on the left is equal to the expression on the right.

NE *Not equal to.* The logical expression is true if the left and right expressions are not equal.

LT *Less than.* The logical expression is true if the expression on the left is less than the expression on the right.

LE *Less than or equal to.* The logical expression is true if the expression on the left is less than or equal to the expression on the right.

GT *Greater than.* The logical expression is true if the expression on the left is greater than the expression on the right.

GE *Greater than or equal to.* The logical expression is true if the expression on the left is greater than or equal to the expression on the right.

Examples of the use of logical expressions are

```
IF (SCORE1+SCORE2 GT TESTA) NEWSCORE=1
```

and

```
IF (LOGINCOM GE 5) CLASS=1
```

Use blanks to separate the relational operator from the expressions. Parentheses are not required around the logical expression.

Joining Relations. You can join two or more relations by using the logical operators AND and OR. For example, the command

```
IF (HOMEWORK GE 85 AND MIDTERM GE 90 AND FINAL GE 90) GRADE=4
```

assigns GRADE the value 4 only when HOMEWORK is at least 85 and MIDTERM and FINAL are at least 90. When AND is specified, the logical expression is true only when *all* relations joined by AND are true. When OR is specified, the logical expression is true when *any* of the relations joined by OR is true. Thus, the command

```
IF ((A EQ 4 AND B EQ 3) OR (A EQ 3 AND B EQ 4)) C=1
```

assigns the value 1 to C for any case that has a value of 4 for A and 3 for B as well as to any case with the value 3 for A and 4 for B.

You must specify operators and expressions explicitly; the specification (X EQ 1 OR 2) in place of (X EQ 1 OR X EQ 2) does not produce the same result.

Reversing the Logic. The NOT logical operator reverses the true or false status of the expression that immediately follows it. For example, the command

```
IF (NOT RACE EQ 1 AND SEX EQ 0) GROUP=1
```

assigns value 1 to GROUP for cases where RACE does not equal 1 and SEX *is* equal to 0. This is not equivalent to the command

```
IF (NOT(RACE EQ 1 AND SEX EQ 0)) GROUP=1
```

which assigns value 1 to GROUP for cases where RACE does not equal 1 and SEX does *not* equal 0.

The Order of Evaluation. Arithmetic operators and functions in a logical expression are evaluated in the same order as in the COMPUTE command (see Section A.36). Functions and arithmetic operators are evaluated first, then relational operators, then NOT, then AND, and then OR. In the expression (NOT SCORESUM/5 EQ 10), the value of SCORESUM is divided by 5, the result compared to 10, and the true-false status of this comparison is reversed by NOT.

If you specify both AND and OR, AND is executed before OR. For example, in the command

```
IF (HOMEWORK GE 90 AND MIDTERM GE 90 OR FINAL GE 95) GRADE=4
```

the logical expression is true for a case with HOMEWORK and MIDTERM values of at least 90, or for a FINAL value of at least 95. You can use parentheses to clarify or change the order of evaluation. Thus, the command

```
IF ((HOMEWORK GE 90 AND MIDTERM GE 90) OR FINAL GE 95) GRADE=4
```

is equivalent to the previous command. The command

```
IF (HOMEWORK GE 90 AND (MIDTERM GE 90 OR FINAL GE 95)) GRADE=4
```

is not equivalent. In this statement, a case must have a score of at least 90 for HOMEWORK, as well as a value of at least 90 for MIDTERM *or* 95 for FINAL, to be assigned the grade 4.

Missing Values in Logical Expressions. If the truth of a logical expression cannot be determined because of missing values, the value of the logical expression is indeterminate (neither true nor false) and is considered missing. In a relation with only one relational operator, the logical expression is indeterminate if the expression on either side of the operator has a missing value. For example, if you specify

```
IF (FINAL GT MIDTERM) TEST=1
```

and either FINAL or MIDTERM is missing for a case, SPSS^X cannot tell whether one variable is greater than the other. In an IF command, SPSS^X simply does not execute the assignment expression. See Section A.42 for missing values and DO IF.

When several relations are joined by AND or OR, SPSS^X automatically returns the missing value if *all* of the relations in the expression have missing values. If any of the relations have valid values, however, SPSS^X tries to evaluate whether the expression can be determined to be true or false according to Table A.44. The outcomes marked with an asterisk are determined even though their expressions contain missing values.

Table A.44 Logical outcome

Expression	Outcome	Expression	Outcome
true AND true	= true	true OR true	= true
true AND false	= false	true OR false	= true
false AND false	= false	false OR false	= false
true AND missing	= missing	true OR missing	= true*
missing AND missing	= missing	missing OR missing	= missing
false AND missing	= false*	false OR missing	= missing

Missing-Value Logical Functions. You can use the functions MISSING and SYSMIS to specify missing values as criteria for performing or not performing transformations. For example, the command

```
IF (SYSMIS(SCORE1)) GRADE=0
```

determines if SCORE1 is system-missing. If it is, GRADE is assigned the value 0.

The command

```
IF (NOT(MISSING(GRADE))) GRADE=1
```

evaluates whether the value of GRADE is not equal to the user- or system-missing values. Each case that has a valid value for GRADE is assigned the value 1 for GRADE.

You can also use the VALUE function on an IF command to ignore the user-missing status of values. For example, the commands

```
RECODE AGE (5 THRU 20 = 1) (20 THRU 65 = 2) (65 THRU HI = 3)
MISSING VALUE AGE (3)
IF (VALUE(AGE) GT 0 ) GRPAGE=1
```

collapse the values of AGE into three values and designate the value 3 as user-missing. The IF command specifies that any case with a value greater than 0 for AGE be given the value 1 for GRPAGE. Because the VALUE keyword on the IF command tells SPSS^X to ignore user-missing values, cases with value 3 for AGE are given the value 1 for GRPAGE.

A.45 Temporary Transformations

The TEMPORARY command makes the transformations that are between it and the next procedure apply only to that procedure. For example, if you want to use recoded and unrecoded versions of variables in the same SPSS^X job, you can specify

```
TEMPORARY
RECODE SODIUM (6 THRU 10=1)(11 THRU 17=2) (18 THRU 27=3)
  /COST (.27 THRU .42=1)(.43 THRU .48=2)(.50 THRU 1.20=3)
CROSSTABS SODIUM BY COST
PLOT PLOT=SODIUM WITH COST
```

SODIUM and COST each will have three values for the CROSSTABS procedure, but both will return to their original unrecoded values for PLOT.

TEMPORARY works for all transformations, including those that select, sample and weight cases (see Sections A.46–A.51). For example, if the commands

```
TEMPORARY
SELECT IF (SEX EQ 1)
FREQUENCIES VARIABLES=TEMP FIRSTEKG SECNDEKG
TEMPORARY
SELECT IF (SEX EQ 2)
FREQUENCIES VARIABLES=TEMP FIRSTEKG SECNDEKG
```

are used, the first FREQUENCIES procedure analyzes only the data for women, and the second FREQUENCIES procedure analyzes only the data for men.

A.46 SELECTING AND SAMPLING CASES

Suppose you are interested in plotting the relationship between cost and alcohol content in the beer data, but you only want the plot to include domestic beers. Or you wish to examine the distribution of calories only for the beers that have been assigned ratings of "very good." These are two examples of situations where you want to select a subset of cases from a file, based on some particular criterion. You can use the SELECT IF command to select a subset of cases for an SPSS^X job.

When there are many cases in a file, you may want to select a random sample of them for processing. This decreases the time needed for analysis and may provide you with useful preliminary results. For example, if you have information on 10,000 cases, you might want to obtain plots or histograms for a random subset of them. These plots should reflect the overall trends present in the data. The SAMPLE command selects a random sample of cases from a file.

To restrict analysis to the first *n* cases in a data set, use the N OF CASES command. This command is particularly useful if you want to get an idea of the display produced by a procedure without having to wait for all cases to be processed. For example, if you are preparing a report and want to make sure that you have included all the necessary information in an appropriate format, running it on a small number of "test" cases is an efficient strategy.

A.47 Selecting Cases

The SELECT IF command selects cases for analysis if they meet criteria you specify. You specify these criteria in a logical expression that SPSS^X can evaluate as true or false. For example, the command

```
SELECT IF (SEX EQ 1)
```

selects cases with the value 1 for SEX for analysis.

You can include the SELECT IF command anywhere in an SPSS^X job, except between the BEGIN DATA and END DATA commands. Once you use SELECT IF, the selection specified is in effect for all subsequent procedures. If you use another SELECT IF command, it selects a subset of cases from the first selected subset rather than from the original data set.

Multiple SELECT IF commands should be used with caution, as you can end up selecting no cases. For example, if the commands

```
SELECT IF (SEX EQ 1)
FREQUENCIES VARIABLES=TEMP FIRSTEKG SECNDEKG
SELECT IF (SEX EQ 2)
FREQUENCIES VARIABLES=TEMP FIRSTEKG SECNDEKG
```

are used, there will be no cases for the second FREQUENCIES procedure to analyze, since SEX cannot equal both 1 and 2. If you want to temporarily select cases for one procedure, use the TEMPORARY command (see Section A.45).

A.48 Specifying the Logical Expression

The logical expression on SELECT IF is specified in the same way as the logical expression on the DO IF and IF commands (see Sections A.41 through A.44). If the logical expression cannot be determined for a case because of missing values, that case is not selected.

To select cases based on missing or nonmissing values for analysis, use the SYSMIS and MISSING functions, as in

```
SELECT IF NOT(MISSING(AGE))
```

This command selects all cases with valid values for AGE.

A.49 Drawing a Sample

The SAMPLE command draws a random subsample of cases. You can include SAMPLE anywhere in an SPSS^X session except between the BEGIN DATA and END DATA commands.

To sample a proportion of cases, specify the proportion on the SAMPLE command, as in

```
SAMPLE .25
```

This command samples approximately one-fourth of the cases.

If you know the total number of cases, you can specify the number of cases to be sampled, as in the command

```
SAMPLE 50 FROM 200
```

This command draws a random sample of 50 cases only if there are exactly 200 total cases. If there are fewer than 200 cases, proportionately fewer cases are sampled. If there are more than 200 cases, the subsample is taken only from the first 200 cases.

Unless preceded by the TEMPORARY command, SAMPLE remains in effect for all subsequent procedures. A second SAMPLE command draws its sample from the sample taken by the first SAMPLE command.

If SAMPLE follows a SELECT IF command, the sample is drawn from the selected subset of cases. Conversely, if SAMPLE precedes SELECT IF, the specified subset of cases is selected from the sample. If you specify more than one SAMPLE command prior to a procedure, each SAMPLE command takes a sample of the previous sample.

A.50 Selecting the First n Cases

The N OF CASES command is used to select the first *n* cases in a file. For example, if your file has 1000 cases, but you want to analyze only the first 100 cases, specify

```
N OF CASES 100
```

You can enter the N OF CASES command at any point in an SPSS^{X} job. If you specify it before the first procedure in a run (or before BEGIN DATA if the data are inline), it limits the cases analyzed by all subsequent procedures. If specified between procedures, it limits the number of cases read for the subsequent procedure only.

The commands SELECT IF and SAMPLE are executed before N OF CASES if the commands occur together (even if N OF CASES is specified first). For example, if you specify

```
N OF CASES 100
SAMPLE .5
```

approximately half of the total cases are sampled, and then the first 100 of these are selected for analysis.

A.51 WEIGHTING CASES

You can adjust the weighting of cases for analysis by using the WEIGHT command. For example, if you have a sample in which males have been oversampled (i.e., there is a much higher proportion of males in the sample than in the population), you may want to give the data for males less weight in your computations.

The only specification on WEIGHT is the name of the variable to be used for weighting, as in the command

```
WEIGHT BY WGHTVAR
```

Only one weighting variable can be specified on the command, and it must be numeric. The values of the weighting variable need not be integers, but missing or negative values are treated as zeros. Most SPSS^{X} procedures can handle noninteger weights, with the exception of PLOT and NPAR TESTS. When weighting is used, files that are saved retain the weighting.

The weighting variable can be an already existing variable or a variable created through transformation statements. For example, suppose men have been oversampled by a factor of 2. To compensate for this, you can weight male cases by .5, as in the commands

```
COMPUTE WT=1
IF (SEX EQ 2) WT=.5
WEIGHT BY WT
```

If you create a weighting variable with an IF command, it is important to first initialize its weight with a COMPUTE command. Otherwise, cases not covered by the IF command will have missing values for the weighting variable. A case weighted by 1 is unaffected when WEIGHT is executed, but a case weighted by 0 or by a missing value is eliminated.

A WEIGHT command stays in effect for the entire job unless followed by another WEIGHT command or turned off with the command

```
WEIGHT OFF
```

Weighting is *not* cumulative. That is, a new WEIGHT command reweights the sample rather than alters previously weighted values. For example, if the commands

```
WEIGHT BY WT1
DESCRIPTIVES ALL 1
WEIGHT BY WT2
DESCRIPTIVES ALL 1
```

are used, the first DESCRIPTIVES procedure computes summary statistics based on cases weighted by WT1, and the second DESCRIPTIVES procedure computes summary statistics based on cases weighted by WT2.

When weighting is in effect, significance tests are usually based on the weighted sample size. If the weighted number of cases exceeds the sample size, the *p*-values given for these tests will be too small. If the weighted number of cases is smaller than the actual sample size, the *p*-values calculated will be too large. You can avoid these problems by using weight factors that add up to the sample size.

A.52 SORTING CASES

You can use the SORT CASES command to reorder your data according to the values of a specified variable or variables. Specify SORT CASES with the BY keyword, followed by the name(s) of the variable(s) to be used for sorting. The variables specified can be numeric or string. String variables are sorted by the alphanumeric sorting order on your computer.

Cases can be sorted in ascending or descending order. Ascending order is the default. To sort cases in descending order (in which the values for the sorting variable are ordered from highest to lowest), you specify (D) after the variable name, as in the command

```
SORT CASES BY SALES(D)
```

(D) is also used to reverse the alphabetical order of string variables.

You can specify (A) after a variable name to explicitly request ascending order. When (D) or (A) appears after a list of otherwise unspecified variables, all are sorted in the order specified. For example, the command

```
SORT CASES BY PRODUCT DEPT SALES(D)
```

requests that PRODUCT, DEPT, and SALES all be sorted in descending order.

When several sorting variables are listed, cases are first sorted according to the first variable named. Cases with the same value for the first sorting variable are then sorted according to the second sorting variable, and so on. For example, the command

```
SORT CASES BY PRODUCT(D) DEPT(A) SALES(D)
```

produces the following sorted values for PRODUCT, DEPT, and SALES:

```
4 1  $9,750
4 2 $18,083
4 2 $15,608
4 2 $15,132
4 2 $12,438
4 2 $11,240
4 2 $10,050
3 1 $17,051
3 2 $39,000
3 2 $19,682
3 2 $13,650
3 2  $9,777
3 2  $9,507
3 2  $8,872
3 2  $8,239
1 1 $35,750
1 1 $17,111
1 1 $13,910
```

[1]With releases before 3.0, replace the DESCRIPTIVES command with the following:

```
CONDESCRIPTIVE ALL
```

Contents

B.1 DATA DEFINITION COMMANDS
B.2 BEGIN DATA and END DATA Commands
B.3 DATA LIST Command
B.4 File Definition on DATA LIST
B.5 Variable Definition on DATA LIST
B.6 REFERRING TO A FILE IN SPSS^X
B.7 FILE LABEL Command
B.8 FILE TYPE|END FILE TYPE Structure
B.9 GET Command
B.10 FILE Subcommand
B.11 RENAME Subcommand
B.12 DROP Subcommand
B.13 KEEP Subcommand
B.14 MAP Subcommand
B.15 MISSING VALUES Command
B.16 SAVE and XSAVE Commands
B.17 OUTFILE Subcommand
B.18 RENAME Subcommand
B.19 DROP Subcommand
B.20 KEEP Subcommand
B.21 MAP Subcommand
B.22 XSAVE Command
B.23 VALUE LABELS Command
B.24 ADD VALUE LABELS Command
B.25 VARIABLE LABELS Command
B.26 UTILITY COMMANDS
B.27 COMMENT Command
B.28 DISPLAY Command
B.29 DOCUMENT Command
B.30 EDIT Command
B.31 FINISH Command
B.32 FORMATS Command
B.33 HELP Command
B.34 INFO Command
B.35 N OF CASES Command
B.36 NUMBERED Command
B.37 PRINT FORMATS Command
B.38 SET and SHOW Commands
B.39 SUBTITLE Command
B.40 TITLE Command
B.41 WRITE FORMATS Command
B.42 DATA TRANSFORMATION COMMANDS
B.43 COMPUTE Command
B.44 Generating Distributions
B.45 COUNT Command
B.46 DO IF|END IF Structure
B.47 IF Command
B.48 RECODE Command
B.49 SAMPLE Command
B.50 SELECT IF Command
B.51 SORT CASES Command
B.52 SPLIT FILE Command
B.53 TEMPORARY Command
B.54 WEIGHT Command
B.55 PROCEDURE COMMANDS

Appendix B

SPSS^X Command Reference

This chapter is an abbreviated guide to the SPSS^X system. It is designed to accompany this book and therefore does not describe the entire SPSS^X language. The *SPSS^X User's Guide,* 3rd ed., documents the entire system as of Release 3.0. (The second edition of the guide documents releases earlier than 3.0. Use the edition that corresponds to the release installed at your computer center.)

The chapter is divided into four sections: data definition commands; job utility commands; data transformation and modification commands; and procedure commands. The commands are organized alphabetically within each section. In the syntax diagrams, square brackets indicate optional specifications not necessary to the completion of the command. Braces enclose alternative specifications. One of these specifications must be entered to complete the specification correctly. Ellipses are used to indicate optional repetition of an element or elements in the specification. This scheme cannot always exactly describe choices and requirements. If you are in doubt, look at examples in the text. Upper-case specifications should be entered as shown; lower-case specifications show information you must provide. The syntax diagram for the current release, 3.0, is given first, followed by the diagram for the previous releases.

B.1 DATA DEFINITION COMMANDS

The data definition commands tell SPSS^X how to read and interpret your data. This involves naming the variables you want to analyze, specifying their location and format within the data for each case, informing SPSS^X of any values that represent missing information, and supplying any labels you want included in your printed output. SPSS^X uses data definition specifications to build a *dictionary* that describes the variables on your file. After you have defined your data, you can save the dictionary and data on an SPSS^X system file and use the system file as input in SPSS^X jobs for additional analysis.

B.2 BEGIN DATA and END DATA Commands

Syntax for all releases:

```
BEGIN DATA
lines of data
END DATA
```

If your data are included as lines in your SPSS^X command file, you must use the BEGIN DATA command immediately before the first line of data and the END DATA command immediately after the last line of data to separate lines containing data from lines containing SPSS^X commands. With in-line data, you can omit the FILE subcommand on the DATA LIST command or specify the default FILE=INLINE. The BEGIN DATA command followed by the data lines and the END DATA command should follow the first procedure command.

B.3 DATA LIST Command

Syntax for all releases:

```
DATA LIST [FILE=file] [{FIXED}] [RECORDS={1}] [{TABLE  }]
                       {FREE }           {n}    {NOTABLE}
                       {LIST }

          [END=varname]

  /{1    } varlist {col location [(format)]  } [varlist ...]
   {rec #}         {(FORTRAN-like format list}

 [/{2    } ...] [/ ...]
   {rec #}
```

Numeric and string formats:

Format	FORTRAN-like format	Data type
(d)	Fw.d	Numeric (default)
(N)	Nw	Restricted numeric
(E,d)	Ew.d	Scientific notation
(COMMA,d)	COMMAw.d	Numeric with commas
(DOT,d)	DOTw.d	Numeric with dots
(DOLLAR,d)	DOLLARw.d	Numeric with commas and dollar sign
(PCT,d)	PCTw.d	Numeric with percent sign
(Z,d)	Zw.d	Zoned decimal
(A)	Aw	String
(AHEX)	AHEXw	Hexadecimal character
(IB,d)	IBw.d	Integer binary
(P,d)	Pw.d	Packed decimal
(PIB,d)	PIBw.d	Unsigned integer binary
(PIBHEX)	PIBHEXw	Hexadecimal unsigned integer binary
(PK,d)	PKw.d	Unsigned packed decimal
(RB)	RBw	Floating point binary
(RBHEX)	RBHEXw	Hexadecimal floating point binary
	Tn	Tabs to column n
	nX	Skips n columns

Some formats may not be available on all implementations of SPSS^X.

The DATA LIST command has two parts: file definition and variable definition. The file definition portion points SPSS^X to the data file and indicates the format of the file and the number of records per case for fixed-format data files. The variable definition portion names the variables and indicates their location and type.

B.4 File Definition on DATA LIST

You can specify four pieces of information describing the file on the DATA LIST command.

FILE Subcommand. Use the FILE subcommand to specify the file for the data described by the DATA LIST command. If the data are included with the SPSS^X commands, omit the FILE subcommand or explicitly specify the default file INLINE.

FIXED, FREE, and LIST Keywords. Use one of the following keywords to indicate the format of the data:

FIXED *Fixed-format data.* Each variable is recorded in the same location on the same record for each case in the data. FIXED is the default.

FREE *Freefield-format data.* The variables are recorded in the same order for each case, but not necessarily in the same location. You can enter multiple cases on the same record with each value separated by one or more blanks or commas. See Section B.5 for an example.

LIST *Freefield data with one case on each record.* The variables are recorded in freefield format as described for keyword FREE except the variables for each case must be recorded on one record. See Section B.5 for an example.

RECORDS Subcommand. Use the RECORDS subcommand with fixed-format data to specify the number of records per case. By default, SPSS^X assumes one record per case for fixed-format data.

TABLE and NOTABLE Subcommands. TABLE, the default for fixed-format files, displays a table that summarizes your file and variable definitions immediately following the DATA LIST command. To suppress this table, specify subcommand NOTABLE.

B.5 Variable Definition on DATA LIST

Use the variable definition portion of the DATA LIST command to assign a name to each variable you intend to analyze and, depending on the format of your file, to provide information about the location and format of the individual variables. For fixed-format data, specify the record number, name, column location, and type of each variable.

FREE or LIST Formats. For FREE and LIST formats, SPSS^X reads the values sequentially in the order that the variables are named on the DATA LIST command. The values must be separated in your data by at least one blank or comma. For example,

```
DATA LIST FREE/ TREAT1 TREAT2 TREAT3
BEGIN DATA
2.90 2.97 2.67 2.56 2.45 2.62 2.88 2.76
1.87 2.73 2.20 2.33 2.50 2.16 1.27 3.18
2.89 2.39 2.83 2.87 2.39
END DATA
```

defines three treatment variables. The first three values build the first case. The value 2.90 is assigned to variable TREAT1, the value 2.97 is assigned to variable TREAT2, and the value 2.67 is assigned to TREAT3. The second case is built from the next three values in the data, and so forth. Altogether, seven cases are built.

In LIST format, each case is recorded on a separate record. To read this data, specify the keyword LIST, as in:

```
DATA LIST LIST/ TREAT1 TREAT2 TREAT3
BEGIN DATA
2.90 2.97 2.67
2.56 2.45 2.62
2.88 2.76 1.87
2.73 2.20 2.33
2.50 2.16 1.27
3.18 2.89 2.39
2.83 2.87 2.39
END DATA
```

The LIST format requires more records in your data file than the FREE format. However, it is less prone to errors in data entry. Since FREE format reads the data as one long series of numbers, if you leave out a value in the data, the values after the missing value are assigned to the incorrect variable for all remaining cases. Since LIST format reads a case from each record, the missing value will affect only the one case.

You cannot use a blank value to indicate missing information in FREE or LIST formatted data. Rather you must assign a value to the missing information and declare the value missing with the MISSING VALUES command.

B.6 REFERRING TO A FILE IN SPSS^X

Specifications differ by implementation of SPSS-X.

SPSS^X can read and write more than one file in a single job. The files include data files, system files, and special files of statistical results. Subcommands that refer to files in SPSS^X are the FILE, OUTFILE, MATRIX, and WRITE subcommands on various procedures.

Not all implementations and releases of SPSS^X use the same method for referring to a file. Some implementations amd releases require both host system commands and the use of the FILE HANDLE command within SPSS^X. Others offer extensions to the ability to reference a file directly on a FILE, OUTFILE, MATRIX, or WRITE subcommand. For instance, some implementations permit the specification of just a portion of a file name and supply defaults for the other portions.

For details on the methods you can use to refer to SPSS^X files at your installation, see the documentation available with keyword LOCAL on the INFO command, discussed in Section B.34.

Examples throughout this manual refer to files by specifying a file handle on the FILE or OUTFILE subcommand of the command being discussed. For example, the GET command uses a FILE subcommand to specify a file, as in

```
GET  FILE=ELECTRIC
```

which gets the SPSS^X system file ELECTRIC.

A file handle cannot exceed eight characters and must begin with an alphabetic character (A–Z) or a $, #, or @. It can also contain numeric characters (0–9), but no embedded blanks are allowed.

On the syntax chart for each command, the file handle is abbreviated to the general term *file*.

B.7 FILE LABEL Command

Syntax for all releases:

```
FILE LABEL label
```

The FILE LABEL command provides a descriptive label for your data file. The file label can contain up to 60 characters and is specified as a literal (see Section B.23). It is printed on the first line of each page of output displayed by SPSS^X and is included in the dictionary of the system file. The command

```
FILE LABEL 'WESTERN ELECTRIC STUDY OF CORONARY HEART DISEASE'
```

assigns a file label to the data file.

B.8 FILE TYPE—END FILE TYPE Structure

Syntax for all releases:

For FILE TYPE MIXED

```
FILE TYPE MIXED [FILE=file] RECORD=[varname] col loc [WILD={NOWARN}]
                                                           {WARN  }
```

For FILE TYPE GROUPED

```
FILE TYPE GROUPED [FILE=file] RECORD=[varname] col loc

 CASE=[varname] col loc [WILD={WARN  }] [DUPLICATE= {WARN  }]
                              {NOWARN}              {NOWARN}

 [MISSING={WARN  }] [ORDERED={YES}]
          {NOWARN}           {NO }
```

For FILE TYPE NESTED

```
FILE TYPE NESTED [FILE=file] RECORD=[varname] col loc

 [CASE=[varname] col loc ] [WILD={NOWARN}] [DUPLICATE={NOWARN}]
                                 {WARN  }             {WARN  }
                                                      {CASE  }

 [MISSING={NOWARN}]
          {WARN  }

END FILE TYPE
```

The FILE TYPE—END FILE TYPE file definition structure is used to read many types of nonrectangular files. *SPSS^X User's Guide,* 3rd ed., discusses all of the features of this file definition facility for nonrectangular files. Another use of the FILE TYPE—END FILE TYPE structure is to check for duplicate, missing, and wild records in a data file with multiple records for each case. This type of file is a rectangular file defined as a GROUPED file.

With the FILE TYPE—END FILE TYPE structure, each record in your file must contain a unique code identifying the record and a code identifying the case for this record. The records for a single case must be together in your file. By default, SPSS^X assumes that the records are in the same sequence within each case. For example, Figure B.8 shows the first nine records from a marketing survey data file.

Figure B.8 Marketing survey data with a missing record

```
001H56277544354435327167566266255344376367355423256144376465577730
001W22356521175255353243575121322442311321265434111311221451411140
002H77111547147174177162242177176511177177177577175123232577757710
003H66222455311346322133433357121464435353324465335311222356477740
003W66177142311375111353131333377116444367321344352211377275222330
004H12132534125477133332343377112433434244133412177144133466355200
004W11277211211374211377277133144374277344211322274277364277314400
005H57254435152577223145366526167422377233166375146266165477522400
005W33235544277577322144355252255535377577166444265255146577533300
```

The first three columns of each record contain the case identifier, and column 4 contains the record identifier. The first two records represent Case 1; the first record is an "H" record type for the husband's record, and the second record is a "W" record type for the wife's record. An error has been introduced into the file: Case 2 has a missing record type W.

You can define this file using FILE TYPE, RECORD TYPE, and END FILE TYPE commands with a DATA LIST command for each record type, as in:

```
FILE TYPE GROUPED FILE=MARKET RECORD=RESPTYP 4 (A) CASE= CASEID 1-3
RECORD TYPE 'H'
DATA LIST   /H1S H10 H1R H2S H20
  H2R H3S H30 H3R H4S H40 H4R H5S H50 H5R H6S H60 H6R H7S H70 H7R
  H8S H80 H8R H9S H90 H9R H10S H100 H10R H11S H110 H11R H12S H120 H12R
  H13S H130 H13R H14S H140 H14R H15S H150 H15R H16S H160 H16R H17S
  H170 H17R H18S H180 H18R H19S H190 H19R H20S H200 H20R VISUAL 5-65
RECORD TYPE 'W'
DATA LIST  /W1S W10 W1R W2S W20
  W2R W3S W30 W3R W4S W40 W4R W5S W50 W5R W6S W60 W6R W7S W70 W7R
  W8S W80 W8R W9S W90 W9R W10S W100 W10R W11S W110 W11R W12S W120 W12R
  W13S W130 W13R W14S W140 W14R W15S W150 W15R W16S W160 W16R  W17S
  W170 W17R W18S W180 W18R W19S W190 W19R W20S W200 W20R 5-64
END FILE TYPE
FREQUENCIES VARIABLES=H1S W1S
```

The FILE TYPE command specifies a grouped file type and identifies MARKET as the data file. The FILE TYPE command also specifies the record identifier variable RESPTYP as a string located in column 4, and the case identifier variable CASEID located in columns 1 through 3. The first RECORD TYPE command specifies record type H as the first record for each case. All type H records are defined by the DATA LIST command following this RECORD TYPE command. The second RECORD TYPE command identifies the type W records, and the following DATA LIST command defines this record type. Records with other values on RESPTYP are reported as errors. If a case has a duplicate record type or if a record type is missing for a case, a warning message is printed. The record missing from Figure B.8 produces the following warning message:

```
>WARNING   518
>A record is missing from the indicated case.  The variables defined on the
>record have been set to the system missing value.

RECORD IDENTIFIER:W
CASE IDENTIFIER :  2
CURRENT CASE NUMBER:       2, CURRENT SPLIT FILE NUMBER:      1.
```

Four types of information are required on the FILE TYPE command for grouped file types.

GROUPED Keyword. GROUPED indicates that the file being described is a grouped file.

FILE Subcommand. FILE names the file to be defined and is required unless your data are included in the command file.

RECORD Subcommand. RECORD names the variable, location, and type of the record identifier. Each record in the file must contain a unique code and the value must be coded in the same location on all records. Specify a variable name, followed by the column location of the variable. If the variable is a string, specify the letter *A* in parentheses after the column location.

CASE Subcommand. CASE names the variable, location, and type of the case identifier. Each case must contain a unique value for this variable. Specify a variable name, followed by the column location of the variable. If the variable is a string, specify an A in parentheses after the column location.

You must include one RECORD TYPE command for each record type containing data that you want to read. The specification on the RECORD TYPE command is the value of the record type variable defined on the RECORD subcommand on the FILE TYPE command. If the record type is a string variable, enclose the value in apostrophes or quotation marks. After each RECORD TYPE command, you must also specify a DATA LIST command describing the variables to be read from that record type. The record types must be specified in the same order as their order within each case.

B.9 GET Command

Syntax for all releases:

```
GET FILE=file

[/KEEP={ALL    }] [/DROP=varlist]
       {varlist}

[/RENAME=(old varlist=new varlist)...]

[/MAP]
```

An SPSS^X system file is a self-documented file containing data and descriptive information, called the dictionary. The dictionary contains variable names, their print and write formats, and optional variable labels, value labels, and missing-value indicators. Use the SAVE command to save a system file (Section B.16) and the GET command to read a system file.

B.10 FILE Subcommand

The only required specification on the GET command is the FILE subcommand, which specifies the system file to be read. For example, to read the Western Electric data, specify:

```
GET FILE=ELECTRIC
```

Optional subcommands rename variables, select a subset of variables, reorder the variables, and display the names of the variables saved. Separate each subcommand from the other subcommands with a slash. A subcommand acts on the results of all the previous subcommands on the GET command.

B.11 RENAME Subcommand

Use the RENAME subcommand to change the names of variables as they are copied from the system file. Variable names are not changed on the system file. The rename specifications are enclosed in parentheses in the form *old=new,* as in:

```
GET FILE=ELECTRIC /RENAME=(EDUYR,DBP58=EDUC,BLOODPR)
```

This command changes the name of variable EDUYR to EDUC, and variable DBP58 to BLOODPR. Use the keyword TO to refer to consecutive variables to be renamed (on the left side of the equals sign) or to generate new variable names (on the right side of the equals sign).

B.12 DROP Subcommand

Use the DROP subcommand to specify variables that you want dropped when SPSS[X] reads the system file. For example, to drop the variables CASEID and FAMHXCVR from the Western Electric data, specify:

```
GET FILE=ELECTRIC/RENAME=(EDUYR,DBP58=EDUC,BLOODPR)
  /DROP=CASEID,FAMHXCVR
```

Note that these variables are not dropped from the system file. Again, you can use the keyword TO to refer to a series of consecutive variables.

B.13 KEEP Subcommand

Use the KEEP subcommand to select a subset of variables and to reorder the variables as they are read from the system file. Specify the variables in the order that you want them copied from the system file. For example, to read only the variables EDUYR (renamed to EDUC), DBP58 (renamed to BLOODPR), and HT58 through DAYOFWK in that order, specify:

```
GET FILE=ELECTRIC/RENAME=(EDUYR,DBP58=EDUC,BLOODPR)
  /KEEP=EDUC,BLOODPR,HT58 TO DAYOFWK
```

Note that the renamed variables are referred to by their new names on the KEEP subcommand. The results of the subcommands are cumulative.

You can reorder all of the variables in your file either by listing the names of all the variables in the order that you want them or by listing the names of the variables that you want at the beginning of the file in the desired order, followed by the keyword ALL. Keyword ALL places all the unnamed variables after the named variables in the same sequence on the active file as they appear in the system file.

B.14 MAP Subcommand

To check the results of the RENAME, DROP, and KEEP subcommands, use the MAP subcommand, as in:

```
GET FILE=ELECTRIC /RENAME=(EDUYR,DBP58=EDUC,BLOODPR)
  /KEEP=EDUC,BLOODPR,HT58 TO DAYOFWK /MAP
```

The MAP subcommand displays the results from the previous subcommands, showing the variables on the active file and their corresponding names on the system file.

B.15 MISSING VALUES Command

Syntax for all releases:

```
MISSING VALUES {varlist(value list) [[/]varlist ...]}
               {ALL(value)                          }
```

Numeric Value List Keywords:

LO, LOWEST, HI, HIGHEST, THRU

Very often, your data file lacks complete information on some cases for some variables. Monitoring equipment can malfunction, interviewers can forget to ask a question or record an answer, respondents can refuse to answer, and so forth. Missing does not always mean the same as unknown or absent. For example, if you record the value 9 for "Refused to answer" and the value 0 for "No answer reported," you might want to specify both of these values as missing.

Use the MISSING VALUES command to declare the missing values for certain variables in your file. The values defined as missing are never changed on the data; they are simply flagged in the dictionary. The SPSS^X statistical procedures and transformation commands recognize this flag, and those cases that contain a user-defined missing value are handled specially. All SPSS^X statistical procedures provide options for handling cases with missing values.

The MISSING VALUES command specifies a variable name or variable list and the missing value or values enclosed in parentheses and separated by a comma or blank. You can specify a maximum of three individual values or one value and a range for each variable. For example, to declare the values 0, 98, and 99 as missing for the variable AGE, specify:

```
MISSING VALUES AGE (0,98,99)
```

You can specify a range of values as missing using the keyword THRU to indicate an inclusive range of values. For example, the command

```
MISSING VALUES AGE (0,98,99) /EDUC (0,97 THRU 99)
```

declares the missing values for AGE and the values 0, 97, 98, and 99 as missing for variable EDUC. Use the keyword HIGHEST or LOWEST with THRU to indicate the highest or lowest value of a variable.

You can define missing values for short string variables. To specify a value of a string variable, enclose the value in apostrophes or quotation marks. The command

```
MISSING VALUES STRING1 ('X','Y')
```

specifies the values X and Y as missing for the single-column string variable STRING1. Value ranges cannot be specified for string variables.

B.16 SAVE and XSAVE Commands

Syntax for all releases:

```
SAVE OUTFILE=file

 [/KEEP={ALL    }] [/DROP=varlist]
        {varlist}

 [/RENAME=(old varlist=new varlist)...]

 [/MAP] [/{COMPRESSED  }]
          {UNCOMPRESSED}


XSAVE† OUTFILE=file

 [/KEEP={ALL    }] [/DROP=varlist]
        {varlist}

 [/RENAME=(old varlist=new varlist)...]

 [/MAP] [/{COMPRESSED  }]
          {UNCOMPRESSED}
```

†Available as of Release 2.0.

An SPSS^X system file is a self-documented file containing data and descriptive information called the dictionary. The dictionary contains variable names, their print and write formats, and optional extended variable labels, value labels, and missing-value indicators. It also contains the file label from the FILE LABEL command and additional documentation supplied on the DOCUMENT command. Use the SAVE command to save a system file (or XSAVE command as of Release 2.0) and the GET command to read a system file (see Section B.9).

B.17 OUTFILE Subcommand

The only required specification on the SAVE command is the OUTFILE subcommand, which specifies the system file to be saved. For example, to save the Western Electric data, specify:

```
DATA LIST FILE=DATA /CASEID 1-4 FIRSTCHD 6 AGE 17-18 DBP58 20-22
  EDUYR 24-25 CHOL58 27-29 CGT58 31-32 HT58 34-37 (1) WT58 39-40
  DAYOFWK 43 VITAL10 45 FAMHXCVR 47 (A) CHD 49
SAVE OUTFILE=ELECTRIC
```

Optional subcommands rename variables, select a subset of variables, reorder the variables, and display the names of the variables saved. Separate each subcommand from the other subcommands with a slash. A subcommand acts on the results of all the previous subcommands on the SAVE command.

B.18 RENAME Subcommand

Use the RENAME subcommand to change the names of variables as they are copied onto the system file. Variable names are not changed on the active file. The rename specifications are enclosed in parentheses in the form *old=new,* as in:

```
SAVE OUTFILE=ELECTRIC /RENAME=(EDUYR,DBP58=EDUC,BLOODPR)
```

This command changes the name of variable EDUYR to EDUC, and the variable DBP58 to BLOODPR. Use the keyword TO to refer to consecutive variables to be renamed (on the left side of the equals sign) or to generate new variable names (on the right side of the equals sign).

B.19 DROP Subcommand

Use the DROP subcommand to specify variables that you want dropped when SPSS^X writes the system file. The variables are not dropped from the active file. For example, to eliminate variables CASEID and FAMHXCVR from the Western Electric system file, specify:

```
SAVE OUTFILE=ELECTRIC /RENAME=(EDUYR,DBP58=EDUC,BLOODPR)
  /DROP=CASEID,FAMHXCVR
```

You can use the keyword TO to drop a series of consecutive variables.

B.20 KEEP Subcommand

Use the KEEP subcommand to select a subset of variables and to reorder the variables as they are written on the system file. Specify the variables in the order that you want them copied from the active file. For example, to save only the variables EDUYR (renamed to EDUC), DBP58 (renamed to BLOODPR), and HT58 through DAYOFWK in that order, specify:

```
SAVE OUTFILE=ELECTRIC /RENAME=(EDUYR,DBP58=EDUC,BLOODPR)
  /KEEP=EDUC,BLOODPR,HT58 TO DAYOFWK
```

Note that the renamed variables are specified by their new names on the KEEP subcommand. The results of the subcommands are cumulative.

You can reorder all of the variables in your system file either by listing the names of all the variables in the order that you want them or by listing the names of the variables that you want at the beginning of the file in the desired order, followed by the keyword ALL. Keyword ALL places all the unnamed variables after the named variables in the same sequence on the system file as they appear in the active file.

B.21 MAP Subcommand

To check the results of the RENAME, DROP, and KEEP subcommands, use the MAP subcommand, as in:

```
SAVE OUTFILE=ELECTRIC /RENAME=(EDUYR,DBP58=EDUC,BLOODPR)
  /KEEP=EDUC,BLOODPR,HT58 TO DAYOFWK /MAP
```

The MAP subcommand displays the results from the previous subcommands, showing the variables saved on the system file and their corresponding names on the active file.

B.22 XSAVE Command

The XSAVE command introduced with Release 2.0 of SPSS^X has the same syntax as the SAVE command. However, unlike SAVE, it is part of the transformation language and does not cause the data to be read. If you are using any procedure to analyze or display data in the same SPSS^X run in which you are saving a system file, simply replace the SAVE command with an XSAVE command before the procedure, and the data will be read only once to accomplish both the XSAVE and the procedure commands.

Also, you can save system files for subsets of your data by using the DO IF structure, as in

```
DO IF SEX EQ 'M'
XSAVE OUTFILE=MEN
ELSE
XSAVE OUTFILE=WOMEN
END IF
CROSSTABS INCOME BY SEX
```

Two system files are saved, one for men and the other for women. The CROSSTABS procedure is needed to execute the DO IF structure.

B.23 VALUE LABELS Command

Syntax for all releases:

```
VALUE LABELS varlist value 'label' value 'label'... [/varlist...]
```

The VALUE LABELS command specifies the variable name or variable list and a list of the values with their associated labels. The labels are specified as literals and must be enclosed in apostrophes or quotation marks, using the same symbol to begin and end the literal. Enter an apostrophe as part of a label by enclosing the literal in quotation marks or by entering the apostrophe twice with no separation. The command

```
VALUE LABELS ANOMIA5 ANOMIA6 ANOMIA7 1 'AGREE' 2 'DISAGREE'
             8 "DON'T KNOW" 9 'NO ANSWER'
```

assigns labels to the values 1, 2, 8, and 9 of variables ANOMIA5, ANOMIA6, and ANOMIA7.

Value labels can be up to 60 characters long and can contain any characters including blanks. However, some procedures print fewer than 60 characters for each label. (See especially the CROSSTABS procedure.) Additional sets of variable names and value labels can be specified on the same command. A slash is required to separate value labels for one variable list from the next.

To assign value labels to short string variables, enclose the value of string variables in apostrophes. The command

```
VALUE LABELS STRING1 'M' 'MALE' 'F' 'FEMALE'
```

assigns value labels to the values M and F of the string variable STRING1.

B.24 ADD VALUE LABELS Command

Syntax for all releases:

```
ADD VALUE LABELS varlist value 'label' value 'label'... [/varlist...]
```

If you assign value labels to any variable that already has value labels assigned to it, the new assignment completely replaces the old assignment. Use the ADD VALUE LABELS command to add value labels to a variable with existing labels.

B.25 VARIABLE LABELS Command

Syntax for all releases:

```
VARIABLE LABELS varname 'label' [/varname...]
```

Use the VARIABLE LABELS command to assign an extended descriptive label to variables. Specify the variable name followed by at least one blank or comma and the associated label enclosed in apostrophes or quotation marks. A variable label applies to one variable only. Each variable label can be up to 40 characters long and can include blanks and any character. The command

```
VARIABLE LABELS ANOMIA5 'LOT OF AVERAGE MAN GETTING WORSE'
                ANOMIA6 'NOT FAIR TO BRING CHILD INTO WORLD'
                ANOMIA7 'OFFICIALS NOT INTERESTED IN AVERAGE MAN'
```

assigns variable labels to the variables ANOMIA5, ANOMIA6, and ANOMIA7.

B.26 UTILITY COMMANDS

Utility commands tell SPSS^X to print titles and subtitles on your printed output, to edit your commands, to display information from the dictionary describing your data, to include document information on the system file, to assign new print and write formats to variables, and to list the values of cases.

B.27 COMMENT Command

Syntax for all releases:

```
COMMENT text
```

Comments help you and others review what you intend to accomplish with the SPSS^X job. You can insert comments by using the COMMENT command or an asterisk (*), or by enclosing the comment within the symbols /* and */ in any command line. Comments are included in the command printback on the display. They are not saved on a system file.

The specification for the COMMENT command is any message you wish, as in:

```
COMMENT    WESTERN ELECTRIC STUDY OF CORONARY HEART DISEASE.
```

Instead of the keyword COMMAND you can use an asterisk, as in:

```
*          WESTERN ELECTRIC STUDY OF CORONARY HEART DISEASE.
```

Alternatively, you can use /* and */ to set off a short comment on a command line, as in:

```
COMPUTE SEXRACE=1   /*CREATE NEW VARIABLE SEXRACE*/
```

If the comment is at the end of the line, the closing */ is optional.

B.28 DISPLAY Command

Syntax for Release 3.0:

```
DISPLAY [SORTED] [{NAMES**   }] [/VARIABLES=varlist]
                  {INDEX      }
                  {VARIABLES  }
                  {LABELS     }
                  {DICTIONARY }

        [MACROS]
        [DOCUMENTS]
```

**Default if subcommand is omitted.

Syntax for releases before 3.0:

```
DISPLAY DOCUMENTS

DISPLAY [SORTED] {DICTIONARY} [/VARIABLES=varlist]
                 {INDEX     }
                 {VARIABLES }
                 {LABELS    }
```

Use the DISPLAY command to display information from the dictionary of a system file. This command is very useful for exploring an unfamiliar or forgotten system file or for producing a printed archive document for a system file.

The following keywords can be specified on the DISPLAY command:

NAMES *Display variable names.* An unsorted list of the variables on the active file is displayed. This is the default.

DOCUMENTS *Display the text provided by the DOCUMENT command.* No error message is issued if there is no documentary information on the system file.

DICTIONARY *Display complete dictionary information for variables.*

INDEX *Display the variable names and positions.*

VARIABLES *Display the variable names, positions, print and write formats, and missing values.*

LABELS *Display the variable names, positions, and variable labels.*

Only one of the above keywords can be specified per DISPLAY command, but you can use as many DISPLAY commands as necessary to obtain the desired information.

In addition, you can use keyword SORTED to display information alphabetically by variable name. SORTED can precede keywords NAMES, DICTIONARY, INDEX, VARIABLES, or LABELS, as in:

```
GET FILE=GSS82
DISPLAY DOCUMENTS
DISPLAY SORTED DICTIONARY
```

The first DISPLAY command displays the document information, and the second displays complete dictionary information for variables sorted alphabetically by variable name.

To limit the display to certain variables, follow the keywords NAMES, DICTIONARY, INDEX, VARIABLES, or LABELS with a slash, the VARIABLES subcommand, an optional equals sign, and a list of variables, as in:

```
GET FILE=GSS82
DISPLAY DOCUMENTS
DISPLAY SORTED DICTIONARY/
  VARIABLES=ANOMIA5 TO ANOMIA6
```

B.29 DOCUMENT Command

Syntax for all releases:

```
DOCUMENT text
```

Use the DOCUMENT command to save a block of text of any length on your system file. For example, the command

```
DOCUMENT  WESTERN ELECTRIC STUDY OF CORONARY HEART DISEASE.
 A LARGE-SCALE, 20-YEAR, PROSPECTIVE STUDY FOLLOWING
 MEN WITHOUT PREVIOUS INCIDENCES OF CORONARY HEART
 DISEASE.  BASE YEAR:  1958.
```

provides information describing the Western Electric data. The block of text is saved on the system file and can be printed using the DISPLAY command (see Section B.28).

B.30 EDIT Command

Syntax for all releases:

```
EDIT
```

Use the EDIT command to check the syntax of your commands without actually reading the data. The EDIT command has no specifications. EDIT is not allowed in interactive mode; in batch mode, EDIT can appear anywhere in your command file. Commands following EDIT are checked. Commands before EDIT are executed.

Since EDIT checks variable names, if you are using a system file in your job, you must make it available so that SPSS^X can read the dictionary. The data portion of the system file is not read. If you are using DATA LIST to define your input data, you do not need to make the data file available. If your job contains data in the command file, you must remove both the data and the BEGIN DATA and END DATA commands for the EDIT job.

The EDIT facility checks syntax for errors but does not detect errors that could occur when the data are read.

B.31 FINISH Command

Syntax for all releases:

```
FINISH
```

The FINISH command has no specifications. In batch mode it is optional and its primary use is to mark the end of a job. In interactive mode it is required to terminate the interactive session.

B.32 FORMATS Command

Syntax for all releases:

```
FORMATS varlist(format) [varlist...]
```

SPSS^X assigns a print and write format to each variable in your file. For variables read with a DATA LIST command, the format used to read the variable is assigned as both the print and write format. For numeric variables created with transformation commands, the format F8.2 (eight print positions with two decimal places) is assigned. These print and write formats are stored for each variable on the dictionary of the system file. SPSS^X uses the print format to display the values and the write format to write the values to a file. Three commands in SPSS^X allow you to change the print and write formats: FORMATS, PRINT FORMATS (Section B.37), and WRITE FORMATS (Section B.41).

Use the FORMATS command to change both the print and write formats for variables. Specify the variable name or variable list followed by the new format specification in parentheses, as in:

```
FORMATS  SCALE1 (F2.0)
```

This command changes the print and write formats for variable SCALE1 to a two-digit integer. The same command can specify different formats for different variables. Separate the specifications for each variable or list with a slash.

The most common format on a FORMATS command is F, used to alter the F8.2 default format for new variables to a more appropriate length and number of decimal places. Formats specified on the FORMATS command are in effect for the remainder of the SPSS^X job and are saved on a system file if a SAVE command is specified.

B.33 HELP Command

When you run SPSS^X in interactive mode, you have an extensive help system available to you. To use HELP, specify HELP or ? at the SPSS-X> prompt and hit return. A menu of help topics displays on your monitor. Alternatively, for help on a specific command, specify HELP or ? and a command name. For example, to get information on the REGRESSION command, type

```
? REGRESSION.
```

and hit return. To request help from a CONTINUE>, DATA>, or HELP> prompt, you must specify the request with a question mark; you cannot use the keyword HELP.

If a help screen has subtopics, a numbered list for you to choose from is provided. For additional help, type the appropriate number from the list of choices and hit the return key. For example, if a help screen has a topic numbered 2, type "2" at the HELP> prompt and hit return (use the key for numeral "2," not the "PF2" key if you have programmable function keys on your keyboard).

You can also go directly to specific screens from any command prompt by entering "? topic subtopic" at the prompt. For example, from any SPSS-X>, CONTINUE>, DATA>, or HELP> prompt, type

```
? REGRESSION STATISTICS.
```

to get help for REGRESSION's STATISTICS subcommand.

In addition to entering subcommand numbers from a command-level screen or typing a complete help request from a command prompt, you can also move from screen to screen using keystrokes. On some systems, the minus (−) and plus (+) keys are available to help you move through a single branch of the help system. The minus key moves you vertically up from a lower level screen to a higher level screen. For example, if you are at a subcommand screen, the minus key moves you up to its parent command screen. The plus key moves you horizontally across screens at the same hierarchical level. For example, if you are at a subcommand screen, the plus key moves you to a different subcommand screen for the same parent command. On some systems, you may be able to scroll among screens using the directional arrow keys.

The help system also has online syntax charts for each SPSS^X command. To see the syntax for a command, type the keyword SYNTAX after the command name, as in:

```
? REGRESSION SYNTAX.
```

which requests syntax for the REGRESSION command.

Exiting HELP. To exit the HELP system and return to your SPSS^X job, just hit the return key at any blank HELP> prompt.

B.34 INFO Command

Syntax for all releases:

```
INFO [OUTFILE = file]
     [OVERVIEW]
     [LOCAL]
     [ERRORS]
     [FACILITIES]
     [PROCEDURES]
     [ALL]
     [procedure name] [/procedure name...]
     [SINCE release number]
```

The INFO command makes available or tells you how to obtain two kinds of documentation not included in this manual or *SPSS^X User's Guide,* 3rd ed., local and update. Local documentation concerns the environment in which you are running SPSS^X. Update documentation includes changes to existing procedures and facilities, new procedures and facilities, and corrections to *SPSS^X User's Guide,* 3rd ed.

You can choose update documentation for facilities (all SPSS^X commands except procedures), for all procedures, or for individual procedures. You can also request documentation produced since a particular release of SPSS^X. To request information via the INFO command, use the following keywords:

OVERVIEW *Overview of available documentation.* This overview includes a table of contents for the documentation available via the INFO command, along with information about documentation available in print.

LOCAL *Local documentation.* Includes commands or job control language for running SPSS^X, conventions for specifying files, conventions for handling tapes and other input/output devices, data formats that SPSS^X reads and writes on your computer, and other information specific to your computer and operating system or to your individual installation.

FACILITIES *Update information for SPSS^X facilities.* This documentation covers all changes, except in procedures, since the publication of this manual and *SPSS^X User's Guide,* 3rd ed. However, unless you use keyword SINCE to specify an earlier release of SPSS^X, you receive updates only for the most current release.

PROCEDURES *Update information for procedures.* This includes full documentation for procedures new in the current release and update information for procedures that existed prior to the current release.

procedure *Documentation for the procedure named.* This is the same information as that produced by the PROCEDURES keyword, but limited to the procedure named. Follow every procedure name with a slash.

ALL *All available documentation.* ALL is equivalent to OVERVIEW, LOCAL, FACILITIES, and PROCEDURES.

Enter as many of these keywords as you wish. If you specify overlapping sets of information, only one copy is printed. The order of specifications is not important and does not affect the order in which the documentation is printed. The following commands produce an overview and documentation for any changes made to system facilities and to the FREQUENCIES and CROSSTABS procedures:

```
INFO  OVERVIEW FACILITIES FREQUENCIES / CROSSTABS
```

Because of possible conflict with procedure names, all keywords in the INFO command must be spelled out in full.

Releases of SPSS^X are numbered by integers, with decimal digits indicating maintenance releases between major releases (so Release 1.1 would be a maintenance release with few changes from Release 1). The release number appears in the heading to each SPSS^X job. Each SPSS^X manual is identified on the title page by the number of the release it documents.

By default, the INFO command produces update information only for the current major release and subsequent maintenance releases. Documentation for earlier releases may also be available, and that fact will be indicated in the INFO overview. To obtain information for earlier releases or to limit the information to maintenance releases since the last major release, use keyword SINCE followed by a release number.

The following command prints documentation for all changes to system facilities and procedures FREQUENCIES and CROSSTABS since Release 3.0.

```
INFO  OVERVIEW FACILITIES FREQUENCIES / CROSSTABS SINCE 3
```

SINCE is not inclusive—SINCE 3 does not include changes made to the system in Release 3.0, though it does include any changes made in Release 3.1. To identify a maintenance release, enter the exact number, with decimal, as in 3.1.

By default, output from the INFO command is included in the display file. If you prefer to send the output to another file, use the OUTFILE subcommand, naming the handle of the file you want to create. The following commands create a file of text comprising an overview, local documentation, changes, and new procedures since Release 3.0:

```
INFO  OUTFILE=SPSSXDOC ALL SINCE 3
```

The characteristics of the output file produced by the INFO command may vary by computer type. As implemented at SPSS Inc., the file includes carriage control, with the maximum length of a page determined by the LENGTH subcommand to the SET command. A printer width of 132 characters is assumed for some examples, though the text is generally much narrower.

B.35 N OF CASES Command

Syntax for all releases:

```
N OF CASES n
```

Use the N OF CASES command to read the first *n* cases from your data file. For example, if your data file contains 1,000 cases and you want to use only the first 100 cases to test your SPSS^X commands, specify:

```
DATA LIST FILE=CITY/1 NAME 1-20 (A) TOTPOP 21-30 MEDSAL 31-40
N OF CASES 100
```

You can also use the N OF CASES command to control the reading of cases from an SPSS^X system file. Place the N OF CASES command after the GET command.

N OF CASES controls the number of cases built on the active file. If you use SAMPLE or SELECT IF with N OF CASES, SPSS^X reads as many records as required to build the specified number of cases. Only one N OF CASES can be used in an SPSS^X job, and it is in effect for the entire job.

B.36 NUMBERED Command

Syntax for all releases:

```
{NUMBERED  }
{UNNUMBERED}
```

It is common practice in some computer environments to reserve columns 73–80 of each input line for line numbers. If your computer system numbers lines this way, SPSS^X includes the line numbers on the printback of commands on the display. The NUMBERED command instructs SPSS^X to check just the first 72 columns for command specifications, and the UNNUMBERED command instructs SPSS^X to check all 80 columns. Neither command has any specifications. If one of the commands is used, it should be the first command in your SPSS^X command file.

The default may vary by installation. Check the local documentation available with the INFO command (Section B.34) for the default at your installation.

B.37 PRINT FORMATS Command

Syntax for all releases:

```
PRINT FORMATS varlist(format) [varlist...]
```

SPSS^X stores a print and write format for each variable in your file (see Section B.32). Use the PRINT FORMATS command to change the print formats for variables. Specify the variable name or variable list followed by the new format specification in parentheses, as in:

```
PRINT FORMATS  SCALE1 (F2.0)
```

This command changes the print format for variable SCALE1 to a two-digit integer. The write format does not change. The same command can specify different formats for different variables. Separate the specifications for each variable or variable list with a slash.

The most common formats are F, COMMA, and DOLLAR. Use the F format to provide a more appropriate length and/or number of decimal positions. Use the COMMA format to include commas for large numbers and DOLLAR to include both commas and the dollar sign. When the COMMA or DOLLAR formats are used, include the commas and the dollar sign in your length calculations. The number 32365.67 in F8.2 format prints as 32,365.67 in COMMA9.2 format and $32,365.67 in DOLLAR10.2 format.

Formats specified on the PRINT FORMATS command are in effect for the remainder of the SPSS^X job and are saved on a system file if a SAVE command is specified.

B.38 SET and SHOW Commands

Syntax for Release 3.0:

```
SET [BLANKS={SYSMIS}]  [BOX={'-I+[++++++++]'}]  [CASE={UPPER}]
            {value }        {X'hexstring   '}         {UPLOW}

  [CCA={'-,,,'         }] [CCB={'-,,,'         }] [CCC={'-,,,'         }]
       {'format-spec'}         {'format-spec'}         {'format-spec'}

  [CCD={'-,,,'         }] [CCE={'-,,,'         }]
       {'format-spec'}         {'format-spec'}

  [COMPRESSION={ON }]  [ENDCMD={'.'     }]  [FORMAT={F8.2}]
               {OFF}           {'string'}          {Fw.d}

  [HEADER={YES}] [JOURNAL=[{ON }] [file]] [LENGTH={59  }]
          {NO }            {OFF}                   {n   }
                                                   {NONE}

  [MEXPAND={ON }]  [MITERATE={1000}]  [MNEST={50}]  [MPRINT={ON }]
           {OFF}             {n   }          {n }           {OFF}

  [MXERRS={40}]     [MXLOOPS={40}]     [MXWARNS={80 }]
          {n }               {n }               {n  }

  [NULLINE={YES}]      [PRINTBACK={YES}]
           {NO }                  {NO }

  [SCRIPTTAB={'@'        }]  [SEED={2000000}]
             {'character'}         {n      }

  [TBFONT={'1234'       }]  [TB1={'-I[++++++++'}]  [TB2={'            '}]
          {X'hexstring'}         {X'hexstring' }         {X'hexstring'}

  [UNDEFINED={WARN   }]  [WIDTH={132}]  [XSORT={YES}]
             {NOWARN}           {n  }          {OFF}
```

Defaults may differ by installation.

```
SHOW [ALL] [BLANKS] [BLKSIZE] [BOX] [BUFNO] [CASE] [CCA] [CCB]

 [CCC] [CCD] [CCE] [COMPRESSION] [ENDCMD] [FORMAT] [HEADER]

 [JOURNAL] [LENGTH] [MEXPAND] [MITERATE] [MNEST] [MPRINT] [MXERRS]

 [MXLOOPS] [MXWARNS] [N] [NULLINE] [NUMBERED] [PRINTBACK]

 [SCOMPRESSION] [SCRIPTTAB] [SEED] [SYSMIS] [TBFONTS] [TB1]

 [TB2] [UNDEFINED] [WEIGHT] [WIDTH] [XSORT] [$VARS]
```

Syntax for releases before 3.0:

```
SET [BLANKS={SYSMIS}]  [BOX={'-I+[++++++++]'}]  [CASE={UPPER}]
            {value }        {X'hexstring   '}         {UPLOW}

  [COMPRESSION={ON }]  [FORMAT={F8.2}]  [LENGTH={59  }]
               {OFF}           {Fw.d}           {n   }
                                                {NONE}

  [MXERRS={40}]  [MXLOOPS={40}]  [MXWARNS={80 }]  [PRINTBACK={YES}]
          {n }            {n }            {n  }              {NO }

  [SEED={2000000}]  [TBFONT={'1234'       }]††  [TB1={'-I[++++++++'}]††
        {n      }           {X'hexstring'}           {X'hexstring' }

  [TB2={'            '}]††  [UNDEFINED={WARN   }]  [WIDTH={132}]
       {X'hexstring'}                  {NOWARN}           {n  }
```

Defaults may differ by installation.

```
SHOW [ALL] [BLANKS] [BLKSIZE] [BOX] [BUFNO] [CASE] [COMPRESSION]

 [FORMAT] [LENGTH] [MXERRS] [MXLOOPS] [MXWARNS] [N] [NUMBERED]

 [PRINTBACK] [SCOMPRESSION] [SEED] [SYSMIS] [TBFONTS]†† [TB1]††

 [TB2]†† [UNDEFINED] [WEIGHT] [WIDTH] [$VARS]
```

††Available as of Release 2.1.

The SET command allows you to choose optional treatments of data on input, properties of the display file, compression of scratch files, the starting point for random number generation, and so on. The SHOW command displays the current settings of those options as well as additional information about the values of system variables, the system-missing value, the variable used to weight cases, and the number of cases currently in the active file, as in

```
SHOW BLANKS /SEED /WEIGHT
```

The slashes between subcommands are optional, but if you omit them, leave at least one blank.

The following list gives the most commonly used keywords available for SET and SHOW along with acceptable arguments.

BLANKS *Value to which blanks read under numeric format should be translated.* The default is the system-missing value.

FORMAT *Default print and write formats for numeric variables created by transformations.* The specification can be any F format. The initial setting is F8.2.

LENGTH *Page length for printed output.* The specification can be any integer in the range 40 through 999,999 inclusive or NONE to suppress page ejects altogether. The default is 59.

N *Unweighted number of cases on the active file.* Available for SHOW only. Prints UNKNOWN if no active file has been created yet.

SEED *Seed for the random number generator.* The specification is a large integer. The default is 2,000,000 but may vary by computer.

WEIGHT *The name of the variable used to weight cases.* Available for SHOW only.

WIDTH *Maximum page width for the display file.* The specification can be any integer from 80 through 132. The default is 132 columns.

ALL *Available for SHOW only.* Displays the settings of all elements available to SHOW.

SET BLANKS. As it reads a data file defined by a DATA LIST command, SPSS^X usually assigns the system-missing value whenever it encounters a completely blank field for a numeric variable. If you want blanks translated to a number, use the BLANKS subcommand, as in

```
SET BLANKS=0
```

Since the command applies only to numeric variables (blanks in strings are taken literally), only numbers are valid specifications.

SET LENGTH. The LENGTH subcommand establishes the maximum length for a printed output page. Initially, the length is set to 59 lines. You can change that to any length from 40 to 999,999 lines with the LENGTH subcommand, as in

```
SET LENGTH=50
```

The length includes the lines from the first printed line on the page to the last that can be printed. The printer you use most likely includes a margin at the top; that margin is not included in the length used by SPSS^X. SPSS^X may occasionally print one line beyond the number specified by LENGTH, so the default 59 lines allows for a ½-inch margin at top and bottom of an 11-inch page printed with 6 lines per inch or an 8 ½-inch page printed with 8 lines per inch.

If you specify a long page length, SPSS^X will continue to give page ejects and titles at the start of each procedure and at logical points in the display, such as between crosstabulation tables. If you want to suppress page ejects altogether, use the NONE keyword, as in

```
SET LENGTH=NONE
```

SPSS^X continues to insert titles at logical points in the display, but the display does not jump to the top of the page when a title is inserted.

SET WIDTH. The WIDTH subcommand allows you to set the maximum width of the display file to any number of characters from 80 through 132, as in

```
SET WIDTH=80
```

The specified width does not include the carriage control character. The default width is 132.

SET FORMAT. The FORMAT subcommand establishes the print and write formats for numeric variables created by transformation commands or read in with the default format on a DATA LIST command specifying LIST or FREE formatted data. The specification must be a simple F format, as in

```
SET FORMAT=F3.0
```

The default is F8.2. The format established by the FORMAT subcommand applies to all numeric variables created by transformation commands and to numeric variables read on a DATA LIST command with LIST or FREE specified, unless the format is specified. You can use the PRINT FORMATS, WRITE FORMATS, and FORMATS commands to specify the print and write formats for individual variables. It is important to note that the actual value maintained on the active file and saved in a system file is not affected by the print or write format.

SET SEED. The pseudo-random number generator that SPSS^X uses in selecting random samples or in creating uniform or normal distributions of random numbers begins with a *seed,* a large integer. Starting with the same seed, the system will repeatedly produce the same sequence of numbers and will select the same sample from a given data file. At the start of each job, the seed is set by SPSS^X to a value that may vary or may be fixed, depending on the implementation. You can set the seed yourself via the SEED subcommand to the SET command, as in

```
SET SEED=987654321
```

The argument can be any integer, preferably a large one, less than 2,000,000,000, which approaches the limit on some machines. The command sets the seed for the next time the random number generator is called. Thus you can reset it following each procedure command in a job if you want to repeat the same random distribution. In the absence of the SEED subcommand, SPSS^X will not reset the seed within a job, so all distributions and samples within the same job will be different.

B.39 SUBTITLE Command

Syntax for all releases:

```
SUBTITLE [']text[']
```

Use the TITLE command (Section B.40) and the SUBTITLE command to place your own heading at the top of each page of your SPSS^X display. With the SUBTITLE command, you can specify a line up to 60 characters long that prints as the second line at the top of each page, as in:

```
SUBTITLE 'FREQUENCIES ON ALL VARIABLES'
```

The subtitle is specified as a literal (see Section B.23).

B.40 TITLE Command

Syntax for all releases:

```
TITLE [']text[']
```

The TITLE command specifies the text for the first line of each page of SPSS^X display. The TITLE command can be used by itself or with the SUBTITLE command. The TITLE command follows the same rules as the SUBTITLE command. For example,

```
TITLE 'BANK EMPLOYMENT STUDY'
SUBTITLE 'FREQUENCIES ON ALL VARIABLES'
```

prints two lines at the top of each page of your display.

B.41 WRITE FORMATS Command

Syntax for all releases:

```
WRITE FORMATS varlist (format) [varlist...]
```

SPSS^X stores a print and write format for each variable in your file (see Section B.32). Use the WRITE FORMATS command to change the write formats for variables. Specify the variable or variable list followed by the new format specification in parentheses, as in:

```
WRITE FORMATS  SCALE1 (F2.0)
```

This command changes the write format for variable SCALE1 to a two-digit integer. The print format does not change. You can use the same command to specify different formats for different variables. Separate the specifications for each variable or variable list with a slash.

The most common format is the F format. Use this format to provide appropriate length and/or decimal positions. Formats specified on the WRITE FORMATS command are in effect for the remainder of the SPSS^X job and are saved on a system file if a SAVE command is specified.

B.42 DATA TRANSFORMATION COMMANDS

The ability to transform data before you analyze it or after preliminary analysis is often as important as the analysis itself. You may want to perform simple data-cleaning checks, correct coding errors, or adjust an inconvenient coding scheme. Or you may want to construct an index from several variables or rescale several variables prior to analysis. You may want to perform an analysis on a sample or selected subset of your file, or weight aggregated data to a population. The SPSS^X transformation language provides these and many other possibilities.

B.43 COMPUTE Command

Syntax for all releases:

```
COMPUTE target variable=expression
```

Use the COMPUTE command to compute a new variable as some combination or transformation of one or more existing variables. The COMPUTE command generates a variable on your active file on a case-by-case basis as an arithmetic or logical transformation of existing variables and constants. To compute a variable, specify the target variable on the left of the equals sign and the expression on the right. For example, the command

```
COMPUTE FAMSCORE=HSSCALE + WSSCALE
```

assigns the sum of existing variables HSSCALE and WSSCALE (the expression) to variable FAMSCORE (the target) for each case. See Appendix A for details.

B.44 Generating Distributions

You can use SPSS^{X} to generate cases without an input data file. For example, to create 100 dummy cases with variable X1 as a uniformly distributed random number and X2 as a normally distributed random number, specify:

```
INPUT PROGRAM
LOOP I=1 TO 100
COMPUTE X1=NORMAL(1)
COMPUTE X2=UNIFORM(1)
END CASE
END LOOP
END FILE
END INPUT PROGRAM

FREQUENCIES VARIABLES=X1,X2 /FORMAT=NOTABLE /HISTOGRAM
```

Explanation of these commands is beyond the scope of this manual. However, if you enter the commands exactly as shown, you will get the histograms for both variables. To change the number of cases generated, change the 100 on the LOOP command to the desired number.

B.45 COUNT Command

Syntax for all releases:

```
COUNT varname=varlist(value list) [/varname=...]
```

Numeric Value List Keywords:
LOWEST, LO, HIGHEST, HI, THRU, MISSING, SYSMIS

The COUNT command is a special data transformation utility used to create a numeric variable that, for each case, counts the occurrences of a value (or list of values) across a list of variables. For example,

```
COUNT READER=NEWSWEEK,TIME,USNEWS(2)
```

creates an index (READER) that indicates the number of times the value 2 (those who read each magazine) is recorded for the three variables for a case. Thus, the value of READER will be either 0, 1, 2, or 3. See Appendix A for details.

B.46 DO IF—END IF Structure

Syntax for all releases:

```
DO IF [(]logical expression[)]

  transformations

[ELSE IF [(]logical expression[)]]

  transformations

[ELSE IF [(]logical expression[)]]
  .
  .
  .
[ELSE]

  transformations

END IF
```

Use the DO IF—END IF structure to conditionally execute a series of transformation commands on the same subset of cases. The DO IF—END IF structure must begin with the DO IF command and end with the END IF command. The structure can be further defined with the ELSE and ELSE IF commands. The DO IF—END IF structure transforms data on subsets of cases defined by the logical expressions on the DO IF and optional ELSE IF commands, as in:

```
DO IF (X EQ 0)
COMPUTE Y=1
ELSE IF (X LT 9)
COMPUTE Y=9
ELSE
COMPUTE Y-2
END IF
```

This structure sets Y equal to 1 when X equals 0; Y equal to 9 when X is less than 9 but not equal to 0; and Y to 2 for all valid values of X greater than 9. Scc Appendix A for details.

B.47 IF Command

Syntax for all releases:

```
IF [(]logical expression[)] target variable=expression
```

Use the IF command to make COMPUTE-like transformations contingent upon logical conditions found in the data. The IF command is followed by a logical expression and an assignment expression, which has the same syntax described in Section B.43 for the COMPUTE command. For example,

```
COMPUTE Y=0
IF (X EQ 0) Y=1
```

computes a new variable Y equal to 0 and changes the variable Y to the value 1 only for cases with value 0 for variable X. The logical expression is X EQ 0 and the assignment expression is Y=1. The parentheses around the logical expression are optional.

B.48 RECODE Command

Syntax for all releases:

For numeric variables:

```
RECODE varlist (value list=value)...(value list-value) [INTO varlist]
       [/varlist...]
```

Input Keywords:
LO, LOWEST, HI, HIGHEST, THRU, MISSING, SYSMIS, ELSE

Output Keywords:
COPY, SYSMIS

For string variables:

```
RECODE varlist [('string',['string'...]='string')][INTO varlist]
      [/varlist...]
```

Input Keywords:
CONVERT, ELSE

Output Keyword:
COPY

Use the RECODE command to change one code for a variable to another as the data are read. The variable or variables to be recoded must already exist and must be specified before the value specifications. Each value specification must be enclosed in parentheses and consists of the input value(s) followed by an equals sign and the output value. For example,

```
RECODE ITEM1 (0=1) (1 THRU 3=2) (8,9=0)
```

changes the original value of 0 for ITEM1 to 1, the original values 1 through 3 inclusive to 2, and the values 8 and 9 to 0. See Appendix A for details.

B.49 SAMPLE Command

Syntax for all releases:

```
SAMPLE {percentage}
       {n FROM m   }
```

Use the SAMPLE command to select a random sample of cases. To select an approximate percentage of cases, specify a decimal value between 0 and 1, as in:

```
SAMPLE .25
```

This command samples approximately 25% of the cases in the active file. When you specify a proportional sample, you usually do not get the exact proportion specified. If you know exactly how many cases are in the active file, you can get an exact-sized random sample by specifying the number of cases to be sampled from the size of the active file, as in:

```
SAMPLE 50 FROM 200
```

The SAMPLE command permanently samples the active file unless a TEMPORARY command precedes it (see Section B.53). Thus, if you use two SAMPLE commands, the second takes a sample of the first.

B.50 SELECT IF Command

Syntax for all releases:

```
SELECT IF [(]logical expression[)]
```

Use the SELECT IF command to select a subset of cases based on logical criteria. The syntax of the logical expression for the SELECT IF command is the same as described for DO IF and IF in Appendix A. If the logical expression is true, the case is selected; if it is false or missing, the case is not selected. For example, the command

```
SELECT IF (VSAT GT 600 OR MSAT GT 600)
```

selects the subset of cases with values greater than 600 on VSAT *or* values greater than 600 on MSAT. The remaining cases are not selected for analysis.

The SELECT IF command permanently selects cases unless preceded by a TEMPORARY command (see Section B.53). If you use multiple SELECT IF commands in your job, they must all be true for a case to be selected.

B.51 SORT CASES Command

Syntax for all releases:

```
SORT CASES [BY] varlist[({A})] [varlist...]
                         {D}
```

Use the SORT CASES command to reorder the sequence of cases in your file. The file is reordered according to the values of the variable or variables specified on the SORT CASES command following the optional keyword BY, as in:

```
SORT CASES BY SEX
```

By default, SPSS^X orders the cases in ascending order: cases with the smallest values for the sort variable or variables are at the front of the file. You can specify the default by following the variable name with (A) or (UP). To sort the cases in descending order—cases with the largest values for the sort variable or variables at the front of the file—specify either (D) or (DOWN) after the variable name, as in:

```
SORT CASES BY SEX (D)
```

You can specify several variables as sort variables. The file is sorted on the first variable mentioned, then within that variable on the next variable, and so forth. You can use string variables as sort keys. The sequence of string variables depends on the character set in use at your installation.

B.52 SPLIT FILE Command

Syntax for all releases:

```
SPLIT FILE {BY varlist}
           {OFF       }
```

During the analysis of a data file, you may want to perform separate analyses on subgroups of your data. Use the SPLIT FILE command to split your file into subgroups that you can analyze separately using SPSS^X. The subgroups are sets of adjacent cases on your file that have the same value(s) for the variable or set of variables. If the cases are not grouped together according to the variable or variables, use SORT CASES to sort the file in the proper order (see Section B.51). Specify the split variable or variables following the keyword BY, as in:

```
SORT CASES BY RACE
SPLIT FILE BY RACE
FREQUENCIES VARIABLES=SALNOW /HISTOGRAM
```

These commands sort the file by the values of the variable RACE and specify split-file processing. The FREQUENCIES command produces a histogram of SALNOW for each value of RACE.

Split-file processing is in effect for the entire SPSS^X job unless you use the TEMPORARY command (see Section B.53). However, split-file definitions are never saved on a system file. You can also turn off split-file processing by specifying the keyword OFF, as in:

```
SPLIT FILE OFF
```

You can change split-file processing by specifying a new SPLIT FILE command.

B.53 TEMPORARY Command

Syntax for all releases:

```
TEMPORARY
```

Use the TEMPORARY command to signal the end of permanent data transformations and the beginning of temporary transformations. Temporary transformations are in effect only through the first procedure after the TEMPORARY command. New variables created after the TEMPORARY command are temporary variables, and any modifications made to existing variables are temporary. All of the transformation commands (RECODE, COMPUTE, IF, COUNT, SELECT IF, SAMPLE, and SPLIT FILE), the DO IF control structure, format declaration commands (FORMATS, PRINT FORMATS, and WRITE FORMATS), labeling commands (VARIABLE LABELS and VALUE LABELS), and the MISSING VALUES command are allowed after the TEMPORARY command.

To make transformations temporary for several procedures, you must respecify the TEMPORARY command for each procedure. Otherwise, transformations between procedures are permanent. Since the SAVE command is a procedure, any transformations following a TEMPORARY command and immediately preceding a SAVE command are saved on the system file.

B.54 WEIGHT Command

Syntax for all releases:

```
WEIGHT {BY varname}
       {OFF       }
```

Use the WEIGHT command to differentially weight cases for analysis. For example, you can use WEIGHT to apply weights to a sample that has some substratum over- or undersampled to obtain population estimates. The WEIGHT command uses the value of a variable to weight the case. Specify the variable name following the keyword BY, as in

```
WEIGHT BY WTFACTOR
```

where the variable WTFACTOR has the appropriate weighting values for each case. The variable may be a weighting factor already coded when the data file was prepared, or you may compute the variable with the transformation language in SPSS^X. SPSS^X does not physically replicate cases. Rather, it arithmetically weights cases when a procedure is executed.

Only one variable can be specified, and the variable must be numeric. Weight values need not be integer. However, negative values or missing values are treated the same as a value of zero. Weighting is in effect for the entire job, and a file saved maintains the weighting unless you use the TEMPORARY command (see Section B.53). In addition, you can turn off weighting with the keyword OFF, as in:

```
WEIGHT OFF
```

To change the weight, use another WEIGHT command specifying a different variable.

B.55 PROCEDURE COMMANDS

A *procedure* is defined as any command that actually reads data. This definition distinguishes a procedure from transformations used to define a file, the PRINT and WRITE utilities used to display a file, and GET used to obtain the data and dictionary from a saved system file. Table B.55 lists procedures within SPSS^X and what they do. Unless otherwise marked, each procedure has been available since Release 1 of SPSS^X.

Procedures in SPSS^X read data from the *active file.* Although you may be defining or manipulating several files during one job, only one file is active at any given point.

Procedures operate on files defined by commands such as DATA LIST, COMPUTE, RECODE, and GET. In fact, procedures execute transformations. Thus, procedures follow blocks of transformations in a job. For example, the commands

```
DATA LIST  /1 SEX 1 SCORE1 TO SCORE10 10-39 GPA 40-42(1)
MISSING VALUES SCORE1 TO SCORE10 (-1)
COMMENT  TRICHOTOMIZE SCORE VARIABLES FOR CROSSTABS
RECODE  SCORE1 TO SCORE10 (0 THRU 33=1)(34 THRU 67=2)(68 THRU 100=3)
VALUE LABELS SCORE1 TO SCORE10 (1) 'LOWER THIRD' (2) 'MIDDLE THIRD'
             (3) 'UPPER THIRD'
CROSSTABS  SCORE1 TO SCORE10 BY SEX
          /CELLS=TOTAL
          /STATISTICS=CHISQ
BEGIN DATA
data records
END DATA
FINISH
```

define variables SEX, SCORE1 to SCORE10, and GPA; flag −1 as missing for variables SCORE1 to SCORE10; recode the values of variables SCORE1 to SCORE10 to range from 1 to 3; and request crosstabular displays of the recoded variables, SCORE1 to SCORE10, by SEX.

Table B.55 SPSS[X] procedures

Command	Function	Release
AGGREGATE	Save an aggregated file	
ALSCAL	Multidimensional scaling	2.1
ANOVA	Factorial analysis of variance	
BOX-JENKINS	Time series analysis	
CLUSTER	Hierarchical clustering	2
CORRELATIONS[1]	Pearson correlations	
CROSSTABS	Contingency table analysis	
DESCRIPTIVES[2]	Univariate descriptive statistics	
DISCRIMINANT	Discriminant analysis	
EXECUTE	Read data file	
EXPORT	Save transportable system file	
FACTOR	Factor analysis	
FREQUENCIES	Frequency tables	
HILOGLINEAR	Hierarchical log-linear analysis	2
LOGLINEAR	Log-linear analysis	
MANOVA	General linear models	
MEANS[3]	Subpopulation means	
MULT RESPONSE	Multiple response tables	
NONPAR CORR	Nonparametric correlations	
NPAR TESTS	Nonparametric tests	
ONEWAY	One-way analysis of variance	
PARTIAL CORR	Partial correlations	
PLOT	Two-dimensional line-printer plots	2
PROBIT	Probit analysis, logistic regression	2
PROXIMITIES	Proximity matrices	2.1
QUICK CLUSTER	Efficient cluster analysis	2
REGRESSION	Multiple regression analysis	
RELIABILITY	Item analysis	
REPORT	Report writer	
SAVE	Save system file	
SORT CASES	Sort cases	
SURVIVAL	Life table analysis	
TABLES	Stub and banner table option	2.1
T-TEST	T test	

[1]Formerly PEARSON CORR. [2]Formerly CONDESCRIPTIVE. [3]Formerly BREAKDOWN.

You can interleave blocks of transformations and procedures. For example, you can define a file, run a procedure, transform that file, and run another procedure on the transformed file. You can analyze data from more than one file in a single job, but only one file can be analyzed at a time. In the following example, two files are analyzed using two different procedures for each.

```
GET FILE=AGENTS /KEEP JUNE JULY AUG TYPE
FREQUENCIES  VARIABLES=JUNE JULY AUG TYPE
             /FORMAT=LIMIT(20) /HBAR
MEANS  JUNE JULY AUG BY TYPE
GET FILE=ACCTS /KEEP REGION TYPE SIZE
FREQUENCIES  VARIABLES=SIZE /FORMAT=NOTABLE
             /HISTOGRAM
MEANS  SIZE BY REGION TYPE
FINISH
```

The first GET command makes the file referenced by AGENTS the active file. The first FREQUENCIES and MEANS procedures analyze this file. The second GET command replaces the active file with the file referenced by ACCTS, and the second set of procedures analyzes this file.

If you make a syntax error on a procedure command, usually that procedure is skipped and subsequent procedures are executed. However, since some procedures save variables on the active file, a procedure that analyzes variables you intended to save with an earlier procedure is also in error.

B.56 Saving Casewise Results

Several procedures in SPSS^X compute and save on the active file new variables that can be analyzed in subsequent procedures. For example, DESCRIPTIVES computes standardized variables with a mean of 0 and a standard deviation of 1 (see Chapter 5). When a variable cannot be computed for a case, SPSS^X supplies the system-missing value. Once the procedure saves these variables on the active file, you can use them in the same way as all other variables on the file. If you save the active file with the SAVE or XSAVE command, new variables are saved on the file.

In the following example, REGRESSION computes standard errors of the predicted values (saved as variable SE), which are then plotted in procedure PLOT.

```
GET FILE=BANK
REGRESSION VARIABLES=SALBEG SALNOW /DEPENDENT=SALNOW /METHOD=ENTER
SALBEG
  /SAVE=SEPRED(SE)
PLOT CUTPOINTS=(1,3,5,10,20) /SYMBOLS='.+*#;;@'
  /PLOT=SE WITH SALBEG
```

See Chapter 2 for the output from the PLOT procedure.

B.57 ANOVA

Syntax for Release 3.0:

```
ANOVA [VARIABLES=] varlist BY varlist(min,max)...varlist(min,max)
  WITH varlist

 [/MISSING={EXCLUDE**} ]
           {INCLUDE  }

 [/FORMAT={LABELS**} ]
          {NOLABELS}

 [/MAXORDERS={ALL**  } ]
             {n      }
             {NONE   }

 [/COVARIATES={FIRST**} ]
              {WITH   }
              {AFTER  }

 [/METHOD={EXPERIMENTAL**} ]
          {UNIQUE        }
          {HIERARCHICAL  }

 [/STATISTICS=[MCA] [REG†] [MEAN] [ALL] [NONE]]
```

**Default if the subcommand is omitted.
†REG (table of regression coefficients) is displayed only if the design is relevant.

Syntax for releases before 3.0:

```
ANOVA varlist BY varlist(min,max) WITH varlist
```

Options:

1	Include missing values	6	Delete five-way terms
2	Suppress labels	7	Covariates with main effects
3	Delete interaction terms	8	Covariates after main effects
4	Delete three-way terms	9	Regression approach
5	Delete four-way terms	10	Hierarchical approach

Statistics:

1 MCA table
2 Unstandardized regression coefficients
3 Cell means

Analysis of variance tests the hypothesis that the group means of the dependent variable are equal. The dependent variable must be interval level, and one or more categorical variables define the groups. These categorical variables are termed *factors*. The ANOVA procedure also allows you to include continuous explanatory variables, termed *covariates*. When there are five or fewer factors, the default model is *full factorial*, meaning that all interaction terms are included. If there are more than five factors, only interaction terms up to order five are included.

The only required subcommand on ANOVA is the VARIABLES subcommand, which specifies the variable list to be analyzed. The actual keyword VARIABLES can be omitted.

B.58 VARIABLES Subcommand

The VARIABLES subcommand names the variable list, and the actual keyword VARIABLES is optional. If you use the VARIABLES keyword, an equals sign must precede the variable list.

The simplest ANOVA command contains one *analysis list* with a *dependent variable list* and a *factor variable list*. In the command

```
ANOVA  VARIABLES=PRESTIGE BY REGION(1,9)
```

PRESTIGE is the dependent variable and REGION is the factor, with minimum and maximum values of 1 and 9.

- Value ranges are not specified for dependent variables.
- The factor variable list follows the keyword BY.
- Every factor variable must have a value range indicating its highest and lowest coded values. The values are separated by a comma and are enclosed in parentheses.
- The factor variables must be integers.

The command

```
ANOVA  VARIABLES=PRESTIGE BY REGION(1,9) SEX(1,2)
```

is a two-way analysis of variance with PRESTIGE as the dependent variable, and REGION and SEX as factors. By default, the model effects are the REGION and SEX main effects and the REGION by SEX interaction.

B.59 Specifying Covariates

The *covariate list* follows the keyword WITH, and you do not specify a value range for the covariates. For example, the command

```
ANOVA VARIABLES=PRESTIGE BY REGION(1,9) SEX(1,2) WITH EDUC
```

names EDUC as the covariate.

B.60 COVARIATES Subcommand

By default, ANOVA assesses the covariates before it assesses the factor main effects.

The COVARIATES subcommand specifies the order for assessing blocks of covariates and factor main effects. The following keywords can be specified on the COVARIATES subcommand:

FIRST *Process covariates before main effects for factors.* This is the default if you omit the COVARIATES subcommand.

WITH *Process covariates concurrently with main effects for factors.*

AFTER *Process covariates after main effects for factors.*

Note that the order of entry is irrelevant when METHOD=UNIQUE (see Section B.62).

B.61 MAXORDERS Subcommand

By default, ANOVA examines all the interaction effects up to and including the fifth order.

The MAXORDERS subcommand suppresses the effects of various orders of interaction. The following keywords can be specified on the MAXORDERS subcommand:

ALL *Examine all the interaction effects up to and including the fifth order.* This is the default if you omit the MAXORDERS subcommand.

n *Examine all the interaction effects up to and including the n-order effect.* For example, if you specify MAXORDERS=3, ANOVA examines all the interaction effects up to and including the third order. All higher order interaction sums of squares are pooled into the error term.

NONE *Delete all interaction terms from the model.* All interaction sums of squares are pooled into the error sum of squares.

The keyword NONE suppresses all interaction terms so only main effects and covariate effects appear in the ANOVA table, with interaction sums of squares pooled into the error (residual) sum of squares. For example, to suppress all interaction effects, specify

```
ANOVA VARIABLES=PRESTIGE BY REGION(1,9) SEX,RACE(1,2)
      /MAXORDERS=NONE
```

B.62 METHOD Subcommand

By default, ANOVA uses what is termed the *classic experimental approach* for decomposing sums of squares. Optionally, you can request the *regression approach* or the *hierarchical approach.*

The METHOD subcommand controls the method for decomposing sums of squares. The following keywords can be specified on the METHOD subcommand:

EXPERIMENTAL *Classic experimental approach.* This is the default if you omit the METHOD subcommand.

UNIQUE *Regression approach.* UNIQUE overrides the WITH and AFTER keywords on the COVARIATES subcommand. All effects are assessed for their partial contribution, so order is irrelevant. The MCA and MEAN specifications on the STATISTICS subcommand are not available with the regression approach.

HIERARCHICAL *Hierarchical approach.*

B.63 STATISTICS Subcommand

By default, ANOVA calculates only the statistics needed for analysis of variance. Optionally, you can request a means and counts table, unstandardized regression coefficients, and multiple classification analysis.

The STATISTICS subcommand requests additional statistics for ANOVA. You can specify the STATISTICS subcommand by itself or with one or more keywords.

If you specify the STATISTICS subcommand with no keywords, ANOVA calculates MEAN and REG (each defined below). If you include a keyword or keywords on the STATISTICS subcommand, ANOVA calculates only the additional statistics you request.

Use keyword MEAN to request means and counts for each dependent variable for groups defined by each factor and each combination of factors up to the fifth level.

Use keyword REG to request unstandardized regression coefficients for covariates. The coefficients are computed at the point where the covariates are entered into the equation. Thus, their values depend on the type of design you have specified.

Use keyword MCA to request multiple classification analysis results. In the MCA table, effects are expressed as deviations from the grand mean. The table includes a listing of unadjusted category effects for each factor, category effects adjusted for other factors, category effects adjusted for all factors and covariates, and eta and beta values.

The following keywords can be specified on the STATISTICS subcommand:

MEAN *Means and counts table.* This statistic is not available with METHOD=UNIQUE.

REG *Unstandardized regression coefficients.* Prints unstandardized regression coefficients for the covariates.

MCA *Multiple classification analysis.* The MCA table is not produced when METHOD=UNIQUE.

ALL *Means and counts table, unstandardized regression coefficients, and multiple classification analysis.*

NONE *No additional statistics.* This is the default if you omit the STATISTICS subcommand.

B.64 MISSING Subcommand

By default, a case that is missing for any variable named in the analysis list is deleted for all analyses specified by that list.

Use the MISSING subcommand to ignore missing-data indicators and to include all cases in the computations. Two keywords can be specified on the MISSING subcommand:

EXCLUDE *Exclude missing data.* This is the default if you omit the MISSING subcommand.

INCLUDE *Include user-defined missing data.*

B.65 FORMAT Subcommand

By default, ANOVA prints variable or value labels if they have been defined.

Use the FORMAT subcommand to suppress variable and value labels. Two keywords can be specified on the FORMAT subcommand:

LABELS *Print variable and value labels.* This is the default if you omit the FORMAT subcommand.

NOLABELS *Suppress variable and value labels.*

B.66 Limitations

The following limitations apply to procedure ANOVA:

- A maximum of 5 ANOVA analysis lists.
- A maximum of 5 dependent variables per analysis list.
- A maximum of 10 independent variables per analysis list.
- A maximum of 10 covariates per analysis list.
- A maximum of 5 interaction levels.
- A maximum of 25 value labels per variable displayed in the MCA table.
- The combined number of categories for all factors in an analysis list plus the number of covariates must be less than the sample size.

B.67 CLUSTER

Syntax for Release 3.0:

```
CLUSTER varlist [/MISSING={LISTWISE**}]
                          {INCLUDE   }

 [/MEASURE={SEUCLID** }] [/METHOD={BAVERAGE**}[(rootname)] [,...]]
           {EUCLID    }           {WAVERAGE  }
           {COSINE    }           {SINGLE    }
           {POWER(p,r)}           {COMPLETE  }
           {BLOCK     }           {CENTROID  }
           {CHEBYCHEV }           {MEDIAN    }
           {DEFAULT   }           {WARD      }

 [/SAVE=CLUSTER({level   })]  [/ID=varname]
                {min,max}

 [/PRINT=[CLUSTER({level   })] [DISTANCE] [SCHEDULE**] [NONE]]
                  {min,max}

 [/PLOT=[VICICLE**[(min[,max[,inc]])]] [DENDROGRAM] [NONE]]
        [HICICLE[(min[,max[,inc]])]]

 [/MATRIX=[IN({file})] [OUT({file})]]
              {*   }        {*   }
```

** Default if the subcommand is omitted.

Syntax for releases before 3.0:

```
CLUSTER† varlist [/MISSING={LISTWISE**}]
                           {INCLUDE   }

 [/READ=[SIMILAR] [{TRIANGLE}]]  [/WRITE[=DISTANCE]]
                   {LOWER   }

 [/MEASURE={SEUCLID** }] [/METHOD={BAVERAGE**}[(rootname)] [,...]]
           {EUCLID    }           {WAVERAGE  }
           {COSINE    }           {SINGLE    }
           {POWER(p,r)}           {COMPLETE  }
           {BLOCK     }           {CENTROID  }
           {CHEBYCHEV }           {MEDIAN    }
           {DEFAULT   }           {WARD      }

 [/SAVE=CLUSTER({level   })]  [/ID=varname]
                {min,max}

 [/PRINT=[CLUSTER({level   })] [DISTANCE] [SCHEDULE**] [NONE††]]
                  {min,max}

 [/PLOT=[VICICLE**[(min[,max[,inc]])]] [DENDROGRAM] [NONE††]]
        [HICICLE[(min[,max[,inc]])]]
```

** Default if the subcommand is omitted.
† Available as of Release 2.0.
†† Available as of Release 2.1.

The complete syntax charts for CLUSTER are included here. Discussion of CLUSTER appears in Chapter 5.

B.68 CORRELATIONS

Syntax for Release 3.0:

```
CORRELATIONS [VARIABLES=] varlist [WITH varlist] [/varlist...]

 [/MISSING={PAIRWISE**}  [INCLUDE]]
           {LISTWISE  }

 [/PRINT={ONETAIL**}  {SIG**}]
         {TWOTAIL  }  {NOSIG}

 [/FORMAT={MATRIX**}]
          {SERIAL  }

 [/MATRIX=OUT({*   })]
              {file}

 [/STATISTICS=[DESCRIPTIVES]  [XPROD]  [ALL]]
```

**Default if the subcommand is omitted.

Syntax for releases before 3.0 (CORRELATIONS was formerly called PEARSON CORR):

```
PEARSON CORR varlist [WITH varlist] [/varlist...]
```

Options:

1 Include missing values
2 Exclude missing values listwise
3 Two-tailed test of significance
4 Write matrix materials to a file
5 Suppress count and significance level
6 Print only nonredundant coefficients
7 Write matrix without n's††

Statistics:

1 Univariate mean, standard deviation, and count
2 Cross-product deviations and covariance

††Available as of Release 2.1.

Procedure CORRELATIONS produces Pearson product-moment correlations with significance levels and, optionally, univariate statistics, covariances, and cross-product deviations. The only required subcommand on CORRELATIONS is the VARIABLES subcommand, which specifies the variable list to be analyzed. The actual keyword VARIABLES can be omitted. Optional subcommands may be entered in any order, provided they appear after the variable list.

B.69 VARIABLES Subcommand

CORRELATIONS prints either a square (symmetric) or rectangular (asymmetric) matrix, depending on how you specify the variable list. Both forms of the specification permit the use of the keyword TO to reference consecutive variables. If you provide a simple list of variables, CORRELATIONS prints the correlations of each variable with every other variable in the list in a square or lower-triangular matrix. The correlation of a variable with itself is always 1.0000 and can be found on the diagonal of the matrix. Each pair of variables appears twice in the matrix (e.g., FOOD with RENT and RENT with FOOD) with identical coefficients, and the upper and lower triangles of the matrix are mirror images.

To obtain the rectangular matrix, specify two variable lists separated by the keyword WITH. SPSS^{X} then prints a rectangular matrix of variables in the first list correlated with variables in the second list. For example,

```
CORRELATIONS  MECHANIC BUS WITH PUBTRANS
```

produces two correlations, MECHANIC with PUBTRANS and BUS with PUBTRANS, while

```
CORRELATIONS  FOOD RENT WITH COOK TEACHER MANAGER ENGINEER
```

produces eight correlations. The variables listed before the keyword WITH define the rows of the matrix and those listed after the keyword WITH define the columns. Unless a variable is in both lists, there are no identity coefficients or redundant coefficients in the matrix.

You can request more than one matrix on a CORRELATIONS command. Use a slash (/) to separate the specifications for each of the requested matrices. For example,

```
CORRELATIONS  FOOD RENT WITH COOK TEACHER MANAGER ENGINEER
   /FOOD TO ENGINEER /PUBTRANS WITH MECHANIC
```

produces three separate correlation matrices. The first matrix contains eight nonredundant coefficients, the second matrix is a square matrix of all the variables from FOOD to ENGINEER, and the third matrix consists of one coefficient for PUBTRANS and MECHANIC.

If all cases have a missing value for a given pair of variables or if they all have the same value for a variable, the coefficient cannot be computed. Since Pearson correlations always have a value in the range −1.00 to 1.00, a period is printed if a coefficient cannot be calculated.

B.70 PRINT Subcommand

By default, CORRELATIONS prints Pearson correlation coefficients based on a one-tailed test. Below each coefficient, it prints both the number of cases and the significance level.

The PRINT subcommand switches to a two-tailed test and/or suppresses the display of the number of cases and the significance level. The following keywords can be specified on the PRINT subcommand:

ONETAIL *One-tailed test of significance.* This test is appropriate when the direction of the relationship between a pair of variables can be specified in advance of the analysis. This is the default.

TWOTAIL *Two-tailed test of significance.* This test is appropriate when the direction of the relationship cannot be determined in advance, as is often the case in exploratory data analysis. (With releases before 3.0, substitute the command OPTION 3.)

SIG *Print the number of cases and significance level.* This is the default for all CORRELATIONS matrices.

NOSIG *Suppress the printing of the number of cases and significance level.* (With releases before 3.0, substitute the command OPTION 5.)

If you use the keyword WITH in the variable list, the display will be a rectangular matrix with the number of cases suppressed and asterisks indicating significance levels.

If you specify both FORMAT=SERIAL and PRINT=NOSIG, only FORMAT=SERIAL will be in effect.

B.71 STATISTICS Subcommand

The correlation coefficient, number of cases, and significance level are automatically printed for every combination of variable pairs in the variable list.

The STATISTICS subcommand provides the following keywords for obtaining additional statistics:

DESCRIPTIVES *Mean, standard deviation, and number of nonmissing cases for each variable.* Missing values are handled on a variable-by-variable basis regardless of the missing-value option in effect for the correlations. (With releases before 3.0, substitute the command STATISTIC 1.)

XPROD *Cross-product deviations and covariance for each pair of variables.* (With releases before 3.0, substitute the command STATISTIC 2.)

ALL *All additional statistics available in CORRELATIONS.* Includes the mean, standard deviation, and number of nonmissing cases for each variable. Also includes the cross-product deviations and covariance for each pair of variables.

B.72 MISSING Subcommand

By default, CORRELATIONS deletes cases with missing values on a pair-by-pair basis. A case missing for one or both of the pair of variables for a specific correlation coefficient is not used for that coefficient. Since each coefficient is based on all cases that have valid codes on that particular pair of variables, the maximum information available is used in every calculation. This can also result in a set of coefficients based on a varying number of cases.

The MISSING subcommand controls missing values. The following keywords can be specified on the MISSING subcommand:

PAIRWISE *Exclude missing values pairwise.* Cases missing for one or both of a pair of variables for a specific correlation coefficient are excluded from the analysis. This is the default.

LISTWISE *Exclude missing values listwise.* Each variable listed on a command is evaluated separately. Cases missing on any variable named in a list are excluded from all analyses. (With releases before 3.0, substitute the command OPTION 2.)

INCLUDE *Include user-defined missing values.* User-missing values are included in the analysis. (With releases before 3.0, substitute the command OPTION 1.)

The PAIRWISE and LISTWISE keywords are mutually exclusive; however, each can be specified with INCLUDE.

B.73 FORMAT Subcommand

By default, CORRELATIONS includes redundant coefficients in the correlation and prints in matrix format. The FORMAT subcommand has two keywords that control matrix format:

MATRIX *Print in matrix format with redundant coefficients.* This is the default.

SERIAL *Print in serial string format with nonredundant coefficients.* (With releases before 3.0, substitute the command OPTION 6.)

B.74 MATRIX Subcommand

Use the MATRIX subcommand to write matrix materials to a system file. The matrix materials include the mean, standard deviation, number of cases used to compute each coefficient, and Pearson correlation coefficient for each variable.

The OUT keyword on MATRIX specifies the file to which the matrix is written. Specify the matrix file in parentheses. There are two options:

(file) *Write the correlation matrix to a system file.* Assign the file name in the parentheses. CORRELATIONS creates a system file containing the matrix materials. The system file is stored on disk and can be retrieved at any time. (With releases before 3.0, use the PROCEDURE OUTPUT command to specify the file, and write the matrix by using either the command OPTION 4 to include case counts or the command OPTION 7 to omit case counts.)

(*) *Replace the active file with the correlation matrix system file.* The matrix materials replace the active file. The correlation matrix is NOT stored on disk. It is resident in the active file.

B.75 Limitations

The following limitations apply to CORRELATIONS:

- A maximum of 40 variable lists.
- A maximum of 500 variables total per CORRELATIONS command.
- A maximum of 250 individual elements. Each unique occurrence of a variable name, keyword, or special delimiter counts as 1 toward this total. Variables implied by the TO keyword do not count toward this total.

B.76 CROSSTABS

Syntax for Release 3.0:

```
CROSSTABS [TABLES=]varlist BY varlist [BY...] [/varlist...]

 [/MISSING={TABLE**} ]
           {INCLUDE}

 [/FORMAT={LABELS**  }  {AVALUE**}  {NOINDEX**}  {TABLES**} ]
          {NOLABELS  }  {DVALUE  }  {INDEX    }  {NOTABLES}
          {NOVALLABS}

 [/CELLS={COUNT**}  [ROW    ]  [EXPECTED]  [SRESID  ]]
         {NONE   }  [COLUMN]  [RESID   ]  [ASRESID]
                    [TOTAL ]              [ALL     ]

 [/WRITE[={NONE** }]]
          {CELLS  }

 [/STATISTICS=[CHISQ]  [LAMBDA]  [BTAU]  [GAMMA]  [ETA ]]
              [PHI  ]  [UC    ]  [CTAU]  [D    ]  [CORR]
              [CC   ]  [NONE  ]                   [ALL ]
```

**Default if the subcommand is omitted.

Syntax for releases before 3.0:

General mode:

```
CROSSTABS [TABLES=]varlist BY varlist [BY...] [/varlist...]
```

Integer mode:

```
CROSSTABS VARIABLES=varlist (min,max) [varlist...]
          /TABLES=varlist BY varlist [BY...] [/varlist...]
```

Options:

1	Include missing values	10	Write cell count for nonempty cells
2	Suppress labels	11	Write cell count for all cells*
3	Add row percentages	12	Suppress tables
4	Add column percentages	13	Suppress cell counts
5	Add total percentages	14	Add expected frequencies
6	Suppress value labels	15	Add residuals
7	Report missing values*	16	Add standardized residuals
8	Order rows by descending value	17	Add adjusted standardized residuals
9	Print index of tables	18	Include all cell information

* *Integer mode only.*

Statistics:

1	Chi-square	5	Uncertainity coefficient	9	Somers' d
2	Phi for 2 × 2 tables, Cramer's V otherwise	6	Kendall's tau-b	10	Eta
		7	Kendall's tau-c	11	Pearson's r
3	Contingency coefficient	8	Gamma		
4	Lambda				

Procedure CROSSTABS produces tables that are the joint distribution of two or more variables that have a limited number of distinct values. The frequency distribution of one variable is subdivided according to the values of one or more variables. The unique combination of values for two variables defines a cell, the basic element of all tables.

B.77 TABLES Subcommand

To run CROSSTABS, use the TABLES subcommand followed by a list of one or more variables, the keyword BY, and another list of one or more variables. You can specify the TABLES subcommand once, only. The actual command keyword TABLES is not required to operate CROSSTABS.

You can specify a list of one or more variables for each dimension. Separate each list with the keyword BY. The first variable list is the list of *row variables* and the variable list following the first BY keyword is the list of *column variables*. Subsequent variable lists following BY keywords specify orders of *control variables*. For example,

```
CROSSTABS  TABLES=FEAR BY SEX BY RACE
```

crosstabulates FEAR by SEX, controlling for RACE. In each subtable, FEAR is the row variable and SEX is the column variable. The first subtable crosstabulates FEAR by SEX within the first category of RACE. The second subtable also crosstabulates FEAR by SEX, but for the next category of RACE. When you use control variables, a subtable is produced for each value of the control variable. The value of the first control variable changes most quickly and the value of the last control variable changes most slowly.

You can specify more than one variable in each dimension. Use the keyword TO to name a set of adjacent variables in the active file, as in:

```
CROSSTABS  TABLES=CONFINAN TO CONARMY BY SEX TO REGION
```

This command will produce CROSSTABS tables for all the variables between and including CONFINAN and CONARMY by all the variables between and including SEX and REGION. You can use similar variables lists to request higher order CROSSTABS tables. The values of the variables to the right of the last BY keyword change most slowly. Within lists separated by the keyword BY, variables rotate from left to right. For example,

```
CROSSTABS  TABLES=CONFINAN TO CONARMY BY SEX BY RACE,REGION
```

will produce CROSSTABS tables for all the variables between and including CONFINAN and CONARMY by SEX, controlling for RACE, and for all the variables between and including CONFINAN and CONARMY, controlling for REGION. If there are five variables implied by the first variables list, the command produces 10 crosstabulations. The first table is CONFINAN by SEX by RACE and the second table is CONFINAN by SEX by REGION. The last table produced is CONARMY by SEX by REGION. The number of values encountered for the control variables determines the total number of subtables. If RACE has two values and REGION has three values, the output from the command will have a total of 25 subtables.

Use a slash to separate tables lists on one CROSSTABS command. For example,

```
CROSSTABS  TABLES=FEAR BY SEX/RACE BY REGION
```

specifies two bivariate tables, FEAR by SEX and RACE by REGION. If you omit a slash between tables lists, CROSSTABS includes the variables as if one tables list had been supplied.

B.78 VARIABLES Subcommand

The VARIABLES subcommand specifies the variables to be used in the crosstabulations. Specify the lowest and highest values in parentheses after each variable. These values must be integers. For example, the command

```
CROSSTABS  VARIABLES=FEAR (1,2) MOBILE16 (1,3)
   /TABLES=FEAR BY MOBILE16
```

produces a table where FEAR has a range from 1 to 2 and MOBILE16 has a range from 1 to 3. Noninteger values are truncated. Cases with values that fall outside the range you specify are not used.

Several variables can have the same range. For example,

```
CROSSTABS  VARIABLES=FEAR SEX RACE (1,2) MOBILE16 (1,3)
   /TABLES=FEAR BY SEX MOBILE16 BY RACE
```

defines 1 as the lowest value and 2 as the highest value for FEAR, SEX, and RACE. Variables may appear in any order.

B.79 CELLS Subcommand

By default, CROSSTABS prints only the number of cases in each cell. The CELLS subcommand prints row, column, or total percentages, and also expected values and residuals. These items are calculated separately for each bivariate table or subtable.

You can specify the CELLS subcommand by itself, or with a keyword or keywords. If you specify the CELLS subcommand by itself, CROSSTABS prints cell counts plus ROW, COLUMN, and TOTAL percentages for each cell. If you specify a keyword or keywords, CROSSTABS prints only the cell information you request.

The following keywords can be specified on the CELLS subcommand:

COUNT *Print cell counts.* This is the default if you omit the CELLS subcommand. (With releases before 3.0, substitute the command OPTION 13.)

ROW *Print row percentages.* Print the number of cases in each cell in a row expressed as a percentage of all cases in that row. (With releases before 3.0, substitute the command OPTION 3.)

COLUMN *Print column percentages.* Print the number of cases in each cell in a column expressed as a percentage of all cases in that column. (With releases before 3.0, substitute the command OPTION 4.)

TOTAL *Print two-way table total percentages.* Print the number of cases in each cell of a subtable expressed as a percentage of all cases in that subtable. (With releases before 3.0, substitute the command OPTION 5.)

EXPECTED *Print expected frequencies.* Print the number of cases expected in each cell if the two variables in the subtable were statistically independent. (With releases before 3.0, substitute the command OPTION 14.)

RESID *Print residuals.* Print the value of the observed cell count minus the expected value. (With releases before 3.0, substitute the command OPTION 15.)

SRESID *Print standardized residuals.* (Haberman, 1978). (With releases before 3.0, substitute the command OPTION 16.)

ASRESID *Print adjusted standardized residuals.* (Haberman, 1978). (With releases before 3.0, substitute the command OPTION 17.)

ALL *Print all cell information.* Print cell count; row, column, and total percentages; expected values; residuals; standardized residuals; and adjusted standardized residuals. (With releases before 3.0, substitute the command OPTION 18.)

NONE *Print no cell information.* Use NONE to write the tables to a procedure file without printed tables. This has the same effect as specifying FORMAT=NOTABLES. (With releases before 3.0, substitute the command OPTION 12.)

B.80 STATISTICS Subcommand

CROSSTABS can calculate a number of summary statistics for each subtable. Unless you specify otherwise, it calculates statistical measures of association for the cases with valid values included in the subtable. If you include user-missing values with the MISSING subcommand, cases with user-defined missing values are included in the tables as well as in the calculation of statistics.

The STATISTICS subcommand requests summary statistics. You can specify the STATISTICS subcommand by itself, or with one or more keywords. If you specify STATISTICS by itself, CROSSTABS calculates CHISQ. If you include a keyword or keywords on the STATISTICS subcommand, CROSSTABS calculates all the statistics you request.

The following keywords can be specified on the STATISTICS subcommand:

CHISQ *Chi-square*. Fisher's exact test is computed using the rounded values of the cell entries when there are fewer than 20 cases in a 2 × 2 table that does not result from missing rows or columns in a larger table; Yates' corrected chi-square is computed for all other 2 × 2 tables. This is the default if you specify the STATISTICS subcommand by itself, with no keywords. (With releases before 3.0, substitute the command STATISTIC 1.)

PHI *Phi for 2 × 2 tables, Cramer's* V *for larger tables*. (With releases before 3.0, substitute the command STATISTIC 2.)

CC *Contingency coefficient*. (With releases before 3.0, substitute the command STATISTIC 3.)

LAMBDA *Lambda, symmetric and asymmetric*. (With releases before 3.0, substitute the command STATISTIC 4.)

UC *Uncertainty coefficient, symmetric and asymmetric*. (With releases before 3.0, substitute the command STATISTIC 5.)

BTAU *Kendall's tau*-b. (With releases before 3.0, substitute the command STATISTIC 6.)

CTAU *Kendall's tau*-c. (With releases before 3.0, substitute the command STATISTIC 7.)

GAMMA *Gamma*. Partial and zero-order gammas for 3-way to 8-way tables are available only if the values of all variables are integers, and you use the VARIABLES subcommand to specify the variables and the minimum and maximum values for building tables. Otherwise, zero-order gammas are printed for 2-way tables and conditional gammas are printed for 3-way to 10-way tables. (With releases before 3.0, substitute the command STATISTIC 8.)

D *Somers'* d, *symmetric and asymmetric*. (With releases before 3.0, substitute the command STATISTIC 9.)

ETA *Eta*. Available for numeric data only. (With releases before 3.0, substitute the command STATISTIC 10.)

CORR *Pearson's* r. Available for numeric data only. (With releases before 3.0, substitute the command STATISTIC 11.)

ALL *All the statistics available for CROSSTABS.*

NONE *No summary statistics*. This is the default if you omit the STATISTICS subcommand.

B.81 MISSING Subcommand

By default, CROSSTABS deletes cases with missing values on a table-by-table basis. A case missing on any of the variables specified for a table is not used either in the printed table or in the calculation of the statistics. When you separate tables requests with a slash, missing values are handled separately for each list. The number of missing cases is always printed at the end of the table, following the last subtable and after any requested statistics.

The MISSING subcommand controls missing values. The following keywords can be specified on the MISSING subcommand:

TABLE *Delete cases with missing values on a table-by-table basis*. This is the default if you omit the MISSING subcommand.

INCLUDE *Include user-defined missing values*. (With releases before 3.0, substitute the command OPTION 1.)

REPORT *Report missing values in the tables*. This option includes missing values in tables but not in the calculation of percentages or statistics. It is only available if the values of all variables are integers, and you use the

VARIABLES subcommand to specify the variables and the minimum and maximum values for building tables. (With releases before 3.0, substitute the command OPTION 7.)

If the missing values are not included in the range specifications on the VARIABLES subcommand, they are excluded from the table regardless of the keyword you specify on MISSING.

B.82 FORMAT Subcommand

By default, CROSSTABS prints tables and subtables with variable labels and value labels when they are available. The values for the row variables print in order from lowest to highest. CROSSTABS uses only the first 16 characters of the value labels. Value labels for the columns print on two lines with eight characters per line.

The FORMAT subcommand modifies the default tables and subtables. The following keywords can be specified on the FORMAT subcommand:

LABELS *Print both variable and value labels for each table.* This is the default.

NOLABELS *Suppress variable and value labels.* (With releases before 3.0, substitute the command OPTION 2.)

NOVALLABS *Suppress value labels, print variable labels.* (With releases before 3.0, substitute the command OPTION 6.)

AVALUE *Print row variables ordered from lowest to highest.* This is the default.

DVALUE *Print row variables ordered from highest to lowest.* (With releases before 3.0, substitute the command OPTION 8.)

NOINDEX *Suppress a table index.* This is the default.

INDEX *Prints an index of tables.* The index lists all tables produced by the CROSSTABS command and the page number where each table begins. The index follows the last page of tables produced by the tables list. (With releases before 3.0, substitute the command OPTION 9.)

TABLES *Print the crosstabs tables.* This is the default.

NOTABLES *Suppress printed tables.* If you use the STATISTICS subcommand (see Section B.80) and specify NOTABLES, only the statistics are printed. If you do not use the STATISTICS subcommand and specify NOTABLES, the CROSSTABS command produces no output. (With releases before 3.0, substitute the command OPTION 12.)

B.83 WRITE Subcommand

The WRITE subcommand writes cell frequencies to a procedure output file (specified on the PROCEDURE OUTPUT command), for subsequent use by SPSS^X or some other program. The output file contains one record per cell.

NONE *Do not write the cell counts to the file.* This is the default if you omit the WRITE subcommand.

CELLS *Write the cell count for nonempty cells to a file.* (With releases before 3.0, substitute the command OPTION 10.)

ALL *Write the cell count for all cells to a file.* This is only available if the values of all variables are integers, and you use the VARIABLES subcommand to specify the variables and the minimum and maximum values for building tables. (With releases before 3.0, substitute the command OPTION 11.)

B.84 Limitations

The following limitations apply to CROSSTABS:

- A maximum of 200 variables total per CROSSTABS command.
- A maximum of 250 nonempty rows or columns printed for each variable.
- A maximum of 20 tables lists per CROSSTABS command.
- A maximum of 10 dimensions per table.
- A maximum of 250 value labels printed on any single table.

B.85 DESCRIPTIVES

Syntax for Release 3.0:

```
DESCRIPTIVES [VARIABLES=] varname[(zname)] [varname...]

 [/MISSING={VARIABLE**}  [INCLUDE]]
           {LISTWISE  }

 [/FORMAT={LABELS** }  {NOINDEX**}  {LINE**}]
          {NOLABELS }  {INDEX    }  {SERIAL}

 [/SAVE]

 [/STATISTICS=[DEFAULT**]  [MEAN**]  [MIN**]  [SKEWNESS]]
              [STDDEV**  ]  [SEMEAN]  [MAX**]  [KURTOSIS]
              [VARIANCE  ]  [SUM   ]  [RANGE]  [ALL]
```

**Default if the subcommand is omitted.

Syntax for releases before 3.0 (DESCRIPTIVES was formerly called CONDESCRIPTIVE):

```
CONDESCRIPTIVE varname [(zname)] [varname...]
```

Options:

1	Include missing values	5	Exclude missing values listwise
2	Suppress variable labels	6	Serial-style formatting
3	Compute Z-scores	7	80-character formatting
4	Reference indexes		

Statistics:

1	Mean	7	Kurtosis	11	Maximum
2	Standard error of mean	8	Skewness	12	Sum
5	Standard deviation	9	Range	13	Mean, standard dev, min, max
6	Variance	10	Minimum		

Procedure DESCRIPTIVES computes univariate summary statistics and standardized variables that are saved on the active file. Although it computes statistics also available in procedure FREQUENCIES (see Section B.94), DESCRIPTIVES computes descriptive statistics for continuous variables more efficiently because it does not sort values into a frequencies table.

DESCRIPTIVES calculates the mean, standard deviation, minimum, and maximum for *numeric* variables, only. You can request optional statistics and *Z*-score transformations.

The only required subcommand on DESCRIPTIVES is the VARIABLES subcommand, which specifies the variable list to be analyzed. The actual keyword VARIABLES can be omitted.

B.86 VARIABLES Subcommand

The variables subcommand names the variable list. The actual keyword VARIABLES is optional. If you explicitly specify keyword VARIABLES, an equals sign must precede the variable list. You can use keyword TO in the list to refer to consecutive variables in the active file. The variables must be numeric.

To request the default summary statistics, specify the VARIABLES subcommand and a simple list of variables, as in:

```
DESCRIPTIVES VARIABLES=NTCPRI FOOD RENT
```

You can also use the keyword ALL to specify all variables in the active file.

You can specify only one variable list with DESCRIPTIVES, but there is no limit to the number of variables named or implied on one command. Variables named more than once will appear in the output more than once. If there is insufficient space to process all the requested variables, DESCRIPTIVES truncates the variable list.

B.87 Z Scores

The *Z*-score variable transformation standardizes variables with different observed scales to the same scale. DESCRIPTIVES generates new variables, each with a mean of 0 and a standard deviation of 1, and stores them on the active file.

B.88 SAVE Subcommand

Use the SAVE subcommand to obtain one *Z*-score variable for each variable specified on the DESCRIPTIVES variable list. The SAVE subcommand calculates standardized variables and stores them on the active file. The commands

```
DESCRIPTIVES VARIABLES=ALL
    /SAVE
```

produce a table of old variables and new *Z*-score variables.

DESCRIPTIVES automatically supplies variable names and labels for the new variables. The new variable name is created by prefixing the letter *Z* to a maximum of seven characters of the variable name. For example, ZNTCPRI is the *Z*-score variable for NTCPRI. When DESCRIPTIVES creates new *Z*-score variables, it prints a table containing the source variable name, new variable name, its label, and the number of cases for which it is computed.

If you want *Z* scores for a subset of the variables listed on DESCRIPTIVES, specify the name of the new variable in parentheses following the source variable on the VARIABLES subcommand, and *do not use the SAVE subcommand.* For example,

```
DESCRIPTIVES VARIABLES=NTCSAL NTCPUR (PURCHZ) NTCPRI (PRICEZ)
```

creates *Z*-score variables for NTCPUR and NTCPRI.

If you specify new names on the VARIABLES subcommand *and* use the SAVE subcommand, DESCRIPTIVES creates one new variable for each variable on the VARIABLES subcommand, using the default names for variables not explicitly assigned names. For example,

```
DESCRIPTIVES VARIABLES=NTCSAL NTCPUR (PURCHZ) NTCPRI (PRICEZ)
            /SAVE
```

creates PURCHZ and PRICEZ and assigns a default name to the *Z*-score variable for NTCSAL. When you specify the name of the new variable yourself, you can use any acceptable eight-character variable name, including any of the default variable names, that is not already part of the active file.

If DESCRIPTIVES cannot use the default naming convention because it would produce duplicate names, it uses an alternative naming convention.

DESCRIPTIVES automatically supplies variable labels for the new variables by prefixing *ZSCORE:* to the first 31 characters of the source variable's label. If it uses a name like ZSC001, it prefixes *ZSCORE(varname)* to the first 31 characters of the source variable's label. If the source variable has no label, it uses *ZSCORE(varname)* for the label.

(With releases before 3.0, substitute the command OPTION 3 for the SAVE subcommand.)

B.89 STATISTICS Subcommand

By default, DESCRIPTIVES prints the mean, standard deviation, minimum, and maximum. If you use the STATISTICS subcommand and any of its keywords, you can specify alternative statistics. When you specify statistics, DESCRIPTIVES prints *only* those statistics you request.

You can use the keyword ALL to obtain all statistics. When requesting the default statistics plus additional statistics, you can specify DEFAULT to obtain the default statistics without having to name MEAN, STDDEV, MIN and MAX.

The following keywords can be specified on the STATISTICS subcommand:

MEAN *Mean.* (With releases before 3.0, substitute the command STATISTIC 1.)

SEMEAN *Standard error of the mean.* (With releases before 3.0, substitute the command STATISTIC 2.)

STDDEV *Standard deviation.* (With releases before 3.0, substitute the command STATISTIC 5.)

VARIANCE *Variance.* (With releases before 3.0, substitute the command STATISTIC 6.)

KURTOSIS *Kurtosis.* Also prints standard error. (With releases before 3.0, substitute the command STATISTIC 7.)

SKEWNESS *Skewness.* Also prints standard error. (With releases before 3.0, substitute the command STATISTIC 8.)

RANGE *Range.* (With releases before 3.0, substitute the command STATISTIC 9.)

MIN *Minimum.* (With releases before 3.0, substitute the command STATISTIC 10.)

MAX *Maximum.* (With releases before 3.0, substitute the command STATISTIC 11.)

SUM *Sum.* (With releases before 3.0, substitute the command STATISTIC 12.)

DEFAULT *Mean, standard deviation, minimum, and maximum.* These are the default statistics if you omit the STATISTICS subcommand. (With releases before 3.0, substitute the command STATISTIC 13.)

ALL *All the statistics available to DESCRIPTIVES.*

B.90 MISSING Subcommand

By default, DESCRIPTIVES deletes cases with missing values on a variable-by-variable basis. A case missing on a variable will not be included in the summary statistics for that variable, but the case *will* be included for variables where it is not missing.

The MISSING subcommand controls missing values, and three keywords can be specified on it:

VARIABLE *Exclude missing values on a variable-by-variable basis.* This is the default if you omit the MISSING subcommand.

LISTWISE *Exclude missing values listwise.* Cases missing on any variable named are excluded from the computation of summary statistics for all variables. (With releases before 3.0, substitute the command OPTION 5.)

INCLUDE *Include user-defined missing values.* (With releases before 3.0, substitute the command OPTION 1.)

The VARIABLE and LISTWISE keywords are mutually exclusive; however, each can be specified with INCLUDE. For example, to include user-missing values in an analysis that excludes missing values listwise, specify

```
DESCRIPTIVES VARIABLES=ALL
  /MISSING=INCLUDE LISTWISE
```

When you use the keyword VARIABLE or the default missing-value treatment, DESCRIPTIVES reports the number of valid cases for each variable. It always displays the number of cases that would be available if listwise deletion of missing values had been selected.

B.91 FORMAT Subcommand

The FORMAT subcommand controls the formatting options available in DESCRIPTIVES, and the following keywords can be specified on it:

LABELS *Print variable labels.* This is the default if you omit the FORMAT subcommand.

NOLABELS *Suppress variable labels.* (With releases before 3.0, substitute the command OPTION 2.)

INDEX *Print reference indexes.* INDEX prints a positional and an alphabetic reference index following the statistical display. The index shows the page location in the output of the statistics for each variable. The variables are listed by their position in the active file and alphabetically. (With releases before 3.0, substitute the command OPTION 4.)

NOINDEX *Suppress reference indexes.* This is the default if you omit the FORMAT subcommand,

LINE *Print statistics in line format.* LINE prints statistics on the same line as the variable name. It is the default if you omit the FORMAT subcommand.

SERIAL *Print statistics in serial format.* SERIAL prints statistics below the variable name, permitting larger field widths and more decimal digits for very large or very small numbers. DESCRIPTIVES automatically forces this format if the number of statistics requested does not fit in the column format. (With releases before 3.0, substitute the command OPTION 6.)

B.92 DISCRIMINANT

Syntax for Release 3.0:

```
DISCRIMINANT GROUPS=varname(min,max) /VARIABLES=varlist

 [/SELECT=varname(value)]

 [/ANALYSIS=varlist(level) [varlist...]]

 [/METHOD={DIRECT**} ] [/TOLERANCE={0.001}]
          {WILKS   }               {t    }
          {MAHAL   }
          {MAXMINF }
          {MINRESID}
          {RAO     }

 [/MAXSTEPS={2v}]
            {m }

 [/FIN={1.0}] [/FOUT={1.0}] [/PIN={1.0**}]
       {fi }         {fo }        {pi   }

 [/POUT={1.0**}] [/VIN={0**}]
        {po   }        {vi }

 [/FUNCTIONS={g-1,100.0,1.0**}] [/PRIORS={EQUAL     }]
             {nf , cp  ,sig  }           {SIZE      }
                                         {value list}

 [/SAVE=[CLASS=varname] [PROBS=rootname] [SCORES=rootname]]

 [/ANALYSIS=...]

 [/MISSING={EXCLUDE**}]
           {INCLUDE  }

 [/MATRIX=[OUT({*   })] [IN({*   })]]
               {file}        {file}

 [/HISTORY={STEP**}  {END** }]
           {NOSTEP}  {NOEND }

 [/ROTATE={NONE**   }]
          {COEFF    }
          {STRUCTURE}

 [/CLASSIFY={NONMISSING  }  {POOLED  }  [MEANSUB]]
            {UNSELECTED  }  {SEPARATE}
            {UNCLASSIFIED}

 [/STATISTICS=[MEAN  ] [COV ] [FPAIR] [RAW  ]  [ALL]]
              [STDDEV] [GCOV] [UNIVF] [COEFF]
              [CORR  ] [TCOV] [BOXM ] [TABLE]

 [/PLOT=[MAP]  [SEPARATE]  [COMBINED]  [CASES]  [ALL]]
```

**Default if the subcommand is omitted.

Syntax for releases before 3.0:

```
DISCRIMINANT GROUPS=varname(min,max) /VARIABLES=varlist

    [/SELECT=varname(value)] [/ANALYSIS=varlist(level) [varlist...]]

    [/METHOD={DIRECT  }] [/TOLERANCE={0.001}] [/MAXSTEPS={2v}]
             {WILKS   }              {t    }             {m }
             {MAHAL   }
             {MAXMINF }
             {MINRESID}
             {RAO     }

    [/FIN={1.0}] [/FOUT={1.0}] [/PIN={1.0}] [/POUT={1.0}] [/VIN={0 }]
          {fi }         {fo }        {pi }         {po }        {vi}

    [/FUNCTIONS={g-1,100.0,1.0}] [/PRIORS={EQUAL     }]
                {nf , cp  ,sig}           {SIZE      }
                                          {value list}

    [/SAVE=[CLASS varname] [PROBS rootname] [SCORES rootname]]

    [/ANALYSIS=...]
```

Options:

1 Include missing values
2 Write matrix materials
3 Read matrix materials
4 Suppress step output
5 Suppress summary table
6 Varimax rotation of funct. matrix
7 Varimax rotation of struct. matrix
8 Include missing during classif
9 Classify only unselected cases
10 Classify only unclassified cases
11 Individual covariance matrices used for classification

Statistics:

1 Group means
2 Group standard deviations
3 Pooled within-groups cov. matrix
4 Pooled within-groups corr. matrix
5 Matrix of pairwise F ratios
6 Univariate F ratios
7 Box's M
8 Group covariance matrices
9 Total covariance matrix
10 Territorial map
11 Unstandardized function coeffs
12 Classification function coeffs
13 Classification results table
14 Casewise materials
15 Combined plot
16 Separate plot

The complete syntax charts for DISCRIMINANT are included here. Discussion of DISCRIMINANT appears in Chapter 3.

B.93 FACTOR

Syntax for Release 3.0:

```
FACTOR VARIABLES=varlist† [/MISSING=[{LISTWISE**}] [INCLUDE]]
                                      {PAIRWISE  }
                                      {MEANSUB   }
                                      {DEFAULT   }

 [/WIDTH={132       }]
         {n         }
         {DEFAULT** }

 [/MATRIX=[IN({COR=file})]  [OUT({COR=file})]]
              {COR=*   }         {COR=*   }
              {FAC=file}         {FAC=file}
              {FAC=*   }         {FAC=*   }

 [/ANALYSIS=varlist...]

 [/PRINT=[DEFAULT**] [INITIAL**] [EXTRACTION**] [ROTATION**]
         [UNIVARIATE**] [CORRELATION] [DET] [INV] [REPR] [AIC] [KMO]
         [FSCORE] [SIG] [ALL]]

 [/PLOT=[EIGEN] [ROTATION (n1,n2)]]

 [/DIAGONAL={value list}]
            {DEFAULT**  }

 [/FORMAT=[SORT] [BLANK(n)] [DEFAULT**]]

 [/CRITERIA=[FACTORS(n)] [MINEIGEN({1.0**})] [ITERATE({25**})]
                                   {eig  }            {ni  }

          [RCONVERGE({0.0001**})] [DELTA({0**})] [{KAISER**}]
                     {r1      }           {d  }    {NOKAISER}

          [ECONVERGE({0.001**})]] [DEFAULT**]
                     {e1     }

 [/EXTRACTION={PC**   }] [/ROTATION={VARIMAX**}]
              {PAF    }             {EQUAMAX  }
              {ALPHA  }             {QUARTIMAX}
              {IMAGE  }             {OBLIMIN  }
              {ULS    }             {NOROTATE }
              {GLS    }             {DEFAULT  }
              {ML     }
              {PA1    }
              {PA2    }
              {DEFAULT}

 [/SAVE=[{REG    } ({ALL} rootname)]]
         {BART   }  {n  }
         {AR     }
         {DEFAULT}

 [/ANALYSIS...]

 [/CRITERIA...]     [/EXTRACTION...]

 [/ROTATION...]     [/SAVE...]
```

**Default if the subcommand is omitted.
†Omit VARIABLES with matrix input.

Syntax for releases before 3.0:

```
FACTOR VARIABLES=varlist [/MISSING={LISTWISE**}]
                                   {PAIRWISE  }
                                   {MEANSUB   }
                                   {INCLUDE   }
                                   {DEFAULT   }

     [/READ={CORRELATION [TRIANGLE]}] [/WRITE={CORRELATION}]
            {FACTOR(n)             }          {FACTOR     }
            {DEFAULT               }          {DEFAULT    }

     [/WIDTH={132}] [/ANALYSIS=varlist...] [/ANALYSIS...]
             {n  }

     [/PRINT=[DEFAULT**] [INITIAL] [EXTRACTION] [ROTATION] [UNIVARIATE]
             [CORRELATION] [DET] [INV] [REPR] [AIC] [KMO] [FSCORE]
             [SIG] [ALL]]

     [/FORMAT=[SORT] [BLANK(n)] [DEFAULT**]]

     [/CRITERIA=[FACTORS(n)] [MINEIGEN({1.0})] [ITERATE({25})]
                                       {eig}            {ni}

               [RCONVERGE({0.0001})] [DELTA({0})] [{KAISER  }]
                          {rl    }          {d}    {NOKAISER}

               [ECONVERGE({0.001})]]
                          {el   }

     [/EXTRACTION={PC**   }] [/ROTATION={VARIMAX**}]
                  {PAF    }             {EQUAMAX  }
                  {ALPHA  }             {QUARTIMAX}
                  {IMAGE  }             {OBLIMIN  }
                  {ULS    }             {NOROTATE }
                  {GLS    }             {DEFAULT  }
                  {ML     }
                  {PA1    }
                  {PA2    }
                  {DEFAULT}

          [/EXTRACTION...] [/ROTATION...]

     [/DIAGONAL=value list] [/PLOT=[EIGEN] [ROTATION (n1,n2)]]

     [/SAVE=[{REG    } ({ALL} rootname)]] [/SAVE...]
             {BART   }  {n  }
             {AR     }
             {DEFAULT}
```

** Default if the subcommand is omitted.

The complete syntax charts for FACTOR are included here. Discussion of FACTOR appears in Chapter 4.

B.94 FREQUENCIES

Syntax for all releases:

```
FREQUENCIES VARIABLES=varlist[(min,max)] [varlist...]

 [/FORMAT=[{CONDENSE}] [{NOTABLE }] [NOLABELS] [WRITE]
           {ONEPAGE }   {LIMIT(n)}

           [{DVALUE}] [DOUBLE] [NEWPAGE] [INDEX]]
            {AFREQ }
            {DFREQ }

 [/MISSING=INCLUDE]

 [/BARCHART=[MINIMUM(n)] [MAXIMUM(n)] [{FREQ(n)    }]]
                                       {PERCENT(n)}

 [/HISTOGRAM=[MINIMUM(n)] [MAXIMUM(n)] [{FREQ(n)    }]
                                        {PERCENT(n)}

             [{NONORMAL}] [INCREMENT(n)]]
              {NORMAL  }

 [/HBAR=same as HISTOGRAM]

 [/NTILES=n]

 [/PERCENTILES=value list]

 [/STATISTICS=[DEFAULT] [MEAN] [STDDEV] [MINIMUM] [MAXIMUM]
              [SEMEAN] [VARIANCE] [SKEWNESS] [SESKEW] [RANGE] [MODE]
              [KURTOSIS] [SEKURT] [MEDIAN] [SUM] [ALL] [NONE]]
```

Procedure FREQUENCIES produces a table of frequency counts and percentages for the values of individual variables. Optionally, you can obtain bar charts for discrete variables, histograms for continuous variables, univariate summary statistics, and percentiles. To produce only statistics on interval-level data, see procedure DESCRIPTIVES (Section B.85).

The only required subcommand on FREQUENCIES is the VARIABLES subcommand, which specifies the variables to be analyzed. Subcommands can be named in any order and are separated from each other by a slash. With the exception of PERCENTILES and NTILES, each subcommand can be used only once per FREQUENCIES command.

B.95 VARIABLES Subcommand

The VARIABLES subcommand names the variables to be analyzed. FREQUENCIES dynamically builds the table, setting up one cell for each unique value encountered in the data.

List the variable names on the VARIABLES subcommand, as in:

```
FREQUENCIES  VARIABLES=POLVIEWS RES16
```

The variable and value labels are printed, if available, followed by the value and the number of cases that have the value. The percentage is based on all the observations, and the valid and cumulative percentages are based on those cases that have valid values. The number of valid and missing observations is also provided. FREQUENCIES tabulates any type of variable, including numeric variables with decimal positions and string variables.

You can use the keyword ALL to name all the variables on the file or the keyword TO to reference a set of consecutive variables on the active file.

B.96 FORMAT Subcommand

The FORMAT subcommand applies to all variables named on the VARIABLES subcommand. You can control the formatting of tables and the order in which values are sorted within the table, suppress tables, produce an index of tables, and write the FREQUENCIES display to another file via keywords on the FORMAT subcommand.

Specify as many formatting options as desired on the FORMAT subcommand. For example,

```
FREQUENCIES  VARIABLES=POLVIEWS PRESTIGE
            /FORMAT=ONEPAGE DVALUE
```

specifies conditional condensed formatting of the tables (keyword ONEPAGE) with values sorted in descending order (keyword DVALUE).

B.97 Table Formats

The following keywords on the FORMAT subcommand control the formatting of tables:

NOLABELS *Do not print variable or value labels.* By default, FREQUENCIES prints variable and value labels defined by the VARIABLE LABELS and VALUE LABELS commands.

DOUBLE *Double-space frequency tables.*

NEWPAGE *Begin each table on a new page.* By default, FREQUENCIES prints as many tables on a page as fit.

CONDENSE *Condensed format.* This format prints frequency counts in three columns. It does not print value labels and percentages for all cases, and it rounds valid and cumulative percentages to integers.

ONEPAGE *Conditional condensed format.* Keyword ONEPAGE uses the condensed format for tables that would require more than one page with the default format. All other tables are printed in default format. If you specify both CONDENSE and ONEPAGE, all tables are printed in condensed format.

B.98 Order of Values

By default, frequency tables are printed in ascending order of values. You can override this order with one of three sorting options on the FORMAT subcommand.

AFREQ *Sort categories in ascending order of frequency.*

DFREQ *Sort categories in descending order of frequency.*

DVALUE *Sort categories in descending order of values.*

B.99 Suppressing Tables

You might be using FREQUENCIES to obtain univariate statistics not available in other procedures, or to print histograms or bar charts, and thus may not be interested in the frequency tables themselves. Or you might want to suppress tables for variables with a large number of values. Two options are available for suppressing tables.

LIMIT(n) *Do not print tables with more categories than the specified value.*

NOTABLE *Suppress all frequency tables.*

If you specify both NOTABLE and LIMIT, NOTABLE overrides LIMIT and no tables are printed.

B.100 Index of Tables

To obtain both a positional index of frequency tables and an index arranged alphabetically by variable name, use the INDEX keyword on the FORMAT subcommand.

INDEX *Index of tables.*

B.101 Bar Charts and Histograms

You can request both bar charts and histograms on one FREQUENCIES command. Use the BARCHART subcommand to produce bar charts for all variables named on the VARIABLES subcommand and the HISTOGRAM subcommand to produce histograms for all variables. Or use the HBAR subcommand to produce bar charts for variables that fit on one page (11 individual categories for the default page length) and histograms for other variables. You can specify only one of these three subcommands on each FREQUENCIES command. If you specify more than one, FREQUENCIES assumes HBAR.

B.102 BARCHART Subcommand

No specifications are required for the BARCHART subcommand. In the default bar chart format, all tabulated values are plotted, and the horizontal axis is scaled in frequencies. The scale is determined by the frequency count of the largest single category plotted. You can specify minimum and maximum bounds for plotting and can request a horizontal scale labeled with percentages or frequencies.

MIN(n) *Lower bound.* Values below the specified minimum are not plotted.

MAX(n) *Upper bound.* Values above the specified maximum are not plotted.

PERCENT(n) *Horizontal axis scaled in percentages.* The *n* specifies the preferred maximum and is not required. If you do not specify an *n* or your *n* is too small, FREQUENCIES chooses 5, 10, 25, 50 or 100, depending on the percentage for the largest category.

FREQ(n) *Horizontal axis scaled in frequencies.* While FREQ is the default scaling method, you can use this keyword to specify a maximum frequency *(n)* for the scale. If you do not specify an *n* or your *n* is too small, FREQUENCIES chooses 10, 20, 50, 100, 200, 500, 1000, 2000, and so forth, depending on the frequency count for the largest category.

You can enter optional specifications in any order, as in

```
FREQUENCIES  VARIABLES=SIBS
            /BARCHART=PERCENT MAX(10)
```

which requests a bar chart on SIBS with values through 10 plotted and the horizontal axis scaled in percentages.

B.103 HISTOGRAM Subcommand

No specifications are required for the HISTOGRAM subcommand. In the default histogram format, all tabulated values are included, and the horizontal axis is scaled by frequencies. The scale is determined by the frequency count of the largest category plotted. The number of intervals plotted is 21 (or fewer if the range of values is less than 21).

You can use all of the formatting options available with BARCHART (MIN, MAX, PERCENT, and FREQ) on the HISTOGRAM subcommand. In addition, you can specify the interval width and superimpose a normal curve on the histogram.

INCREMENT(n) *Interval width.* By default, values are collected into 21 intervals for plotting. You can override the default by specifying the actual interval width. For example, if a variable ranges from 1 to 100 and you specify INCREMENT(2), the width of each interval is 2, producing 50 intervals.

NORMAL *Superimpose the normal curve.* The normal curve is based on all valid values for the variable and includes values excluded by MIN and MAX. The default is NONORMAL.

You can enter the optional specifications in any order, as in

```
FREQUENCIES  VARIABLES=PRESTIGE
            /HISTOGRAM=NORMAL INCREMENT(4)
```

which produces a histogram of PRESTIGE with a superimposed normal curve and an interval width of four.

B.104 HBAR Subcommand

The HBAR subcommand produces either bar charts or histograms, depending upon the number of values encountered in the data. If a bar chart for a variable fits on a page, HBAR produces a bar chart; otherwise, it produces a histogram. For the default page length of 59, a bar chart is displayed for variables with fewer than 12 categories. Histograms are displayed for all other variables specified on the VARIABLES subcommand. All specifications for HISTOGRAM and BARCHART also work with HBAR.

B.105 Percentiles and Ntiles

You can use either the PERCENTILES or NTILES subcommands to print percentiles for all variables specified on the VARIABLES subcommand. If two or more PERCENTILES and NTILES subcommands are specified, FREQUENCIES prints one table with the values for all requested percentiles.

B.106 PERCENTILES Subcommand

Percentiles are the values below which a given percentage of cases fall. Use the PERCENTILES subcommand followed by an optional equals sign and a list of percentiles between 0 and 100 to print the values for each percentile. For example, to request the values for percentiles 10, 25, 33.3, 66.7, and 75 for variable PRESTIGE, specify:

```
FREQUENCIES  VARIABLES=PRESTIGE
            /PERCENTILES=10 25 33.3 66.7 75
```

B.107 NTILES Subcommand

*N*tiles are the values that divide the sample into groups of equal numbers of cases. To print the values for each *n*tile, use the NTILES subcommand followed by an optional equals sign and one integer value specifying the number of subgroups. For example, to request quartiles for PRESTIGE, specify:

```
FREQUENCIES VARIABLES=PRESTIGE /NTILES=4
```

SPSS^X prints one less percentile than the number specified on the NTILES subcommand. If a requested percentile cannot be calculated, SPSS^X prints a period (.) as the value associated with that percentile.

B.108 STATISTICS Subcommand

The STATISTICS subcommand specifies univariate statistics for all variables named on the VARIABLES subcommand.

MEAN *Mean.*

SEMEAN *Standard error of the mean.*

MEDIAN *Median.* The median is defined as the value below which half the cases fall. If there is an even number of cases, the median is the average of the (nth/2) and (nth/2+1) cases when the cases are sorted in ascending order. The median is not available if you specify AFREQ or DFREQ on the FORMAT subcommand.

MODE *Mode.*

STDDEV *Standard deviation.*

VARIANCE *Variance.*

SKEWNESS *Skewness.*

SESKEW *Standard error of the skewness statistic.*

KURTOSIS *Kurtosis.*

SEKURT *Standard error of the kurtosis statistic.*

RANGE *Range.*

MINIMUM *Minimum.*

MAXIMUM *Maximum.*

SUM *Sum.*

DEFAULT *Mean, standard deviation, minimum, and maximum.* You can use DEFAULT jointly with other statistics.

ALL *All available statistics.*

NONE *No statistics.*

You can specify as many keywords as you wish on the STATISTICS subcommand. For example,

```
FREQUENCIES  VARIABLES=PRESTIGE POLVIEWS
            /STATISTICS=MEDIAN DEFAULT
```

prints the median and the default statistics (the mean, standard deviation, minimum, and maximum). If you use the STATISTICS subcommand with no specifications, the default statistics are printed.

B.109 MISSING Subcommand

FREQUENCIES recognizes three types of missing values: user-missing, system-missing, and, if you specify on the VARIABLE subcommand a value range for each variable, out-of-range values. Both user- and system-missing values are included in frequency tables. They are labeled as missing and are not included in the valid and cumulative percentages. Missing values are not used in the calculation of descriptive statistics, nor do they appear in bar charts and histograms.

To treat user-missing values as valid values, use the MISSING subcommand, which has one specification, INCLUDE. For example,

```
MISSING VALUES  SATFAM TO HAPPY(8,9)
FREQUENCIES  VARIABLES=SATFAM HAPPY (0,9)
            /BARCHART
            /MISSING=INCLUDE
```

includes values 8 and 9 (which were previously defined as missing with the MISSING VALUES command) in the bar charts.

B.110 Limitations

The following limitations apply to FREQUENCIES:

- A maximum of 500 variables total per FREQUENCIES command.
- A maximum of 32,767 observed values over all variables.

B.111 HILOGLINEAR

Syntax for all releases:

```
HILOGLINEAR† varlist (min,max) [varlist (min,max)...]

 [/MISSING = {LISTWISE}] [INCLUDE]
             {DEFAULT }

 [/CWEIGHT = {varname }]
             {(matrix)}

 [/PRINT = [DEFAULT]  [ASSOCIATION]
           [FREQ]     [RESID]
           [ESTIM]    [ALL]
           [NONE††]]

 [/PLOT = [DEFAULT]  [RESID]
          [NORMPROB] [NONE ]]

 [/CRITERIA = [CONVERGE({0.25})] [ITERATE({20})] [P({0.05})]
                        {n   }            {n }      {prob}

          [DELTA({0.5})]††† [MAXSTEPS({10})] [DEFAULT]]
                 {d  }                {n }

 [/METHOD [= BACKWARD]]

 [/MAXORDER = k]

 [/DESIGN = effectname effectname*effectname ...]

 [/DESIGN = ... ]
```

†Available as of Release 2.0.
††Available as of Release 2.1.
†††Available as of Release 2.2.

The complete syntax charts for HILOGLINEAR are included here. Procedure HILOGLINEAR is fully described in Chapter 8.

B.112 INPUT MATRIX

INPUT MATRIX is not used in Release 3.0. See the MATRIX subcommand of individual procedures when using matrix materials with Release 3.0. Syntax for releases before 3.0:

```
INPUT MATRIX [FILE=handle] [/FREE]
```

Use the INPUT MATRIX command *only with releases before 3.0* to indicate that matrix materials are to be read.

If you are using only matrix materials in your job, you must use the NUMERIC command to provide variable names, and you must enclose the

NUMERIC and INPUT MATRIX commands in an INPUT PROGRAM—END INPUT PROGRAM structure. The commands should immediately precede the procedure command to which they apply, as shown in the example below:

```
UNNUMBERED
INPUT PROGRAM
N OF CASES 88
NUMERIC POPSTABL NEWSCIRC FEMEMPLD FARMERS RETAILNG COMMERCL INDUSTZN
  HEALTH CHLDNEGL COMMEFFC DWELGNEW MIGRNPOP UNEMPLOY MENTALIL
INPUT MATRIX FREE
END INPUT PROGRAM
FACTOR READ=CORRELATION TRIANGLE
  /VARIABLES=POPSTABL TO MENTALIL
  /PRINT=CORRELATION
BEGIN DATA
1.
-.175 1.
-.276 .616 1.
 .369 -.625 -.637 1.
etc.
END DATA
```

The UNNUMBERED command is required (only if the default is NUMBERED) when the matrix is included with the commands (between the BEGIN DATA and END DATA commands) if the matrix uses the full 80 columns.

The INPUT PROGRAM and END INPUT PROGRAM surround the NUMERIC command that supplies the variable names associated with the matrix. The variable names must be listed in exactly the order in which the matrix was organized in the original source.

The N OF CASES supplies the number of cases on which the matrix is based in order to compute degrees of freedom. (See the discussion of PEARSON CORR under PROCEDURE OUTPUT for matrix materials that include this information.) The N OF CASES command does not have to be enclosed within the INPUT PROGRAM—END INPUT PROGRAM structure.

The INPUT MATRIX command in the proceding example has no FILE subcommand, which means that the matrix is expected following BEGIN DATA in the command file. The FREE subcommand indicates that the matrix is in freefield format. With matrix materials included in the command file, the BEGIN DATA command must follow the procedure that reads the matrix and the matrix must be followed by the END DATA command. If matrix materials are included in the command file and are formatted, use the INPUT MATRIX command with no specifications.

You can also read a matrix from a separate file, as in

```
FILE HANDLE REGMAT /file specifications
INPUT PROGRAM
NUMERIC NTCPRI FOOD SERVICE RENT
INPUT MATRIX FILE=REGMAT
END INPUT PROGRAM
REGRESSION READ=N CORR
  /VARIABLES=NTCPRI FOOD SERVICE RENT /DEPENDENT=NTCPRI
/METHOD=STEPWISE
```

The FILE HANDLE command defines the file handle for the file containing the matrix materials. The INPUT PROGRAM and END INPUT PROGRAM commands enclose the commands defining the matrix file. The NUMERIC command defines variable names for the variables in the matrix, and the FILE subcommand on the INPUT MATRIX command indicates that the matrix materials are to be read from the file referenced by handle REGMAT.

You can use both matrix materials and a file of cases as input to DISCRIMINANT and REGRESSION procedures. See the *SPSS^X User's Guide* for instructions.

B.113 LIST

Syntax for all releases:

```
LIST [VARIABLES={ALL    }] [/FORMAT=[{WRAP  }] [{UNNUMBERED}]]
                {varlist}             {SINGLE}    {NUMBERED  }

 [/CASES=[FROM {1}] [TO {eof}] [BY {1}]]
               {n}      {n  }      {n}
```

The LIST procedure displays the values of variables for cases in the active file in an automatic format. The simplest LIST command is the command alone implying all variables, as in:

```
DATA LIST  FILE=HUBDATA RECORDS=3
  /1 MOHIRED YRHIRED 12-15 DEPT82 19
  /2 SALARY79 TO SALARY82 6-25
  /3 NAME 25-48 (A)
LIST
```

LIST uses the dictionary print formats assigned when the variables are defined on a DATA LIST, PRINT FORMATS, or FORMATS command, or the formats assigned when the variables are created with transformation commands.

LIST may require more than one line to display each case, depending on the page width. Values for each case are always displayed with a blank space between the variables.

Each execution of LIST begins at the top of a new page. If SPLIT FILE is in effect (Section B.52), each split also begins at the top of a new page.

B.114 VARIABLES Subcommand

The default specification for the VARIABLES subcommand is keyword ALL. You can limit the listing to specific variables using the VARIABLES subcommand, as in:

```
DATA LIST  FILE=HUBDATA RECORDS=3
  /1 EMPLOYID 1-5 MOHIRED YRHIRED 12-15 DEPT79 TO DEPT82 SEX 16-20
  /2 SALARY79 TO SALARY82 6-25 HOURLY81 HOURLY82 40-53(2) PROMO81 72
     AGE 54-55 RAISE82 66-70
  /3 JOBCAT 6 NAME 25-48 (A)
LIST VARIABLES=MOHIRED YRHIRED DEPT82 NAME
```

Variables named must already exist. Because LIST is a procedure, variables named cannot be scratch or system variables. You can use the TO convention for naming consecutive variables, as in:

```
LIST VARIABLES=MOHIRED YRHIRED DEPT82 SALARY79 TO SALARY82 NAME
```

If you specify more variables than can be printed on one line, the line wraps. If all the variables fit on a single line, SPSS^X prints a heading using the variable name and prints a single line per case. When the variable name is longer than the print width, SPSS^X centers numeric variables in the column.

B.115 CASES Subcommand

Use the CASES subcommand to limit the number and pattern of cases listed. Subcommand CASES must be followed by at least one of the following keywords:

FROM n *The case number of the first case to be listed.* The specification CASES FROM 100 starts listing cases at the 100th sequential case. If LIST is preceded by SAMPLE or SELECT IF, the first case listed is the 100th case selected. The default is 1, which means listing begins with the first selected case.

TO n *Upper limit on the cases to be listed.* The specification CASES TO 1000 limits listing to the 1000th selected case or the end of the file, whichever comes first. The default is to list until the end of the file. If LIST encounters the CASE subcommand followed by a single number, TO is assumed. For example, CASES 100 is interpreted as CASES TO 100.

BY n *Increment used to choose cases for listing.* The specification CASES BY 5 lists every fifth selected case. The default is 1, which means every case is listed.

You need only specify one of these keywords, but you can specify any two or all three, as in:

```
LIST VARIABLES=MOHIRED YRHIRED DEPT82 SALARY79 TO SALARY82 NAME
  /CASES FROM 50 TO 100 BY 5
```

If SPLIT FILE is in effect, case selections specified via the CASE subcommand are restarted for each split.

B.116 FORMAT Subcommand

The default specifications for the FORMAT subcommand are WRAP and UNNUMBERED. If the page width cannot accommodate your entire variable list, keyword WRAP wraps the listing in multiple lines per case.

When the list requires more than one line per case, SPSS^{X} prints the name of the first variable listed in that line. To locate the values of a particular variable, consult the table produced before the listing.

If there is enough space, keyword WRAP implies one line per case. To tell SPSS^{X} to use the single-line format only, specify the keyword SINGLE, as in:

```
LIST VARIABLES=MOHIRED YRHIRED DEPT82 SALARY79 TO SALARY82 NAME
  /CASES FROM 50 TO 100 BY 5 /FORMAT=SINGLE
```

If there is not enough room within the line width, SPSS^{X} issues an error message and does not execute the listing. Therefore, use SINGLE only when you want one line per case or nothing.

If you want LIST to number the cases that are being listed, specify keyword NUMBERED, as in:

```
LIST VARIABLES=MOHIRED YRHIRED DEPT82 SALARY79 TO SALARY82 NAME
  /CASES FROM 50 TO 100 BY 5 /FORMAT=SINGLE,NUMBERED
```

B.117 LOGLINEAR

Syntax for Release 3.0:

```
LOGLINEAR varlist(min,max)...[BY] varlist(min,max)

          [WITH covariate varlist]

 [/MISSING={LISTWISE**}] [INCLUDE]
           {DEFAULT   }

 [/WIDTH={132}]
         { 72}

 [/CWEIGHT={varname }] [/CWEIGHT=(matrix)...]
           {(matrix)}

 [/GRESID={varlist }]  [/GRESID=...]
          {(matrix)}

 [/PRINT={DEFAULT**}] [/NOPRINT={ESTIM**  }]
         {FREQ**   }            {COR**    }
         {RESID**  }            {DESIGN** }
         {DESIGN   }            {RESID    }
         {ESTIM    }            {FREQ     }
         {COR      }            {DEFAULT  }
         {ALL      }            {ALL      }
         {NONE     }
```

```
 [/PLOT={DEFAULT  }
        {RESID    }
        {NORMPROB }
        {NONE**   }

                        {DEVIATION [(refcat)]         }
                        {DIFFERENCE                   }
                        {HELMERT                      }
 [/CONTRAST (varname)={SIMPLE [(refcat)]            }]...[/CONTRAST...]
                        {REPEATED                     }
                        {POLYNOMIAL [({1,2,3,...})]   }
                        {              {metric     }  }
                        {[BASIS] SPECIAL(matrix)      }

 [/CRITERIA=[CONVERGE({0.001**})] [ITERATE({20**})] [DELTA({0.5**})]
                       {eps    }           {n   }         {d    }

           [DEFAULT]]

 [/DESIGN=effect effect... effect BY effect...] [/DESIGN...]
```

**Default if the subcommand is omitted.

Syntax for releases before 3.0:

```
LOGLINEAR varlist(min,max)...[BY] varlist(min,max)
          [WITH covariate varlist]

 [/WIDTH={132}]
         { 72}

 [/CWEIGHT={varname }] [/CWEIGHT=(matrix)...]
           {(matrix)}

 [/GRESID={varlist }]  [/GRESID=...]
          {(matrix)}

 [/PRINT={DEFAULT**}] [/NOPRINT={ESTIM** }]
         {FREQ**   }            {COR**   }
         {RESID**  }            {DESIGN**}
         {DESIGN   }            {RESID   }
         {ESTIM    }            {FREQ    }
         {COR      }            {DEFAULT }
         {ALL      }            {ALL     }
         {NONE††   }

 [/PLOT={DEFAULT  }
        {RESID    }
        {NORMPROB }
        {NONE**   }

                        {DEVIATION [(refcat)]††       }
                        {DIFFERENCE                   }
                        {HELMERT                      }
 [/CONTRAST (varname)={SIMPLE [(refcat)]            }]...[/CONTRAST...]
                        {REPEATED                     }
                        {POLYNOMIAL [({1,2,3,...})]   }
                        {              {metric     }  }
                        {[BASIS]†† SPECIAL(matrix)    }

 [/CRITERIA=[CONVERGE({0.001**})] [ITERATE({20**})] [DELTA({0.5**})]
                       {eps    }           {n   }         {d    }

           [DEFAULT]]

 [/DESIGN=effect effect... effect BY effect...] [/DESIGN...]
```

Options:

1 Include missing values

**Default if the subcommand is omitted.
††Available or modified as of Release 2.1.

The complete syntax charts for LOGLINEAR are included here. Procedure LOGLINEAR is fully described in Chapter 9.

B.118 MANOVA

Syntax for Releases 2.2 and 3.0:

```
MANOVA dependent varlist [BY factor list (min,max) [factor list...]
                         [WITH covariate list]]

 [/WSFACTORS=name (levels) name...]

 [/TRANSFORM [(varlist [/varlist])]=[ORTHONORM] [{CONTRAST}]]
      [{DEVIATIONS (refcat)  }]                  {BASIS   }
       {DIFFERENCE           }
       {HELMERT              }
       {SIMPLE (refcat)      }
       {REPEATED             }
       {POLYNOMIAL [(metric)]}
       {SPECIAL (matrix)     }

 [/WSDESIGN=effect effect...]

 [/MEASURE=newname newname...]

 [/RENAME={newname} {newname}...]
          {*      } {*      }

 [/MISSING=[LISTWISE] [INCLUDE]]

 [/{PRINT   }= [CELLINFO ([MEANS] [SSCP] [COV] [COR] [ALL])]]
   {NOPRINT }

      [HOMOGENEITY ([BARTLETT] [COCHRAN] [BOXM] [ALL])]

      [DESIGN ([ONEWAY] [OVERALL] [DECOMP] [BIAS] [SOLUTION]
               [REDUNDANCY] [COLLINEARITY] [ALL])]

      [ERROR ([SSCP] [COV] [COR] [STDDEV] [ALL])]

      [SIGNIF ([MULTIV] [EIGEN] [DIMENR] [UNIV] [HYPOTH]
               [AVERF] [AVONLY] [HF] [GG] [EFSIZE]
               [SINGLEDF] [BRIEF] [STEPDOWN] [ALL] [NONE])]

      [PARAMETERS ([ESTIM] [ORTHO] [COR] [NEGSUM] [ALL])]
                   [EFSIZE] [OPTIMAL]]

 [/PLOT=[CELLPLOTS] [STEMLEAF] [ZCORR] [NORMAL] [BOXPLOTS]]
        [ALL]

 [/PCOMPS [COR] [NCOMP(n)] [MINEIGEN(eigencut)]
          [COV] [ROTATE(rottype)] [ALL]]

 [/DISCRIM [RAW] [STAN] [ESTIM] [COR] [ALL]
           [ROTATE(rottype)] [ALPHA({.25})]]
                                   {  a}

 [/OMEANS [VARIABLES(varlist)] [TABLES ({factor name     })]]
                                        {factor BY factor}
                                        {CONSTANT        }
 [/PMEANS [VARIABLES(varlist)] [TABLES ({factor name     })]]
                                        {factor BY factor}
           [PLOT]                       {CONSTANT        }
```

```
[/RESIDUALS [CASEWISE] [PLOT]]
[/METHOD=[MODELTYPE ({MEANS       })]
                     {OBSERVATIONS}

   [ESTIMATION ({QR      } {NOLASTRES} {NOBALANCED} {CONSTANT  })]
                {CHOLESKY} {LASTRES  } {BALANCED  } {NOCONSTANT}

   [SSTYPE ({UNIQUE    })]]
            {SEQUENTIAL}

[/MATRIX=[IN({file})]  [OUT({file})]]†
             {*   }          {*   }

[/ANALYSIS [({CONDITIONAL  })]=dependent varlist
             {UNCONDITIONAL}    [WITH covariate varlist]
                                [/dependent varlist...]]

[/PARTITION (factorname)[=({1,1...  })]]
                           {df,df...}

                            {DEVIATION [(refcat)]       }
                            {SIMPLE [(refcat)]          }
                            {DIFFERENCE                 }
[/CONTRAST (factorname)={HELMERT                    }]
                            {REPEATED                   }
                            {POLYNOMIAL[({1,2,3...})]]}
                            {             {metric  }    }
                            {SPECIAL (matrix)           }

[/CRITERIA=[ZETA ({1.0E-8})] [EPS ({1.0E-8})]]
                  {zeta  }         {eps   }

         {WITHIN           }     {W }
[/ERROR={RESIDUAL         }  or {R }]
         {WITHIN + RESIDUAL}     {WR}
         {n                }

[/POWER=[T({.05})] [F({.05})] [{APPROXIMATE}]]
           {  a}      {  a}    {EXACT      }

[/CINTERVAL=[{INDIVIDUAL}][({.95}) ]] [UNIVARIATE ({BONFER })]
             {JOINT     }   {  a}                  {SCHEFFE}

                                    [MULTIVARIATE  ({ROY      })]]
                                                    {PILLAI   }
                                                    {BONFER   }
                                                    {HOTELLING}
                                                    {WILKS    }

          {[CONSTANT...]                                              }
          {[effect effect...]                                         }
          {[POOL (varlist)...]                                        }
          {[effects BY effects...]                                    }
[/DESIGN={[effects {WITHIN} effects...]                              }]
          {          {W     }                                         }
          {[effect + effect...]                                       }
          {[factor (level)... [WITHIN factor (partition)...]]         }
          {[MUPLUS...]                                                }
          {[MWITHIN...]                                               }
          {[{terms-to-be-tested} {AGAINST} {WITHIN  }  or {W }]      }
          { {term=n            } {VS     } {RESIDUAL}     {R }        }
          {                                {WR      }     {RW}        }
          {                                {n       }                 }
```

†For Release 2.2, use the READ and WRITE subcommands (see syntax chart on following page).

Syntax for releases before 2.2:

```
MANOVA dependent varlist [BY factor list (min,max) [factor list...]
                          [WITH covariate list]]

 [/WSFACTORS=name (levels) name...]

 [/TRANSFORM [(varlist [/varlist])]=[ORTHONORM] [{DEVIATIONS (refcat)   }]]
                                                {DIFFERENCE             }
                                  [{CONTRAST}]  {HELMERT                }
                                   {BASIS   }   {SIMPLE (refcat)        }
                                                {REPEATED               }
                                                {POLYNOMIAL [(metric)]  }
                                                {SPECIAL (matrix)       }
 [/WSDESIGN=effect effect...]

 [/MEASURE=newname newname...]

 [/RENAME={newname} {newname}...]
          {*      } {*      }

             {[CELLINFO ([MEANS] [SSCP] [COV] [COR])]                          }
             {                                                                 }
             {[HOMOGENEITY ([BARTLETT] [COCHRAN] [BOXM])]                      }
             {                                                                 }
             {[FORMAT ({WIDE  })]                                              }
             {         {NARROW}                                                }
             {                                                                 }
             {[DESIGN ([ONEWAY] [OVERALL] [DECOMP] [BIAS] [SOLUTION])]         }
             {                                                                 }
             {[PRINTCOMPS ([COR] [NCOMP(n)] [MINEIGEN(eigencut)]               }
             {             [COV] [ROTATE(rottype)])]                           }
             {                                                                 }
 [/{PRINT  }={[ERROR ([SSCP] [COV] [COR] [STDDEV])]                            }]
   {NOPRINT} {                                                                 }
             {[SIGNIF ([MULTIV] [EIGEN] [DIMENR] [UNIV] [HYPOTH]               }
             {         [STEPDOWN] [AVERF] [BRIEF] [AVONLY] [SINGLEDF])]        }
             {                                                                 }
             {[DISCRIM ([RAW] [STAN] [ESTIM] [COR]                             }
             {          [ROTATE(rottype)] [ALPHA(alpha)])]                     }
             {                                                                 }
             {[PARAMETERS ([ESTIM] [ORTHO] [COR] [NEGSUM])]                    }
             {                                                                 }
             {[OMEANS ([VARIABLES(varlist)] [TABLES ({factor name     })])]    }
             {                                       {factor BY factor}        }
             {                                       {CONSTANT        }        }
             {                                                                 }
             {[PMEANS ([VARIABLES(varlist)] [TABLES ({factor name     })])]    }
             {                                       {factor BY factor}        }
             {         [ERROR(erroron)]              {CONSTANT        }        }
             {                                                                 }
             {[POBS [ERROR(erroron)]]         [TRANSFORM]                      }

 [/PLOT=[CELLPLOTS] [STEMLEAF] [ZCORR]      [SIZE ({40  },{25   })]]
        [POBS] [NORMAL] [BOXPLOTS] [PMEANS]        {nhor} {nvert}

 [/METHOD=[MODELTYPE ({MEANS       })]
                      {OBSERVATIONS}

         [ESTIMATION ({QR      } {NOLASTRES} {NOBALANCED} {CONSTANT  })]
                      {CHOLESKY} {LASTRES  } {BALANCED  } {NOCONSTANT}

         [SSTYPE ({UNIQUE    })]]
                  {SEQUENTIAL}
```

```
[/READ[=SUMMARY]]  [/WRITE[=SUMMARY]]

[/ANALYSIS [([REPEATED] {CONDITIONAL  })]=dependent varlist
                        {UNCONDITIONAL}    [WITH covariate varlist]
                                           [/dependent varlist...]]

[/PARTITION (factorname)[=({1,1...   })]]
                           {df,df...}

                           {DEVIATION [(refcat)]      }
                           {SIMPLE [(refcat)]         }
                           {DIFFERENCE                }
[/CONTRAST (factorname)={HELMERT                   }]
                           {REPEATED                  }
                           {POLYNOMIAL[({1,2,3...})]}
                           {             {metric  }   }
                           {SPECIAL (matrix)          }

[/SETCONST=[ZETA ({1.0}-}8})] [EPS ({1.0}-}8})]]
                  {zeta }            {eps  }

          {WITHIN             }    {W }
[/ERROR={RESIDUAL           } or {R }]
          {WITHIN + RESIDUAL}    {WR}
          {n                  }

           {[CONSTANT...]                                              }
           {[effect effect...]                                         }
           {[CONTIN (varlist)...]                                      }
           {[effects BY effects...]                                    }
[/DESIGN={[effects {WITHIN} effects...]                             }]
           {          {W     }                                         }
           {[effect + effect...]                                       }
           {[factor (level)... [WITHIN factor (partition)...]]        }
           {[CONPLUS...]                                               }
           {[MWITHIN...]                                               }
           {[{terms-to-be-tested} {AGAINST} {WITHIN  }    {W }]}
           { {term=n            } {VS     } {RESIDUAL} or {R } }
           {                                {WR      }    {RW} }
           {                                {n       }         }
```

Options:

1 Include missing values

The complete syntax charts for MANOVA are included here. Procedure MANOVA is fully described in Chapters 6 and 7.

B.119 MEANS

Syntax for Release 3.0:

```
MEANS [TABLES=]varlist BY varlist [BY...] [/varlist...]

 [/MISSING={TABLE**    }]
           {INCLUDE    }
           {DEPENDENT}

 [/FORMAT={LABELS**   }  {NAMES**}  {VALUES**}   {TABLE**}]
          {NOLABELS   }  {NONAMES}  {NOVALUES}   {TREE   }
          {NOCATLABS}

 [/CELLS=[DEFAULT**]  [MEAN**   ]  [ALL]]
         [COUNT**  ]  [STDDEV** ]
         [SUM      ]  [VARIANCE]

 [/STATISTICS=[ANOVA] [LINEARITY] [ALL] [NONE] ]
```

**Default if the subcommand is omitted.

Syntax for releases before 3.0 (MEANS was formerly called BREAKDOWN):

General mode:

```
BREAKDOWN [TABLES=]varlist BY varlist [BY...] [/varlist...]
```

Integer mode:

```
BREAKDOWN VARIABLES=varlist ({min,max       }) [varlist...]
                             {LOWEST,HIGHEST}

        /{TABLES     }=varlist BY varlist [BY...] [/varlist...]
         {CROSSBREAK}
```

Options:

1	Include missing values	7	Suppress cell standard deviations
2	Exclude missing for dependent only	8	Suppress value labels
3	Suppress variable and value labels	9	Suppress independent variable names†
4	Tree format (general mode only)	10	Suppress independent variable values†
5	Suppress cell frequencies	11	Suppress mean†
6	Print cell sums†	12	Print variance†

Statistics:

1 Oneway analysis of variance 2 Test of linearity

†Available or modified as of Release 2.0.

MEANS calculates means and variances for a criterion or dependent variable over subgroups of cases defined by independent or control variables. This operation is similar to crosstabulation, where each mean and standard deviation summarize the distribution of a complete row or column of a contingency table.

B.120 TABLES Subcommand

Use the TABLES subcommand followed by one or more dependent variables, the keyword BY, and one or more independent variables. The actual command keyword TABLES is not required.

A maximum of six dimensions can be specified on an analysis list: one dependent variable and up to five independent variables separated by the keyword BY. For example,

```
MEANS  TABLES=RAISE81 BY DEPT81 BY GRADE81S
```

breaks down RAISE81 by DEPT81 and by GRADE81S within DEPT81. The first variable always becomes the dependent or criterion variable. The independent variables are entered into the table in the order in which they appear following the TABLES subcommand, proceeding from left to right. The values of the last variable change most quickly. MEANS prints subpopulation statistics for each category of the first independent variable. However, for subsequent variables, it prints statistics only for each category of the variable within a category of the preceding independent variable.

You can specify more than one dependent variable and more than one independent variable in each dimension. Use the keyword TO to name a set of adjacent variables in the active file, as in:

```
MEANS  TABLES=RAISE79 TO RAISE81 BY DEPT TO AGE
```

This command will produce MEANS tables for all the variables between and including RAISE79 and RAISE81 by all the variables between and including DEPT and AGE. You can also use variable lists to request higher-order breakdowns. The variables to the right of the last BY change most quickly. Within lists separated with a BY, variables rotate from left to right. For example,

```
MEANS  TABLES=VAR1 TO VAR3 BY VAR4 VAR5 BY VAR6 TO VAR8
```

produces 18 tables. The first table is VAR1 by VAR4 by VAR6 and the second is VAR1 by VAR4 by VAR7. The combinations of VAR1 and VAR5 follow the combinations of VAR1 and VAR4. The last table produced is VAR3 by VAR5 by VAR8.

Use multiple TABLES subcommands, or a slash to separate tables lists on one TABLES subcommand. For example,

```
MEANS  TABLES=RAISE82 BY GRADE/SALARY BY DEPT
```

specifies two tables, RAISE82 by GRADE and SALARY by DEPT. If you omit a slash between tables lists, MEANS includes the variables as if one analysis list had been supplied.

B.121 VARIABLES Subcommand

The VARIABLES subcommand is followed by a list of variables. This list identifies variables to be included on the TABLES subcommand. Specify the lowest and highest values in parentheses after each variable. These values must be integers. You can *not* use LOWEST, LO, HIGHEST, HI with independent variables. For example, the command

```
MEANS  VARIABLES=DEPT81(1,4) EEO81(1,9) RAISE81(LO,HI)
  /TABLES=RAISE81 BY DEPT81 BY EEO81
```

produces a table where RAISE81 has a range from the lowest to the highest value, DEPT81 has a range from 1 to 4, and EEO81 has a range from 1 to 9. The final variable or set of variables and their range must be followed by a slash.

You do not have to specify an explicit range for dependent variables because they are usually continuous and are not assumed to be integers. However, you must provide bounds. Use keywords LOWEST (or LO) and HIGHEST (or HI) for criterion variables. You can also use explicit bounds to eliminate outliers from the calculation of the summary statistics. Explicit numeric bounds must be specified as integers. For example, (0,HI) excludes nonnegative values.

Several variables can have the same range. For example,

```
MEANS  VARIABLES=DEPT80 DEPT81 DEPT82 (1,3) GRADE81S (1,4)
                 SALARY82 (LO,HI)
      /TABLES=SALARY82 BY DEPT80 TO DEPT82 BY GRADE81S
```

defines 1 as the lowest value and 3 as the highest value for DEPT80, DEPT81, and DEPT82. Variables may appear in any order. However, the order in which you place them on the VARIABLES subcommand affects their implied order on the TABLES subcommand.

B.122 CROSSBREAK Subcommand

To print tables in a crosstabular form when the values of all independent variables are integers, use the VARIABLES subcommand to specify the variables to be used and the minimum and maximum values for building tables, and use the CROSSBREAK subcommand in place of the TABLES subcommand. CROSSBREAK has exactly the same specification field as the TABLES subcommand.

Tables printed in crossbreak form resemble CROSSTABS tables, but their contents are considerably different. The cells contain means, counts, and standard deviations for the dependent variable. The first independent variable defines the rows and the second independent variable defines the columns. The CROSSBREAK format is especially suited to breakdowns with two control variables. The CROSSBREAK subcommand prints separate subtables for each combination of values when you specify three or more dimensions.

B.123 CELLS Subcommand

By default, MEANS prints the means, standard deviations, and cell counts in each cell. Use the CELLS subcommand to modify cell information.

You can specify the CELLS subcommand by itself, or with a keyword or keywords. If you specify the CELLS subcommand with no keywords, MEANS prints ALL cell information (defined below). If you specify a keyword or keywords, MEANS prints only the information you request.

The following keywords can be specified on the CELLS subcommand:

DEFAULT *Print the means, standard deviations, and cell counts in each cell.* This is the default if you omit the CELL subcommand.

MEAN *Print cell means.* (With releases before 3.0, substitute the command OPTION 11.)

STDDEV *Print cell standard deviations.* (With releases before 3.0, substitute the command OPTION 7.)

COUNT *Print cell frequencies.* (With releases before 3.0, substitute the command OPTION 5.)

SUM *Print cell sums.* (With releases before 3.0, substitute the command OPTION 6.)

VARIANCE *Print variances.* (With releases before 3.0, substitute the command OPTION 12.)

ALL *Print the means, counts, standard deviations, sums, and variances in each cell.* This is the default if you specify the CELLS subcommand with no keyword(s).

B.124 STATISTICS Subcommand

MEANS automatically computes means, standard deviations, and counts for subpopulations. Optionally, you can obtain a one-way analysis of variance for each table as well as a test of linearity. The STATISTICS subcommand computes additional statistics. Statistics you request on the STATISTICS subcommand are computed *in addition to* the default statistics or those you request on the CELLS subcommand.

You can use the STATISTICS subcommand by itself or with a keyword or keywords. If you use the STATISTICS subcommand with no keyword, MEANS computes ANOVA (defined below). If you specify a keyword, MEANS computes the additional statistics you request.

The following keywords can be specified on the STATISTICS subcommand:

ANOVA *Analysis of variance.* Prints a standard analysis of variance table and calculates *ETA* and ETA^2. This is the default if you specify the STATISTICS subcommand with no keyword. (With releases before 3.0, substitute the command STATISTIC 1.)

LINEARITY *Test of linearity.* Calculates the sums of squares, degrees of freedom, and mean square associated with linear and nonlinear components, as well as the F ratio, Pearson's r, and r^2. ANOVA *must* be requested to obtain LINEARITY. LINEARITY is ignored if the control variable is a short string. (With releases before 3.0, substitute the command STATISTIC 2.)

ALL *Both ANOVA and LINEARITY.*

NONE *No additional statistics.* This is the default if you omit the STATISTICS subcommand.

If you specify a two-way or higher-order breakdown, the second and subsequent dimensions are ignored in the analysis of variance table. To obtain a two-way and higher analysis of variance, use procedure ANOVA (see Section B.57).

B.125 MISSING Subcommand

By default, MEANS deletes cases with missing values on a tablewide basis. A case missing on any of the variables specified for a table is not used. Every case contained in a table will have a complete set of nonmissing values for all variables in that table. When you separate tables requests with a slash, missing values are handled separately for each list.

The MISSING subcommand controls missing values, and the following keywords can be specified on it:

TABLE *Delete cases with missing values on a tablewide basis.* This is the default if you omit the MISSING subcommand.

INCLUDE *Include user-defined missing values.* Handles user-defined missing values as if they were not missing. (With releases before 3.0, substitute the command OPTION 1.)

DEPENDENT *Exclude cases with missing values for the dependent variable only.* A case is included if it has a valid value for the dependent variable, although it may have missing values for the independent variables. Missing values are ignored for control variables. (With releases before 3.0, substitute the command OPTION 2.)

B.126 FORMAT Subcommand

By default, MEANS prints variable and value labels and the names and values of independent variables. All tables print in report format.

The FORMAT subcommand controls table formats, and the following keywords can be specified on it:

LABELS *Print both variable and value labels for each table.* This is the default if you omit the FORMAT subcommand.

NOLABELS *Suppress variable and value labels.* (With releases before 3.0, substitute the command OPTION 3.)

NOCATLABS *Suppress value (category) labels.* (With releases before 3.0, substitute the command OPTION 8.)

NAMES *Print the names of independent variables.* This is the default if you omit the FORMAT subcommand.

NONAMES *Suppress names of independent variables.* (With releases before 3.0, substitute the command OPTION 9.)

VALUES *Print the values of independent variables.* This is the default if you omit the FORMAT subcommand.

NOVALUES *Suppress values of independent variables.* This is useful when there are category labels. (With releases before 3.0, substitute the command OPTION 10.)

TABLE *Print each table in report format.* This is the default if you omit the FORMAT subcommand.

TREE *Print each table in tree format.* (With releases before 3.0, substitute the command OPTION 4.)

B.127 Limitations

The following limitations apply to MEANS:

- A maximum of 200 variables total per MEANS command.
- A maximum of 250 tables.
- A maximum of 6 dimensions per table.
- A maximum of 30 tables lists per MEANS command.
- A maximum of 200 value labels printed on any single table.

B.128 ONEWAY

Syntax for Release 3.0:

```
ONEWAY  varlist BY varname(min,max)

 [/POLYNOMIAL=n]  [/CONTRAST=coefficient list] [/CONSTRAST=...]

 [/RANGES={LSD          }({0.05 }) ] [/RANGES=...]
          {DUNCAN       } {alpha}
          {SNK          }
          {TUKEYB       }
          {TUKEY        }
          {LSDMOD       }
          {SCHEFFE      }
          {ranges values}

 [/MISSING={ANALYSIS**}  [{EXCLUDE**}]]
           {LISTWISE  }   {INCLUDE  }

 [/HARMONIC={NONE** or PAIR}]
            {ALL           }

 [/FORMAT={NOLABELS**}]
          {LABELS    }

 [/MATRIX =[NONE**] [IN({*    })] [OUT({*    })]]
                        {file}           {file}

 [/STATISTICS=[NONE       **]]
              [DESCRIPTIVES]
              [EFFECTS     ]
              [HOMOGENEITY ]
              [ALL         ]
```

**Default if the subcommand is omitted.

Syntax for releases before 3.0:

```
ONEWAY varlist BY varname(min,max)

       [/POLYNOMIAL=n]  [/CONTRAST=coefficient list]

       [/RANGES={LSD          }({0.05 })]
                {DUNCAN       } {alpha}
                {SNK          }
                {TUKEYB       }
                {TUKEY        }
                {LSDMOD       }
                {SCHEFFE      }
                {ranges values}
```

Options:

1 Include missing
2 Exclude missing listwise
3 Suppress variable labels
4 Matrix output of counts, means, standard deviations
6 Value labels as group labels
7 Matrix input of counts, means, standard deviations
8 Matrix input of counts, means, pooled variance, degrees of freedom
10 Harmonic mean for range tests

Statistics:

1 Descriptive statistics
2 Fixed- and random-effects measures
3 Homogeneity-of-variance tests

Procedure ONEWAY produces a one-way analysis of variance for an interval-level variable by one independent variable. You can test for trends across categories, specify contrasts, and use a variety of range tests. Procedure ONEWAY requires a dependent variable list and the independent variable with its range of integer values. All ONEWAY subcommands are optional and may be entered in any order, provided they appear after the variable list.

B.129 Specifying the Design

A ONEWAY analysis list contains a dependent variable list and one independent (grouping) variable with its minimum and maximum values. Use only one analysis list per ONEWAY command. Dependent variables must be numeric. The independent variable follows the keyword BY, and you must include a value range specifying the highest and lowest values to be used in the analysis. These values are separated by a comma and are enclosed in parentheses.

While you can specify any number of categories for the independent variable, contrasts and multiple comparison tests are not available for more than 50 groups. ONEWAY deletes empty groups for the analysis of variance and range tests. The independent variable must have integer values. Noninteger values encountered in the independent variable are truncated.

B.130 POLYNOMIAL Subcommand

The POLYNOMIAL subcommand partitions the between-groups sum of squares into linear, quadratic, cubic, or higher-order trend components. Specify this subcommand after the analysis specification, as in:

```
ONEWAY  WELL BY EDUC6 (1,6)
  /POLYNOMIAL = 2
```

The value specified in the POLYNOMIAL subcommand denotes the highest degree polynomial to be used. This value must be a positive integer less than or equal to 5 and less than the number of groups. Use only one POLYNOMIAL subcommand per ONEWAY command.

When you use the POLYNOMIAL subcommand with balanced designs, ONEWAY computes the sum of squares for each order polynomial from weighted polynomial contrasts, using the group code as the metric. These contrasts are orthogonal; hence the sum of squares for each order polynomial is statistically independent. If the design is unbalanced and there is equal spacing between groups, ONEWAY also computes sums of squares using the unweighted polynomial contrasts. These contrasts are not orthogonal. The deviation sums of squares are always calculated from the weighted sums of squares (Speed, 1976).

B.131 CONTRAST Subcommand

The CONTRAST subcommand specifies a priori contrasts to be tested by the *t* statistic. The specification for the CONTRAST subcommand is a vector of coefficients, with each coefficient corresponding to a category of the grouping variable. For example, the command

```
ONEWAY  WELL BY EDUC6(1,6)
  /CONTRAST = -1 -1 -1 -1 2 2
```

contrasts the combination of the first four groups with the combination of the last two groups.

You can also specify fractional weights, as in:

```
/CONTRAST = -1 0 0 0 .5 .5
```

This subcommand contrasts Group 1 and the combination of Groups 5 and 6.

For most applications, the coefficients should sum to zero. Those sets that do not sum to zero are used, but a warning message is printed. In addition, you can use the repeat notation $n * c$ to specify the same coefficient for a consecutive set of means. For example,

```
/CONTRAST = 1 4*0 -1
```

specifies a contrast coefficient of 1 for Group 1, 0 for Groups 2 through 5, and −1 for Group 6. You must specify a contrast for every group implied by the range specification in the analysis list, even if a group is empty. However, you do not have to specify trailing zeros. For example,

```
/CONTRAST = -1 2*0 1 2*0

/CONTRAST = -1 0 0 1 0 0

/CONTRAST = -1 2*0 1
```

all specify the same set of contrast coefficients for a six-group analysis.

You can specify only one set of contrast coefficients per CONTRAST subcommand and no more than 50 coefficients per set. Output for each contrast list includes the value of the contrast, the standard error of the contrast, the *t* statistic, the degrees of freedom for *t*, and the two-tailed probability of *t*. Both pooled- and separate-variance estimates are printed.

B.132 RANGES Subcommand

The RANGES subcommand specifies any of seven different tests appropriate for multiple comparisons between means. Each RANGES subcommand specifies one test. For example,

```
ONEWAY  WELL BY EDUC6 (1,6)
  /POLYNOMIAL = 2
  /CONTRAST = 2*-1,2*1
  /CONTRAST = 2*0, 2-*1, 2*1
  /CONTRAST = 2*-1,2*0,2*1
  /RANGES = SNK
  /RANGES = SCHEFFE (.01)
```

produces two range tests. RANGES subcommands cannot be separated by CONTRAST or POLYNOMIAL subcommands. The available tests are

LSD *Least-significant difference.* Any alpha between 0 and 1 can be specified. The default is 0.05.

DUNCAN *Duncan's multiple range test.* The default alpha is 0.05. Only 0.01, 0.05, and 0.10 are used. DUNCAN uses 0.01 if the alpha specified is less than 0.05; 0.05 if the alpha specified is greater than or equal to 0.05 but less than 0.10; and 0.10 if the alpha specified is greater than or equal to 0.10.

SNK *Student-Newman-Keuls.* Only 0.05 is available as the alpha value.

TUKEYB *Tukey's alternate procedure.* Only 0.05 is available as the alpha value.

TUKEY *Honestly significant difference.* Only 0.05 is available as the alpha value.

LSDMOD *Modified LSD.* Any alpha between 0 and 1 can be specified. The default alpha is 0.05.

SCHEFFE *Scheffé's test.* Any alpha between 0 and 1 can be specified. The default alpha is 0.05.

Range tests always produce multiple comparisons between all groups. Nonempty group means are sorted in ascending order. Asterisks in the matrix indicate significantly different group means. In addition to this output, homogeneous subsets are calculated for balanced designs and for all designs that use either the Duncan (DUNCAN) or the Student-Newman-Keuls (SNK) procedure to calculate multiple range tests.

B.133 User-Specified Ranges

You can specify any other type of range by coding specific range values. You can specify up to $k - 1$ range values in ascending order, where k is the number of groups and where the range value times the standard error of the combined subset is the critical value. If fewer than $k - 1$ values are specified, the last value specified is used for the remaining ones. You can also specify n repetitions of the same value with the form $n * r$. To use a single critical value for all subsets, specify one range value, as in:

```
ONEWAY  WELL BY EDUC6(1,6)
  /RANGES=5.53
```

B.134 HARMONIC Subcommand

The HARMONIC subcommand determines the sample size estimate to be used when the N's are not equal in all groups. Either only the sample sizes in the two groups being compared are used, or an average sample size of all groups is used.

The default keyword for HARMONIC is NONE, which uses the harmonic mean of the sizes of just the two groups being compared. To use the harmonic mean of *all* group sizes, specify keyword ALL. If ALL is used, ONEWAY calculates homogeneous subsets for SCHEFFE, TUKEY, TUKEYB, and LSDMOD tests on unbalanced designs. Specify only one keyword on the HARMONIC subcommand.

NONE *Harmonic mean of the sizes of the two groups being compared.* You may also use keyword PAIR as an alias for NONE.

ALL *Harmonic mean of group sizes as sample sizes for range tests.* If the harmonic mean is used for unbalanced designs, ONEWAY determines homogeneous subsets for all range tests. (With releases before 3.0, substitute the command OPTION 10.)

B.135 STATISTICS Subcommand

By default ONEWAY calculates the analysis of variance table. It also calculates any statistics specified by the CONTRASTS and RANGES subcommands.

Use the STATISTICS subcommand to request additional statistics. The default keyword for STATISTICS is NONE, for no additional statistics. You can specify any one or all of the following statistics:

NONE *No optional statistics.* This is the default.

DESCRIPTIVES *Group descriptive statistics.* Prints the number of cases, mean, standard deviation, standard error, minimum, maximum, and 95% confidence interval for each dependent variable for each group. (With releases before 3.0, substitute the command STATISTIC 1.)

EFFECTS *Fixed- and random-effects statistics.* Prints the standard deviation, standard error, and 95% confidence interval for the fixed-effects model, and the standard error, 95% confidence interval, and estimate of between-component variance for the random-effects model. (With releases before 3.0, substitute the command STATISTIC 2.)

HOMOGENEITY *Homogeneity-of-variance tests.* Prints Cochran's *C*, the Bartlett-Box *F*, and Hartley's *F* max. (With releases before 3.0, substitute the command STATISTIC 3.)

ALL *All statistics available for ONEWAY.*

B.136 MISSING Subcommand

The MISSING subcommand controls missing values. Its default keywords are ANALYSIS and EXCLUDE. ANALYSIS excludes cases with missing values on an analysis-by-analysis basis. Use keyword LISTWISE to delete cases on a variable-by-variable basis. EXCLUDE determines that user-missing values are not used in the analysis. Use keyword INCLUDE to treat user-missing values as valid.

ANALYSIS *Exclude missing values on a pair-by-pair basis.* A case missing on either the dependent variable or grouping variable for a given analysis is not used for that analysis. Also, a case outside the range specified for the grouping variable is not used. This is the default.

LISTWISE *Exclude missing values listwise.* Cases missing on any variable named are excluded from all analyses. (With releases before 3.0, substitute the command OPTION 2.)

EXCLUDE *Exclude user-missing values.* This is the default.

INCLUDE *Include user-missing values.* User-defined missing values are included in the analysis. (With releases before 3.0, substitute the command OPTION 1.)

Keywords ANALYSIS and LISTWISE are mutually exclusive. Each can be used with either INCLUDE or EXCLUDE.

B.137 FORMAT Subcommand

By default, ONEWAY identifies groups as GRP1, GRP2, GRP3, etc. Use the FORMAT subcommand to identify the groups by their value labels. The FORMAT subcommand has only two keywords, NOLABELS and LABELS. NOLABELS is the default.

NOLABELS *Suppress value labels.* This is the default.

LABELS *Use the first eight characters from value labels for group labels.* The value labels are those defined for the independent variable. (With releases before 3.0, substitute the command OPTION 6.)

B.138 MATRIX Subcommand

ONEWAY writes means, standard deviations, and frequencies to a matrix system file that can be used by subsequent ONEWAY procedures. In addition, it reads means, frequencies, pooled variance, and degrees of freedom for the pooled variance.

The OUT keyword on MATRIX specifies the file to which the matrix is written. The IN keyword specifies the file from which the matrix is read. In both cases, specify the matrix file in parentheses, with one of the following options:

(file) *Write the correlation matrix to, or read it from, the system file specified in the parentheses.* (With releases before 3.0, when writing a matrix, use the PROCEDURE OUTPUT command to specify the file, and the command OPTION 4. When reading a matrix, use the INPUT MATRIX command, and either the command OPTION 7 to read frequencies, means, and standard deviations, or the command OPTION 8 to read means, frequencies, pooled variance, and degrees of freedom for the pooled variance.)

(*) *Replace the active file with the correlation matrix, or read the matrix from the active file.*

In addition to OUT and IN, ONEWAY allows the keyword NONE, to explicitly indicate that the data are not matrix materials.

B.139 Limitations

The following limitations apply to ONEWAY:

- A maximum of 100 dependent variables and 1 independent variable.
- An unlimited number of categories for the independent variable. However, contrasts and range tests are not performed if the actual number of nonempty categories exceeds 50.
- Only 1 POLYNOMIAL subcommand.
- A maximum of 10 CONTRAST subcommands and 10 RANGES subcommands.
- Any alpha values between 0 and 1 are permitted for the LSD, LSDMOD, and SCHEFFE range tests. SNK, TUKEY, and TUKEYB use an alpha value of 0.05, regardless of what is specified. DUNCAN uses an alpha value of 0.01 if the alpha specified is less than 0.05; 0.05 if the alpha specified is greater than or equal to 0.05 but less than 0.10; 0.10 if the alpha specified is greater than or equal to 0.10; or 0.05 if no alpha is specified.

B.140 OPTIONS and STATISTICS

OPTIONS and STATISTICS are not used in Release 3.0. See individual procedures for subcommand and keyword specifications when using Release 3.0. Syntax for releases before 3.0:

```
OPTIONS option numbers

STATISTICS {statistics numbers}
           {ALL               }
```

Use the OPTIONS and STATISTICS commands *only with releases before 3.0.*

In releases before 3.0, there are two types of syntax for procedures in SPSS^X. Some procedures are entirely self-contained. In these procedures, you use subcommands to specify analyses, formatting options, missing-data options, additional statistics, and so forth. REGRESSION, FACTOR, CLUSTER, HILOGLINEAR, and LOGLINEAR are examples of subcommand-driven procedures. Other procedures use associated OPTIONS and STATISTICS commands to produce nondefault output. DISCRIMINANT uses both and MANOVA has a single OPTION. For example, to include missing data in procedure DISCRIMINANT, you must use an OPTIONS command.

The OPTIONS and STATISTICS commands immediately follow the procedure command to which they apply. They can be specified in either order. The specification field for either command contains one or more numbers corresponding to specific options or statistics available for the procedure. In addition, you can use the keyword ALL on the STATISTICS command to request all optional statistics.

Some options and statistics are not available in combination with other options or statistics. If you specify an illegal combination of options or statistics, SPSS^X usually overrides the conflict and prints a warning message indicating the action taken.

B.141 PLOT

Syntax for all releases:

```
PLOT† [HSIZE = {80**}]
               {n   }

 [/VSIZE = {40**}]
           {n   }

 [/CUTPOINT = {EVERY({1**})}]
              {      {n  } }
              {value list  }

 [/SYMBOLS = {ALPHANUMERIC**                        }]
             {NUMERIC                               }
             {'symbols'[,'overplot symbols']        }
             {X'hexsymbs'[,'overplot hexsymbs']     }
             {DEFAULT                               }

 [/MISSING = [{PLOTWISE**}] [INCLUDE]]
              {LISTWISE  }

 [/FORMAT = {DEFAULT**       }]
            {CONTOUR[({10})] }
            {         {n } } }
            {OVERLAY         }
            {REGRESSION      }

 [/TITLE = 'title']

 [/HORIZONTAL = ['title'] [STANDARDIZE] [REFERENCE(value list)]
                [MIN(min)] [MAX(max)] [UNIFORM]]

 [/VERTICAL = ['title'] [STANDARDIZE] [REFERENCE(value list)]
              [MIN(min)] [MAX(max)] [UNIFORM]]

 /PLOT = varlist WITH varlist [(PAIR)] [BY varname] [;varlist...]

 [/PLOT=...]
```

†Available as of Release 2.0.
**Default if the subcommand is omitted.

Procedure PLOT produces two-dimensional line-printer plots. You can request simple scatterplots, scatterplots with a control variable and/or regression statistics, contour plots, and overlay plots.

The only required subcommand on PLOT is the PLOT subcommand. There are two types of optional subcommands: global subcommands (HSIZE, VSIZE, CUTPOINT, SYMBOLS, and MISSING) and local subcommands (FORMAT, TITLE, HORIZONTAL, and VERTICAL).

You can specify each of the global subcommands only once, and each must be prior to the first occurrence of the PLOT subcommand. You can use the PLOT subcommand and accompanying local subcommands more than once within a PLOT command. However, local subcommands apply only to the *immediately following* PLOT subcommand. A PLOT subcommand must be the last subcommand you specify. Use a slash to separate every subcommand from the next.

This abbreviated command reference does not discuss the character overstrike capabilities on the SYMBOLS subcommand. This feature is not essential to the operation of PLOT as described in this book. However, these features are fully discussed in the *SPSS^X User's Guide*, 3rd ed.

B.142 PLOT Subcommand

Use the PLOT subcommand to specify the variables to plot. Specify the variables for the vertical (Y) axis, then the keyword WITH, then the variables for the horizontal (X) axis.

By default, PLOT creates separate plots for all combinations formed by each variable on the left side of the WITH keyword with each variable on the right. However, you can choose to plot only corresponding pairs of variables by using the keyword PAIR in parentheses. In the following,

```
/PLOT = Y1 Y2  WITH  X1 X2
/PLOT = Y1 Y2  WITH  X1 X2 (PAIR)
```

the first PLOT subcommand specifies four plots, showing Y1 with X1, Y1 with X2, Y2 with X1, and Y2 with X2. The second PLOT subcommand specifies only two plots, showing Y1 with X1 and Y2 with X2.

Use semicolons to separate multiple plot lists. For example,

```
/PLOT = BONUS WITH TENURE SALNOW;SALNOW WITH SALBEG
```

requests three scatterplots. The first request produces plots of BONUS with TENURE and BONUS with SALNOW. The second request produces the plot of SALNOW with SALBEG.

In the output, an information table precedes the plots you request on a PLOT subcommand. This table shows the number of cases used, the size of the plot, and a list of symbols and frequencies.

B.143 Control and Contour Variables

Use the BY keyword on a PLOT subcommand's variable list to specify a control variable or a contour variable for a set of plots. You can specify only one such variable on any plot list. Producing a contour plot requires the FORMAT subcommand (see Section B.148).

PLOT uses the first character of the control variable's value label as the plot symbol. If no value labels are supplied, PLOT uses the first character of the actual value. For the numeric value 28, the symbol would be 2; for the string value MALE, the symbol would be M. PLOT does not check uniqueness of symbols, but you can use the VALUE LABELS command to create appropriate value labels that prevent ambiguity.

B.144 TITLE Subcommand

You can provide a title for a plot with the TITLE subcommand. Enclose your own descriptive title for a plot in apostrophes on the TITLE subcommand. The default title of a plot uses either the names of the variables for a bivariate plot or the type of plot requested on the FORMAT subcommand (see Section B.146). The command

```
PLOT TITLE='Plot of Beginning Salary on Current Salary'
 /PLOT=SALNOW WITH SALBEG
```

requests a title that overrides the default.

A title can contain up to 60 characters. A title longer than the horizontal width specified on the HSIZE subcommand (see Section B.151) will be truncated.

B.145 VERTICAL and HORIZONTAL Subcommands

You can specify axis labels with the HORIZONTAL and VERTICAL subcommands. These two subcommands also control minimum and maximum values plotted, standardization of axes, provisions for reference lines, and whether the axes have uniform scales on different plots. Adjusting minimum and maximum values is especially useful when you want to focus on a subset of a larger plot. The minimum and maximum value specifications function like a TEMPORARY SELECT IF transformation (see Section B.50). PLOT excludes values outside the specified range from the immediately following PLOT subcommand. PLOT scales the axes to include the specified values. However, to ensure that integers or simple decimals are on the axes, PLOT may extend the scales slightly beyond the specified minimum and maximum.

You can also use the VERTICAL or HORIZONTAL subcommand to designate a label for each axis, to choose the positions of reference lines, and to specify standardization of values.

The VERTICAL and HORIZONTAL subcommands have the same keyword specifications:

'label' *Label of axis.* You can specify a label of up to 40 characters. The default is the variable label for the variable on the axis. If there is no variable label, PLOT uses the variable name. If you specify a label longer or wider than the plot frame size (see Section B.151), the label will be truncated.

MIN(min) *Minimum value included on axis.* The default is the minimum observed value. With the MIN option, only data values greater than or equal to *min* are plotted. The axis scale includes this value.

MAX(max) *Maximum value included on axis.* The default is the maximum observed value. With the MAX option, only data values less than or equal to *max* are plotted. The axis scale includes this value.

UNIFORM *Uniform values on axis.* This option specifies that all plots will have scales with the same values on the (vertical or horizontal) axis. Uniform scales also result if you specify both MIN and MAX. If you specify UNIFORM but not MIN and MAX, PLOT determines the minimum and maximum across all variables for the axis.

REFERENCE(value list) *Reference lines for axis.* For either axis, this option specifies values at which to draw reference lines perpendicular to the axis.

STANDARDIZE *Standardize variables on axis.* With this option, PLOT standardizes variables to have a mean of 0 and a standard deviation of 1. This option is useful if you want to overlay plots of variables that otherwise would have different scales.

The command

```
PLOT TITLE='Annual Salary by Age, XYZ Corporation  1983'
    /VERTICAL='Annual salary before taxes' MIN (500) MAX (75000)
      REFERENCE(25000,50000)
    /HORIZONTAL='Age of employee' MIN (18) MAX (65)
      REFERENCE (33,48)
       /PLOT=INCOME WITH AGE
```

produces a bivariate scatterplot with labeled axes that include values of INCOME between 500 and 75,000 and values of AGE between 18 and 65. The keyword REFERENCE requests reference lines at 25,000 and 50,000 on the vertical axis and at 33 and 48 on the horizontal axis.

B.146 FORMAT Subcommand

Procedure PLOT produces four main types of plots: scatterplots, contour plots, overlay plots, and regression plots. The FORMAT subcommand specifies the plot type for the immediately following PLOT subcommand.

B.147 Bivariate Scatterplots

The default plot is a bivariate scatterplot. To obtain a bivariate scatterplot, you can omit the FORMAT subcommand or specify FORMAT=DEFAULT.

B.148 Contour Plots

A contour plot is similar to a control plot in that symbols on either plot indicate values of the control variable for the cases represented at the positions of the symbols. However, the control variable for a contour plot is a continuous variable. You specify a contour variable after the BY keyword on the PLOT subcommand (see Section B.143).

The CONTOUR keyword on the FORMAT subcommand requests a recoding of the control variable into *n* equal-width intervals corresponding to *n* plotting symbols. When more than one contour level occurs at a print position, PLOT prints the symbol for the highest level. You can specify a maximum of 35 contour levels for each contour plot. If you do not specify the number of levels the number defaults to 10.

The command

```
PLOT FORMAT=CONTOUR(10)
 /TITLE 'SOLUBILITY OF AMMONIA IN WATER'
 /HORIZONTAL='ATMOSPHERIC PRESSURE'
 /VERTICAL='TEMPERATURE'
 /PLOT=TEMP WITH PRESSURE BY CONCENT
```

requests a contour plot with ten levels of the variables named on the PLOT subcommand. Labels are specified for the HORIZONTAL and VERTICAL axes. The boundary values of each level of the control variable appear below the plot.

B.149 Overlay Plots

The OVERLAY keyword on the FORMAT subcommand tells SPSS^X to put all plots specified on the following PLOT subcommand in one frame. You can overlay only bivariate plots (simple scatterplots and regression plots), not control or contour plots. PLOT selects a unique symbol for each plot to be overlaid, plus a symbol to represent multiple plots in one print position.

You can overlay plots by specifying groups of variables on either side of the keyword WITH. The command

```
PLOT FORMAT=OVERLAY
 /TITLE 'MARRIAGE AND DIVORCE RATES  1900-1983'
 /VERTICAL='RATES PER 1000 POPULATION'
 /HORIZONTAL='YEAR' REFERENCE (1918,1945) MIN (1900) MAX (1983)
 /PLOT=MARRATE DIVRATE WITH YEAR
```

requests two plots to be overlaid in one frame. The TITLE specification provides a title for the plot. The VERTICAL subcommand provides a label for the vertical axis. The HORIZONTAL subcommand provides a label, specifies that reference lines be drawn perpendicular to points 1918 and 1945, and specifies 1900 and 1983 as minimum and maximum data values to plot. The PLOT subcommand specifies the variables for the overlay.

B.150 Regression Plots

With the REGRESSION keyword, PLOT calculates and prints statistics for the regression of the vertical-axis variable on the horizontal-axis variable. PLOT produces a scatterplot and marks regression-line intercepts with the letter R. For example, the command

```
PLOT TITLE='SALARY REGRESSION'
 /VERTICAL='CURRENT ANNUAL SALARY'
 /HORIZONTAL= 'ANNUAL STARTING SALARY'
 /FORMAT=REGRESSION
 /PLOT=SALNOW WITH SALBEG
```

requests a fully labeled regression plot of SALNOW with SALBEG.

You can also request regression plots with control variables. For example, the command

```
PLOT FORMAT=REGRESSION
 /PLOT=A B C WITH D; Y WITH X BY Z
```

requests regression statistics for three bivariate plots and one control plot. In a control plot, you do not get separate regression statistics for each control category. Instead, regression statistics are pooled over all categories.

B.151 HSIZE and VSIZE Subcommands

Use the HSIZE and VSIZE subcommands to specify dimensions for your plots. The HSIZE and VSIZE subcommands must precede all PLOT subcommands and can be specified only once. All plots requested on one PLOT command are drawn to the same specified size.

The default size of your plot depends on current page size. With a typical computer page, the default width is 80 positions and the default length is 40 lines. You can override the defaults by using the VSIZE and HSIZE subcommands. The VSIZE subcommand specifies the vertical frame size (length) of the plot, and the HSIZE subcommand specifies the horizontal frame size (width). For example,

```
PLOT VSIZE=30/HSIZE=70
 /PLOT= Y WITH X
```

requests a length of 30 print lines and a width of 70 print positions. The specified size does *not* include print lines for the plot frames or for auxiliary information such as titles, axis scale numbers, regression statistics, or the symbol table.

B.152 HSIZE and VSIZE with HORIZONTAL and VERTICAL

When you specify HSIZE or VSIZE in conjunction with a HORIZONTAL or VERTICAL minimum value, PLOT uses the minimum value as the starting point of the axis. To provide equal-interval, integer scale values, PLOT may extend an axis beyond the minimum and maximum values specified on the HORIZONTAL or VERTICAL subcommand. For example, the command

```
PLOT VSIZE=30 /HSIZE=70
 /FORMAT=OVERLAY
 /TITLE 'MARRIAGE AND DIVORCE RATES  1900-1983'
 /VERTICAL='RATES PER 1000 POPULATION'
 /HORIZONTAL='YEAR' REFERENCE (1918,1945) MIN (1900) MAX (1983)
 /PLOT=MARRATE DIVRATE WITH YEAR
```

produces a plot whose area is 30 lines by 70 characters. The values on the horizontal axis starts at 1900, and the maximum value on the horizontal axis is slightly greater than 1983.

B.153 Controlling Plot Symbols

Two subcommands, CUTPOINT and SYMBOLS, control the frequencies that plotted symbols represent and the characters for the symbols in plots.

Use the CUTPOINT subcommand to adjust the frequencies represented by each plot symbol in bivariate plots (simple scatterplots and regression plots). The SYMBOLS subcommand lets you specify which characters represent a given frequency value in bivariate scatter and regression plots, overlay, and contour plots. Both CUTPOINT and SYMBOLS must precede the first PLOT subcommand and can be specified only once on a PLOT command. All requested plots use the same cutpoint values and symbols.

You cannot use SYMBOLS specifications for scatterplots with control variables or for regression plots with control variables. For these plots, procedure PLOT assigns the symbols. However, you can determine what the symbols will be by giving the control variables appropriate names or value labels (see Section B.143). Table B.153 summarizes the subcommands affecting plot symbols.

Table B.153 Subcommands for symbol control

Plot type	Meaning of each symbol	Subcommand(s) for controlling symbols
Bivariate scatter or regression	Frequency of cases	CUTPOINT SYMBOLS
Control	Value of control variable	None (see Section B.143)
Overlay	Identity of overlaid plot	SYMBOLS
Contour	Level of contour variable	SYMBOLS FORMAT (for number of levels)

B.154 SYMBOLS Subcommand

Use the SYMBOLS subcommand to specify the plotting symbols. The SYMBOLS subcommand applies to bivariate, overlay, and contour plots. It does not apply to control plots. You can use only one SYMBOL subcommand on a PLOT command. The available keywords are:

ALPHANUMERIC *Alphanumeric plotting symbols.* PLOT uses the characters 1–9, A–Z, and * as plot symbols. Thus, * represents 36 or more cases at a print position. This is the default symbol set.

NUMERIC *Numeric plotting symbols.* PLOT uses the characters 1–9 and * as plot symbols. Thus, * represents 10 or more cases at a print position.

'symbols'[,'ovprnt'] *List of plot symbols.* You can provide your own list of symbols enclosed in apostrophes. Optionally, you can specify a second list of overprinting symbols separated from the first list by a comma or space. The overprinting symbols can be either hexadecimal representations (preceded by an X) or keyboard characters.

X'hexsym'[,'ovprnt'] *List of hexadecimal plot symbols.* Indicate hexadecimal symbols by specifying X before the hexadecimal representation list enclosed in apostrophes. Optionally, you can specify a second list of overprinting symbols separated from the first list by a comma or space. The overprinting symbols can be either hexadecimal representations or keyboard characters.

B.155 CUTPOINT Subcommand

By default, frequency plots use successive symbols in print positions corresponding to 1, 2, 3... cases, respectively. To define your own set of frequency values for the successive symbols, use the CUTPOINT subcommand. You can specify the desired interval width on the EVERY keyword, or you can use a value list in parentheses to specify cutpoints:

EVERY(n) *Frequency intervals of width* n. The default is an interval size of 1, meaning that each individual frequency up to 35 has a different symbol. The last default frequency interval includes all frequencies greater than 35. If you specify SYMBOLS as well as EVERY, the last symbol specified will represent all frequencies greater than those for the next-to-last symbol.

(value list) *Cutpoints at the values specified.*

You can specify only one CUTPOINT subcommand on a PLOT command, and it applies only to bivariate plots, not to control, overlay, or contour plots. If you specify

```
PLOT  CUTPOINT=EVERY(4)
 /PLOT = Y WITH X
```

1 will represent 1 to 4 cases at a print position, 2 will represent 5 to 8 cases, and so forth. If you specify

```
PLOT  CUTPOINT= (4, 10, 25)
 /PLOT = Y WITH X
```

1 will represent 1 to 4 cases at a print position, 2 will represent 5 to 10 cases, 3 will represent 11 to 25 cases, and 4 will represent 26 or more cases.

B.156 MISSING Subcommand

Use the MISSING subcommand to change or make explicit the treatment of cases with missing values. You can use only one MISSING subcommand on a PLOT command. Three specifications are available:

PLOTWISE *Exclude cases with missing values plotwise.* For each plot within a single frame, cases are deleted that have missing values on any variable for that plot. This is the default.

LISTWISE *Exclude cases with missing values listwise.* Cases with missing values on any variable named on any PLOT subcommand are deleted from all plots specified on the PLOT command.

INCLUDE *Include user-defined missing values as valid.*

If you specify

```
PLOT MISSING = LISTWISE
 /FORMAT=REGRESSION
 /PLOT = Y WITH A; Z WITH B
```

PLOT excludes cases with missing values on any of the variables Y, A, Z, and B.

For overlay plots, plotwise deletion applies to each subplot requested, not to the full list specified on the PLOT subcommand. With the command

```
PLOT FORMAT=OVERLAY
 /PLOT = INCOME82 TAXES82 WITH YEAR82
```

cases with missing values on INCOME82 or YEAR82 will be deleted from that subplot only, and cases with missing values on TAXES82 or YEAR82 will be deleted from the other subplot. The complete overlay plot may have a different number of cases for each subplot that is overlaid. The number of cases plotted in each subplot is stated below the plot frame.

B.157 Limitations

There are no limitations on the number of plots requested or on the number of variables specified on a PLOT command. The following limitations apply to the optional subcommands:

- A maximum of 60 characters for a title specified on the TITLE subcommand.
- A maximum of 36 symbols per SYMBOLS subcommand.
- A maximum of 35 cutpoints per CUTPOINT subcommand.
- A maximum of 10 reference points on each HORIZONTAL or VERTICAL subcommand.
- A maximum of 40 characters per label on each HORIZONTAL or VERTICAL subcommand.

B.158 PROCEDURE OUTPUT

Syntax for all releases:

```
PROCEDURE OUTPUT OUTFILE=file
```

Some procedures in SPSS^X write output files, whose organization prevents them from being added directly to the active file. Included among these files are the various types of matrix materials. Table B.158 lists procedures that create output files.

Table B.158 Procedures that write output files

Procedure	Type of File
CLUSTER	Distance matrix
CROSSTABS	Cell counts
DISCRIMINANT	Matrix materials
FACTOR	Matrix materials
FREQUENCIES	Display file
MANOVA	Matrix materials
NONPAR CORR	Matrix materials
PARTIAL CORR	Matrix materials
PEARSON CORR	Matrix materials
QUICK CLUSTER	Final cluster centers
REGRESSION	Matrix materials
RELIABILITY	Matrix materials
SURVIVAL	Life table records

With Release 3.0, you must specify the PROCEDURE OUTPUT command only before the CROSSTABS, FREQUENCIES, and SURVIVAL procedures when they write output files. With releases before 3.0, you must specify the PROCEDURE OUTPUT command before *any* procedure that writes a file. (With Release 3.0, matrix materials written by procedures are controlled by the MATRIX subcommand.)

PROCEDURE OUTPUT has one subcommand, OUTFILE, which names the file to which the output is directed. (With releases before 3.0, you must also define the file handle on a previous FILE HANDLE command.)

B.159 PROXIMITIES

Syntax for Release 3.0:

```
PROXIMITIES  varlist

 [/MISSING={LISTWISE**} ]
           {INCLUDE   }

 [/STANDARDIZE=[{VARIABLE}] [{NONE**  }] ]
               [{CASE    }]  {Z       }
                             {SD      }
                             {RANGE   }
                             {MAX     }
                             {MEAN    }
                             {RESCALE }

 [/VIEW={CASE**   } ]
        {VARIABLE}

 [/MEASURE=[{NONE                  }] [ABSOLUTE] [REVERSE] [RESCALE]
            {EUCLID**              }
            {SEUCLID               }
            {COSINE                }
            {CORR                  }
            {BLOCK                 }
            {CHEBYCHEV             }
            {POWER(p,r)            }
            {MINKOWSKI(p)          }
            {CHISQ                 }
            {PH2                   }
            {RR[(p[,np])]          }
            {SM[(p[,np])]          }
            {JACCARD[(p[,np])]     }
            {DICE[(p[,np])]        }
            {SS1[(p[,np])]         }
            {RT[(p[,np])]          }
            {SS2[(p[,np])]         }
            {K1[(p[,np])]          }
            {SS3[(p[,np])]         }
            {K2[(p[,np])]          }
            {SS4[(p[,np])]         }
            {HAMANN[(p[,np])]      }
            {OCHIAI[(p[,np])]      }
            {SS5[(p[,np])]         }
            {PHI[(p[,np])]         }
            {LAMBDA[(p[,np])]      }
            {D[(p[,np])]           }
            {Y[(p[,np])]           }
            {Q[(p[,np])]           }
            {BEUCLID[(p[,np])]     }
            {SIZE[(p[,np])]        }
            {PATTERN[(p[,np])]     }
            {BSEUCLID[(p[,np])]    }
            {BSHAPE[(p[,np])]      }
            {DISPER[(p[,np])]      }
            {VARIANCE[(p[,np])]    }
            {BLWMN[(p[,np])]       }

 [/ID=varname ]

 [/PRINT [={PROXIMITIES**}] ]
           {NONE         }

 [/MATRIX=[IN({file})] [OUT({file})]]
              {*   }        {*   }
```

**Default if the subcommand is omitted.

Syntax for releases before 3.0:

```
PROXIMITIES†† varlist

 [/MISSING={LISTWISE**} ]
           {INCLUDE   }

 [/READ=[SIMILAR] [{SQUARE      }]]
                   {TRIANGULAR  }
                   {SUBDIAGONAL}

 [/STANDARDIZE=[{VARIABLE}] [{NONE**  }] ]
               [{CASE    }]  {Z       }
                             {SD      }
                             {RANGE   }
                             {MAX     }
                             {MEAN    }
                             {RESCALE}

 [/VIEW={CASE**   } ]
        {VARIABLE}

 [/MEASURE=[{NONE                    }] [ABSOLUTE] [REVERSE] [RESCALE]
            {EUCLID**                }
            {SEUCLID                 }
            {COSINE                  }
            {CORR                    }
            {BLOCK                   }
            {CHEBYCHEV               }
            {POWER(p,r)              }
            {MINKOWSKI(p)            }
            {CHISQ                   }
            {PH2                     }
            {RR[(p[,np])]            }
            {SM[(p[,np])]            }
            {JACCARD[(p[,np])]       }
            {DICE[(p[,np])]          }
            {SS1[(p[,np])]           }
            {RT[(p[,np])]            }
            {SS2[(p[,np])]           }
            {K1[(p[,np])]            }
            {SS3[(p[,np])]           }
            {K2[(p[,np])]            }
            {SS4[(p[,np])]           }
            {HAMANN[(p[,np])]        }
            {OCHIAI[(p[,np])]        }
            {SS5[(p[,np])]           }
            {PHI[(p[,np])]           }
            {LAMBDA[(p[,np])]        }
            {D[(p[,np])]             }
            {Y[(p[,np])]             }
            {Q[(p[,np])]             }
            {BEUCLID[(p[,np])]       }
            {SIZE[(p[,np])]          }
            {PATTERN[(p[,np])]       }
            {BSEUCLID[(p[,np])]      }
            {BSHAPE[(p[,np])]        }
            {DISPER[(p[,np])]        }
            {VARIANCE[(p[,np])]      }
            {BLWMN[(p[,np])]         }

 [/ID=varname ]

 [/PRINT [={PROXIMITIES**}] ]
           {NONE         }

 [/WRITE [=PROXIMITIES]]

 [/OUTFILE [={  *   }]]
             {handle}
```

††Available as of Release 2.1.
**Default if the subcommand is omitted.

PROXIMITIES produces distance, dissimilarity, or similarity matrices for a small to moderate number of cases and variables. You can compute the proximity measures between pairs of either cases or variables. You can standardize the data by case or by variable using any of several methods before computing proximities. You can specify any one of several similarity, dissimilarity, and distance measures. PROXIMITIES provides measures for quantitative, frequency count, and binary data. You can also write out the proximity matrices to be input to procedures ALSCAL and CLUSTER.

B.160 Variable Specification

You need only a PROXIMITIES variable specification to produce a default matrix of Euclidean distances between cases. You can use the PROXIMITIES variable specification in three distinct ways. First, you can use the PROXIMITIES variable specification to identify the variables used to compute similarities or distances between cases. Second, you can use it to identify the variables for which to compute distances, dissimilarities or similarities. Finally, you can use the PROXIMITIES variable specification to identify (provide labels for) the items represented in a similarity or distance matrix read from the matrix input file. For example,

```
PROXIMITIES A B C
```

would compute Euclidean distances between cases based on the values of variables A, B, and C.

B.161 MISSING Subcommand

You can use the MISSING subcommand to change or to make explicit the treatment of cases with missing values. You can specify either of two keywords with the MISSING subcommand. The default treatment is listwise deletion of cases with missing values.

LISTWISE *Delete cases with missing values listwise.* This is the default.

INCLUDE *Include user-missing values as valid.* This deletes only cases with system-missing values in a listwise fashion.

B.162 STANDARDIZE Subcommand

Use the STANDARDIZE subcommand to standardize data values for either cases or variables before computing proximities. Specify one of two options to control standardization by case or by variable.

VARIABLE *Standardize the values for each variable.* This is the default if you specify the STANDARDIZE subcommand without an explicit standardization mode option.

CASE *Standardize the values within each case.*

You have a choice of several means of standardization. These allow you to equalize selected properties of the values. You may specify only one standardization method option.

Z *Standardize values to z-scores having zero mean and unit standard deviation.*

SD *Standardize values to unit standard deviation.*

RANGE *Standardize values to unit range.*

MEAN *Standardize values to unit mean.*

MAX *Standardize values to a maximum magnitude of one.*

RESCALE *Standardize values to range from zero to one.*

NONE *No standardization, compute proximities using the data in its original form.* This is the default if you do not specify the STANDARDIZE subcommand.

B.163 VIEW Subcommand

Use the VIEW subcommand to indicate whether to compute proximities between cases or between variables. In either case, PROXIMITIES keeps the raw data matrix for the current split file group in memory. This restricts the use of PROXIMITIES to small to moderate sized data sets.

CASE *Compute proximity values between cases.* This is the default.

VARIABLE *Compute proximity values between variables.*

B.164 MEASURE Subcommand

You can use the MEASURE subcommand to select the distance, dissimilarity, or similarity measure to compute. There are measures for continuous, frequency count, and binary data. There is also a NONE keyword to allow you to transform the values in an existing proximity matrix.

NONE *Do not compute proximity coefficients.* Use the NONE specification only if you input an existing proximity matrix using the READ subcommand.

You can use any of seven keywords with the MEASURE subcommand to obtain proximities for continuous data.

EUCLID *Euclidean distances.* The distance between two cases is the square root of the sum of the squared differences in values on each variable. This is the default.

SEUCLID *Squared Euclidean distances.* The distance between two cases is the sum of the squared differences in values on each variable.

COSINE *Cosine of vectors of values.* This is a pattern similarity measure.

CORRELATION *Correlation vectors of values.* This is a pattern similarity measure.

BLOCK *City-block or Manhattan distances.* The distance between two cases is the sum of the absolute differences in values on each variable.

CHEBYCHEV *Chebychev distance metric.* The distance between two cases is the maximum absolute difference in values for any variable.

POWER(p,r) *Distances in an absolute power metric.* The distance between two cases is the *r*th root of the sum of the absolute differences to the *p*th power in values on each variable.

MINKOWSKI(p) *Distances in an absolute Minkowski power metric.* The distance between two cases is the *p*th root of the sum of the absolute differences to the *p*th power in values on each variable.

You can use either of two keywords with the MEASURE subcommand to obtain proximities for frequency count data.

CHISQ *Chi-square test of equality for two sets of frequencies.* The magnitude of this similarity measure depends on the total frequencies of the two cases or variables whose proximity is computed. Expected values are from the model of independence of cases (or variables), X and Y.

PH2 *Phi-squared between sets of frequencies.* This is the CHISQ measure normalized by the square root of the combined frequency. Therefore its values do not depend on the total frequencies of the two cases or variables whose proximity is computed.

There are many measures for binary data. These measures emphasize different aspects of the relation between the sets of binary values. You specify each measure in the same way. Each measure has two optional integer-valued parameters, p (present code) and a (absent code). If you specify no parameters, PROXIMITIES assumes that a value of 1 indicates a characteristic is present, and a 0 represents it is absent. If you specify only the first parameter, PROXIMITIES uses its value to indicate that a characteristic is present, and all other values to indicate it is absent. If you specify both parameters, PROXIMITIES uses the first value to identify the characteristics that are present, the second value to identify those absent, and skips all other values. The binary measures are:

RR[(p[,a])] *Russel & Rao similarity measure.* This is the binary dot product. It has a range from 0 to 1 and is a similarity measure.

SM[(p[,a])] *Simple matching similarity measure.* This is the ratio of number of matches to total number of items. It has a monotonic relation to the SS1 and RT coefficients. It has a range from 0 to 1 and is a similarity measure.

JACCARD[(p[,a])] *Jaccard similarity measure.* This is also known as the similarity ratio. It has a monotonic relation to the DICE and SS2 coefficients. It has a range from 0 to 1 and is a similarity measure.

DICE[(p[,a])] *Dice or Czekanowski similarity measure.* It has a monotonic relation to the JACCARD and SS2 coefficients. It has a range from 0 to 1 and is a similarity measure.

SS1[(p[,a])] *Sokal & Sneath similarity measure 1.* It has a monotonic relation to the SM and RT coefficients. It has a range from 0 to 1 and is a similarity measure.

RT[(p[,a])] *Rogers & Tanimoto similarity measure.* It has a monotonic relation to the SM and SS1 coefficients. It has a range from 0 to 1 and is a similarity measure.

SS2[(p[,a])] *Sokal & Sneath similarity measure 2.* It has a monotonic relation to the JACCARD and DICE coefficients. It has a range from 0 to 1 and is a similarity measure.

K1[(p[,a])] *Kulczynski similarity measure 1.* It has a range from 0 to no upper limit and is a similarity measure.

SS3[(p[,a])] *Sokal & Sneath similarity measure 3.* It has a range from 0 to no upper limit and is a similarity measure.

Other binary measures yield values that one can interpret as conditional probabilities.

K2[(p[,a])] *Kulczynski similarity measure 2.* This gives the conditional probability one item is present given the other item is present. It is averaged over each item acting as the predictor. It has a range from 0 to 1 and is a similarity measure.

SS4[(p[,a])] *Sokal & Sneath similarity measure 4.* This gives the conditional probability that one item has a state (present or absent) given the other item has that state. It is averaged over each item acting as the predictor. It has a range from 0 to 1 and is a similarity measure.

HAMANN[(p[,a])] *Hammann similarity measure.* This gives the probability that both items have the same state (both present or both absent) minus the probability the items have different states (one absent and one present). This measure has a monotonic relation to the SM, SS1, and RT coefficients. It has a range from -1 to «1 and is a similarity measure.

Other binary measures assess the association between binary items as the predictability on one item given the other.

LAMBDA[(p[,a])] *Goodman & Kruskal lambda (similarity).* This coefficient assesses the predictability of the state of an item (present or absent) given the state of the other. It has a range from 0 to 1 and is a similarity measure.

D[(p[,a])] *Anderberg's D (similarity).* This coefficient assesses the predictability of the state of an item (present or absent) given the state of the other. It has a range from 0 to 1 and is a similarity measure.

Y[(p[,a])] *Yule's Y coefficient of colligation (similarity).* It is a function of the cross ratio for a two by two table. It has a range from -1 to «1 and is a similarity measure.

Q[(p[,a])] *Yule's Q (similarity).* This is the 2 X 2 version of Goodman and Kruskal's ordinal measure *gamma*. It is a function of the cross ratio for a two by two table. It has a range from -1 to «1 and is a similarity measure.

The remaining binary measures are either the binary equivalents of association measures for continuous variables or measure special properties of the relation between items.

OCHIAI[(p[,a])] *Ochiai similarity measure.* This is the binary form of the cosine. It has a range from 0 to 1 and is a similarity measure.

SS5[(p[,a])] *Sokal & Sneath similarity measure 5.* It has a range from 0 to 1 and is a similarity measure.

PHI[(p[,a])] *Fourfold point correlation (similarity).* This is the binary form of the Pearson product moment correlation coefficient. It has a range from −1 to +1 and is a similarity measure.

BEUCLID[(p[,a])] *Binary Euclidean distance.* It has a range from 0 to no upper limit and is a distance measure.

BSEUCLID[(p[,a])] *Binary squared Euclidean distance.* It has a range from 0 to no upper limit and is a distance measure.

SIZE[(p[,a])] *Size difference.* It has a range from 0 to no upper limit and is a dissimilarity measure.

PATTERN[(p[,a])] *Pattern difference.* It has a range from 0 to 1 and is a dissimilarity measure.

BSHAPE[(p[,a])] *Binary shape difference.* It has no upper nor lower limit and is a dissimilarity measure.

DISPER[(p[,a])] *Dispersion similarity measure.* It has a range from -1 to «1 and is a similarity measure.

VARIANCE[(p[,a])] *Variance dissimilarity measure.* It has a range from 0 to no upper limit and is a dissimilarity measure.

BLWMN[(p[,a])] *Binary Lance & Williams nonmetric dissimilarity measure.* This is also known as the Bray-Curtis nonmetric coefficient. It has a range from 0 to 1 and is a dissimilarity measure.

In addition to the specifications for kind of measure, three additional specifications transform the coefficient values PROXIMITIES reads or computes.

ABSOLUTE *Take the absolute values of the proximities.*

REVERSE *Transform similarity values into dissimilarities or vice-versa.* Specify this keyword to reverse the ordering of the proximities by negating the coefficients.

RESCALE *Rescales the proximity values to a range of 0 to 1.*

If you specify more than one transformation, they are done in the above order: first take the absolute values, then reverse, and finally rescale.

B.165 ID Subcommand

Use the ID subcommand to specify an identifying string variable for cases. You can name any string variable on your file as the identifier. PROXIMITIES uses the value of this variable to identify cases in procedure output. By default, the procedure identifies cases by case number alone.

B.166 PRINT Subcommand

PROXIMITIES always prints the name of the similarity or distance measure it computes, and the number of cases. You can use the PRINT subcommand with any of the following keywords to obtain additional output:

PROXIMITIES *Matrix of proximities between items.*

NONE *Do not print matrix of proximity values.*

B.167 MATRIX Subcommand

PROXIMITIES can both read and write matrix materials. It writes proximity type matrices that can be used by PROXIMITIES or other procedures. Procedures CLUSTER and ALSCAL can read a proximity matrix directly. Procedure FACTOR can read a correlation matrix written by PROXIMITY, but you must first use RECODE to change the ROWTYPE_ value PROX to a ROWTYPE_ value CORR. Also, if using a proximity matrix in FACTOR, you may *not* use the ID subcommand in PROXIMITIES.

The OUT keyword on MATRIX specifies the file to which the matrix is written. The IN keyword specifies the file from which the matrix is read. In both cases, specify the matrix file in parentheses, with one of the following options:

(file) *Write the correlation matrix to a system file.* Assign the file name in the parentheses. CORRELATIONS creates a system file containing the matrix materials. The system file is stored on disk and can be retrieved at any time.

(*) *Replace the active file with the correlation matrix system file.* The matrix materials replace the active file. The correlation matrix is NOT stored on disk. It is resident in the active file.

With releases before 3.0, instead of the MATRIX subcommand, use the READ subcommand to obtain a similarity or distance matrix from a matrix input file. You can, for example, read a correlation matrix created by CORRELATIONS or another SPSS^X procedure. This permits you to apply the ABSOLUTE, REVERSE, and/or RESCALE transformations to an existing matrix of proximity values. When you specify the READ subcommand, PROXIMITIES assumes MEASURE=NONE. Three keywords are available with this subcommand.

SIMILAR *Matrix contains similarity values.*

SQUARE *Matrix is in full, square form.* This is the default.

TRIANGULAR *Matrix is in lower-triangular form.* This is similar to SUBDIAGONAL but includes the diagonal elements.

SUBDIAGONAL *Matrix is in subdiagonal form.* This is the same as TRIANGULAR but excludes the diagonal elements.

You can specify either SQUARE or TRIANGULAR or SUBDIAGONAL, but not more than one of these specifications.

With releases before 3.0, instead of the MATRIX subcommand, use the WRITE subcommand to save a computed similarity or distance matrix on the procedure output file. You can use the optional keyword PROXIMITIES on this subcommand.

B.168 OUTFILE Subcommand

With releases before 3.0, you use the OUTFILE subcommand to save a computed similarity, dissimilarity, or distance matrix to an SPSS^X system file or to the active file. If you specify nothing or an asterisk (*) PROXIMITIES writes the proximity matrix and any split file variables to the active file. This new active file can be used directly by ALSCAL. To write to a separate SPSS^X system file, you must specify a file handle on the subcommand.

B.169 Limitations

PROXIMITIES stores both cases and a lower-triangular matrix of similarities or distances in memory when computing a matrix of distances between either cases or variables. Storage requirements increase rapidly with number of cases and number of items (cases or variables) for which proximities are computed. You should be able to compute a distance matrix for 150 cases using a small number of variables in an 80K byte workspace.

PROXIMITIES ignores case weights when computing coefficients.

B.170 REGRESSION

Syntax for Release 3.0:

```
REGRESSION [MATRIX=[IN({file})]  [OUT({file})]]
                       {*   }         {*   }

 [/WIDTH={132**}]
         {n    }

 [/SELECT={varname relation value}

 [/MISSING={LISTWISE**       }] [INCLUDE]]
           {PAIRWISE         }
           {MEANSUBSTITUTION}

 [/DESCRIPTIVES=[DEFAULTS] [MEAN] [STDDEV] [CORR] [COV]
                [VARIANCE] [XPROD] [SIG] [N] [BADCORR]
                [ALL] [NONE**]]

 [/VARIABLES={varlist     }]
             {(COLLECT)**}
             {ALL         }

 [/CRITERIA=[DEFAULTS**] [TOLERANCE({0.0001**})] [MAXSTEPS(n)]
                                    {value    }

             [PIN({0.05**})] [POUT({0.10**})]
                  {value }         {value }

             [FIN({3.84 })] [FOUT({2.71 })]]
                  {value}          {value}

 [/STATISTICS=[DEFAULTS**] [R**] [COEFF**] [ANOVA**] [OUTS**]
              [ZPP] [LABEL] [CHA] [CI] [F] [BCOV] [SES] [LINE]
              [HISTORY] [XTX] [COND] [END] [TOL] [ALL]]

 [/{NOORIGIN**}]
   {ORIGIN    }

 [/REGWGT=varname]

 /DEPENDENT=varlist

 [/METHOD=]{STEPWISE [varlist]          } [...] [/...]
           {FORWARD [varlist]           }
           {BACKWARD [varlist]          }
           {ENTER [varlist]             }
           {REMOVE varlist              }
           {TEST(varlist)(varlist)...}

 [/RESIDUALS=[DEFAULTS] [ID(varname)] [DURBIN] [{SEPARATE}]
                                                 {POOLED  }
              [HISTOGRAM({ZRESID      })] [OUTLIERS({ZRESID      })]
                         {tempvarlist}              {tempvarlist}

              [NORMPROB({ZRESID      })]  [SIZE({LARGE})]]
                        {tempvarlist}           {SMALL}

 [/CASEWISE=[DEFAULTS] [{OUTLIERS({  3  })}]
                        {         {value} }
                        {ALL              }

             [PLOT({ZRESID })]   [{DEPENDENT PRED RESID}]]
                   {tempvar}      {tempvarlist          }

 [/SCATTERPLOT=[SIZE({SMALL})] (varname,varname)...]
                     {LARGE}

 [/PARTIALPLOT=[{ALL     }] [SIZE({SMALL})]]
                {varlist}         {LARGE}

 [/SAVE=tempvar(newname) tempvar(newname)...]
```

Temporary variables for residuals analysis are: PRED, ADJPRED, SRESID, MAHAL, RESID, ZPRED, SDRESID, COOK, DRESID, ZRESID, SEPRED, LEVER.
**Default if the subcommand is omitted.

Syntax for releases before 3.0:

```
REGRESSION [READ=[DEFAULTS] [MEAN] [STDDEV] [CORR] [N]
                 [VARIANCE] [COV] [INDEX]]

 [/WIDTH={132**}]
         {n    }

 [/SELECT={(ALL)**                  }]
          {varname relation value}

 [/MISSING={LISTWISE**        }] [INCLUDE]]
           {PAIRWISE          }
           {MEANSUBSTITUTION}

 [/DESCRIPTIVES=[DEFAULTS] [MEAN] [STDDEV] [CORR] [COV]
                [VARIANCE] [XPROD] [SIG] [N] [BADCORR]
                [ALL] [NONE**]]

 [/WRITE=[DEFAULTS] [MEAN] [STDDEV] [CORR]
         [VARIANCE] [COV] [N] [NONE]]

 /VARIABLES†† ={varlist   }]
               {(COLLECT)}
               {ALL       }

 [/CRITERIA=[DEFAULTS**] [TOLERANCE({0.0001**})] [MAXSTEPS(n)]
                                    {value   }

            [PIN({0.05**})] [POUT({0.10**})]
                 {value }         {value }

            [FIN({3.84 })] [FOUT({2.71 })]]
                 {value}          {value}

 [/STATISTICS=[DEFAULTS**] [R] [COEFF] [ANOVA] [OUTS]
              [ZPP] [LABEL] [CHA] [CI] [F] [BCOV] [SES] [LINE]
              [HISTORY] [XTX] [COND] [END] [TOL] [ALL]]

 [/{NOORIGIN**}]
   {ORIGIN    }

 /DEPENDENT=varlist

 [/METHOD=]{STEPWISE [varlist]          } [...] [/...]
           {FORWARD [varlist]           }
           {BACKWARD [varlist]          }
           {ENTER [varlist]             }
           {REMOVE varlist              }
           {TEST(varlist)(varlist)...}

 [/RESIDUALS†† =[DEFAULTS] [ID(varname)] [DURBIN] [{SEPARATE}]
                                                   {POOLED  }
               [HISTOGRAM({ZRESID       })] [OUTLIERS({ZRESID       })]
                          {tempvarlist}               {tempvarlist}

              [NORMPROB({ZRESID       })]  [SIZE({LARGE})]]
                       {tempvarlist}            {SMALL}

 [/CASEWISE†† =[DEFAULTS] [{OUTLIERS({  3  })}]
                          {          {value} }
                          {ALL                }

               [PLOT({ZRESID })]  [{DEPENDENT PRED RESID}]]
                     {tempvar}     {tempvarlist           }

 [/SCATTERPLOT=[SIZE({SMALL})] (varname,varname)...]
                     {LARGE}

 [/PARTIALPLOT=[{ALL     }] [SIZE({SMALL})]]
                {varlist}         {LARGE}

 [/SAVE=tempvar(newname) tempvar(newname)...]
```

Temporary variables for residuals analysis are: PRED, ADJPRED, SRESID, MAHAL, RESID, ZPRED, SDRESID, COOK, DRESID, ZRESID, SEPRED, LEVER.

††Modified as of Release 2.1.
**Default if the subcommand is omitted.

The complete syntax charts for REGRESSION are included here. Procedure REGRESSION is fully described in Chapter 2.

B.171 T-TEST

Syntax for Release 3.0:

Independent samples:

```
T-TEST GROUPS=varname ({1,2**       }) /VARIABLES=varlist
                       {value       }
                       {value,value}

 [/MISSING={ANALYSIS**}  [INCLUDE]]
           {LISTWISE  }

 [/FORMAT={LABELS**} ]
          {NOLABELS}
```

Paired samples:

```
T-TEST PAIRS=varlist [WITH varlist [(PAIRED)]] [/varlist ...]

 [/MISSING={ANALYSIS**}  [INCLUDE]]
           {LISTWISE  }

 [/FORMAT={LABELS**} ]
          {NOLABELS}
```

**Default if the subcommand is omitted.

Syntax for releases before 3.0:

Independent Samples:

```
T-TEST GROUPS=varname ({1,2        }) /VARIABLES=varlist
                       {value      }
                       {value,value}
```

Paired Samples:

```
T-TEST PAIRS=varlist [WITH varlist] [/varlist ...]
```

Options:

1 Include missing values	4 Narrow formatting
2 Exclude missing values listwise	5 Special pairing for WITH†
3 Suppress variable labels	

†Available as of Release 2.0.

T-TEST compares sample means by calculating Student's *t* and tests the significance of the difference between the means. It tests either independent samples (different groups of cases) or paired samples (different variables). T-TEST subcommands can be used in any order.

B.172 Independent Samples

An independent-samples test divides the cases into two groups and compares the group means on a single variable. This test requires the GROUPS and VARIABLES subcommands. You can specify only one independent-samples test per T-TEST command.

B.173 GROUPS Subcommand

The GROUPS subcommand names the variable and the criterion for dividing the cases into two groups. You can name only one variable. You can use any of three different methods to define the two groups. In the first method, a single value in parentheses groups all cases with a code equal to or greater than the value into one group and the remaining cases into the other group. For example, the command

```
T-TEST GROUPS=WORLD(2) /VARIABLES=NTCPUR
```

groups together all cases with the value of WORLD greater than or equal to 2. The remaining cases go into the other group.

Alternatively, if you specify two values in parentheses, one group includes cases with the first value on the grouping variable, and the other includes cases with the second value, as in:

```
T-TEST  GROUPS=WORLD(1,3) /VARIABLES=NTCPUR
```

In this example, cases with values other than 1 or 3 for variable WORLD are not used.

If the grouping variable has only two values, coded 1 and 2, respectively, you do not have to specify a value list. For example, the command

```
T-TEST  GROUPS=SEX /VARIABLES=GRADES
```

groups all cases having the value 1 for SEX into one group and cases having the value 2 for SEX into the other group. All other cases are not used.

B.174 VARIABLES Subcommand

The VARIABLES subcommand names the variables being analyzed. You can use only numeric variables. The command

```
T-TEST  GROUPS=WORLD(1,3) /VARIABLES=NTCPRI NTCSAL NTCPUR
```

compares the means of the two groups defined by WORLD for the variables NTCPRI, NTCSAL, and NTCPUR, while

```
T-TEST  GROUPS=WORLD(1,3) /VARIABLES=NTCPRI TO MCLOTHES
```

compares the means of the groups defined by WORLD for all variables between and including NTCPRI and MCLOTHES.

B.175 PAIRS Subcommand

A typical application of a paired-samples test is the comparison of pre- and post-course test scores for students in a class. To obtain a paired-samples *t* test, use the PAIRS subcommand, as in:

```
T-TEST  PAIRS=WCLOTHES MCLOTHES
```

You can name only numeric variables. If you specify a list of variables, each variable is compared with every other variable. For example, the command

```
T-TEST PAIRS=TEACHER CONSTRUC MANAGER
```

compares TEACHER with CONSTRUC, TEACHER with MANAGER, and CONSTRUC with MANAGER.

You can use the keyword WITH to request a test comparing every variable to the left of the keyword with every variable to the right of the keyword. For example,

```
T-TEST  PAIRS=TEACHER MANAGER WITH CONSTRUC ENGINEER
```

compares TEACHER with CONSTRUC, TEACHER with ENGINEER, MANAGER with CONSTRUC, and MANAGER with ENGINEER. TEACHER is not compared with MANAGER, and CONSTRUC is not compared with ENGINEER.

You can use the slash to separate analysis lists, as in

```
T-TEST  PAIRS=WCLOTHES MCLOTHES/NTCPRI WITH NTCPUR NTCSAL
```

which specifies two analysis lists.

(PAIRED) Keyword. Use the keyword (PAIRED) for testing paired samples. If you specify the keyword (PAIRED) in addition to the keyword WITH on the PAIRS subcommand, as in

```
T-TEST  PAIRS=TEACHER MANAGER WITH CONSTRUC ENGINEER (PAIRED)
```

TEACHER is paired with CONSTRUC and MANAGER is paired with ENGINEER. You must name or imply the same number of variables on each side of the keyword WITH. If the number of variables is not equal, SPSS^X will generate as many T-TESTS as it can and will then issue a warning indicating the number of variables is not equal.

(With releases before 3.0, substitute the command OPTION 5 for the (PAIRED) keyword.)

B.176 Independent and Paired Designs

You can request both independent- and paired-samples tests on a single T-TEST command. To do so, specify the GROUPS, VARIABLES, and PAIRS subcommands.

```
T-TEST GROUPS= WORLD(1,3) /VARIABLES=NTCPRI NTCSAL NTCPUR
      /PAIRS=WCLOTHES MCLOTHES
```

B.177 One-Tailed Significance Levels

By default, the probability is based on the two-tailed test. This is appropriate when significant differences in either direction are of interest. When theoretical considerations predict that the difference will be in a given direction (such as the Group 1 mean will be higher than the Group 2 mean), a one-tailed test is appropriate. To calculate the one-tailed probability, divide the two-tailed probability by 2.

B.178 MISSING Subcommand

By default, T-TEST deletes cases with missing values on an analysis-by-analysis basis. For independent-samples tests, cases missing on either the grouping variable or the analysis variable are excluded from the analysis of that variable. For paired-samples tests, a case missing on either of the variables in a given pair is excluded from the analysis of that pair. The following keyword options are available using the MISSING subcommand:

ANALYSIS *Delete cases with missing values on an analysis-by-analysis basis.* This is the default if you omit the MISSING subcommand.

LISTWISE *Exclude missing values listwise.* A case missing for any variable specified on either the GROUPS or the VARIABLES subcommand is excluded from any independent sample analysis. A case missing for any variable specified on the PAIRS subcommand is excluded from any paired sample analysis. (With releases before 3.0, substitute the command OPTION 2.)

INCLUDE *Include user-defined missing values.* User-missing values are included in the analysis. (With releases before 3.0, substitute the command OPTION 1.)

The ANALYSIS and LISTWISE keywords are mutually exclusive; however, each can be specified with INCLUDE.

B.179 FORMAT Subcommand

By default, T-TEST prints variable labels. You can suppress variable labels by specifying NOLABELS on the FORMAT subcommand:

LABELS *Print variable labels.* This is the default if you omit the FORMAT subcommand.

NOLABELS *Suppress variable labels.* (With releases before 3.0, substitute the command OPTION 3.)

B.180 Limitations

The following limitation applies to procedure T-TEST:

- A maximum of 1 GROUPS and 1 VARIABLES subcommand per T-TEST command. Otherwise, T-TEST is constrained only by the amount of work space available on your computer.

Appendix C

Answers to Exercises

Chapter 2

Syntax

1. a. The METHOD subcommand must follow the DEPENDENT subcommand. The METHOD keyword is optional as of Release 2.1 but is an error in earlier releases. Specify the variable-entry keyword alone.

```
>ERROR   10505  LINE  15, COLUMN  4, TEXT: METHOD
>MISPLACED REGRESSION METHOD SUBCOMMAND--The METHOD subcommand must follow a
>DEPENDENT subcommand or another METHOD subcommand.  It cannot follow any other
>subcommand.  Check for a missing DEPENDENT subcommand.
>THIS COMMAND NOT EXECUTED.
```

   b. The CRITERIA subcommand must precede the METHOD subcommand.

```
>ERROR   10595  LINE  17, (END OF COMMAND)
>INVALID REGRESSION SUBCOMMAND ORDER--CRITERIA, STATISTICS, ORIGIN or NOORIGIN
>subcommands should be placed directly before the DEPENDENT subcommand for the
>equation to which they apply.  They should not be placed before the position
>indicated above.
>THIS COMMAND NOT EXECUTED.
```

   Specifications can be split across command lines (see DESCRIPTIVES). The equals sign following a subcommand keyword is optional (see METHOD).

   c. There is no DEPENDENT subcommand.

```
>ERROR   10505  LINE  15, COLUMN  4, TEXT: METHOD
>MISPLACED REGRESSION METHOD SUBCOMMAND--The METHOD subcommand must follow a
>DEPENDENT subcommand or another METHOD subcommand.  It cannot follow any other
>subcommand.  Check for a missing DEPENDENT subcommand.
>THIS COMMAND NOT EXECUTED.
```

   The slash that separates subcommands can either follow one subcommand or precede the other.

   d. The SCATTERPLOT subcommand must follow the METHOD subcommand.

```
>ERROR   10508  LINE  10, COLUMN  4, TEXT: SCATTER
>MISPLACED SUBCOMMAND ON REGRESSION COMMAND--Only the METHOD subcommand can
>follow a DEPENDENT subcommand.
>THIS COMMAND NOT EXECUTED.
```

   Except for the first or only command words, keywords can be truncated up to the first three characters (see DEP, SCATTER, STEP, etc.)

2.
```
REGRESSION SELECT MARITAL EQ 1
  /DESCRIPTIVES
  /VARIABLES=JOBSATIS STRESS INCOME HOMEOWNR RACE EXERCISE
             SEX DIETYPE OVERWGHT PETS AGE ILLFREQ
  /DEPENDENT=ILLFREQ
  /METHOD=STEPWISE
  /CASEWISE=OUTLIERS(2) PLOT(ZRESID)
```

3. a. REMOVE must be followed by a variable list.

```
>ERROR   10524  LINE  25, (END OF COMMAND)
>MISSING VARIABLE LIST ON REGRESSION METHOD SUBCOMMAND--The REMOVE method
>requires a variable list.
>THIS COMMAND NOT EXECUTED.
```

   Misspelling DEPENDENT has no effect since the error occurs beyond the third character.

   b. The SCATTERPLOT subcommand should specify the residual and predicted value names preceded by an asterisk to distinguish them from regular variables, as in

```
/SCATTERPLOT=(*RESID,*PRED)
```

```
>ERROR   10543  LINE  12, COLUMN 17, TEXT: RESID
>INVALID VARIABLE NAME ON REGRESSION SCATTERPLOT OR PARTIALPLOT subcommand.
>The variable specified does not exist on the file.  Check for a misspelled
>name.
>THIS COMMAND NOT EXECUTED.
```

c. OVERWGHT is not listed in the VARIABLES subcommand.

```
>ERROR     714  LINE  13, COLUMN 17, TEXT: OVERWGHT
>A variable was not named or implied on the primary variable list.
>THIS COMMAND NOT EXECUTED.
```

d. The STATISTICS subcommand must precede the DEPENDENT subcommand.

```
>ERROR   10508  LINE  11, COLUMN  5, TEXT: STATISTICS
>MISPLACED SUBCOMMAND ON REGRESSION COMMAND--Only the METHOD subcommand can
>follow a DEPENDENT subcommand.
>THIS COMMAND NOT EXECUTED.
```

4.
```
REGRESSION VARIABLES=DISTRICT PCTHOMES PCTBUSNS BUSNSTYP
             AVGINCOM PCTSNGLE CATALOGS SALESPN TVADS RADIOADS
             NEWSPADS SALES
  /STATISTICS=COEFF HISTORY CI
  /DEPENDENT=SALES
  /METHOD=FORWARD
  /RESIDUALS=HISTOGRAM(RESID)
  /SCATTERPLOT=(*RESID,*PRED)
```

5. No. Since the TOLERANCE keyword belongs on the CRITERIA subcommand, the correct command is

```
REGRESSION VARIABLES=MATHTEST IQ MTHANXTY SEX
             OCCUPATN EDUCATN
  /CRITERIA=TOLERANCE(.001)
  /DEPENDENT=MATHTEST
  /METHOD=BACKWARD
```

Or, if you a running a release of SPSS^X prior to Release 2.1, the method subcommand is

```
/BACKWARD
```

Statistical Concepts

1. This hypothesis is of interest because it specifies that there is no linear relationship between the dependent variable and the independent variables.
2. You are checking the assumption of independence of errors when you examine a casewise serial plot.
3. a. H_0: $\beta_1=\beta_2= \ldots \beta_k=0$
   b. The coefficients for the variables entered at this step are 0, or the increase in R^2 for the population when these variables are entered is 0.
4. Multiple R^2 cannot decrease as additional variables are entered into an equation.
5. No. The band must be narrowest at the mean, $\overline{X}$.
6. You can make the best predictions of the mean of Y at the mean of the X's. The best predictions of values of Y are also at $\overline{X}$.
7. a. The assumption of equality of variance appears to be violated. As the predicted values increase in magnitude, so does the spread of the residuals.
   b. Since there is definite curvature in the residuals, the assumption of linearity appears to be violated.
   c. There appears to be a pattern to the residuals. Groups of negative residuals are followed by groups of positive residuals, suggesting that the observations are not independent.
   d. The assumption of normality appears to be violated since the histogram of residuals is definitely not normal.
   e. The normal probability plot suggests that the normality assumption is violated.
8. The variable SEX would be the next to enter since it has the largest F value and this value exceeds 3.84.
9. The variable WORK would be removed next since it has the smallest F value and the F value is less than 3.
10. When several variables are very highly correlated, including all of them in a regression model can lead to computational difficulties and unstable coefficients. In this case the squared multiple correlation between X4 and the other independent variables, X1 and X3, is greater than 0.9999.
11. $R^2 = 28.9/49.2 = 0.587$

```
ANALYSIS OF VARIANCE
                    DF        SUM OF SQUARES       MEAN SQUARE
REGRESSION           1              28.90000          28.90000
RESIDUAL             3              20.30000           6.76667

F =         4.27094         SIGNIF F =  .1307
```

12.
```
CASEWISE PLOT OF STANDARDIZED RESIDUAL

*: SELECTED  M: MISSING

              -3.0            0.0            3.0
  CASE # X    O:..............:..............:O   Y        *PRED       *RESID
     1 1      .               . *            .    7       6.0000       1.0000
     2 2      .               . *            .    9       7.7000       1.3000
     3 3      .        *      .              .    6       9.4000      -3.4000
     4 4      .              *.              .   10      11.1000      -1.1000
     5 5      .               .    *         .   15      12.8000       2.2000
  CASE # X    O:..............:..............:O   Y        *PRED       *RESID
              -3.0            0.0            3.0
```

13.
```
------------------ VARIABLES IN THE EQUATION ------------------

VARIABLE             B         SE B          T   SIG T

WORK             23.78        21.56       1.10    .271
MINORITY       -939.86       252.80      -3.72    .000
SEX           -1617.53       240.70      -6.72    .000
EDLEVEL         630.05        40.78      15.45    .000
AGE              33.43        15.43       2.17    .031
(CONSTANT)    -2183.79       775.24      -2.82    .005
```

14. a.
```
CASE SEQ     COOKS' DISTANCE

       1              .0007
       4             2.2982
```

b. Case 4.

c. Yes. If Case 4 is excluded, there is little relationship between X and Y.

15. a.
```
SEQNUM        AGE     MAHALANOBIS' DISTANCE

     2         27               2.3169
     3         60               2.3169
     4         41                .0532
     5         76               8.9889
```

b. Case 5.

16. Yes, because X1 and X2 are uncorrelated and the coefficients are standardized. X2 would be the most important variable by itself for predicting Y.

17. The FIN value is less than the FOUT value. SPSS^X issues the following warning and proceeds.

```
>WARNING 10554  LINE   7, COMMAND NAME: REGRESSION
>CONFLICTING CRITERIA ON REGRESSION CRITERIA SUBCOMMAND--FOUT (F-to-enter) is
>greater than FIN (F-to-enter).  REGRESSION has reset FOUT to 0.9*FIN.  If FOUT
>is NOT less than FIN and the STEPWISE method is used, the same variable might
>be entered and then removed in a cycle that continues until it exceeds the
>number of steps allowed for the equation.
```

Chapter 3

Syntax

1. The first METHOD subcommand is not preceded by an ANALYSIS subcommand. This is not an error, but you are warned that the entire variable list is used. Since the ANALYSIS subcommand that is specified names the complete variable list, the TO convention is more convenient. The real error is that the sum of the PRIORS values is not 1. Therefore, a correct command is

```
DISCRIMINANT GROUPS=CRMEVICT(1,3)
   /VARIABLES=SES SEX RACE NBRHOOD DEMEANOR MARITAL AGE
    PBLCTRAN INCOME
   /ANALYSIS=SES TO INCOME
   /METHOD=DIRECT
   /ANALYSIS=SES TO INCOME
   /METHOD=WILKS
   /TOLERANCE=0.05
   /PRIORS=0.5 0.3 0.2
   /STATISTICS=TABLE
   /PLOT=CASES [1]
```

```
SINCE ANALYSIS= WAS OMITTED FOR THE FIRST ANALYSIS ALL VARIABLES
ON THE VARIABLES= LIST WILL BE ENTERED AT LEVEL 1.
WARNING.  THE SUM OF PRIOR PROBABILITIES IS    1.100000, NOT 1.0.
```

Leading zeroes in value specifications are optional (see TOLERANCE and PRIORS).

[1]With releases before 3.0, replace the DISCRIMINANT command with the following:

```
DISCRIMINANT GROUPS=CRMEVICT(1,3)
  /VARIABLES=SES SEX RACE NBRHOOD DEMEANOR MARITAL AGE
   PBLCTRAN INCOME
  /ANALYSIS=SES TO INCOME
  /METHOD=DIRECT
  /ANALYSIS=SES TO INCOME
  /METHOD=WILKS
  /TOLERANCE=0.05
  /PRIORS=0.5 0.3 0.2
STATISTICS 13 14
```

2.
```
DISCRIMINANT GROUPS=RISK(1,3)
 /VARIABLES=INCOME CREDIT AGEHEAD CHILDREN JOBTIME
  RESTIME HOMEOWNR
 /METHOD=MAHAL
 /TOLERANCE=.01
 /PRIORS=.3 .2 .5
 /STATISTICS=BOXM TABLE
 /PLOT=MAP SEPARATE
```
[2]

3.
```
DISCRIMINANT GROUPS=EMOTION(1,2)
  /VARIABLES=ETHNIC SEX IQ SES EMOTINDX INCOME EDUCATN
  /METHOD=WILKS
  /PIN=.01
  /POUT=.01
  /PRIORS=SIZE
  /STATISTICS=RAW TABLE
  /PLOT=CASES
```
[3]

4. a. Only one GROUPS subcommand can be used per DISCRIMINANT command.

```
>ERROR   10439  LINE  28, COLUMN 11, TEXT: GRADEMPL
>Unrecognized text appears on the DISCRIMINANT command.  The only recognized
>subcommands are: GROUPS, VARIABLES, SELECT, ANALYSIS, METHOD, TOLERANCE,
>MAXSTEPS, FIN, FOUT, PIN, POUT, VIN, FUNCTIONS, PRIORS, SAVE, PROBS, and
>SCORES.
>THIS COMMAND NOT EXECUTED.
```

   b. EXERCISE is not listed in the VARIABLES subcommand.

```
>ERROR     711  LINE  35, COLUMN 39, TEXT: EXERCISE
>Undefined variable name.  Check spelling, verify the existence of this
>variable.
>THIS COMMAND NOT EXECUTED.
```

   c. There are only three PRIORS probabilities, and four are needed.

```
>ERROR   10436  LINE  42, (END OF COMMAND)
>You specified an invalid value on the PRIORS subcommand on the DISCRIMINANT
>command.  Each value should lie in the range 0 to 1, there should be as many
>values as groups, and the sum of the values should be one.
>THIS COMMAND NOT EXECUTED.
```

   d. The GROUPS subcommand must specify two integer values of a range.

```
>ERROR   10468  LINE  44, COLUMN 31, TEXT: )
>You specified an invalid range in the GROUPS subcommand in a DISCRIMINANT
>command.  Specify an integer pair in which the first number is small than the
>second.
>THIS COMMAND NOT EXECUTED.
```

Statistical Concepts

1.

CASE SEQ	DISCRIMINANT SCORE
1	109.87
2	129.26
3	122.24

2. No. When the discriminating variables are correlated, a standardized discriminant-function coeffiecient indicates only the importance of the variable when the other variables are also included in the discriminant function.

3. a. Eta^2=0.3183. It is the proportion of the total variance in the discriminant scores attributable to differences between the groups.
   b. Eigenvalue=0.4668. It is the ratio of between-groups variability to within-groups variability.
   c. Wilks' lambda=0.6817. It is the proportion of the total variance in the discriminant scores not accounted for by differences between the groups.

---

[2]With releasese before 3.0, replace the DISCRIMINANT command with the following:

```
DISCRIMINANT GROUPS=RISK(1,3)
  /VARIABLES=INCOME CREDIT AGEHEAD CHILDREN JOBTIME
   RESTIME HOMEOWNR
  /METHOD=MAHAL
  /TOLERANCE=.01
  /PRIORS=.3 .2 .5
STATISTICS 7 13 10 16
```

[3]With release before 3.0, replace the DISCRIMINANT command with the following:

```
DISCRIMINANT GROUPS=EMOTION(1,2)
 /VARIABLES=ETHNIC SEX IQ SES EMOTINDX INCOME EDUCATN
 /METHOD=WILKS
 /PIN=.01
 /POUT=.01
 /PRIORS=SIZE
STATISTICS 11 13 14
```

4.

VARIABLE	B DISCRIMINANT	B REGRESSION
WEIGHT	-.8963	-.3543
HEIGHT	.0544	.0215
AGE	-2.8958	-1.1446
BLOODPRS	-4.2636	-1.6852

5. X5.

6. The program is working very badly. The "eigenvalue" is negative, "Wilks' lambda" is greater than 1, and "eta^2" is not the square of the canonical correlation.

7. a. False.
   b. True.
   c. False.
   d. True.
   e. False.
   f. True.

8. X1, X3, and X7.

9.

CASE SEQ	P(FEMALE|D)	P(MALE|D)	GROUP CLASSIFICATION
8	.3277	.6723	MALE
9	.5338	.4662	FEMALE
10	.6130	.3870	FEMALE
11	.4957	.5043	MALE
12	.0166	.9834	MALE

10. Function B, because it separates the two groups better than Function A.

11.

FUNCTION A		NO. OF CASES	PREDICTED GROUP MEMBERSHIP 1	2
GROUP EUROPEAN ORIGIN	1	17	16	1
			94.12%	5.88%
GROUP ASIAN ORIGIN	2	42	0	42
			0.0%	100.0%

PERCENT OF GROUPED CASES CORRECTLY CLASSIFIED: 98.31%

FUNCTION B		NO. OF CASES	PREDICTED GROUP MEMBERSHIP 1	2
GROUP EUROPEAN ORIGIN	1	17	15	2
			88.24%	11.76%
GROUP ASIAN ORIGIN	2	42	2	40
			4.76%	95.24%

PERCENT OF GROUPED CASES CORRECTLY CLASSIFIED: 93.22%

Function B, because it has fewer variables and a misclassification rate only slightly higher than that for Function A.

12. a. 32.22%.
    b. Yes, since the function correctly classifies 75% of the frequent users and doesn't misclassify any of the other users as frequent users.

13. a.

CANONICAL DISCRIMINANT FUNCTIONS

FUNCTION	EIGENVALUE	PERCENT OF VARIANCE	CUMULATIVE PERCENT	CANONICAL CORRELATION	AFTER FUNCTION	WILKS' LAMBDA
1	4.8490	65.20	65.20	.9105	0	.0336
2	1.7056	22.93	88.13	.7940	1	.1963
3	0.8826	11.87	100.00	.6847	2	.5312

    b. Function 3.

14. a. False.
    b. False.
    c. True.
    d. False.
    e. False.
    f. True.

15. Yes. Given the small sample sizes, these histograms are reasonably consistent with the assumption of multivariate normality.

16. *F*-to-enter = 58.218. PRODUCT should be included.

17.
```
CASE SEQ     CLASSIFICATION

   10              3
   11              3
   12              2
   13              3
   14              1
```

Chapter 4

Syntax

1.
```
FACTOR VARIABLES=PCTHOMES PASTSALE DSTRCTYP AVGINCOM
       PCTBUSNS BUSNSTYP PCTFAMLY AVGAGE AVGEDUC
       PRICE
  /EXTRACTION=ML
  /PRINT=DEFAULT REPR
  /PLOT=EIGEN ROTATION(1,2)
  /ROTATION=NOROTATE
  /CRITERIA=DELTA(-.5)
  /ROTATION=OBLIMIN
```

2. a. The VARIABLES subcommand is missing.

```
>ERROR   11295  LINE  12, COLUMN  8, TEXT: ANALYSIS
>The required VARIABLES subcommand is missing.
>THIS COMMAND NOT EXECUTED.
```

A correct version of the command is

```
FACTOR VARIABLES=IQ GPA TESTSCOR STRESS SAT PSYCHTST ANXIETY
                 DEPRESSN HOSTILTY CONFDNCE PASTSCOR
  /ANALYSIS=IQ TO PSYCHTST
  /EXTRACTION=ML
  /ROTATION=VARIMAX
  /ANALYSIS=TESTSCOR ANXIETY TO PASTSCOR
  /EXTRACTION=ML
  /ROTATION=EQUAMAX
```

The variable lists on the two ANALYSIS subcommands use the shorter TO convention based on the order of variables named on the VARIABLES subcommand.

b. The SES variable named on the second ANALYSIS subcommand is not named on the VARIABLES subcommand.

```
>ERROR     714  LINE  21, COLUMN 40, TEXT: SES
>A variable was not named or implied on the primary variable list.
>THIS COMMAND NOT EXECUTED.
```

A correct version is

```
FACTOR VARIABLES=SES IQ GPA TESTSCOR STRESS
       SAT PSYCHTST NBRHOOD
  /ANALYSIS=IQ TO PSYCHTST
  /PLOT=ROTATION(2,3)
  /ANALYSIS=ALL
  /ROTATION=EQUAMAX
```

The second ANALYSIS subcommand uses keyword ALL to request the entire list of variables named on the VARIABLES subcommand.

c. The order of variables indicated by the keyword TO on the first ANALYSIS subcommand should refer to their order on the VARIABLES subcommand.

```
>ERROR     713  LINE  24, COLUMN 27, TEXT: TESTSCOR
>The form VARX TO VARY to refer to a range of variables has been used
>incorrectly.
>THIS COMMAND NOT EXECUTED.
```

d. The SCREE keyword does not exist.

```
>ERROR   11217  LINE  30, COLUMN  9, TEXT: SCREE
>An invalid keyword is used on the PLOT subcommand.  Valid keywords are EIGEN
>and ROTATION.
>THIS COMMAND NOT EXECUTED.
```

The correct keyword is EIGEN, as in

```
FACTOR VARIABLES=IQ GPA TESTSCOR STRESS SAT
       PSYCHTST NBRHOOD SES
  /EXTRACTION=ML
  /ROTATION=OBLIMIN
  /PRINT=REPR KMO
  /PLOT=EIGEN
```

The absence of an ANALYSIS subcommand is not an error. However, it generates the message

```
>NOTE    11284
>Since the ANALYSIS subcommand is not used, all variables on the VARIABLES
>subcommand will be used for the first analysis.
```

3.
```
FACTOR VARIABLES=DRUGUSE PEERS FAMSTABL NBRHOOD SCHLACHV
       ALCOHOL ALIENATN RECREATN SPORTS SES AGE
       CRIME
  /PRINT=CORRELATION EXTRACTION ROTATION
  /ROTATION=QUARTIMAX
```

4. a. Only one VARIABLES subcommand can be used per FACTOR command.

   b. The person who wrote the command apparently wants to obtain two factor analyses using different variables. The correct command needed is

```
FACTOR VARIABLES=IQ GPA TESTSCOR SAT EDUCATN SES NBRHOOD
  /ANALYSIS=IQ TO EDUCATN
  /EXTRACTION=ML
  /ANALYSIS=ALL
  /EXTRACTION=ML
```

5. No. Both factor analyses will use extraction based on a minimum eigenvalue of 1.5, since the CRITERIA subcommand applies to both ANALYSIS subcommands. She needs a second CRITERIA subcommand following the second ANALYSIS subcommand to reestablish the default.

6.
```
FACTOR VARIABLES=WORDLNTH PARLNTH VOCAB COMPRHSN TOPIC
                 INTEREST BCKGRND IQ EDUCATN
  /ANALYSIS=ALL
  /PLOT=EIGEN ROTATION(1,2)
  /ROTATION=QUARTIMAX
  /ANALYSIS=ALL
  /PLOT=ROTATION(3,4)
  /ROTATION=QUARTIMAX
  /ANALYSIS=ALL
  /EXTRACTION=ML
  /PLOT=EIGEN ROTATION(1,2)
  /ROTATION=VARIMAX
  /ANALYSIS=ALL
  /PLOT=ROTATION(3,4)
  /ROTATION=VARIMAX
```

The problem poses four analyses, two to plot each two-factor plot for a principal components extraction and quartimax rotation, and two with maximum-likelihood extraction and varimax rotation. The ROTATION keyword on the PLOT subcommand can be specified only once per analysis.

Statistical Concepts

1. Factor 1 appears to represent recreational interests, while Factor 2 seems to represent status. Political activity and IQ seem to have nothing to do with either factor.

2. a. $TESTSCOR=0.41127F_1+0.34432F_2-0.14892F_3$
   $PSYCHTST=0.11383F_1+0.11524F_2+0.89989F_3$

   b. Factor 1 appears to represent mental capabilities, Factor 2 represents status, and Factor 3 represents psychological state. Variables GPA, SAT, and TESTSCORE, which are achievement scores, don't seem to relate to any of the factors.

3. a.

VARIABLE	COMMUNALITY	FACTOR	EIGENVALUE	PCT OF VAR	CUM PCT
AGE	1.00000	1	2.27	32.4	32.4
MEDHIST	1.00000	2	2.05	29.3	61.7
BLOODPRS	1.00000	3	1.73	24.7	86.4
WEIGHT	1.00000	4	.64	9.1	95.5
IQ	1.00000	5	.15	2.1	97.6
PSYCHTST	1.00000	6	.10	1.4	99.0
STRESS	1.00000	7	.07	1.0	100.0

   b.

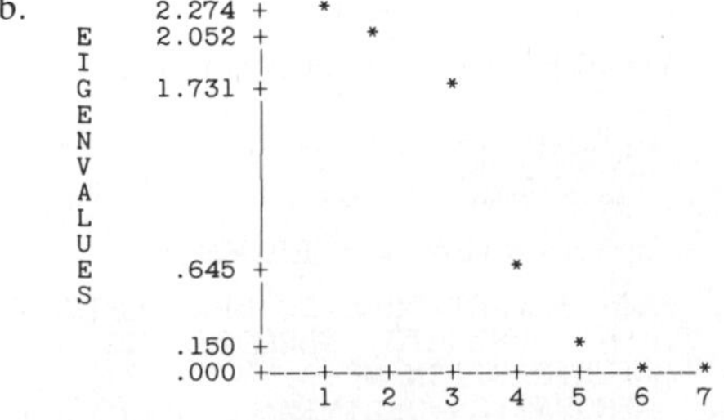

   c. Factors 1, 2, and 3, since each accounts for a substantial portion of the variance and the other four factors account for only 13.6% of the variance.

4. a.

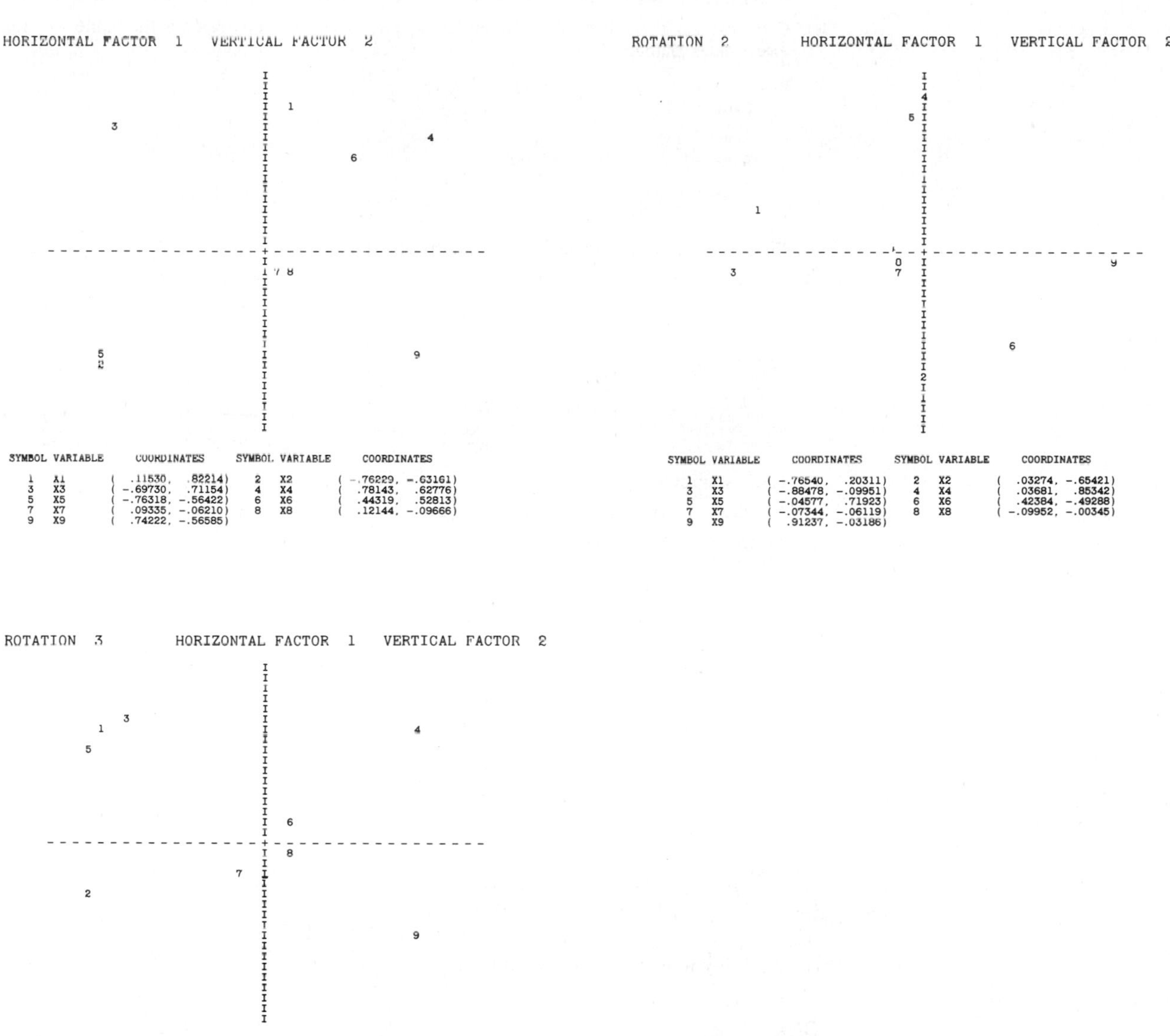

SYMBOL	VARIABLE	COORDINATES	SYMBOL	VARIABLE	COORDINATES
1	X1	(.11530, .82214)	2	X2	(-.76229, -.63161)
3	X3	(-.69730, .71154)	4	X4	(.78143, .62776)
5	X5	(-.76318, -.56422)	6	X6	(.44319, .52813)
7	X7	(.09335, -.06210)	8	X8	(.12144, -.09666)
9	X9	(.74222, -.56585)			

SYMBOL	VARIABLE	COORDINATES	SYMBOL	VARIABLE	COORDINATES
1	X1	(-.76540, .20311)	2	X2	(.03274, -.65421)
3	X3	(-.88478, -.09951)	4	X4	(.03681, .85342)
5	X5	(-.04577, .71923)	6	X6	(.42384, -.49288)
7	X7	(-.07344, -.06119)	8	X8	(-.09952, -.00345)
9	X9	(.91237, -.03186)			

SYMBOL	VARIABLE	COORDINATES	SYMBOL	VARIABLE	COORDINATES
1	X1	(-.72702, .61164)	2	X2	(-.81423, -.24321)
3	X3	(-.60819, .71522)	4	X4	(.71828, .62192)
5	X5	(-.79945, .50163)	6	X6	(.11281, .10554)
7	X7	(-.09282, -.12812)	8	X8	(.13230, -.03941)
9	X9	(.73359, -.50152)			

b. Rotation 2 produces the most easily interpreted factors.

5. No. The Factor 1 "loading " of 1.04930 on X5 is not possible.
6. The first factor correlation matrix.
7. PASTSALE, OCCUPATN, URBAN, INCOME, EDUCATN, AGE, RECREATN, SEX.
8. Only part of the table can be completed. The communalities remain the same but the eigenvalues change.
9. a. True.
   b. False.
   c. True.
   d. False.
   e. False.
   f. True.
10. Figure 2 cannot be completed with the information given.
11. FACTOR MATRIX:

	FACTOR 1	FACTOR 2	FACTOR 3
DEPRESSN	.070	.702	-.050
ANXIETY	-.087	.810	.074
STRESS	.216	.733	.326
CONFDNCE	.027	-.049	-.882
PERFORM	-.080	.063	-.742
AGGRESSN	.879	.131	.011
HOSTILTY	.917	.178	-.078
AUTHORTN	.909	-.065	.062

FINAL STATISTICS

VARIABLE	COMMUNALITY
DEPRESSN	.500
ANXIETY	.669
STRESS	.690
CONFDNCE	.781
PERFORM	.561
AGGRESSN	.790
HOSTILTY	.879
AUTHORTN	.834

12. FINAL STATISTICS

VARIABLE	COMMUNALITY	FACTOR	EIGENVALUE	PCT OF VAR	CUM PCT
PROGOVT	.85284	1	2.37	33.9	33.9
INCOME	.60793	2	1.85	26.4	60.3
EDUCATN	.88507	3	1.66	23.7	84.0
RACE	.88403				
UNEMPLOY	.82279				
HOMEOWNR	.91417				
CONSERV	.91287				

13. a. ESTIMATED CORRELATIONS

	X1	X2	X3	X4
X1	1.000			
X2	.495	1.000		
X3	.705	.375	1.000	
X4	.573	.275	.571	1.000

b. RESIDUALS

	X1	X2	X3	X4
X1	******			
X2	.042	******		
X3	.195	-.040	******	
X4	-.015	-.007	.039	******

c. 1.

d. Fairly well, given the answer to (c).

Chapter 5

Syntax

1. a. An inappropriate distance measure is requested.

```
>WARNING 14220
>CENTROID, MEDIAN and WARD agglomerative methods are recommended for use with
>squared euclidean measure.
```

b. Noninteger POWER parameters are specified and the CLUSTER minimum and maximum values are reversed.

```
>ERROR   14209  LINE   23, COLUMN 18, TEXT: .5
>The POWER specification is invalid.  The correct format is POWER(p,r), where p
>is the power and r is the root of the Minkowski measure.
>THIS COMMAND NOT EXECUTED.

>ERROR   14212  LINE  24, COLUMN 29, TEXT: 1
>The level specification of CLUSTER in subcommand PRINT is invalid.  The
>correct format is CLUSTER(min,max) or just CLUSTER(n).
```

c. Noninteger HICICLE parameters are specified and MEANSUB is not a valid keyword for the MISSING subcommand.

```
>ERROR   14216  LINE  31, COLUMN 23, TEXT: .5
>The PLOT specification is invalid.  The valid keywords are: VICICLE(optional
>level specification), HICICLE(optional level specification) and DENDOGRAM.
>The optional level specification can be one, two or three numbers.
>THIS COMMAND NOT EXECUTED.

>ERROR   14204  LINE  32, COLUMN 12, TEXT: MEANSUB
>The MISSING specification is invalid.  The valid keywords are: LISTWISE,
>INCLUDE and DEFAULT.
```

d. Only one distance measure can be specified. Also, the CLUSTER keyword specifies too many values.

```
>ERROR   14209  LINE  26, COLUMN 19, TEXT: BLOCK
>Only one distance measure is allowed.
>THIS COMMAND NOT EXECUTED.
>ERROR   14212  LINE  27, COLUMN 23, TEXT: 2
>The level specification of CLUSTER in subcommand PRINT is invalid.  The
>correct format is CLUSTER(min,max) or just CLUSTER(n).
```

2. HICICLE and DENDROGRAM belong on the PLOT subcommand.

```
CLUSTER SWEETNES TARNESS SALTINES BTTRNESS CALORIES PROTEIN
        CARBHYDR FAT PALTBLTY
  /METHOD=BAVERAGE WAVERAGE SINGEL COMPLETE
  /MEASURE=DEFAULT
  /PRINT=SCHEDULE CLUSTER(1,9) DISTANCE
  /PLOT=HICICLE(1,9,1) DENDROGRAM
  /ID=TYPE
  /MATRIX=IN(*)4
```

3.

```
CLUSTER WINGSPAN BEAKCURV BEAKWDTH MIGRLNTH MATELNTH
        FSHDIET INSDIET GRNDIET
  /METHOD=WAVERAGE SINGLE COMPLETE
  /MEASURE=POWER(4,4)
  /PRINT=CLUSTER(5,20)
  /PLOT=HICICLE(5,20,1)
  /ID=BIRD
```

4. No. The METHOD subcommand can be specified only once.

```
>ERROR   14203  LINE  52, COLUMN  4, TEXT: MEASURE
>Subcommand can only appear once.
>THIS COMMAND NOT EXECUTED.
```

The solution is to specify two CLUSTER commands, as in

```
CLUSTER WEIGHT LENGTH WIDTH HGHTLEN WINDOWS CHROME DOODADS
  /METHOD SINGLE
  /MEASURE EUCLID
  /PRINT CLUSTER(5,10)
  /PLOT HICICLE(5,10,1)
CLUSTER WEIGHT LENGTH WIDTH HGHTLEN WINDOWS CHROME DOODADS
  /METHOD COMPLETE
  /MEASURE BLOCK
  /PRINT CLUSTER(5,10)
  /PLOT HICICLE(5,10,1)
```

Statistical Concepts

1. a. Squared Euclidean Dissimilarity Coefficient Matrix

Case	1	2	3
2	37.5100		
3	11.8900	29.5400	
4	15.6600	39.2900	1.1300

b. Cases 3 and 4.

2. a. Cluster 1: SWISS, BLUE. Cluster 2: FARMERS, COTTAGE. Cluster 3: All other cheeses.

b. Cluster 1: SWISS, BLUE. Cluster 2: FARMERS, COTTAGE. Cluster 3: COLBY. Cluster 4: MONTEREY JACK, CHEDDAR. Cluster 5: EDAM, GOUDA, MOZZARELLA.

c. Cluster 1: FARMERS, COTTAGE. Cluster 2: MOZZARELLA, GOUDA, EDAM. Each remaining case constitutes a single cluster.

---

[4]With releases before 3.0, replace the CLUSTER command with the following:

```
CLUSTER SWEETNES TARNESS SALTINES BTTRNESS CALORIES PROTEIN
        CARBHYDR FAT PALTBLTY
  /METHOD=BAVERAGE WAVERAGE SINGEL COMPLETE
  /MEASURE=DEFAULT
  /PRINT=SCHEDULE CLUSTER(1,9) DISTANCE
  /PLOT=HICICLE(1,9,1) DENDROGRAM
  /ID=TYPE
  /READ=SIMILAR LOWER
```

3. a.

```
Agglomeration Schedule using Complete Linkage

        Clusters  Combined               Stage Cluster 1st Appears    Next
Stage   Cluster 1 Cluster 2  Coefficient   Cluster 1  Cluster 2       Stage

  1         2         3        .494757        0          0             2
  2         1         2        .582524        0          1             6
  3         4         5       1.146706        0          0             8
  4         6         8       1.247115        0          0             6
  5         9        10       1.912980        0          0             9
  6         1         6       3.659030        2          4             7
  7         1         7       6.030436        6          0             8
  8         1         4      16.585556        7          3             9
  9         1         9      25.452454        8          5             0
```

b. Stage 5.

4. a.

```
Dendrogram using Complete Linkage

                              Rescaled Distance Cluster Combine

         C A S E          0         5        10        15        20        25
Label              Seq    +---------+---------+---------+---------+---------+

CHEMIST             3     -+-------------------------------+
BIOCHMST            4     -+                               +-------------+
PHYSICST            5     ---+-----------------------------+             |
ENGINEER            6     ---+                                           |
PHYSICAN            1     -+-----------------------------------------------+
VETRNARN            2     -+
```

b. Three.

5. a.

```
Agglomeration Schedule using Complete Linkage

        Clusters  Combined               Stage Cluster 1st Appears    Next
Stage   Cluster 1 Cluster 2  Coefficient   Cluster 1  Cluster 2       Stage

  1         1         4        .560000        0          0             3
  2         2         5        .680000        0          0             3
  3         1         2      13.210000        1          2             4
  4         1         3      15.840000        3          0             0


Vertical Icicle Plot using Complete Linkage

    (Down) Number of Clusters  (Across) Case Label and number

      3  5  2  4  1
   1 +XXXXXXXXXXXXX
   2 +X  XXXXXXXXXX
   3 +X  XXXX  XXXX
   4 +X  X  X  XXXX
```

b. Three.

6. You shouldn't. At Stages 8 and 9, an existing cluster was split into two clusters.

7. a. False.
   b. False.
   c. False.
   d. False.
   e. False.
   f. False.

8.

```
Cluster Membership of Cases using Complete Linkage

                                      Number of Clusters

Label                    Case      6    5    4    3    2

CANDIDE                    1       1    1    1    1    1
BLEAK HOUSE                2       1    1    1    1    1
ANNA KARENINA              3       1    1    1    1    1
ODYSSEY                    4       2    2    2    2    2
TOM JONES                  5       3    3    1    1    1
OLIVER TWIST               6       4    4    3    3    1
MADAM BOVARY               7       1    1    1    1    1
PORTRAIT OF A LADY         8       1    1    1    1    1
MOBY DICK                  9       5    5    4    2    2
GREAT EXPECTATIONS        10       6    4    3    3    1
```

Chapter 6

Syntax

1. a. The BY keyword is needed between ESTEEM and SEX.

```
>ERROR    702  LINE   8, COLUMN 18, TEXT: (
>Unrecognized text was found where a variable list was expected.
>THIS COMMAND NOT EXECUTED.
```

b. A factor may not be changed to a covariate.

```
>ERROR   12106  LINE  11, COLUMN 25, TEXT: AGE
>The covariate list is incorrect in the ANALYSIS specification.
>THIS COMMAND NOT EXECUTED.
```

c. Only one ANALYSIS subcommand may be used per DESIGN subcommand.

```
>ERROR   12041  LINE  14, COLUMN  4, TEXT: ANALYSIS
>There are two ANALYSIS specifications that are not separated by a DESIGN
>specification.  Use ANALYSIS = ( list1/ list2/ .../ ) / in order to specify
>more than one analysis with the same design.  Alternatively, specify a design,
>e.g.  ANALYSIS(REPEATED)/, followed by DESIGN/, before the next ANALYSIS
>specification.
>THIS COMMAND NOT EXECUTED.
```

d. The ANALYSIS subcommand may not be used to specify factors.

```
>ERROR   12107  LINE  20, COLUMN 22, TEXT: BY
>There is an error in one of the following: dependent variable list,
>ANALYSIS(REPEATED), ANALYSIS(CONDITIONAL), or ANALYSIS(UNCONDITIONAL).
>THIS COMMAND NOT EXECUTED.
```

e. A slash is needed between the variable list and the first ANALYSIS command.

```
>ERROR     701  LINE  23, COLUMN  8, TEXT: ANALYSIS
>An undefined variable name, or a scratch or system variable was specified in a
>variable list which accepts only standard variables.  Check spelling, and
>verify the existence of this variable.
>THIS COMMAND NOT EXECUTED.
```

f. Only one BY keyword may be used.

```
>ERROR     702  LINE  29, COLUMN 43, TEXT: BY
>Unrecognized text was found where a variable list was expected.
>THIS COMMAND NOT EXECUTED.
```

g. The variable lists in an ANALYSIS subcommand may not overlap.

```
\ERROR   12043  LINE  33, (END OF COMMAND)
\A variable appears twice in the ANALYSIS specification.  To use the same
\variable more than once in the ANALYSIS, specify multiple ANALYSIS
\subcommands.
\THIS COMMAND NOT EXECUTED.
```

2. No. Only the main effects and two-way interactions have been specified in the DESIGN subcommand.
3. AGE is nested within the two-way interaction RACE by SEX.
4. All interaction terms.
5.

```
   /PARTITION(AGGRESSN)=(1,2,1,1)
```

6.

```
MANOVA STRESS PAIN ATTITUDE BY SURGERY(1,2) DRUG(1,4)
          ILLNESS(1,3) WITH STAYTIME
  /DESIGN=SURGERY DRUG ILLNESS SURGERY BY DRUG SURGERY
          BY ILLNESS DESIGN BY ILLNESS
  /PRINT=HOMOGENEITY(BARTLETT) CELLINFO(MEANS SSCP)
          ERROR(COR) SIGNIF(UNIV) PARAMETERS(ESTIM)
  /PCOMPS=COR ROTATE(VARIMAX)
  /DISCRIM=STAN 5
  /PLOT=BOXPLOTS NORMAL
```

7.

```
   /DESIGN=ANGER BY SEX + TEST BY SEX BY ANGER
```

8.

```
MANOVA GENRLATT PURCHASE NEED INCOME BY SEX
        FOLLOWUP HOMEOWNR(1,2)
  /ANALYSIS=(GENRLATT/PURCHASE WITH INTEREST/NEED)
        WITH INCOME
  /DESIGN
```

Statistical Concepts

1. a. True
   b. False
   c. False
   d. True
   e. False
   f. False

[5]With releases before 2.2, replace the MANOVA command with the following:

```
MANOVA STRESS PAIN ATTITUDE BY SURGERY(1,2) DRUG(1,4)
        ILLNESS(1,3) WITH STAYTIME
  /DESIGN=SURGERY DRUG ILLNESS SURGERY BY DRUG SURGERY
        BY ILLNESS DESIGN BY ILLNESS
  /PRINT=HOMOGENEITY(BARTLETT) CELLINFO(MEANS SSCP)
        ERROR(COR) PRINCOMPS(COR ROTATE(VARIMAX))
        SIGNIF(UNIV) PARAMETERS(ESTIM) DISRIM(STAN)
  /PLOT=BOXPLOTS NORMAL
```

2. EFFECT .. UNEMPLOY

Univariate F-tests with (1,398) D. F.

Variable	Hypoth. SS	Error SS	Hypoth. MS	Error MS	F	Sig. of F
HLTHSCOR	31.963	5058.182	31.963	12.709	2.515	.113
FAMILY	167.100	10006.914	167.100	25.143	6.646	.010
ALCOHOL	10.260	610.134	10.260	1.533	6.693	.010

3. a. One-sample t-test.
   b. One-way analysis of variance.
   c. Two-independent-samples, pooled-variance t-test.

4. a. There appears to be a curvilinear relationship, with the means decreasing as the variances increase.

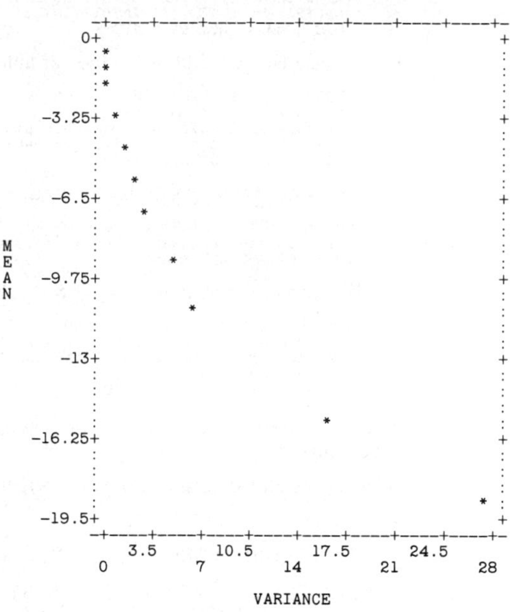

   b. The means are proportional to the standard deviations, with MEAN=−4*STTDEV (approximately).

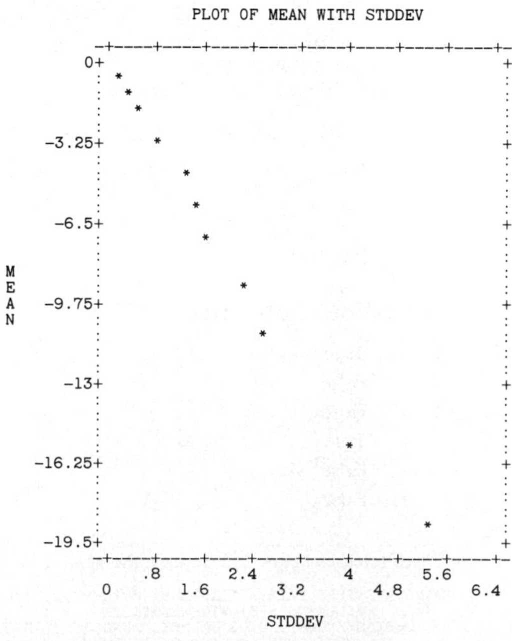

   c. MANOVA requires equality of variances.

5. Dimension Reduction Analysis

Roots	Wilks Lambda	F	Hypoth. DF	Error DF	Sig. of F
1 TO 1	.868	6.997	1.00	46	.011

6. No. The distribution of the scores appears to be bimodal and skewed to the left.

```
 1 . 8
 2 . 7
 3 .
 4 . 1
 5 . 2378
 6 . 011113559
 7 . 1167
 8 . 24
 9 . 113488899
10 . 00
```

7. EFFECT .. INDEPDCE BY BACKGRND

Univariate F-tests with (4,136) D. F.

Variable	Hypoth. SS	Error SS	Hypoth. MS	Error MS	F	Sig. of F
CREATVTY	11.833	49.223	2.958	0.362	8.172	.000
SAT	1283.427	11438.150	320.857	84.104	3.815	.004
POLITICS	.084	3.497	.021	.026	.804	.501
PREDJDCE	.682	10.895	.170	.080	2.131	.093

8. a.

	IQ	ALIENATN	PREDJDCE	NEWSINFO
IQ	6729.50			
ALIENATN	3136.13	1461.52		
PREDJDCE	-10699.43	-4986.22	17011.32	
NEWSINFO	13093.22	6101.79	-20817.27	25474.73

b.

	DESEGRTN	NUKEFREZ	GAYRGHTS
DESEGRTN	1785.00		
NUKEFREZ	3710.42	7712.73	
GAYRGHTS	5109.86	10621.70	14627.83

9. No. The diagonal terms must be nonnegative

10. a. Group 1.
    b. Group 3.
    c. Group 3.
    d. No. The spread for Group 3 is about three times larger than the spread for Group 4.

11.

Estimates for HLTHINFO

CONSTANT

Parameter	Coeff.
1	36.06

INCOME

Parameter	Coeff.
2	-5.58

Estimates for HLTHCARE

CONSTANT

Parameter	Coeff.
1	30.33

INCOME

Parameter	Coeff.
2	-9.44

Estimates for HEALTH

CONSTANT

Parameter	Coeff.
1	23.88

INCOME

Parameter	Coeff.
2	-4.43

12. a. Plots 1 and 2.
    b. Plots 2, 3, and 4.

13. a. Estimates of effects for canonical variables

	Canonical Variable			
Parameter	A	B	C	D
2	.309	.882	.590	.833

b. B contributes most. A contributes least.

14. Yes. All of the variables are highly loaded on the first component, indicating that one (or more) of the variables may be nearly a linear combination of the others.

15. No. The two statistics are equivalent when there is only one dependent variable.

Chapter 7

Syntax

1. The within-subjects factors are EXAMTIME and SEASON, the between-subjects factor is PROGRAM, and the covariate is GENENTH.

2.
```
MANOVA RELIEF1 TO RELIEF18 BY SEX(1,2) ETHNIC(1,4)
        WITH AGE1 TO AGE18
  /WSFACTORS=INJECTN(2) DOSE(3) TIME(3)
  /WSDESIGN=INJECTN DOSE TIME INJECTN BY DOSE INJECTN
        BY TIME DOSE BY TIME
  /DESIGN=SEX ETHNIC
```
[6]

3. a. The HUMOR covariate must be repeated 12 times.

```
>ERROR   12064  LINE  12, COLUMN  4, TEXT: WSDESIGN
>The wrong number of levels was specified in WSFACTOR.  The product of levels
>of within-subject factors must be either an integral multiple or divisor of
>the number of dependent variables and/or covariates in the MANOVA
>specification.
>THIS COMMAND NOT EXECUTED.
```

(With releases before 2.2, you also need a WSDESIGN subcommand followed by an ANALYSIS(REPEATED) subcommand.)

b. The WSDESIGN subcommand specifies 6 dependent variables, but only 5 dependent variables are listed.

```
>ERROR   12042
>The number of dependent variables in the MANOVA specification is less than the
>product of the levels of the within-subject factors defined in WSFACTOR.
>THIS COMMAND NOT EXECUTED.
```

c. Correct.

d. The between-subjects factors are listed on the WSFACTORS subcommand, and the number of levels for the within-subjects factor ROOM is not specified.

```
>ERROR   12014  LINE  26, (END OF COMMAND)
>The WSFACTOR subcommand is invalid.  An integer greater than or equal to 2
>should appear in parentheses after each factor name.
>THIS COMMAND NOT EXECUTED.
```

(With releases before 2.2, you also need a WSDESIGN subcommand followed by an ANALYSIS(REPEATED) subcommand.)

e. The value ranges are not specified for the between-subjects factors, value ranges are given instead of the number of levels in the WSFACTORS subcommand, and the CONTRAST subcommand should appear before the WSDESIGN subcommand.

```
>ERROR   12003  LINE  27, COLUMN 43, TEXT: WITH
>A parenthesized value range is required for every factor in the factor list.
>The lowest and highest values of the factor must be specified.  Any cases
>outside of this range will be rejected.
>THIS COMMAND NOT EXECUTED.
```

(With releases before 2.2, you also need a WSDESIGN subcommand followed by an ANALYSIS(REPEATED) subcommand.)

4.
```
MANOVA FUNNY1 TO FUNNY4 BY SEX(1,2) RACE(1,2)
  /WSFACTORS=OBSCENE(2) SEXIST(2)
  /RENAME=CONSTANT TOBSDIFF TSEXDIFF OBSSEX
  /WSDESIGN=OBSCENE SEXIST
  /DESIGN=SEX RACE
```

5.
```
MANOVA ADWINS NOADWINS ADSPRS NOASPRS ADSUMS NOADSUMS
        ADFALS NOADSFAL ADWINC NOADWINC ADSPRC NOADSPRC
        ADSUMC NOADSUMC ADFALC NOADFALC BY
        SEX(1,2) RACE(1,3) WITH INCOME1 TO INCOME8
  /WSFACTORS=SEASON(4) ADS(2)
  /PRINT=HOMOGENEITY(BOXM) SIGNIF(AVERF)
  /NOPRINT=PARAMETERS(ESTIM)
```
[7]

---

[6]With releases before 2.2, replace the MANOVA command with the following:

```
MANOVA RELIEF1 TO RELIEF18 BY SEX(1,2) ETHNIC(1,4)
        WITH AGE1 TO AGE18
  /WSFACTORS=INJECTN(2) DOSE(3) TIME(3)
  /WSDESIGN=INJECTN DOSE TIME INJECTN BY DOSE INJECTN
        BY TIME DOSE BY TIME
  /ANALYSIS(REPEATED)
  /DESIGN=SEX ETHNIC
```

[7]With releases before 2.2, replace the MANOVA command with the following:

```
MANOVA ADWINS NOADWINS ADSPRS NOASPRS ADSUMS NOADSUMS
        ADFALS NOADSFAL ADWINC NOADWINC ADSPRC NOADSPRC
        ADSUMC NOADSUMC ADFALC NOADFALC BY
        SEX(1,2) RACE(1,3) WITH INCOME1 TO INCOME8
  /WSFACTORS=SEASON(4) ADS(2)
  /PRINT=HOMOGENEITY(BOXM) SIGNIF(AVERF)
  /NOPRINT=PARAMETERS(ESTIM)
  /ANALYSIS(REPEATED)
```

Statistical Concepts

1. a. Independent-samples analysis of variance.
   b. Repeated measures analysis of variance.
   c. Neither.
   d. Independent-samples analysis of variance.

2. AVERAGED Tests of Significance for MEAS.1 using UNIQUE Sums of Squares

Source of Variation	Sum of Squares	DF	Mean Square	F	Sig. of F
WITHIN CELLS	41778	82	509		
CLASS	47408	2	23704	47	.000

3. $$\text{TCONDIFF} = 0.40825 \times (\bar{X}_{\text{DIGIT=1,COND=PRES}} + \bar{X}_{\text{DIGIT=2,COND=PRES}} + \bar{X}_{\text{DIGIT=3,COND=ABS}}) - 0.40825 \times (\bar{X}_{\text{DIGIT=1,COND=ABS}} + \bar{X}_{\text{DIGIT=2,COND=ABS}} + \bar{X}_{\text{DIGIT=3,COND=ABS}})$$

$$\text{TDIG1} = 0.5 \times (\bar{X}_{\text{DIGIT=2,COND=PRES}} + \bar{X}_{\text{DIGIT=2,COND=ABS}}) - 0.5 \times (\bar{X}_{\text{DIGIT=1,COND=PRES}} + \bar{X}_{\text{DIGIT=1,COND=ABS}})$$

$$\text{TDIG2} = 0.57735 \times (\bar{X}_{\text{DIGIT=3,COND=PRES}} + \bar{X}_{\text{DIGIT=3,COND=ABS}}) - 0.28868 \times (\bar{X}_{\text{DIGIT=1,COND=PRES}} + \bar{X}_{\text{DIGIT=1,COND=ABS}} + \bar{X}_{\text{DIGIT=2,COND=PRES}} + \bar{X}_{\text{DIGIT=2,COND=ABS}})$$

$$\text{TINT1} = 0.5 \times (\bar{X}_{\text{DIGIT=2,COND=PRES}} + \bar{X}_{\text{DIGIT=1,COND=ABS}}) - 0.5 \times (\bar{X}_{\text{DIGIT=1,COND=PRES}} + \bar{X}_{\text{DIGIT=2,COND=ABS}}$$

$$\text{TINT2} = 0.57735 \times \bar{X}_{\text{DIGIT=3,COND=PRES}} + 0.28868 \times (\bar{X}_{\text{DIGIT=1,COND=ABS}} + \bar{X}_{\text{DIGIT=2,COND=ABS}}) - 0.28868 \times (\bar{X}_{\text{DIGIT=1,COND=PRES}} + \bar{X}_{\text{DIGIT=2,COND=PRES}}) - 0.57736 \times \bar{X}_{\text{DIGIT=3,COND=ABS}}$$

4. a. For each column, square the coefficients and add them. The result will be 1 (plus or minus rounding error).
   b. Contrast 1 and Constrast 3

   $.57735(-.408 - .408 + .816) = 0$

   Constrast 2 and Contrast 3

   $(-.70711 \times -.40825) + (.70711 \times -.40825) = 0$

5. Tests of Significance for CONS using UNIQUE Sums of Squares

Source of Variation	Sum of Squares	DF	Mean Square	F	Sig. of F
WITHIN CELLS	2642130	45	58714		
CONSTANT	18905908	1	18905908	322	.000

- -

Estimates for CONS

CONSTANT

Parameter	Coeff.	Std. Err.	T-Value	Sig. of T	Lower 95% CL	Upper 95% CL
1	774	43	18	.000	686	862

6. Univariate, since Mauchley's (or Bartlett's for releases before 2.2) test of sphericity gives us no reason to reject the hypothesis that the population correlation matrix is an identity matrix.

7. No HOSPITAL effect is evident.

Estimates for CONS

CONSTANT

Parameter	Coeff.	Std. Err.	T-Value	Sig. of T	Lower 95% CL	Upper 95% CL
1	54	20	2.7	.007	15	93

HOSPITAL

Parameter	Coeff.	Std. Err.	T-Value	Sig. of T	Lower 95% CL	Upper 95% CL
2	-12	8.6	1.4	.162	-29	5

8. The test of the hypothesis that the covariate coefficient is 0 must have the same significance level as the test of the regression effect in the analysis of variance table.

9. a. No. The results could also be explained by a learning effect from one interview to the next.
   b. Yes. Three groups of students could have been used, with each student randomly assigned to one of the drug groups.

10. a. False.
    b. False.
    c. True.
    d. False.
    e. False.
11. Within-subjects factors: Weightlifters (present or absent), coach (present or absent). Between-subjects factors: Film (shown or not shown), warm-up (done or not done). Covariate: Overall initial strength.
12. a. Yes.
    b. Pre-tour support for spay and neuter programs is lowest with Film 1, highest with Film 3, and intermediate with Film 2. When Film 1 is used, a dramatic increase in support occurs after the tour. When Film 2 is used, the tour produces a fairly large increase in support, but only about half of the increase when Film 1 is used. When Film 3 is used, the increase in support after the tour is small. After the tour, there is no difference in average support between the groups who saw Films 1 and 2. However, the group that saw Film 3 has a higher average support.
    c. Use of Film 3 without the tour.
13.

```
Regression analysis for WITHIN CELLS error term

Dependent variable .. CONS

Covariate          B        Beta      Std. Err.     T-Value      Sig. of T  Lower 95% CL  Upper

TC1              -3.7       -.62           .74          -5          .0005         -5.15
```

Chapter 8

Syntax

1. a. There are several errors in this command. First, VARIABLES is an unacceptable keyword in HILOGLINEAR.

```
>WARNING   708  LINE   2, COLUMN 13, TEXT: VARIABLES
>A variable name is more than 8 characters long.  Only the first 8 characters
>will be used.

>ERROR     701  LINE   2, COLUMN 13, TEXT: VARIABLES
>An undefined variable name, or a scratch or system variable was specified in a
>variable list which accepts only standard variables.  Check spelling, and
>verify the existence of this variable.
>THIS COMMAND NOT EXECUTED.

>ERROR     702  LINE   2, COLUMN 22, TEXT: =
>Unrecognized text was found where a variable list was expected.
```

Second, variable SEASON is missing a range of values.

```
>ERROR   12703  LINE   6, COLUMN  5, TEXT: /
>There was no parenthesized value range after a list of factor variables in a
>LOGLINEAR command model specification.
>THIS COMMAND NOT EXECUTED.
```

Finally, MAXORDER is not an acceptable subcommand for the DESIGN specification. Since there are three variables, the maximum order possible is three.

```
>ERROR   13838  LINE   8, COLUMN 13, TEXT: MAXORDER
>There is an unrecognized symbol in the DESIGN specification.  This factor name
>is not defined.
>THIS COMMAND NOT EXECUTED.
```

An acceptable specification might be:

```
HILOGLINEAR JOY(1,2) DAY(1,7) SEASON(1,4)
    /MAXORDER=2
```

which would fit the hierarchical model with all second-order interactions.

b. This command would generate the following error message:

```
>ERROR   13841  LINE  10, COLUMN 17, TEXT: A
>The specification of the generating class of the model is incorrect.  It could
>be that factor name appeared twice or the incorrect inclusion of lower order
>terms.
>THIS COMMAND NOT EXECUTED.
```

This error occurs because the main effects A and B are part of the model specified by the generating class A*B. Specifying them individually and as part of the model generated by A*B leads to the message that they are included twice. Since the saturated model is the default, the correct specification is either:

```
HILOGLINEAR A B(1,2)
    /DESIGN
```

or

```
HILOGLINEAR A B(1,2)
    /DESIGN A*B
```

c. This command would generate the following error message:

```
>ERROR   13835  LINE  12, (END OF COMMAND)
>The matrix specified in the CWEIGHT subcommand is not correct.
>THIS COMMAND NOT EXECUTED.
```

If CWEIGHT is used a weight must be specified for every cell of the table. In this case there are 4 cells but only three weights assigned. A correct specification that assigns a weight of 0 to the first cell and weight of 1 to the remaining cells is

```
/DESIGN A B(1,2)
/CWEIGHT (0 3*1)
```

d. STEP is not a valid option for the METHOD subcommand. Only BACKWARD elimination is available.

```
>ERROR   13852  LINE  14, COLUMN 13, TEXT: STEP
>The METHOD specification is invalid.  The only valid keyword is BACKWARD.
>THIS COMMAND NOT EXECUTED.
```

2. a. False.
   b. False.
   c. True.
   d. False.

3. a. `/DESIGN A B C`
   b. `/DESIGN A*B A*C B*C`
   c. `/DESIGN C A*B`
   d. This is not a hierarchical model since it does not include the main effects and cannot be fit in HILOGLINEAR.
   e. This is not a hierarchical model since the C main effect is not included and cannot be fit in the HILOGLINEAR procedure.

4. a. `/DESIGN A*B A*C A*D B*C B*D C*D`
   b. `/DESIGN A B C D`
   c. `/DESIGN A*B*C A*B*D B*C*D A*C*D`
   d. `/DESIGN`

   or

   `/DESIGN A*B*C*D`

5. a.
```
HILOGLINEAR SAT(1,3) SEX MARITAL(0,1)
  /PRINT ESTIM FREQ ASSOCIATION
  /DESIGN
```
   b.
```
HILOGLINEAR SAT(1,3) SEX MARITAL(0,1)
  /PRINT FREQ RESID
  /PLOT NORMPLOT
  /DESIGN SATIS*SEX MARITAL*SATIS)
```

Statistical Concepts

1. a. Not hierarchical; AGE needed.
   b. Not hierarchical; CHILDREN*SEX and SEX*ABORTION needed.
   c. Not hierarchical; ALIVE1*MARITAL*RELATIVES, ALIVE1*RELATIVES*SOCIALFE, MARITAL*RELATIVES, and MARITAL*RELATIVES*SOCIALFE needed.
   d. Hierarchical.

2. a. A, B, C, D, E, A*B, A*C, B*C, A*D, A*E, D*E, A*B*C, A*D*E
   b. A, B, C, D, A*B, A*C, A*D, B*C, B*D, C*D, A*B*C, A*B*D, A*C*D, B*C*D, A*B*C*D
   c. A, B, C, D, E, A*B, A*C, A*D, B*C, B*D, C*D, A*E, D*E, A*B*C, A*B*D, A*C*D, B*C*D, A*B*C*D
   d. A, B, C, D, E, A*B, A*C, A*D, B*C, B*D, C*D, A*E, B*E, C*E, D*E, A*B*C, A*B*D, A*C*D, B*C*D, A*B*C*D
3. a. CRIMETYP*GANGMEMB*AGE, CRIMETYP*SEX, CRIMETYP*RACE
   b. DIVNLABR*LAWTYPE*SOLIDRTY, DIVNLABR*DEVIANCE*RITUALS, LAWTYPE*SOLIDRTY*DEVIANCE, SOLIDRTY*DEVIANCE*RITUALS, LAWTYPE*RITUALS
   c. HEALTH*MARITAL, HEALTH*PETS, HEALTH*INCOME, PETS*INCOME
   d. HIGHBP*SEX*STRESS, HIGHBP*SALT*SUGAR, HIGHBP*AGE
4. a. AGE*DIETFAT
   b.. $\chi^2 = 41.117$, with 56 DF
5.

Table A

Tests that K-way and higher order effects are zero.

K	DF	L.R. Chisq	Prob
4	4	2.290	.683
3	16	33.746	.006
2	29	167.442	.000
1	35	234.101	.000

Table B

Tests that K-way effects are zero.

K	DF	L.R. Chisq	Prob
1	6	66.659	.000
2	13	133.696	.000
3	12	31.456	.002
4	4	2.290	.683

6. Tests of PARTIAL associations.

Effect Name	DF	Partial Chisq	Prob
STRESS*TEST	4	15.765	.0034
TEST*PASSFAIL	2	63.824	.0000
STRESS*PASSFAIL	2	4.958	.0838
TEST	2	271.257	.0000
STRESS	2	139.910	.0000
PASSFAIL	1	17.980	.0000

7. a. False.
   b. True.
   c. True.
   d. False.
   e. False.
   f. False.
8. a. It decreases happiness.
   b. It's reasonably safe to assume that there is no effect, given the small *Z* value.
   c. It decreases prestige.
9. a.

Parameter	Coefficient
λ^{SALE}_{NO}	-0.682
$\lambda^{DISTRICT}_{3}$	0.497
$\lambda^{DISTRICT—SALE}_{2—NO}$	-0.486
$\lambda^{DISTRICT—SALE}_{1—NO}$	0.281

   b. District 2.
10. No. The log cell frequencies, log F_{ijkl}, are what the model predicts.

11. Estimates for Parameters

SEX*AUTOPREF

Parameter	Coeff.	Std. Err.	Z-Value	Lower 95 CI	Upper 95 CI
1	-1.06	.20	-4.08	-1.56	-.55
2	.09	.28	.32	-.46	.64

SEX

Parameter	Coeff.	Std. Err.	Z-Value	Lower 95 CI	Upper 95 CI
1	1.11	.25	4.44	.62	1.60

AUTOPREF

Parameter	Coeff.	Std. Err.	Z-Value	Lower 95 CI	Upper 95 CI
1	.79	.26	3.04	.28	1.30
2	.40	.28	1.42	-.15	.95

12. 6 DF, since there are 2×4×3=24 cells in the table and 18 independent parameters.

13. Pearson χ^2=5.041 with 2 DF and p=.08.

14. a. Observed, Expected Frequencies and Residuals

Factor	Code	OBS. count & PCT.	EXP. count & PCT.	Residual	Std. Resid.
BREED	1				
TRNABLTY	1				
SOCLZATN	1	4.00 (9.76)	3.12 (7.62)	.88	.498
SOCLZATN	2	1.00 (2.44)	1.87 (4.57)	-.87	-.636
TRNABLTY	2				
SOCLZATN	1	7.00 (17.07)	6.18 (15.06)	.82	.330
SOCLZATN	2	8.00 (19.51)	8.82 (21.52)	-.82	-.276
BREED	2				
TRNABLTY	1				
SOCLZATN	1	11.00 (26.83)	11.87 (28.96)	-.87	-.253
SOCLZATN	2	8.00 (19.51)	7.12 (17.38)	.88	.330
TRNABLTY	2				
SOCLZATN	1	.00 (.00)	.82 (2.01)	-.82	-.905
SOCLZATN	2	2.00 (4.88)	1.18 (2.87)	.82	.755

b. Yes.

15. a. No, because of the pattern in the residuals. The model overpredicts frequencies for Jackson and underpredicts frequencies for Maxwell.

b. (A) The model underpredicts all but one of the frequencies.
(B) The model predicts best for higher frequencies.
(C) The model overpredicts for frequencies less than 30 and underpredicts for the other frequencies.
(D) No deficiencies of the model show up in this plot.

Chapter 9

Syntax

1. a. Covariates, the variables specified after the WITH keyword, cannot have value ranges following them.

```
>ERROR    702  LINE   2, COLUMN 31, TEXT: (
>Unrecognized text was found where a variable list was expected.
>THIS COMMAND NOT EXECUTED.

>ERROR    702  LINE   2, COLUMN 32, TEXT: 1
>Unrecognized text was found where a variable list was expected.

>ERROR    702  LINE   2, COLUMN 34, TEXT: 4
>Unrecognized text was found where a variable list was expected.

>ERROR    702  LINE   2, COLUMN 35, TEXT: )
>Unrecognized text was found where a variable list was expected.
```

b. Procedure LOGLINEAR does not allow asterisks (*) in the design specification. A model can be specified only by enumerating all terms to be included. Generating classes are not accepted.

```
>ERROR   12738  LINE   6, COLUMN 12, TEXT: *
>There is an unrecognized symbol in the DESIGN specification.  This effect name
>is not defined.
>THIS COMMAND NOT EXECUTED.
```

c. In the specification of a logit model, only one BY keyword is allowed. All variables following the single BY keyword are considered independent variables.

```
>ERROR    702  LINE   7, COLUMN 32, TEXT: (
>Unrecognized text was found where a variable list was expected.
>THIS COMMAND NOT EXECUTED.

>ERROR    702  LINE   7, COLUMN 33, TEXT: 1
>Unrecognized text was found where a variable list was expected.

>ERROR    702  LINE   7, COLUMN 35, TEXT: 2
>Unrecognized text was found where a variable list was expected.

>ERROR    702  LINE   7, COLUMN 36, TEXT: )
>Unrecognized text was found where a variable list was expected.
```

d. A variable that does not appear on the LOGLINEAR command occurs on the design specification.

```
>ERROR  12738  LINE  10, COLUMN 22, TEXT: D
>There is an unrecognized symbol in the DESIGN specification.  This effect name
>is not defined.
>THIS COMMAND NOT EXECUTED.
```

2. a.
```
/CWEIGHT (0 1 1
          1 0 1
          1 1 0)
```
b.
```
/CONTRAST(A)=POLY
```
c.
```
/GRESID= (1 1 1
          0 0 0
          0 0 C
/GRESID= (0 0 0
          1 1 1
          0 0 0)
/GRESID= (0 0 0
          0 0 0
          1 1 1)
```
or
```
/GRESID = (3*1 6*0)
/GRESID = (3*0 3*1 3*0)
/RESIDd = (6*0 3*1)
```
d.
```
/DESIGN A B
```
e.
```
/DESIGN
```
or
```
/DESIGN A B A BY B
```

3. a.
```
/DESIGN
```
or
```
/DESIGN A B C A BY B A BY C B BY C A BY B BY C
```
b.
```
/DESIGN A B C A BY B A BY C B BY C
```
c.
```
/DESIGN A B C B BY C
```

4. a.
```
LOGLINEAR JOY(0,1) DAY(1,7) SEASON(1,4)
     /DESIGN JOY DAY SEASON
```
b.
```
LOGLINEAR JOY(0,1) DAY(1,7) SEASON(1,4)
     /DESIGN JOY DAY SEASON JOY BY DAY JOY BY SEASON
      SEASON BY DAY
```
c.
```
LOGLINEAR JOY(0,1) DAY(1,7) SEASON(1,4)
     /DESIGN JOY DAY SEASON JOY BY SEASON JOY BY DAY
```
d.
```
     /DESIGN JOY
```
e.
```
COMPUTE X=1
LOGLINEAR JOY(0,1) WITH X
     /DESIGN X
```

5. a.
```
LOGLINEAR PARTY IDEOL (1,3)
    /DESIGN PARTY IDEOL
```
b.
```
COMPUTE COV=IDEOL
LOGLINEAR PARTY IDEOL (1,3) WITH COV
    /DESIGN PARTY IDEOL PARTY BY COV
```
or
```
LOGLINEAR PARTY IDEOL (1,3)
    /CONTRAST(IDEOL)=POLY
    /DESIGN PARTY IDEOL PARTY BY IDEOL(1)
```
c.
```
COMPUTE COV=PARTY
LOGLINEAR PARTY IDEOL (1,3) WITH COV
    /DESIGN PARTY IDEOL IDEOL BY COV
```
or
```
LOGLINEAR PARTY IDEOL (1,3)
    /CONTRAST(PARTY)=POLY
    /DESIGN PARTY IDEOL IDEOL BY PARTY(1)
```
d.
```
COMPUTE B1=PARTY
COMPUTE B2=IDEOL
LOGLINEAR PARTY IDEOL(1,3) WITH B1 B2
    /DESIGN PARTY IDEOL B1 BY B2
```
or
```
LOGLINEAR PARTY IDEOL(1,3)
    /CONTRAST(PARTY)=POLY
    /CONTRAST(IDEOL)=POLY
    /DESIGN PARTY IDEOL PARTY(1) BY IDEOL(1)
```

Statistical Concepts

1. a.
```
COMPUTE X=1
LOGLINEAR CARS(2,6) WITH X
  /DESIGN X
```
b.

Observed, Expected Frequencies and Residuals

Factor	Code	OBS. count & PCT.	EXP. count & PCT.	Residual	Std. Resid.	Adj. Resid.
CARS	2	40.00 (40.00)	20.00 (20.00)	20.0000	4.4721	5.0000
CARS	3	25.00 (25.00)	20.00 (20.00)	5.0000	1.1180	1.2500
CARS	4	20.00 (20.00)	20.00 (20.00)	.0000	.0000	.0000
CARS	5	10.00 (10.00)	20.00 (20.00)	-10.0000	-2.2361	-2.5000
CARS	6	5.00 (5.00)	20.00 (20.00)	-15.0000	-3.3541	-3.7500

Goodness-of-Fit test statistics

```
Likelihood Ratio Chi Square =   38.88306   DF = 4  P =  .000
        Pearson Chi Square =   37.50000   DF = 4  P =  .000
```

c. Yes.

d.
```
LOGLINEAR CARS(2,6)
  /CONTRAST (CARS)=POLY
  /DESIGN CARS(1)
```
e.

Observed, Expected Frequencies and Residuals

Factor	Code	OBS. count & PCT.	EXP. count & PCT.	Residual	Std. Resid.	Adj. Resid.
CARS	2	40.00 (40.00)	41.13 (41.13)	-1.1321	-.1765	-.3634
CARS	3	25.00 (25.00)	25.88 (25.88)	-.8828	-.1735	-.2021
CARS	4	20.00 (20.00)	16.29 (16.29)	3.7129	.9200	1.0548
CARS	5	10.00 (10.00)	10.25 (10.25)	-.2488	-.0777	-.0949
CARS	6	5.00 (5.00)	6.45 (6.45)	-1.4492	-.5706	-.7393

f. No.

2. a.
```
LOGLINEAR HAPPY(1,2) HEALTH(1,4)
     /CONTRAST(HEALTH)=POLY
     /DESIGN HAPPY HEALTH
```
   b. Reject the null hypothesis.
   c.
```
LOGLINEAR HAPPY(1,2) HEALTH(1,4)
     /CONTRAST(HEALTH)=POLY
     /DESIGN HAPPY HEALTH HEALTH(1) BY HAPPY
```
   d. The model appears to fit well.

3.
```
HEALTH     (DEVIATION PARAMETER ESTIMATES)

 Parameter          Coeff.        Std. Err.          Z-Value      Lower 95 CI      Upper 95 CI

        2     -.0627405043          .06625          -.94702         -.19259           .06711
        3      .6045689791          .04365         13.84909          .51901           .69013
        4      .1323719052          .05911          2.23936          .01651           .24823

HEALTH     (SIMPLE PARAMETER ESTIMATES)

 Parameter          Coeff.        Std. Err.          Z-Value      Lower 95 CI      Upper 95 CI

        2      .6114598758          .13166          4.64429          .35341           .86951
        3     1.2787693592          .11133         11.48590         1.06056          1.49698
        4      .8065722853          .11472          7.03068          .58172          1.03143

HEALTH     (DIFFERENCE PARAMETER ESTIMATES)

 Parameter          Coeff.        Std. Err.          Z-Value      Lower 95 CI      Upper 95 CI

        2      .6673094834          .07431          8.98025          .52166           .81295
        3     -.1385423322          .08504         -1.62912         -.30522           .02814
        4     -.8989338401          .10849         -8.28612        -1.11157          -.68630
```

4. a.
```
LOGLINEAR HAPPY(1,2) BY INCOME(1,3) HEALTH(1,4)
  /DESIGN HAPPY HAPPY BY INCOME HAPPY BY HEALTH
```
   or since the default is a saturated model:
```
  /DESIGN
```
   b.
```
LOGLINEAR HAPPY(1,2) INCOME(1,3) HEALTH(1,4)
  /DESIGN HAPPY INCOME HEALTH
          HAPPY BY INCOME
          HAPPY BY HEALTH
          INCOME BY HEALTH
          HAPPY BY INCOME BY HEALTH
```
   or
```
  /DESIGN
```
   c.
```
Goodness-of-Fit test statistics

  Likelihood Ratio Chi Square =      .00000    DF = 0  P = 1.000
           Pearson Chi Square =      .00000    DF = 0  P = 1.000
```
   d. They would not differ.
   e. `/DESIGN HAPPY HAPPY BY INCOME HAPPY BY HEALTH`
   f.
```
/DESIGN HAPPY INCOME HEALTH
        HAPPY BY INCOME
        HAPPY BY HEALTH
        INCOME BY HEALTH
```

Bibliography

Afifi, A. A., and V. Clark. *Computer-aided Multivariate Analysis.* Belmont, California: Lifetime Learning Publications, 1984.

Agresti, A. *Analysis of Ordinal Categorical Data.* New York: John Wiley and Sons, 1984.

Anderberg, M. R. *Cluster Analysis for Applications.* New York: Academic Press, 1973.

Andrews, D.F., R. Gnanadesikan, and J. L. Warner. Methods for assessing multivariate normality. In: *Multivariate Analysis III.* ed. P. R. Krishnaiah. New York: Academic Press, 1973.

Bacon, L. Unpublished data, 1980.

Barcikowski, R. S., and R. R. Robey. Decisions in single group repeated measures analysis: statistical tests and three computer packages. *American Statistician,* 38:2 (1984), 148-50.

Barnard, R. M. *Field-dependent Independence and Selected Motor Abilities,* Ph.D. diss. School of Education of New York University, 1973.

Belsley, D. A., E. Kuh, and R. E. Welsch *Regression Diagnostics: Identifying Influential Data and Sources of Collinearity.* New York: John Wiley and Sons, 1980.

Benedetti, J. K., and M. B. Brown. Strategies for the selection of log-linear models. *Biometrics,* 34 (1978), 680 686.

Berk, K. N. Comparing subset regression procedures. *Technometrics,* 20 (1978), 1-6.

——. Tolerance and condition in regression computation. *American Statistical Association,* 72 (1977), 863-866.

Bishop, Y. M. M., S. E. Feinberg, and P. W. Holland. *Discrete Multivariate Analysis: Theory and Practice.* Cambridge, Mass: MIT Press, 1975.

Bock, R. D. *Multivariate Statistical Methods in Behavioral Research.* New York: McGraw-Hill, 1975.

Burns, P R. *Multiple Comparison Methods in MANOVA.* Proceedings 7th SPSS Users and Coordinators Conference, 1984.

Cattell, R. B. The meaning and strategic use of factor analysis. In *Handbook of Multivariate Experimental Psychology,* ed. R. B. Catell. Chicago: Rand McNally, 1966.

Churchill, G. A., Jr. *Marketing Research: Methodological Foundations.* Hinsdale, Illinois: Dryden Press, 1979

Cochran, W. G., and G. M. Cox. *Experimental Designs.* 2nd ed. New York: John Wiley and Sons, 1957.

Consumer Reports, July 1983.

Cook, R. D. Detection of influential observations in lincar regression. *Technometrics, 19 (1977), 15-18.*

Draper, N. R., and H. Smith *Applied Regression Analysis.* New York: John Wiley and Sons, 1981.

Everitt, B. S. *The Analysis of Contingency Tables.* London: Chapman and Hall, 1977.

——. *Cluster Analysis.* 2nd ed. London: Heineman Educational Books Ltd., 1980.

——. *Graphical Techniques for Multivariate Data.* New York: North-Holland, 1978.

Eysenck, M.W. *Human Memory: Theory, Research and Individual Differences.* New York: Pergamon Press, 1977.

Fienberg, S. E. *The Analysis of Cross-Classified Categorical Data.* Cambridge, Mass: MIT Press, 1977.

Finn, J. D. *A General Model for Multivariate Analysis.* New York: Holt, Rinehart, and Winston, 1974.

Frane, J. W. Some simple procedures for handling missing data in multivariate analysis. *Psychometrika,* 41 (1976), 409-415.

——. A note on checking tolerance in matrix inversion and regression. *Technometrics,* 19 (1977), 513-514.

Freund, R. J. The case of the missing cell. *The American Statistician,* 34 (1980), 94-98.

Gilbert, E. S. On discrimination using qualitative variables. *Journal of the American Statistical Association,* 63 (1968), 1399-1412.

Goldstein, M., and W. R. Dillon. *Discrete Discriminant Analysis.* New York: Wiley and Sons, 1978.

Goodman, L. A. *The Analysis of Cross-Classified Data Having Ordered Categories.* Cambridge: Harvard University Press, 1984.

Green, B. F. The two kinds of linear discriminant functions and their relationship. *Journal of Educational Statistics,* 4:3 (1979), 247-263.

Green, P. E. *Analyzing Multivariate Data.* Hinsdale, Illinois: Dryden Press, 1978.

Greenhouse, S. W., and S. Geisser. On methods in analysis of profile data. *Psychometrika,* 24 (1959), 95-112.

Gunst, R. F., and R. L. Mason *Regression Analysis and its Application: A Data-Oriented Approach.* New York: Marcel Dekker, 1980.

Haberman, S. J. Analysis of dispersion of multinomial responses. *Journal of the American Statistical Association,* 77 (1982), 568-580.

——. *Analysis of Qualitative Data,* Vol 1. London: Academic Press, 1978.

——. *Analysis of Qualitative Data,* Vol 2. New York: Academic Press, 1979.

Hand, D. J. *Discrimination and Classification.* New York: Wiley and Sons, 1981.

Harman, H. H. *Modern Factor Analysis.* 2nd ed. Chicago: University of Chicago Press, 1967.

Horton, R. L. *The General Linear Model.* New York: McGraw-Hill, 1978.

Huynh, H., and L. S. Feldt. Estimation of the Box correction for degrees of freedom from sample data in randomized block and split-plot designs. *Journal of Educational Statistics, 1 (1976), 69-82.*

Jonassen, C. T., and S. H. Peres. *Interrelationships of Dimensions of Community Systems.* Columbus: Ohio State University Press, 1960.

Kaiser, H. F. An index of factorial simplicity. *Psychometrika* 39 (1974), 31-36.

Kim, J. O., and C. W. Mueller. *Introduction to Factor Analysis.* Beverly Hills: Sage Press, 1978.

Kleinbaum, D. G., and L. L. Kupper. *Applied Regression Analysis and Other Multivariate Methods.* North Scituate, Mass: Duxbury Press, 1978.

Kshirsagar, A. M., and E. Arseven. A note on the equivalency of two discrimination procedures. *The American Statistician,* 29 (1975), 38-39.

Lachenbruch, P. A. *Discriminant Analysis.* New York: Hafner Press, 1975.

Meehl, P. E. Configural scoring. *Journal of Consulting Psychology,* 14 (1950), 165.

Meyer, L. S., and M. S. Younger. Estimation of standardized coefficients. *Journal of the American Statistical Association,* 71 (1976), 154-157.

Miller, R. G. *Simultaneous Statistical Inference.* 2nd ed. New York: Springer-Verlag, 1981.

Milligan, G. W., and P. D. Isaac. The validation of four ultrametric clustering algorithms. *Pattern Recognition,* 12 (1980), 41-50.

Milliken, G. W., and D. E. Johnson. *Analysis of Messy Data.* Belmont, California: Lifetime Learning Publications, 1984.

Moore, D. H. Evaluation of five discrimination procedures for binary variables. *Journal of the American Statistical Association,* 68 (1973), 399.

Morrison, D. F. *Multivariate Statistical Methods.* New York: McGraw-Hill, 1967.

Neter, J., and W. Wasserman. *Applied Linear Statistical Models.* Homewood, Illinois: Richard D Irwin Inc., 1974.

Norusis, M. J. *SPSS^X Introductory Statistics Guide.* New York: McGraw-Hill, 1983.

Olsen, C. L. On choosing a test statistic in multivariate analysis of variance. *Psychological Bulletin,* 83 (1976), 579-586.

Roberts, H. V. Statistical bases in the measurement of employment discrimination. In E. Robert Livernash, ed., *Comparable Worth: Issues and Alternatives.* Washington D.C.: Equal Employment Advisory Council, 1980, 173-195.

Romesburg, H. C. *Cluster Analysis for Researchers.* Belmont, California: Lifetime Learning Publications, 1984.

Searle, S. R. *Linear Models.* New York: John Wiley and Sons, 1971.

Sneath, P. H. A., and R. R. Sokal. *Numerical Taxonomy.* San Francisco: W.H. Freeman and Co., 1973.

SPSS Inc. *SPSS^X User's Guide.* New York: McGraw-Hill, 1983.

SPSS Inc. *SPSS^X Statistical Algorithms.* Chicago: SPSS Inc., 1983.

Stoetzel, J. A factor analysis of liquor preference of French consumers. *Journal of Advertising Research,* 1:1 (1960), 7-11.

Tatsuoka, M. M. *Multivariate Analysis.* New York: John Wiley and Sons, 1971.

Timm, N. H. *Multivariate Analysis with Applications in Education and Psychology.* Monterey: Brooks/Cole, 1975.

Tucker, L. R. Relations of factor score estimates to their use. *Psychometrika,* 36 (1971), 427-436.

Tucker, R. F., R. F. Koopman, and R. L. Linn. Evaluation of factor analytic research procedures by means of simulated correlation matrices. *Psychometrika,* 34 (1969), 421-459.

Van Vliet, P. K. J., and J. M. Gupta. *THAM v. sodium bicarbonate in idiopathic Respiratory Distress Syndrome* Archives of Disease in Childhood, 48 (1973), 249-255.

Wahl, P. W. and R. A. Kronmal. Discriminant functions when covariances are unequal and sample sizes are moderate. *Biometrics,* 33 (1977), 479-484.

Winer, B. J. *Statistical Principles in Experimental Design.* New York: McGraw-Hill, 1971.

Witkin, H. A., et al. *Personality Through Perception.* New York: Harper and Brothers, 1954.

Index

A (format)
fixed-format data, 377
freefield-format data, 377, 378
A (keyword)
SORT CASES command, 399
ABS (function), 387
absolute value, 387
ADD VALUE LABELS (command), 411
syntax, 411
addition, 386
ADJPRED (temporary variable)
REGRESSION command, 61
adjusted predicted value, 31
adjusted quasi-symmetry model
log-linear analysis, 350
adjusted R^2, 17-18, 20, 44
AFREQ (keyword)
FREQUENCIES command, 449
AFTER (keyword)
ANOVA command, 429
AGAINST (keyword)
MANOVA command, 237
agglomeration schedule, 175-176
agglomerative hierarchical clustering, 169
AIC (keyword)
FACTOR command, 155
ALL (keyword)
ANOVA command, 430, 431
CORRELATIONS command, 435
CROSSTABS command, 438, 440
DESCRIPTIVES command, 443
FREQUENCIES command, 452
MEANS command, 464
ONEWAY command, 469-470
reserved keyword, 376
all-groups histogram, 107
ALPHA (keyword)
FACTOR command, 153
MANOVA command, 244
ALPHANUMERIC (keyword)
PLOT command, 477
alphanumeric variable, 368, 377
ANALYSIS (keyword)
ONEWAY command, 470
T-TEST command, 491
ANALYSIS (subcommand)
DISCRIMINANT command, 110
FACTOR command, 152
MANOVA command, 234-235
analysis of variance, 18-20, 195-246, 257-288, 428-431
in MEANS command, 464
ANALYSIS(REPEATED) (subcommand)
MANOVA command, 287
AND (keyword)
logical operator, 394
reserved keyword, 376
ANOVA (command), 7, 428-431
covariates, 429
COVARIATES subcommand, 429
FORMAT subcommand, 431
full factorial models, 429
interaction effects, 430
limitations, 431
MAXORDERS subcommand, 430
METHOD subcommand, 430
MISSING subcommand, 431
sums of squares, 430
syntax, 428
ANOVA (keyword)
MEANS command, 464
REGRESSION command, 58
ANY (function), 388
AR (keyword)
FACTOR command, 156
arcsine, 387
arctangent, 387
argument, 387-389
arithmetic operator, 386-387
ARSIN (function), 387
ARTAN (function), 387
ASRESID (keyword)
CROSSTABS command, 438
assignment expression
in COMPUTE command, 385
in IF command, 393
ASSOCIATION (keyword)
HILOGLINEAR command, 317
AVALUE (keyword)
CROSSTABS command, 440
averaged F test, 207
AVERF (keyword)
MANOVA command, 243, 287
AVONLY (keyword)
MANOVA command, 243

BACKWARD (keyword)
HILOGLINEAR command, 316
REGRESSION command, 56
backward elimination
discriminant, 111
log-linear models, 312-314
regression, 47-48
BADCORR (keyword)
REGRESSION command, 60
BALANCED (keyword)
MANOVA command, 240
bar charts, 3
BARCHART (subcommand)
FREQUENCIES command, 450
BART (keyword)
FACTOR command, 156
BARTLETT (keyword)
MANOVA command, 242, 288
Bartlett-Box F
in ONEWAY command, 470
Bartlett's test of sphericity, 128, 138, 155, 203-204, 218, 267
BASIS (keyword)
(LOGLINEAR command), 360
MANOVA command, 239
BAVERAGE (keyword)
CLUSTER command, 184
Bayes' rule, 82
BCOV (keyword)
REGRESSION command, 58
BEGIN DATA (command), 380-381, 401
syntax, 401
Beta coefficient, 14, 39
between-groups F, 98
BIAS (keyword)
MANOVA command, 242
BLANK (keyword)
FACTOR command, 155
blanks
reading, 380, 419, 419
BLANKS (keyword)
SET command, 419
SHOW command, 419
BLOCK (keyword)
CLUSTER command, 184
box-and-whisker plots, 208-209
Box's M test, 108, 276
BOXM (keyword)
MANOVA command, 242, 288
BOXPLOTS (keyword)
MANOVA command, 245
BREAKDOWN (command), see MEANS
BRIEF (keyword)
MANOVA command, 243
BTAU (keyword)
CROSSTABS command, 439
BY (keyword)
CROSSTABS command, 437
LIST command, 456
LOGLINEAR command, 356, 356
MANOVA command, 236

MEANS command, 462-463
PLOT command, 473
reserved keyword, 376
SORT CASES command, 399

canonical correlation, 89-90, 104-105, 213
carry-over effect
repeated measures, 257-258
case, 367-368
case identifier, 368
CASES (subcommand)
LIST command, 455-456
CASEWISE (keyword)
MANOVA command, 245
CASEWISE (subcommand)
REGRESSION command, 62-63
casewise plot, 23
CC (keyword)
CROSSTABS command, 439
CDFNORM (function), 389
CELLINFO (keyword)
MANOVA command, 242
CELLPLOTS (keyword)
MANOVA command, 245
CELLS (subcommand)
CROSSTABS command, 438
MEANS command, 464
CENTROID (keyword)
CLUSTER command, 184
CFVAR (function), 388
CHA (keyword)
REGRESSION command, 58
CHEBYCHEV (keyword)
CLUSTER command, 184
chi-square
change in, 309-310
chi-square test, 439
CHISQ (keyword)
CROSSTABS command, 439
CHOLESKY (keyword)
MANOVA command, 240
CI (keyword)
REGRESSION command, 58
CLASS (keyword)
DISCRIMINANT command, 113
classification of cases, 100-103
CLASSIFY (subcommand)
DISCRIMINANT command, 114-115
CLUSTER (command), 167-186, 432
cluster membership variables, 186
ID subcommand, 186
MATRIX subcommand, 186
MEASURE subcommand, 184-185
METHOD subcommand, 184
MISSING subcommand, 186
PLOT subcommand, 185
PRINT subcommand, 185
SAVE subcommand, 186
syntax, 432
variable list, 183
CLUSTER (keyword)
CLUSTER command, 185
cluster analysis, 2, 167-183
COCHRAN (keyword)
MANOVA command, 242, 288
Cochran's C
in ONEWAY command, 470

COEFF (keyword)
REGRESSION command, 58
coefficient of determination, 17-18
coefficient of variation, 388
COLUMN (keyword)
CROSSTABS command, 438
COMMA (format), 386
command file
defined, 374
COMMENT (command), 411-412
syntax, 411
common factor, 126
communality, 130, 133-134
COMPLETE (keyword)
CLUSTER command, 184
complete linkage criterion, 169
COMPUTE (command), 4, 385-391, 421-422
syntax, 421
with DO IF command, 392
COND (keyword)
REGRESSION command, 58
CONDENSE (keyword)
FREQUENCIES command, 449
CONDESCRIPTIVE, see DESCRIPTIVES
conditional probability, 83
conditional transformation, 392-396
confusion matrix, 85
CONSTANT (keyword)
MANOVA command, 237, 241
CONSTRAST (subcommand)
MANOVA command, 286
CONTIN (keyword)
MANOVA command, 236
contingency coefficient, 439
contour plots
PLOT command, 475
CONTRAST (keyword)
MANOVA command, 239
CONTRAST (subcommand)
LOGLINEAR command, 360-361
MANOVA command, 242
ONEWAY command, 467-468
CONVERGE (keyword)
HILOGLINEAR command, 316
LOGLINEAR command, 361
convergence criterion
log-linear models, 303, 361
COOK (temporary variable)
REGRESSION command, 61
Cook's distance, 30-32
COPY (keyword)
RECODE command, 383, 385
COR (keyword)
LOGLINEAR command, 359
MANOVA command, 242, 243, 243, 243, 244, 288
CORR (keyword)
CROSSTABS command, 440
CORRELATION (keyword)
FACTOR command, 155
REGRESSION command, 60
correlation matrix, 204
discriminant, 79-80
factor, 127, 127-128
missing data, 36-37

CORRELATIONS (command), 7, 433-436
FORMAT subcommand, 435
limitations, 436
MATRIX subcommand, 435
MISSING subcommand, 435
PRINT subcommand, 434
significance tests, 434
STATISTICS subcommand, 434-435
syntax, 433
VARIABLES subcommand, 433-434
COS (function), 387
cosine, 387
COSINE (keyword)
CLUSTER command, 184
COUNT (command), 391-392, 422
syntax, 422
COUNT (keyword)
CROSSTABS command, 438
MEANS command, 464
COV (keyword)
MANOVA command, 242, 242, 243
REGRESSION command, 61
covariates
in ANOVA command, 429
COVARIATES (subcommand)
ANOVA command, 429
Cramer's V, 439
CRITERIA (subcommand)
FACTOR command, 153-154
HILOGLINEAR command, 316
LOGLINEAR command, 361
MANOVA command, 246
REGRESSION command, 57-58
CROSSBREAK (subcommand)
MEANS command, 463
CROSSTABS (command), 5, 436-440
cell contents, 438
cell percentages, 438
CELLS subcommand, 438
expected values, 438
FORMAT subcommand, 440
indexing tables, 440
limitations, 440
MISSING subcommand, 440
residuals, 438
STATISTICS subcommand, 438-440
syntax, 436
TABLES subcommand, 437-438
VARIABLES subcommand, 437-438
WRITE subcommand, 440
crosstabulation
defined, 436-437
in CROSSTABS command, 436-438
in MEANS command, 463
CTAU (keyword)
CROSSTABS command, 439
cumulative distribution function, 389
CUTPOINT (subcommand)
PLOT command, 477-478
CWEIGHT (subcommand)
HILOGLINEAR command, 317
LOGLINEAR command, 357-358

d
Somers, 440
D (keyword)
CROSSTABS command, 440
SORT CASES command, 399

data definition commands, 375-382, 401-411
DATA LIST (command), 375-379, 402-403
  file definition, 402-403
  FILE subcommand, 375, 402
  syntax, 402
  variable definition, 403
  variables, 375-376
data preparation, 367-370
data transformation commands, 421-426
date function, 389
DECOMP (keyword)
  MANOVA command, 242
DEFAULT (keyword)
  DESCRIPTIVES command, 443
  FREQUENCIES command, 452
  MEANS command, 464
deleted residual, 30-32
delta, 147
DELTA (keyword)
  FACTOR command, 154
  HILOGLINEAR command, 316
  LOGLINEAR command, 361
dendrogram, 175-177
DENDROGRAM (keyword)
  CLUSTER command, 185
DEPENDENT (keyword)
  MEANS command, 465
DEPENDENT (subcommand)
  REGRESSION command, 56
DESCRIPTIVES (command), 441-444
  compared to FREQUENCIES, 441
  FORMAT subcommand, 443-444
  MISSING subcommand, 443
  SAVE subcommand, 442
  STATISTICS subcommand, 442-443
  syntax, 441
  variable list, 441
  Z scores, 442
DESCRIPTIVES (keyword)
  CORRELATIONS command, 435
  ONEWAY command, 469
DESCRIPTIVES (subcommand)
  REGRESSION command, 60-61
DESIGN (keyword)
  LOGLINEAR command, 359
  MANOVA command, 242
DESIGN (subcommand)
  HILOGLINEAR command, 315
  LOGLINEAR command, 356
  MANOVA command, 235-237
design matrix
  log-linear analysis, 353-355
  multivariate analysis of variance, 205
DET (keyword)
  FACTOR command, 155
detrended normal plot, 200-201
DEVIATION (keyword)
  LOGLINEAR command, 360
  MANOVA command, 239, 242
deviation contrasts, 215-216, 216
DFREQ (keyword)
  FREQUENCIES command, 449
DIAGONAL (subcommand)
  FACTOR command, 153
dictionary, 378
DIFFERENCE (keyword)
  LOGLINEAR command, 360
  MANOVA command, 239, 242
DIMENR (keyword)
  MANOVA command, 243
dimension reduction analysis, 224
DIRECT (keyword)
  DISCRIMINANT command, 110
DISCRIM (subcommand)
  MANOVA command, 243-244
DISCRIMINANT (command), 75-116, 444-445
  ANALYSIS subcommand, 110
  CLASSIFY subcommand, 114-115
  FIN subcommand, 112
  FOUT subcommand, 112
  FUNCTIONS subcommand, 112
  GROUPS subcommand, 109
  HISTORY subcommand, 114
  inclusion levels, 111
  MATRIX subcommand, 114
  MAXSTEPS subcommand, 111
  METHOD subcommand, 110-111
  MISSING subcommand, 114
  PIN subcommand, 112
  PLOT subcommand, 115-116
  POUT subcommand, 112
  PRIORS subcommand, 113
  ROTATE subcommand, 114
  SAVE subcommand, 113-114
  SELECT subcommand, 112
  STATISTICS subcommand, 115
  syntax, 444-445
  TOLERANCE subcommand, 112
  VARIABLES subcommand, 110
  VIN subcommand, 112
discriminant analysis, 2, 75-116, 167, 213-215, 223-224
discriminant function coefficients, 213-214
discriminant scores, 81-82
disk file, 367
DISPLAY (command), 412-413
  DICTIONARY keyword, 412
  DOCUMENTS keyword, 412
  INDEX keyword, 412
  LABELS keyword, 412
  NAMES keyword, 412
  SORTED keyword, 412-413
  syntax, 412
  VARIABLES keyword, 412
display file
  defined, 374
  length, 419
  width, 419-420
DISTANCE (keyword)
  CLUSTER command, 185
distance measure, 168-169, 179-181
division, 386
divisive hierarchical clustering, 169
DO IF (command), 393, 422-423
  missing values, 393
  syntax, 422
DOCUMENT (command), 413
  syntax, 413
documentation
  local, 415
  new facilities, 415
  new procedures, 416
  new releases, 416
DOLLAR (format), 386
DOUBLE (keyword)
  FREQUENCIES command, 449
DRESID (temporary variable)
  REGRESSION command, 61
DUNCAN (keyword)
  ONEWAY command, 468
DURBIN (keyword)
  REGRESSION command, 62
Durbin-Watson statistic, 27
DVALUE (keyword)
  CROSSTABS command, 440
  FREQUENCIES command, 449

ECONVERGE (keyword)
  FACTOR command, 154
EDIT (command), 413
  syntax, 413
EFFECTS (keyword)
  ONEWAY command, 469-470
EIGEN (keyword)
  FACTOR command, 155
  MANOVA command, 243
eigenvalues, 213
  and canonical correlations, 224
  discriminant analysis, 89
ELSE (command), 392-393
ELSE (keyword)
  RECODE command, 383
ELSE IF (command), 393
END (keyword)
  REGRESSION command, 59
END DATA (command), 380-381, 401
  syntax, 401
END FILE TYPE (command), 405-406
  syntax, 405
END IF (command), 393
ENTER (keyword)
  REGRESSION command, 56
EPS (keyword)
  MANOVA command, 246
EQ (keyword)
  relational operator, 394
  reserved keyword, 376
EQUAL (keyword)
  DISCRIMINANT command, 113
EQUAMAX (keyword)
  FACTOR command, 154
  MANOVA command, 243, 244
equamax rotation, 141
equiprobability model, 357
  log-linear analysis, 329-330
ERROR (keyword)
  MANOVA command, 242-243, 288
ERROR (subcommand)
  MANOVA command, 238
error sums-of-squares and cross-products matrix, 221
ESTIM (keyword)
  HILOGLINEAR command, 317
  LOGLINEAR command, 359
  MANOVA command, 243, 244
ESTIMATION (keyword)
  MANOVA command, 240-241
ETA (keyword)
  CROSSTABS command, 440
eta coefficient, 440, 464
EUCLID (keyword)
  CLUSTER command, 184
EVERY (keyword)
  PLOT command, 478
EXCLUDE (keyword)
  ANOVA command, 431

MANOVA command, 246
ONEWAY command, 470
EXP (function), 387
EXPECTED (keyword)
CROSSTABS command, 438
expected misclassification rate, 88
EXPERIMENTAL (keyword)
ANOVA command, 430
exponent function, 387
exponentiation, 386
EXPORT (command), 382
EXTRACTION (keyword)
FACTOR command, 155
EXTRACTION (subcommand)
FACTOR command, 153
extraction phase, 130-138

F (keyword)
REGRESSION command, 58
F test
averages, 207
F-to-enter, 45
F-to-remove, 47
FACTOR (command), 125-157, 446-447
analysis block subcommands, 150-151
ANALYSIS subcommand, 152
CRITERIA subcommand, 153-154
DIAGONAL subcommand, 153
EXTRACTION subcommand, 153
factor scores, 156
FORMAT subcommand, 155
global subcommands, 150-151
MATRIX subcommand, 157
MISSING subcommand, 151-152
PLOT subcommand, 155-156
PRINT subcommand, 154-155
ROTATION subcommand, 154
SAVE subcommand, 156
syntax, 446-447
VARIABLES subcommand, 151
WIDTH subcommand, 152
factor analysis, 2, 125-157
extraction, 130-138
factor scores, 148-150
loading, 133
rotation, 139-148
factor matrix, 133-134
factor pattern matrix, 133
factor scores
Anderson-Rubin method, 156
Bartlett method, 156
regression method, 156
factor structure matrix, 133
oblique rotation, 146-147
FACTORS (keyword)
FACTOR command, 153
FILE (subcommand)
INPUT MATRIX command, 453-454
FILE HANDLE (command), 375
FILE LABEL (command), 404-405
syntax, 404
file specifications, 404
FILE TYPE (command), 405-406
syntax, 405
FIN (keyword)
REGRESSION command, 57
FIN (subcommand)
DISCRIMINANT command, 112
FINISH (command), 413
syntax, 413

FIRST (keyword)
ANOVA command, 429
Fisher's classification function
coefficients, 92
Fisher's exact test, 439
fixed zero cell, 345
fixed-format data, 369-370
FORMAT (keyword)
SET command, 419, 420
SHOW command, 419
FORMAT (subcommand)
ANOVA command, 431
CORRELATIONS command, 435
CROSSTABS command, 440
DESCRIPTIVES command, 443-444
FACTOR command, 155
FREQUENCIES command, 449
LIST command, 456
MEANS command, 465
ONEWAY command, 470
PLOT command, 475-476
T-TEST command, 491
FORMATS (command), 378, 379, 386, 413-414
syntax, 413
FORWARD (keyword)
REGRESSION command, 56
forward selection, 45-47
FOUT (keyword)
REGRESSION command, 57
FOUT (subcommand)
DISCRIMINANT command, 112
FREE (keyword)
DATA LIST command, 378-379
INPUT MATRIX command, 453-454
freefield-format data, 370, 378-379
FREQ (keyword)
FREQUENCIES command, 450
HILOGLINEAR command, 317
LOGLINEAR command, 359
FREQUENCIES (command), 2-5, 448-452
BARCHART subcommand, 450
compared to DESCRIPTIVES, 441
FORMAT subcommand, 449
HBAR subcommand, 451
HISTOGRAM subcommand, 450-451
limitations, 452
MISSING subcommand, 452
NTILES subcommand, 451
PERCENTILES subcommand, 451
STATISTICS subcommand, 451-452
syntax, 448
VARIABLES subcommand, 448
FROM (keyword)
LIST command, 455
SAMPLE command, 397
FSCORE (keyword)
FACTOR command, 155
function, 387-389
FUNCTIONS (subcommand)
DISCRIMINANT command, 112
furthest neighbor criterion, 169

gamma, 439-440
GAMMA (keyword)
CROSSTABS command, 439-440
GE (keyword)
relational operator, 394
reserved keyword, 376

generalized residuals, 330-331
generating class
log-linear models, 307-308
generating distributions
COMPUTE command, 422
GET (command), 381, 406-407
DROP subcommand, 407
FILE subcommand, 406
KEEP subcommand, 407
MAP subcommand, 407
RENAME subcommand, 407
syntax, 406
Gini's concentration measure, 336
GLS (keyword)
FACTOR command, 153
GRESID (subcommand)
LOGLINEAR command, 358-359
group centroid, 85-86
GROUPS (subcommand)
DISCRIMINANT command, 109
T-TEST command, 489-490
GT (keyword)
relational operator, 394
reserved keyword, 376

HARMONIC (subcommand)
ONEWAY command, 469
Hartley's F, 470
HBAR (subcommand)
FREQUENCIES command, 451
HELMERT (keyword)
LOGLINEAR command, 360
MANOVA command, 239, 242
HELP (command), 414-415
syntax charts, 415
HICICLE (keyword)
CLUSTER command, 185
HIERARCHICAL (keyword)
ANOVA command, 430
hierarchical clustering, 169
hierarchical model, 297-318
log-linear models, 307-308
HIGHEST (keyword)
COUNT command, 392
RECODE command, 384
HILOGLINEAR (command), 297-318, 453
CRITERIA subcommand, 316
CWEIGHT subcommand, 317
DESIGN subcommand, 315
MAXORDER subcommand, 315-316
METHOD subcommand, 316
MISSING subcommand, 318
PLOT subcommand, 318
PRINT subcommand, 317
syntax, 453
variable list, 314-315
HISTOGRAM (keyword)
REGRESSION command, 61
HISTOGRAM (subcommand)
FREQUENCIES command, 450-451
histograms, 3-4
HISTORY (keyword)
REGRESSION command, 59
HISTORY (subcommand)
DISCRIMINANT command, 114
HOMOGENEITY (keyword)
MANOVA command, 242, 288
ONEWAY command, 470

homogeneity-of-variance tests
  in ONEWAY command, 470
HORIZONTAL (subcommand)
  PLOT command, 474-475
Hotelling's T^2, 205, 211-212
Hotelling's trace, 220
Householder transformations
  MANOVA command, 240
HSIZE (subcommand)
  PLOT command, 476-477
HYPOTH (keyword)
  MANOVA command, 243
hypothesis sums-of-squares
  and cross-products matrix, 211-212, 221-222

icicle plot, 171-174
ID (keyword)
  REGRESSION command, 62
ID (subcommand)
  CLUSTER command, 186
  PROXIMITIES command, 485
IF (command), 393-396, 423
  syntax, 423
IMAGE (keyword)
  FACTOR command, 153
implied decimal place, 378
IMPORT (command), 382
IN (keyword)
  MANOVA command, 245-246
INCLUDE (keyword)
  ANOVA command, 431
  CLUSTER command, 186
  CORRELATIONS command, 435
  CROSSTABS command, 440
  DESCRIPTIVES command, 443
  FACTOR command, 151
  HILOGLINEAR command, 318
  MANOVA command, 246
  MEANS command, 465
  ONEWAY command, 470
  PLOT command, 478
  REGRESSION command, 60
  T-TEST command, 491
incomplete tables
  log-linear analysis, 345-350
INCREMENT (keyword)
  FREQUENCIES command, 450
independence model
  log-linear models, 302-304
independent-samples test, 489-490
INDEX (keyword)
  CROSSTABS command, 440
  DESCRIPTIVES command, 443
  FREQUENCIES command, 449
indicator variables, 35
INFO (command), 415-416
  FACILITIES keyword, 415
  local documentation, 415
  LOCAL keyword, 415
  new facilities, 415
  new procedures, 416
  new releases, 416
  OUTFILE subcommand, 416
  OVERVIEW keyword, 415
  PROCEDURES keyword, 415
  syntax, 415
INITIAL (keyword)
  FACTOR command, 155
inline data, 380-381
input data file
  defined, 374
INPUT MATRIX (command), 453-454
  FILE subcommand, 453-454
  FREE keyword, 453-454
  syntax, 453
  with NUMERIC command, 453-454
INPUT PROGRAM (command)
  with INPUT MATRIX command, 453-454
intercept, 13, 15
INTO (keyword)
  RECODE command, 384-385
INV (keyword)
  FACTOR command, 155
ITERATE (keyword)
  FACTOR command, 153
  HILOGLINEAR command, 316
ITERATION (keyword)
  LOGLINEAR command, 361

jackknife, 87

KAISER (keyword)
  FACTOR command, 154
Kaiser-Meyer-Olkin test, 129, 138, 155
Kendall's tau-b, 439
Kendall's tau-c, 439
KMO (keyword)
  FACTOR command, 155
KURTOSIS (keyword)
  DESCRIPTIVES command, 443
  FREQUENCIES command, 452

LABELS (keyword)
  ANOVA command, 431
  CROSSTABS command, 440
  DESCRIPTIVES command, 443
  MEANS command, 465
  ONEWAY command, 470
  T-TEST command, 491
LAG (function), 388
lambda, 439
LAMBDA (keyword)
  CROSSTABS command, 439
LASTRES (keyword)
  MANOVA command, 240-241
latent effect
  repeated measures, 258
LE (keyword)
  relational operator, 394
  reserved keyword, 376
learning effect
  repeated measures, 258
least squares, 13
LENGTH (keyword)
  SET command, 419, 419
  SHOW command, 419
LEVER (temporary variable)
  REGRESSION command, 61
LG10 (function), 387
LIMIT (keyword)
  FREQUENCIES command, 449
limitations, see entries under individual procedures
LINE (keyword)
  DESCRIPTIVES command, 444
  REGRESSION command, 58
linear-by-linear association model
  log-linear analysis, 342-343
LINEARITY (keyword)
  MEANS command, 464
LIST (command), 455-456
  CASES subcommand, 455-456
  FORMAT subcommand, 456
  syntax, 455
  VARIABLES subcommand, 455
LISTWISE (keyword)
  CLUSTER command, 186
  CORRELATIONS command, 435
  DESCRIPTIVES command, 443
  FACTOR command, 151
  HILOGLINEAR command, 318
  MANOVA command, 246
  ONEWAY command, 470
  PLOT command, 478
  REGRESSION command, 60
  T-TEST command, 491
listwise missing-value treatment, 36
LN (function), 387
loadings, 219
local documentation
  INFO command, 415
log-linear analysis, 2, 297-318, 329-361
logarithm
  base e, 387
  base 10, 387
logical expression, 393-396
  in DO IF command, 392
  in ELSE IF (command), 393
  in IF command, 393-396
  in SELECT IF command, 397
logical functions, 388
logical operator, 394
logit model, 356
  log-linear analysis, 334-337
  parameter estimates, 336, 340-341
LOGLINEAR (command), 329-361, 456-457
  CONTRAST subcommand, 360-361
  CRITERIA subcommand, 361
  CWEIGHT subcommand, 357-358
  DESIGN subcommand, 356
  GRESID subcommand, 358-359
  logit model, 356
  MISSING (subcommand), 361
  NOPRINT subcommand, 359
  PLOT subcommand, 359-360
  PRINT subcommand, 359
  syntax, 456-457
  variable specification, 355-356
  WIDTH subcommand, 361
LOWEST (keyword)
  COUNT command, 392
  RECODE command, 384
LSD (keyword)
  ONEWAY command, 468
LSDMOD (keyword)
  ONEWAY command, 468
LT (keyword)
  relational operator, 394
  reserved keyword, 376

MAHAL (keyword)
  DISCRIMINANT command, 110
MAHAL (temporary variable)
  REGRESSION command, 61
Mahalanobis' distance, 29-32, 98

MANOVA (command), 195-246, 458-461
ANALYSIS subcommand, 234-235
ANALYSIS(REPEATED) subcommand, 287
constant covariate, 283-284
CONTRAST (Subcommand), 286
CONTRAST subcommand, 242
covariate list, 234
CRITERIA subcommand, 246
dependent variable list, 233
DESIGN subcommand, 235-237
ERROR subcommand, 238
factor variable list, 233-234
matrix input, 245-246
matrix output, 245-246
MATRIX subcommand, 245-246
MEASURE subcommand, 285-286, 287
METHOD subcommand, 240-241
MISSING subcommand, 246
NEGSUM keyword, 228
NOPRINT subcommand, 242-245
PARTITION subcommand, 241
PCOMPS subcommand, 243
PLOT subcommand, 245
predicted means, 245
principal components analysis, 243
PRINT subcommand, 242-245, 287-288
RENAME subcommand, 240, 285
repeated measures, 257-288
RESIDUALS subcommand, 245
SEQUENTIAL keyword, 227
syntax, 458-461
TRANSFORM subcommand, 239-240
UNIQUE keyword, 227
WSDESIGN subcommand, 286-287
WSFACTORS subcommand, 284-285
matrices
correlation, 245-246
covariance, 435
reading, 453-454
writing, 479
MATRIX (keyword)
CORRELATIONS command, 435
DATA LIST command, 381
MATRIX (subcommand)
CLUSTER command, 186
CORRELATIONS command, 435
DISCRIMINANT command, 114
FACTOR command, 157
MANOVA command, 245-246
ONEWAY command, 470-471
PROXIMITIES command, 486
REGRESSION command, 64
Mauchly's test of sphericity, 267-268
MAX (function), 388
MAX (keyword)
DESCRIPTIVES command, 443
FREQUENCIES command, 450
PLOT command, 474
MAXIMUM (keyword)
FREQUENCIES command, 452
maximum function, 388
MAXMINF (keyword)
DISCRIMINANT command, 110
MAXORDER (subcommand)
HILOGLINEAR command, 315-316
MAXORDERS (subcommand)
ANOVA command, 430
MAXSTEPS (keyword)
HILOGLINEAR command, 316
REGRESSION command, 57
MAXSTEPS (subcommand)
DISCRIMINANT command, 111
MCA (keyword)
ANOVA command, 431
MEAN (function), 388
MEAN (keyword)
ANOVA command, 431
DESCRIPTIVES command, 442
FREQUENCIES command, 451
MEANS command, 464
REGRESSION command, 60
mean square, 19
MEANS (command), 6, 461-465
CELLS subcommand, 464
CROSSBREAK subcommand, 463
crosstabulation, 463
FORMAT subcommand, 465
limitations, 465
MISSING subcommand, 465
STATISTICS subcommand, 464
syntax, 461-462
TABLES subcommand, 462-463
VARIABLES subcommand, 463
MEANS (keyword)
MANOVA command, 240, 242
MEANSUBSTITUTION (keyword)
FACTOR command, 151
REGRESSION command, 60
MEASURE (subcommand)
CLUSTER command, 184-185
MANOVA command, 285-286, 287
PROXIMITIES command, 483
measures of dispersion and association, 336-337
MEDIAN (keyword)
CLUSTER command, 184
FREQUENCIES command, 451
METHOD (subcommand)
ANOVA command, 430
CLUSTER command, 184
DISCRIMINANT command, 110-111
HILOGLINEAR command, 316
MANOVA command, 240-241
REGRESSION command, 56-57
MIN (function), 388
MIN (keyword)
DESCRIPTIVES command, 443
FREQUENCIES command, 450
PLOT command, 474
MINEIGEN (keyword)
FACTOR command, 153
MANOVA command, 243
MINIMUM (keyword)
FREQUENCIES command, 452
minimum function, 388
MINRESID (keyword)
DISCRIMINANT command, 110
MISSING (function), 388
in IF command, 395-396
in SELECT IF command, 397
MISSING (keyword)
COUNT command, 392
RECODE command, 384
MISSING (subcommand)
ANOVA command, 431
CLUSTER command, 186
CORRELATIONS command, 435
CROSSTABS command, 440
DESCRIPTIVES command, 443
DISCRIMINANT command, 114
FACTOR command, 151-152
FREQUENCIES command, 452
HILOGLINEAR command, 318
LOGLINEAR command, 361
MANOVA command, 246
MEANS command, 465
ONEWAY command, 470
PLOT command, 478-479
PROXIMITIES command, 482
REGRESSION command, 60
T-TEST command, 491
missing values, 367-368, see entries under individual procedures
functions, 388, 389
in DO IF command, 393
MISSING function, 388
NMISS function, 388
suffix, 388
SYSMIS function, 388
VALUE function, 388
MISSING VALUES (command), 380, 407-408
syntax, 407
mixed-model approach, 267
ML (keyword)
FACTOR command, 153
MOD (function), 387
MODE (keyword)
FREQUENCIES command, 452
models for ordinal data
log-linear analysis, 341-345
MODELTYPE (keyword)
MANOVA command, 240
modulo, 387
multicollinearity, 54-55
multiple comparison tests, 45
multiple linear regression analysis, 2
multiple R, 17-18
multiplication, 386
MULTIV (keyword)
MANOVA command, 243
MUPLUS (keyword)
MANOVA command, 236-237

N (keyword)
ANOVA command, 430
REGRESSION command, 61
SHOW command, 419
N OF CASES (command), 398, 416-417
syntax, 416
with SAMPLE command, 398
with SELECT IF command, 398
NAMES (keyword)
MEANS command, 465
NCOMP (keyword)
MANOVA command, 243
NE (keyword)
relational operator, 394
reserved keyword, 376
nearest neighbor criterion, 169
NEGSUM (keyword)
MANOVA command, 243

NEWPAGE (keyword)
  FREQUENCIES command, 449
Newton-Raphson algorithm, 361
NMISS (function), 388
NOBALANCED (keyword)
  MANOVA command, 240
NOCATLABS (keyword)
  MEANS command, 465
NOCONSTANT (keyword)
  MANOVA command, 241
NOINDEX (keyword)
  CROSSTABS command, 440
  DESCRIPTIVES command, 443
NOKAISER (keyword)
  FACTOR command, 154
NOLABELS (keyword)
  ANOVA command, 431
  CROSSTABS command, 440
  DESCRIPTIVES command, 443
  FREQUENCIES command, 449
  MEANS command, 465
  ONEWAY command, 470
  T-TEST command, 491
NOLASTRES (keyword)
  MANOVA command, 240-241
NONAMES (keyword)
  MEANS command, 465
NONE (keyword)
  ANOVA command, 430, 431
  CROSSTABS command, 438, 440
  FREQUENCIES command, 452
  LOGLINEAR command, 359
  MEANS command, 464
  ONEWAY command, 469
NONPAR CORR (command), 7
NOORIGIN (subcommand)
  REGRESSION command, 59
NOPRINT (subcommand)
  LOGLINEAR command, 359
  MANOVA command, 242-245
NORMAL (function), 389
NORMAL (keyword)
  FREQUENCIES command, 450
  MANOVA command, 245
normal probability plot, 28, 200
NORMPLOT (keyword)
  HILOGLINEAR command, 318
NORMPROB (keyword)
  LOGLINEAR command, 359
  REGRESSION command, 61-62
NOROTATE (keyword)
  FACTOR command, 154
  MANOVA command, 243
NOSIG (keyword)
  CORRELATIONS command, 434
NOT (keyword)
  logical operator, 394
  reserved keyword, 376
NOTABLE (keyword)
  FREQUENCIES command, 449
NOTABLES (keyword)
  CROSSTABS command, 440
NOVALLABS (keyword)
  CROSSTABS command, 440
NOVALUES (keyword)
  MEANS command, 465
NTILES (subcommand)
  FREQUENCIES command, 451
NUMBERED (command), 417
  syntax, 417
NUMERIC (command)
  with INPUT MATRIX command, 453-454
NUMERIC (keyword)
  PLOT command, 477
numeric function, 387-389
numeric variable, 377
NVALID (function), 388

OBLIMIN (keyword)
  FACTOR command, 154
oblimin method, 147
oblique rotation, 139-140, 145-148
observation, see case
OBSERVATIONS (keyword)
  MANOVA command, 240
OFF (keyword)
  WEIGHT command, 398-399
OMEANS (subcommand)
  MANOVA command, 244
ONEPAGE (keyword)
  FREQUENCIES command, 449
ONETAIL (keyword)
  CORRELATIONS command, 434
ONEWAY (command), 7, 466-471
  CONTRAST subcommand, 467-468
  FORMAT subcommand, 470
  HARMONIC subcommand, 469
  limitations, 471
  MATRIX subcommand, 470-471
  MISSING subcommand, 470
  POLYNOMIAL subcommand, 467
  RANGES subcommand, 468-469
  STATISTICS subcommand, 469-470
  syntax, 466
  value labels, 470
ONEWAY (keyword)
  MANOVA command, 242
OPTIONS (command), 471
  syntax, 471
OR (keyword)
  logical operator, 394
  reserved keyword, 376
ORIGIN (subcommand)
  REGRESSION command, 59
ORTHO (keyword)
  MANOVA command, 243
orthogonal polynomial contrasts, 216
orthogonal rotation, 139-143
ORTHONORM (keyword)
  MANOVA command, 239
orthonormalized contrasts, 261
OUT (keyword)
  CORRELATIONS command, 435
  MANOVA command, 245-246
  ONEWAY command, 470-471
  PROXIMITIES command, 486
OUTFILE (subcommand)
  PROCEDURE OUTPUT command, 479
  PROXIMITIES command, 486
outlier, 12, 28-29
OUTLIERS (keyword)
  REGRESSION command, 61-62
output file
  defined, 375
OUTS (keyword)
  REGRESSION command, 58
OVERALL (keyword)
  MANOVA command, 242
overlay plots
  PLOT command, 475-476

P (keyword)
  HILOGLINEAR command, 316
PAF (keyword)
  FACTOR command, 153
page size, see SET command
PAIRED (keyword)
  T-TEST command, 490-491
paired-samples [t] test, 490-491
PAIRS (subcommand)
  T-TEST command, 490-491
PAIRWISE (keyword)
  CORRELATIONS command, 435
  FACTOR command, 151
  REGRESSION command, 60
pairwise missing-value treatment, 37
parameter estimates
  linear-by-linear association model, 343
  log-linear analysis, 351-353
  logit model, 336, 340-341
  multivariate analysis of variance, 215-217
  row- and column-effects models, 344
PARAMETERS (keyword)
  MANOVA command, 243
part coefficient, 39-40
partial [F] test, 42-43
partial chi-square, 311-312
partial coefficient, 39-40
PARTIAL CORR (command), 7
partial regression coefficient, 37-38
PARTIALPLOT (subcommand)
  REGRESSION command, 64
PARTITION (subcommand)
  MANOVA command, 241
PC (keyword)
  FACTOR command, 153
PCOMPS (subcommand)
  MANOVA command, 243
Pearson chi-square
  log-linear models, 304-305
PEARSON CORR (command)
  see CORRELATIONS, 7
Pearson correlation coefficient, 440, 464
PERCENT (keyword)
  FREQUENCIES command, 450
PERCENTILES (subcommand)
  FREQUENCIES command, 451
period missing value specification suffix, 388
PHI (keyword)
  CROSSTABS command, 439
phi coefficient, 439
Pillai's trace, 220
PIN (keyword)
  REGRESSION command, 57
PIN (subcommand)
  DISCRIMINANT command, 112
PLOT (command), 6-7, 472-479
  contour plots, 475
  CUTPOINT subcommand, 477-478
  FORMAT subcommand, 475-476
  HORIZONTAL subcommand, 474-475
  HSIZE subcommand, 476-477
  limitations, 479
  MISSING subcommand, 478-479

overlay plots, 475-476
PLOT subcommand, 473
regression plots, 476
SYMBOLS subcommand, 477-478
syntax, 472
TITLE subcommand, 474
VERTICAL subcommand, 474-475
VSIZE subcommand, 476-477
PLOT (keyword)
MANOVA command, 245
REGRESSION command, 62
PLOT (subcommand)
CLUSTER command, 185
DISCRIMINANT command, 115-116
FACTOR command, 155-156
HILOGLINEAR command, 318
LOGLINEAR command, 359-360
MANOVA command, 245
PLOT command, 473
PLOTWISE (keyword)
PLOT command, 478
PMEANS (subcommand)
MANOVA command, 244
POLYNOMIAL (keyword)
LOGLINEAR command, 360
MANOVA command, 239, 242
POLYNOMIAL (subcommand)
ONEWAY command, 467
POOLED (keyword)
REGRESSION command, 62
pooled within-groups correlation matrix, 79-80
portable file, 381-382
posterior probability, 83
POUT (keyword)
REGRESSION command, 57
POUT (subcommand)
DISCRIMINANT command, 112
POWER (keyword)
CLUSTER command, 185
PRED (temporary variable)
REGRESSION command, 61
predicted means, 231-232
principal components analysis, 130-134, 218-220, 243
PRINCOMPS (keyword)
MANOVA command, 242-243
PRINT (subcommand)
CLUSTER command, 185
CORRELATIONS command, 434
FACTOR command, 154-155
HILOGLINEAR command, 317
LOGLINEAR command, 359
MANOVA command, 242-245, 287-288
PROXIMITIES command, 485
print formats, 378
setting default, 420
PRINT FORMATS (command), 417
syntax, 417
prior probability, 82-83
PRIORS (subcommand)
DISCRIMINANT command, 113
PROBIT (function), 389
PROBS (keyword)
DISCRIMINANT command, 113
procedure commands, 426-491
PROCEDURE OUTPUT (command), 479
matrix output, 479
OUTFILE subcommand, 479
syntax, 479
procedures
creating new variables, 428
matrix files, 453-454
output files, 479
update documentation, 416
PROXIMITIES (command), 183, 480-486
ID subcommand, 485
limitations, 486
MATRIX subcommand, 486
MEASURE subcommand, 483
MISSING subcommand, 482
OUTFILE subcommand, 486
PRINT subcommand, 485
READ subcommand, 486
STANDARDIZE subcommand, 482
syntax, 480-481
variable specification, 482
VIEW subcommand, 483
WRITE subcommand, 486
proximity matrices, 480-486

QR (keyword)
MANOVA command, 240
QUARTIMAX (keyword)
FACTOR command, 154
MANOVA command, 243, 244
quartimax rotation, 141
quasi-independence model
log-linear analysis, 346-347

R (keyword)
REGRESSION command, 58
R^2, 17-18, 20, 44
random numbers
setting seed, 420
random zeroes, 345
RANGE (function), 388
RANGE (keyword)
DESCRIPTIVES command, 443
FREQUENCIES command, 452
RANGES (subcommand)
ONEWAY command, 468-469
RAO (keyword)
DISCRIMINANT command, 110
Rao's V, 98
RAW (keyword)
MANOVA command, 244
RCONVERGE (keyword)
FACTOR command, 154
READ (subcommand)
PROXIMITIES command, 486
RECODE (command), 382-385, 423-424
syntax, 423
record, 368-369
record identifier, 370
rectangular file, 370
REFERENCE (keyword)
PLOT command, 474
REG (keyword)
ANOVA command, 431
FACTOR command, 156
regression, 11-55
assumptions, 14-15, 24-35, 48-53
transformations, 32-35
REGRESSION (command), 11-65
CASEWISE subcommand, 62-63
CRITERIA subcommand, 57-58
DEPENDENT subcommand, 56
DESCRIPTIVES subcommand, 60-61
MATRIX subcommand, 64
METHOD subcommand, 56-57
MISSING subcommand, 60
NOORIGIN subcommand, 59
ORIGIN subcommand, 59
PARTIALPLOT subcommand, 64
regression sum of squares, 18-19
REGWGT subcommand, 64
RESIDUALS subcommand, 61-62
SAVE subcommand, 64
SCATTERPLOT subcommand, 63
SELECT subcommand, 59-60
STATISTICS subcommand, 58-59
syntax, 487-488
VARIABLES subcommand, 56
WIDTH subcommand, 64-65
REGRESSION (keyword)
PLOT command, 476
regression method
for calculating sums of squares, 227
regression plots
PLOT command, 476
REGWGT (subcommand)
REGRESSION command, 64
relational operator, 393-394
remainder, 387
REMOVE (keyword)
REGRESSION command, 56
RENAME (subcommand)
MANOVA command, 240, 285
REPEATED (keyword)
LOGLINEAR command, 360
MANOVA command, 239, 242
repeated measures analysis of variance, 257-288
REPORT (keyword)
CROSSTABS command, 440
REPR (keyword)
FACTOR command, 155
reproduced correlation matrix, 134
reserved keyword, 376
RESID (keyword), see RESIDUAL keyword
CROSSTABS command, 438
HILOGLINEAR command, 317, 318
RESID (temporary variable)
REGRESSION command, 61
residual
hierarchical log-linear models, 305-307
log-linear, 329-330
multivariate analysis of variance, 227-231
regression, 16, 18-19, 24
RESIDUAL (keyword)
LOGLINEAR command, 359, 359
MANOVA command, 237, 238
RESIDUALS (subcommand)
MANOVA command, 245
REGRESSION command, 61-62
RND (function), 387
ROTATE (keyword)
MANOVA command, 243, 244
ROTATE (subcommand)
DISCRIMINANT command, 114

ROTATION (keyword)
FACTOR command, 155, 155
ROTATION (subcommand)
FACTOR command, 154
rotation phase, 139-148
ROW (keyword)
CROSSTABS command, 438
row- and column-effects models
log-linear analysis, 344-345
Roy-Bargman step-down
MANOVA command, 243
Roy's largest root, 220, 222

SAMPLE (command), 397, 424
syntax, 424
saturated model
log-linear models, 298-300
SAVE (command), 381, 408-410
DROP subcommand, 409
KEEP subcommand, 409-410
MAP subcommand, 410
RENAME subcommand, 409
syntax, 408
SAVE (subcommand)
CLUSTER command, 186
DESCRIPTIVES command, 442
DISCRIMINANT command, 113-114
FACTOR command, 156
REGRESSION command, 64
scatterplot, 11-12
SCATTERPLOT (subcommand)
REGRESSION command, 63
SCHEDULE (keyword)
CLUSTER command, 185
SCHEFFE (keyword)
ONEWAY command, 468
scientific notation, 39, 41
SCORES (keyword)
DISCRIMINANT command, 113
scree plot, 131-132
in FACTOR command, 155
SD (function), 388
SDRESID (temporary variable)
REGRESSION command, 61
SEED (keyword)
SET command, 419, 420
SHOW command, 419
SEKURT (keyword)
FREQUENCIES command, 452
SELECT (subcommand)
DISCRIMINANT command, 112
REGRESSION command, 59-60
SELECT IF (command), 396-397, 424
missing values, 397
syntax, 424
SEMEAN (keyword)
DESCRIPTIVES command, 442
FREQUENCIES command, 451
SEPRED (temporary variable)
REGRESSION command, 61
SEQUENTIAL (keyword)
MANOVA command, 241
sequential method
for calculating sums of squares, 227
SERIAL (keyword)
CORRELATIONS command, 435
DESCRIPTIVES command, 444
SES (keyword)
REGRESSION command, 58
SESKEW (keyword)
FREQUENCIES command, 452

SET (command), 418-420
syntax, 418
SEUCLID (keyword)
CLUSTER command, 184
Shannon's entropy measure, 336
SHOW (command), 418-420
syntax, 418
SIG (keyword)
CORRELATIONS command, 434
FACTOR command, 155
REGRESSION command, 60
SIGNIF (keyword)
MANOVA command, 243, 287
similarity measure, 168-169
SIMPLE (keyword)
LOGLINEAR command, 360
MANOVA command, 239, 242
simple contrasts, 216
SIN (function), 387
SINGLE (keyword)
CLUSTER command, 184
single linkage criterion, 169
SINGLEDF (keyword)
MANOVA command, 243
SIZE (keyword)
DISCRIMINANT command, 113
REGRESSION command, 61-62, 63, 64
SKEWNESS (keyword)
DESCRIPTIVES command, 443
FREQUENCIES command, 452
slope, 13, 15-16
SNK (keyword)
ONEWAY command, 468
SOLUTION (keyword)
MANOVA command, 242
solution matrix, 227
Somers d, 440
SORT (keyword)
FACTOR command, 155
SORT CASES (command), 399, 424-425
syntax, 424
SPECIAL (keyword)
LOGLINEAR command, 360
MANOVA command, 239, 242
SPLIT FILE (command), 425
syntax, 425
SQRT (function), 387
squared Euclidean distance, 168
SRESID (keyword)
CROSSTABS command, 438
SRESID (temporary variable)
REGRESSION command, 61
SSCP (keyword)
MANOVA command, 242, 242
SSTYPE (keyword)
MANOVA command, 241
STAN (keyword)
MANOVA command, 244
standard deviation function, 388
standard error of the estimate, 16, 20, 23
STANDARDIZE (keyword)
PLOT command, 474
STANDARDIZE (subcommand)
PROXIMITIES command, 482
standardized discriminant function coefficients, 90, 213-214, 223
standardized regression coefficient, 14

standardized residual
hierarchical log-linear models, 305-307
regression, 24
standardized scores, see Z scores
STATISTICS (command), 471
syntax, 471
STATISTICS (subcommand)
CORRELATIONS command, 434-435
CROSSTABS command, 438-440
DISCRIMINANT command, 115
FREQUENCIES command, 451-452
MEANS command, 464
ONEWAY command, 469-470
REGRESSION command, 58-59
STDDEV (keyword)
DESCRIPTIVES command, 443
FREQUENCIES command, 452
MANOVA command, 243
MEANS command, 464
REGRESSION command, 60
stem-and-leaf plot, 199
STEMLEAF (keyword)
MANOVA command, 245
STEPDOWN (keyword)
MANOVA command, 243
stepdown F tests, 225-226
STEPWISE (keyword)
REGRESSION command, 56
stepwise variable selection, 48, 93
string variable, 368, 377
in COUNT command, 391-392
structure coefficients, 214
Studentized deleted residual, 31-32
Studentized residual, 24
SUBTITLE (command), 420
syntax, 420
subtraction, 386
SUM (function), 388
SUM (keyword)
DESCRIPTIVES command, 443
FREQUENCIES command, 452
MEANS command, 464
SYMBOLS (subcommand)
PLOT command, 477-478
symmetry models
log-linear analysis, 347-349
SYSMIS (function), 388
in IF command, 395-396
in SELECT IF command, 397
SYSMIS (keyword)
COUNT command, 392
RECODE command, 384
system file, 381
system-missing value, 380

T-TEST (command), 7, 489-491
FORMAT subcommand, 491
GROUPS subcommand, 489-490
limitations, 491
MISSING subcommand, 491
PAIRS subcommand, 490-491
significance tests, 491
syntax, 489
VARIABLES subcommand, 490
TABLE (keyword)
CROSSTABS command, 440
MEANS command, 465
TABLES (keyword)
CROSSTABS command, 440
MANOVA command, 244, 244

TABLES (subcommand)
  CROSSTABS command, 437-438
  MEANS command, 462
tau statistics, 439
TEMPORARY (command), 396, 425
  syntax, 425
TEST (keyword)
  REGRESSION command, 56
test of linearity, 464
THRU (keyword)
  COUNT command, 392
  RECODE command, 384
TITLE (command), 420-421
  syntax, 420
TITLE (subcommand)
  PLOT command, 474
TO (keyword)
  DATA LIST command, 376
  LIST command, 456
  reserved keyword, 376
tolerance, 55, 94
TOLERANCE (keyword)
  REGRESSION command, 57-58
TOLERANCE (subcommand)
  DISCRIMINANT command, 112
TOTAL (keyword)
  CROSSTABS command, 438
total correlation matrix, 79-80
TRANSFORM (keyword)
  MANOVA command, 243, 287
TRANSFORM (subcommand)
  MANOVA command, 239-240
TREE (keyword)
  MEANS command, 465
TRUNC (function), 387
truncate, 387
TUKEY (keyword)
  ONEWAY command, 468
TUKEYB (keyword)
  ONEWAY command, 468
TWOTAIL (keyword)
  CORRELATIONS command, 434

UC (keyword)
  CROSSTABS command, 439
ULS (keyword)
  FACTOR command, 153
uncertainty coefficient, 439
UNIFORM (function), 389
UNIFORM (keyword)
  PLOT command, 474
UNIQUE (keyword)
  ANOVA command, 430
  MANOVA command, 241
unique factor, 126
UNIV (keyword)
  MANOVA command, 243
UNIVARIATE (keyword)
  FACTOR command, 154
user-missing value, 380
utility commands, 411-421

V
  Cramer's, 439
value, 367-368
VALUE (function), 388
  in IF command, 395-396
VALUE LABELS (command), 379, 410-411
  syntax, 410
VALUES (keyword)
  MEANS command, 465
variable, 367-368, 375-376
VARIABLE (keyword)
  DESCRIPTIVES command, 443
variable clustering, 181-183
variable definition, 375-380
VARIABLE LABELS (command), 379, 411
  syntax, 411
VARIABLES (keyword)
  MANOVA command, 244, 244
VARIABLES (subcommand)
  CORRELATIONS command, 433-434
  CROSSTABS command, 437-438
  DISCRIMINANT command, 110
  FACTOR command, 151
  FREQUENCIES command, 448
  LIST command, 455
  MEANS command, 463
  REGRESSION command, 56
  T-TEST command, 490
VARIANCE (function), 388
VARIANCE (keyword)
  DESCRIPTIVES command, 443
  FREQUENCIES command, 452
  MEANS command, 464
  REGRESSION command, 60
VARIMAX (keyword)
  FACTOR command, 154
  MANOVA command, 243, 244
varimax rotation, 140-143
VERTICAL (subcommand)
  PLOT command, 474-475
VICICLE (keyword)
  CLUSTER command, 185
VIEW (subcommand)
  PROXIMITIES command, 483
VIN (subcommand)
  DISCRIMINANT command, 112
VS (keyword)
  MANOVA command, 237
VSIZE (subcommand)
  PLOT command, 476-477

WARD (keyword)
  CLUSTER command, 184
WAVERAGE (keyword)
  CLUSTER command, 184
WEIGHT (command), 398-399, 426
  missing values, 398
  syntax, 426
WEIGHT (keyword)
  SHOW command, 419
WIDTH (keyword)
  SET command, 419, 420
  SHOW command, 419
WIDTH (subcommand)
  FACTOR command, 152
  LOGLINEAR command, 361
  REGRESSION command, 64-65
WILKS (keyword)
  DISCRIMINANT command, 110
Wilks' lambda, 90, 213, 220
WITH (keyword)
  ANOVA command, 429
  LOGLINEAR command, 356, 356-357
  PLOT command, 473
  reserved keyword, 376
WITHIN (keyword)
  MANOVA command, 237, 238
within-cells correlation matrix, 203-204, 219
WR (keyword)
  MANOVA command, 237, 238
WRITE (subcommand)
  CROSSTABS command, 440
  PROXIMITIES command, 486
write formats
  setting default, 420
WRITE FORMATS (command), 421
  syntax, 421
WSDESIGN (subcommand)
  MANOVA command, 286-287
WSFACTORS (subcommand)
  MANOVA command, 284-285

XPROD (keyword)
  CORRELATIONS command, 435
  REGRESSION command, 61
XSAVE (command), 408-410
  syntax, 408
XTX (keyword)
  REGRESSION command, 58

Yates' corrected chi-square test, 439
YRMODA (function), 389

Z scores
  in DESCRIPTIVES command, 442
Z scores, 14
ZCORR (keyword)
  MANOVA command, 245
ZETA (keyword)
  MANOVA command, 246
ZPP (keyword)
  REGRESSION command, 58
ZPRED (temporary variable)
  REGRESSION command, 61
ZRESID (temporary variable)
  REGRESSION command, 61